GNVQ Advanced

Information Technology

Geoffrey Knott BA, AIB, Cert Ed

Nick Waites BSc, MSc, Cert Ed

Business Education Publishers

1995

©Geoffrey Knott and Nick Waites

ISBN 0-907679-80-3

First Published 1995
Reprinted 1995
Reprinted 1996

Published in Great Britain by

Business Education Publishers Limited,
Leighton House,
10 Grange Crescent,
Stockton Road,
Sunderland
SR2 7BN.

Tel 0191 567 4963
Fax 0191 514 3277

British Cataloguing-in-Publications Data
A catalogue record for this book is available from the British Library

Printed in Great Britain by The Bath Press, Bath

To Anne and Carolyn with love

Acknowledgements

We would like to thank Tony Seals at National Instruments for helping to produce the material relating to the LabVIEW graphical programming language, Rachel Knott for proof reading the book and Carolyn and Rachel Knott for providing the encouragement and coffee to keep us going through the long hours.

All errors and omissions remain the responsibility of the authors.

GK
NW
Durham
July 1995

The Authors

Geoffrey Knott is a Lecturer in Computing and Information Technology at New College Durham. He has wide experience of teaching and developing BTEC and GNVQ courses and extensive practical experience in Computing and Information Technology before entering teaching. He is the co-author of *Computer Studies for BTEC, Information Processing for BTEC, Computing for A Level, BTEC and First Degree, Business GNVQ Advanced, Core Skills for GNVQ* and is the author of *Small Business Computer Systems* and *Information Technology Skills*.

Nick Waites is Senior Lecturer in Computing at New College Durham. He has taught Computing and Information Technology for many years and is currently responsible for staff development in computing and IT. He is the co-author of *Computer Studies for BTEC, Information Processing for BTEC, Computing for A Level, BTEC and First Degree, Business GNVQ Advanced* and *Core Skills for GNVQ* and is the author of *GCSE Information Systems*. He lives in the North East of England in an old chapel which he has converted to a Martial Arts Centre.

How to use this book

The integrated nature of the *GNVQ Advanced Information Technology* units imposes a major constraint on the structure of a course text: the subject material cannot easily be presented in a form which allows it have a one-to-one correspondence with the course specification. The course units have been designed to encourage students to explore topics which draw together many different areas of information technology. Thus, for example, Unit 2 *Using Information Technology* involves the use of a word processor to design a range of documents, the use of graphic and computer-aided design software, the study of computer models and simulation, the use of a spreadsheet or other software to develop computer models, and finally it involves an exploration of computer control systems! This is an enormously broad range of knowledge and skills to acquire for a single unit. Of course many of the skills required in this unit are also required in others, suggesting that perhaps an early grounding in skills required by a number of units might be a good preparation for covering the course requirements.

Hence, our strategy has been to divide this textbook into three parts:

Part 1 - Knowledge Resource

Contains material to cover the range statements for each unit thoroughly, though the subject matter is organised in terms of topic areas rather than by unit.

Part 2 - Skills Resource

Contains detailed information for the acquisition of practical skills necessary to achieve many of the performance criteria stated in the unit specifications. The skills covered are word processing, using spreadsheets, database design and use, using graphics programs, using local area networks and electronic communication, automated procedures and team and project skills. Two additional sections deal with program design and programming in Pascal; though these skills are not required for the mandatory units, we felt that they are likely to form part of a computing course such as this, perhaps in the guise of an option or additional unit.

Part 3 - Study Programme

The Study Programme provides numerous, unit-based activities, designed to allow the student to achieve all of the performance criteria required for the Mandatory Units. The activities have also been designed to allow the student to achieve many of the Core Skills performance criteria. All the performance criteria that we consider achievable by an activity are identified by number, element and unit. The master grid, *PC/Study Component Matrix* on the next two pages, maps Performance Criteria to the Study Components for the complete programme. By marking performance criteria, as they are attained, the matrix provides a convenient method of tracking progress over the duration of an IT GNVQ Advanced course of study.

The matrix can be used to determine which Study Components are needed to cover particular Performance Criteria, or perhaps more usefully, to identify which Performance Criteria are covered by any one of the Study Components. The Study Programme has the following features:

- *24 Study Components*, each of which deals with a topic area, often spanning more than one Unit. Relevant Knowledge and Skill Resources for each Study Component are identified, allowing the appropriate knowledge and skills to be acquired prior to attempting the listed activities;

- *Initial Study Components* which deal with the acquisition of skills relating to general-purpose application packages, so that these skills may be applied in activities which require them.

The Study Components thus provide the focus by which the skills and knowledge relating to a topic may be acquired in a methodical manner. Activities within a Study Component allow the student to explore important aspects of the topic and, at the same time, satisfy related performance criteria.

In addition to the Study Components, four case studies are included as further material to supplement the programme of activities. Two of these case studies, Barford Properties and Pilcon Polymers are actually used in a number of the activities.

PC / Study Component Matrix — Study Component

Element	PC	1	2	3	4	5	6	7	8	9	10	11	12	13	14	15	16	17	18	19	20	21	22	23	24
1.1	1										■														
	2										■														
	3										■														
	4										■														
	5																								
1.2	1															■									
	2																								
	3																								
1.3	1																■								
	2																■								
	3																■								
	4																								
1.4	1				■																				
	2				■																				
	3				■																				
	4				■																				
	5				■																				
2.1	1					■	■	■	■	■	■	■	■	■	■										
	2					■	■		■	■	■	■	■	■	■										
	3					■	■	■	■	■	■	■	■	■	■										
	4					■	■	■	■	■	■	■	■	■	■										
	5					■	■	■	■	■	■	■	■	■	■										
	6					■		■	■	■		■	■	■	■										
2.2	1					■	■		■	■	■		■	■	■	■	■	■	■						
	2					■	■		■	■	■		■	■	■	■	■	■	■						
	3					■		■	■		■		■	■	■	■	■	■	■						
	4					■	■		■		■		■	■	■	■	■	■	■						
	5					■	■		■		■		■	■	■	■	■	■	■						
	6					■	■		■		■		■	■	■	■	■	■	■						
2.3	1																			■					
	2																			■					
	3																			■					
	4																			■					
	5																			■					
2.4	1																							■	
	2																							■	
	3																							■	
	4																							■	
	5																							■	
	6																							■	
3.1	1						■					■													
	2						■					■													
	3						■					■													
	4											■													
3.2	1												■												
	2												■												
	3												■												
	4												■												
	5																								
3.3	1									■															
	2									■															
	3									■															
	4									■															
3.4	1									■															
	2														■										
	3									■					■										
	4																								
4.1	1																	■							
	2					■																			
	3					■																			
4.2	1					■																			
	2					■																			
	3					■																			
	4					■																			
	5					■																			
	6					■																			

Study Component		1	2	3	4	5	6	7	8	9	10	11	12	13	14	15	16	17	18	19	20	21	22	23	24
Element	PC																								
4.3	1																		■						
	2																		■						
	3																		■						
	4																		■						
	5																		■						
	6																								
4.4	1					■																			
	2					■																			
	3					■																			
	4					■																			
	5					■																			
	6					■																			
5.1	1								■																
	2							■																	
	3							■																	
	4								■																
	5								■																
	6								■																
5.2	1							■																	
	2							■																	
	3							■																	
	4							■																	
	5							■																	
5.3	1								■																
	2								■																
	3								■																
	4								■																
	5								■																
6.1	1																				■				
	2																					■			
	3																					■			
	4																					■			
6.2	1																					■			
	2																					■			
	3																					■			
	4																				■				
	5																								
6.3	1																						■		
	2																						■		
	3																						■		
	4																						■		
	5																						■		
7.1	1									■															
	2									■															
	3									■															
7.2	1									■															
	2									■															
	3									■															
	4									■															
7.3	1									■															
	2									■															
	3									■															
	4									■															
8.1	1																								■
	2																								■
	3																								■
	4																								■
8.2	1													■					■						■
	2																		■						■
	3													■											■
	4																								■
8.3	1																								■
	2																								■
	3																								■

Contents

PART 1 Knowledge Resource

Chapter 1
Information Technology

Chapter 2
Software

Chapter 3
Computer Files

Chapter 4
Types of Computers

Chapter 5
Computer Hardware

Chapter 6
Computer Systems Architecture

Chapter 7
Data Communications

Chapter 8
Computer Networks

Chapter 9
Information Flow in Organisations

Chapter 10
Data Handling Systems

Chapter 11
System Development

Chapter 12
The Feasibility Study

Chapter 13
Systems Analysis and Design

Chapter 14
Data Control and Security

Chapter 15
Privacy, Fraud and
Copyright

Chapter 16
Health and Safety

Chapter 17
Relational Database
Management Systems

Chapter 18
High-level Languages

Chapter 19
Modelling and Simulation

Chapter 20
Control Systems

PART 2 Skills Resource

Chapter 21
Word Processing

Chapter 22
Spreadsheets

Chapter 23
Spreadsheet Graphics

Chapter 24
Graphics

Chapter 25
Database Construction and Operation

Chapter 26
Local Area Network Operation

Chapter 27
Data Communications System Operation

Chapter 28
Automated Procedures

Chapter 29
Program Design

Chapter 30
Programming in Pascal

Chapter 31
Information Technology
Team Projects

Chapter 32
Developing Simple Control Systems

PART 3 Study Programme

Study Components

Case Studies

Index

Chapter 1

Information Technology

Introduction

Information technology is a term used to describe the range of products and systems which handle, manage, process and produce information, using computer and/or telecommunications technologies. When we use the word information, we do not just mean the kinds produced by administrative systems, such as payroll and accounting (*data handling systems*). We also mean the information used by a robot to assemble components and spot weld car bodies. Such dedicated systems (they only carry out a single or small range of specified tasks) also include those for car engine management, rocket control and washing machine operation. Information technology also covers, for example, enhanced telephone systems and cell phones, fax machines and modems (for transmitting computer data over telephone lines). Despite the fact that the term information technology covers a huge range of systems it is possible to identify some common features, which are described in the rest of this chapter. For ease of explanation, they mainly refer to *information* or *data handling* systems.

Information Systems

An *information system* is usually defined as a collection of people, equipment and procedures designed to collect, record, process, store, retrieve and present information. For example, the electricity board has a system which consists of:

- *people* to collect information by recording meter readings, to maintain the electricity supply to customers, to supervise and control the production of bills, to deal with customer queries, to maintain the generating equipment and so on;

- *equipment* in the form of generators, power lines and electricity meters in addition to computers;

- *procedures* for collecting and recording customers' electricity usage and for calculating, producing and distributing bills, for maintaining current electricity supplies and for providing new supplies, for dealing with customer queries and complaints, for producing employee pay slips etc.

The structure of an information technology system is illustrated in Figure 1.1. To use the electricity board example once more, information systems receive as inputs *raw data* such as meter readings, *transactions* such as payments and *messages* such as customer correspondence. These inputs are processed by the computer system or dealt with manually depending on the type of input. An *interface* provides the means by which people can actually use the system. For example, data in the form of customer meter readings must be collected and converted into a form that can be fed into the computer system so that bills can be generated. The procedures and devices used to do this are aspects of the electricity board's information system interface. Similarly, information provided by the system, customer bills or management reports for example, needs to be presented, by means of the interface, in a form understandable to the appropriate people. In addition to the computer system are numerous *manual procedures* which require the direct attention of the organisation's employees. For

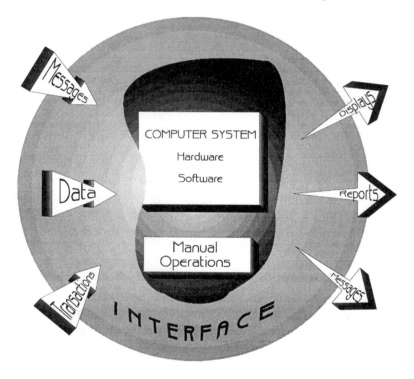

Figure 1.1. *The structure of an information system*

instance, meter readers must visit customers in order to record meter readings; other employees must deal with customer queries; and some must control, maintain and program the computer systems that the organisation uses.

Though only one component of an information system, the computer is of central importance; without it the information processing requirements of large and complex organisations would be almost impossible to deal with effectively. What we normally mean when we talk about a computer is a *digital computer system*, a collection of complex devices, (or *hardware)*, which, under the control of *computer programs* (or *software),* process data. Such is their remarkable usefulness, speed and versatility that computer systems now perform invaluable services in all areas of modern society. Sometimes their presence is not at all obvious: televisions, hi fi's, washing machines and even cars often contain very small, dedicated computers called *micro-processors*; other domestic computers, such as games consoles or PCs, are much more apparent; large service industry organisations, such as banks, depend on large, powerful computers called *mainframes* to perform the huge amount of data processing required.

Whatever their size or form, computers are essentially devices for performing high speed operations on data to produce some useful result. The data is usually provided by an input device such as a keyboard or some type of sensor, and the result is presented by an output device such as a printer or a digital display. Systems which involve the use of computers are called information systems, since the result, or output, from a computer system is information of some kind. A data processing computer system uses raw data, in the form of numbers or text, to produce data that we can understand more easily and use; in other words, such a system produces *information*.

Computer Hardware

The electronic and mechanical devices that together comprise the hardware of a computer system fall into a number of categories, as illustrated in Figure 1.2. The diagram shows a small selection of devices commonly used in personal computer systems (PCs), though similar devices are used in other types of computer systems such as those based on large, mainframe computers.

In general terms, the hardware of a computer system consists of a *central processing unit* (CPU) connected to a number of external devices collectively called *peripherals*. The CPU is the heart of the computer system and it contains an amount of fast memory in the form of ROM (*R*ead *O*nly *M*emory) and RAM (*R*andom *A*ccess *M*emory) for storing data and programs, a *control unit* which co-ordinates the flow of data within the computer system, and an *arithmetic logic unit* (ALU) which performs calculations of various types.

Peripheral devices are often grouped according to their functions as follows:

- input device such as a keyboard or a mouse
- output device such as a monitor or a printer
- data storage device such as a floppy disk drive

An input device, such as a keyboard, converts keystrokes representing letters or numbers into electrical signals which the CPU can 'understand'. Conversely, an output device such as a printer or a monitor converts electrical signals produced by the CPU into a form that we can readily understand. As a storage device, a floppy disk drive allows large amounts of data to be stored in a magnetic form (a bit like the way a domestic tape recorder stores music) thus; data is not lost when the computer is switched off, and the data can be read back into the computer at some later date. The CPU controls the operation of these peripheral devices according to instructions temporarily stored in its memory. Another of its main functions is to perform calculations on data also stored in its memory.

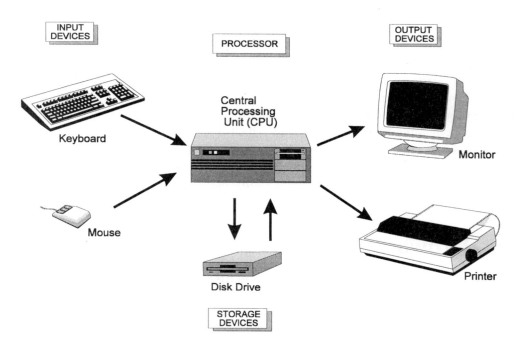

Figure 1.2. *A Computer System*

The total operation of the computer is controlled by a sequence of numeric codes called a *computer program*. The program, stored inside the computer system, and consisting of combinations of a set of very simple operations, or steps (sometimes hundreds of thousands of them), is executed at enormous speed (typically several million steps each second) so that the computer appears to be performing very complex, sophisticated operations. In fact, as we shall see, computers perform only very simple tasks, but do so without mistake (most of the time!) at great speed. Computer programs are created using *programming languages,* such as *BASIC* and *Pascal*. They allow computer programmers to express their requirements in a form closely related to the type of task being programmed. For example, *COBOL* is frequently used for data processing tasks, *FORTRAN* is used for mathematical and scientific applications, and *Prolog* is often used for writing knowledge-based systems.

Computer Software

Computer programs are often known as *software*, but the term software is usually connected with sets of programs covering fairly broad application areas. Examples of terms that occur frequently in computer-related texts are:

- system software;

- mathematical and scientific software;

- computer-aided design (CAD) software;

- applications software.

An information system will normally use a number of different types of software: the *operating system,* a component of system software, controls the overall operation of all the components of the computer system; *applications software* perform or aid commonly required tasks, such as word processing, accountancy and the calculation and production of customer bills; *database managers*, also a type of system software, allow databases to be created, modified and searched.

Computer Processing Methods

Another aspect of an information system is the manner in which the computer system is organised or used. Here are some common examples:

- *batch processing* - tasks are grouped and processed on the basis of some common requirement, usually at a predetermined time. For example, customer electricity bills and employee wages would usually be processed as separate batches.

- *interactive* - a number of users are connected to the computer via terminals consisting of a keyboard and a display screen. The computer shares its processing time between the separate users by giving each one in turn a time 'slice'. For instance, a research centre might have a number of researchers, each with his or her own terminal connected to a high-powered computer. Because it would be tedious for a researcher to have to wait in a sort of queue until his or her turn to gain access to the computer, a time-sharing system, in which each person would be given a small amount of processing time in a cycle, would be much more appropriate.

- *real-time* - again this is where a number of users might require simultaneous access to the computer, but each request for the use of the computer is acted upon with as little delay as possible. A typical example of this type of information system is for airline reservations in which a number of travel agents would be connected to a central computer providing access to the airline's flight database.

- *distributed systems* - these are systems which rely on computer *networks*. With increasing frequency, companies with a number of computers will connect them together to form computer networks in order to share hardware and software resources. In other words, both the hardware and software of the information system may be distributed over some large area rather than being located in a single room. *Local area networks* (*LANs*) connect computers that are close to each other (on the same site, for example) and *wide area networks* (*WANs*) connect together computers, that are distant from each other, by means of telephone lines or satellite links.

Chapter 2
Software

Introduction

Software is the general term used to describe the complete range of computer *programs* which will convert a general-purpose digital computer system into one capable of performing a large variety of specific functions. The term software implies its flexible, changeable nature, in contrast to the more permanent characteristics of the equipment or *hardware* which it controls. The particular type, or types, of software controlling the computer system at any particular moment will determine the manner in which the system functions. For example, a certain type of software might cause the computer to behave like a wordprocessor, another might allow it to keep company accounts or to perform stock control functions.

Computer Programs

At the level at which the computer operates, a program is simply a sequence of numeric codes stored in the memory. Each of these codes can be directly translated by the computer's electronic circuits into some simple operation such as transferring an item of data from the memory into the processor, or adding the contents of two memory locations and storing the result in a third area of memory. It may take many thousands of elementary operations to perform a task, but because each operation can be completed in a tiny fraction of a second, even complex calculations can be performed almost instantaneously. Computer programs, in this fundamental numerical form, are termed *machine code*, that is code which is directly 'understandable' by the computer's processing unit.

The numeric codes of the program are in binary form, or at least the electrical equivalent of binary, and they are stored in the *immediate access store,* that is the *memory*, of the computer. Because this memory is volatile (in other words, it is temporary and can be changed), it is possible to exchange the program currently held in the memory for another when the computer is required to perform a different function. For this reason the term *stored program* is often used to describe this fundamental characteristic of the modern digital computer.

The collection of numeric codes which directs the computer to perform such simple operations as those mentioned above is called the *instruction set*. A typical computer would have all of the following types of instructions and, in addition, other more specialised instructions:

- *Data transfer*. The movement of data within the processor or between the processor and the memory of the computer system.
- *Input-output*. The movement of data between the processor and external devices such as printers, disk drives, VDUs and keyboards.
- *Arithmetic and logic operations*. Such instructions direct the computer to perform arithmetic functions such as addition, subtraction, multiplication, division, increment, decrement, comparison, and logical operations such as AND, OR, NOT and EXCLUSIVE OR.
- *Transfer of control*. This directs the machine to skip one or more instructions or repeat a previous block of instructions.

Programming Languages

When it is considered that a typical program might contain tens of thousands of machine code instructions, it might seem that programming is a formidable task, well beyond the capabilities of all but the most determined and meticulous of computer professionals. Indeed, if machine code were the only computer language in use, it is extremely unlikely that society would today be experiencing such a widespread presence of computers in almost every aspect of industrial, commercial, domestic and social life. Fortunately for the computer industry, however, programming techniques have evolved along with advances in hardware. There is now a proliferation of programming languages designed to allow the programmer to concentrate most of his attention on solving the problem rather than on the tedious task of converting the solution to machine code form.

Computer programming languages fall into two main categories: *low-level languages* and *high-level languages*. Low-level languages are those that have a form which is closely related to the basic numeric codes required by a computer when executing a program. Machine code and *assembly languages* are examples of low-level languages. A program written in an assembly language is much more readable and understandable than its equivalent in machine code; the problem arises, however, that it is no longer directly executable by the computer. Because the computer is unable to decode instructions in this form they must first be converted into the equivalent machine code. An *assembler* is a machine code program which performs this function. It accepts an assembly language program as data and produces as output the required machine code program.

High-level languages are often termed 'procedure orientated' or 'programmer orientated' languages because they are designed for the benefit of the programmer interested in a certain type of application or procedure. For instance some languages, notably COBOL, are particularly suitable for business applications, others for scientific programming (FORTRAN, for instance) and others for educational use (Pascal and Logo, for example). A high-level language is almost entirely constructed of generalised sets of instructions or *statements*. A single statement, for instance, in a high-level language can specify the evaluation of a complex arithmetic expression requiring many machine code instructions. The translator required for such a language is therefore much more complex than an assembler since each statement will generally generate many machine code instructions. High-level language translators, or language processors as they are sometimes known, are of two main types, namely *interpreters* and *compilers*. These are described later in the chapter in a section which deals with high-level languages in some detail.

The majority of computer programs are written in high-level languages because they are relatively easy to write, test and modify, thus reducing the time and money required to produce reliable software. Programs which are required to operate at very high speeds are sometimes written in assembly languages which allow the programmer to optimise program code so that it executes as fast as possible, but the need for such programming is diminishing with the steady increase in computer operating speeds.

Categories of Software

The tree diagram in Figure 2.1 illustrates the different categories of software and, to some extent, their relationships to each other. This section begins by examining the distinction between *systems software* and *applications software*.

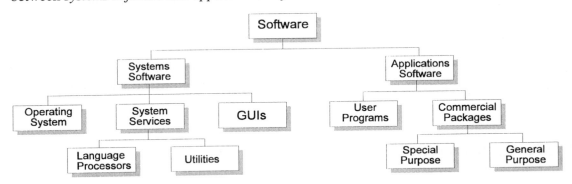

Figure 2.1. *Categories of software*

The term *systems software* covers the collection of programs usually supplied by the manufacturer of the computer. These programs protect the user from the enormous complexity of the computer system, and enable the computer to be used to maximum effect by a wide variety of people, many of whom will know very little about the inner workings of computers. Without systems software a modern digital computer would be virtually impossible to use; as computer hardware has evolved, so systems software has been forced to become more and more complex in order to make effective use of it.

Broadly speaking, systems software consists of three elements:

- those programs concerned with the internal control and co-ordination of all aspects of the computer system, namely the Operating System;
- a number of other programs providing various services to users. These services include translators for any languages supported by the system and utility programs such as program editors and other aids to programming.

- *graphical user interfaces* (GUIs) providing intuitive, easily learned methods for using microcomputer systems,

Applications software refers to programs which have some direct value to the organisation, and will normally include those programs for which the computer system was specifically purchased. For example, a mail order company might acquire a computer system initially for stock control and accounting purposes when its volume of business begins to make these functions too difficult to cope with by manual means.

Applications programs would be required to record and process customers' orders, update the stock file according to goods sent or received, make appropriate entries in the various accounts ledgers, etc.

Commercially produced applications software falls into two main categories:

- *special-purpose* packages, such as a company payroll program used to store employee details and generate details of pay for each individual employee.
- *general-purpose* packages which may be used for a wide variety of purposes. An example of a general-purpose package is a *word processor*, a program which allows the computer to be used somewhat like an electronic typewriter and is therefore appropriate to numerous processing tasks.

User programs are those written by people within the organisation for specific needs which cannot be satisfied by other sources of software. These program writers may be professional programmers employed by the organisation, or other casual users with programming expertise.

Systems Software

First generation computers are normally defined in hardware terms, in that they were constructed using valve technology, but another important characteristic of this generation of computers was the equally primitive software support provided for programmers and other users. Modern computers perform automatically many of the tasks that programmers in those days had to handle themselves: writing routines to control peripheral devices, allocating programs to main store, executing programs, checking peripheral devices for availability, as well as many other routine tasks.

In subsequent generations of computers, manufacturers started addressing themselves to the problem of improving the programming environment by providing standard programs for many routine tasks. Many of these routines became linked together under the control of a single program called the *executive*, *supervisor*, or *monitor*, whose function was to supervise the running of user programs and, in general, to control and co-ordinate the functioning of the whole computer system, both hardware and software. Early programs of this type have evolved into the sophisticated programs collectively known as *operating systems*.

Systems software has four important functions, namely to:

- facilitate the running of user programs;
- optimise the performance of the computer system;

- provide assistance with program development;
- simplify the use of the computer system.

The operating system takes care of the first two requirements, *system services* provide assistance with program development and *graphical user interfaces*(GUIs) simplify the use of the computer system.

Operating Systems

If a computer system is viewed as a set of resources, comprising elements of both hardware and software, then it is the job of the collection of programs known as the *operating system* to manage these resources as efficiently as possible. In so doing , the operating system acts as a buffer between the user and the complexities of the computer itself. One way of regarding the operating system is to think of it as a program which allows the user to deal with a simplified computer, but without losing any of the computational power of the machine. In this way the computer system becomes a virtual system, its enormous complexity hidden and controlled by the operating system and through which the user communicates with the real system.

The Main Functions of Operating Systems

Earlier it was stated that the function of an operating system is to manage the resources of the computer system. These resources generally fall into the following categories:

Central Processing Unit (CPU)
Since only one program can be executed at any one time, if the computer system is such that several users are allowed access to the system simultaneously, in other words a *multi-user* system, then access to the CPU must be carefully controlled and monitored. In a *timesharing* multi-user system each user is given a small time-slice of processor time before passing on to the next user in a continuously repeating sequence. Another common scheme is to assign priorities to users so that the system is able to determine which user should have control of the CPU next.

Memory
Programs (or parts of programs) must be loaded into the memory before they can be executed, and moved out of the memory when no longer required there. Storage space must be provided for data generated by programs, and provision must be made for the temporary storage of data, caused by data transfer operations involving devices such as printers and disk drives.

Input/Output (I/O) Devices
Programs will request the use of these devices during the course of their execution and in a multi-user system conflicts are bound to arise, when a device being utilised by one program is requested by another. The operating system will control allocation of I/O devices and attempt to resolve any conflicts which arise. It will also monitor the state of each I/O device and signal any faults detected.

Backing Store

Programs and data files will usually be held on mass storage devices such as magnetic disk and tape drives. The operating system will supervise data transfers to and from these devices and memory and deal with requests from programs for space on them.

Files

These may be regarded as a limited resource in the sense that several users may wish to share the same data file at the same time in multi-user systems. The operating system facilitates access to files and ensures restricted access to one program at any one time for those files which are to be written to.

Resource allocation is closely linked to one part of the operating system called the *scheduler*. The term *scheduling* refers to the question of when, in a multi-user system, should a new process be introduced into the system and in which order the processes should be run.

The above is by no means an exhaustive list of the functions of an operating system. Other functions include:

- interpretation of the command language by which operators can communicate with it;
- error handling. For example, detecting and reporting inoperative or malfunctioning peripherals;
- protection of data files and programs from corruption by other users;
- protection of data files and programs from unauthorised use;
- accounting and logging of the use of the computer resources.

MS-DOS Operating System

The Command Line and Shell Interfaces

All MS-DOS commands can be entered through the *command line* (C:/> prompt), or through the operating system's *shell*. Figure 2.2 illustrates the graphical nature of the shell interface. Instead of keying in a command, character by character, a user can select it from the range of menu options. An on-line, Help facility can be accessed as required. The shell is regarded as 'user friendly' and supports the use of a mouse. The command line tends to be used only by experienced users. Commands are available for the control of every aspect of the computer system's resources. The most commonly used commands are concerned with the management of *file storage* space and the running of *applications*. The functions of some of these commands are described in this chapter. Where example commands are given, they relate to the use of the C:/> prompt, rather than the operating system's shell. All operating system commands are dealt with by the *command line interpreter*. Some commands are *memory resident* or *internal* and are continually available once MS-DOS has been loaded. Other, less frequently used commands, are called from disk as required. Apart from the management of disk space, MS-DOS provides facilities for *optimising* the use of *main memory* and this topic is briefly examined at the end of the chapter.

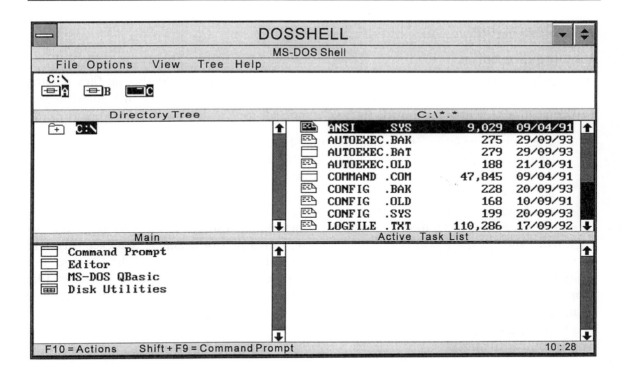

Figure 2.2. *The DOS shell window*

File Management Facilities

Each *file name* is held in a *directory* together with its size (expressed in bytes) and the date and time it was created or last modified (the previous figure shows a typical directory listing). Most microcomputer systems keep track of the current date and time (even when the machine is switched off) with CMOS memory (Chapter 5). Directories are used to divide disk space into a number of user or application areas. A floppy disk with 720Kb (kilobytes) capacity may contain, say, 30 or 40 files at most, so it is quite easy for a user to scan a single directory in the search a particular file name. A hard disk, with a capacity of hundreds of megabytes, may contain thousands of files and managing them all in a single directory is virtually impossible. For this reason, MS-DOS allows the creation of *sub-directories* to which groups of files can be assigned. When the operating system's attention is directed to a particular directory, it is known as the *current* or *working* directory. MS-DOS keeps track of files on disk with the use of a *file allocation table* (FAT). When a disk is formatted, MS-DOS initially sets up two system areas, one for the FAT and the other for the main or *root* directory. The FAT has an entry for each *cluster* (a cluster is group of sectors). Clusters containing only part of a file have a FAT entry which points to the next cluster relating to that file, or, if it is the last part of a file, a special indicator. Thus, MS-DOS can find a complete file by reference to the pointers in each cluster containing a part of it. Empty clusters have a zero entry in the FAT.

File Operations

Viewing directories

As explained earlier, it is essential to organise file storage space and to allocate files relating to a single application into, at least, one separate sub-directory. To view the contents of a particular directory may require the entry of commands to:

- select the *drive letter*. If a system has a hard disk and two floppy disk drives, these are labelled as C, A and B, respectively. Sometimes, if the hard disk is partitioned into several areas (or there are other drives attached to the system), additional drive letters may be used - D, E, F and so on.
- switch to the working directory.

The previous figures show the C:/> and DOS shell views of drives and directories. Note that each row details, from left to right, the *file name*, *extension* (for example, autoexec.bat), size of file in bytes and the date it was last modified. The file extension indicates the file type. For example, BAT indicates a *batch* file (see later) and EXE an *executable program* file. Applications packages add their own file extension to any file created with the package. For example, if a user creates a worksheet with the Excel package and names it `BUDGET`, the file will appear in the directory as BUDGET.XLS. The details of a named file can also be viewed by the command

```
dir a:budget.xls
```

Using a Wild Card

A wild card allows the user to broaden the scope of a command. For example, to display details of files beginning with the file name 'TEST', on drive B, could be entered as

```
dir b:test*
```

The wild card can be used with some other commands, including the COPY command, which is explained in the next section.

Other File and Disk Commands

- *erase* - to remove a named file (or, using the wild card, group of files) from disk. DEL has the same effect.
- *undelete*. Available with MS-DOS 5.0 (and later versions) this command recovers a file which has been accidentally deleted. Deleted files are only marked as such and are recoverable with this command, unless MS-DOS has subsequently used the area for another file. The command cannot be used if the directory which contained the deleted file has been removed (see later).
- *copy* - to a named file or group of files to another disk and/or directory.
- *attrib* - protects a file by setting it to 'read only'. For example, `attrib +r budget.xls` prevents any write operation of the named file (`attrib -r budget.xls` removes the protection).
- *comp* - compares the contents of two files or two groups of files.

- *diskcomp* - compares the contents of two disks on a track-by-track basis, rather than by reference to particular files.
- *diskcopy* - allows the copying of a complete disk onto another. It is generally used to carry out security backups.
- *format* - formats the disk in the specified drive. All new disks must be formatted to accept MS-DOS files before use (a similar command exists in all operating systems). The command initialises the directory and file allocation tables on disk. It destroys any existing files as the complete disk contents are wiped. File protection attributes provide no protection. The only protection against accidental formatting of diskettes is to use the appropriate write protection mechanism. Hard disks cannot be write-protected but more recent versions of MS-DOS provide more user warnings if the specified drive contains the hard disk. The accidental wiping of a 200 megabyte hard disk could be catastrophic.
- *print* - initiates a primitive form of 'spooling' and prints a named text file on the attached printer while other commands are processed.
- *recover* - recovers a file or entire disk containing some 'bad' or corrupted sectors. The command causes MS-DOS to read the file sector by sector and skips the bad sectors, marking them to ensure that they are not used again. Thus, the uncorrupted parts of a file can be recovered.
- *type* - displays the contents of a file on screen. For example, `type a:test.dat`, displays the contents of the file named `test.dat` and stored on drive `A:\>`. A wild card cannot be used with this command.

Directory Creation and Handling

If a computer is used by more than one user, or a single user is working on a number of different projects, it is advisable to organise files accordingly into different directories. This is similar to separating manual files by placing them into different drawers or sections of a filing cabinet. Although it may be common practice to maintain all files in the *root directory* of a floppy disk, it is virtually essential, if any proper control is to be maintained, to organise files on hard disk into different directories. A user has to decide what logical divisions can be made, to divide files into groups. For example, there may be one directory for a spreadsheet program, another for the word processing program and another for the accounts programs. Each of these directories may contain further sub-directories for the work files associated with each of the applications programs. Organising files in this way makes use of what is termed a *multi-level directory structure*. This topic of creating and handling directories is dealt with in Chapter 26.

Batch File - an Automated Procedure

Batch files are special files used for the automatic execution of regularly used sequences of commands (see also Automated Procedures in Chapter 28). Any valid sequence of commands can be included and the operating system will execute them in the same way as if they had been entered one at a time from the keyboard. To be recognised by the operating system as a batch file, MS-DOS requires the filename extension .BAT to be used. To execute a batch file, only the filename, without the extension .BAT, is typed. One particular type of batch file called *autoexec.bat* has a special significance which is explained later in this section.

Creating a Batch File

A batch file is created with a text editor. The sequence of commands shown below could form a batch file to run the Lotus 123 spreadsheet.

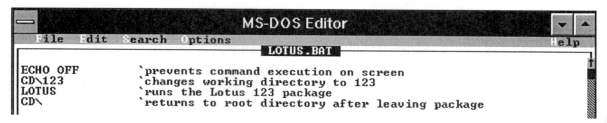

It is assumed that the program files are held in a directory called 123. If the batch file were created with the name *lotus.bat,* then the user would simply type 'lotus' at the keyboard, to execute the commands.

Batch File Example - File Copying

A batch file called `movfile.bat` could also be used to automate a file copying operation. The following sequence of commands creates a new directory called `second`, copies a file `bumph.dat` from its location in the directory called `first`, deletes the original and then displays the contents of directory `second` (which now contains `bumph.dat`). The word `rem` means remark or comment and is used to document the file; `rem` is ignored by MS-DOS.

```
rem prevents command execution of screen
@echo off
rem creates the new directory
md c:\second
rem copies the bumph.dat file to the new directory
copy c:\first\bumph.dat c:\second
rem deletes the original file
erase c:\first\bumph.dat
rem displays the contents of the new directory
dir c:\second
rem displays the message shown
echo Here is the file in the new directory
```

Figure 2.3 *Batch file to copy a specific file*

The drawback of the batch file shown in Figure 2.3, is that it only deals with two particular directories and one named file. MS-DOS allows *replaceable parameters* to be entered with the batch file name. This means that movfile.bat can be modified to allow the user to specify directory names and filenames before the batch file is executed. The modified commands are shown in Figure 2.4. The replaceable parameters are represented by %1 and %2.

If the command, `movfile c:\second c:\first\bumph.dat`, is entered, MS-DOS executes the batch file called `movfile` and replaces %1 with `c:\second` and %2 with c:\first\bumph.dat. If you trace these replacements through the command sequence in Figure 2.4, you will see that its effect is the same as that in Figure 2.3. Of course, you can enter other parameters to use the batch file for any new directory and file or files to be moved to it. For example, movfile c:\newplace c:\oldplace*.doc would move a set of files, with the same file extension .doc, from the existing directory oldplace to the new directory newplace.

```
echo off
md %1
copy %2 %1
erase %2
dir %2
echo Contents of new directory
```

Figure 2.4. *Batch file with replaceable parameters*

Creating a Menu with Batch Files

Menu Example 1

The examples which follow are designed to allow the user to run one of three applications, through a simple menu display, shown in Figure 2.5.

```
rem prevents command execution on screen
@echo off
rem clears the screen
cls
rem displays menu text on screen
echo                     Applications Menu
echo                     * * * * * * * * * * * * * * * *
rem displays blank line
echo.
echo                 W. Word Processor
echo                 S. Spreadsheet
echo                 D. Database
echo                 Q. Quit
echo.
Rem displays message and waits for entry of W, S, D or Q
prompt                  Type W, S, D, or Q and then ENTER:
rem letter runs batch file W.BAT, S.BAT, D.BAT or Q.BAT.
```

Figure 2.5. *Batch file called* appsmenu.bat

Figure 2.5 is a batch file named appsmenu.bat, which prompts for the entry of a letter, which is identified with one of the menu choices. The batch file has to be executed with a replaceable parameter, as appsmenu %1.

When the user enters one of the letters in the menu, the replaceable parameter (%1) takes this value. There are four other batch files, called w.bat, s.bat, d.bat and q.bat. Depending on which letter is entered, on of these batch files is executed. These batch files are shown in Figures 2.6 to 2.9.

```
@echo off
cls
rem changes the directory to the user's work area
cd\workfile\wpwork
rem gives the path to run the pcwrite word processor
c:\wp\pcwrite
rem changes the directory back to the root
cd\
rem runs the menu batch file again
appsmenu
```

Figure 2.6. *Batch file* **w.bat**

```
@echo off
cls
cd\workfile\sswork
c:\ss\easycalc
cd\
appsmenu
```

Figure 2.7. *Batch file* s.bat

```
@echo off
cls
cd\workfile\dbwork
c:\db\dbase
cd\
appsmenu
```

Figure 2.8. *Batch file* **d.bat**

```
rem sets the MS-DOS command prompt to current
rem drive letter,with > sign (for example, C:\>)
prompt $p$g
cls
```

Figure 2.9. *Batch file* q.bat

As you can see from Figure 2.6, which is the batch file for the word processor option, the sequence of commands, swaps to the user's directory and then executes the word processing program (the path is provided to its directory). When the user quits the word processor, the commands to change back to the root directory and runs appsmenu.bat again. The batch files for the spreadsheet and database options (Figures 2.7 and 2.8) operate in a similar manner. The q.bat file in Figure 2.9 returns the user to the operating system prompt.

Menu Example 2

The previous menu example involved the use of five batch files, but the batch files w.bat, s.bat, d.bat and q.bat can be combined by using if and goto commands. Figure 2.10 shows the modified appsmenu.bat file, this time with numbered menu items. Another batch file choice.bat is executed when the user responds to the prompt.

```
@echo off
cls
echo                        Applications Menu
echo                        * * * * * * * * * * * * * * * *
echo.
echo                        1. Word Processor
echo                        2. Spreadsheet
echo                        3. Database
echo                        4. Quit
echo.
echo     Enter "choice", followed by 1, 2, 3, or 4
echo     For example, "choice 3", at the ? prompt.
rem  response  executes  the  choice.bat  file  with  a
replaceable
rem parameter (% takes a value of 1, 2, 3, or 4)
prompt   ?:
```

Figure 2.10. *Batch file* **appsmenu.bat** *for menu example 2*

As you can see from Figure 2.10, the user has to enter the word "choice" followed by 1, 2, 3, or 4, for example, choice 3 executes the choice.bat file with the replaceable parameter having a value of 3. Figure 2.11 shows the choice.bat file.

```
@echo off
rem if commands used to test value of response entered
rem in appsmenu.bat and branch to appropriate command
if "%1"=="1" goto wordproc
if "%1"=="2" goto sprdshet
if "%1"=="3" goto database
if "%1"=="4" goto baktodos
rem calls a batch file to deal with an invalid entry
rem and then returns to next command in this file
call notvalid
rem if replaceable parameter has value of "1"
rem jump to here and execute word processing option
:wordproc
```

```
cd\workfile\wpwork
c:\wp\pcwrite
rem show menu again
goto showmenu
rem jump to here if "2" entered
:sprdshet
cd\workfile\sswork
c:\ss\easycalc
goto showmenu
rem jump to here if "3" entered
:database
cd\workfile\dbwork
c:\db\dbase
rem jumps here after quitting option 1, 2, or 3
:showmenu
cd\
appmenu2
rem jump to here if "4" entered
:baktodos
cd\
prompt $p$g
cls
```

Figure 2.11. *Batch file* `choice.bat`

The remarks in Figure 2.11 explain its operation. Another batch file `notvalid.bat` is called if the user follows the word "choice" with a value other than 1, 2, 3, or 4. The batch file is shown in Figure 2.12.

```
@echo off
cls
echo     Not a valid choice
rem displays "Press any key when ready" and waits
rem until user taps a key
pause
```

Figure 2.12. *Batch file* `notvalid.bat`, *to deal with an invalid response*

As you can see, `notvalid.bat` simply displays an error message and then, with the pause command displays the message "Press any key when ready" and waits for the user to respond. Because the batch file is executed from a `call` command in `choice.bat`, it acts as a subprogram and returns to execute the next command in `choice.bat`.

The Function of Autoexec.bat Files

An autoexec.bat file can be used to customise a computer for a particular purpose at system 'start up'. Thus, for example, a computer which is used for one particular package can be automated to load that package when MS-DOS is started. Because the autoexec.bat file is executed when the operating system is first loaded, it must reside in the root directory.

The automatic starting of the Windows GUI (see later) provides a popular example of such customisation. This is because users of the GUI tend to use software packages which are controlled by it. Similarly, the appsmenu.bat could be included to automatically display the menu in Menu Examples 1 and 2. Autoexec.bat files can include numerous, advanced command sequences, but a simple example is provided in Figure 2.13.

```
echo off
rem loads Uk keyboard driver
keyb uk
rem provides path to DOS commands and programs
path c:\dos;c:\word
rem loads mouse driver
mouse
rem opens the MS-DOS shell
dosshell
```

Figure 2.13. *An example* `autoexec.bat` *file*

Configuring a System with the Config.sys File

The *config.sys* file is also stored in the root directory and is automatically executed when the system is switched on. It contains commands which configure the computer system for particular installation requirements. Figure 2.14 shows a sample config.sys file.

```
rem identifies the mouse driver
device=c:\mouse\mouse.sys
rem sets number of files which can be open at any one
rem time. Normal set-up allows only 8. An application
rem which requires more is likely to indicate the fact.
files =20
rem these are disk buffers in which MS-DOS can hold data
rem being read from or written to disk, when the amount
rem of data is not an exact multiple of sector size. Word
rem processors which use the disk intensively perform
rem better with 10 to 20 buffers. If a large number of
rem directories is created, then 20 to 30 buffers
rem may improve performance.
Buffers=20
rem this selects the time, date and currency format.
rem The code 044 is for the UK.
Country=044
```

Figure 2.14. *Sample* `config.sys` *file*

Multi-tasking Operating Systems

Multi-tasking is a technique which allows a computer to carry out tasks in a similar fashion to a human worker. For example, the Financial Director of a business may be composing a financial report which requires the use of a dictaphone, occasional reference to various financial summaries and telephone calls to other executive staff in the business. Although these tasks are not carried on at exactly the same time, the director is periodically switching from one to another, as they all contribute to the completion of the financial report. At certain times, an unrelated task may have to be completed, for example, the answering of a brief query from a member of staff. This does not require complete abandonment of the other tasks in hand and the main work continues from the point at which it was left. Computer multi-tasking requires that the system can accommodate several tasks in memory at one time and that these tasks can be run concurrently, by rapidly switching the processor's attention between them.

The fact that almost all office tasks can benefit from computerisation puts an increased demand on computer resources which may be satisfied by a *multi-user* system. This can be achieved with a local area network (LAN). The hardware and software requirements for LAN construction are described in Chapters 8 and 26.

This section looks at two operating systems which provide a multi-tasking environment for small business computer systems:

- OS/2 (Operating System/2) Version 2.1

- Windows NT (New Technology) Version 3.1

OS/2 Version 2.1

OS/2 Version 1.0 was announced by IBM and Microsoft in April 1987, as a multi-tasking operating system. Since then the collaboration between these two companies has broken down and Microsoft has produced its highly successful Windows GUI (see later). Numerous improvements have been made to the original version of OS/2, but it is still failing to make any significant impression in the PC software market. In an effort to take an increased share of this market, IBM has ensured that OS/2 is able to run applications developed for MS-DOS and Windows, as well as OS/2 itself.

Workplace Shell - the OS/2 GUI

Workplace Shell has the main features of a conventional GUI, with windows that can be moved and re-sized, scroll bars (for viewing different areas of work within the available window), dialogue boxes, etc. Unlike the Windows GUI (see later), it does not allocate file management to a separate component. Instead, users are encouraged to view data files as the entry point for applications (rather than the other way around). Workplace Shell can be described as *object orientated*. An object can be a program, a data file, a folder (directory) or device (such as a printer). When an object is selected, a pop-up menu offers options appropriate to the object. For example, a program object menu includes a 'run' option.

Similarly, a data file object provides options concerning, for example, the printing or copying of the file. When running Microsoft Windows applications, the desktop is presented accordingly, with the Program Manager window.

32-bit Applications

For brevity, OS/2 Version 2.1 is referred to simply as OS/2. As a 32-bit operating system, OS/2 can take full advantage of the current 32-bit processors and 32-bit software. Handling data in 32-bit units, rather than 16 bits at a time, contributes to quicker system performance. To ensure its compatibility with a huge section of the PC software market, OS/2 can run 16-bit software; virtually all MS-DOS and a few Windows applications are designed to retain backward compatibility with the 16-bit 80286 processor. Windows 3.1 also runs 32-bit applications (using an i386, or later, processor), when it is operating in *enhanced mode*.

Multi-tasking

OS/2 allocates a separate, private, area of memory to each application. It also provides facilities to protect one application from the activities of another. Device drivers (disk controllers, screen and printer drivers) operate at a higher level of privilege within memory, because they have to remain accessible to all current applications.

OS/2 uses *pre-emptive* multi-tasking. This means that the operating system controls the amount of processor time each application receives, before switching activity to one of the others. The amount of time received by a task, depends on its urgency (the user can specify priorities). OS/2 can *multi-thread* separate processes; for example, it can a initiate the printing of a document by a word processor and then immediately return to its previous task. The user can continue working on another task, while the document is being printed in the background.

File Management

OS/2 offers two file management systems. Users have to choose which one to install. The choice depends largely on the capacity of the drive and whether or not MS-DOS applications are to be used.

- an enhanced File Allocation Table (FAT) system, which can be read by MS-DOS;

- a High Performance File System (HPFS).

The HPFS is completely different from the FAT system and is designed to manage, more effectively, the higher capacity (measured in gigabytes) hard drives. HPFS file names can be up to 254 characters in length (compared with the 8 permitted by MS-DOS). Both filing systems allow up to 64Kb of *attribute data* to be attached to each file; the data can comprise text and images. This permits extensive labelling of a file, describing its contents and perhaps associations with other files or applications. Effectively, this means that longer file names can also be used with the enhanced FAT system.

Both systems (like Windows 3.1) support *write caching* (see Chapter 6), which means that writing to disk can be delayed if the processors is busy. The mechanism can be disabled, as there is a small risk that data may be lost (while it waits in the cache memory) if there is a sudden power cut.

Windows NT

Microsoft's Windows NT operating system first became available in September 1993. It is a 32-bit multi-tasking operating system and competes directly with OS/2. Its hardware requirements are greater than those needed for the Windows 3.1 GUI and it is not seen as a replacement for it. Windows NT needs a minimum of 12Mb of main memory and 75Mb of free disk space. Machines based on RISC processors (Chapter 6) require 16Mb of main memory and 92Mb free disk space to run Windows NT. The operating system includes facilities for networking, enabling machines to be used as print and file *servers* (Chapter 26).

There are three main parts to Windows NT:

- NT *executive*, which is the operating system and controls the hardware;

- Win32 sub-system, which the NT executive runs as an application. Win32 provides the Windows GUI;

- MS-DOS, OS/2 and Portable UNIX sub-systems, which allows the running of software written for these operating systems. Concerning OS/2, only applications written for the character-based interface are supported. Software written for Windows 3.1 (see earlier) will also run under Windows NT. These sub-systems can only operate through the Win32 sub-system.

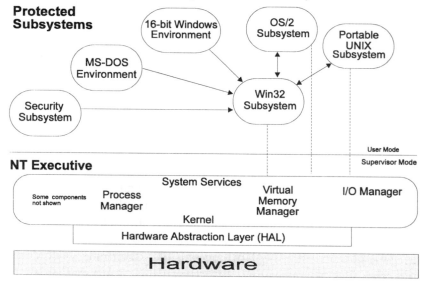

Figure 2.15. *Windows NT*

Figure 2.15 illustrates the main components in the structure and their relationship one another and to the hardware.

- The Virtual Memory Manager controls the allocation of main memory to applications and ensures that each is protected from other processes. When there is insufficient main memory space, some memory contents are paged to disk (*virtual memory*) until room becomes available (when they are paged back in). This protection does not apply to Windows 3.1 applications (run through the Windows sub-system) which can, at times, clash for memory space and crash.

- The Process Manager controls the multi-tasking process. Windows NT (like OS/2) can carry out 'fine grained' multi-tasking. This enables the concurrent processing of tasks within the same application. For example, new records could be entered into a database, while a database sort is being executed in the background.

- The Input/Output Manager handles file reading and writing operations, at the physical machine level. It provides a File Allocation Table (FAT) system, compatible with the MS-DOS system and a High Performance File System (HPFS) to handle OS/2 applications. NT's own file system (NTFS) allows the use of long file names and the storage of files up to 17 billion gigabytes in size.

- The *kernel* handles signals from the hardware, indicating conditions such as, the completion of data transfer through a communications port (Chapter 27).

Portability

The MS-DOS and OS/2 operating systems are designed to make particular use of the Intel series of processors (Chapter 6). Apart from the kernel, the Windows NT operating system does not relate specifically to the architecture of any particular processor; to some extent it is 'processor independent' and can be used on non-Intel processor machines. This independence is achieved with the use of a Hardware Abstraction Layer (HAL), which comes between the hardware and the NT Executive.

System Services

Often a manufacturer will provide a number of programs designed specifically for program or application development. Three such aids are:

Language Processors

These are computer programs designed to convert high-level language programs into machine code, that is, into a form directly usable by a computer. Common types of language processors are *compilers* and *interpreters* which are described in the chapter on high-level languages.

Utility Programs

As part of the systems software provided with a computer system there are a number of utility programs specifically designed to aid program development and testing. These include:

Editors. These permit the creation and modification of source programs and data files. The facilities offered by these programs usually include such things as character, word and line insertion and deletion, automatic line numbering, line tabulation for languages which require program instructions to be spaced in a specific manner, the storage and retrieval of files from backing storage, and the printing of programs or other files.

Debugging aids. Programs in which the appropriate translator can find no fault will often contain errors in logic, known as 'bugs', which only become apparent when the program is run, producing results which are contrary to expectations, or even causing the computer to cease functioning. These bugs are often very difficult to detect and may lead to long delays in the implementation of the program. Debugging aids help programmers to isolate and identify the cause of bugs.

File Managers. These simplify and facilitate a number of operations connected with program development and maintenance such as:

- keeping backup copies of important files;
- deleting files and creating space for new ones;
- merging files;
- providing details of current files held on backing storage;
- sorting file names into specified orders.

Without the help of special utility programs, operations such as those described above could be extremely time-consuming and consequently expensive.

Graphical User Interfaces(GUIs)

The vast majority of microcomputer users are interested merely in using a computer as a tool, without any real interest in the technical details of its operation. A typical user will probably want to run one or more common general-purpose applications, organise files into directories, delete files and format disks. Though the operating system will provide these services, the user needs to have a certain amount of technical knowledge to perform these tasks. Graphical

user interfaces (or GUIs, pronounced *Gooeys*) provide a more intuitive means of performing common tasks. They usually make use of a pointing device, typically a *mouse* (see Chapter 5), by means of which a *pointer* is moved around the monitor screen on which small pictures (or *icons*) are displayed. These icons represent, among other things, programs which can be run by moving the mouse pointer over the icon and then clicking one of the buttons on the mouse. Applications run in their own self-contained areas called *windows*. In addition, it is usually possible to activate *pull-down menus* which provide access to standard functions.

When a GUI uses **W**indows, **I**cons, **M**ouse, **P**ointers and **P**ull-down menus, it is referred to as a WIMP environment. Figure 2.16 shows an example of a GUI produced by Microsoft, namely, Microsoft Windows.

Three windows are shown in the figure:

1. A window running a Program Manager containing icons representing available applications programs. An application is run by positioning the pointer over the application's icon and clicking one of the mouse buttons, a very simple, easily remembered operation. This is really a utility window rather than an application.
2. A window running CorelDRAW, a graphic design program.
3. A window running the word processor, Microsoft Word for Windows.

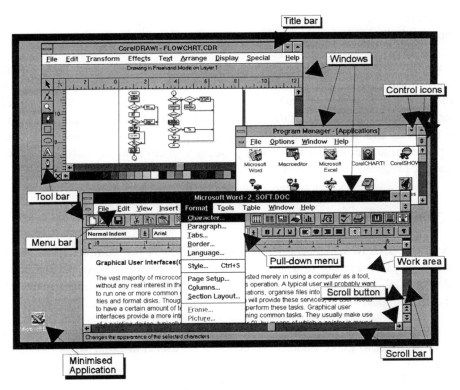

Figure 2.16. *Windows Environment*

Only Microsoft Word, in the window with the black title bar, is active, that is, currently in use. Either of the other two can be made the active window by merely positioning the pointer in the window and clicking the mouse. Thus it is possible to be working on several applications at the same time, switching from one to the other very quickly and with minimum effort.

All such windows, no matter what the application, have a number of common features, including:

- a title bar with the name of the particular application and the name of the document being edited or created by that application;
- a menu bar containing the names of a number of pull-down menus;
- horizontal and vertical scroll bars providing access to parts of the document not shown in the window;
- a number of control icons for sizing, maximising (making the current window occupy the whole screen), minimising (reducing the window to an icon such as that shown in the bottom left-hand corner of Figure 2.16) and closing the window;
- a tool bar containing icons which, when selected, perform frequently required tasks, such as saving documents to disk or printing documents as in the case of Word for Windows, or drawing tools in the case of CorelDRAW.
- a help facility accessed from the menu bar and providing detailed information on the operation of all aspects of the application on the screen while the application is running.

The major advantage of applications having these common features is that, having learned how one application operates, it is possible to use much of the same knowledge with other windows applications, thus significantly reducing the time required to become proficient in the use of unfamiliar applications. In addition, numerical, textual and graphical data can be freely transferred between the applications. For example, it is possible to design a diagram in a graphics application and embed it in a word processor document, or include a table produced by a spreadsheet program in a document.

Applications Software

An analysis of the uses to which companies and individuals put computers would reveal that the same types of tasks appear time and time again. Many organisations use computers for payroll calculations, others to perform stock control functions, accounting procedures, management information tasks and numerous other common functions.

These types of programs are classed as *applications software*, software which is applied to practical tasks in order to make them more efficient or useful in other ways. Systems software is merely there to support the running, development and maintenance of applications software.

An organisation wishing to implement one of these tasks (or any other vital to its efficient operation) on a computer has several alternatives:

- Ask a software house, that is, a company specialising in the production of software, to take on the task of writing a specific program for the organisation's needs.
- Use its own programming staff to produce the software 'in house'.
- Buy a commercially available program 'off the shelf' and hope that it already fulfils, or can be modified to fulfil, the organisation's requirements.
- Buy a general purpose program, such as a database or spreadsheet package, that has the potential to perform the required functions.

The final choice will depend on such factors as the urgency of the requirements, financial constraints, size of the company and the equipment available. It is beyond the scope of this chapter to enter into a discussion regarding either the strategy for making such a decision or to investigate specific items of software available for specific applications but, with the immense and growing, popularity of these programs, particularly for personal microcomputer systems, it is worth looking in more detail at general-purpose packages. Note that the **use** of typical general-purpose packages is addressed in the skills section of this book; here we look at the general characteristics of this category of software.

General Purpose Packages for Microcomputers

Discussion of this class of software will be restricted here to the following headings, though they are not intended to represent an exhaustive of all the categories of general purpose packages which are available:

- Word processors
- Spreadsheets
- Databases
- Graphics packages, including desktop publishing(DTP), business graphics, graphic design and computer aided drawing(CAD)
- Knowledge-based systems
- Hypertext systems

What characterises these software packages is that they have been designed to be very flexible and applicable to a wide range of different tasks. For instance, a spreadsheet can be used as easily for simple accountancy procedures as for stock control; a database can be used with equal facility to store information on technical papers from journals, stock item details or personnel details for payroll purposes. In fact, particularly in respect of modern personal computer software, the trend is for general-purpose packages to do more and more. For example, recent word processors, such as Microsoft's *Word for Windows* and *WordPerfect*, include facilities for creating or embedding drawings, graphs and spreadsheets, in addition to the normal functions associated with a word processor; the graphic design package *CorelDRAW!*, includes some word processing functions and graph drawing functions; the spreadsheet *Excel* has a number of facilities normally associated with database packages. Fierce market competition has resulted in the major software houses continually improving on their last version of a piece of software, attempting to outdo their competitors.

The suitability of a particular general-purpose package for a specific application will be largely dependent on the particular characteristics of the package. Though the general facilities afforded, for instance, by different database packages may be roughly equivalent, each manufacturer will adopt its own style of presentation and will provide certain services not offered by its competitors. A prospective buyer should have a clear idea of the main uses for which the package is to be purchased right at the outset, because some packages may be much more suitable than others.

Some advantages of general-purpose software compared to other forms of applications software are as follows:

- Because large numbers of the package are sold, prices are relatively low.
- They are appropriate to a wide variety of applications.
- As they already have been thoroughly tested, they provide a great reduction in the time and costs necessary for development and testing.
- They are suitable for people with little or no computing experience.
- They are very easy to use.
- Most packages of this type are provided with extensive documentation.

However, there are also a number of disadvantages:

- Sometimes the package will allow only a clumsy solution to the task in question.
- The user must still develop the application in the case of a spreadsheet or database for example. This requires a thorough knowledge of the capabilities of the package, which are frequently extensive, and how to make the best use of them.
- The user will need to provide his own documentation for the particular application for which the package has been tailored.
- Unless the software is used regularly, it is easy to forget the correct command sequences to operate the package, particularly for people inexperienced in the use of computer software of this type.
- The user must take responsibility for his own security measures to ensure that vital data is not lost, or to prevent unauthorised personnel gaining access to the data.

Word processors

The word processor performs much the same function as a typewriter, but it offers a large number of very useful additional features. Basically, a word processor is a computer with a keyboard for entering text, a monitor for display purposes, one or more disk drives for storage of files produced by applications and a printer to provide the permanent output on paper. A word processor is really nothing more than a computer system with a special piece of software to make it perform the required word processing functions; some such systems have hardware configurations specifically for the purpose (such as special keyboards and letter-quality printers) but the majority are merely the result of obtaining an appropriate word processor application package.

Word processors can be used to produce:

- letters
- legal documents
- booklets
- articles
- mailing lists

and in fact any type of textual material.

Here are some of the advantages they have over ordinary typewriters:

- typing errors can be corrected before printing the final version;
- the availability of such automatic features as page numbering, the placing of page headers and footers and word/line counting;
- whole document editing, such as replacing every incidence of a certain combination of characters with another set of characters. For instance, replacing each occurrence of the name 'Mr. Smith' by 'Mrs. Jones';
- printing multiple copies all to the same high quality;
- documents can be saved and printed out at some later date without any additional effort.

However, word processors do have some drawbacks. For instance, prolonged viewing of display monitors can produce eyestrain. They are generally considerably more expensive than good typewriters, and to be used properly, a certain amount of special training is required.

On the whole, word processors are now firmly established in the so-called 'electronic office' and there is no reason to suppose that their use will not continue to expand.

Features of Word Processors

A typical word processing package will provide most of the following facilities:

Word Wrap

As text is typed, a word is moved automatically to the start of a new line if there is insufficient room for it at the right-hand margin. With this facility, the only time that the <Enter> key needs to be pressed, to move the cursor to the beginning of a new line, is at the end of paragraphs or when a blank line is required.

Scrolling

Once the bottom of the screen is reached during text entry, the top of the text moves, line by line, up out of view as each new line of text is entered. This ensures that the line being entered is always visible on screen. The directional arrow keys on a standard keyboard allow scrolling to be carried out at will to view various parts of the document.

Deletion

This facility allows the deletion of characters, words, lines or complete blocks of text.

Insertion

This is concerned with the insertion of single letters or a block of text.

Block Marking

This allows the marking or highlighting of text to be dealt with separately from the rest of the document. The marked text, often shown by changing its colour, may be moved, deleted, copied or displayed in a different style - in italics or bold print, for example.

Text Movement or Copying

The user may need to move or copy a marked block of text to a different part of the document. A *cut and paste* system is often used for these operations: marked text is placed on a 'clipboard', from which it subsequently can be copied, or *pasted*, to another part of the document.

Tabulation

Tabulation markers can be set to allow the cursor to be moved directly to column positions with the use of the TAB key. This is useful when text or figures are to be presented in columns.

Formatting

Text can be *aligned left*, with a straight left margin and a ragged right margin:

```
XXXX XXX XXXXX X XXXX XXXXXXXXXX XXX XXXXXXX XXXX XXXXXXX XXX
XXXXXX XX XXXXXXX X XXXXX XXXXXXX XX XXXX X XXX XXXXXXXXXXX XXX
XXX XXXXXXX X XXXXXXX XXX XXXXX XXXXX X XXXX X XX XXXXXX X
XXXXXXXXXXXXXX XXX XXXXXXX XX XXXXXX XXX XXXXXX XXXX
XXXXXXXXX XXXX XXXXX XXX X XXXXXXXXXX XXXXXX XXX XXXXXXXXX XX
XXXXXXXXXXXXXX XXXX X.
```

or it can be *justified* so that it has a straight left and right margin:

```
XXXX XXX XXXXX X XXXX XXXXXXXXXX XXX XXXXXXX XXXX XXXXXXX XXX
XXXXXX XX XXXXXXX X XXXXX XXXXXXX XX XXXX X XXX XXXXXXXXXXX
XXXXXXXXXXXXXX   XXX   XXXXXXX   XX   XXXXXX   XXX   XXXXXX   XXXX
XXXXXXXXX XXXX XXXXX XXX X XXXXXXXXXX XXXXXX XXX XXXXXXXXX XX
XXXXXXXXXXXXXX XXXX X.
```

or it can be *right aligned* with a straight right margin only:

```
XXXX XXX XXXXX X XXXX XXXXXXXXXX XXX XXXXXXX XXXX XXXXXXX XXX
XXXXXX XX XXXXXXX X XXXXX XXXXXXX XX XXXX X XXX XXXXXXXXXXX XXX
XXX XXXXXXX X XXXXXXX XXX XXXXX XXXXX X XXXX X XX XXXXXX X
XXXXXXXXXXXXXX XXX XXXXXXX XX XXXXXX XXX XXXXXX XXXX
XXXXXXXXX XXXX XXXXX XXX X XXXXXXXXXX XXXXXX XXX XXXXXXXXX XX
XXXXXXXXXXXXXX XXXX X.
```

or it can be *centred*:

```
XXXX XXX XXXXX X XXXX XXXXXXXXXX XXX XXXXXXX XXXX XXXXX XXX XX
XXXXXXX X XXXXX XXXXXXX XX XXXX X XXX XXXXXXXXXXX XXX XXX
XXXXXXX X XXXXXXX XXX XXXXX XXXXX X XXXX X XX XXXXXX X
XXXXXXXXXXXXXX XXX XXXXXXX XX XXXXXX XXX XXXXXX XXXX
XXXXXXXXX XXXX XXXXX XXX X XXXXXXXXXX XXXXXX XXX XXXXXXXXX XX
XXXXXXXXXXXXXX XXXX X.
```

Printing Styles

Text can be printed in a variety of styles, including **boldface**, *italic* or <u>underlined</u>. Most word processors allow these styles to be displayed on the screen as well as on the printer and are known as WYSIWYG (What You See Is What You Get) packages.

Various fonts and sizes of characters

Different character fonts, that is variations in the shapes of characters, and sizes of characters can be mixed in the same document:

This is called Bahamas 12 pt

This is Courier New 8pt

This is Times New Roman 14 pt

THIS IS UMBRELLA 14PT

Mailing Lists

This allows a user to personalise standard letters. The mailing list is, in effect, a file of names and addresses, details from which can be inserted into marked points in a standard letter. The word processor prints multiple copies of the standard letter selected by the user and personalises each with data extracted from the mailing list.

Additional Features

These include facilities for the checking of spelling in a document by reference to a dictionary held on disk, the import of text and figures from other packages such as spreadsheets, the incorporation of graphics and the export of text to other packages. Some word processors also contain a programming language to allow a wide variety of tasks to be automated. Menus and toolbars can often be tailored to reflect a users particular preferences.

Windows-based Word Processors

Programs like Microsoft's *Word for Windows* and other windows-based word processors are rapidly taking over from those that do not operate in a window's environment. These latest word processors allow the use of a mouse to move the cursor around documents quickly, to edit text and to provide easy access to commonly used functions such as saving and printing work, opening existing documents and creating tables. All the other advantages of windows-based programs also apply. The use of this type of word processor is dealt with in the skills section of this book.

Spreadsheets

Just as word processors are designed to manipulate text, spreadsheets are designed to do the equivalent with numerical information. A spreadsheet program presents the user with a blank grid of 'cells' each of which is capable of containing one of three types of information:

1. Labels consisting of alphanumeric characters. These allow the user to make the spreadsheet more readable and easier to understand.

2. Numbers which can be used in calculations.
3. Formulas, which usually will make reference to other cells. These allow calculations to be performed on data in other cells or on the results from other formulas.

These three types of information are sufficient to allow a wide range of applications to be implemented in a very convenient and easily understandable way. Figure 2.17 shows an example of a simple *Excel* spreadsheet, to give you an idea of what a spreadsheet looks like. The grid is labelled with column letters along the top and with row numbers down the left-hand side. A cell is referenced by naming its column and row. In the figure, the cell D8 contains the formula =C8*20/100 which produces the value 199.80 by using the number in C8 (999.00). Refer to the skills section for an explanation of the structure and operation of spreadsheets.

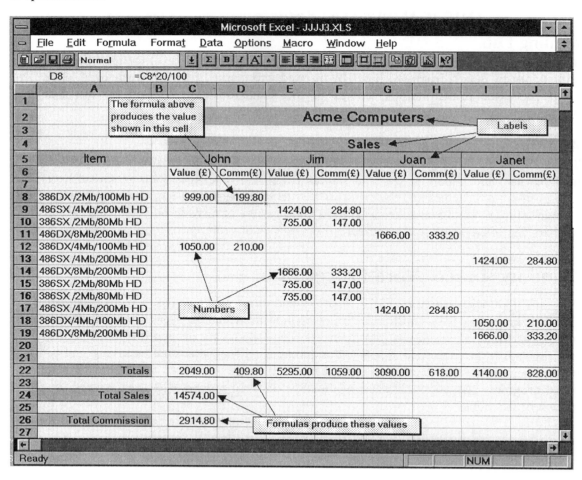

Figure 2.17. *An Excel spreadsheet*

Typical Spreadsheet Facilities

Apart from the entry of labels, numbers and formulas, a spreadsheet package normally provides various facilities accessed via a menu bar to handle the data stored on the worksheet. Typically, spreadsheets offer the following facilities:

Filing. So that spreadsheets can be saved, retrieved and printed.

Editing. This allows areas of the spreadsheet to be moved, copied or deleted using cut and paste.

Formatting. A cell entry can be centred, or left or right justified within a cell. Numeric values can be displayed in a variety of formats including fixed decimal, integer, percent and scientific or as money values prefixed by a $ or £ sign to 2 decimal places. Individual formats can be selected 'globally', that is throughout a worksheet or for selected ranges of cells;

Functions. Built-in functions can be used in formulas. For example, in Excel, `=SUM(range)` adds the contents of a specified range of cells, `=AVERAGE(range)` calculates the average value in a specified range of cells, `=MIN(range)` extracts the minimum value held in a specified range of cells, and `=SQRT(cell)` returns the square root of a value in a specified cell. The full range of functions usually include those used in mathematics, trigonometry, finance and statistics.

Macros. Frequently used or complex sequences of spreadsheet operations can be stored and executed automatically by using macros. Sometimes a macro can be invoked by special keys or by icons appearing on the toolbar of windows-based spreadsheets. Macros can greatly speed up or simplify spreadsheet operations. Macros can also be useful when the spreadsheet has been tailored for a particular application which may be used by inexperienced people. Without macros, each user would have to be completely familiar with the spreadsheet commands needed. With macros, one experienced user can tailor the spreadsheet so that training time for other staff is minimised.

Graphs. Numerical data can be displayed in a variety of graphical forms, including bar charts, line graphs, scatter diagrams and pie charts. The range and quality of graphs vary greatly from one package to another. With the use of a colour printer, very attractive and presentable graphs can be produced to illustrate business reports.

Consolidation. This feature allows the merging of several spreadsheets into a summary sheet, whilst keeping the original spreadsheets intact.

Other Facilities. These include, amongst others, cell protection facilities to prevent alteration of certain entries, the alteration of individual column widths and the display of cell contents as formulae instead of the results of their calculation.

Spreadsheets have a number of attractive features compared to traditional programming solutions to processing needs:

- designed for laymen;
- easy to learn and use;

- wide range of uses;
- relatively cheap;
- easily modified;
- well tried and tested;
- provide quick development time.

On the debit side, they tend to be:

- too general purpose and therefore they tend to provide satisfactory rather than ideal solutions;
- the problem must still be analysed and a solution method identified.

Database

At one time database programs, or *Database Management Systems* (DBMS) as they are often called, were restricted to mainframe computers because of the large memory requirements demanded of such applications. Currently, however, even personal business microcomputers have sufficient internal memory (8 megabytes - roughly 4 million characters of storage - is common) and backing storage capacity to make such applications not only feasible but also extremely powerful.

These programs allow files, comprising collections of records, to be created, modified, searched and printed.

Here are just a few examples of database applications:

- names and addresses of possible customers for a mail order firm;
- details of the books in a library giving author, title and subject are covered by each book, to aid with locating books of a certain type;
- details of the items stored in a warehouse, giving location, cost, number currently in stock and supplier;
- lists of people on the electoral register for a certain region;
- details of the employees of a large firm.

Typical database facilities

A typical database program will offer, as a minimum, the following facilities:

- user-definable record format allowing the user to specify the fields within the record;
- user-definable input format to allow the user to define the way the data is to be entered into the computer;
- file searching capabilities for extracting records satisfying certain criteria from a file;
- file sorting capabilities so that records can be ordered according to the contents of a certain field;
- calculations on fields within records for inclusion in reports;
- user-definable report formats, so that different types of reports containing different combinations of record fields may be produced.

Database Packages for Microcomputers

These packages fall broadly into two groups, *card index* and *relational*. Generally, card index systems are simpler to set up and operate but they provide less sophisticated data manipulation and search facilities than do the relational type. Further, the relational type provide a programming language which allows the development of 'user friendly', tailored applications. Thus, a user can be protected from the complexities of package operation by being presented with, for example, a menu-driven system with options for record insertion, modification, deletion and retrieval and perhaps the production of summary reports. The card index type cannot be programmed in this way, so the user must have a more detailed knowledge of package operation. On the other hand, card index packages tend to be easier to use. The superior data management facilities provided by the relational type tend to be under-used unless professional database designers and programmers are involved in the development of the database application. The business executive who plans to use the database as a personal tool without such professional help, will probably be well advised to purchase a card index package rather than a relational database package.

Graphics Packages

Graphics packages are designed to create and manipulate images. These images vary considerably in form and so a particular graphics package will often be geared towards a certain type of image. The following is a list of common types of software packages for graphics applications:

- business graphics;
- graphic design;
- desktop publishing;
- computer aided design.

Some graphics packages will to a greater or lesser degree cater for all of these applications, but many are designed specifically for only one of them.

Business graphics packages allow the production of such things as bar charts, line graphs and pie diagrams, that is, diagrams of a statistical nature likely to be included in business reports.

Packages for **graphic design** consist of a collection of special functions aimed at aiding the graphic designer. The artist uses the screen as his canvas and a light-pen, mouse or equivalent device as his brush. They generally allow work of professional quality to be produced in a relatively short amount of time, and include such facilities as

- providing a large colour palette;
- geometric figure drawing, e.g. lines, rectangles, circles;
- filling areas with colour or patterns;
- undoing mistakes;
- moving/copying/deleting/saving areas of the screen display;
- choice of a variety of character fonts;
- printing the finished design;

- provide a large number of pre-drawn pictures for inclusion in designs. This is called 'clip-art'.

Graphic design programs are usually one of two distinct types: those that simulate the tools that traditionally would be used by an artist and allow pictures such as digitised photographs to be edited at the pixel level - these are called bit-map graphics packages- and those that are object-based in which images are built up from lines, rectangles, circles and other geometrical shapes which can be filled with colour, overlapped and manipulated in various ways.

Desktop publishing programs are designed to facilitate the production of posters, illustrated articles, books and other forms of documents which combine large amounts of text with illustrations. As such they tend to contain a number of facilities in common with graphic design packages and word processors, but in particular they emphasise page layout and the management of large documents. These packages place a lot of emphasis on being able to experiment with arranging sections of the document and seeing its overall appearance. Text is also given more importance; a rudimentary word processor may be provided, or text may be imported from a prepared file, and the user is generally able to experiment with different type fonts on text already displayed on the screen.

Typically, a DTP package will have facilities for:

- modifying text by means of using different fonts and type styles;
- importing text from word processors;
- displaying text in columns;
- importing pictures/diagrams from graphic design packages;
- re-sizing pictures;
- producing simple geometrical shapes such as lines, rectangles and circles;
- mixing text and graphics;
- handling very large documents
- applying heading and paragraph styles consistently throughout a large document;

Computer-aided design constitutes perhaps one of the most widely used commercial applications of computer graphics. Here the user simulates real-world geometrical objects using various software drawing tools. Often these tools are selected and used in a WIMP style environment. Sometimes a graphics tablet is used in conjunction with a pressure-operated stylus, or a light-pen might be used to draw electronically on the VDU screen. Whatever the physical method of using the system, the types of software tools and facilities available are fairly standard, providing tools for operations such as:

- drawing common objects (lines, curves, circles, ellipses, rectangles, polygons etc);
- editing objects (modifying or deleting objects);
- filling shapes with patterns or colours;
- generating three-dimensional objects;
- rotating two-dimensional and three-dimensional objects;
- viewing three-dimensional objects from different directions;
- displaying three-dimensional objects in wireframe or solid form;
- applying different texturing effects to solid objects.

Applications of CAD programs include:

- engineering drawing;
- architectural design;
- interior design;
- printed-circuit and integrated circuit design;
- advertising material;
- computer animation for tv advertising;
- special effects in films.

Knowledge-based Systems

A knowledge-based system embodies human knowledge in a form suited to processing by a computer program. Such a system will store facts about a certain subject area, and relationships, often in the form of rules, which will allow conclusions to be drawn from the facts. A Prolog program is a good example of a knowledge base, and a Prolog translator executing such a program could be classed as a knowledge-based system.

The most common type of knowledge-based system is the *expert system*, and this is discussed in some detail in the following section.

Expert Systems

Pure research in the field of artificial intelligence has had a number of practical spin-offs. One such spin-off has been the development of programs known as *expert systems,* or *intelligent knowledge based systems*. These are programs designed to be able to give the same sort of help or advice, or make decisions, as a human expert in some narrow field of expertise. For instance, a program called PROSPECTOR is capable of predicting the existence of mineral ores given various pieces of information gathered from physical locations. In the same way that, given certain evidence, an expert might say that a particular site looked favourable for containing ore, PROSPECTOR indicates the probability of the existence of the ore. PROSPECTOR is in fact attributed with the discovery of an extremely valuable quantity of molybdenum which had previously been overlooked by human experts.

Expert systems have been developed in numerous areas which traditionally have been the province of human experts. For example, several expert systems have been developed to aid medical diagnosis and treatment. However, decisions in areas such as this are often so critical that it would be foolish to blindly accept the pronouncement of a computer. For this reason, expert systems have the built-in ability to justify the chain of logical reasoning leading to any conclusion, so that it can be checked and verified (or rejected) by a human.

Another characteristic of many expert systems is the use of fuzzy logic which allows degrees of uncertainty to be built in to logical deduction processes. Such expert systems are able to state conclusions which are qualified by a probability value indicating the probability of the conclusion being correct.

Other successful expert systems include:

- MYCIN - diagnosis of infections
- HEURISTIC DENDRAL - identifies organic compounds
- XCON - for configuring (VAX) computer systems
- SACON - for advice on structural analysis

An expert system has three main components:

1. A *knowledge base* consisting of rules which use facts supplied by some external source, typically a user.
2. An *inference engine* which processes the knowledge base.
3. A *user interface* to facilitate communication with the user.

As an example, the following knowledge base is for a simple botanical expert system to identify whether a particular plant is a shrub, tree, herb or vine.

Four rules are to be used:

```
1.IF STEM IS GREEN THEN TYPE IS HERB.
2.IF STEM IS WOODY AND ATTITUDE IS CREEPING THEN TYPE IS VINE.
3.IF STEM IS WOODY AND ATTITUDE IS UPRIGHT AND ONE MAIN TRUNK
  IS TRUE THEN TYPE IS TREE.
4.IF STEM IS WOODY AND ATTITUDE IS UPRIGHT AND ONE MAIN TRUNK
  IS FALSE THEN TYPE IS SHRUB.
```

This forms the knowledge base.

The inference engine starts by attempting to satisfy a primary goal, in this instance to determine the TYPE of the plant. To this end, it searches its knowledge base for the goal by looking for a rule containing the word TYPE in the conclusion part of the rule (after the THEN part of a rule). This process of examining conclusions to rules while attempting to resolve goals is called *backward chaining* (or goal-driven inference).

Rule 1 satisfies this requirement, but in order to establish if the plant is a HERB, the system must obtain information regarding the STEM. Initially this information will not be available and must be supplied by the user. Consequently, obtaining the STEM information is added to a list of subgoals to be evaluated, along with rule 1, and the system looks for another rule containing the goal in its conclusion. The subgoal list also notes the rule which generated the subgoal in question.

After the remaining rules have been processed in a similar fashion, the system must then attempt to satisfy the subgoal list. Consequently, the user interface is invoked. This generates a question of the form

```
IS THE STEM OF THE PLANT GREEN?
```

Let us suppose that the plant is a SHRUB (which has a woody stem, grows upright, and has more than one main trunk). The user answers NO which is stored as a fact relating to the stem of the plant.

Having succeeded with a subgoal, the inference engine again searches for a rule conclusion containing TYPE. It can attempt to evaluate the first rule now that it has all the necessary information. The rule does not produce a conclusion since the STEM is not green. This rule is therefore discarded since it can never cause the primary goal to succeed in this particular consultation.

Examination of the second rule reveals to the inference engine that it cannot be resolved until the ATTITUDE of the plant is in its list of facts, so this is added to its list of subgoals.

Eventually, all the necessary facts are available and the inference engine is able to discard all rules except rule 4 which establishes that the plant is a SHRUB.

In the course of a consultation the user might wish to know why the system is asking a certain question. The information required to answer this question is easy to find: the subgoal generating the question being asked was stored along with the rule from which it came, and this contains all the necessary information. For example, if the inference engine was attempting to resolve rule 4 by asking about the number of TRUNKS, the user interface might respond,

```
I am trying to determine the TYPE.
I know that the STEM is woody.
I know that the ATTITUDE is upright.
If ONE MAIN TRUNK is false then I will know that the TYPE
is SHRUB.
```

Expert System Shells

The term *shell* is given to expert systems which have been given no specific knowledge base, only the inference engine and user interface; the knowledge base has to be provided by the user. A single expert system shell can thus be used to provide advice or help in a number of areas of expertise, providing it is given the appropriate knowledge base for each area.

For example, an expert system shell could be used to give advice on the procedures and sequence of steps necessary for selling a house (what solicitors call 'conveyancing'), or to give advice about possible causes and cures of diseases in houseplants, or diagnosing faults in cars. Not only could these applications be of practical use, but they could also be instructive because the user could ask for and obtain the reasons behind any conclusions.

One of the problems of using such shells is the determination of the rules which represent the wisdom of a human expert; many experts are not consciously aware of the precise reasoning processes they themselves use in order to come to some conclusion, yet in order to produce an expert program, these processes must be defined in a form that is usable. The process of determining the knowledge base rules is known as 'knowledge elicitation' or 'knowledge acquisition' and is performed by 'knowledge engineers'.

Hypertext

Hypertext, also called 'linked text' and 'extended text', systems are concerned with classifying and categorising text. Such systems allow blocks of text to be linked together in various ways for the purpose of establishing a chain of connected topics. Blocks of text may be established as a connected set of nodes or subsections of text nodes can be linked to other subsections or to other nodes.

A hypertext system does not rearrange the text in its database; it merely allows a user to define a method of organising it. For example, an author engaged in researching for a book may read many papers and reference books and in the course of doing so may make notes in a notebook to summarise their contents. A hypertext notebook would, for example, allow the author to link his own annotations to references, and link references to other references. Obviously this would greatly simplify the task of collecting together material relevant to writing about a particular topic. Hypertext systems usually allow the user to browse through a hypertext document, adding, deleting or modifying links between nodes and points. Software on-line help facilities are usually based on hypertext ideas.

Current hypertext systems which allow the inclusion graphical or even sound nodes in addition to text are termed *hypermedia* systems. The World Wide Web, a major information source on Internet, offers globally distributed hypermedia pages. Internet users are able to obtain hypermedia pages on an enormous variety of subjects from all over the world.

Chapter 3

Computer Files

Introduction

A *file*, in computer terms, refers to a collection of data stored on a backing storage device such as a magnetic disk or tape drive. This data, however, can be in numerous different forms. For instance, a file could contain:

- the output from a program such as a word processor, spreadsheet or drawing package;
- a database of personnel records or customer details, for example;
- a program written in a language such as BASIC or COBOL;
- an application program such as a word processor, spreadsheet, database package, DTP or CAD program.

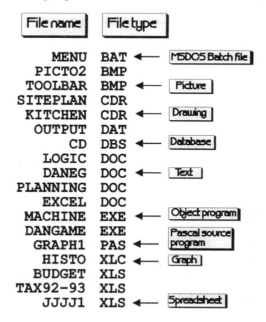

Figure 3.1. *Examples of different types of files*

The form of file is often indicated by the name under which it has been stored. In the operating system MS-DOS, three extra characters (*file extension*) are allowed in the file name for the purpose of identifying the type of file. If you were to view a list of files held on a disk you might see something like that shown in Figure 3.1. Files with the extension BAT or EXE can be executed by the operating system directly, but all the rest are used in conjunction with programs of various types. Many files have no particular structure. For instance, a picture file which contains colour information for the pixels comprising the picture is simply a list of colour codes in the order that they appear on a display screen; a text file from a word processor is a list of codes for letters and special characters such as tabs and paragraph marks; data files produced by other programs can contain mixtures of numbers and characters. Many files, for example those used in business and commercial processing, do have a common type of structure.

The Structure of Data files

Figure 3.2 shows how a data file of book records might be organised. The *file* is a collection of *records*, one for each book. Each record contains details of the book's title, its author(s), ISBN number, publisher, date of publication and cost: these categories of data are called *fields*, and each field contains a maximum number of characters of a certain type.

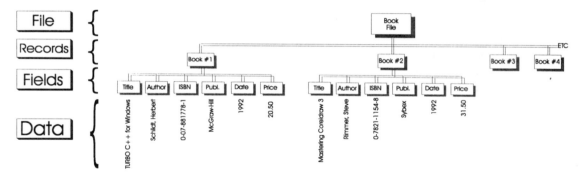

Figure 3.2. *Data file structure*

The size and type of the fields (see Relational Database Management Systems) need to be determined when the file is being planned, whether it will eventually be created by a database package or a purpose-written program using a language such as COBOL.

Types of Data File

The remainder of this chapter is concerned with structured data files, as used in business and commercial data processing. Common examples are stock, payroll, personnel and customer files. These files can be categorised by the ways in which they are used and there are generally recognised to be four such categories.

Master Files

They are used for the storage of permanent data which is used in applications such as stock, sales or payroll. Some of the fields tend to contain data which is fairly static, for example, customer name and address, whilst data in some fields is continually changing, for example, customer balance, as transactions are applied to the file. Such updating is carried out, either through the direct entry (on-line) of individual transactions, or from an accumulated set of entries stored on a transaction file.

Transaction Files

These are transient and only exist to allow the updating of master files. Each transaction record contains the key field value of the master record it is to update (to allow correct matching with its relevant master record), together with data gathered from source documents, for example, invoice amounts which update the balance field in customer accounts.

Reference Files

These contain data used for reference or look-up purposes, such as price catalogue and customer name and address files.

Archival or Historical Files

These contain data which, for legal or organisational reasons, must be kept and tend to be used on an ad hoc basis and may be referred to only occasionally.

Primary and Secondary Record Keys

In most organisations, when an information system is operational it will be necessary to identify each record uniquely. In a personnel file system, for example, it might be thought that it is possible to identify each individual record simply by the employee's surname; this would be satisfactory as long as no two employees had the same surname. In reality, many organisations will of course have several employees with the same surnames, so to ensure uniqueness, each employee is assigned a unique code, such as a Works Number. The works number field is then used as the primary key in the filing system, each individual having his or her own unique Works Number.

There are certain circumstances when the primary key may be a *composite* key, that is, one made up of more than one field and the following example shows how a pair of fields, which individually may not be unique, can be combined to provide a unique identifier.

Table 3.1 shows an extract from a file which details suppliers' quotations for a number of different products. There is a need for a composite key, (consisting of SupplierCode and PartCode) because there may be a number of quotations from one supplier (in this case, supplier 41192 and 23783) and a number of quotations for the same part (in this instance, part number A112).

SupplierNo	PartNo	Price	DeliveryDate
23783	A361	1452.75	31/01/95
37643	B452	341.50	29/01/95
23783	A112	2345.29	30/01/95
41192	A112	2474.29	28/01/95
41192	C345	122.15	30/01/95

Table 3.1. *Extract for quotation file with composite primary key*

It is necessary, therefore, to use both Supplier-No and Part-No to identify one quotation record uniquely. Uniqueness is not always necessary. For example, if it is required to retrieve records which fulfil a criterion, or several criteria, secondary keys may be used. Thus, for example, in an information retrieval system on Personnel, the secondary key Department may be used to retrieve the records of all employees who work in, say, the Sales Department. This topic is examined in detail in the chapters on databases, in both the Knowledge and Skills Resources.

File Storage Media

File storage media may be classified according to the kind of access they provide

- serial access;
- direct access.

Serial Access Media

Serial access means that in order to identify and retrieve a particular record, it is necessary to 'read' all the records which precede it in the relevant file. Magnetic tape (Chapter 5) is a serial access medium. One of the difficulties is that there are no, readily identifiable, physical areas on the medium which can be addressed. In other words, it is not possible to give a name or code and refer this to a particular location. It is said to be *non-addressable*. To look for an individual record stored on magnetic tape requires the software to examine each record's primary key field (or, sometimes a secondary key when searching for records with a particular value in that field) in sequence from the beginning of the file until the required record is found.

Direct Access Media

Magnetic and CD-ROM disks allow direct access to individual records, without reference to the rest of the relevant file. They have physical divisions which can be identified by computer software (and sometimes hardware) and are *addressable*, so that particular locations can be referred to by a name or code to retrieve a record which is stored at that location. Retrieval of an individual record is achieved (depending on the way the file is organised) by specifying the relevant primary key field value, thus providing the software with a means of finding and retrieving the specific individual record directly.

Physical and Logical Records

Because of the physical characteristics of magnetic tape it is necessary, when processing a file, that the tape unit (the device onto which a tape is loaded for processing) starts to read the tape at the beginning of the reel. As there are no specific physical locations on the tape which can be identified and referred to by the computer (except of course the beginning and end), the only way it can find a particular record is by reading the whole file. Unless the whole tape is to be processed, it may only be necessary to read up to the point where the specific record it is seeking is found. There may well be more than one logical file on a tape but these will have to be read in the sequence that they appear on the tape. As the tape is read, the computer will compare the key field value of each record which it comes to, with the specified key value, until the required record is found. Figure 3.3 illustrates the way in which a file is arranged on tape both logically and physically.

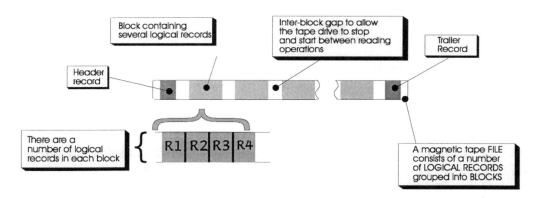

Figure 3.3. *Logical records in physical blocks on tape*

You should note from Figure 3.3 that records R1, R2, R3 and R4 are instances of logical records. For example, if this were a stock file, each logical record would relate to one commodity held in stock. On the other hand each physical block consists, in this illustration, of 4 logical records. The reason for making the distinction between logical and physical records stems from the fact that data is transferred between the computer's internal memory and the tape storage medium in manageable blocks, the optimum size of each depending on factors such as the size of the computer's internal memory.

Magnetic disk provides file storage facilities which are more flexible and powerful than those provided by magnetic tape. As an addressable medium, the surface of the disk is divided into physical locations which are illustrated in Figure 3.4. The address of any one physical location on a single disk incorporates a track number, and within that track, a sector number. A sector is the smallest physical area on the disk which can be addressed, each addressable unit being referred to as a block or physical record. The size of the block is normally determined by the systems designer through the use of systems software, although some disk storage systems use hard sectoring (the block size cannot be altered). The number of logical records which can be accommodated in a particular block obviously depends upon the physical size of the block and the length of each logical record.

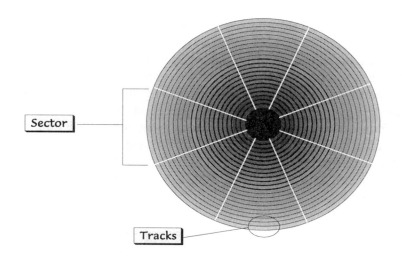

Figure 3.4. *Address structure of magnetic disk*

Updating Master Files

Another common requirement with such data files as stock or customer account files is to update the file using another one containing transactions. The *transaction file* contains information which will be used to update (that is, bring up to date or modify in some way) a *master file*.

For example, a mail order club specialising in music CDs might keep its members' details on a file which is updated on a daily basis. Each member record in the membership file might include the fields shown in Table 3.2. The membership number is the primary key.

Field	Type	Max size
Name	alphanum	20 char
Membership number	alphanum	6 char
Date of joining	alphanum	6 char
Address line 1	alphanum	20 char
Address line 2	alphanum	20 char
Address line 3	alphanum	20 char
Address line 4	alphanum	20 char
Post code	alphanum	8 char
Balance of account	numeric	6 figures
No. of items ordered to date	numeric	3 figures
Last item ordered (code)	alphanum	5 char

Table 3.2. *CD Club membership record*

Details of payments received by post from members will be used to update the members file so that accurate statements of balances can be produced when necessary. In addition to payments, however, members could also send in changes of address or membership cancellations, and new members will also need to have their details added to the file. All of these different types of transactions will be stored in a file and used to modify the master members file. Table 3.3 identifies some possible types of transactions and how they will affect the master file.

Transaction type	Master file action to be taken
1. Payment	Subtract payment from current balance
2. Order	Add price of CD to current balance
3. Change of address	Change address field in customer record
4. Cancellation of membership	Delete membership details from file

Table 3.3. *Transaction types to update master file*

The transaction file might therefore have a different record format for each type of transaction, as shown in Table 3.4.

Notice that the transaction code appears on each type of transaction so that the program processing the transactions can make the appropriate changes to the master file, depending on whether the code is 1, 2, 3 or 4. The membership number must also appear on the transaction in order to locate the correct member's record.

Transaction type	Field	Type	Size
Payment	Transaction code	Value 1	
	Membership number	alphanum	6 char
	Amount paid	numeric	6 figures
	Date received	date	6 char
Order	Transaction code	Value 2	
	Membership number	alphanum	6 char
	Item order code	alphanum	6 char
	Date received	date	6 char
Change of address	Transaction code	Value 3	
	Membership number	alphanum	6 char
	Address line 1	alphanum	20 char
	Address line 2	alphanum	20 char
	Address line 3	alphanum	20 char
	Post code	alphanum	8 char
Cancel membership	Transaction code	Value 4	
	Membership number	alphanum	6 char

Table 3.4. *Record format for each transaction type*

Organising and Accessing Files

Before a record from a data file can be updated, it must first be located on the backing storage device and then transferred into the main memory of the computer. The method employed to locate a record depends on the type of backing storage device and how the file has been organised.

Sequential access

With files held on magnetic tape, the method of organising the records in a file is limited to arranging the records according to some *sequence*, such as storing them in ascending order of key field.

Transaction file		Master file	Action
Membership number	Type	Membership number	
		123456	No transaction: copy record to new master file
		123457	No transaction: copy record to new master file
123458	1	123458	Subtract payment from balance Copy record to new master file
		123459	No transaction: copy record to new master file
123460	1	123460	Subtract payment from balance Copy record to new master file
123461	2	123461	Add cost of CD to balance Copy to new master file
123462	3	123462	Change address Copy to new master file
		123463	No transaction: copy record to new master file
123464	1	123464	Subtract payment from balance Copy record to new master file
		123465	No transaction: copy record to new master file
		123466	No transaction: copy record to new master file
123467	4	123467	Delete record: record not copied to new master file
etc.		etc.	

Table 3.5. *Sample transactions to update master file*

For example, in the CD club example above, the members' records would be held in order of membership number, from the lowest to the highest. In a personnel file of a large company, employees records would probably be held in order of works number. Processing a magnetic tape file involves reading each record in turn in the order that they are stored on the tape.

This is termed *sequential access*. Using a transaction file to update such a master file requires that it too is *sorted* into the same order. In our CD club example, transactions held on magnetic tape would also be sorted into ascending order of membership number. The usual processing method is to create a new master file from the old one rather than just changing the existing file; the old master file is retained for security purposes (see chapter on System Controls). Table 3.5 shows how the master file is processed using a number of transactions. Note that there doesn't have to be a transaction for every record in the master file.

Where there is no transaction for a record on the master file, the record is simply copied to the new master file; when there is a transaction, the modification to the record is made and then the modified record is written to the new master file; if a record is to be deleted from the master file, it simply is not written to the new file.

Direct Access

The processing method just described for magnetic tape files could also be used for files held on magnetic disk, but the latter also allows *direct access* to be used. In direct access, the location at which a record is stored on the magnetic disk is related to its key field. For example, using the membership numbers in the previous table, the last three digits of this key field could be used to specify the location of the member's record. Thus in the membership number *123456*, the last three digits, that is *456*, might give the location of the record as *track 4*, *surface 5* and *sector 6* on a particular multiple disk pack. Given the method of calculating its location, a record can be accessed directly without the need to process all the preceding records on the disk; this can save a great deal of time. For instance, if a customer rings up with a query about his or her account, a customer services clerk sitting at a computer workstation would be able to key in the customer's account number and view the record immediately. Direct access organisation is particularly useful for this type of information retrieval application.

Processing a transaction file for a direct access master file does not require either of the files to be sorted. The key field provided in a transaction record will allow the

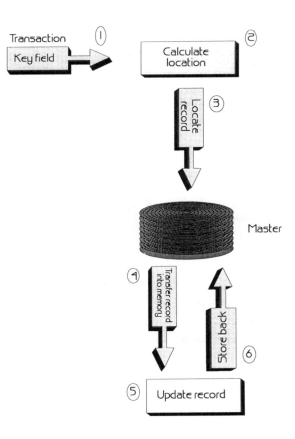

Figure 3.5. *Updating a record directly*

appropriate master file record to be retrieved directly and written back to the same storage area. Figure 3.5 illustrates direct access transaction processing

A rough guide to deciding whether to use sequential or direct access is that if only about 10% or fewer records are likely to be accessed during a typical processing run, then direct access should be used; if over 40% of records are likely to be accessed then sequential organisation is appropriate; between 10% and 40% will require other factors to be taken into account, such as file size, whether the file will be modified or just read, and how frequently it will be processed.

A third way of accessing records is by means of an index in which the keys of the records, along with their locations, are stored. When a record is required, the index is searched sequentially until its key is found. The location of the record is then available so that the record can be retrieved directly. The most commonly used form of indexed organisation is called *indexed sequential*. In this variation, records are stored in order in groups called *blocks*. So, if a block was large enough to contain a maximum of, say, ten records, these ten records would be stored in some order of the key field, and the highest key value of the block of records would be stored in the index, together with the location of the start of the block. Since only one key is stored, the size of the index can be significantly reduced. When a record is required, the index is searched until a larger key is found. The record must therefore be stored in the location pointed to by the previous key in the index. Figure 3.6 illustrates indexed sequential organisation.

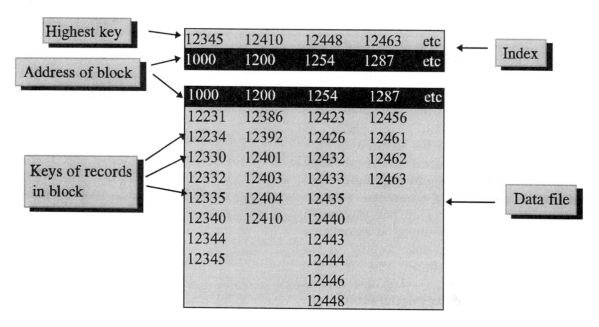

Figure 3.6. *Indexed sequential file organisation*

Chapter 4

Types of Computers

Introduction

As well as computers being used in a variety of ways, the internal structure, or *architecture* of computers varies widely. The largest, most complex and most expensive computers are known as *mainframes*, and these are used for large scale operations requiring a great deal of processing power, flexibility and speed. *Minicomputers* are generally slower, smaller and cheaper than mainframes, but they are still capable of supporting a number of on-line users. At the bottom of the scale are microprocessor-based computer systems, so-called *workstations* or *microcomputers*, which are able only to handle single users or relatively simple tasks. As computer technology continues to advance, the distinction between these three categories is becoming less clear.

A further class of computer system has been given the name *supercomputer*, a term usually reserved for the largest and fastest computers existing. These computers are usually used for very advanced and specialised applications requiring enormous computing power which cannot be provided even by mainframe computers.

Mainframes

Though the term *mainframe* has in recent years come to mean medium to large-scale computers, it originally referred to the 'frame', or rack, which held the main electronics boards and wiring of a large computer. In modern mainframe computers, the CPU and memory are usually housed in the same cabinet to improve memory access speeds; the speed of modern processors is such that the distance which data has to travel to and from the CPU can significantly affect the performance of the computer system.

Mainframes are used for applications requiring extensive data files which need to be accessed by many users, and which require a very fast response time. For example, an airline booking system will use a mainframe to cope with storing and providing access to all of its flights and recording passenger details. Such systems can be used by numerous and widely dispersed travel agents, all needing fast access to the flights database. Banks and building societies use mainframes to cope with the great number of customer transactions which they need to process, and because of the greatly varied processing tasks involved in these types of businesses.

The main characteristics of mainframes are:

- large physical size - they usually occupy a large room with air-conditioning to dissipate the heat which they generate;
- very fast;
- very expensive;
- use a wide range of sophisticated hardware and software, and they have a very large amount of RAM (hundreds of megabytes, for instance);
- used by large organisations.

Minicomputers

In price and capability, minicomputers lie somewhere between microcomputers and mainframes. Minicomputers are often used to provide a processing service in a multi-user environment, that is, where a number of users are connected on-line to a central processor. Such systems are often termed *time-sharing* services because the processor in such a system allocates a small amount of time, a *time slice*, to each user in turn. This sharing of time happens so rapidly that users are generally unaware that there are others using the system. Figure 4.1 is a simplified illustration of a time-sharing system. The diagram shows four users

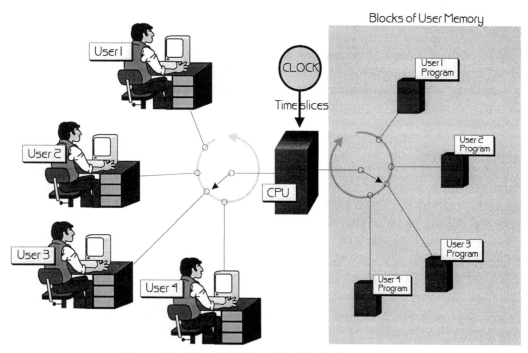

Figure 4.1. *A simplified view of a time-sharing system*

simultaneously using the minicomputer system. Each user has been allocated a block of memory for his program and data and currently *User 3* has control of the processor. A system clock is used to interrupt the current user after a certain time slice has elapsed and the next user then has control. This process repeats for every user on the system in a continuous cycle.

Though microcomputer-based local area networks have to some extent replaced the use of minicomputers, there are still multi-user applications, such as those involving databases, which require the fast access and processing power of minicomputers. The other major use of the minicomputer is as a standalone real-time processor for complex control systems.

Microprocessors and Microcomputers

A *microprocessor*, manufactured using a single integrated circuit (IC), contains circuitry to control the execution of program instructions stored in external memory, an arithmetic logic unit to perform calculations and other operations on data, and a number of registers to hold data and instructions temporarily. Microprocessors vary greatly in speed and capability: some of the simplest types are used in electronic devices such as printers, photocopiers, cameras, toys, watches and washing machines, to control their operation, while other more sophisticated microprocessors are used in very powerful microcomputer and minicomputer systems.

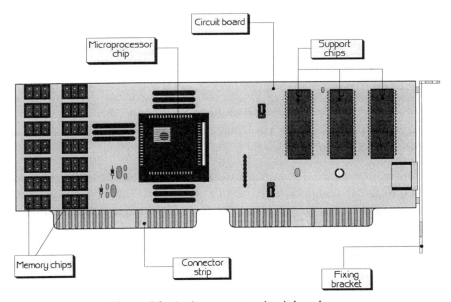

Figure 4.2. *A microcomputer circuit board*

A *microcomputer* is a more complete device containing, in addition to a microprocessor, memory for storing programs and data, and interfaces for connecting it to input and output devices such as keyboards, monitors, mice and printers. A microcomputer typically consists of a collection of integrated circuits on one or more circuit boards about the size of A4 sheets of paper (see Figure 4.2). The circuit boards for a PC will include support ICs for controlling a printer, a graphics display, one or more disk drives, a mouse and a keyboard.

Types of Personal Computers (PCs)

As explained above, a personal computer, or *PC*, is based on a microprocessor, and is usually purchased as a complete system comprising a monitor, capable of displaying graphic images in colour, a main processor case which also houses one or more floppy disc drives, one or more hard disc drives, and a number of circuit boards, a full sized keyboard and a mouse. A typical system based on an Intel 80486 32 bit microprocessor would have a 3½ inch floppy disc drive, an internal hard drive with a capacity of 200 Megabytes and 8 Megabytes of RAM. Such a system will usually come complete with operating system software (such as MS-DOS and MS Windows) and a word processor program already installed on the hard disc, and would cost in the region of £800. Printers are usually supplied separately.

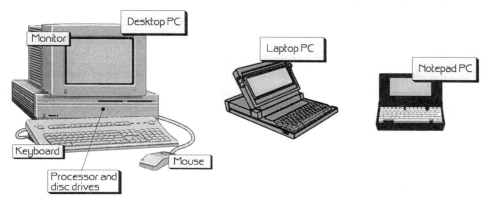

Figure 4.3. *Different types of PCs*

A *laptop* PC is a small, portable microcomputer system which has a liquid crystal display screen, a full sized keyboard, a floppy disc drive and a hard disc drive all built into a single case. The flat screen is usually hinged so that it can be set at a convenient viewing angle when the computer is being used. Laptops are battery powered but there is usually the facility also to run them from mains power supplies by using a special adapter.

Because of recent advances in miniaturisation, laptops have almost completely been superseded by *notebook* computers. Notebook computers are typically 280mm wide by 230mm long and 45mm deep, that is, about the size of a sheet of A4 paper and weighing only 4-6lbs. This is about half the size of a laptop computer. They use the latest microcomputer technology to achieve the processing capabilities of full sized microcomputer systems. These machines frequently have an inbuilt tracker ball as a compact alternative to a mouse. Prices range from under £1000 for a machine with a monochrome screen to over £3000 for a machine with a colour monitor and high capacity (over 300 MB) hard disc drive.

Personal digital assistant (*PDA*) computers take miniaturisation even further in microcomputers which are small enough to fit in your pocket. They achieve this small size by replacing a keyboard with a pen-like device which allows you to write on the special display screen. The *pen computing* incorporated in this style of machine, uses a pen-like stylus to draw on a special LCD display which can detect the position of the pen, and pass that information to the microprocessor. Pen computers are provided with special software which is capable of recognising handwriting and storing it as if it had been entered using a keyboard. The lack of a keyboard allows these devices to be made so small and light that they can be operated while standing or even walking. Standard program functions represented by icons or menus (see the section on graphical user interfaces in Chapter 2) are selected by tapping them with the tip of the pen or by pressing a pressure-sensitive button on the pen's shaft. Pen computers are currently marketed mainly as electronic versions of personal organisers, but they have uses in other areas, including recording patient information by mobile workers such as doctors and nurses while they are on their rounds, and by police for recording the details of incidents or crimes on the spot, and for warehouse staff to note stock details.

Uses of Microprocessors and Microcomputers

Microprocessors are used extensively in general-purpose computing systems, including minicomputers and mainframes, because of their low cost, small size, low power consumption and increasingly impressive speed and processing power. Only the very highest performance computers with very complex or specialised structures need to use CPUs manufactured from separate components rather than on a single chip.

Microcomputers are often used in more complex computer systems as additional controllers for peripherals and disk drives, graphics processors or for monitoring keyboards. However, the great majority of microcomputers are used in *embedded systems* in which the microcomputer is dedicated to performing a special function within a complex device. In embedded control systems, the microcomputer typically consists of a microprocessor combined with some read only memory (ROM) containing a pre-written program, and a small amount of random access memory (RAM) to store data and results. In this context, standard microprocessors are used as cheap substitutes for otherwise expensive and complex purpose-built electronic circuits.

Applications of embedded control systems range from domestic appliances and cars to missiles and space probes. Modern defence systems use microprocessors extensively. For example, they are used in

- missiles for aiming and guidance purposes; some missiles have stored contour maps which are used by microprocessors to keep the missile as close to the ground as possible;
- fighter aircraft for navigation, radar displays and weapon systems;
- radar systems on fast patrol boats for tracking enemy aircraft and for aiming guns and guiding missiles.

Microprocessors and microcomputers are being used with increasing frequency in the transportation industries. Examples of such uses include:

- in cars and lorries for controlling fuel and air flow to improve performance and fuel economy, controlling the operation of brakes to prevent skidding, monitoring and controlling shock absorbers to provide a more comfortable ride, processing traffic information to give advice to drivers on suitable routes avoiding traffic congestion;
- monitoring the number of vehicles arriving at traffic lights to regulate traffic flow;
- in aircraft for monitoring and reporting their current status to the main flight computers;
- in flight simulators used for training pilots.

In the home, microprocessors are embedded in devices such as:

- video recorders which can automatically record programs on different channels at different times;
- microwave ovens with digital controls for setting different cooking programmes;
- cameras which have digital displays and automatic focusing, exposure and flash functions;
- watches which can store and display telephone numbers;
- chess games which record a person's move and provide their own moves to high standards of play;
- washing machines and tumble dryers with complex programmes which can be set from digital keypads;
- games consoles which provide arcade quality graphics;
- compact disc players which allow the playing order of CDs to be pre-programmed;
- personal computers (PCs) which provide enormous computing power at low cost;
- door chimes which contain digitally stored tunes and play a different one each time the bell is pushed.

Microprocessors are also used in:

- controllers for robot arms in factories;
- devices which control air conditioners, lights and access to restricted areas in offices;
- fax machines and modems;
- bar code readers;
- scanners used for generating three dimensional images of the body for medical purposes;
- portable cellular telephones.

Microcomputers and microprocessors have been used to enhance the operation of all manner of electronic device, and there is no reason to suppose that their use will not continue to increase.

Supercomputers

The term *Supercomputer* is usually reserved for the most advanced computers available at any particular time. They are very large and fast and usually are capable of performing complex calculations such as those required in computer simulations. For example, computers have been used to simulate weather patterns in order to be able to perform forecasts. Such simulations involve setting up very complex mathematical equations to represent changes in temperature and pressure over areas of the earth's surface; these equations require so much computer time to evaluate that, even for the fastest supercomputers, predictions are limited to just a few hours.

Supercomputers achieve their processing power and speed in various ways, though they almost invariably have the principle of parallel organisation in common. Most computers perform tasks in a certain order, one after the other but an alternative approach is to identify tasks which can be performed at the same time, that is in parallel, and assign separate hardware units to each parallel task. One common way of doing this is to write programs that separate tasks which can be processed at the same time, and provide a processor for each. This is termed *multiprocessing*.

Perhaps the most well known supercomputers are manufactured by Cray. The Cray Research C-90 supercomputer was designed in 1992 to have the following characteristics:

Number of parallel processors	16
Memory size	4096 Megabytes
Speed	16 billion calculations per second

In comparison, a modern high-performance microcomputer typically might be able to perform at most a few million similar calculations per second, and have perhaps 16 Megabytes of memory.

Chapter 5

Computer Hardware

Introduction

The term *hardware* embraces the complete range of physical devices used in a computer system. We can separate these devices into a number of convenient categories as shown in Figure 5.1.

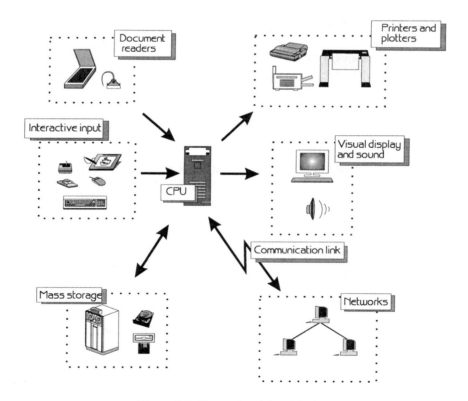

Figure 5.1. *Types of peripheral device*

- The *Central Processing Unit* (CPU) which consists of the Control Unit, the Arithmetic and Logic Unit (ALU) and the Immediate Access Store (IAS), or memory.

- *Interactive input devices* such as keyboards, light pens, mice and graphics tablets.
- *Document readers* such as bar code readers, scanners/digitizers, optical character readers (OCR), and magnetic ink character readers (MICR).
- Output devices such as visual display units(VDU), voice synthesisers and sound systems.
- *Printers* and *plotters.*
- *Mass* (or *backing*) *storage devices* such as microfiche, microfilm, floppy disk drives, hard disk drives, magnetic tape drives, streamers and CD-ROM drives.
- *Communication devices* such as acoustic couplers and modems.

In this chapter we will describe how each of these hardware devices works and how they are used in practice where relevant.

The CPU (Central Processing Unit)

The heart of any computer system is the *Central Processing Unit*, or *CPU*. Typically, the CPU consists of a *Control Unit*, an *Arithmetic Logic Unit*, or *ALU,* and the *Immediate Access Store*, or *IAS*, also known as *Memory*. In the case of personal computers, the memory is usually classed as being separate from the control unit and the ALU, both of which are contained on a single chip called a *microprocessor*. Figure 5.2 shows a typical arrangement of a CPU.

The control unit co-ordinates the flow of data both within the CPU and to and from peripheral devices such as printers, disc drives and keyboards. The control unit is somewhat like a telephone exchange, ensuring that, under the control of the program currently held in memory, the correct connections are made between the various components. Each instruction within the program is examined by the control unit, which then sends messages, in the form of electrical control signals, to the appropriate parts of the computer system. For example, the control unit will allow data from input devices to be transferred to memory for storage, or it will open pathways between memory and output devices, or it will cause data to be transferred to and from the ALU.

The control unit supervises the *fetch-execute* cycle, in which program instructions (for the program currently stored in memory) are transferred one by one from memory into the control unit for decoding. There will normally be quite a few types of instructions which the control unit must deal with. The collection of such instructions is called the *instruction set* of the CPU and it will normally contain instructions for the following types of operations

- *Data transfer* - copying data from memory into special areas called *registers,* within the control unit, or the ALU so that it can perform arithmetic operations on them, or copying data from one part of memory to another, or transferring data from registers to memory.

- *Input/output* - transferring data from memory to an external output device such as a printer, or transferring data obtained from an input device such as a keyboard to memory.

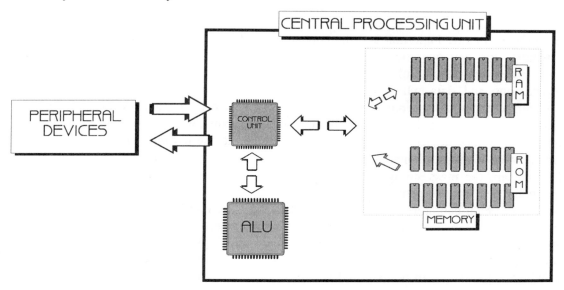

Figure 5.2. *The components of the central processing unit*

- *Transfer of control* - the result of a previous operation (for instance, if the most recent subtraction of two numbers gave a negative answer) can be used to skip to another part of the program without having to execute the instructions in between. These instructions are also called *branching*, or *jump* instructions. They work in conjunction with special registers called *flags* which automatically keep track of certain things which can happen when a program is being executed. For example, one flag, often called the *zero flag*, might be given a value of 1 if the last arithmetic operation gave an answer of zero, or a value of 0 if the last arithmetic operation gave a value not equal to zero; another flag, the *sign flag*, might record in a similar way whether the last instruction to be executed produced a positive or a negative result. Programmers use the state of these flags with transfer of control instructions to allow their programs to cope with things which occur while a program is running. The chapter on programming explains this idea in more detail.
- *Arithmetic* - performing addition, subtraction, multiplication and division on numbers stored in memory or in registers.
- *Logic* - comparing two values held in registers or in memory, or combining two values bit by bit using rules like those governing the output from gates with two inputs.
- *Shift* - moving the bits of a binary number, one or more places to the left or to the right.

The *arithmetic and logic unit* contains circuitry for performing important tasks such as the addition, subtraction, multiplication and division of two numbers held in memory or in registers. It is also able to compare two numbers and determine whether or not they are equal, and to perform other logical operations such as *AND*, *OR* and *NOT*. It is able to do these operations at enormously high speed; even the slowest of processors are able to do hundreds of thousands of arithmetic operations each second, and the fastest can do several millions per second.

Both the arithmetic logic unit and the control unit rely heavily on the immediate access store (memory) for their operation. The ALU uses numbers held in memory for calculations and it also stores the results of calculations in memory; the control unit processes program instructions and data which must be held in memory. Computer programs are usually transferred to memory from a mass storage device such as a magnetic disk as part of the initial setting up procedure for the running of a program. So far, we have mentioned three types of memory devices used in computer systems: at one extreme are *registers* which are small, very high speed memory units used within the control unit and ALU; at the other extreme are the mass storage devices, also known as *backing* or *auxiliary* storage, such as magnetic disk or magnetic tape drives (see later in this chapter for a description of these devices), which can store vast amounts of data but which are relatively slow; the *immediate access store*, or *memory* shown in Figure 5.2 is somewhere in the middle in terms of size and speed. Because of the importance of main memory, a great deal of effort has gone into producing different types of very fast memory devices since it is often the case that the speed at which a program can be executed is determined mainly by the time it takes to access data and instructions held in memory.

The two most important categories of memory are *Random Access Memory* (RAM) and *Read Only Memory* (ROM). RAM is a type of memory which allows data to be stored and retrieved directly. It is generally organised into a large array of units of storage called *words*. Typically, a word might be anything from eight to sixty-four bits (binary digits) long, but it will almost always be one or more bytes in length. Memory is usually specified as a number of bytes of storage rather than a number of words. For example, you might read that a personal computer has 512KB of memory meaning 512 blocks of 1024 bytes (KB=*kilobyte*=1024 bytes), or that it has 8MB (MB=*megabyte*=1024x1024 bytes - about a million).

Each word of storage has its own address, somewhat like a house number, which uniquely identifies it. This allows data to be stored or retrieved from a block of memory, containing perhaps millions of words, very rapidly. RAM used for main memory usually requires a small amount of electrical power for its operation. This means that when the computer system is switched off, the contents of the RAM will be lost, and consequently RAM is usually employed as a temporary store for such things as data, programs and graphics images. The term *volatile*, meaning subject to rapid change, is often used to describe this type of memory.

ROM is a type of memory designed to hold data more permanently than RAM. With most types of ROM, the data is built into the memory at the time of its manufacture and it cannot be changed. Because of this, the data is not lost when there is no electrical power to the memory, and it therefore called *non-volatile*. It has two main advantages over RAM:

- the data contained in it is not lost when the computer is switched off, and is therefore immediately available when the computer is switched on;

- it is simpler to manufacture and consequently it is cheaper and faster than RAM.

ROM is often used for holding a program called a *bootstrap loader* which runs as soon as the computer is switched on, causing a program called the *operating system* (see Chapter 2) to be copied from backing storage into the main RAM memory.

Input Devices

Input devices provide a convenient means of transferring information into a computer so that it may be processed in some way or stored permanently on magnetic media. Whatever its particular purpose, each type of input device is an *interface*, a means of bridging the gap between the human user and the electronic computer. For example, an input device such as computer *keyboard* converts the pressing of a key into an electrical signal representing a particular binary code; this code could represent a character within a word processing document, or it could be part of a response to a question posed by the current computer program. An interactive device such as a *mouse* or a *touch screen* provides a convenient method of communicating actions to a computer. Other input devices, such as *scanners* and *optical mark readers*, allow typed or hand-written documents to be read into a computer. In this section we describe several categories of input devices, namely *interactive devices*, *analogue to digital converters*, and *document readers*.

Interactive input devices

Interactive input devices are used in conjunction with visual display units so that the user is provided with immediate feedback on the task being performed by the computer. For example, the movement of a mouse or tracker ball is shown by a pointer on a display screen, and when a key is pressed on a keyboard, the appropriate character appears on the screen.

Computer Keyboard

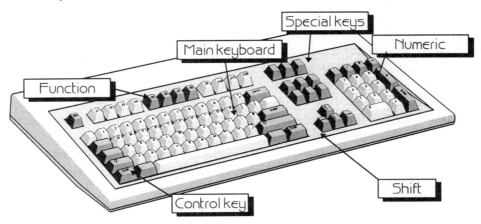

Figure 5.3. *A typical computer keyboard*

A typical computer keyboard, such as that commonly used in personal computer systems, is shown in Figure 5.3. The main section of a computer keyboard is similar to a typewriter keyboard, with the usual alphabetic and punctuation characters. The *shift* keys are used to switch between upper case (capital) letters and lower case (small) letters. The *control* keys are sometimes used to change the operation of a normal key. For example, holding down one of the control keys while hitting the *F* key might activate a menu. The separate *numeric keypad* is useful when data includes a high proportion of numeric characters. The *function* keys are used by application programs for special purposes, so the operation of a function key will often be different from one program to another, but quite frequently function key *F1* is used to gain access to a help facility if one is provided.

A keyboard is usually detachable, enabling the operator to position it to suit personal comfort, but it remains physically connected by a coiled cable. The desirable qualities of a keyboard are reliability, quietness and light operating pressure and in these terms keyboards vary considerably.

Keyboards are commonly used for the following types of tasks:

- entering alphanumeric information (that is, combinations of alphabetic, numeric and special characters such as punctuation marks) into the computer. A typical example of this is the use of a keyboard for word processing;
- interactively communicating with a program which asks the user questions and responds to the answers. A good example of this is an expert system (see Chapter 2) which provides advice on some area of interest after asking the user a sequence of questions;
- controlling animated graphics characters in computer games;
- entering commands to an operating system such as MS-DOS.

Mouse

A mouse is a small, hand-held device which the user can move on a flat surface to direct a pointer on the computer screen. It has two or more buttons which work in conjunction with software packages, allowing the user to draw, erase, select and format textual and graphical images. The most common type incorporates a ball which makes contact with the flat surface on which the mouse is moved and turns

Figure 5.4. *A typical mouse*

two rollers, one tracking vertical movements on screen, the other horizontal. The movement of the rollers is detected by sensors which continually send electrical signals through the mouse cable to the computer, reporting the location of the mouse. The software then uses these signals to adjust the pointer's position on the computer screen so that the pointer follows the movement of the mouse. Another type of mouse detects movement purely by optical sensors which work in conjunction with a special mouse pad, and some are cable-less, using infra-red to transfer signals to the computer in a way similar to the use of remote controls for TVs.

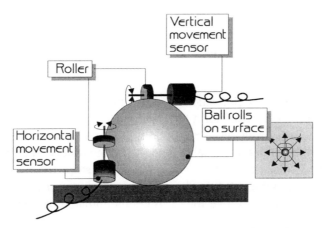

Figure 5.5. *How the mouse movement is detected*

Most computer systems are equipped with a mouse facility and many packages, including those for art, design, word processing and desktop publishing can only be operated effectively with a mouse. Graphical user interfaces (GUIs - see Chapter 2) such as Microsoft Windows also depend heavily on its use.

Tracker ball

A tracker ball is another variation of a mouse and is used for the same purposes. As shown in Figure 5.6, a tracker ball is a bit like an upside-down mouse, with the ball visible on the top of the base. To use a tracker ball you simply move the ball in the required direction using your fingers. Buttons are supplied just like on a mouse. Like joysticks, tracker balls have the advantage over mice that a flat surface is not required for its operation, and for this reason they are often used with portable computers.

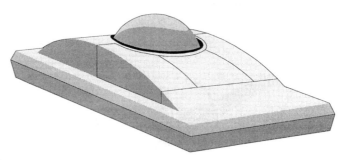

Figure 5.6. *A tracker ball*

Touch Screen

A touch screen is a touch-sensitive display, used to read the position of a fingertip. The screen displays options which a user can select simply by touching them. The computer detects the position touched and performs the appropriate action. The range of input values which can be selected will normally be small (a finger is not a very precise pointing device), so a touch screen might typically be used by a tourist agency to allow visitors to request information on, for example, local accommodation, entertainment and tourist attractions, or by a bank to allow customers to view details of banking services. The main components of a touch screen are a special film coating on the surface of the screen and a controlling microprocessor which determines the co-ordinates of the finger's contact point and displays the required information.

Digitising Tablet

A *digitising tablet* consists of a flat surface, containing an active area, typically 250mm square, which has a grid of very fine horizontal and vertical wires embedded into it. Attached to the tablet is a *stylus* which produces a magnetic field at its tip. The grid of wires allows the position of the stylus on the tablet to be determined very accurately (the grid can contain up to 1000 points per inch), so that the computer can track and store the movement of the stylus. As the user 'draws' on the tablet the results appear on the computer screen. Drawings are stored in the computer's memory so that they can be manipulated or displayed.

Digitising tablets are useful for entering drawings consisting of lines - engineering drawings or maps for example - into the computer. The line drawing can be placed on the tablet and the stylus used to trace the outline or locate key points. Usually the tablet can also be used as a device for selecting options in a similar way to the concept keyboard described earlier, but with the capability of providing many more options. Computer-aided drawing programs often allow templates of pre-defined shapes - electrical circuit components for example - to be overlaid on the tablet so that the user can select a shape which will then appear on the screen ready to be used in a drawing.

Figure 5.7. *A digitising tablet with stylus*

Light Pen

A light pen has an optical sensor in its tip and can only be used in conjunction with a *cathode ray tube* (CRT) display which creates images on screen through the use of a scanning electron beam; as the beam creates the screen images line by line (see the section on Visual Display Units), the light pen's optical sensor detects the exact moment when the beam passes beneath it and, from this, its position at any particular moment. By displaying functions at particular locations on the screen, the controlling program can allow the light pen to be used to make selections from several alternatives. It may also be used in conjunction with a drawing package to create, edit or manipulate images on screen. Though similar to the operation of a graphics tablet and stylus, a light pen is not capable of the same high accuracy, but it is generally cheaper. LCD (liquid crystal display) displays used in laptop, notebook and palmtop computers do not make use of electron beam scanning and cannot, therefore, support the use of light pens.

Analogue to Digital Converters (ADCs)

Data is often not in *digital* format but is instead a measurement of, for example, temperature or light intensity. These are called *analogue* forms of data and, before they can be used by a digital computer, they must be converted into digital format. A device which converts analogue data into digital data is called an *analogue to digital converter*(ADC).

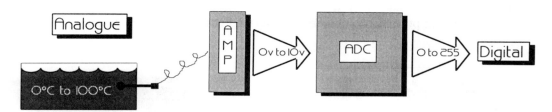

Figure 5.8. *An example of analogue to digital conversion*

If, for example, a certain microprocessor-controlled washing machine allowed you to select several temperature settings for the water, it might use a temperature sensor in conjunction with an ADC to convert water temperatures between 0°C and 100°C to a binary signal in the range 0 to 255, as illustrated in Figure 5.8. The diagram shows a temperature sensor immersed in the water. This will produce a small electrical signal, proportional to the water temperature, which must be amplified so that it produces a voltage in the range 0 volts to 10 volts, for example. The ADC then converts this voltage to a binary signal in the range 0 to 255 (11111111 in binary), so that 0°C is represented by 0 and 100°C is represented by 255. Thus a temperature of 25°C would produce about 2.5 volts from the amplifier and this would translate to binary 63 (00111111).

The term *digitiser* is usually reserved for more complex ADCs used for converting whole frames of photographic film into digital images which, with the aid of suitable software, can be displayed on a computer screen and edited. The output from a video camera, or medical scanning equipment can also be digitised for use in a computer. Digitisers which are designed for textual or graphical documents are usually termed *scanners* which are described in the next section.

Document readers

There are a number of devices designed to capture information, in the form of pictures or text, already printed on paper. Examples of such devices are *scanners, optical character readers* (OCRs), *optical mark readers* (OMRs), *magnetic ink character readers* (MICRs) and *bar code readers*

Scanners

Scanners allow whole documents to be scanned optically and converted into digital images. These vary from small hand-held devices which are manually moved slowly over the document (Figure 5.9), to machines which allow whole sheets of paper to be fed in and scanned automatically (Figure 5.10). Versions of both of these types of scanners are capable of dealing with colour images as well as black and white, though these machines tend to be significantly more expensive. Special scanners are available to convert textual documents, typed or hand-written, into the sort of format used by word processors. These devices perform *optical character recognition*(OCR*)* and have special software which processes the images once they have been converted into a computer-processable form. The software which can handle handwriting tends to be distinct from that for typed text, and is now commonly available for pen-based portable computers as described in a later section in this chapter.

Figure 5.10. *A full page scanner*

Figure 5.9. *A hand-held scanner being used to scan a document*

Optical Character Reader

As described earlier, these devices perform *optical character recognition* (OCR), the process of converting images of printed or hand-written material into a format suitable for computer processing. Figure 5.11 shows the main components of an optical character reader designed for printed documents. The document is illuminated and scanned by a strong light source and the lens concentrates the document's image onto a detector. The detector passes the image data to the OCR software which processes each character of the image, individually matching each character against stored data of the character set. Non-text regions containing graphics for example are often separated out and saved separately from the text which is output in a format which can be processed by an application program such as a word processor. Most commercial general-purpose OCR devices read machine-written text, but a few can cope with hand-printed text. Special-purpose OCR readers are available for such tasks as reading data on pre-printed forms or processing gas and electricity meter readings.

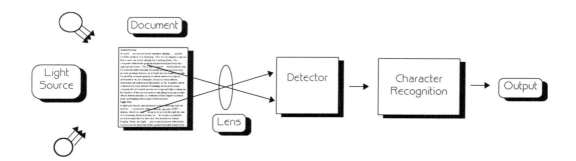

Figure 5.11. *The components of an OCR system*

Optical Mark Reader (OMR)

An OMR is designed to read simple marks placed in pre-set positions on a document. The document is pre-printed and the values which can be entered are usually limited to marks placed in specially placed boxes. Thus, a suitable application for OMR is a multi-choice examination paper, where the answer to each question has to be indicated by a pencil mark in one of several boxes located after the question number. The OMR scans the answer sheet for boxes containing pencil marks and thus identifies the answers, allowing the associated software to determine automatically the grade which the candidate has obtained. Optical mark readers can read up to 10,000 A4 documents per hour.

Magnetic Ink Character Reader (MICR)

This particular device is employed almost exclusively by the banking industry, where it is used for sorting and processing huge volumes of cheques. The millions of cheques which pass through the London Clearing System could not possibly be sorted and processed without the use of devices such as MICRs. Highly stylised characters, such as those illustrated below, are printed along the bottom of the cheques by a special printer, using ink containing iron oxide.

The characters are first magnetised as the cheque passes through the MICR which then electronically reads the magnetised characters. A high degree of reliability

0 1 2 3 4 5 6 7 8 9

Figure 5.12. *MICR characters*

and accuracy is possible, partly because of the stylised font, but also because the characters are not affected by dirty marks. This is obviously important when cheques may pass through several hands before reaching their destination. Such marks could cause problems for an optical character reader.

Bar Code Readers

A *Bar code* usually consists of a series of black bars of varying thickness with varying gaps between. These bars and gaps are used to represent data, which are often printed underneath in human-readable form. Using a laser scanner, the beam passes over the code noting the occasions when light is reflected by a bar and when it is absorbed by a space; the feedback is then converted by the scanner to a computer-readable code. Several standard codes are in use, each having particular features which are appropriate to certain application areas. One very common code is the Universal Product Code (UPC), a purely numeric code which, as the name suggests, is associated with supermarkets and general product distribution.

Bar codes are commonly used to store a variety of data such as prices and stock codes relating to products in shops and supermarkets. A sticker with the relevant bar code (itself produced by computer) is attached to each product, or alternatively, the packaging may be pre-coded. By using the data from the code, the cash register can identify the item, look up its latest price and print the information on the customer's receipt.

Figure 5.13. *A Universal Product Code*

Another useful application is for the recording of library issues. A bar code sticker is placed inside the book cover and at the time of issue or return it can be scanned and the library stock record updated. By providing each library user with a bar-coded library card, the information relating to an individual borrower can be linked with the book's details at the time of borrowing.

Output Devices

Just as input devices allow human beings to communicate with computers, so output devices allow computers to present electronically stored, binary coded data in a form which we can comprehend. In this section we describe *visual display units*, a number of different types of *printers*, and two types of *plotters*.

Visual Display Unit

The most commonly used device for communicating with a computer is the *visual display unit* (VDU). Input of text is usually by means of a full alphanumeric keyboard and output is displayed on a viewing screen similar to a television. The term VDU *terminal* is normally used to describe the screen and keyboard as a combined facility for input and output. On its own, the screen is called a *monitor* or *display*. So that an operator can see what is being typed in through the keyboard, input is also displayed on the screen. A square of light called a *cursor* indicates where the next character to be typed by the operator will be placed. Keyboards are described in the section on input devices.

Text and Graphics Modes

All modern display screens operate in either *text* or *graphics mode*. Text consists of letters (upper and lower case), numbers and special characters such as punctuation marks. Most applications require some text display, although it is safe to say that even basic word processors rely almost entirely on the graphics capability of modern screens to permit the use of various character styles or *fonts*. Despite this, the term *graphics* generally refers to picture images, such as maps, charts or drawings produced using graphic design programs, or even photographic images captured with an appropriate *digitising* device (see section earlier in this chapter).

Text Mode Dot Matrix Characters

In text mode (see preceding section), characters are formed using a matrix of *pixels* as shown in the adjacent example and the clarity of individual characters is determined by the number of pixels used. Selected dots within the matrix are illuminated to display particular characters. A 9 x 16 matrix obviously gives greater clarity and definition than an 8 x 8 matrix. Although both upper and lower case can be accommodated in a particular size matrix, it is usual to add extra rows for the 'tails' of lower case letters such as *g*, *p*, *y* and *j*. There are two main text modes, each defined according to the number of characters which

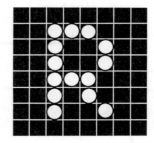

Figure 5.14 .*A capital R in an 8x8 dot matrix*

can be displayed on a single line and the number of rows accommodated within the screen's height; they are, 40 characters x 25 rows and 80 characters x 25 rows. The highest *resolution* (see next section) display standard uses 132 characters by 25 or 43 rows,

Screen Resolution and Size

A screen's *resolution* determines the clarity or sharpness of the displayed text or graphics characters. The achievement of high quality graphics generally requires a higher resolution or sharper image than is required for text display. Images are formed on the screen with pixels or tiny dots of light and the density with which they are packed determines the screen's resolution. A typical high-resolution screen provides a pixel density of 1024 columns by 768 rows, a total of 786,432 pixels.

Most microcomputer screens are 14-inch (across the diagonal) but larger screens are often used for applications such as computer-aided design (CAD), where the level of detail on some designs cannot be properly seen on a standard screen, and desktop publishing (DTP) to allow a complete page to be displayed at one time using characters of a readable size. Typical screen sizes are 15, 17, 20 and 21-inch.

Graphics Display with Bit Mapping

To provide maximum control over the screen display, each pixel can be individually controlled by the programmer to give maximum flexibility in the design of individual images. Several *bits* of memory store the colour information for each pixel on the screen; the more colours which are required to be displayed, the more bits which are required per pixel, and the total amount of memory needed for a complete screen depends on the screen resolution, that is, the number of pixels to be displayed. An image, built up in memory pixel by pixel, is used to automatically generate the screen display. This is termed *bit mapping*, which is illustrated in Figure 5.15. With black and white images for example, only one bit per pixel is needed: logic 0 to represent black and logic 1 for white; with four colours, black, red, yellow and white for instance, two bits are needed (00=black, 01=red, 10=yellow, 11=white); three bits are necessary for eight colours, and so on.

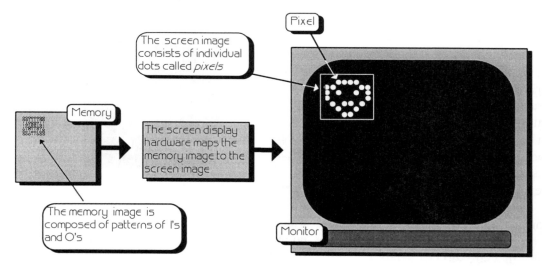

Figure 5.15. *How a bit mapped image is formed*

Where movement is required, for example in computer games, this is achieved in a similar manner to filmed cartoons - smooth movement is simulated by altering the contents of the appropriate memory locations to make small changes to the shape and location of the image. In addition to animation, bit mapping allows the drawing of extremely detailed and life-like pictures and is therefore used by many graphic design and drawing packages. Even word processors or other text-orientated packages make use of bit mapping to allow the display of different character styles and sizes as well as the *icon* images commonly used in WIMP-based *graphical user interfaces* or GUIs (see Chapter 2).

Monochrome and Colour

A monochrome screen uses one colour for the foreground and another for the background. White on black is not generally used because of indications from various research studies which users suffer greater eye fatigue than is the case with combinations such as green on black or amber on black.

Colour displays require more memory than monochrome, and as we explained earlier, the greater the number of colours available for a particular screen resolution, the more memory that is needed. However, a greater range of colours can obtained by using a process called *dithering*. Close to one another, two different colours appear to merge into a new colour, so by carefully 'mixing' pixels of different colours on the screen, many new colours can be created from the true ones available. Though colour displays require a great deal of memory, over recent years the fall in memory costs and the improvements in screen resolution and quality are making them the norm rather than the exception.

Printers

Printers are classed as being either *impact* or *non-impact* devices, but within these two categories there are large variations in speed of operation and quality of print. Speed of operation is largely dependent on whether the printer produces a character, a line or a page at a time. Impact printing uses a print head to strike an inked ribbon which is located between the print head and the paper. Individual characters can be printed, either by a *dot-matrix* mechanism, or by print heads which contain each character as a separate font (*solid font* type). Non-impact printers do not use mechanical hammers. Though non-impact *ink* and *bubble jet printers* use dot matrix heads similar to some impact printers, the method of transferring the ink to the paper is different, and *laser printers* work on a different principle entirely, a technology closely related to that used in photocopiers.

Dot Matrix Printers

Characters can be formed from a matrix of dots (see the section on VDUs) and the density of the matrix largely determines the quality of the print. The impact is carried out by a number of tiny pins (typically nine or twenty-four) each of which can be projected or withdrawn according to the pattern which is required.

A *ROM* (*Read Only Memory*) 'chip' inside the printer provides it with one or more character sets, and character styles, or *fonts*. Other fonts may be provided by plug-in cartridges or by software. Most printers now provide a range of print qualities and styles which can be selected through a keypad on the casing.

Increased density of print is achieved by passing the print head over a line twice (*double-striking*). Because the individual pins of dot matrix printers can usually be controlled by software, such printers are capable of producing graphical images as well as text. Some matrix-dot printers have special mechanisms and ink ribbons which enable them to produce colour images.

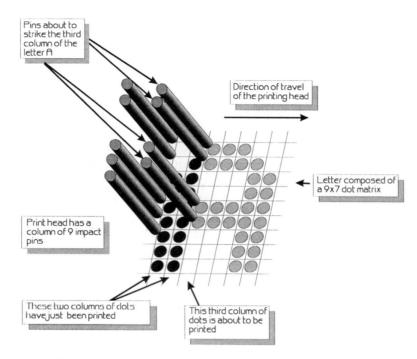

Figure 5.16. *How a character is formed by a dot matrix printer*

Barrel Printer

The barrel printer has a band with a complete set of characters at each print position, of which there are usually 132. Each print position has a hammer to impact the print ribbon against the paper. The mechanism is illustrated in Figure 5.17.

One complete revolution of the barrel exposes all the characters to each print position, so a complete line can be printed in one revolution. The characters on the barrel are arranged so that all characters of the same type are in the same horizontal position. Thus, for example, any required *A*s can be printed, then *B*s and so on, until the complete line is printed. The barrel revolves continuously during printing, the paper being fed through and the process repeated for each line of print. Typical printing speeds are 100 to 400 lines per minute. Barrel printers are used for high volume text output.

Line printers are expensive compared with character printers but may be necessary where large volume text output is required. Printing speeds of up to 3000 lines per minute are achieved with impact line printers. Even higher speeds are possible with non-impact printers.

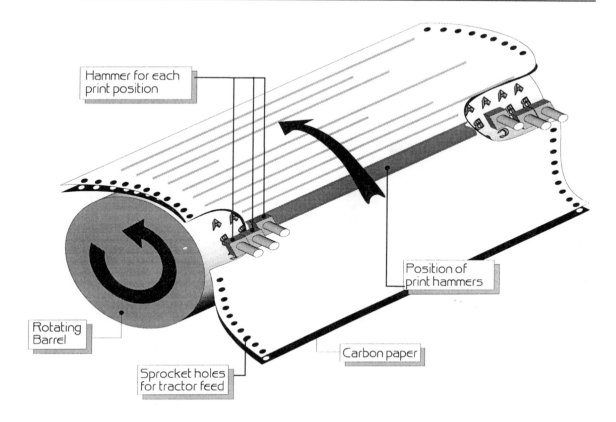

Figure 5.17. *How a barrel printer works*

Ink Jet Printers

Ink jet printers spray high-speed streams of ink droplets from individual nozzles in the print head onto the paper to form characters. There are two different approaches to propelling the ink onto the paper. In *thermal* ink jet printers (see Figure 5.18) electric heating elements are used to heat the ink and form vapour bubbles, which force the ink through fine nozzles onto the paper; the empty nozzles then refill. The other main approach is to use the *piezo-electric effect*. Here, a small electrical signal causes a special type of crystal to alter in size, thus creating a pump-like action which forces the ink through the nozzle. Otherwise, the action of this printer is essentially the same as for the thermal type. As for a impact dot matrix printer, characters are formed by the print head printing a number of columns of dots, but because the ink nozzles can be made so small, the separation of the individual dots is much smaller, thus producing much higher quality output. (Typically, there are between 40 and 60 such nozzles). By a series of passes and adjustments to the head's position, graphical images can be produced.

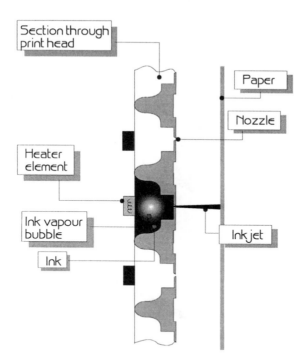

Figure 5.18. *Part of the print head of an inkjet printer*

Ink jet printers produce output much more slowly than laser printers. However, printing quality is very high and they provide a relatively cheap alternative to the laser printer, particularly so when colour output is required.

Laser Printers

Laser printers use a combination of two technologies: electro-photographic printing used in photo-copying, and high-intensity lasers. Figure 5.19 illustrates the operation of a laser printer. Once the image to be printed has been transferred to the printer's memory, a microprocessor inside the printer converts the image, line by line, into a sequence of signals which switch a laser beam on and off. Each laser beam pulse, representing a single dot of the image, is reflected by a rotating mirror to the surface of a drum. The special surface of the drum is given an electrical charge wherever the laser beam strikes. After a horizontal line of the image has been transferred to the drum in this manner, the drum rotates so that the next line can be built up. As the drum rotates, it comes into contact with plastic ink powder, called *toner*, which is attracted to the electrically charged areas of the drum. Because the printer paper has been given an electrical charge greater than that of the drum, the toner is transferred to the paper as the latter comes into contact with the drum. Finally, the toner is permanently bonded to the paper by means of heated rollers.

Achieving print speeds of 500 pages per minute (ppm), the most expensive laser printers are used in very large systems which require exceptionally high speed output. Effectively, complete pages are printed at one time.

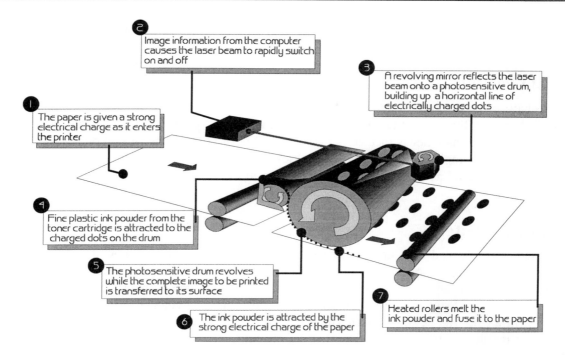

Figure 5.19. *How a laser printer works*

Although more costly than dot matrix and ink jet printers, laser printers offer greater speed and quality. Typically, speeds range from 6 to 26 pages per minute. Printing definition, or *resolution*, is measured in *dots-per-inch* or *dpi*; until recently the norm has been 300 dpi but more expensive machines producing 600 dpi are becoming increasingly common. The high quality of the printed image makes the laser printer highly suitable for producing the camera-ready copy used in book and magazine publishing.

Other types of printers

Liquid Crystal Shutter Printer

A liquid crystal shutter uses a very similar technology to that of a laser printer, but instead of a laser it contains a powerful halogen light source. In laser printers, the laser is fixed in one position, so to complete an image the width of a page, the beam is reflected from a rotating mirror which moves the laser beam horizontally across the drum (see previous section). This scanning action involves some complicated mechanical machinery which, together with the laser, form a major part of the component costs. Liquid crystal shutter printers, on the other hand, use a halogen light bulb as their light source and an array of liquid crystal shutters (the same technology used for liquid crystal displays (LCD) on watches and portable computer display screens) to control which positions on the photo-sensitive drum are exposed at any one time. Typically, the array contains 2400 shutters, sufficient to produce a full page-width line of ink dots at one time. In a liquid crystal shutter printer, moving parts are limited to the revolving drum and the paper and this makes the machine simpler and cheaper to service than its laser counterpart.

Chain Printer

In a chain printer several complete sets of characters are held on a continuous chain which moves horizontally across the paper. The ribbon is situated between the chain and the paper and an individual hammer is located at each of the 132 print positions. A complete line can be printed as one complete set of characters passes across the paper. Thus, in one pass as many lines can be printed as there are sets of characters in the chain. Printing speeds are therefore very high.

Thermal Printers

Characters are burned onto heat-sensitive thermographic paper, which is white and develops colour when heated above a particular temperature. The heat is generated by rods in the dot-matrix print head. By selective heating of the rods, individual characters can be formed from the matrix. Printing can be carried out serially, one character at a time or, by several heads, on a line-by-line basis. Serial thermal printing is slow but speeds of more than 1000 lines per minute are possible with line thermal printing.

Electro-sensitive Printers

This type produces characters in a similar fashion to the thermal printer except that the paper used has a thin coating of aluminium which covers a layer of black, blue or red dye. Low voltage electrical discharges in the matrix rods produce sparks which selectively remove the aluminium coating to reveal the layer of dye underneath. Operated as line printers with heads at each print position, printing speeds of more than 3000 lines per minute are achieved.

Summary of Printers

Generally, smaller, low-speed character printers are of use with microcomputer systems, but the increasing popularity of the latter has demanded increased sophistication in small printers. Features which have improved speeds of character printers include *bi-directional* printing (in two directions) and *logic-seeking,* which allows the printer to cut short a traverse across the paper if only a few characters are required on a line. The most popular printers for microcomputers are impact dot-matrix, ink-jet and laser.

Plotters

A plotter is a device designed to produce charts, drawings, maps and other forms of graphical information on paper. The images may be produced by *pens, electro-statically* or *ink jets* (see Printers section). Electrostatic plotters are quicker but the quality of the image is inferior to that produced with the pen type. Ink jet plotters, though expensive, produce the best quality drawings. Pen plotters use an ink pen or pens to create images on paper. There are two types, *flatbed* and *drum.*

Drum Plotter

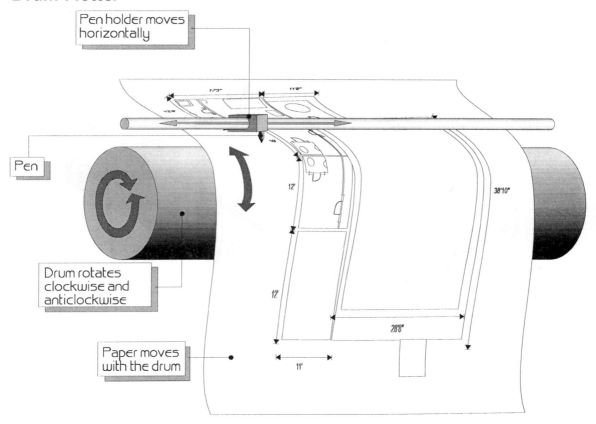

Figure 5.20. *How a drum plotter works*

A drum plotter has a different drawing mechanism. Instead of the paper remaining still, it moves to produce one of the lateral movements whilst the pens move to execute the other movements. To control the paper, the drum plotter uses sprocket wheels to interlock with the paper. The main advantage of the drum plotter is its ability to handle large sheets of paper. The operation of a drum plotter is illustrated in Figure 5.20. Plotters are commonly used in conjunction with computer-aided design (CAD) systems for the production of engineering and architectural drawings.

Flatbed plotter

This type of plotter looks like a drafting board with pens mounted on a carriage which moves along guide tracks. The paper is placed on the 'bed'. The pens can be raised or lowered as the image being created requires and different coloured pens can be brought into use at various stages of the process. Drawing movements are executed by movement of the carriage along the tracks and by the pens along the carriage. The size of paper which can be accommodated is limited by the size of the plotter 'bed', but this can be extremely large.

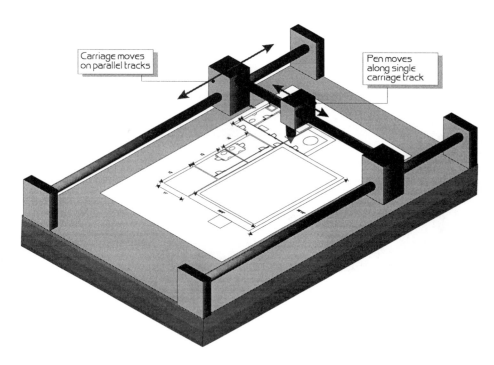

Figure 5.21. *How a flatbed plotter works*

Backing Storage

All backing storage systems consist of two main components, a *device* and a *medium*. For example, a disk drive is a device and a magnetic disk is a storage medium. Under program control, data can be transferred between main memory and the storage medium by way of a storage device connected on-line to the CPU. Although conventional magnetic tape and magnetic disk systems still account for the majority of data storage, a number of new products are now available, particularly in the area of removable disk systems. This section of the chapter describes:

- magnetic tape, including reel-to-reel and streamer systems
- magnetic disk (conventional hard and floppy)
- CD-ROM

Magnetic Tape

Despite the continued evolution of disk storage, magnetic tape is still used in most large scale computer installations as a cheap and secure method of storing large volumes of data. The problem with using magnetic tape, however, is that the data stored on it can only be accessed *serially*, that is, in the order in which it was stored. This is similar to the way that a domestic music cassette tape is 'processed', because to hear a track in the middle of the cassette tape, you must either listen to, or wind the tape past, the preceding tracks - in general, you can't get instant access to a particular track.

For many applications, for example, in the processing of an organisation's payroll where the data relating to each person must be used, serial processing is not a disadvantage. In applications such as this, the data items stored on the tape are simply processed from the first to the last in that order. Tape is also useful for the storage of historical or *archival* data where rapid access to data is not essential. The Police National Computer system for example, stores old, *inactive* criminal records in magnetic tape libraries, whilst millions of records of current criminal activities are kept *on-line* so that they are immediately available using fast magnetic disk devices (see the next section on magnetic disk). When an inactive record needs to be retrieved, the relevant tape is removed from the tape library, placed in the magnetic tape device and searched until the required data is found. It would be inefficient and expensive to keep all records, no matter how old, on-line (that is, connected to the computer) all the time.

However, there are a large number of applications, requiring fast, direct access to data, for which magnetic tape is not suitable. Other backing storage devices, such as those described later in this section, are used in such circumstances.

General Features of Magnetic Tape

The type of tape used on large mainframe and minicomputer systems is stored on a detachable reel approximately 1 foot in diameter. A tape is a long ribbon of plastic film coated with a

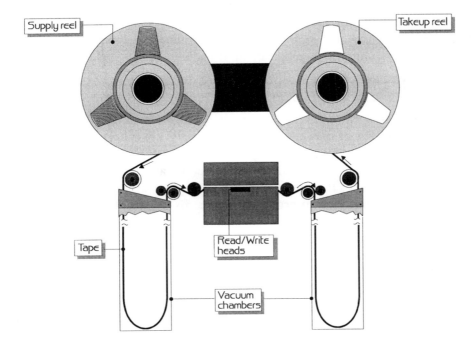

Figure 5.22. *A reel-to-reel magnetic tape system*

substance which can be magnetised. Typically, a tape is 2400 feet long and half an inch wide. Before a tape can be accessed by a computer system it must be loaded into an on-line *tape unit*, the main features of which are shown in Figure 5.22.

It can be seen from the figure that there are two reels, the *supply* reel containing the tape which is to be *read* from or *written* to by the computer system and the *take-up* reel which collects the tape as it is unwound from the supply reel. During processing, the tape is rapidly propelled past separate *read* and *write heads* at high speed and data is transferred between tape and main memory in units of data called *blocks*. A small gap (*inter-block gap*) is left between each block, so that following the transfer of a block, the tape can decelerate and stop and then accelerate again to the speed required for transfer of the next block, without any loss of data. To keep the tape at the proper tension, even during acceleration and deceleration, vacuum chambers are used to allow some slack in the tape beneath each reel. When processing is finished, the tape is re-wound onto the supply reel, which is then removed from the tape unit. The take-up reel remains in the unit.

Data Storage on Magnetic Tape

Figure 5.23 shows how data is stored on magnetic tape. Each character is represented by a group of binary digits (nine for example), across the width of the tape. As the figure shows, each 0-bit or 1-bit is stored as a magnetic 'dot' in a single *track* along the length of the tape and each group of bits representing one character occupies one *frame* across the tape. Data stored on tape are frequently organised as a *file* of *records*. For example, a company's personnel file, used for payroll purposes, would contain one record for every employee. Each employee's record would contain a number of *fields*, such as works number, name, address, data of birth, department etc., and each field would contain a number of characters, or *frames*, in binary form, providing the appropriate information.

In order to process a file held on magnetic tape, each record in turn must be copied into the memory of the computer. Though this transfer of data from the magnetic tape device to the computer's immediate access store takes place very quickly (thousands of characters per second), it is inefficient to transfer only one record at a time. This is because gaps containing no data must be left on the tape to allow the tape drive to halt the tape after the record has been read and to restart it in order to read the next record, and this stopping and starting cannot take place instantaneously. If there were to be a gap after every record, far too much tape would be wasted. The solution is to group a few records together into a *block* and leave an *inter-block gap*. This means that rather than one record at a time being read, a block containing several records is transferred into a special area of memory called a *buffer* where they are available for processing. When a block of records has been processed, the next block is read into the buffer.

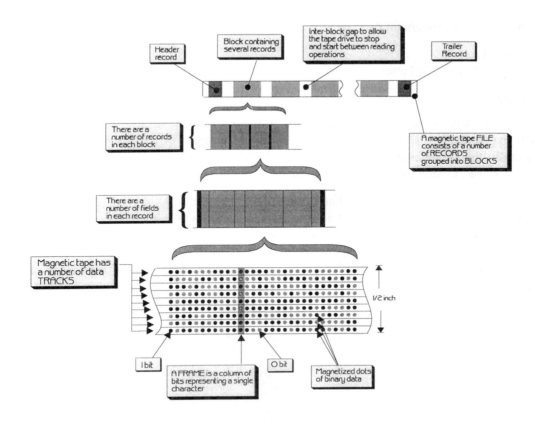

Figure 5.23. *Data storage on magnetic tape*

Streamer tapes

These look like cassette tapes, but are slightly larger, and are often used to *back-up* (copy for security purposes) hard disks on microcomputer systems. The tape back-up device may be built into the computer's system unit, but frequently it is purchased as a separate item. Streamer tapes have huge capacity, typically hundreds of megabytes, and can copy the contents of a hard disk in less than half an hour.

Magnetic Disks

Many computer applications require quick, *direct access* to data or programs, that is, without the need to search through data not of immediate interest before locating a particular item. Remember that this is not the case when data are stored on magnetic tape - if the required item is in the middle of the tape, the computer must read all the preceding data first in order to locate it. The facility provided by magnetic disk, allowing an item to be located directly, is the main reason for it being the most important backing storage medium in use today.

Two popular types of magnetic disk are:

- hard disks
- floppy disks or diskettes.

Hard Disks

The disk is usually made of aluminium with a special coating which allows data to be recorded magnetically. Data are stored in concentric rings or *tracks*. The storage is fundamentally the same as that for tape, except that the magnetic states representing binary patterns are stored in single-file around the tracks.

Figure 5.24 illustrates these features. Each track is divided into a number of *sectors* and each sector has a certain storage capacity. Each track, and sector within the track, has a number, or *address*, recorded on it which can be used by software to locate a particular item stored on the disk. A common method of using these addresses is to use part of the disk for an index containing the names and track/sector addresses of every item stored on the remainder of the

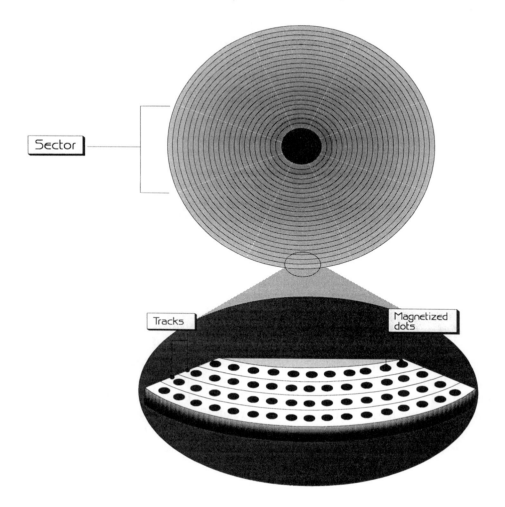

Figure 5.24. *How data is stored on magnetic disk*

disk. So, whenever a particular item needs to be used by the computer, the item's address is first retrieved from the index so that the read-write head can be directly positioned over the track containing the item's sector address.

The number of tracks and sectors available on a disk's surface is known as its *format*. The sector size can either be fixed permanently by a physical marker on the surface of the disk, or it can be set by software. The former is known as *hard* sectoring and the latter as *soft* sectoring. All microcomputer systems use soft sectoring, so that a disk employed in such a system must always be *formatted* before it can be used. This involves writing track and sector information to the disk according to the requirements of the particular disk operating system concerned. A sector of a track, in a similar way to a block on magnetic tape, is the unit of data transferred between a disk drive and the computer.

Figure 5.25. *A microcomputer system hard disk drive*

Figure 5.25 illustrates the construction of a microcomputer hard disk drive. During computer operation, the disk rotates continuously. The read-write head does not touch the disk's surface as this would result in rapid wear of the surface and the head. Instead, the head flies just above the surface of the disk, so that information can be recorded onto or read from the concentric tracks. The head is specially shaped so that as the disk passes beneath it at high speed, a flow of air forces the head to rise a tiny distance above the surface.

The most common approach to the design of the read-write head's access mechanism is by means of a single *movable* head per disk surface as illustrated in Figure 5.25. To increase on-line storage capacity, a number of disks, or *platters*, may be mounted on the same spindle, each surface of the disk having its own read-write head.

Exchangeable disk packs

Some disk drives, particularly those used in large-scale computer installations, are capable of using removable sets of disks called *exchangeable disk packs* containing six, eight, ten or twelve platters mounted on a central spindle which rotates all the disks at the same speed. There is sufficient gap between each surface to allow read-write heads to move in and out between the disks. Only one head will be reading or writing at any one time. The disk pack is enclosed in a plastic shell, to protect the disk surfaces from dust. Figure 5.26 illustrates the disk pack and the access mechanism.

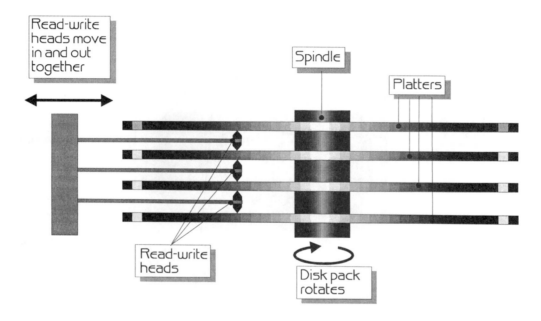

Figure 5.26. *An exchangeable disk pack*

Winchester Disks

When first introduced, Winchester disks were designed for large computer systems and are still popular on such systems. Virtually all microcomputer systems now include a *hard drive* or *hard disk unit* as standard, because its large storage capacity and quick data access times are essential for the use of modern software. Winchester disk systems consist of packs of hard disks, stacked in the same way as the exchangeable disk pack systems described earlier. The disks are not removable and are sealed inside the storage units together with the read-write mechanism. The contamination-free environment in which the disks are stored allows very high speeds of rotation, typically, 3600 revolutions per minute. Storage capacities are increasing as technology advances, but commonly available systems for microcomputers are measured in hundreds of megabytes.

Floppy Disks or Diskettes

Apart from a built-in hard disk unit, a microcomputer has at least one, and possibly two, floppy disk drives to enable the installation of new software onto the hard disk and to allow the copying of files for security purposes. Floppy disks, as their name suggests, are flexible plastic disks coated in a magnetisable material and encased in a square, plastic, protective casing. The diskette revolves inside the casing at approximately 360 revolutions per minute (rpm), which is much slower than a hard disk. The casing is lined with a soft material which helps to clean the diskette as it revolves. The read-write head makes contact with the diskette surface when data transfer is in progress and withdraws at other times to reduce wear. Unlike a hard disk, the diskette does not rotate continuously - it only rotates when data is being transferred to or from the computer. A diskette will eventually wear out after about 500 to 600 hours of contact.

There are two commonly used types of floppy disk: $3\frac{1}{2}$ inch and $5\frac{1}{4}$ inch. Figure 5.27 shows the component parts of the $3\frac{1}{2}$ inch diskette, which all new microcomputer systems now use in favour of its less robust and lower capacity $5\frac{1}{4}$ inch forerunner. To allow users to transfer data from both types, manufacturers usually offer systems with two drive units, one for each.

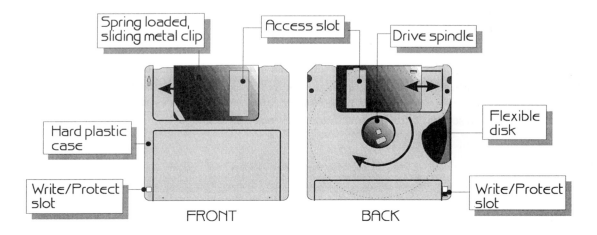

Figure 5.27. *A $3\frac{1}{2}$ inch floppy disk*

The $3\frac{1}{2}$ inch disk is stored in a rigid plastic casing which makes it more robust than its $5\frac{1}{4}$ inch counterpart. A metal sliding shutter, covering the slot which provides access to the recording surface, slides open when the disk is placed in the drive unit. The greater protection provided by this rigid casing allows data to be recorded more densely, up to 1.44 megabytes (Mb), than is generally practicable with the $5\frac{1}{4}$ inch variety (maximum 1.2 Mb).

A small hole with a sliding shutter is located in one corner of the casing and acts as the write-protect slot. The drive unit uses an infra-red light source to determine whether the slot is open, indicating that the disk is *read only,* or closed allowing data to be both written to the disk or read from it. The figure shows the disk with the slot in the open, read-only, state. This is opposite to the condition used with a **5 ¼** inch floppy disk drive when a covered notch in the side of the jacket indicates 'read only'.

CD-ROM (Compact Disk-Read Only Memory)

This type of optical disk uses laser beam technology to allow data to be recorded and read. Data is again recorded as bit-patterns represented by tiny holes in the surface of the disk produced by high-intensity laser beams. The data can then be read from the disk using a laser beam of reduced intensity. The majority of CD-ROM drives, just like domestic CD music players, are capable only of reading CDs, but much more expensive machines exist which allow reading and writing, and it is likely that in the near future they will become as common as the current read-only drives.

Typically, a single CD-ROM disk can store an enormous 600 Mb of data, sufficient space for storing video sequences and digitised sound such as speech. *Multimedia* systems, which use a microcomputer with sophisticated sound capabilities, a CD-ROM drive and a high resolution colour screen, are becoming increasingly popular as a result. These systems use computer programs which combine music and speech with full motion video for such applications as computer-based training (CBT) and interactive games. CD-ROM is also used for storing and providing access to reference material such as dictionaries, encyclopaedias and graphic images such as clip art. A number of manufacturers are marketing machines specially designed for multimedia applications.

Compared to magnetic disk, CD-ROM currently has two major drawbacks: it is significantly slower, and it is read-only. For these reasons magnetic disk drives are preferable in a great number of areas, but it is very likely that further technological advances will increase the popularity of CD-based backing storage in the very near future.

Chapter 6

Computer Systems Architecture

Introduction

As explained in the chapter on Computer Hardware, all computers have the same basic functional components, but the architectural details in some are far more complex than in others. This chapter begins with a study of some typical architectural features to be found in microcomputer systems. The final part of this chapter describes some approaches to parallel processing (the simultaneous processing of data by multiple processors).

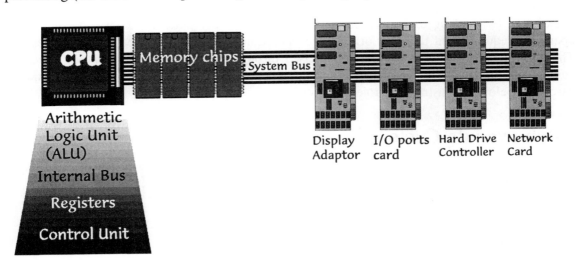

Figure 6.1. *Microcomputer system components*

The features examined are:

- the processor or CPU;
- memory (both RAM and ROM);
- bus architecture;
- file storage.

External, peripheral components, including screen displays, keyboards, printers and other devices are dealt with in Computer Hardware.

Processor

The processor is a CPU (Central Processing Unit) on a 'chip' and provides the central base for a machine's power. The following section describes the main features of processor design and examines more recent advances which have enabled huge increases in processor power. The main features of a processor are its:

- clock speed;
- word length;
- architecture.

Clock Speed

As the initiator of all the activities in a computer, the processor has a wide range of tasks to perform and to ensure that these tasks are properly synchronised, an internal clock mechanism is used. The speed of the clock is one determinant of how quickly a processor can *execute* instructions.

A *program* (a set of instructions designed to make the computer perform in a particular way) is executed by *fetching* each instruction in turn from the computer's memory, *decoding* the operation required and then performing the operation under the direction of the processor. The control of *program execution* is exercised through the processor's *automatic sequence control mechanism*. The activity it controls is known as the *fetch-execute cycle* and is described below to illustrate the role of the clock.

Fetch-execute Cycle

Data can take various forms when stored as a *memory word* (the contents of a memory location) namely:

- pure binary;
- coded binary, for example, binary-coded decimal (BCD);
- character codes, for example, ASCII.

All the above are considered to be data and can be interpreted as such by the CPU, but in order to perform any tasks, it has to have access to *computer instructions*. During processing, data currently being processed and the instructions needed to process the data, are stored in main memory.

Thus, a memory word can also form an instruction, in which case, it is referred to as an *instruction word*; one formed of data is known as a *data word*.

The CPU has a number of registers which it can use to temporarily store a number of words read from memory. These registers are used to apply meaning to memory words. It should be noted that memory words cannot be determined as being data or instructions simply by examination of the code. The CPU differentiates between data and instructions by locating:

- instructions in an *instruction register*;
- data in *data registers*.

A computer program stored in main memory comprises a sequence of instructions, each of which is transferred, in turn, into the CPU's instruction register, thus identifying the next operation the CPU is to perform. The instructions are retrieved from consecutive memory locations, unless the last instruction executed requires the next instruction to be fetched from a different location. Instructions dealing with the latter circumstance are called *branch* or *jump* instructions. The process of fetching, interpreting and executing instructions is called the fetch-execute cycle but may also be referred to as the instruction cycle or automatic sequence control. The fetch-execute cycle involves the use of a number of *registers* (special storage locations) within the processor.

Program Counter (PC)

The Program Counter (PC) keeps track of the memory locations, where program instructions are stored. At any one time, during a program's execution, the PC holds the memory address of the next instruction to be executed. Its operation is possible because the instructions forming a computer program are stored in adjacent memory locations, so that the next instruction will, normally (except when a *branch* instruction is encountered), be stored in an address a single increment more than the address of the last instruction to be fetched. By incrementing the address in the PC each time an instruction is received, the PC always has the address of the next instruction.

Memory Buffer Register (MBR)

All transfers (both data and instructions) between memory and the processor must pass through the Memory Buffer Register (MBR).

Memory Address Register (MAR)

The Memory Address Register (MAR) holds the address of the next memory word to be fetched (whether it contains data or an instruction) and during the fetching of program instructions will contain the address of the next instruction (the value copied from the PC).

Current Instruction Register (CIR)

The Current Instruction Register (CIR) stores the current instruction for decoding and execution.

Accumulators and General-purpose Registers

These registers are situated within the arithmetic/logic unit (ALU) and provide a working area for data fetched from memory. Values about to be added or subtracted can be copied, through the MBR, into the accumulators. The arithmetic result can be placed in one accumulator and copied from there into the required memory location.

Figure 6.2 shows the CPU registers (apart from the general-purpose) and a group of instructions in contiguous memory locations.

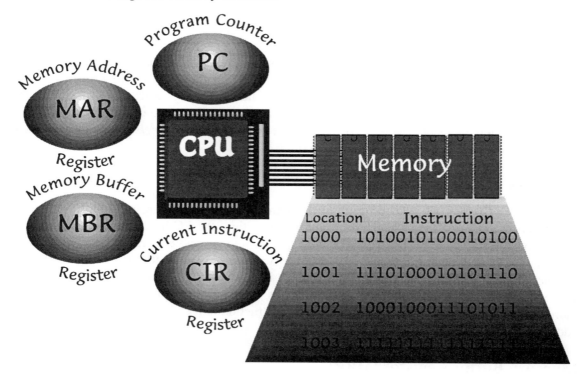

Figure 6.2. *Processor registers used in Fetch Execute Cycle and program in memory*

To fetch an instruction from memory, the CPU places its address in the MAR and then carries out a memory read. The instruction is then copied into the MBR and from there, into the CIR. Similarly, an instruction which itself requires the reading of a particular *data word* causes the address of the data word to be placed into the MAR. The execution of a memory read then copies the addressed data word into the MBR, from where it can be accessed by the CPU. To summarise, the fetch-execute cycle involves a number of discrete steps:

1.   the contents of the PC are copied into the MAR; the MAR now contains the address of the next instruction to be fetched and a memory read is initiated to transfer the instruction from memory into the MBR;

2.   the PC is incremented and now contains the address of the next instruction;

3.   the instruction is transferred from the MBR into the CIR;

4.   the instruction in the CIR is decoded and executed;

5.   unless the instruction is a STOP instruction then the cycle is repeated.

Certain steps in the fetch-execute cycle must wait until the previous step is completed. For example, during the fetching of a program instruction from memory the instruction cannot be moved from the Memory Buffer Register (MBR) to the Current Instruction Register (CIR) until the transfer from memory to MBR has been completed. The time taken for the latter transfer is dependent on the speed of the memory read operation. Not all activities are dependent on the prior completion of another or others. For example, once the value of the Program Counter (PC) has been copied to the Memory Address Register (MAR), the PC can be incremented at any time during the fetch-execute cycle.

Synchronising Operations

To synchronise the processor's operations, the clock generates regularly timed 'pulses', usually at a rate between 33 and 100 million per second. A technical specification will express this rating in MHz (Megahertz or million *cycles* per second). For example a 90 MHz processor operates with a clock running at 90 million pulses or cycles per second.

Different processor activities take different times to complete. For example, it takes longer to read the contents of a memory location (a *memory read*) than to increment a value stored in one of the registers within the processor. Any such processor activity must be synchronised with a clock cycle. The number of clock cycles which the processor needs to complete an operation will depend on the type of operation. For example, one operation may be completed within a single clock cycle, whilst another may take several cycles.

Wait State

When a processor handles data more quickly than it can be accessed from main memory, a memory read may take more than one clock cycle to complete. Each additional clock cycle is known as a wait state. The topic is referred to in more detail later, in the section on *cache memory*.

Subject to certain limitations to be explained later, the greater the clock rate, the quicker the computer system (as a whole) will perform. For example, a 100 MHz processor will carry out processing more quickly than a 66 MHz processor.

Word Length

Any given processor is designed to handle a particular number of bits as a unit, typically, 8, 16 or 32. The size of this unit is known as the processor's *word length*. A processor with a word length of, for example, 32 bits, uses that unit size during the execution of arithmetic, logic, data transfer or input/output instructions. In addition, any working registers within the processor are also equal to the word length of the processor.

Other Processor Registers

Apart from the registers used in the fetch-execute cycle, most processors have a number which are general-purpose and as such, can be used by the *low-level programmer* to store intermediate results of processing. *Index* registers can be used to hold offset values to allow *indexed indirect* addressing methods or can be used as *counters*. Another register contains the *stack pointer*, which is used to store the address of the next available location in a special area of memory called a *stack*. A *flag* or *status register* is used for the storage of various flag bits which can be set to 1 or cleared to 0 depending on some condition, and typically include:

- sign flag (positive or negative) indicating the sign of the result of the last arithmetic operation; this would be copied from the sign bit of the result of this last operation;
- carry flag, set to 1 if the last arithmetic operation produced a carry;
- zero flag, set to 1 if the result of the last arithmetic operation was zero and to 0 if the result was non-zero;
- overflow flag to indicate the occurrence of arithmetic overflow in the last operation;
- break status, set to 1 if a break instruction has been executed;
- interrupt disable flag, set to 1 if interrupts are disabled.

Data Bus

Within the processor, data are transmitted along a set of parallel lines called an *internal data bus*. An *external data bus* acts as the interface with the system's *motherboard*. The motherboard is a circuit board into which the system components (Figure 6.1) are plugged. If the board is designed for the needs of a particular processor, the data path between the processor and memory components is at least as wide as the processor's internal bus. Thus, a motherboard designed to take a 32 bit processor has a 32 bit data path to connect it to other processor or memory chips. The processor's external data bus (which connects with the motherboard) is also 32 bits wide. The motherboard is connected to a *system data bus,* which acts as the communication channel between the motherboard and the other system components. It is worth mentioning that the ISA (Industry Standard Architecture - first used in the IBM AT) design, which is still used in most PCs, has a system data bus which is only 16 bits wide. It also operates at a clock speed of 8 MHz, which is too slow for modern processors. Such imbalance affects the performance of a computer system as a whole (see Bus Architecture). Table 6.1 shows the word lengths of generations of Intel processors.

Processor	Word Length	Internal	External
8080	8 bits	8 bits	8 bits
8088	16 bits	16 bits	8 bits
8086	16 bits	16 bits	16 bits
80286	16 bits	16 bits	16 bits
i386	32 bits	32 bits	32 bits
i486	32 bits	32 bits	32 bits
P24T	32 bits	64 bits	32 bits
Pentium	32 bits	64 bits	64 bits

Table 6.1. *Generations of processors showing word lengths*

Maths Co-processors

Most processors have an associated faster processor (known as a maths co-processor) which can radically improve the performance of processor-intensive applications, such as spreadsheets and computer-aided design (CAD). For example, associated with the Intel processors mentioned earlier are the 8087, 80287, i387 and i487. The Intel i386DX, i486DX and Pentium processors, on the other hand, house a maths co-processor on the same chip; data flow is much faster than is possible with a separate co-processor (the SX versions of the i386 and i486 processors do not incorporate a co-processor, and can be upgraded with the i387 and i487, respectively). The co-processor can only improve system performance if the software recognises and makes use of it.

Processor Architecture

The internal structure of a processor is generally referred to as its *architecture*. Within the integrated circuits that form the processor, are contained a complex collection of component units, including registers, counters, arithmetic and logic circuits and memory elements. Although the details of such architecture are mainly of concern to the programmer working at machine code level, two main approaches to processor design are briefly described below. All the instructions available with a particular processor are known as its *instruction set*. CISC is an acronym for *complex instruction set computer* and RISC stands for *reduced instruction set computer*.

CISC Architecture

For some time, the view was that longer word lengths should be used to create more complex instruction sets and thus, more powerful processors. This approach has given way to the RISC design, which makes more effective use of the increased word lengths available in modern processors.

RISC Architecture

A RISC processor exhibits a number of particular design features:

- a reduced instruction set processor, as the name suggests, is one which provides only a small number of different instructions compared with the prevailing standards for its CISC competitors. Research into conventional CISC architecture has suggested that the average processor spends most of its time executing only a handful of simple instructions. Each instruction type in a RISC processor can be executed in only one clock pulse. More complex instructions can take several clock pulses.
- superscalar execution. This is the ability to execute more that one instruction at once (in parallel pipelines). Thus, for example, a floating point arithmetic calculation can be executed in one pipeline, at the same time as an integer operation in the other. A separate arithmetic unit is available to deal with each. Intel's Pentium processor can, therefore, execute two instructions in one clock pulse, compared with its predecessor's (the i486) one.
- integral cache memory. The topic of cache memory is examined later, but the location of this component on the processor provides faster data flow than is possible with a separate cache memory component.
- branch prediction. The processor contains circuitry to predict the outcome of conditional branch instructions (when a certain condition is true, the program branches to an instruction out of the usual sequence) before they even enter the pipeline. Predictions are based on previous execution history. A correct prediction avoids retrieval of irrelevant instructions into the pipeline; instead, the valid instruction is fetched from the branch target address. An incorrect prediction means that the pipeline has to be cleared, but the algorithms for prediction achieve a high success rate, which makes the technique worthwhile.

A British microcomputer manufacturer, Acorn, was among the first to produce a RISC microcomputer called the ARM (Acorn RISC Machine). Now, all the world's major computer manufacturers produce their own RISC-based machines. Notable examples of modern RISC processors include the IBM 'RISC/6000' series, IBM/Motorola 'PowerPC601', DEC 'Alpha AXP' and the Sun Microsystems/Texas Instruments 'SuperSparc'. Such processors are designed for high performance systems, to be used as *file servers* or *workstations* in networks (see Chapter 17), rather than as stand-alone machines, where the power would be wasted. Unlike the Alpha, PowerPC and SuperSparc processors, which have been designed purely as RISC processors, the Intel i486 and Pentium processors have had to retain some CISC features, to remain compatible with the huge range of PC software designed for the i386 and its predecessors. The Alpha, PowerPC and SuperSparc processors are pure RISC processors and not compatible with software designed for the Intel range. This means that they are excluded from the lucrative PC software market. Although the Pentium still includes some complex instruction support, its design includes all the RISC features outlined earlier.

Memory

There are two types of internal computer memory - RAM (Random Access Memory) and ROM (Read Only Memory).

RAM

Functions

RAM constitutes the working area of the computer and is used for storage of program(s) and data currently in use. Computer memory is measured in 'Kb' (kilobytes), where 1 Kb is 1024 bytes; for larger memory, the unit of measurement is 'Mb' (megabyte), which is 1024 Kb. Generally, the performance of a computer system can be improved by the addition of more memory. Other upgrading measures, such as the addition of a hard disk controller (see later) will make less impact on system performance if main memory capacity is inadequate. If there is too little memory, more frequent access to disk is required. As a hard disk drive (see Disk) is a relatively slow component, compared with main memory, frequent disk accesses slow down overall system performance. Large main memory enables the system to keep *resident*, all the files it needs for an application.

Because RAM is 'volatile' (the current contents are lost when power is removed or different programs and data are entered), all programs and data files are held more permanently on a magnetic storage medium; invariably this is 'floppy' or hard disk.

Technical Features

RAM is directly accessible by the processor and memory/processor transfers which occur during a program's execution have to be made as quickly as possible to maximise the use of the processor's power. The previous section on processors describes the use of a `clock' which generates regularly timed pulses to synchronise the activities of the processor and explains that different activities take different numbers of clock pulses. Memory/processor transfers, although extremely quick, typically 80 to 100 nanoseconds (ns) for a read from RAM, constitute a penalty in terms of using the processor's power. Thus, the quicker the transfer can be carried out, the less time that the processor spends unoccupied. One quality RAM should possess, therefore, is speed. Predictably, the higher the speed, the greater is the cost.

Types of RAM

Broadly, two types of RAM are used in computers. They are:

- Static RAM (SRAM);
- Dynamic RAM (DRAM).

A number of comparisons can be drawn between the two types:

- DRAMs are easier to make than SRAMs;

- More DRAM can be packed onto a single integrated circuit or `chip' than is possible with SRAM;
- DRAM consumes less power than SRAM;
- Static RAM, as the term suggests, retains its contents as long as power is maintained, whereas Dynamic RAM needs to be 'refreshed' (the contents of each location are rewritten) at intervals not exceeding 2 milliseconds (ms);
- SRAM can be written to and read from more quickly, but is more expensive than DRAM.

The most important features for comparison relate to speed of access and cost. To maximise use of a powerful processor SRAM is the obvious choice. Unfortunately, the needs of modern software for large main memory would make computer systems based wholly on SRAM very expensive. The use of *graphical user interfaces*, such as Microsoft Windows and the increasing sophistication of software packages, calls for a minimum of 8 to 16 Mb of RAM. As software becomes more sophisticated even more memory will be needed. So, for economic reasons, main memory consists of DRAM chips grouped together on a memory board. For example, 8Mb of RAM may consist of 8 x 1Mb memory chips. A conflict exists between processor speed and memory cost. Doubling the clock speed of a processor from 33 MHz to 66 MHz does not necessarily double the speed of the computer's overall operation because of other factors, including *disk access* time and memory read time. To help improve the speed of memory accesses and still keep down the cost of memory, a system of *cache memory* can be used.

Cache Memory

To understand the function of cache memory it is necessary to refer to a feature identified in the section on the processor, namely *wait-state*. A wait-state is an extra clock pulse added to a processor cycle when it accesses memory. The slower the memory, the more wait-states which have to be added to processor cycles to give the memory time to respond. The greater the number of wait-states, the lower the overall computer system performance. Thus, a high performance processor is wasted if it is used with a slow memory system which requires many wait-states. A memory system which requires zero wait-states will allow the system (ignoring peripheral device performance) to function at the maximum performance of the processor. It must be emphasised that overall system performance depends on all components forming a computer system and that *disk access time* also plays a major part in determining such performance. The topic of disk storage is dealt with in a later section. A cache memory system aims to provide the performance of fast Static RAM (SRAM) but at the lower cost of Dynamic RAM (DRAM).

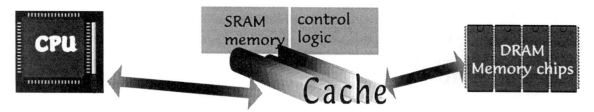

Figure 6.3. *Cache memory*

A cache is a small amount of very fast SRAM located between the processor and main memory. Figure 6.3 illustrates the relationship between main memory, the processor and the cache.

The cache size is typically 64Kb to 256Kb and its purpose is to hold a copy of frequently used code and data. Instead of accessing the slower main memory (consisting of DRAM) for such data, the processor can go directly to the cache memory without incurring any wait-states. The effectiveness of cache memory is based on the principle that once a memory location has been accessed, it is likely to be accessed again soon. This means that after the initial access, subsequent accesses to the same memory location need go only to the cache. Much computer processing is repetitive, so a high 'hit rate' in the cache can be anticipated. The cache hit rate is simply the ratio of cache 'hits' to the total number of memory accesses required by the processor. Systems using cache memory may achieve an 85 to 90 per cent hit rate. Thus, system performance can be radically improved beyond that possible with other systems using the same processor but lacking a cache memory system.

Cache memory aims to improve memory access times and keep down memory costs. The larger the cache, the greater the hit rate but the greater the cost of the memory. For example, a cache the same size as the main memory would obviously give a 100 per cent hit rate but would defeat the object of having a cache.

Modern processors have an integral cache (on the same chip) which provides even better cache performance.

ROM

Function

ROM (Read Only Memory) is a permanent storage area for special programs and data which have been installed during the process of computer manufacture. The contents are 'hard-wired' and cannot be altered by software.

The software contained within ROM is fairly standard for most machines and generally includes part of the BIOS (Basic Input/Output System). As the name suggests, the BIOS handles the basic hardware operations of input and output. The aim of the BIOS is to provide an interface between the programmer and the computer. The interface relieves the programmer of concern about the physical characteristics of the hardware devices which form the system. As such, the BIOS is machine orientated and will vary from one make of machine to another.

Bus Architecture

This concerns the internal structure of a computer, that is the way in which the various components are connected and communicate with one another. As technological advances improve the performance of certain components, so the architecture has to change to take advantage of these improvements. A brief summary of some architectural standards, which aim to improve *overall system performance*, is provided later. These standards are:

- IBM's Micro Channel Architecture (MCA)
- Extended Industry Standard Architecture (EISA)
- Local Bus (VESA and PCI)

To begin with, however, we will look at bus component and its various functions.

Types of Bus

A bus connects different parts of the computer system, including the processor, RAM, disk drive controller and input/output (I/O) ports, allowing the transfer of data between them (see Figure 1). A number of features concerning buses can be identified:

- a bus is a group of parallel wires, one for each bit of a word, along which data can flow (as electrical signals);
- the system bus comprises a number of such communication channels, connecting a computer's processor and its associated components of memory and input/output(I/O) devices.
- a single bus may carry data for different functions at separate times or it may be dedicated to one function. A computer will usually have several buses, used for specific purposes, for example, the I/O bus or main memory to processor bus.
- the width of a bus determines the length of word which can be handled at one time. For example, a processor which used a 16-bit bus, but required a 32-bit word to address memory, would have to concatenate two 16-bit words in two separate fetch operations.

Communication is required within a processor, to allow movement of data between its various registers between the processor and memory and for I/O transfers. In a *single bus* system, I/O and memory transfers share the same communication channel, whereas in a *two-bus* system, I/O and memory transfers are carried out independently; similarly, in small systems with few I/O devices, they may share the same bus, a larger system requiring several I/O buses to ensure efficient operation.

Each of the separately identified functions of memory, register-to-register and I/O transfers must have the use of the following bus types.

Data Bus

This is for the transfer of data subject to processing or manipulation in the machine.

Address Bus

This carries the address of the location for the required data. For example, a memory word to be read from RAM (the details of memory addressing as part of the fetch-execute cycle are described earlier), or the output port (and thus connected device) to which a character is to be transmitted.

Control Bus

As the name suggests, a control bus carries signals concerning the timing of various operations, such as memory write, memory read and I/O operations.

All signals on a bus follow strict timing sequences, some operations taking longer than others. All processor operations are synchronised by a *clock*, the operation of which is described earlier.

Input/Output Ports

To allow an I/O device to communicate with the I/O bus, for example, to place data entered through a keyboard onto the data bus, requires the use of an I/O *port*. A number of I/O ports are usually available, the number and types depending on the range of devices which the system is designed to support. Each port has an interfacing role which must convert the data signals, as presented by the connected device, into the form required by the processor, as well as the converse for output data. Thus, for example, the *external ASCII* code used for data storage on a particular tape storage system, will probably have to be converted by the interface into the machine's particular *internal* code.

Expansion Slots

These are slots into which expansion boards or can be plugged, to add extra features to a system. For example, a user may wish to install a sound card, to allow full use of multi-media software, or an additional serial port (see Chapter 27) to connect to a modem. Expansion slots are connected to the system bus (it makes electrical contact), so when an expansion card is plugged in, it becomes part of the system.

Micro Channel Architecture (MCA)

MCA aims to overcome the limitations of the old, Industry Standard Architecture (ISA), IBM AT (Advanced Technology) machines as well as a myriad of 'clones' produced by IBM's competitors. IBM use MCA in their 32-bit PS/2 (Personal System 2) range.

System Bus Width and System Performance

One of the many differences with the MCA approach concerns the width of the *system bus*. This bus is a communication link between the processor and system components and is an essential, but passive, part of system architecture. The active components, such as the processor, disk controller and other peripherals are the primary determinants of system performance. As long as the data transfer speed along the bus matches the requirements of these devices and does not create a 'bottleneck', the bus does not affect system performance. The MCA bus is 32 bits, compared with the AT's 16 bits, and the wider data path allows components within the system to be accessed twice as quickly. The MCA bus also uses bus-mastering controllers to handle data transfers more quickly. The wider bus is also compatible with the 32-bit external bus used on more recent processors (see Processor - Word Length).

The bus can be controlled by separate 'bus master' processors, relieving the main processor of this task.

MCA is also radically different from AT architecture in many other respects. For example, the expansion slots in the PS/2 range which allow the user to insert extra features, perhaps for networking or for extra memory, are physically different from those in the AT and PC machines and their expansion cards will not fit in the PS/2 machines. The problem for existing AT and PC users is that they cannot buy new PS/2 machines and still make use of their existing expansion cards. This incompatibility has also meant that few manufacturers have produced MCA versions of their expansion cards.

IBM and Apricot are the biggest proponents of the MCA standard, but the fact that IBM is continuing to release ISA models is possibly an admission that MCA is unlikely to become the dominant architecture.

Extended Industry Standard Architecture (EISA)

A consortium of IBM's competitors including Compaq, Zenith, NEC and Olivetti amongst others, established a new architecture (EISA - Extended Industry Standard Architecture) which aims to give the benefits of MCA and to retain compatibility with existing AT expansion cards. EISA also uses a 32-bit bus, thus providing the same data transfer benefits as MCA, particularly for hard disk controllers (a very important contributor to overall system performance).

Both EISA and MCA machines are more expensive than the ISA-based microcomputers, and tend to be used where extra power is needed, as *file servers* (Chapters 8 and 26) in networked systems. Most small business users find that ISA machines are adequate for their needs, particularly as the use of *local bus* technology is further increasing their power.

Local Bus

A local bus is a high speed data path connecting the processor with a peripheral. Local bus design is used, primarily, to speed communications with hard disk (see later) controllers and display adapters. The need for local bus derives from the imbalance between the clock speed of a 32-bit processor (typically, 33, 66 or 100MHz) and the ISA 16-bit system bus (operating at 8 MHz). The ISA system is illustrated in Figure 6.4.

This imbalance can result in the processor idling while waiting for data to be transferred from disk, or the display adapter waiting for screen data. The widespread use of Windows, a *graphical user interface* and software packages which make intensive use of the hard disk (such as databases) and screen graphics (computer-aided design), has highlighted the deficiencies of such 'unbalanced' computer systems. A local bus provides a wider data path, currently 32 bits and an increased clock speed, typically 33MHz or more. The first local bus systems appeared in 1992, with manufacturers following a standard referred to as *VL-bus*, developed by VESA (Video Electronics Standards Association). Figure 6.5 illustrates the broad principle of a local bus system. In 1993, Intel backed the development of a new industry standard called *PCI*.

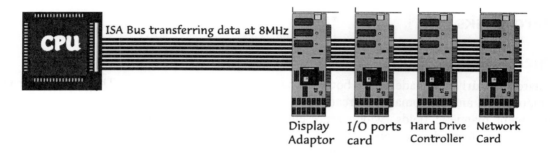

Figure 6.4. *ISA 8MHz bus and high speed processor imbalance*

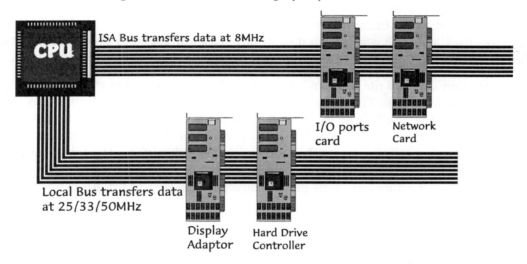

Figure 6.5. Local bus to high speed display and hard drive devices

The standard is in competition with VL-bus and aims to encourage the development of computer systems which allow local bus connection to any high-speed peripheral. Apart from speeding communication with screen graphics controllers, PCI local bus can be used with, for example, hard disk, network and motion video controllers (up to 10 devices in total).

Disk Storage

A business microcomputer system incorporates:

- an integral (fixed inside the system unit casing) *hard disk*, which is the system's primary backing storage device;
- one or two *floppy disk drives* (one for 5.25 inch and the other for 3.5 inch diskettes).

The following section examines hard drive operation and the effect it has on system performance. The techniques of disk caching and defragmentation, to improve performance, are also described.

Hard Disks

Operating Principles

A hard disk drive is made up of both mechanical and electronic parts. The main electronic component is an electromagnetic read/write head, which converts digital impulses into semi-permanent magnetic fields, which represent binary coded data (known as *writing* to disk); *reading* data from disk reverses this process. A hard disk unit comprises a *pack* of several disks (or *platters*) stacked on a central *drive spindle* which *rotates* at high speed; a speed of 3600 revolutions per minute (rpm) is typical for a standard drive unit, but higher performance units revolve at speeds up to 7200 rpm. The rotation speed is a major factor in determining the rate at which data can be transferred to or from disk (the *data transfer rate*). A read/write head moves back and forth across each disk surface, to allow access to every *track*. Rotation of the disks gives access to individual *sectors* (see Computer Hardware) within each track.

The gap between a read/write head and the disk surface is minute; the smaller the gap, the better the data transfer rate. The faster the rotation speed, the less time the system has to wait for the disk to position itself correctly, to read or write the data. A possible drawback of high performance hard drives is the increased risk of a *head crash*. The faster the rotation rate, the harder will be the impact, if a read/write head strikes the disk surface. Hard disk crashes are usually costly, resulting in loss of data (hopefully secured on other media) and replacement of an expensive piece of equipment (some manufacturers of high speed hard drives offer a 5 year warranty).

The disks are usually made from aluminium, but some manufacturers are using glass substrate, which can improve data recording densities and data access times. Glass disks are lighter and thus, need less power to rotate them (desirable for 'green' technology and in portable computers running on battery power). Glass substrate disks are more resistant to damage from a head crash, which makes them particularly suitable for *notebooks* and other portable computers (head crashes are more likely in a portable system).

Storage Capacity and Performance

Storage capacity is measured in megabytes or Mb (roughly 1 million bytes) or gigabytes (Gb - approximately a thousand million bytes). At the time of writing, typical storage capacities range from 120 Mb to 2 Gb. *Disk array* systems offer even larger capacity, measured in hundreds of gigabytes. Traditionally, track recording density (the amount of data packed into a single track) is dictated by the amount of data which can be recorded in the innermost (the shortest) track. All the other tracks then use the same recording density. A technique called *variable zone recording* or *zoned-bit recording* (ZBR) stores more information in the longer, outer tracks. In this way, the storage capacity of the entire hard disk is radically increased.

The performance of a particular drive involves a measurement of its *overall response time*, measured in milliseconds. Different kinds of *disk access* take different times, so a quoted response time should be an aggregate of the time taken for a range of typical operational activities. In practice, this means running a system with a range of commonly used applications; currently, this includes use of MS-DOS and Windows applications. Typical response times range, approximately, from 19 ms to 10 ms.

Disk Access Time

Disk access time has three main components:

- seek time - locating the read/write head over the correct track;
- rotational delay - waiting for the correct sector to arrive under the head;
- data transfer time - transmitting the data via the read/write head into memory.

Seek time places the greatest burden on disk access time, in that it involves extensive mechanical movement of the read/write head. The quicker the head can be moved to the required track, the quicker the data can be retrieved. To ensure operational efficiency, hard disks are enclosed in a sealed unit (referred to as Winchester technology) to prevent contamination with dust or other impurities which may cause a head crash.

Hard disk performance may be improved with the use of:

- a hardware caching controller;
- software caching
- de-fragmentation software.

Hardware Caching Controller

A hardware caching controller improves the rate at which data can be *written* to or *read* from a hard disk. As an electro-mechanical component of the computer system, the hard disk can access data at speeds measured in milliseconds (thousandths of a second), compared with the processor and main memory speeds, which can be measured in nanoseconds (thousand millionths of a second). A high performance processor may remain idle while waiting for the hard drive to complete a write or read operation. A hardware caching controller uses a separate memory chip, plugged into the drive's controller board (see Figure 6.1). The cache memory is used to store data in anticipation of a read or write operation.

- *Write caching* is the drive's attempt to accept data before the write head is correctly positioned to record it. A write operation starts with the computer signalling the drive that it has begun the process. Instantly, the drive starts to move the read/write heads over the correct track. At the same time, the data to be transferred is copied from main memory to the RAM cache within the drive. Once the copy has been completed, the system is free to continue with other tasks, leaving the drive to complete the write operation (using the copy of the data held in the RAM cache). The 'write operation completed' signal is issued while the drive is still recording (as soon as the copy to the cache is completed); otherwise, the system would still be delayed while the cache copy is written to disk. There is a theoretical risk of data loss, but, for most applications, there is none. Write caching is particularly effective for sequential file processing, where data is recorded into contiguous locations on disk (a complete track is filled before the head moves to the next track). Several write operations can be carried out without any head movement and seek time (the most significant contributor to the slowing of access speeds) is minimised. The opportunities for overlapping write operations are maximised.

- *Read caching*. The drive attempts to fetch data before the application requests it. The principles are the same as for main memory caching (see Memory Cache).

The memory chip used as the RAM cache is held within the drive unit and does not, therefore, take any part of the system's main memory capacity. A hardware caching controller can radically improve the performance of a hard drive, although other advances in design, such as increased rotation speed may be more significant.

In any event, improvement in hard disk performance leads to a speed imbalance within the typical microcomputer. Computer systems using the ISA standard (see Bus Architecture) *system bus* and a high performance hard drive are not well balanced. Many hard drives can handle data up to five times faster than the ISA bus. This can lead to a system 'bottleneck', which local bus technology (see Bus Architecture) seeks to overcome.

Software Caching

A hard disk without a hardware caching controller will probably slow down a system, which in other respects is classed as a high performance system. An effective alternative, commonly used for systems operating Microsoft Windows, is to use a software caching system, such as SmartDrive, Super PC-Kwik and Norton NCache. This uses part of the computer's own main memory as the cache and thus reduces the amount available for applications software and data. Without a hardware caching controller, software caching is an essential component for must business systems.

De-fragmentation

The MS-DOS operating system, for example, keeps track of every stored file by following chains of *clusters* through a *file allocation table* (FAT). A cluster is a group of, up to, 32 sectors, which the operating system uses as a file *allocation unit*. A filename entry in the FAT is followed by the address of the first cluster containing the file. If the file occupies more than one cluster, the first cluster contains a pointer to the next, which contains a pointer to the one after that, and so on, until the end of the file is reached (the last cluster contains a special marker). This system was adopted to allow disk space to be taken by new files when old ones are deleted. If a file cannot be fitted into a vacant space, it becomes *fragmented* (distributed over different parts of the disk). The operating system is still able to keep track of the complete file through the cluster linking mechanism, but read and write times become extended. This is because of the increased head movement (see Seek Time).

De-fragmentation software, such as that provided with MS-DOS 6.0 operating system, re-organises the disk space, such that each file occupies contiguous (no gaps) clusters. The frequency with which de-fragmentation should be carried out depends on the level of file activity and the application. If the application results in frequent changes to the size of files, system performance may be noticeably affected as fragmentation increases.

Parallel Processing Architectures

The potential for increasing computation speed through parallelism has long been recognised, its first real manifestation being in the change from computers which handled data serially bit by bit with a single processor to those manipulating parallel bit groupings or words, albeit still with only one processor. Parallelism as described here is concerned with the use, in a variety of approaches, of multiple processors to act upon either single or multiple streams of data. A number of factors have permitted the research and development of parallel processing architectures, which previously had not been cost-effective.

Factors Encouraging Development

The development of VLSI (Very Large Scale Integration) circuits has allowed tremendous progress to be made in the miniaturisation of computer components, most significantly in terms of processor and memory chips, but although users have felt the benefits of significant speed improvements, they have not been of the same order. They continue to improve, but it has been apparent for some time that the power needs of some applications go beyond single processor systems. It is also recognised that the greatest increases in speed can be obtained through changes in system architecture. The RISC (Reduced Instruction Set Computer) approach is already bringing about significant benefits, but parallel architectures, despite the particular difficulties they present for the design of software which can take full advantage, probably hold the greatest potential for radical performance gains. Parallel hardware is, of course, only half the solution and it must be also possible to write programs which can execute in parallel. The Occam programming language developed by Inmos, addresses the special requirements of writing code for arrays of transputers (see end section).

Architectural Approaches to Parallelism

The following sections provide information on some of the ways in which degrees of parallelism may be achieved.

Pipelining

This term refers to the activities of a 'pipeline' of processors each of which performs a mathematical operation on a single vector stream of data. The approach is based on the premise that any arithmetic process incorporates a number of distinct stages which can be separately allocated to individual processors.

Each processor has an associated register, isolated from the rest, and permitting parallel computation on the data. A clock pulse synchronises the activities of all processors in the pipeline, so that the data moves through it, step by step with each clock pulse. As an illustrative example, floating point addition requires the performance of a sequence of three operations, namely to:

(i)   equalise the exponents, adjusting one mantissa as necessary;
(ii) add the mantissas;
(iii) normalise the result.

New sets of numbers to be added can be fed into the pipeline as each set moves through it to produce the sum.

Instruction pipeline. Pipeline processing can also be applied to the instruction stream. Using the buffering principle, consecutive instructions are read from memory into the pipeline, while preceding instructions are executed by the processor. Complications arise when an instruction causes a branch out of sequence, at which point the pipe must be cleared and all instructions read from memory, but not yet processed, are discarded. The overall effect of such queuing is to reduce the average memory access time for reading instructions.

Although pipelining can be described as a parallel architecture, the processors are only operating on a single vector stream of data and the acronym SISD (Single Instruction Single Data-stream) is frequently used to describe its mode of operation.

A major advantage of pipeline architecture is that program code developed for von Neumann architecture, that is serial code, can be run without modification, whilst improvements in the performance of programs particularly suited to pipeline processing can be changed accordingly. This requires the identification of discrete processing stages and the division of particularly processor-hungry sections of code for allocation to separate processors. A number of manufacturers have produced powerful machines of this type.

Processor Arrays

Processors connected in a pipeline can be described as forming a linear array, but the following section is concerned with two and three-dimensional processor arrays, for which the Inmos transputer was specifically designed

SIMD (Single Instruction Multiple Data-stream)

In a two-dimensional array, for example, 4096 processors may be connected in a 64 x 64 square, so that each one has 4 neighbouring elements.

Known as SIMD architecture, each program instruction is transmitted simultaneously to all the processors in the array, so each can then execute the instruction using its locally stored set of data. Because all processors are executing the same instruction at any one time, existing serial code can be used, provided the data can be conveniently divided. By the parallel processing of large numbers of data sets at one time, massive increases in job processing speed can be achieved. Of course, not all processors in the array are necessarily concerned with a particular processing stage and data may have to be passed on to the next relevant processor through a number of array elements which have no interest in the data. The length of such communications paths can have a significant effect on system performance and in efforts to reduce the number of processors handling data with which they have no concern, a number of geometrical designs (beyond the requirements of this text) are in use.

MIMD (Multiple Instruction Multiple Data-stream)

This also permits the parallel processing of separate sets of data, but each processor is at a different stage in the program's execution. More complex than the SIMD approach, it requires firstly, the vectoring of the program code into separate processes, each with the potential for execution on a separate processor and secondly in some systems, the division of data into local (available to a particular processor) and global (available to all). Each processor can be viewed as dealing with a particular part of the overall program and a particular data set, as well as having access to certain data available globally to all processors. In order that they can be executed in parallel, each of the processes should be substantially independent of the rest, although in general, they need to communicate with one another. If global memory is used for such communication, co-ordination difficulties can arise. In the Cray 2 system for example, passing data from one processor to another via global memory, requires the synchronisation of the write operation by the transmitting processor and the subsequent read by the receiving one.

The transputer incorporates serial links which allow communications between processors and the concept of global memory is not used.

Transputers

The Transputer is effectively a 'building block' for parallel processing architectures; while it contains its own memory and processing elements, it also features unique serial links which allow it to communicate with other Transputers. A matrix of Transputers can be created with each one solving a small part of a complete task. The addition of extra Transputers to a system incrementally adds the full power of each unit to the overall system performance. In theory, if one Transputer operates at 10 million instructions per second (mips), then two will give a system performance of 20 mips, 10 will give 100 mips and so on. In practice, the problem still remains of splitting computer processing problems into separate parts for each of the transputers to handle.

Applications

A number of applications likely to benefit particularly from parallel processing are outlined below.

- *Weather forecasting*, which requires 'number crunching' operations on huge volumes of data, gathered globally and from monitoring satellites, in time to produce accurate weather forecasts, rather than comments on existing weather conditions!
- *Graphics applications*. Ray tracing, for example, where a set of descriptors of three-dimensional objects in three-dimensional space is mapped onto a flat screen complete with shadows, refraction and reflections, needs considerable computation to trace where the light on each screen pixel came from. The

application is most easily implemented on pipeline architecture, where it benefits from both the faster maths and the faster communication. With about 10 million calculations to generate a single screen picture, speed is vital when generating sequences of images. A major application is in aircraft flight simulators, where the scenes to be shown are not known exactly in advance, as they depend on the pilot's actions. To be of any use they need to be generated virtually instantaneously in real-time.

- *Simulation*. Engineering design problems benefit hugely from computer simulation. The designers of North Sea oil platforms could ill afford to build prototypes to test to destruction, so they carry out all the structural analysis on a Cray supercomputer costing around 20 million; the process only takes about 9 hours, but the time taken still makes extensive prototyping very expensive. A car body designer using a 1 million mainframe has to wait about 20 hours for a typical run to complete. These lengthy run-times mean that computer simulation tends to be used to validate designs already completed, rather than as a development tool.

- *Image processing*. A particularly exciting example involves the use of computers to assist the plastic surgeon in the repair of facial injuries or deformities. The patient's head is scanned by cameras and the image digitised for display on a computer screen. This image can be rotated or tilted on screen by the surgeon and experimental 'cuts' made, the results of which can then be viewed on screen from any angle. In this way, a plastic surgeon can study the results of a variety of strategies before making a single mark on the patient. The complexity of such image processing requires parallel processing if rapid response to user input is to be achieved. Industrial processes frequently require robots which can recognise different shaped components and possess sufficient 'spatial awareness' to allow accurate assembly to take place. Artificial intelligence techniques are applied to both these areas, so that robots can 'learn' and the power of parallel processing greatly enhances the opportunity for such developments;

- *Speech recognition* is an enormously complex process if a system is to be capable of handling a wide range of vocabulary, pronunciation and intonation, let alone the meaning of phrases and even sentences. Artificial intelligence techniques are being applied to the speech recognition process and parallel processing power greatly improves the opportunities for its evolution.

- *Financial and economic system modelling*. To make realistic assessments of the effectiveness of various economic strategies requires the processing of huge volumes of raw data.

Multi-processing. Parallel processing should not be confused with multi-processing architectures which allow the simultaneous running of several, separate programs, but with each program only having control of one processor at a time.

Chapter 7
Data Communications

Telecommunications and Data Communications

The word *telecommunications* can be applied to any system capable of transmitting text, sounds, graphical images or indeed, data of any kind, in electronic form. The signals may travel along wires or they may be radio signals, which require no wires, but can travel through the atmosphere and space. Currently, not all aspects of telecommunications system are digital, so sometimes, data may be transmitted in *analogue* form. Computer data is represented in *digital* form, so where the telecommunications systems support it, data is moved between remote computer systems as digitised signals. The topic of analogue and digital signals is dealt with later. The combination of computer and telecommunications technologies has profoundly affected the way computer systems are used. To a computer, text, sounds and graphical images all constitute data, which it represents digitally, using the *binary* coding system. Although not all transmissions of digital data involve general-purpose computers, they are often generated and controlled by digital computer technology. Data generated by a computer is already in digital form, but other data (the term is used in its broadest sense), such as sounds of human speech, or a photograph, need to be digitally encoded before transmission over a digital network. The term *data communications* can be applied to systems that combine the use of telecommunications and computer technologies.

Standards Authorities

The data communications industry has always had to deal with problems of *incompatible* standards. As explained later, standards have to do with all aspects of a communications system, including, for example, the *hardware devices*, the *encoding* of data and the forms of *signals* used. At first, the only computer systems available for use in data communications systems were mainframes and later, minicomputers. These computer systems were produced by a small number of very large manufacturers, the most important being IBM; they also produced the communications devices that worked with their computers. In competition with one another, each manufacturer set the standards for use with its equipment. These *closed* systems prevented a customer from using equipment, produced by different manufacturers, in the same data communications system.

The huge expansion in the uses of data communications, both nationally and internationally has been made possible through the adoption of some common standards. Common standards lead to *open* systems, which allow users to use components from more than one manufacturer. A number of bodies are concerned with the establishment of international standards and these are listed below. Frequently, a standard arises initially from the work of a particular manufacturer, and then, often because of the importance of the manufacturer, it is included in the recommendations of the standards authorities.

- CCITT. This is an acronym for 'Comité Consultatif Internationale de Télégraphie et Téléphonie' an organisation that has its headquarters in Geneva, Switzerland. It is part of the United Nations' International Telecommunications Union (ITU). The CCITT makes recommendations on most aspects of data communications, for example, modems (see Data Circuit Termination Equipment), networks and facsimile transmission or FAX and publishes them every four years. These recommendations usually obtain world-wide acceptance and are applied to modems, networks, and facsimile transmission. CCITT's V series of standards cover equipment used on telephone lines and its X series relate to digital packet transmission standards. Some examples of these standards are mentioned later in this element.

- ANSI is the acronym for American National Standards Institute. ANSI has long maintained a strong influence on standards in the computer and data communications industries. It is formed from industrial and business groups and is a member of the International Standards Organisation (ISO). Examples of its influence can be found in the fields of computer hardware and programming languages. For example, by conforming to ANSI standards, the FORTRAN, COBOL and C languages enable the production of computer software, which is largely *portable*. In other words, because each language is more or less 'universal', a program written in, for example, COBOL can be readily translated for use on any make of computer. For further explanation of this topic, refer to Chapter 18. In the area of microcomputer hardware, the ANSI standards define the SCSI (an acronym for Small Computer System Interface) parallel interface, for the connection of peripherals, such as disk drives and printers. The institute is also responsible for the ANSI.SYS *device driver*, a program that provides facilities for greater control of a computer console (screen and keyboard), than is possible with the MS-DOS operating system (see Chapter 2).

- IEEE is the acronym for the Institute of Electrical and Electronic Engineers. The organisation has set numerous standards for various aspects of telecommunications and computing. Notably, the IEEE has defined standards for local area network (LAN) protocols (see Chapter 8).

- The ISO (International Standards Organisation), has its headquarters in Geneva, Switzerland and is responsible for the definition of the Open Systems Interconnection (OSI) model. This model aims to ensure that any computer terminal is able to connect to any network and communicate with any other terminal, whether it is connected to the same or any other linked network. The OSI model is examined in greater detail in the section on Communications Protocols.

Public Telecommunications Authorities

The main telecommunications network in the United Kingdom is the public switched telephone network (*pstn*), which is owned by British Telecom (BT). Although BT owns the network, Mercury Communications (a competitor *public telecommunications operator* or PTO), is able to use the pstn to provide telephone and network services. Competition also comes from the independent providers of cellular telephone services.

Types of Communications Networks

Public Switched Telephone Network (pstn)

The *pstn* is the main telecommunications network for the United Kingdom. It was originally designed for voice transmission, using analogue electrical signals; these electrical signals represent what is spoken and heard at each end of a link. A telephone mouthpiece contains a diaphragm, which vibrates when struck by sound waves. The vibrations are converted into electrical impulses and are sent over the network to the earpiece on the receiving telephone; a diaphragm in the earpiece converts the impulses back into sound.

Much of the pstn is now digital, in particular the national trunk network and call switching exchanges; the analogue connections are mainly confined to the pstn's local links to homes and businesses. Digital voice transmission uses coded patterns of digital impulses, which are similar to those used to represent computer data. To transmit computer data over analogue sections of the pstn, requires use of a *modem* (see Data Circuit Termination Equipment or DCE). This device converts the computer's digital signal into an appropriate analogue form before transmission; a modem at the receiving end converts the analogue signal back to the digital form required by the computer.

Types of Telecommunications Lines
- *Dedicated lines*. These can be leased from British Telecom and provide a permanent connection for devices in a network. They provide high transmission rates and are relatively error-free. They are only cost-effective for high volume data transmission, or when a permanent link is vital to the users. Charging is by a flat rate rather than when calls are made.
- *Dial-up* or switched lines. These are cheaper, but support lower transmission rates than leased lines. They are more cost effective than leased lines for low-volume work and allow the operator to choose the destination of transmissions.

Digital Network Systems

Public Switched Data Network (psdn) or Switchstream

The psdn, owned by British Telecom (BT) and named *Switchstream*, is a *packet switching* (see next section) network. Modems are not required and transmission performance is better than that achievable over the partially analogue pstn. Switchstream is one of four digital services, collectively known as X-Stream; the other services are Kilostream, Megastream and Satstream.

Switchstream conforms to the CCITT (see Standards Authorities) standard known as the X.25 protocol; for this reason, the network is often referred to as the X.25 network. A major benefit of using this CCITT standard is that the network can be used for international communications.

Packet Switching

Figure 1 illustrates the main components of a packet switching network: high speed data lines; packet switching exchanges (PSEs); packet assembler/disassembler (PAD); packet terminal; character terminal.

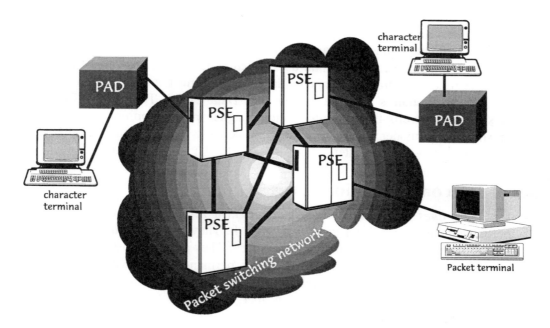

Figure 7.1. Packet Switching Network

With the use of a specialised computer, called a *packet terminal*, a customer can create the packets and connect directly to the network through a dedicated dataline. If the customer is not using a packet terminal (Figure 7.1 shows two simple character terminals), a dial-up connection is used and the data has to go through a *packet assembler/disassembler* (PAD).

This device converts data to and from the network's protocol as it enters and leaves the network.

The principles of packet switching are as follows. Messages are divided into data packets, which are then directed through the network to their destination under computer control. Besides a *message* portion, each packet contains data concerning:

- the destination address;
- the source identification;
- the sequence of the packet in the complete message;
- the detection and control of transmission errors.

The progress of a packet is monitored and controlled by *packet switching exchanges* (PSE) located at each *node* in the network. A node is a junction of network lines, which could be a computer or a computer terminal or other device.

As a packet arrives at a node, the exchange checks the addressing instructions and unless it corresponds to its present location, forwards it on the *most appropriate route*. Each node has an *input queue*, into which all arriving packets are entered (even those which are addressed to the node itself) and a number of *output queues* (to allow for the possibility of network congestion). Figure 7.2 shows the queue features of a packet switching exchange.

Figure 7.2. *Packet Switching Exchange (PSE) Queues*

The route on which a packet is then transmitted may be determined by one of a number of *routing strategies*:

- hot potato. The packet is sent as quickly as possible to the shortest output queue; such packets are not unduly delayed, although they may not be transmitted on the most direct route;
- pre-determined routing. With this method, the routing details are included in the packet itself, each switching exchange forwarding the packet according to the embedded instructions;
- directory routing. Each switching exchange has a copy of a routing table to which it refers before forwarding each packet. The appropriate output queue is determined from the table and the packet destination.

Network traffic information is continually transmitted between the various nodes, so that each switching computer has information to allow, for example, the avoidance of congested routes. Figure 7.3 illustrates how a network structure provides alternative routes by which a packet may reach its destination.

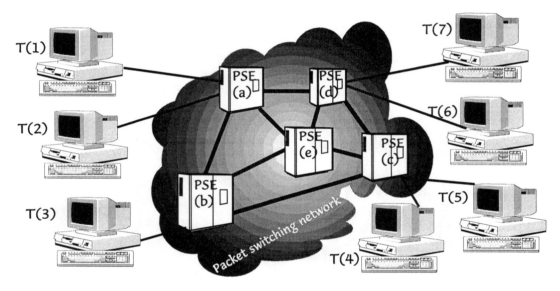

Figure 7.3. *Routing in a packet switching network*

If a network is structured as shown in Figure 7.3, a packet sent from terminal T(2) to terminal T(6), would go into the input queue of packet switching exchange PSE (a). Depending on the routing strategy and network traffic conditions, the packet could be directed to an output queue leading to any of the other PSEs. If PSE (e) was inoperative, the alternative routes would be cut drastically; in fact the packet would either have to go through PSEs (b), (c) and (d), in that sequence, or direct from PSE (a) to PSE (d). Packet switching allows packets relating to a single message, to be transmitted on different routes. This may be necessary, either because of the breakdown of some routes, or because of variations in traffic conditions over different routes.

The X.25 Protocol

As already mentioned, the psdn uses a packet switching protocol, known as X.25. The CCITT (see Standards Authorities) provide the X.25 protocol for interfacing terminals with a psdn. The protocol provides users with the following facilities.

1. Division of a message into packets.

2. Error checking and re-transmission of any packet effected by an error.

3. An addressing format that allows international transmission.

4. The PSEs control the transmission of packets through the network.

Kilostream

An alternative to packet switching is to use *multiplexing*. The Kilostream service uses this technique for data transmission. The service provides a high speed direct link between two points. Data can pass in both directions at the same time; this is known as *full duplex* mode. The main link can transmit data at a rate of 2·048 megabits per second (Mbits/s); this allows a number of low speed terminals to be connected to the high speed link through separate low speed links, each transmitting at either 12·8 kilobits per second (Kb/s) or 64 Kb/s. The signals from each terminal can then be merged for transmission along the high speed link, using a technique known as *time division multiplexing* (TDM). The process of multiplexing is carried out by a *terminal multiplexer*. At the receiving end of the link, the signals are separated out for transmission along low speed lines connected to their respective terminals. The terminal multiplexer at each end of the link can carry out the functions of multiplexing (combining signals) and demultiplexing (separating the signals). The is obviously necessary for full duplex operation.

Multiplexers fall into two broad categories according to the methods used to combine signals and separate them:

- *Frequency Division Multiplexing (FDM)* differentiates between the data signals sent from different devices by using a different *frequency range* for each. This can be likened to tuning a radio or television to receive particular programmes. So that any given radio programme does not interfere with the transmissions of another (although, they sometimes do), it is assigned a frequency that is not too close to the other assigned frequencies. In the same way, when a data transmission channel is multiplexed to accommodate signals from separate devices, some space must be left between the frequency ranges to avoid confusion of signals. Spaces between the different frequency ranges are know as *guard bands*.
- *Time Division Multiplexing (TDM)*, as the term suggests, provides a *time slice* on the higher-speed line for each terminal. The multiplexer has a number of registers, one per low-speed channel. Each register can store one character. The multiplexer scans each register in sequence, emptying the contents into a continuous stream of data to be transmitted. A multiplexer will send a null character whenever it finds an empty slot.

Figure 7.4 illustrates the multiplexing of signals from three terminals to a remote mainframe computer.

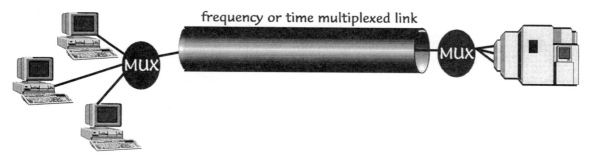

Figure 7.4. *Multiplexers used to allow several terminals to use a single link*

Megastream

This service is similar to Kilostream, except that no terminal multiplexing equipment is provided. Data can be transmitted at 2·048, 8, 34 or 140 Mbits/s. A user can choose to use the high speed circuit directly or multiplex the circuit, such that a number of low speed channels are made available across the link. Each separate lower speed channel can then be used to carry data or some may be left for the transmission of digitised speech.

Satstream

This digital data service provides customers with a small dish aerial to allow radio transmission of data, through a communications satellite. Customers are thus able to connect with networks in Western Europe.

Integrated Services Digital Network (ISDN)

Many forms of data, including text, voice and video images, can be digitised and an Integrated Services Digital Network (ISDN) is designed to allow the *integrated* transmission of these various data forms over the same network (Figure 7.5). An Integrated Services Digital Network exists in various forms in different countries, although the ultimate aim is to achieve an international system. It is defined as a wholly *digital* system, with end-to-end digital connections and digital exchanges throughout. ISDN has become achievable because the telephone network has become largely digital. The public telephone network is, by far, the largest communications network, so once it is fully digitised, every business and home user will have access to ISDN services. Figure 7.5 illustrates the main features of an ISDN. British Telecom's ISDN began with a pilot scheme in 1985, which was extended in 1986 and has continued to develop since. The network provides three types of access:

- *single-line* IDA (integrated digital access). The user gains access with *Network Terminating Equipment* (NTE);

- *line adapter module* (LAMs). A LAM allows two terminals to simultaneously share the same, two-wire, connection; this could provide a cheap method of communicating with a remote computer system;
- *multi-line* IDA, which provides 30 independent channels, each being capable of transmitting voice or data.

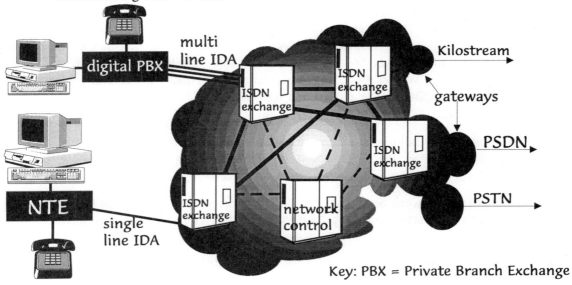

Figure 7.5. *ISDN network with gateways to other network systems*

Broadcast Networks

Data communications networks also support:

- television and radio broadcasting;
- cellular telephone systems.

Television and Radio Broadcasting

When a television studio broadcasts a programme, the signals are carried to television receivers through a network of transmitters; radio programmes are broadcast from a studio in a similar fashion. An out-of-date term for a radio is a 'wireless'; thus the transmissions in these broadcast networks are all carried out without the use of 'wires', that is, as *radio waves*. Radio waves vary in *frequency* and different frequency bands are used for different kinds of broadcasting. It is beyond the scope of this text to go into detail concerning these frequency bands, but the abbreviations VHF (very high frequency) and UHF (ultra-high frequency) should be familiar. The term *broadcast* is used because the radio wave signals can be received by any number of receivers within the broadcast area. The geographical area which can be reached by a broadcasting station depends on whether the method, namely:

- *cable* connections; this is an exception here as it clearly involves the use of wire or cable;

- *terrestrial* transmitters;
- *communications satellites*

A broadcasting company may use a combination of cable, terrestrial and satellite transmitters to distribute its programmes. For example, the American company WTBS, in Atlanta, Georgia uses satellite to transmit low-cost sports and entertainment programmes to cable systems across the USA. Cable broadcasting, as the term indicates, uses physical cabling and is only economic over a limited area, such as a large city. However, in combination with satellite broadcasting, cable television plays an important role. Although terrestrial transmitters allow a much larger broadcast area than cable, satellites are essential to modern television broadcasting. Within the UK, pictures and monophonic sound are transmitted as analogue signals. The BBC has developed and transmits, NICAM stereo sound, using digital encoding techniques.

Television broadcasting allows the transmission of *moving pictures*, *sound* and *data* to television receivers within the area served by a broadcasting station. Database services provided by television are *one-way* only, to television receivers and are collectively known as

- *Teletext* (see Network Services). The BBC teletext service is known as Ceefax and ITV's as Oracle. To access these services a television receiver must have a Teletext *decoder*.

Microwave Transmissions and Communications Satellites

Microwaves are super-high frequency (SHF) radio waves and can be used where transmitter and receiver are not 'in sight' of one another. The communication path must be relatively obstruction-free. Microwaves can also be transmitted, through earth transmitters, to communications satellites; microwaves can penetrate cloud. Earth stations must be no more than 25-30 miles apart, because humidity in the atmosphere interferes with microwave signals. Each station in a communication path acts as a *repeater* station. Obviously, it is impractical to build sufficient repeater stations to deal with all transmissions, so communications satellites are essential. Once a satellite has received a signal, it amplifies it and sends it back to earth. Satellite communications are now fairly common and provide a cheaper and better trans-ocean transmission medium than undersea cable. Apart from television broadcasting, satellites form an essential part of the international telephone network. Voice and data messages are digitally transmitted as packets (see Packet Switching). Numerous transmission channels can be created using *frequency division multiplexing* (see Kilostream).

Cellular Telephone Networks

These networks use *cellular radio* communications, which operate in the UHF (ultra-high frequency) band. Local *base stations* allow cellphone (hand-held or vehicle-based) users to access the pstn. Each base station covers a *cell site*, an area within which it can pick up cellphone signals. Within the UHF band, signals can penetrate buildings and other barriers, but a user must be within a few miles of a transmitter, particularly in urban areas, where the largest numbers of users tend to be found. Thus, a base station in a rural area, serving fewer users, can cover a larger cell site than is possible in an urban area. Computers are used to allow links to be maintained even while the caller is moving from one transmission area to another. Thus, when a base station receives a signal from a cellphone, it monitors the strength of the signal continuously to determine if it is still the most suitable base station to handle the transmission. Obviously, if the user is driving while making a call, a different base station may be handling the call at different points on the journey. The only effect of these changes is a brief (about one-fifth of a second) interruption to the call as the switch is made to a different base station. Two major cellular radio operators in the UK are Cellnet and Vodaphone.

Modes of Data Communication

Direction of Transmission

Communications media can be classified according to whether *two-way transmission* is supported.

- *Simplex* mode allows communication in one direction only.
- *Half-duplex* supports communications in both directions, but not at the same time; in other words there is only a single channel and the direction is switched after completion of transmission in the other direction.
- *Duplex* mode allows communication in both directions at the same time, as there are two channels permanently available. In interactive systems, where two way communication is continuously required, duplex is the only suitable mode.
- *Asymmetric duplex* is the same as duplex, except that the transmission speed in one direction is different from that of the other.

Devices differ in the ways they communicate or 'talk' with each other. One such difference is in the number of *conductors* or lines they use to transmit data.

Serial Transmission

With serial transmission, the binary signals representing the data are transmitted one after another in a serial fashion. Serial data transmission is normally used, except for very short connections between a peripheral and a computer, where parallel techniques are employed. The technique is illustrated in Figure 7.6.

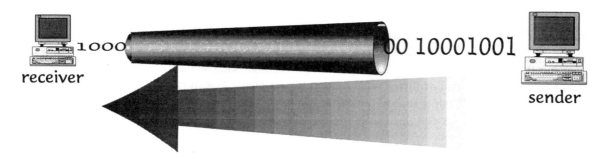

Figure 7.6 *Serial transmission between two devices*

Parallel Transmission

As the term makes obvious, data bits are transmitted as groups in parallel; Figure 7.7 illustrates this form.

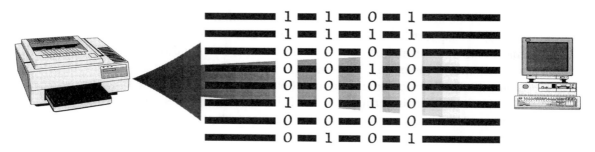

Figure 7.7. *Parallel transmission between a computer and a local printer*

This is obviously quicker than sending them serially, but it is only practicable over short distances. Communication between a computer and its nearby peripherals can be carried out using parallel transmission, which is particularly important where high-speed devices, such as disk or tape units, are concerned. Microcomputer systems often use parallel transmission to communicate with a nearby printer. The number of lines needed for a parallel connection defines its *bus width*. As explained in the later section on Connectors or Interfaces, each line has a particular function. Thus, apart from the 8 bits needed for the data (see Data Representation), *handshaking* (Protocols) signals are needed to control the transfer of data between a computer and a terminal, which operate at different speeds. Additional handshake lines are needed to carry these signals.

Asynchronous Serial Transmission

When a sending device transmits characters at irregular intervals, as does for example, a keyboard device, it is said to be transmitting *asynchronously*.

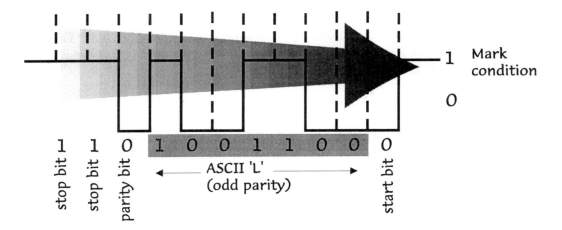

Figure 7.8. *Asynchronous character format*

Although the characters are not sent at regular intervals, the bits within each character must be sent at regularly timed intervals. An example of asynchronous character format is shown in Figure 7.8. It can be seen from the Figure 7.8 that the line has two electrical states, representing 1 and 0. Between characters, the line is in the *idle* state, a 1 or *mark* condition.

The first or *start bit*, set to 0, indicates the start of a character, whilst a *stop bit* marks the end. The receiving machine 'listens' to the line for a start bit. When it senses this it counts off the regularly timed bits that form the character. When a stop bit is reached, the receiver switches back to its 'listening' state. The presence of start and stop bits for each character permits the time interval between characters to be irregular, or asynchronous.

Synchronous Serial Transmission

The start and stop bits used in asynchronous transmission are wasteful, in that they do not contain information. With higher speed devices or *buffered* low-speed devices, data can be transmitted in more efficient, timed, or *synchronous* blocks. Figure 7.9 illustrates the technique.

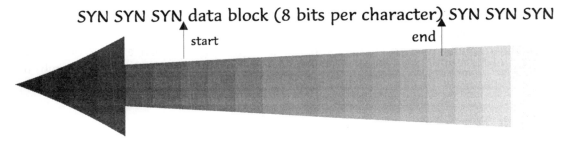

Figure 7.9. *Synchronous character format*

A variety of formats may be used, each having their operating rules or protocol. Communications protocols are dealt with later in this Chapter.

In synchronous transmission, a data stream may be very long, so it is vital that the timing between transmitter and receiver is synchronised and that individual characters are separated. This is done by using a *clock lead* from the transmitter. Synchronisation (*syn*) characters are placed at the beginning of each data block and, in case timing is lost by line disturbance, several syn characters may be situated at intervals within the data block. Thus if timing is lost, the receiver can re-time its bit groupings from the last syn character. Like the start and stop bits used in asynchronous transmission, syn characters constitute an overhead and have to be 'stripped' out by the receiver. Synchronous transmission is generally used for data speeds of 2400 bps or more. Some VDU terminals are designed for high speed data transmission and use synchronous transmission; many others use asynchronous transmission.

Parallel-Serial Conversion (UART and USRT)

As data moves around a computer system in parallel form, it needs to be converted to serial form for transmission though a telecommunications link and from serial to parallel, when the transmission is inward. These conversion processes are carried out by a hardware device called a *universal asynchronous transmitter and receiver* (UART) or *universal synchronous transmitter and receiver* (USRT), depending on the type of computer being used.

Devices

Data Terminal Equipment (DTE)

All the external devices attached to a network may be referred to collectively as data terminal equipment (DTE). Examples of DTE equipment are: computer terminals, including microcomputers used for that function; minicomputers; bank cash dispensers; printers.

Dumb Terminal

The DTE may be a *dumb* terminal, that is, one which has no processing power of its own, possibly no storage, and is entirely dependent on a controlling computer. As soon as each character is entered by the operator, it is transmitted over the communications link, to the controlling computer; this makes editing extremely difficult and slow. The remote computer, to which the terminal is connected, has to use an *input buffer* (small amount of memory assigned to that purpose) to store characters as they arrive. Because the terminal is dumb, the remote computer must regularly *poll* the line to determine the presence of data.

Intelligent Terminal

An *intelligent* terminal (it may be a microcomputer) has memory and processing power, so an operator can use it to store, edit and manipulate data, independently of any other connected computer. For example, a document could be retrieved from a remote computer, be edited within the intelligent terminal and then, in its updated form, be transmitted back to the remote computer. The intelligent terminal's processing facility is provided by an internal processor, usually a microprocessor; its internal memory allows data to be held and manipulated before transmission. The facility may also include local backing storage and a printer. Intelligent terminals can use either EBCDIC or ASCII code (see Standards for Data Representation), but a dumb terminal can only use ASCII.

Two points need to be made concerning the methods used to transmit data and the type of terminal used.

- Dumb terminals, having no processing power and no buffer memory have to use a *point-to-point* connection with the remote, controlling computer. Such terminals transmit data asynchronously. The characters are not evenly separated, because the transmission of characters is determined by the typing speed of the operator and the characters will obviously not be transmitted at precise, regular intervals.
- Intelligent terminals, having a buffer store, can accumulate the keyed characters and send them in blocks or streams. The remote computer signals when transmission of a data stream can begin, thus allowing line sharing by numerous communicating devices. Such line sharing is carried out by multiplexing, a technique described in the earlier section on Packet Switching Networks.

Data Circuit Termination Equipment (DCE)

The intervening connections of a network are leased from the main telecommunications provider, which in the UK is British Telecom. The equipment that allows the DTE to be connected to and interfaced with the network is known as *data circuit termination equipment* (DCE). The CCITT (see Standards Authorities) use the term *data communication equipment* (also DCE). An example of DCE is a *modem*, which allows computer data to be transmitted over sections of the pstn (usually local connections to homes and businesses) which still use analogue signalling.

Modem

Even though much of the public switched telephone network (pstn) uses digital transmission techniques, local connections to homes and businesses still use analogue signals. To allow transmission of computer data (which is digital) over these analogue links, a device called a *modem* is needed to *modulate* and *demodulate* the computer's signals. The modem for the transmitter device has to modulate the digital signal into the corresponding analogue form for transmission along the telephone line. The modem at the receiver device has to carry out the reverse operation. Modems are capable of both functions, so that two way communications are supported. Modems are examined in more detail in the section on Protocols. Figure 7.10 illustrates the role of the modem in a data telecommunications link.

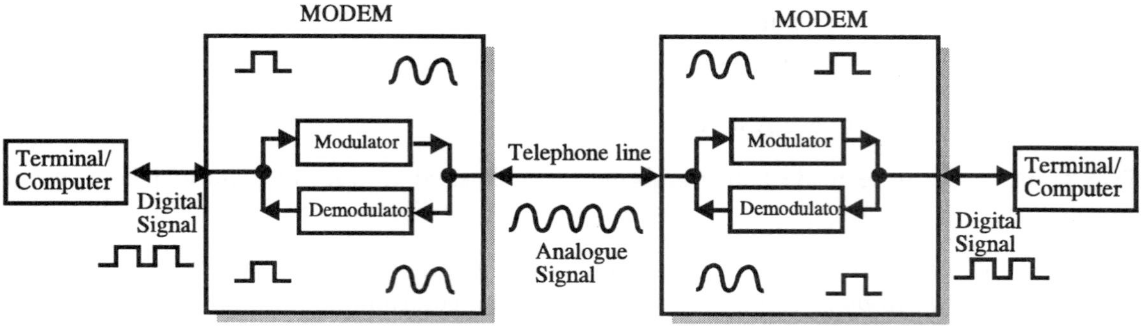

Figure 7.10. *Modems in a data communications link*

Telephone-Modem Connections

To allow computer communication through a telephone line, the user must obtain a modem, of which there are two main types:

- asynchronous (irregularly transmitted characters) serial modems. Each character requires *start* and *stop bits* to separate one character from another.
- synchronous (regularly timed transmission of data blocks) serial modems. Start and stop bits are not required, because the transmitting and receiving modems are synchronised.

Modem Speeds

Baud rate indicates the number of signal changes or pulses per second supported by a communication link. The term used to be synonymous with *bits per second* (bps), but improved data encoding techniques mean, for example, that a 2400 baud link can support data transfer rates from 2400 bps to 14,400 bps. These bps speeds can be converted to characters per second (cps). An asynchronous link (without error correction) sends each character with start and stop bits, a total of 10 bits. Therefore, 2400 bps is equivalent to 240 cps for that type of link. A synchronous modem does not need to use start and stop bits and with error correction, requires a different conversion rate; 8 bits per character means that 2400 bps equates with 300 cps. Different modems provide different data transmission rates, measured in bits per second (bps or baud).

Computer-Modem Connection

To make use of a modem, the microcomputer should have a serial communication (RS232) port. However, there are two possible alternatives; an adapter card with a serial port capability; a communications board (this fits in an expansion slot, located inside the computer's system casing), which combines the functions of the serial port and the modem.

Connectors or Interfaces

Interface devices (or connectors - the terms are interchangeable) are designed to allow various pieces of equipment to work with one another. For this reason, they normally conform to certain standards, of which there are a number. For example, to connect a computer to a modem requires an interface that will allow:

- the movement of data, in both directions, between the two devices;
- select the transmission rate for data to pass through the telephone line;
- synchronisation of the two devices (with clock timing signals).

Standards (usually recommended by one of the Standards Authorities), applied to the design of the interface, may relate to, for example, the number and arrangement of pins, their functions and the signals that are applied to each. This topic is examined further in the following section on Data Communications Standards. The following sections examine several types of interfaces. Interfaces can be categorised according to whether they are designed to handle *serial* or *parallel* transmission of data.

Data Communications Standards

Data Representation

Before transmission, characters must be coded into a code recognised by the sending and receiving devices. Almost all terminals are designed to use either the ASCII or EBCDIC codes.

The ASCII (American Standard Code for Information Interchange) code uses seven binary digits (*bits*), plus a *parity bit* (see Error Detection) to represent a full range of characters. It is defined by the International Standards Organisation (ISO). The 8-bit EBCDIC (Extended Binary-coded Decimal Interchange Code) character code has a 256 character set and is generally used with IBM and IBM-compatible equipment.

Parallel Interfaces

Centronics Parallel Interface

This interface has become a world-wide standard for parallel data transmission between computers and peripherals. It was originally developed by the American printer manufacturer Centronics, Inc. The Centronics parallel interface includes eight parallel data lines and additional lines for control and status information. The eight data lines are the minimum required for transmission of one complete character at a time; an ASCII coded character consists of 8 bits (including the parity bit). The control and status lines are needed for the 'conversation' between the device and the computer. For example, when a printer is *on-line* it sends a ready signal to the computer and when the computer is ready to send a character, it *initialises* the printer, which clears the printer's buffer memory. A *character* printer (ink jet or dot matrix, for example) has a small amount of memory called buffer memory, which it uses to temporarily store a line of characters, before they are printed. Laser printers, which print a complete page at a time, need sufficient buffer memory to store all the data (both text and graphics) on a page, before the page is printed. The signals and processes that enable printing through a Centronics interface are, briefly, as follows.

1. Once the printer is on-line, it sends a *ready* signal to the computer.

2. The computer sends a response, which *initialises* the printer; this has the effect of alerting the printer and clearing its small buffer memory.

3. After the printer is initialised, the computer places the data bits (8), for the first character to be printed, on the data lines.

4. The computer sends a *strobe* signal, which sends the 8 data bits, in parallel, to the printer's buffer memory.

5. Once the data is received by the printer, it is acknowledged with an *acknowledge* signal to the computer.

6. The process continues, until the computer has no more characters to send. The printer may, at times, send a *busy* signal, if it is not ready for the next character; the computer then has to wait for the all clear, before sending the next character. A printer may also interrupt the process, if, for example, it is out of paper.

SCSI (Small Computer Systems Interface)

SCSI (pronounced 'scusi') is a high speed, parallel interface standard, defined by ANSI (see Standards Authorities). SCSI interfaces are widely available for connecting microcomputers to a range of peripheral devices, including hard disks and printers; SCSI interfaces are also used for connecting computers to one another, and to local area networks (see Chapter 8). Separate *ports* (a port is a location for passing data in or out of a computer) do not have to be used for each attached device. Instead one device can be connected directly to a SCSI port in the computer and other devices (a maximum total of seven) can be linked to the first, in a "daisy chain". Only one device can communicate through the SCSI port at any one time, so each device in a chain is given a separate logical address, which indicates its priority. The device with the highest address is given top priority.

Macintosh computers and some computers in the IBM range include an SCSI port as standard. IBM PCs and 'compatibles' can be upgraded to include an SCSI port, with the use of an expansion card. The SCSI interface is of particular value for the attachment of high speed devices, such as hard disk drives. The interface allows more rapid data transfer than is the norm for the IDE (Industry Device Electronics) based hard drives, used in most PCs.

Serial Interfaces

Serial interfaces are used for the connection of modems, terminals and printers. Physically, they are recognisable by the shape of the plug and socket, which are D-shaped. The most common are the 9-pin and 25-pin. Figure 7.11 illustrates a 25-pin D-connector.

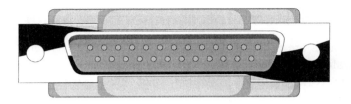

Figure 7.11. *25-pin D-connector*

RS232 and V24 Serial Interfaces

Both these standards relate to an interface for serial transmission between a computer or terminal and a modem. RS232 is a Recommended Standard (RS) of the American Electrical Industries Association (EIA). There have been 4 versions of this standard, the most recent being the RS232D (sometimes known as EIA 232D), although the previous version, RS232C is still the most widely used. The main purpose of the revision was toV24 is the CCITT's equivalent of the RS232C. The V24 standard does not define the physical characteristics of the connection (the RS232 standard does), but only the characteristics of the control signals (see Flow Control) and how they are to be used; nevertheless, the V24 standard is usually used with the 25-pin D-connector (see Figure 7.11). This connector is defined by the International Standards Organisation (ISO - see Standards Authorities).

Communications Protocols

A protocol is a set of rules for the transmission of data between two devices. A protocol may include rules to deal with:

1. the establishment of which device currently has *control of the communications link*;

2. *error detection and correction*;

3. *data flow control*; this is to ensure that data transmission flows smoothly, that the communications channel is not overloaded and that the transmitting device does not send data more quickly than the receiver can handle.

Protocols are often developed by manufacturers and then become recommended by Standards Authorities, but sometimes, they are developed by the latter. Not all protocols cover all three items listed above. For example, the V24 (CCITT standard) and RS232 protocols, which are computer-modem interfaces (see Connectors or Interfaces), do not provide error detection facilities; they are *low level* protocols. Similarly, the X25 interface is a protocol and interface standard for connection to a packet switching network; there are a whole series of X protocols established by the CCITT relating to packet switching networks. A higher level protocol, such as V42 (see Example Protocols) includes error detection and correction facilities. The rest of this section aims to give a brief introduction to this very complex area of data communications.

The OSI (Open Systems Interconnection) Model

Many computer devices are now designed for use in networked systems. Manufacturers are now tending to conform to standard protocols that make their equipment compatible with a variety of user networks. *Closed* networks, that are restricted to one manufacturer's equipment and standards, are not attractive to the user, because it restricts the choice of equipment which can be used. The aim of standardisation is to achieve more open systems which allow users to select from a wider range of manufacturer's products. A Reference Model for Open Systems Interconnection (OSI) has been under development by the International Standards Organisation (ISO) since 1977. Other standards, including SNA (IBM's System Network Architecture) and Ethernet, are largely incompatible with one another. Certain standards in the OSI model have been set by manufacturers as their commercial products have gained in popularity.

The OSI reference model for communications protocol identifies a hierarchy of seven layers. The layers and their functions are briefly described below.

Application Layer

This is the highest layer in that it is closest to the user. It supports the transfer of information between end-users, applications programs and devices. Several types of protocol exist in this layer, including those for specific applications and those for more generalised applications, such as accounting, entry control and user identification. The applications layer 'hides' the physical network from the user, presenting a user-orientated view instead. For example, the user need not know that several physical computers are involved when accessing a database.

Presentation Layer

This layer covers standards on how data is presented to the end-user devices. The aim is to ensure that different devices, which may be using data in different formats, can communicate with one another. The presentation layer can, for example, handle conversions between ASCII and EBCDIC character codes. It may also carry out encryption to ensure data security during transmission over vulnerable telecommunication links. The presentation layer also attempts to deal with conversions between terminals which use different line and screen lengths and different character sets.

Session Layer

The session layer is concerned with the exchange of information between different applications and users; it is the user's interface into the network. When a user requests a particular service from the network, the session layer handles the dialogue.

Transport Layer

The data transmission system on any network will have its own peculiarities and the function of the transport layer is to 'mask' out any undesirable features which may prevent a high quality transmission for the network.

Network Layer

The function of the network layer is to perform the routing of information around the network and also to connect one network to another. The software can also carry out accounting functions to enable the network owner to charge users.

Data Link Layer

The physical data transmission media used in a network are subject to interference which can corrupt data and other signals. The data link layer handles data transmission errors and thus improves the quality of the network. The techniques used, for example, for the receipt and acknowledgement of data by a receiver device, are determined by the data link layer. The CCITT V42bis protocol, with its error detection and correction facilities falls into this level.

Physical Layer

The physical layer provides the means to connect the physical medium and is concerned with the transmission of binary data within the communication channel. Standards are set regarding the mechanical, electrical and procedural aspects of interface devices. For example, standards are set for the number of pins a network connector should have and the function and position of each pin. The RS232 and V24 protocols are within this level.

Handshaking

Synchronisation of data transmission between communicating devices is essential, primarily because they often operate at different speeds, and sometimes, a device may have to wait because the other device is not ready. For example, if a file is being transferred from a remote terminal to a receiving computer, and the file is too large to fit into the computer's memory, then it will have to save sections of the file at intervals. If the computer has no multi-tasking capability, then data may be lost if it is transmitted during a save operation. To prevent such data loss, the flow of data has to be controlled and the activities of the communicating devices need to be properly synchronised. Handshaking is necessary for both parallel and serial transmissions and involves acknowledgement signals between devices that they are ready to communicate with one another. The process of handshaking can be software or hardware controlled. A hardware handshake, for example, between a computer and a printer, involves the exchange of signals, through dedicated lines or conductors; the signals indicate the readiness of each device to send or receive data. A software handshake, usually employed for serial transmissions through modems, enables each device to establish the particular protocols which will be used for transmissions. Error control and data compression (to improve the transmission rate) can be built into the modem's specification and thus be hardware controlled, or they can be provided by a communications package.

Flow Control

Flow control enables communicating modems to pause and restart data transmission, as necessary. The need for pauses and restarts stems from the fact that a receiving modem has to use buffer memory (of limited capacity) and may not be able to empty it (pass it on) as quickly as it is being filled. This could be because the computer to which it is connected is busy with another task, such as printing. If transmission is not paused once the buffer is full, data will be lost. To exert flow control, the receiving modem must signal the sending modem that transmission has to be temporarily interrupted. This can be done, either by the modem or the terminal software (see Chapter 27).

Error Detection

Parity Checking of Codes

The ASCII code is a 7-bit code. An additional bit, known as the *parity bit* (in the left-most or most significant bit position), is used to detect *single bit* errors which may occur during data transfer.

data	odd	even
1001010	**0**1001010	**1**1001010
0010010	**1**0010010	**0**0010010
0101101	**1**0101101	**0**0101101

Table 7.1. *Parity Control*

The parity scheme used for detecting single bit errors is fairly straightforward. There are two types of parity, *odd* and *even*, though it is of little significance which is used. If odd parity is used, the parity bit is set to binary 1 or 0, such that there is an odd number of binary 1s in the group. Conversely, even parity requires that there is an even number of binary 1s in the group. Examples of these two forms of parity are provided in Table 7.1. The parity bit for each group is in **bold**. If even parity is being used and main memory receives the grouping 10010100 then the presence of an odd number of binary 1s indicates an error in transmission. Provided that the number of bits corrupted is odd, all transmission errors will be detected. However, an even number of bits in error will not affect the parity condition and thus will not be revealed. Additional controls can be implemented to detect multiple bit errors; these controls make use of parity checks on blocks of characters; known *as block check characters* (BCC), they are used extensively in data transmission control and are described in the following paragraphs.

Block Check Characters (BCC)

The idea of even and odd parity bits for each character is introduced in the previous paragraph and is shown to be inadequate for the detection of even numbers of bit errors. Block check characters (BCCs) aim to conquer this problem by checking the parity of blocks of characters within a data transmission stream. BCCs may carry out *longitudinal* or *cyclic* redundancy checks.

Longitudinal Redundancy Checking (LRC)

Each BCC consists of a group of parity bits which carry out LRC. However, each LRC bit is a parity check on the corresponding bits in all the characters in a block. Thus, the first parity bit in the BCC relates to the bits which occupy the first position in each character in the block, the second parity bit in the BCC relates to the second position bits in each character in the block and so on. LRC ensures that multiple errors, whether even or odd, are likely to be discovered, so at the receiver end of the transmission, the parity of individual characters and blocks of characters is checked. By reference to Figure 7.12, the principles of LRC can be explained as follows.

VRC parity (each character) bit 7   Bit position

7	6	5	4	3	2	1	0
0	1	0	0	1	0	1	1
0	1	0	0	1	1	1	0
1	1	0	0	1	1	1	1
1	1	0	1	0	1	0	0
1	1	0	1	0	1	0	0
1	1	0	1	0	1	1	1
0	1	0	0	0	0	0	1
1	1	0	0	1	0	0	1
1	1	0	1	0	1	0	0
1	1	0	0	0	1	0	1
0	1	0	1	0	0	1	1
1	1	0	1	0	1	1	1	BCC

LRC parity (per block)

Figure 7.12. *Vertical (VRC) and longitudinal redundancy checks (LRC)*

Cyclic Redundancy Checking (CRC)

The BCCs described previously treat a data block as a set of characters, whereas cyclic redundancy checking (CRC) uses a BCC which views each data block as a continuous *stream* of bits.

Firstly, the data block is regarded as one large binary number. That number is divided by an another agreed binary number, the quotient is discarded and the remainder (sometimes referred to as a *checksum*) is attached to the data block as a BCC. Upon receipt of the data block, the receiver repeats the calculation used to generate the BCC and compares the result with the BCC attached by the transmitter; any difference between them indicates some corruption of the block.

Echoplex (Echo Checking)

Echoplex is used in asynchronous communications, for low speed, *dumb* (see Devices) terminals connected to a remote host computer. When a character is transmitted (in other words, when a key is pressed) the host device immediately sends it back to be displayed on the dumb terminal's screen. If the displayed character does not match the character selected from the keyboard, the operator should detect this; the host device can be advised, by the terminal operator, to ignore the incorrect character, be the sending of an agreed *control* character. Clearly, the method is slow and crude. A character could have been received correctly by the host device and an error could corrupt it on its way back. The operator has no way of knowing how and at what point an error occurred. Another disadvantage is that error correction is manual; in an interactive system, the user needs to rely on automatic error control and correction.

Error Correction

Automatic Repeat Request (ARQ)

When a receiver detects an error it must tell the sending device to re-transmit the erroneous data; this is known as *automatic repeat request* (ARQ). The technique is most appropriate to the handling of data streams, that is, synchronous communications, in conjunction with cyclic redundancy checking (CRC - see earlier). ARQ can take one of three forms:

- *Stop and wait ARQ* or *ACK and NAK*. With this form the receiver acknowledges every block of data, with ACK if it detects no error and NAK if an error is detected. The sending device cannot send the next block until an acknowledgement is received. Any NAK block is re-transmitted repeatedly, if necessary, until an ACK is received.
- *Go-back N ARQ*. With this form, a block is only acknowledged if an error is detected. The sending device can continue transmitting without waiting for an acknowledgement. When a NAK is received, the block in which the error occurred is identified and that block, plus any transmitted since (N blocks), must be re-transmitted.
- *Selective-repeat ARQ*. This is the most sophisticated form of ARQ, in that blocks transmitted since the erroneous block (correct ones are not acknowledged), do not have to be sent again. Thus the sender only re-transmits the identified block and then continues from where it left off, when the NAK was received.

File Transfer Protocols

File transfer is the process of transmitting complete files (see Computer Files for different types) from one computer to another. To achieve a successful transfer, both sending and receiving devices must establish the protocol (the set of rules) by which they will communicate. Various protocols are commonly recognised, but they vary in their performance and suitability for particular tasks. Some examples are described below.

ASCII

This is only appropriate for *text* files, which contain no control characters. Thus it cannot be used to transfer files produced with a word processor, spreadsheet or graphics package. Neither can it transfer command (COM) or executable (EXE) files, or files in compressed (ZIP, or example) form. Apart from this, the protocol is not good at controlling errors.

Xmodem

This is a file-transfer protocol used for asynchronous communications. It is commonly used in communications packages. The Xmodem protocol transfers data in blocks of 128 bytes, giving each transmitted *frame* a sequential block number; this number is used to identify the location of errors. A *checksum* (see Block Check Characters) is attached to each block to check transmission errors. Its ability to find and correct errors makes it suitable for the transfer of files, which must retain their integrity, such as program files.

Zmodem

This is one of the most advanced protocols, being much faster than Xmodem. Its error correction controls are absolutely reliable.

CCITT V42bis

This protocol includes a *data compression* (through encoding, data is reduced in volume) technique and error detection and correction. Both the sending and receiving modem must possess the error correction facility.

Transmission Media

When data is transmitted between two hardware devices in a network, a communication medium is used. The commonly used media are, *twisted-pair* cable, *coaxial* cable and *optical fibre*. Where a physical connection is not practical, then radio, infra-red, microwave and laser technologies may be used.

Twisted-pair Cable

Twisted-pair cable is formed from strands of wire twisted in pairs. It predates any other method and is still extensively used for standard telephone or telex terminals. Each twisted pair can carry a single telephone call between two people or two machines. Although twisted-pair cable is generally used for analogue signal transmission, it can be used successfully for digital transmission. Variation in the lengths of wire within pairs can result in signals being received out of phase, but this can be overcome by the frequent use of repeaters. The repeaters 'refresh' the signal as it passes to maintain its consistency. Although transmission rates permitted by such cable are lower than for some other media, they are acceptable for many computer applications.

Coaxial Cable

Coaxial cable is resistant to the transmission interference which can corrupt data transmitted via twisted-pairs cable. It thus provides a fast, relatively interference-free transmission medium. Its construction consists of a central conductor core which is surrounded by a layer of insulating material. The insulating layer is covered by a conducting shield, which is itself protected by another insulating layer. During network installation, the cable can be cut and connections made, without affecting its transmission quality. The quality of cable can vary and some low quality cable is unsuitable for data transmission over long distances. On the other hand, high quality cable can be quite rigid and difficult to install in local networks, where space is limited. Despite this difficulty, it is an extremely popular choice for LANs.

Optical Fibre Cable

Optical fibre cable consists of thousands of clear glass fibre strands which transmit light or infra-red rays instead of electrical signals. The data is transmitted by a light-emitting diode (two-state signals) or injection-laser diode. Transmission speeds of billions of bits per second are achieved. Repeaters are only required after several miles. The other end of the cable has a detector which converts the light pulses into electrical pulses suitable for the attached device. Optical fibre cable is more expensive than electrical cable but is finding increasing use in LANs. However, its main application is for long-distance communications.

Transmission Rates

Baud rate indicates the number of signal changes or pulses per second of a communications link. The term used to be synonymous with *bits per second* (bps), but improved *data compression* techniques mean, for example, that a 2400 baud link can support data transfer rates from 2400 bps to 14,400 bps. These bps speeds can be converted *to characters per second* (cps) rate. For example, an asynchronous modem (without error correction) sends each character with a start and stop bit, a total of 10 bits. Therefore, 2400 bps is equivalent to 240 cps for that type of link. A synchronous modem does not need to use start and stop bits and with error correction, requires a different conversion rate; 8 bits per character means that 2400 bps equates with 300 cps. The effective transmission rate depends on a variety of factors, including the type of communications link, the transmitting and receiving devices and the protocols being used.

Network Services

Many networks, both private and public, provide additional services which give them the collective name of *value-added networks* or VANs. Switchstream, Megastream and Satstream (see Digital Network Systems) are VANs provided by British Telecom. Other VANs provide specific services, such as *videotext* (see later), electronic mail, facsimile transmission, bulletin boards and bibliographic databases, for use by academics and researchers.

Gateways

Gateways allow different types of computer to communicate with one another, even if they use different communications protocols or transfer data at different speeds. For example, the mainframe computers of the main holiday tour operators can be accessed by travel agents, through a Prestel gateway.

Bibliographic Databases

These databases provide information on specialised or widely ranging topics. For example, BLAISE, which is provided by the British Library, gives information on British book publications. Euronet Diane (Direct Information Access Network in Europe) provides information extracted from publications, research documents and so on, which may be of interest to specialists, such as scientists, engineers, economists and lawyers. Each extract provides the relevant bibliographic references to allow users to access the original sources more fully.

Bulletin Boards

A bulletin board (BB) is simply a means by which, users can, for example, exchange ideas, pass on information and buy or sell items to one another. Frequently, no charge is made. Chat lines are often included; this means that two users can carry on a conversation, through the use of screen and keyboard. Where more than two users are 'conversing', a form of *teleconferencing* can occur; any user wishing to contribute to the discussion has their contribution placed in a queue, from where it will be displayed on each contributor's screen.

Telex

Telex is a well established communications system which, rather like the public telephone network, allows subscribers to communicate with one another. There are over a million subscribers in this country at present. Each subscriber is given a telex code (you will often see it at the top of business letter headings next to the telephone number) and must have a teleprinter which is a combination of keyboard and printer. There is no screen, so all messages sent or received are printed onto hard copy. The transmission rate of approximately 6 characters per second is slow compared with more modern telecommunications systems, but the limitations of keyboard entry and printer speed on the teleprinter, make any faster speed unnecessary. The main benefit of telex is that a permanent record of communications is kept and the receiver does not have to be 'on the spot' when the message arrives. Its main disadvantage is that there is no storage facility for messages. Any transmission has to be printed as soon as it is transmitted so that if the receiver is faulty, the system comes to a halt. Although it is inferior to e-mail (see next section), it is still the only method (apart from telephone) of instant communication with less developed countries, where Telex machines are still widely used.

Electronic Mail (E-Mail) Services

E-mail systems based on computer networks are paper-less (except when a user requires hard copy). A major advantage is the facility for message storage if a destination terminal is busy, or has a temporary fault. When it is free, the message can be transmitted.

Certain basic features can be identified as being common to all e-mail systems:

- a terminal for preparing, entering and storing messages. The terminal will be 'intelligent', possibly a microcomputer, mainframe terminal or dedicated word processor. In any event, it should have some word processing or text editing facilities to allow messages to be changed on screen before transmission. A printer may also be available for printing out messages received over the system;
- an electronic communication link with other workstations in the network and with the central computer controlling the system;
- a directory containing the electronic addresses of all network users;
- a central mailbox facility (usually the controlling computer) for the storage of messages in transit or waiting to be retrieved.
- Ideally, the following facilities are available to e-mail users:
- messages are automatically dated upon transmission;
- messages are automatically acknowledged as being received when the recipient first accesses it from the terminal;
- multiple addressing, that is the facility to address a message to an identified group, without addressing each member of the group individually;
- priority rating to allow messages to be allocated different priorities according to their importance.

Networks require two particular features in order to support e-mail:

- a message storage facility to allow messages to be forwarded when the recipient is available;
- compatibility with a wide range of manufacturers' equipment. Devices attached to a network have to be able to 'talk' to the communications network using protocols or standards of communication.

Benefits of E-Mail

The following major benefits are generally claimed for e-mail systems:

- savings in stationery and telephone costs;
- more rapid transmission than is possible with conventional mail;
- e-mail can be integrated with other computer-based systems used in an organisation;
- all transmissions are recorded, so costs can be carefully controlled;
- e-mail allows staff to 'telework', that is, to work from home via a terminal;
- the recipient does not have to be present when a message is sent. Messages can be retrieved from the central 'mailbox' when convenient.

Teletex

Teletex is nothing to do with teletext systems, such as Ceefax and Oracle (see Videotex). Teletex is similar to Telex, except that transmissions are quicker and cheaper and text is not restricted to upper case characters. It uses the pstn, but can also access packet switching networks and the Telex system through *gateways*. Teletex standards have been internationally agreed through the CCITT (see Standards Authorities) and Teletex is now used in many countries throughout the world.

Electronic Data Interchange (EDI)

Similar to E-mail, EDI allows users to exchange business documents, such as invoices, delivery notes, orders and receipts over the telephone network. EDI can drastically reduce the volume of paperwork and business can be transacted much more quickly than is possible through the normal postal system. UK examples of EDI systems are:

- Tradanet, linking manufacturers, wholesalers, distributors and retailers;
- Brokernet, which links insurance companies and brokers;
- Drugnet, linking medical practices to pharmaceutical companies, allowing the provision of current information on various products;
- Factornet allows firms to deal with *factors* who buy outstanding customer bills at a discount; the factors then obtain payment from the debtor. Small firms find this service particularly useful as it enables them to improve their cash flow.

EFTPOS (Electronic Funds Transfer at Point-of-Sale)

This service provides for the automatic debiting of customers' bank accounts at the checkout or point of sale. Many garages now have a device for reading the magnetic strip details on bank and credit cards. The system saves considerable time when contrasted with payments by cheque and as an alternative to cash, reduces the likelihood of theft. The retailer also has the assurance that the payment is authorised before the sale is made. Usually, a retailer will have a 'floor' limit, or amount above which a telephone call needs to be made to the credit card company for authorisation of payment.

EFT (Electronic Funds Transfer)

This system is used to transfer money between the branches of the same bank and between different banks. In the UK, the system is known as the Banker's Automated Clearing Service (BACS). The service is not restricted to bank use; organisations can pay their employees' salaries directly into their bank or building society accounts. Business accounts can also be settled through this EFT system. Apart from the banks, other users usually link into the pstn through a dial-up connection (unless the volume of data justifies a leased line).

Facsimile Transmission (FAX)

This service allows the transmission of facsimiles or exact copies of documents or pictures through a data communications network. Using a fax machine connected to a telephone line, the user simply dials the fax number of the recipient, waits for the correct signal and the document is fed though the fax machine and transmitted. The fax machine sends picture elements or pixels obtained by scanning the document in a series of parallel lines; a synchronised fax machine at the other end prints a facsimile from those pixels.

Teletext

Teletext systems, such as Ceefax and Oracle, provide a public service based on a central computer database, which users can access via an ordinary television set with special adapter and keypad. The database consists of thousands of 'pages' or frames of information which are kept up to date by Information Providers. Pages can be accessed and displayed on the television screen through the use of the keypad, directly via page number or through a series of hierarchical indexes. Major subject areas include Sport, News, Business, Leisure and Entertainment, Finance and Travel. Pages are transmitted using spare bandwidth unused by television pictures, in 'carousels' or groups. The user may have to wait some time while the carousel containing the required page is transmitted. Its major drawback is that communication is *one-way*. The user cannot send messages to the database, only receive.

Viewdata or Videotex

A viewdata system is based on a central computer database, which provides 'pages' of information on a variety of subjects, including sport, travel and business, for access by subscribers. As an *interactive* system, users typically access services using simple, low cost, viewdata terminals, or microcomputer systems equipped with special software. Users connect with a viewdata *gateway* through the public telephone network. The major public viewdata system in the UK is *Prestel*. It uses the Teletext *alpha mosaic* character set. The graphics it produces appear similar to Lego building blocks. Developed by British Telecom, Prestel is now technologically out of date and is used, mainly, as a *gateway* to third party databases, for example, Electronic Yellow Pages, and CitiService (a financial database). Apart from information provision, the following services may be available through a viewdata system.

- Electronic mail. Viewdata users can transmit electronic messages to other users in the system, using such things as bulletin boards and 'chat lines'. The British Campus 2000, which links together schools in Britain and other countries is an example of a viewdata electronic mail system.
- Paying bills, purchasing tickets, ordering goods and other such transactions.
- The distribution of computer programs. Centrally stored computer programs can be transferred to users' microcomputer systems so that they can later be used independently of the viewdata system. This is sometimes referred to as *telesoftware*.

In France, a combined teletext and viewdata system is called Antiope, and another viewdata system, available since 1984, is called Teletel. The latter system is very widely used, with more than eight million terminals attached to the system. The US service is called Prodigy and in Japan it is called Captain.

File Transfer

A file can be a data file or a program file; the data could be a document prepared on a word processor and a program file could be a program of any kind. A file transfer service allows the use of one computer to retrieve a file from another computer, through a telecommunications link. Equally, a file can be transmitted in the opposite direction. E-mail is a special kind of file transfer facility, but to most users, the facility is used to retrieve documentary information from remote databases, or software from, for example, bulletin boards. To be transferred correctly, and this is particularly important in the case of program files (it can't be executed if the code is corrupted), requires the use of file transfer protocols. A modem suited to the purpose will use a particular file transfer protocol and whatever communications package is used, it must be able to use that protocol.

The Internet

Overview

The Internet is a world-wide network derived from DARPANET (Defense Advanced Research Projects Agency Network) which was developed, during the 1960s, initially as a military defence project for the U.S. Department of Defense. Later, with universities and other academic institutions making unauthorised use of the network for private electronic mail, the name was changed to ARPANET. A packet switching protocol called NCP (network control protocol) had its initial development in the UK and this was adopted as the network protocol. Since 1984, the number of host computers connected to the network has grown from 500 to more than 3 million; it is estimated that the number of users, world-wide is over 30 million. This figure is likely to increase exponentially.

World Wide Web (WWW)

Although accessing the network is not difficult, finding specific information can be, considering the number of host computers connected to it. In 1990, the European Laboratory of Particle Physics in Switzerland, developed a *hypertext* (see Chapter 2) based user interface. This interface allows a user to move from one Internet resource to another by way of, for example, topic searches, without knowing in advance, the precise location of each piece of information.

Service Providers

To gain access to Internet, microcomputer users need to use a *service provider*. These are organisations which not only provide the necessary software to gain access to the network, but provide some of the additional services outlined in the previous section; in particular, the services cover e-mail, file transfer and access to bibliographic databases. Listed below are some of the UK service providers, some providing more sophisticated facilities than others.

- BBC Networking Club.
- CityScape.
- CIX (Compulink Information Exchange).
- Demon Internet.
- EasyNet.

A major American service provider is CompuServe.

Chapter 8
Computer Networks

Types of Network

Networking computer systems has the effect of decentralising computer processing and improving communications within and between organisations and between organisations and individuals. Some computer networks use dedicated intelligent terminals or microcomputer systems to permit some independent processing power at sites remote from the *host* computer, to which they are connected. Other networks distribute even more processing power by linking microcomputer, minicomputer, mainframe and supercomputer systems. They are sometimes referred to as *distributed processing* systems. Networks can be configured to suit almost any application, from the provision of a world-wide airline reservation system to home banking. *Nodes* (connection points in the network) may only be a few feet apart and limited to a single building, or they may be several thousand miles apart.

Local and Wide Area Networks

Computer networks can be classified according to their geographical spread. A network confined to, say, one building, with microcomputer workstations distributed in different rooms, is known as a *local area network* (LAN). One particular type, known as a ring network can extend over a diameter of around five miles. A computer network distributed nationally or even internationally makes use of telephone and sometimes, satellite links, and is referred to as a *wide area network* (WAN). In large organisations with several branches, it is common practice to maintain a LAN at each branch for local processing requirements and to link each LAN into a WAN covering the whole organisation. In this way, branches of an organisation can have control over their own processing and yet have access to the organisation's main database at headquarters. In addition, inter-branch communication is possible.

Network Architecture

The architecture of any network includes definition of:

- its *components*, both hardware and software, identified by *name* and *function*
- the ways the *components* are *connected* and communicate with one another.

The architecture of wide area networks (WANs) is described in Chapter 7 and the following primarily relates to local area networks (LANs). However, the section on Network Topologies does relate, in part, to WANs.

LAN Architecture

It is important that the components are combined in such a way that the LAN can be:

- *extended*. The LAN must be capable of providing for new users and new equipment, as the need arises;
- *upgraded* to take advantage of new technologies which can improve network performance;
- *connected* to other LANs, both local and remote and Wide Area Networks.

LAN architecture comprises hardware and software, both for the control of the LAN communications and as an interface between the LAN and its users. In order that all components are compatible and operate as a coherent system, it is important that they conform to agreed standards (Chapter 7). This means that LAN producers have to take account of generally agreed standards for equipment linking and data communications, so that as new products come onto the market, the user is not left with a system which cannot take advantage of them. Unfortunately, a number of different standards exist and this means that the decision on which type of LAN to purchase is not always straightforward.

Hardware Components

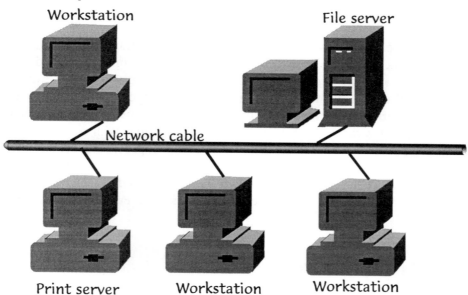

Figure 8.1. *Main components of client-server network*

Figure 8.1 shows a simple client-server (see later) LAN and identifies the main hardware components of:

- workstation;
- file server;
- printer server;
- network cabling;

The way in which they are connected defines its general *topology* or physical shape.

LAN Workstation

A *workstation* gives a user access to a LAN and its facilities. A workstation comprises:

- a microcomputer;
- a *network card* (Chapter 26), which fits into an *expansion slot* inside its system casing. The network card enables workstations to communicate across the network, and with the *file server* (see later). The card converts computer-generated data into a form suitable for transmission over the LAN and as such is an *interface* (Chapter 7). The card is operated with a network card *driver* (see Software Components).

Servers

The general function of servers is to allocate shared resources to other nodes on the network. There are a number of different types of server, which can be categorised according to the resources they control.

File Server

The file server is usually a specially configured microcomputer, with a network card, more memory and disk storage, as well as a more powerful processor than is needed for a workstation. It has to control access to shared storage, directories and files. In addition, it controls the exchange of files between network users. Most network software provides *multiple device* support. This means that file servers can support several disks, allowing file storage capacity on the LAN to be increased beyond that of the file server's integral hard disk. A LAN can also consist of several file servers; indeed except for the smallest of networks, this is normally the case.

Print Server

A print server (there may be several) accepts and queues jobs from workstations; the user may be informed when printing is complete. The print server may also provide certain print management functions, for example, to attach priorities to different print jobs so that certain jobs are printed before others, no matter what their positions in the queue. A print server will be configured to:

- support the use of particular printers;
- service particular printer queues; users with the right to use a particular print queue can then place their jobs in that queue.

Communications Server

If a LAN is to have access to external networks or databases, a communications server is required. Generally, the communications server can establish a temporary link with remote computers or users on other networks (see Remote Inter-networking).

Network Topologies

Computer networks can be categorised according to their physical shape or topology. Each terminal in a network is known as a *node*. If a central computer controls the network it is known as the *host* computer. The topology of a network is the *arrangement* of the nodes and the ways they are interconnected. The communication system within a network is known as the *subnet*. Data can be transmitted around the subnet either on a *point-to-point* basis or through a *broadcast* channel.

- If point-to-point transmission is used, the data passes through each device in the network. Thus, if two devices wish to communicate, they must do it indirectly, via any intervening devices. Each device must have the facility to store the entire message and forward it when the output channel is free.
- If a broadcast channel is used, a common communication channel is shared by all devices in the network. This means that any message sent by a device is received by all devices. The message contains the address of the device intended to receive it, so that the other devices can ignore it.

There are a number of recognised network topologies and some of the most common are described below.

Star Network

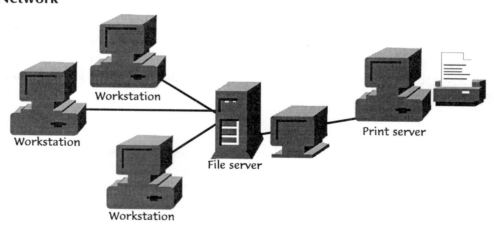

Figure 8.2. *Star topology*

A star topology means that each node is connected, by separate connections to a computer at the centre, known as the *hub*. Figure 8.2 shows a LAN in a star topology. It is also a popular ~~n~~ology for a WAN. In this structure, all messages pass through the host (probably a ~~fr~~ame or minicomputer) computer, which interconnects the different devices on the ~~networ~~k. So, in this topology the host computer at the hub has a *message switching* function.

Messages are transmitted point-to-point. The topology is particularly useful for intercommunications between pairs of users on the network (via the host). The network may consist of numerous computer systems (the nodes), connected to a larger host computer which switches data and programs between them.

The star computer network is by far the most popular for WANs, because most large organisations start with a central computer at the head office, from which branch computer facilities are provided through the telephone network. The main aim is to provide computer communication between the branches and head office. Most other network topologies aim to provide communication between all devices on a network. The star topology can also be used for a LAN.

The *advantages* of a star network topology are as follow:

- It is suitable for WANs where organisations rely on a central computer for the bulk of processing tasks, perhaps limiting the nodes to their local processing needs and the validation of data, prior to transmission to the central computer;
- Centralised control of message switching allows a high degree of security control;
- Each spoke in the star is independent of the rest and a fault in a link or device in one spoke, can be identified by the computer at the hub;
- The data transmission speeds used can vary from one *spoke* (a link from the hub to a node) to another. This is important if some spokes transmit using high speed devices, such as disk, whilst others transmit from low speed keyboard devices. The method of transmission may also vary. For example, one node may only require access to the network at the end of each day, in which case a *dial-up* connection may be sufficient. A dial-up connection uses the public telephone network and the user only pays for the time taken for transmission. Alternatively, other nodes may require the link for most of the working day, in which case a permanent *leased line* is appropriate. Leased lines provide a more reliable transmission medium and also allow higher speeds of data transmission.

The main *disadvantages* inherent in star networks are as follow:

- The network is vulnerable to hub failures which affect all users. As a distributed processing system, some processing is still possible at the nodes but inter-node communication is lost when the host computer fails;
- For a WAN, the control of communications in the network requires expensive technology at the hub, probably a mini or mainframe computer. Complex operating and communications software is needed to control the network.

Ring Network

The ring topology is specifically designed for use with a LAN and is not suitable for a WAN. A ring network connects all the nodes in a ring, as illustrated in Figure 8.3.

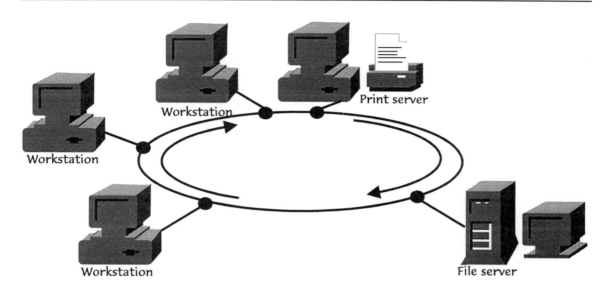

Figure 8.3. *Ring topology*

The *Cambridge Ring*, developed at Cambridge University, has no host computer and none of the nodes need have overall control of access to the network. In practice, a monitoring station is used for the control of data transmission in the network. Messages in a ring network flow in one direction, from node to node.

The ring consists of a series of repeaters, which are joined by the physical transmission medium (twisted pair, co-axial, or fibre-optic cable - see Chapter 7). The choice of medium depends on the distances to be covered and the desired transmission rates. Fibre-optic cable allows the greatest distances to be covered and the highest transmission rates. Repeaters are used to regenerate messages as they pass around the network. The use of repeaters allows a ring network to cover larger distances than is possible for other topologies. In fact, recent developments using fibre optic cable allow a ring with a range of about 100 kilometres, which makes it a *metropolitan area network* (MAN). The user devices are connected to the repeaters. A message from one node, addressed to another, is passed continually around the ring until the receiving node flags that it is ready to accept it. Acceptance of a message is determined by its *destination address*, which is examined by each node it passes. If the destination address matches the node's own address, the node takes the message; otherwise, the node repeater regenerates the signal to be passed to the next node in the ring. Data is transmitted in mini-packets of about 40 bits and contains the address of the sending node, the address of the destination node and some control bits. A variation on the Cambridge ring is the IBM ring, which uses a different protocol to allow better control of message flow on the network; the two protocols, *empty slot* and *token passing* are described in the section on Network Access Protocols. The ring network presents particular advantages:

- There is no dependence on a central host computer as data transmission around the network is supported by all the devices in the ring. Each node device has sufficient intelligence to control the transmission of data from and to its own node;

- Very high transmission rates are possible; 10 megabits/sec is typical.
- Routing between devices is relatively simple because messages normally travel in one direction only around the ring;
- The transmission facility is shared equally amongst the users.

The main disadvantages are as follows:

- The system depends on the reliability of the whole ring and the repeaters, although it can be designed to bypass any failed node.
- It may be difficult to extend the length of the ring because the physical installation of any new cable must ensure that the ring topology is preserved.

Star/Ring Network - IBM Token Ring

The *IBM Token Ring* Network is a star-based topology, with a hub or *multiple access unit* (MAU) to which all the workstations are connected. The movement of data is, however in a *logical ring*. All signals between workstations are through the MAU. The star/ring structure has a major advantage over the basic ring. If one workstation breaks down, or the connection with the MAU is broken, other workstations are not affected (except that they cannot communicate with the damaged workstation). Failure of the MAU will prevent operation of the network. The Cambridge ring structure, described earlier, is prone to complete failure if one workstation fails (the continuous ring is broken).

Bus Network

With a bus topology, the workstations are connected to a main cable (known as the *bus* or trunk), along which data travels. The ends of a bus are not connected, so that data has to travel in both directions to reach the various nodes on the network. The bus topology makes the addition of new devices straightforward, either by attachment to the existing cable or to cable which can be added at either end. The main bus standard is known as *Ethernet*. The term *station* tends to be used rather than node for this type of network. The communications subnet uses a *broadcast* channel, so all attached stations can 'hear' every transmission. As is the case in the ring network, there is no host computer and all stations have equal priority in using the network to transmit. The maximum length of a single bus *segment* is 500 metres and 100 stations can be attached to it. Segments can be specially linked to form larger configurations, up to a maximum of about 12 kilometres. Transmission speeds of 10 megabits/second are obtainable. The topology is illustrated in the Figure 8.4.

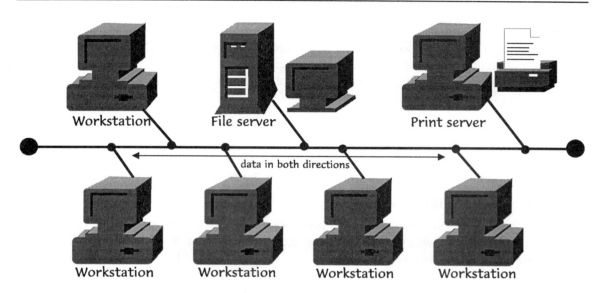

Figure 8.4. *Bus topology*

The bus network provides certain benefits:

- If a node malfunctions, it simply stops communicating; it doesn't prevent the rest of the network from working;
- The attachment of devices is straightforward and the cable can be extended, if necessary; additional *segments* can be linked to extend the network.

The main drawback is that:

- if a part of the Ethernet cabling develops a fault, the whole network (assuming it consists of a single segment) fails.

Mesh Network

The nodes of a mesh network are fully interconnected, as shown in Figure 7.3 in Chapter 7. The mesh topology is not found in LANs, but is typical of the public switched telephone network (pstn) and WANs. Its complexity requires the use of switching techniques to route data through the network (see Packet Switching in Chapter 7).

Network Cabling - the Transmission Medium

In order to share resources on a network, servers, workstations and other devices must be connected; although 'wireless' radio media are possible, most LANs use physical cabling, which acts as the *transmission medium*. The physical layout of the cabling should conform to one of the basic *topologies*: star, ring or bus. The type of cable used depends on the chosen topology and the rules governing the transmission of data through the cable (the *protocol*). The cabling standards of Ethernet and Token Ring, described below, are also LAN protocols.

Ethernet Cabling

Ethernet is one the two most widely accepted standards (the other is Token Ring) for specifying how data is placed on and retrieved from a LAN. An Ethernet-equivalent standard is IEEE 802.3 (see Chapter 7, Standards Authorities), which also uses Ethernet cable, but packets data slightly differently for transmission through the cable. Ethernet cable falls into two main categories:

- *Thick Ethernet* coaxial cable, with a diameter of 10mm has a solid copper core conductor. A single network segment can be 500 metres and supports the attachment of 100 devices. The cabling conforms to the "IEEE 802.3 Type 10Base5" standard. The transmission rate is 10 megabits (1,000,000 bits) per second (Mb/s).
- *Thin Ethernet*, which is 10 millimetres diameter, has a core of stranded cable. The maximum length of cable which can be used in a single network segment is around 180 metres and the maximum number of workstations is around 30. The cabling conforms to the "IEEE 802.3 Type 10Base2" standard. The cable supports a maximum transmission rate of 2 Mb/s.
- *10BaseT* Standard Ethernet. The "T" stands for *twisted pair*. This cable is much cheaper than the thick Ethernet cabling, but provides the same transmission rate of 10 Mb/s; being the same as most telephone cabling, it is easier to install.

Token Ring Cabling

Used in *IBM token ring* networks use twisted pair cabling, either two pairs or four, depending on data transmission requirements. A single IBM Token Ring network will support up to 260 network devices at rates of 4 Mb/s or 16 Mb/s. Up to eight rings can be connected using *bridges*.

Fibre-optic Cabling

See Chapter 7. Cable of this type is available for use with any of the network types, but provides greater *bandwidth* and permits transmission over greater distances, without the use of *repeaters*.

Cable Bandwidth

There are two different methods of utilising a LAN cable for the transmission of data; *baseband* and *broadband*.

- Baseband. In a baseband network, a transmitting device uses the whole bandwidth (frequency range), so only one signal can be carried at any one time. This means that, for a brief moment, a transmitting device has exclusive use of the transmission medium. In general, broadband networks are suitable for networks which only transmit data signals.
- Broadband. Broadband networks provide a number of frequency bands or channels within the total bandwidth (*frequency division multiplexing*) and thus allow simultaneous use by different devices on the network. Generally, one channel is dedicated to the user workstations, leaving others free for transmitting video pictures for the security system, voice communication, television pictures and so on.

Cable-Device Connection

A number of different devices are used to make the connection between network devices, such as workstations and servers, and the transmission medium. The particular components used will depend on the type of network (for example, Ethernet or Token Ring); even for the same type of network, there are a range of connection alternatives. The following section only details the main categories of connection component.

- network card (adapter), which is the *interface* for linking a network device to all other resources on the network; this is fitted into an expansion slot inside each workstation and other network devices. A device attaching to a Token ring network needs a different type of network card, from one attaching to an Ethernet network. A notebook or portable computer can be connected using its PCMCIA (Personal Computer Memory Card International Association) slot and a special network adapter.
- Ethernet transceiver; this device implements the CSMA/CD access protocol (see Access protocols). It is external from the network device and is connected to the network card and the Ethernet network cable. Although most network cards already contain a transceiver chip, *thick* Ethernet connections need an external transceiver. Thin Ethernet connections simply use the transceiver chip on the network card.
- BNC connector; this is one of several types of connector used for *thin* Ethernet cable. There are BNC 'male' and 'female' connectors for linking sections of cable and 'T' connectors for attaching devices to the cable. *Thick* Ethernet cabling uses a stronger screw coupling for cable connections (N-series connectors). Figure 8.5 illustrates its appearance.
- *terminator*; this is an electrical resistor which must be attached to each end of an Ethernet network segment (see Bus Topology).
- Multiple Access Unit (MAU). This is the central component of a star/ring topology and is used in the IBM Token Ring network (see Star/Ring Network).

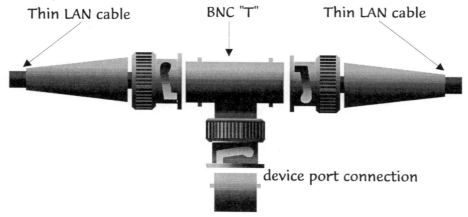

Thin LAN cable   BNC "T"   Thin LAN cable

device port connection

Figure 8.5. *BNC "T" connector*

Connecting and Extending LANs

Although there are limitations to the range of a LAN and the number of devices which can be attached, imposed by the performance ability of the network transmission medium, networks can be connected to one another and extended. LANs set up separately can be connected permanently, or data transmission between them can be restricted, for special user or system requirements. The functions of the main devices used in this area of LAN architecture are described below.

Repeater

Repeaters allow the effective length of an Ethernet segment to be increased. The maximum length of an Ethernet segment is restricted because of signal loss and distortion which occurs as a data packet travels along the cable. A repeater re-strengthens, that is, *re-amplifies* the signal and resets its timing, so that the effective length of the segment can be increased. It is also used to enable a signal to travel to another segment of a network. A repeater can normally connect any kind of cable medium: thick or thin Ethernet, twisted pair or optical fibre. Figure 8.6 illustrates the role of a repeater in connecting a thick Ethernet "backbone", to thin Ethernet segments. In relation to the Open Systems Inter-connection (OSI) model, referred to in Chapter 7, a repeater works at the Physical level and only needs to know how to interact with the physical transmission medium.

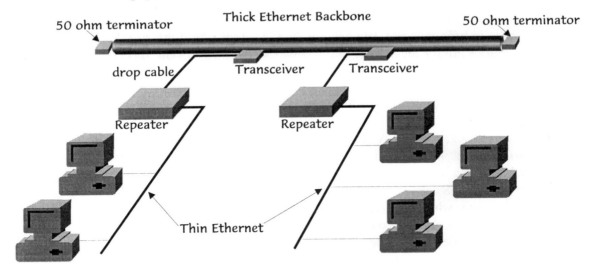

Figure 8.6. *Repeaters linking thick Ethernet backbone to thin Ethernet segments*

Bridge

A bridge is used to connect two LANs of the same type, that is, two token ring or two Ethernet LANs. This is known as *local inter-networking*. Packets crossing such a link are *forwarded* by the bridge device. Bridges are *protocol transparent*. Thus, the otherwise similar networks can be using different protocols, for example, IPX (Novell) or TCP/IP (Macintosh). They can also divide large networks into smaller segments. Segmenting large networks can improve administrative control and the performance of the separate segments. In the latter case, the bridge can be configured such that only data which needs to cross the bridge actually does. For example, if there are two segments, one for the Sales department and the other for Accounts, the data traffic for each function will be isolated within the respective segments, except when data needs to travel between the two. This improves the performance of each segment and thus the effectiveness of the whole network.

Software Components

Apart from the physical components identified in the previous section, the following software in needed to run a network (see Chapter 26 for more detail):

- a *network operating system* resident in the file server. A major commercial example is Novell Netware;
- a *local operating system* within each workstation, for example, MS-DOS, MS Windows, OS/2, UNIX or Apple Macintosh.
- *network connection software*; this must be loaded at a workstation before it can communicate with the network.

Network Operating System

A network operating system typically includes functional components to set-up, monitor and administer:

- the *directory* and *file* system on the server; directories are used to organise the storage of programs and data held on the file server's hard drive(s). Some directories are for the storage of the network operating system; others contain application programs and some directory space is allocated for the storage of users' data. Chapter 26 provides an example of a file server's directory structure; each directory is labelled to identify the nature of the files it contains.
- user *login* and activity. A user must be identified by the network operating system before being given access to the network. The supervisor *creates* users and assigns a user-id to each. A user may also be assigned to a *user-group*, for example, Sales or Marketing. To access a network, a user must login at a workstation, which will require the entry of a *user-id* and possibly, a *password*. The precise conditions can be set by the network supervisor: certain time periods can be set when users are not allowed to log into the network; the time restrictions can be applied to all users, specific groups or individuals. The resources available to any given user can also be controlled through the login procedure.
- *user access* to applications and data files. Typically, users are assigned *rights*, sometimes as individuals, but more usually as members of a group. These rights relate to directories and files; in other words, the rights determine whether, for example, a user is allowed to delete or copy files in a particular directory. Access rights to *network executables*, that is application programs, only allow the programs to be run.

- network *printing*; users can be given access to a shared printer, through a print *queue*; each queue is controlled by a printer server, which directs the jobs to a network printer under its control.
- *electronic messaging*; this is a LAN version of electronic mail and provides a mailbox facility for inter-user communication.
- network *backup*. This task, although important to users, because it may prevent the loss of important work, or network facilities, is a task carried out on a regular basis by the network supervisor.

All these tasks are the responsibility of the *network supervisor* or *administrator* who has special rights of access, not available to others. Usually, these tasks are carried out through a system console; any computer on the network can be used for this purpose, but, usually it will be secure in a separate location. Although printing, electronic messaging, applications and limited file management are available to users, their rights should not extend to the amendment of these facilities. A more detailed examination of some of the functional operating system components (listed above) is made in Chapter 26.

Workstation Operating System

Each workstation must have its own local operating system, such as MS-DOS to control processing; once an application is retrieved from the file server, the workstation must be able to run it.

Network Connection Software

The network connection software must be loaded into the workstation RAM (usually from the its integral hard drive, during start-up), before the workstation can be logged onto the network. This software remains in the workstation RAM as long as it is logged onto the network. A program which remains resident like this is referred to as a TSR (terminate and stay resident) program. There are usually several components to the connection software, each having a separate function. Two major functional components are the:

(i) *communication protocol*. This is the set of rules for transmitting data through the network; it ensures that devices can successfully communicate with one another by using the same 'language'. Example protocols are: IPX (Novell Netware); TCP/IP (Macintosh); SNA (IBM).

(ii) *LAN driver*, which controls the network card fixed inside the workstation. LAN drivers which conform to the ODI (Open Data-link Interface) standard can accept data from the network in any of the standard communication protocols, listed in (i). This means that workstations of different operating system types (MS-DOS, Macintosh, UNIX etc.) can be attached to the same LAN and share its resources.

Figure 26.1, in Chapter 26, illustrates the location of each of these components.

Network Access Protocols

Empty Slot Technique

This system is appropriate for networks in the shape of rings or loops, where messages are passed point-to-point in one direction. One or more empty *slots* or *packets* circulate continuously around the ring. When a device has information to transmit, it loads it into the slot, which carries it to its destination. At the time of loading, the destination address is placed in the slot and a 'full-empty' flag is set to 'full'. As the slot is passed from one repeater to another, no attempt will be made to load the slot as long as the flag is set to 'full'. When the slot reaches the destination device, the device's repeater reads the information without clearing the slot. Before passing it on, the repeater sets a 'received message' flag in the slot. When the slot again reaches the sending device, the flag is set to 'empty'. The destination device can check that the message was received by checking the 'received' flag. If the message was not successfully received, perhaps because the destination device was not 'listening', the sender device can check the acknowledgement flag and re-transmit in the next slot.

Token Passing Technique

This technique is also used for ring networks. An imaginary *token* is passed continuously around the ring. The token is recognised as such by the devices, as a unique character sequence. If a device is waiting to transmit, it catches the token and with it, the authority to send data. As long as one device has the token, no other device can send data. A receiving device acknowledges the receipt of a message by inverting a 1-bit field. Token Ring (IEEE 802.5 Standard) employs this access method.

Carrier Sense Multiple Access (CSMA)

This method of access control is used on broadcast systems such as the bus network. Each device is theoretically free to transmit data to any other device at any time. Before attempting to transmit, a device's network card polls the network path to ensure that the destination device is free to receive data and that the communications channel is free. A device wishing to transmit must wait until both conditions exist. Generally such delay will be no more than a few millionths of a second.

- CSMA *Collision Detection* (CSMA-CD). Because of the possibility of collision through simultaneous transmission, a collision detection mechanism is used. When collision does occur, the devices involved cease transmission and try again some time later. In order to avoid the same collision, each device involved is made to wait a different time. If a number of retries prove unsuccessful, an error will be reported to the user. Ethernet (IEEE 802.3 Standard) networks (see Network Cabling) uses a form of CSMA/CD.
- CSMA *Collision Avoidance* (CSMA-CA). This strategy attempts to improve on that of CSMA-CD, which allows a device to place a packet onto the network path as soon as its network card detects it as being free. In the time between the test (measured in fractions of a microsecond) and the placing of

the packet onto the path, another device's network card may have detected the path as free and be about to place another packet onto it. CSMA-CA seeks to remedy this problem by requiring a device's network card to test the path *twice*, once to see if the path is free and a second time, after alerting the device that it may use the network, but before the packet is placed onto the path.

Remote Inter-networking

The term "inter-networking" is used to describe the formation of integrated network systems, through the connection of separate networks, locally and remotely. This enables organisations to construct organisation-wide information and communications systems, even if sections of it are a few or thousands of miles apart. This section looks at the devices used to make connections between LANs which are remote from one another and necessarily therefore, between LANs and wide area networks; these may be, for example, public switched telephone and data networks (see Chapter 7). In general, these devices deal with the:

- connection of networks operating on different protocols;
- connection of LANs to WANs;
- connection of networks of different architecture, cabling and protocol;
- routing of packets along the most efficient path;
- conversion between different packet formats, protocols and transmission speeds.

Computer networking is a relatively new industry and terminology is not entirely standardised. For this reason, definitions of terms, such as bridge, router and gateway can vary from one manufacturer's specification to another. Some devices, for example, combine the features of bridges and routers and are referred to as "bridge/routers". Bearing this in mind, the following definitions are generally accepted.

Gateway or Router

A gateway, or router, is used to connect two LANs of different (they don't have to be) type ; thus, for example, an Ethernet LAN can be connected to a Token Ring LAN, or the connection may be Ethernet to Ethernet. The LANs may be remotely connected through, for example, British Telecom's Kilostream (Chapter 7) WAN, with a gateway at each LAN's entry point to the WAN. The term *router* is used to signify that the device is more 'intelligent' than a bridge (see Connecting and Extending LANs), in that it makes decisions about the route a data packet (by reference to its destination address) should follow to reach its destination; in this way, packets can be made to take the most efficient path. It may determine an alternative route for a packet, in the event of, for example, congestion or breakdown on a particular link. Networks may have different architectures and protocols. A LAN using IPX (Novell) protocol can use a gateway to allow users access to, for example, a remote IBM network, which uses SNA protocol, through the Kilostream packet (X.25 protocol) switching network.

Multiplexer

Low speed terminals, such as those with keyboards, transmit at about 300 bps, whereas voice-grade telephone lines can support transmission speeds of up to 14,400 bps. A multiplexer allows a number of low-speed devices to share a high-speed line. The messages from several low-speed lines are combined into one high-speed channel and then separated out at the other end by a demultiplexor. In two-way transmissions, both these functions are carried out in one unit at each end of the higher speed channel. The operation of a multiplexer linking several remote terminals to a host computer is illustrated in Figure 7.4, in Chapter 7. Multiplexers use different methods to combine signals and separate them out: *frequency division multiplexing* (FDM) and *time division multiplexing* (TDM).

Concentrator

A concentrator greatly increases data throughput by increasing the number of low-speed channels and instead of transmitting a null character, empties the contents of the next full register. The data from each low-speed device is identified by extra identification bits and this constitutes an overhead.

Front-End-Processors (FEP)

A front-end-processor is the most sophisticated type of device for communications control and is usually a minicomputer held at the site of a mainframe host computer. Its main task is to handle all the communications traffic, leaving the mainframe free to concentrate on other processing tasks. Its main tasks include:

- parity checking;
- 'stripping' of overhead characters from serial transmission, start-stop bits and SYN (synchronous transmission - see Chapter 7) characters;
- conversion from serial to parallel transmission and vice versa;
- network control;
- network accounting;
- character conversion.

Benefits of Computer Networks

The general benefits are:

- sharing of appropriate *software*, *hardware resources* and common *data*;
- sharing of *processing* activity;
- *connectivity*; this is a very broad term used to categorise facilities and devices which support connection and communication between otherwise incompatible systems or devices. For example, a *terminal emulation* card, which enables a microcomputer to communicate with a remote IBM host computer, falls into this category;
- accessible services for *security*, *user support* and *system maintenance*.

Sharing Hardware and Software

In a LAN, particularly, there are opportunities to share hardware and software. This is because, resources tend to be distributed over a small area; it is reasonable to ask users to share a printing resource if the printers serving them are within the same room, or perhaps in an adjacent room. It could be argued that the rapid fall in hardware costs has, to a certain extent, reduced the need for sharing peripherals, such as hard disk drives and printers. Although the prices of hard drives have fallen, the heavy demands of modern software and the increasing number of applications, ensures matching increases in demand for on-line storage. It is now common for microcomputer systems, even at the cheaper end of the market, to have their own hard disk storage with capacities measured in hundreds of megabytes. Although printers are becoming much cheaper, an increasing number of users are demanding the high quality output (and sometimes colour) provided by top quality printers; printers at the top of the quality range are still relatively expensive. In summary, a number of factors concerning computer usage, storage and printing confirm that resource sharing remains a major purpose of a LAN.

- Applications. The range of computer applications and the number of users is continually increasing;
- Software packages. The increasing sophistication of software means that large amounts of disk space are needed for each package. Network versions of a package are cheaper (per user) than those for stand-alone systems;
- Storage technologies. Optical storage and high performance hard drives are capable of storing thousands of megabytes (gigabytes or gb) and are still relatively expensive. Individual users, each with their own hard disk-based microcomputer, are unlikely to make use of the several hundred megabytes available on each machine. A shared, large volume, hard or optical drive can satisfy the storage needs of all users.
- Printers. Most users require only occasional use of a printer, so there is little point in providing one for each. This is particularly the case for colour printers. A laser printer can produce the high quality output demanded by many applications and it operates at speeds which allow sharing to take place, without unreasonable delay for users;
- Other devices, such as scanners and plotters are relatively expensive and are likely to be used only occasionally.

Sharing Data

A major benefit of all types of network concerns the sharing of data, frequently from centralised databases. This purpose is made particularly clear by the expansion of Internet, the world-wide network described in Chapter 8. Data can also be regarded as a resource, so sharing it can bring similar benefits to those available from sharing hardware. For example, a common data store supports the use of a *database* system, which itself reduces the need for data duplication. Traditional computer processing methods require that each application has its own files and this results in the duplication of many data items and the updating process. For example, in a retail business both the stock control and purchasing departments make use of commodity details such as Stock Codes, Descriptions and Prices; if separate files are maintained by each department, a change in, for example, the Price of a commodity requires more than one input. A database system allows these details (a single copy of each commodity's Stock Code, Description and Price) to be shared by all departments that need them. Even if database methods are not used, the storage of the various application files in a common disk store, means that they can, if desired, be made available to all users on a network. For an organisation with numerous branches, each with its own processing facility, there needs to be a central resource, where the results of processing at branches can be merged (and possibly re-distributed) to give corporate (across the organisation, as a whole) information.

Limiting Access to Shared Storage

The sharing of data files presents some problems which need to be tackled. Firstly, access to some data may have to be restricted to particular users. Although the aim of networks is to provide computer access to as many users as possible, procedural and software controls can be built in to limit entry to the system, or to particular files or processes. Network software allows the network administrator to vary the rights of users, according to the kinds of access they require to particular applications or files. Another problem with sharing files is that several users may attempt to update the same data at the same time. This can lead to corruption of data. To combat this problem, network software usually provides a facility for locking individual records while they are being updated. Thus, if a particular record is being altered, it is locked and made inaccessible by any other user until the updating process is complete.

Sharing Processing Activity

Host Computer with Intelligent Terminals

A host computer with intelligent terminals allows processing to be carried out at remote sites; as such it comes under the heading of WAN. The distribution of processing work may be very limited, such that the majority is processed by a central computer. For example, terminals connected to a remote host computer often have their own processing power, file storage and printing facilities. Usually, before being transmitted to the host computer for the updating of files, *transaction* data will require some *validation* and other accuracy checks and this can be done at the terminal. Microcomputers equipped with suitable software are often used to *emulate* mainframe intelligent terminals, with the added advantage of being useable as stand-alone systems, when not communicating with the mainframe.

Alternatively, the work may be equally shared amongst a number of powerful computer systems, which then merge the results of their separate efforts.

Client-Server Network

A *client-server* LAN aims to exploit the full processing power of each computer in the network, including the *file server* and the user workstations or *clients*. This is effected by dividing the processing tasks between a client and a server. The client, a microcomputer in its own right (as opposed to the *dumb* terminal found in older mainframe systems) provides the user with a completely separate facility for running applications. The file server which could be a microcomputer, minicomputer, or mainframe, enhances the client component by providing additional services. These services are traditionally offered by minicomputer and mainframe systems operating a *time-sharing* (see Chapter 4); they include shared file management, data sharing between users, network administration and security. The major benefit of a client-server network is that the power of the client and server machines is used jointly to carry out the processing of an application. Interactive activities, for example, construction of a spreadsheet or the word processing of a report, are carried out by the client machine; having logged onto the network, the user can load the required applications software from the file server. Matters of backup and file sharing security, relating to the application, can be handled by the server. Printing tasks can also be queued and handled as a shared printer becomes available. This task is handled by one or more *print servers*, which can be dedicated devices, or microcomputers assigned to the task. Except for very small LANs, most operate on the client-server principle.

Peer-to-Peer Network

With a peer-to-peer configuration, it is not necessary to have a file server; instead all the workstations on the network contribute to control of the network. Thus, any workstation can supply or use resources of others, as required. Unfortunately, this has the effect of slowing performance; in addition it means that files are not held centrally and this complicates file management. *Novell Personal Netware* and *LANtastic 6.0* are popular examples of peer-to-peer networking products. The peer-to-peer approach is highly suitable for very small networks, but both the products mentioned allow the system to be developed to introduce some file server control. Facilities are also included to allow users to share resources in groups; the name of another peer-to-peer networking product illustrates this feature: *Windows for Workgroups*; up to 10 users can be networked.

Support and Maintenance Services

A major purpose of computer networks is to provide a range of support and maintenance services to enable users to make effective use of computer resources. The operation of computer networks, both small and large, requires a range of specialist support and maintenance services. Conversely, an organisation which computerises its work through the use of numerous, stand-alone microcomputer systems, may have to rely on the expertise of the users themselves, to manage their own systems. A LAN requires investment in specialist hardware, a network operating system and the employment of one or more persons to *manage*, *maintain* and *develop* (as user requirements change) the network. The provision of computer facilities through a shared resource, such as a LAN, means that all the users have access to the support services it provides. If an organisation has a LAN at each of its branches and links them together through a packet switching network, such as British Telecom's Switchstream, then it can use the support services of BT when, for example, deciding on the purchase of necessary communications equipment, the selection of other data transmission services or on ways of securing the transmission of particularly sensitive data.

The following list provides some typical examples of support and maintenance services:

- user training, both in the use of the network and applications available through it;
- installation of new applications required by users;
- development of different user menus to give appropriate access to network facilities; thus, some users may only require access to a particular word processor, whilst others may need to use a variety of applications and data files;
- provision of printing services appropriate to user applications; this can be done by assigning user output (identified by a user code) to a printer of a particular type; this can be done through the network management software, so that all users have potential access to all printer attached to the network.

Efficiency, Reliability and Fault Control

An efficient and reliable network should:

- be accessible (for all services, including shared storage, processing, printing and communication) when users need it;
- not lose or corrupt data that users wish to keep;
- be able to recover full operation following, for example, hardware fault or power failure;
- be used by properly trained users who follow 'in-house' standards for network use and know how to optimise use of its resources, in the performance of their work;
- be regularly maintained and modified to ensure it continues to fulfil the purposes of the organisation.

Achieving Efficiency and Reliability

In aiming for such efficiency and reliability, an organisation may use the following guidelines and suggestions for network administration, staff training and the use of fault control systems.

- Use hardware and software which conforms to a Standard; this should ensure that equipment from different sources is compatible and works properly with other network components;
- Obtain a service and support contract with the supplier of the network, or some other organisation which specialises in the system in use; the 'call out' response times, to attend to faults or repairs, should meet the needs of the network owner.
- Ensure that fully trained staff are employed to install, configure, monitor, and develop the network;
- Make use of devices to protect against, for example, power failure; an Uninterruptible Power Supply or *UPS* device automatically provides several

minutes of power, in the even of a power cut, to allow work to be saved and the network to be shut down safely.

- Train users to use the system properly and not to, for example, attempt to reconfigure a workstation's network software;
- Employ security to prevent unauthorised access, and entry of viruses to the file server. Virus protection software can help, but users should not be able to bring disks or software from machines at home or other locations; diskless workstations can be used to prevent such abuse of the network.
- Ensure regular *backup* of the file server, using, for example, tape streamer devices.
- Use a technique, such as *disk mirroring*, whereby two file server disks operate in tandem. Each block of data written to the main disk is also written to the mirror disk; if one fails, the other continues supporting the network without interrupt.

Connectivity

Numerous devices are available to connect different types of system to one another; examples include:

- network cards for Macintosh machines to connect to Ethernet or Token Ring networks, which are primarily designed for PCs based on the MS-DOS operating system;
- terminal emulator cards and gateway software, for the attachment of, for example, a Novell LAN, to an IBM 3270 mainframe within an SNA (Systems Network Architecture) network;

Access to network services

To ensure that network users have the access they need to printing, file storage, communications and applications, the following example network requirements may be given consideration.

- The network needs to be constructed with components of the necessary power and capacity; the speed of the servers and workstations is crucial to the speed of the network. The speed requirement concerns the response times users experience in accessing the different services. Retrieval of applications and data files from the server should be such that each user feels as if he or she is the sole user of the equipment.
- The type of network and transmission medium is also an important determinant of network performance. For example, a Token Ring network generally performs more quickly than an Ethernet bus network. Similarly, data transmissions over packet switching networks are higher than those possible over voice grade telephone lines.
- Printing services need to include the quality that is required for particular applications. For example, an internal memorandum can probably be printed by an ink jet printer, but this will be inadequate for a graphical image to be printed in a magazine. Not all work will need to be printed immediately, but

facilities should exist for urgent work to be given the necessary priority on a shared printer.

- If large volumes of data need to be transferred from a remote database, then the communications software and equipment must allow transfers to be carried out as quickly as possible; rental time on a packet switching network can be very expensive.

Support of mixed traffic

"Mixed traffic" is a collective phrase to describe the different kinds of information which may be transmitted over computer networks and telecommunications links. These different kinds of information include, audio and video images, as well as computer data (text, numbers and other characters). If an organisation wishes to have a mixed traffic system, it will require a *broadband* (see Broadband) network.

Management Activities

A computer network requires significant capital expenditure and an organisation needs to ensure that it is used for the defined purposes. This requires a range of monitoring systems, which are outlined below.

Monitoring Activity Levels

The word 'activity' is used to refer to various aspects of network use and operation, for example, traffic volumes and patterns. There may be particular times when the volume of data moving around the network significantly reduces its performance; this may indicate a need to re-organise the work patterns of users or to modify the network structure (perhaps by dividing it into smaller segments according to user function, for example Sales and Accounts - see Bridge).

System Reporting

A network operating system will normally include various software *utilities* to allow the system administrator or supervisor to monitor and receive reports on various network conditions. For example, the system may report when a workstation has become inoperable or a fault has been detected on the server, or that certain system files have become corrupted and need repair. System reporting can help to ensure network reliability in that the supervisor is notified of such conditions.

Storage Control

An important aspect of network management is the control of file storage space on the network. In a client-server (see Client Server Network), applications and data files are held on the file server and its space needs to be managed efficiently to ensure that required files remain accessible and that redundant files are removed (*purged*) and, if necessary, *archived* (copies held on another disk or tape medium, in case they are needed). If redundant files are not removed, space is wasted and the task of retrieving other files becomes more difficult (searching through redundant files for those required). The topic of directory and file management is dealt with in more detail in Chapters 2 and 26.

System Configuration

Any network has a particular *configuration*; that is to say, particular types of components are used, they are connected and communicate in a particular way, and particular facilities are provided. The configuration of a network affects the way it works, not only electronically in terms of its hardware and software components, but also in its relationship with users. Thus, the network can be configured concerning:

- *user passwords*. A user may be required to enter a *password* before he or she is logged onto the network and given access to its resources;
- *user access rights*. The supervisor can assign rights to users in respect of particular directories or files on the file server. Such rights determine what a user can do with those resources. For example, in their own user directories, users may be able to create, copy, delete and rename data files; this would be essential if users were able to store work produced with various applications packages. In contrast, users rights within the directory containing applications software (*executable* files), would be very restricted and only sufficient to allow them to run the programs. Some groups of users may have no rights to particular applications programs. For example, a sales clerk would be unlikely to have rights to run the personnel management software.
- *job queues*. The shared servers (print and communications servers, for example) can be assigned work from particular users or groups of users, through a system of queues. Thus, a print server manages print queues, which are jobs from users awaiting printing on a shared printer. The configuration determines the printing devices to which jobs are assigned and their priority, if any, in a queue. Access to, for example, a laser printer, may be restricted to a small group of users.

The topics of passwords, rights and queues are examined in more detail in Chapter 26 and other security matters are dealt with in Chapters 14 and 15.

Chapter 9

Information Flow in Organisations

Introduction

This Chapter examines the *structure* of organisations, their *functional areas* and the *information flows*, which they need to operate. For example, a building materials supplier needs to maintain proper records of its stocks of goods, its customers and the goods they order, if it is to operate efficiently and profitably. Current stock levels and supplier delivery times need to be communicated to sales staff, so that they can ensure fulfilment of customer orders, or if stocks are insufficient, give accurate information on likely delivery dates. Details of sales need to be communicated to staff in the Accounts department, so that they can update the customers' accounts. The primary aim of some organisations is to provide a service, rather than to make a profit. For example, a local government Social Services Department, which is an example of a *public service* organisation, must maintain up-to-date records of children 'at risk' from abuse or neglect. Information on such children may be gathered from various sources, such as school teachers, health visitors and police, and it needs to be stored in such a way that all the information relevant to a particular child is passed to the relevant social worker. With proper information, social work staff should be more effective in protecting those children for whom they have responsibility. Systems designed to produce information may be variously described as: 'data handling systems'; 'data processing systems'; and 'information processing systems', but they all require that data is captured, input, processed, output and distributed to those who need it. The flow of information is the 'lifeblood' of an organisation and if it stops flowing, the organisation cannot operate and will collapse. For example, if the Sales staff do not pass on details of sales to the Accounts Department, it cannot invoice its customers for the money they owe. Similarly, if a Social Services Department receives information that a particular young child is being left alone at night and does not pass this on to the relevant social worker, he or she will not be prompted to question the parents on the matter. Today, most organisations make use of information technology to support the production and flow of information.

A Classification of Organisations

Initially, it is convenient to categorise organisations as follows:

- *public service*;
- *commercial and industrial*.

Public Service Organisations

Many public services are provided by central and local government (the public sector) Central government takes responsibility for a wide range of services and has specific organisations, referred to as Departments, to manage each. Thus, there are separate departments, each responsible for the provision of, amongst others, health, education, defence and social welfare services. The role of local government is continually changing as successive governments pursue policies which tend to centralise power, or devolve it to locally elected council bodies. The provision of water, electricity and gas services used to be provided by 'public utilities', but they have been 'privatised' and now operate as commercial and industrial businesses. Some services, traditionally provided by the public sector, are now partly in the private sector; for example, some prisons are privately owned and the work of refuse collection may be carried out by private companies. Even so, overall control of such services is still the responsibility of central and local government departments.

Table 9.1 lists some major central government organisations and briefly describes the responsibilities of each. Table 9.2 does the same, in respect of local government.

Central Government	Responsibilities
Education	Schools
Transport	Road and building
Home Office	Law and order, including police and prison services policy
Health	Hospitals,
Trade and Industry	Business and industrial policy
Social Security	Benefits such as income support, unemployment benefit.
Treasury	Economic policy
Defence	Armed Forces

Table 9.1. *Central Government Departments and Responsibilities*

It should be noted that although the government departments retain overall responsibility for the areas listed in Table 9.1, some of the work is carried out by private companies. For example, some hospitals, prisons and schools are privately owned. As part of the government's 'privatisation' programme, local councils have to allow private businesses to tender for (compete for) work traditionally carried out by their own departments; this is called Compulsory Competitive Tendering (CCT).

Local Government	Responsibilities
Social Services	Home helps, children's homes, meals on wheels, day nurseries, residential homes and day centres for the mentally ill.
Education	Nursery, and secondary schools.
Housing	Council housing provides affordable accommodation for those who cannot buy their own homes.
Environmental Services	Refuse collection and disposal, street sweeping and pollution control.
Police and Fire Services	Although there is co-operation between forces, these services are still locally controlled.
Planning and Building Control	Consider applications for local building and enforce regulations on building standards.

Table 9.2. *Local Government Departments and Responsibilities*

For example, private businesses can tender for contracts to carry out street sweeping or refuse collection. In addition, some schools have 'opted out' and receive their funding directly from central governments.

Industry and Commerce

The term 'industry' covers a wide range of organisations which form part of a country's economy. We tend to link factories with the idea of industry, but the term also covers:

- extraction industries, such as coal-mining and fishing;
- manufacturing businesses which take raw materials and process them into finished products, such as cars and clothing, as well as those assembling ready-made components into, for example, computers and televisions.
- retail and wholesale businesses, concerned with buying, selling and distributing goods for personal and business consumption.
- service industries, such as hotel, catering, travel and banking.

The word 'commerce' overlaps with 'industry' and includes all forms of trading organisation and those which support trade, such as banking and insurance.

Organisational Structures

A structure can be defined as having component parts, which are connected in a particular way. Structures are designed to fulfil purposes. For example, a house is a structure, consisting of rooms, windows, floors, ceilings, doors and connection passages; the mix of these component parts and the way they are put together determines the design of the house. Two main types of organisational structure are considered here:

- hierarchical;
- flat;

Hierarchical Structure

An organisation with a hierarchical structure includes different levels of authority and responsibility. Heads of Department may be directly responsible to one of the Directors. For example, the Accounts Department Head may be subject to the authority of the Financial Director. Such authority relates to the operation of the organisation and enables tasks to be completed. There may be Section Supervisors who are responsible to their respective Heads of Department for particular functions within departments. Each section supervisor may have authority over a number of clerks. Generally, there are more 'indians' than 'chiefs', so a hierarchical structure can be viewed as a pyramid, as shown in Figure 9.1; the lower down the pyramid you descend, the larger the number of staff you are likely to find employed. The jobs at the top of the pyramid carry the most authority and the greatest responsibility for the success or failure of the organisation. Operatives and clerical staff are unlikely to have any authority in the organisation, but they have responsibility for the completion of their own jobs.

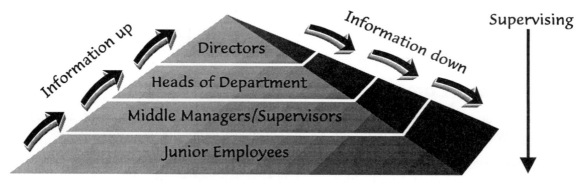

Figure 9.1. *Hierarchy of authority and responsibility and information flow*

Downward Communication

Figure 9.1, shows that, within the pyramid, communications go up and down. Policy decisions taken at board level by the directors are implemented by instructing the relevant departmental heads to see that the policy is carried out. They will then brief middle managers for whom they are responsible, and the final stage in the process is the communication between middle managers and junior staff.

Upward Communications

The communication also passes from the bottom upwards. Staff provide feedback to their seniors. This may take many forms; it may involve monitoring shortages of materials, absences of staff, production problems, grievances and suggestions for improving work methods. Anything which requires the authority or approval of someone further up the organisational hierarchy and which has been generated or identified below, will pass back up the system. Only in extreme circumstances is it likely that an issue arising at the bottom of the pyramid will pass right back to the top for consideration and decision. For the most part, an immediate senior is likely to have sufficient authority to make a decision; ultimately however, it is a question of the extent of *delegated* responsibility held by senior employees that determines whether they can deal with it personally, or must pass it back to their own superiors.

As organisations grow bigger it is inevitable that communications have much further to travel. This is not ideal since it is likely to take longer to transmit information and there is greater distancing between the giver and the receiver, which can lead to a 'them and us' view of the organisation by junior staff. However, it is clear that as the organisation grows, so its communication system must be become increasingly refined. Information technology support is crucial to the efficiency of communications and the support it can provide is examined in the final part of this Chapter.

Line and Functional Authority

Line authority is the direct relationship between a superior and his or her subordinates. It is shown in an organisation chart by a vertical line, indicating direct authority. Functional authority indicates the responsibility for specialist functional areas, such as personnel, purchasing and production. Organisation charts are an attempt to record formal structure, showing some of the relationships, the downward flow of authority and responsibility and the main lines of communication.

Flat Structure

In contrast to a hierarchy, a flat structure generally has a single level of management, as shown in Figure 9.2. Except for the smallest organisations, very few will have an entirely flat structure. It is possible, that an organisation wishes to avoid a cumbersome hierarchy and attempts to keep the number of management levels to a minimum; they are thus aiming for a 'flatter' structure. As mentioned earlier, hierarchies with many levels of authority can make communication difficult. A flatter structure can encourage 'team spirit' through the avoidance of the 'them and us' feelings, which can be characteristic of hierarchies. Figure 9.2 represents a firm of solicitors, where each partner has the same level of authority and responsibility, specialises in a particular aspect of the law and has joint authority over the Office Manager and articled clerks ('apprentice' solicitors). The Office Manager is responsible for supervision of the clerical staff. Although there are hierarchical elements in the organisation, its structure is fairly 'flat'.

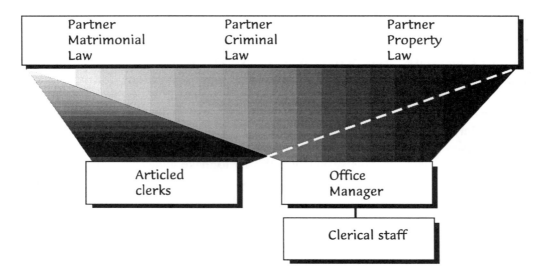

Figure 9.2. *'Flatter' structure in a firm of solicitors*

Functional Areas

This section investigates some of the main functional areas to be found in organisations, namely: cost and management accounting; financial accounting (sales; purchasing and general ledger); invoicing; stock control; marketing; payroll; personnel; design; production; services.

Accounting

Cost and Management Accounting

The financial accounting function is largely concerned with past events. The cost and management accounting function aims to provide management with information to support their decisions on the planning of future business activity. The information should enable management to:

- establish and monitor the financial targets of the business. One target may be to increase sales of a particular product by 10 per cent over the next six months. A parallel target could be to cut, by 5 per cent, its unit production cost. Targets are usually fairly specific so that their achievement, or otherwise, can be determined;
- control income and expenditure within the business. Financial accounting is concerned with the whole of the business whereas cost accounting identifies cost centres (for different parts of the business). Analysing costs and revenues in this way allows a business to allocate financial budgets for various areas of the business and determine the contribution of each area to the profitability of the business.

Financial Accounting

Financial accounting or 'book-keeping' is the process of recording financial transactions arising from the day-to-day operation of a business. The sale of goods to a customer and the subsequent settlement of the debt are two examples of financial transactions. Apart from their function as a control mechanism over the financial transactions of a business, accounting records can be analysed to provide information on the performance of a business over a period. Typically, such information is extracted annually or every six months, in the form of a *balance sheet* and *trading and profit and loss account*. These financial statements are also required by *external agencies*, such as the Inland Revenue (for tax assessment) and the bank, if loan facilities are required.

Financial accounts need to record:

- *debtor* transactions; debtors are people or organisations who owe money to the business for goods or services provided (credit sales);
- *creditor* transactions; creditors are people or organisations to whom the business owes money, for the supply of goods (credit purchases).

These transactions are recorded in the *sales ledger* and the *purchases ledger* respectively. A third ledger, the *nominal* (or *general*) ledger is used to record the overall income and expenditure of the business, with each transaction classified according to its purpose.

Sales Accounting

When credit sales are made to customers, a record needs to be kept of amounts owing and paid. Payment is normally requested with an invoice, which gives details of goods supplied, quantities, prices and VAT. Credit sales are usually made on for example, a 14, 21 or 28 day basis, which means that the customer has to pay within the specified period to obtain any discounts offered. Overdue payments need to be chased, so sales accounting systems normally produce reports analysing the indebtedness of different customers. Debt control is vital to business profitability and computerised systems can produce prompt and up-to-date reports as a by-product of the main application.

Purchase Accounting

This function is concerned with controlling amounts owed and payments made to suppliers of services, goods or materials, which are used in the main business of the company. For example, a car manufacturer will need to keep records of amounts owing to suppliers of car components and sheet steel manufacturers. Delayed payments to suppliers may help cash flow, but can harm an organisation's image, or even cut off a source of supply when a supplier refuses to deliver any more goods until payment is made.

General Ledger

The general ledger keeps control of financial summaries, including those originating from payroll, sales and purchase accounting and acts as a balance in a double entry system. Computerised systems can automatically produce reports at the end of financial periods, including a trial balance, trading and profit and loss account and balance sheet.

Other Finance-related Functions

Stock Control

Any organisation which keeps stocks of raw materials or finished goods needs to operate a stock control system. Although stock constitutes an asset, it ties up cash resources that could be invested in other aspects of the business. Equally, a company must keep sufficient quantities of items to satisfy customer demand or manufacturing requirements. To maintain this balance a stock control system should provide up-to-date information on quantities, prices, minimum stock levels, and re-order quantities. It should also give warning of excessively high, or dangerously low levels of stock. In the latter case, orders may be produced automatically. A stock control system may also generate valuable management reports on, for example, sales patterns, slow-moving items, and overdue orders.

Sales order processing

This function will normally be concerned with:

- the validation of orders, checking, for example, that the goods ordered are supplied by the business or that the customer's credit status warrants the order's completion;
- the identification of individual items ordered. A customer may request several different items on the same order form and any particular item will probably appear on many different order forms, so the quantities for each are totalled to produce picking lists to enable warehouse staff to retrieve the goods for despatch;
- the monitoring of back orders. If an order cannot be fulfilled, it may be held in abeyance until new stocks arrive, so all outstanding back orders need to be available on request.

Invoicing

This function deals with the production of customer invoices, requesting payment for goods or services delivered. Information stored in the customer files and stock files is used to produce invoices, usually on pre-printed continuous stationery.

Payroll

Payroll systems are concerned with the production of payslips for employees and the maintenance of records required for taxation and other deductions. In a manual system, the preparation of payroll figures and the maintenance of payroll records is a labour intensive task. Although tedious and repetitive, it is a vitally important task. Most employees naturally regard pay as being the main reason for work and resent delays in payment or incorrect payments, unless of course it is in their favour! The repetitive nature of the task makes it a popular candidate for computerisation, especially with organisations which employ large numbers of people. The automatic production of reports for taxation purposes also provides a valuable benefit. Smaller organisations with only several employees probably do not regard payroll as a high priority application for computerisation. The benefits are not as great if the payroll can be carried out by one or two employees who also carry out a number of other tasks.

Personnel

The personnel function is responsible for the selection (usually by interview), recruitment, training and development of staff. Personnel records will store all the information needed by Salaries and Wages to make the correct payments to employees; this will include details of, for example, gross salary, tax code, statutory sick pay and holiday entitlement. Depending on the size of the organisation, information may also be held concerning: qualifications, courses attended; personal and career development plans.

Design

The design function is present where an organisation develops its own products and services; a trader, who simply buys and sells goods has no need of a design team. Design is part of the research and development (R & D) function, which is vital to organisations wishing to radically develop their product range. The nature of design teams depends on the product or service being designed. The skills and talents of a car design team are clearly very different from those of a team designing a cover for a magazine.

Production

The production function should, ideally, be driven by the market for the business's products. In other words, it should be geared to produce the necessary mix and quantities of products required by customers. If goods are perishable within a short time, and large reserve stocks cannot be held, then production should be flexible and responsive to the day-to-day sales requirements. Of course, this is an ideal and production plans cannot always be changed at short notice; ships and other large items take months or years to build. The production department must know exactly what is required and when; it must also have the staff with the necessary skills and any machinery must have the appropriate facilities and production capacity. For example, a production department which is geared to produce 1000 units of a product per day, will probably find it difficult to produce 2000 units, without modification of the system of production.

Marketing

A marketing function is a vital part of many large national and international businesses; it aims to generate information, from a wide range of data sources, to support marketing decisions. Three such decision areas are:

- *strategic* and relating to, for example, expansion of the company's existing market share the identification of new marketable products;
- *tactical*, for example, planning the marketing mix;
- *operational*, for example, day-to-day planning of sales calls and ad hoc promotions.

At the operational level, for example, data gathered from sales invoices, sales force staff and accounting information can be used to establish customer types. Thus, customers can be classified as 'low', 'medium' or 'high' volume users according to the frequency and volume of their orders. This information can help sales staff to target particular categories of customer and to plan the timing of sales calls.

At the tactical level, a invoices provide information on sales variance between different market segments over time or sales projections based on current patterns.

Information Needs

To operate, different functions within an organisation need access to particular types of information, some examples of which are briefly described below.

- *Design specifications*; before a product is manufactured a specification is produced detailing, for example, the types, qualities and quantities of required materials, physical features, performance requirements (such as for a car) and so on. Some products, such as computer software, need to include design features concerning, for example, the user interface.
- *Construction drawings*. As the term indicates, these are used to guide the person or persons building or constructing the product. An architect produces construction drawings for the house builder to follow; design specification details are also included, so that the builder knows the types and quantities of materials.
- *Market research*. This information is often gathered through surveys, either using questionnaires or monitoring consumer buying patterns. A company should carry out market research before beginning the production or sale of a new product in its range.
- *Advertising* is essential to any organisation wishing to promote its image or product range. Advertising uses market research information to target the most appropriate areas of the population. For example, market research may

indicate that a product is most likely to be bought by professional people living in the south of England; advertising can be directed, perhaps through mails shots, to that section of the population.

- *Sales orders* detail customer order requirements, including item details, quantities and delivery dates; *purchase orders* detail the organisation's purchase requirements from suppliers.
- *Payments and receipts*. These may relate to sales orders or purchase orders. Receipts are amounts received from debtors. Payments are made by a business to settle debts with creditors (suppliers to the business).
- *Transport requirements*. This information will detail, for example, a goods list, the delivery address, special requirements, such as refrigeration and possibly the route to be taken.

Information Flow Diagrams

Figure 9.3 illustrates some information flows within a typical manufacturing and wholesaling organisation.

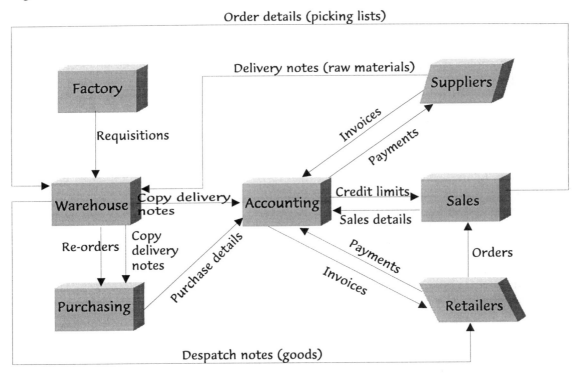

Figure 9.3. *Information flow diagram for a manufacturing and wholesale business*

An examination of Figure 9.3 shows that each functional area is dependent on one or more other areas for the information it needs to operate. For example, to charge the retail outlets (their customers) for the goods supplied, the Accounting function requires the necessary sales information, which is supplied by the Sales function. The information allows the Accounting function to prepare the necessary invoices to send to customers. Similarly, Purchasing must be kept informed by the Warehouse (stock control) of raw materials which need re-ordering from suppliers, to replenish stocks.

These examples of *operational* information allow day-to-day decisions to be made on the operation of the business. To keep the diagram in Figure 9.3 fairly simple, certain vital functions, such as Production Control and Marketing, are not shown. Obviously, their inclusion would increase the number of information flows and the complexity of the diagram.

The information flows shown in Figure 9.3 are all 'triggered' by *events*. For example:

- a customer order is generated when a customer orders goods;
- credit limit details flow from Accounting to Sales, when a customer order is checked;
- an invoice is raised when goods are despatched to a customer;
- a payment to a supplier is triggered when the invoice payment falls due.

IT Support of Information Flows

To illustrate the role of IT in managing information flow, we use a simple example of a small electrical company, Wingrove Electrical Ltd, based on the outskirts of London. It employs 38 people and produces electrical components for use in central heating equipment. The following examples of activities and information flows are used to show the potential benefits of using IT.

An Enquiry from a Potential Buyer

A telephone enquiry from a potential customer is received by the company's telephonist, who attempts to connect the caller with the company sales manager, who is out of the office. She makes a note of the caller's name and the nature of the enquiry and promises to pass these details on to the sales manager when she returns to the office. Unfortunately, the paper with the message is lost and so is the potential order.

Clearly, the system could have been improved by a number of methods.

- If Wingrove had a local area network, the telephonist could have obtained sufficient product information to meet the initial enquiry of the potential buyer;
- The message could have been transmitted through the electronic mail system, for the sales manager to access when she returned.
- If the sales manager used a notebook computer, she could download such messages remotely, though the telecommunications network. In any event, it is extremely likely that she would be carrying a mobile telephone or pager and could have been contacted.

Receipt of an Order

Wingrove receives a substantial order by post. The manual procedures involve copying the order, sending a copy to Accounting and a copy attached to a 'job sheet' to Production. When the order is completed and despatched, Accounting will invoice the customer and await payment. Unfortunately, when the customer eventually pays, he submits a cheque for an incorrect amount, but the clerk fails to notice that the amount on the invoice and the amount on the cheque do not agree; as a result, he processes the invoice as paid. Wingrove has thus lost some of its profit.

- The company could improve its financial control by installing a computerised order processing and invoice verification system.
- As each order is received into the company, the appropriate details, such as customer, item, quantity, price and so on, are entered into its computer, which automatically generates an invoice, statements and increasingly harshly worded reminders, until the customer settles the debt.
- When the cheque arrives, its value is also entered and the program automatically checks to ensure that the amount matches both the original price quoted and the invoice value.
- As protection against the miskeying of the cheque amount, a further check involves the automatic reconciliation, each month, of totals for paid and unpaid invoices.

Production of a Quotation

Wingrove's managing director is informed that Birmingham City Council is intending to replace the central heating systems in all its public buildings, over the next three years and is seeking tenders for the component parts of the system. Wingrove would very much like to gain the contract and decide to submit a detailed quotation document.

The quotation is 28 pages long and contains an extensive amount of technical detail, as well as product specifications, prices and delivery details. Typed manually, reference would have to be made to numerous files for component specifications and prices and the inevitable modifications to the tender would involve extensive re-typing.

- Using a word processor and quotation template, the task can be completed much more quickly.
- Layout alterations and editing can easily be accomplished before a final copy is printed.
- A high quality printer, possibly with colour facility will contribute to a highly professional appearance and improve the image of the company.
- Component specification and price data can be imported from the company's database of such information, directly into the document.
- If speed is important, the document can be sent by fax or e-mail to Birmingham City Council.

Forms of Information

The information flows shown in Figure 9.3 may be transmitted verbally, on paper (documents) or electronically.

Chapter 10

Data Handling Systems

The Data Processing Cycle

Computer-based data handling systems employed at the *operational* level of an organisation, for example, in the areas of payroll calculation or sales order processing, frequently involve a repeated cycle of events, which can be identified as follows:

- data collection and input;
- processing of the data, including reference to and the updating of relevant files;
- reporting of output.

Data Collection

Depending on the application, this stage in the cycle may include one or more of the following procedures.

Source Document Preparation

To ensure standardisation of practice and to facilitate checking, data collected for input, for example, customer orders, are transcribed onto source documents specially designed for the purpose.

Data Transmission

If the computer centre is geographically remote from the data collection point, the source documents may be physically transported there, or be keyed and transmitted through a terminal and *telecommunications network* to the computer.

Data Encoding and Verification

This involves the transcription, usually through a keyboard device, of the data onto a storage medium such as magnetic tape or disk; a process of machine verification, accompanied by a repeated keying operation assists the checking of keying accuracy. *Key-to disk* and *key-to-tape* systems are used for encoding, commonly making use of diskette and cassette tape storage, from which media the data is then merged onto a large reel of magnetic tape or onto magnetic disk for rapid subsequent input.

Data Input and Validation

Data validation is a computer-controlled process that checks the data for its validity according to certain pre-defined standards. For example, an account number may have to comprise 6 digits and be within the range 500000 to 900000.

Sorting

To improve the efficiency of processing sequentially organised files, input data is sorted into a sequence determined by the *primary key* of each record in the relevant master file.

Processing, Storage and Retrieval

This stage is entirely computer controlled and involves the processing of *input* data according to the requirements of the program currently in use. Thus, for example, in payroll processing, data on hours worked for each employee may be input and processed against information regarding rates of pay and tax codes held on the payroll *master file*, to produce the necessary payslips. In addition, the payroll information regarding, for example, pay to date and tax paid to date is updated on the master file.

Reporting of Output

The destination of the results of processing also depends on the application and the requirements of the users. Output may be in the form of thousands of printed payslips or invoices or it may be simply a screen display of information in response to a user enquiry.

Processing Methods

Data handling systems make use of one or more processing methods, depending on the requirements of the application. The methods can be categorised according to the ways in which data is controlled, stored and passed through the system; the major categories are:

- batch processing;
- on-line processing, which includes real-time and time-share processing;
- distributed processing and centralised processing

To allow particular methods of processing a computer must have the necessary *operating system* software (Chapter 2); thus any particular computer system is equipped with, for example, a batch processing or real-time operating system, or even a combination of types, depending on the needs of the user organisation.

Batch Processing Systems

Such systems process *batches* of data at regular intervals. The data is usually in large volumes and of identical type. Examples of such data are customer orders, current weekly payroll details and stock issues or receipts. Although associated with large organisations using mainframe or minicomputer systems, the technique can be used by a small business using a microcomputer.

The procedure can be illustrated with the example of payroll, which is a typical application for batch processing. Each pay date, whether it is every week or every month, the payroll details, such as hours worked, overtime earned or sickness days claimed, are gathered for each employee (these details are referred to as *transactions*) and processed in batches against the payroll *master file*. The computer then produces payslips for all employees in the company. A major feature of this and similar applications is that a large percentage of the payroll records in the master file are processed during the payroll 'run'. This percentage is known as the *hit rate*. Generally, high hit rate processing is suitable for batch processing and if, as is usual, the master file is organised sequentially, then the *transaction file* will be sorted into the same sequence as the master file. In the case of magnetic tape, transactions must be sorted because the medium only allows *serial* (one record after another in their physical order) access.

Batch processing method closely resembles manual methods of data handling, in that transactions are collected together into batches, sent to the computer centre, sorted into the order of the master file and processed. Such systems are known as 'traditional' data processing systems. There is normally an intermediate stage in the process when the data must be encoded using a *key-to-tape* or *key-to-disk* system.

A disadvantage of batch processing is the delay, often of hours or days, between collecting the transactions and receiving the results of processing and this has to be remembered when an organisation is considering whether batch processing is suitable for a particular application. Conversely, batch processing has the advantage of providing many opportunities for controlling the accuracy of data (Chapter 14) and thus is commonly used when the immediate updating of files is not crucial.

On-line Processing Systems

If a peripheral, such as a Visual Display Unit or keyboard, is *on-line*, it is under the control of the computer's processor or Central Processing Unit (CPU). On-line processing systems therefore, are those where all peripherals in use are connected to the CPU of the main computer. Transactions can be keyed in directly. The main advantage of an on-line system is the reduction in time between the collection and processing of data.

There are two main methods of on-line processing:

- real-time processing;
- time-share processing.

Real-time processing

Process Control in Real-time

Real-time processing originally referred only to process control systems where, for example, the temperature of a gas furnace is monitored and controlled by a computer. The computer, through an appropriate sensing device, responds immediately to the boiler's variations outside pre-set temperature limits, by switching the boiler on and off to keep the temperature within those limits.

Real-time processing is now used in everyday consumer goods, such as video cameras, because of the development of the 'computer on a chip', more properly called the *microprocessor*. The important feature common to all real-time applications is that the speed of the computer allows almost immediate response to external changes.

Information Processing in Real-time

To be acceptable as a real-time information processing system, the *response-time* (that is the time between the entry of a transaction or enquiry at a VDU terminal, the processing of the data and the computer's response) must meet the needs of the user. The delay or response time may vary from a fraction of a second to 2-3 seconds depending on the nature of the transaction and the size of the computer. Any delay beyond these times would generally be unacceptable and would indicate the need for the system to be updated.

There are two types of information processing systems which can be operated in real-time. These are: transaction processing; information storage and retrieval.

Transaction Processing

This type of system handles clearly defined transactions one at a time, each transaction being processed completely, including the updating of files, before the next transaction is dealt with. The amount of data input for each transaction is small and is usually entered on an *interactive* basis through a VDU. In this way, the user can enter queries through the keyboard and receive a response, or the computer can display a prompt on the screen to which the user responds. Such 'conversations' are usually heavily structured and in a fixed format and so do not allow users to ask any question they wish.

A typical example of transaction processing is provided by an *airline booking system* (see Booking Systems, later).

Information Storage and Retrieval

This type of system differs from transaction processing in that, although the information is updated in real-time, the number of updates and the number of sources of updating is relatively small.

Consider, for example, the medical records system in a hospital. A record is maintained for each patient currently undergoing treatment in the hospital. Medical staff require the patient's medical history to be available at any time and the system must also have a facility for entering new information as the patient undergoes treatment in hospital. Sources of information are likely to include a doctor, nurses and perhaps a surgeon, and new entries probably do not number more than one or two per day.

This is an entirely different situation from an airline booking system where the number of entries for one flight record may be 200-300 and they could be made from many different booking offices throughout the world. A further example of a library system is provided later (see Library Systems)

Time-share Processing

The term *time sharing* refers to the activity of the computer's processor in allocating *time-slices* to a number of users who are given access through terminals to centralised computer resources. The aim of the system is to give each user a good *response time*. These systems are commonly used where a number of users require computer time for different information processing tasks. The processor time-slices are allocated and controlled by a time-share operating system. The CPU is able to operate at such speed that, provided the system is not overloaded by too many users, each user has the impression that he or she is the sole user of the system.

A particular computer system will be designed to support a maximum number of user terminals. If the number is exceeded or the applications being run on the system are 'heavy' on CPU time the response time will become lengthy and unacceptable. Time-share systems are possible because of the extreme speed of the CPU in comparison with peripheral devices such as keyboards, VDU screens and printers. Most information processing tasks consist largely of input and output operations which do not occupy the CPU, leaving it free to do any processing required on other users' tasks.

Distributed Processing

As the term suggests, a distributed processing system is one which spreads the processing tasks of an organisation across several computer systems; frequently, these systems are connected and *share resources* (this may relate to common access to files or programs, or even the processing of a single complex task) through a data communications system (Chapter 7). Each computer system in the network must be able to process independently, so a central computer with a number of remote intelligent terminals cannot be classified as distributed, even though some limited validation of data may be carried out separately from the main computer. Examples of distributed systems include mini or mainframe computers interconnected by way of *wide area networks*, or a number of *local area networks* similarly linked.

Distributed systems provide a number of benefits:

- *Economy*. The transmission of data over telecommunications systems can be costly and local database storage and processing facilities can reduce costs. The radical reduction in computer hardware costs has favoured the expansion of distributed systems against centralised systems;

- *Minicomputers and microcomputers*. The availability of minicomputer and microcomputer systems with data transmission facilities has made distributed processing economically viable. An increasingly popular option, in large multi-sited organisations, is to set up local area networks of microcomputers at each site and connect them through communications networks to each other and/or to a central mainframe computer at the Head Office. This provides each site with the advantages of local processing power, local and inter-site communications through *electronic mail* (Chapter 7) and access to a central mainframe for the main filing and database systems;
- *Local management control*. It is not always convenient, particularly where an organisation controls diverse activities, to have all information processing centralised. Local management control means that the information systems will be developed by people with direct knowledge of their own information needs. Responsibility for the success or otherwise of their division of the organisation may be placed with local management, so it is desirable that they have control over the accuracy and reliability of the data they use.

Centralised Systems

With this type of system, all processing is carried out centrally, generally by a mainframe computer. The continuing reduction in hardware costs and the increase in computer power has led the move towards distributed processing systems. This is achieved through computer networks.

Financial Accounting Systems

The following section describes the various financial accounting systems of a typical business and the packaged software available to support them. Financial systems support the main accounting functions of a business.

The Ledgers

Business accounts are needed to record:

- *debtor* transactions; debtors are people or organisations who owe money to the business for goods or services provided (credit sales);
- *creditor* transactions; creditors are people or organisations to whom the business owes money, for the supply of goods (credit purchases).

These transactions are recorded in the *sales ledger* and the *purchases ledger* respectively. A third ledger, the Nominal (or General) Ledger is used to record the overall income and expenditure of the business, with each transaction classified according to its purpose.

Sales Ledger

General Description

The purpose of the sales ledger is to keep a record of amounts owed to a business by its trading customers or clients. It contains a record for each customer with a credit arrangement. Most businesses permit their customers to buy goods on credit. The goods are usually supplied on the understanding that, once payment has been requested, the debt will be paid for within a specified period of, for example, 14 or 30 days. Payment is requested with the use of an *invoice* addressed to the customer and containing details of goods supplied, the amount owing and credit days given. Once a customer order has been accepted and processed, the total amount due for the order is recorded in the relevant customer's account in the sales ledger and the balance owing is increased accordingly. When a payment is received from the customer, the amount is entered to the customer's account and the balance owing is decreased by the appropriate amount.

There are two main approaches to sales ledger maintenance, *balance forward* and *open item*.

- Balance forward. This method provides: an opening balance (the amount owing at the beginning of the month); the transactions for that month, giving the date, type (for example, goods sold or payment received); the amount of each transaction; a closing balance. The closing balance at the end of the month is carried forward as the opening balance for the next month. A *statement of account*, detailing all the transactions for the month will normally be sent to the customer and a copy filed away for business records. The customer's account in the sales ledger will not then contain details of the previous month's transactions so any query will require reference to the filed statements of account.
- Open item. The open item method is more complicated in that each invoice is identified by a code and requires payments from customers to be matched against the relevant invoices. All payments received and relating to a particular invoice are recorded against it until it is completely paid off. This method can make control difficult as some customers may make part payments, which cannot be tied to a particular invoice. If a customer does not specify to which invoice a particular payment relates it is normally assigned to the oldest invoice(s). Once an invoice has been completely settled it is cleared from the ledger and any subsequent statements of account.

Package Requirements and Facilities

Customer Master File

When setting up the Sales Ledger system, one of the first tasks is to open an account for each customer. These accounts are maintained in a sales ledger *master file*, which is updated by sales and account settlement transactions. A typical package should provide as a minimum, the following data item types for each customer record:

- *account number* - used to identify uniquely a customer record;

- *name and address* - this will normally be the customer's address to which statements of account and invoices are sent;
- *credit limit* - the maximum amount of credit to be allowed to the customer at any one time. This is checked by sales staff before an order is authorised for processing;
- *balance* - this is the balance of the customer's account at any one time.

A choice is usually provided to select the form of sales ledger required, either open item or balance forward (see previous section). Normally, when the file is first created, a zero balance is recorded and outstanding transactions are entered to produce a current balance. An open item system stores details of any unpaid invoices. Each invoice can be associated with a particular customer account through the account number.

Transaction Entries

Transactions may be applied directly to customer accounts in the sales ledger (*transaction processing*) or they may be initially stored as a transaction file for a *batch* updating run. Whichever method the package uses, it should allow for the entry of the following transaction types:

- *invoice* - this is sent to the customer requesting payment concerning a particular order. The amount of the invoice is debited to the customer's account in the sales ledger, thus increasing the amount owing;
- *credit note*. If, for example, goods are returned by a customer or there is a dispute concerning the goods, a credit note is issued by the business to the customer. The amount of the credit note will be credited to the customer's account in the sales ledger, thus reducing the balance owing. Credit notes are often printed in red to distinguish them from invoices;
- *receipt* - this is any payment or remittance received from a customer in whole or partial settlement of an invoice. Such an entry will be credited to the customer's account and reduce the balance owing accordingly.

The following data may be entered with each type of transaction:

- *account number* - essential to identify the computer record. Although some packages allow for the entry of a shortened customer name (if the account number has been forgotten) the account number is still necessary to identify uniquely a record;
- *date of transaction*;
- *amount of transaction*;
- *transaction reference* - normally this is the invoice number to which the transaction relates.

Outputs

The following facilities may be expected:

- *single account enquiry* - details of an individual customer's account can be displayed on screen. Retrieval may be by account number or a search facility, using a shortened version of the customer name. If more than one record is retrieved by this method they may be scanned through on screen until the required record is found;

- *customer statement printing* - it is essential that the system can produce monthly statements for sending to customers;
- *debtors' age analysis* - this provides a schedule of the total amounts owing by customers, categorised according to the time various portions of the total debt have been outstanding (unpaid). It is important for a business to make financial provision for the possibility of *bad debts*. These are debts which are unlikely to be settled and may have to be taken out of business profits.

From their own experience of the trade, the proprietor of business should be able to estimate the percentage of each debt that is likely to become bad. Generally, the longer the debt has been outstanding, the greater the likelihood that it will remain unpaid.

- *customers over credit limit* - this may form the basis of a `black list' of customers. Any new order from one of these customers has to be authorised by management. On the other hand, the appearance of certain customers on the list may suggest that some increased credit limits are needed. When a business is successful, it often needs more credit to expand further.
- *dormant account list* - if there has been no activity on an account for some time, it may warrant removal from the file. Alternatively, it may be useful to contact the customer to see if further business may be forthcoming.

Validation and Control

The package should provide for careful validation of transactions and the protection of records from unauthorised access or amendment. Generally, for example, a customer record cannot be removed from the sales ledger while the account is still 'live' (there is a balance outstanding). More details of validation and control are given in Chapter 14 on Data Control and Security.

Purchase Ledger

General Description

The purchase ledger function mirrors that of the sales ledger, except that it contains an account for each *supplier*, from whom the business buys goods. When trading with a supplier, it is usually through credit arrangements, similar to those provided by the business for its own customers. Thus, the business receives an invoice requesting payment, within a certain period, for goods purchased. The amount of the invoice is credited to the supplier's account and the balance owing to the supplier is increased accordingly. When payment is made to a supplier, in full or part settlement of an invoice, the supplier's account is debited by the appropriate amount and the balance is decreased. Most purchase ledger systems operate on an open item basis. Each supplier invoice is given a reference number and when payment is made to a supplier, the reference number can be used to allocate the payment to a particular invoice.

Package Requirements and Facilities

Supplier Master File

The supplier master file contains the suppliers' (*creditors*) accounts. It is updated by supplier invoices and payments to suppliers. A typical package should provide, as a minimum, the following data item types for each supplier record:

- *account number-* used to identify uniquely a supplier record;
- *name and address* - the name and address of the supplier business;
- *credit limit* - the maximum amount of credit allowed to the business by the supplier at any one time. A check should be kept on this to avoid rejection of orders;
- *settlement discount* - this is the amount of discount given by a supplier if an invoice is settled within a specified discount period;
- *due date* - the system may issue a reminder when payment is due. A report may be printed, on request, listing all invoice amounts due for payment within, say, 7 days;
- *balance* - the current balance on the account.

A choice is usually provided to select the form of purchase ledger required (either open item or balance forward).

Transactions

Transactions may update the supplier accounts directly (transaction processing) or they may be initially stored as a transaction file for a later updating run. A purchase ledger package should allow for the following transactions:

- *supplier invoices* - before entry, each invoice must be checked against the appropriate order and then against the relevant delivery note, for actual receipt of goods. The balance on a supplier's account (the amount owed to the supplier) is increased by an invoice entry. Some packages allow unsatisfactory (there may be doubt about the delivery of the goods) invoices to be held in abeyance until cleared;
- *approved payments* - once an invoice has been cleared for payment, a voucher may be raised to ensure payment, on or before a due date, and discount for prompt payment. The entry of the payment value decreases the balance of a supplier's account and thus the amount owed by the business to the supplier. Cheques may be produced automatically on the due date, but there should be some checking procedure to ensure that payments are properly authorised;
- *adjustments* - to reverse entries made in error.

Outputs

The following output facilities may be expected:

- *single account enquiries* - details of an individual supplier's account can be displayed on screen; retrieval may be through a supplier code;

- *payment advice slip* - this may be produced to accompany a payment to a supplier. Each payment slip details the invoice reference, the amount due and the value of the payment remitted. Payment advice slips help the supplier, who may be using an open item sales ledger system;
- *automatic cheques* - the package may, with the use of pre-printed stationery, produce cheques for payment to suppliers, as and when invoices fall due. There must be a careful checking and authorisation procedure to prevent incorrect payments being made;
- *unpaid invoices* - a list of all outstanding invoices, together with details of supplier, amount owing and due date;
- *creditors' age analysis* - this is the supplier equivalent of debtors' age analysis. The report provides a schedule of total balances owing to suppliers, analysed according to the time the debt has been outstanding. The report may be used to determine which payments should be given priority over others.

Nominal Ledger

General Description

The nominal ledger is used to record the income and expenditure of a business, classified according to purpose. Thus, for example, it contains an account for *sales*; sales totals are entered on a daily basis. The sales ledger analyses sales by customer, whereas the *sales account* provides a cumulative total for sales, as the accounting year progresses. The *purchases account* in the nominal ledger fulfils a similar purpose for purchases by the business. Other income and expenditure accounts recorded in the nominal ledger may include, for example, *rent*, *heating* and *wages*. If some items of income and expenditure are too small to warrant separate analysis, there may also be *sundry income* and *sundry expenditure* accounts. The information held in the nominal ledger accounts is used to draw up a *profit and loss account*. This account provides information on the trading performance of the business over the year. A *balance sheet* can then be produced to give a `snapshot' view of the business's assets and liabilities, on a particular date.

Package Requirements and Facilities

Nominal Accounts Master File

When an account is opened in the nominal ledger, the following data item types should be available:

- *account code* - each account is given a code, to allow the allocation of transactions. For example, an entry for a gas bill payment may be directed to the Heating account by the code 012;
- *account name* - for example, Sales, Heating, Rent;
- *balance*.

Associated with each account are a number of transactions processed during the current accounting period.

Transactions

- *sales and purchases* - these may be entered periodically as accumulated totals or, in an integrated accounts system, values may be posted automatically, at the same time as they update customer and supplier accounts in the sales ledger and purchase ledger;
- *other income and expenditure* - entries concerning, for example, wages, rent, rates or heating.

Outputs

Typical output facilities include:

- *trial balance* - this is a list of debit and credit balances categorised by account. The balances are taken from the nominal ledger and the total of debit balances should agree with the total of credit balances.
- *transaction report* - a full list of transactions which may be used for error checking purposes, or as an audit trail, to allow the validity of transactions to be checked by an external auditor. The topic of auditing is described in more detail in Chapter 14 on Data Control and Security;
- *trading and profit and loss account* - a statement of the trading performance of the business over a given period;
- *balance sheet* - a statement of the business's assets and liabilities at a particular date.

The major benefit of the computerised nominal ledger is that these reports can be produced easily and upon request. The manual production of a trial balance, trading and profit and loss statement and balance sheet can be a laborious and time consuming task. Many small businesses, operating manual systems, have difficulty in completing their annual accounts promptly for annual tax assessment.

Other Business Applications

Apart from the basic ledgers described in the previous section, there are other applications which can benefit from computerisation. They include:

- stock control;
- sales order processing and invoicing.

Stock Control

General Description

Different businesses hold different kinds of stock. For example, a grocer holds some perishable and some non-perishable stocks of food and a clothing manufacturer holds stocks of materials and finished articles of clothing. Any trader's stock needs to be controlled, but the reasons for control may vary from one business to another. For example, a grocer wants to keep the full range of food items that customers expect, but does not want to be left with stocks of unsold items, especially if they are perishable. A clothing manufacturer's stocks will not perish if they are unsold, but space occupied by unwanted goods could be occupied by more popular items. On the other hand, if the manufacturer runs out of raw materials the production process can be slowed or even halted. Apart from such differences, there are some common reasons for wanting efficient stock control:

- excessive stock levels tie up valuable cash resources and increase business costs. The cash could be used to finance further business;
- inability to satisfy customer orders promptly because of insufficient stocks, can often lead to loss of custom.

It is possible to identify some typical objectives of a stock control system and these can be used to measure the usefulness of facilities commonly offered by computer packages:

- to maintain levels of stock which will be sufficient to meet customer demand promptly;
- to provide a mechanism which removes the need for excessively high safety margins of stock to cover customer demand. This is usually effected by setting minimum stock levels which the computer can use to report variations outside these levels;
- to provide automatic re-ordering of stock items which fall below minimum levels;
- to provide management with up-to-date information on stock levels and values of stock held. Stock valuation is also needed for accounting purposes.

Stock control requires that an individual record is maintained for each type of stock item held. Apart from details concerning the description and price of the stock item, each record should have a balance indicating the number of units held. A unit may be, for example, a box, 500 grammes or a tonne. The balance is adjusted whenever units of that particular stock item are sold or purchased. Manual or computerised records can only give recorded levels of stock. Physical stock checks need to be carried out to determine the actual levels. If there is a difference between the recorded stock level of an item and the actual stock of that item, it could be because of pilferage or damage. Alternatively, some transactions for the item may not have been applied to the stock file.

Package Requirements and Facilities

Stock Master File

The stock master file contains records for each item of stock and each record may usefully contain the following data item types:

Stock code or reference - each stock item type should have a unique reference, for example, A0035. The code should be designed so that it is useful to the user. For example, an initial alphabetic character may be used to differentiate between raw materials (R) and finished goods (F) and the remaining digits may have ranges which indicate particular product groupings. The stock file may also be used to record any consumable items used by a business, for example, stationery and printer ribbons. The initial character of the stock code could be used to identify such a grouping. The number and type of characters in a code, as well as its format, are usually limited by the package because the code will also be used by the software to determine a record's location within the file;

- *Description* - although users may become used to referring to individual products by their codes or references, a description is needed for the production of, for example, purchase orders or customer invoices;
- *Analysis code* - this may be used in conjunction with sales orders so that they can be analysed by product group. If, for example, a clothing manufacturer produces different types of anorak, it is important for production planning purposes to know the relative popularity of each type;
- *Unit size* - for example, box, metre, tonne, kilo;
- *Re-order level* - this is the stock level at which an item is to be re-ordered, for example, 30 boxes. Reaching this level may trigger an automatic re-order when the appropriate program option is run. Alternatively it may be necessary to request a summary report which highlights all items at or below their re-order level. The decision on what the re-order level should be for any particular item will depend on the *sales turnover* (the number of units sold per day or week) and the *lead time* (the time taken for delivery after a purchase order is placed with a supplier). Seasonal changes in sales figures will require that re-order levels for individual items are changed for time to time;
- *Re-order quantity* - this is the number of item units to be re-ordered from a supplier when new stock is required;
- *Bin reference* - this may be used to indicate the physical location of stock items within, for example, a warehouse;
- *Minimum stock level* - when an item falls to this level, a warning is given that the stock level of the item is dangerously low. As with the re-order level, the warning may be produced by a request for a special summary report which highlights such items. Even though the re-order level warning may have already been given, it is possible that no new stocks were ordered or that the supplier was unusually slow with deliveries;
- *Cost price* - the price paid by the business for the stock item;
- *Sale price* - the price charged to the customer. The package may allow the storage of more than one sale price to differentiate between, for example, retail and wholesale customers;
- *VAT code* - different items may attract different rates of Value Added Tax (VAT);
- *Supplier code* - if orders can be produced automatically, then the supplier code may be used to access a supplier file, for the address and other details needed to produce an order;
- *Quantity issued* - generally, several values may be entered, so that the turnover of an item can be viewed for different periods, for example, from 3 months ago to date, the preceding 3 month period and so on;
- *Stock allocated* - a quantity may not have been issued but may have been allocated to a customer order or factory requisition;

- *Quantity in stock* - the current recorded level of stock. This will change whenever an issue, receipt or adjustment transaction is entered.

Transactions

- *Goods received* - stock received from a supplier;
- *Goods returned* - for example, stock returned by a customer or unused raw materials returned from the factory;
- *Goods issued* - this may result from a customer order or from a factory requisition, if the business has a manufacturing process;
- *Stock allocated* - this will not reduce the quantity in stock figure but the amount allocated should be used to offset the quantity in stock when judging what is available;
- *Amendments* - for, example, there may be amendments to price, re-order level or supplier code.

The method used to update the stock master file will depend on how up-to-date the figures need to be (this will depend on how `tight' stock levels are) and how often the data entry operator can get at the computer. To keep the file up-to-date throughout the day, physical stock changes have to be notified immediately to stock control and the transactions have to be entered as they occur. Unfortunately, this means that a single-user system would be unavailable to any other users, such as sales staff, who needed to know quantities in stock. A networked system with central file storage, would allow continual updating and enquiry access. If the stock levels are sufficiently high to allow differences to arise between physical and `book' totals without risking shortages, then daily batch updating may be acceptable. In such a situation, an enquiry on a stock item may reveal, for example, a `book' stock of 200 units, when the physical stock is only 120 units (80 having been issued since the last update at the end of the preceding day).

Outputs

Typical outputs from a stock control package include:

- *Stock enquiry* - details concerning a stock item may be displayed on screen, or printed;
- *Stock out report* - a list of stock items which have reached a level of zero;
- *Re-order report* - a list of stock items which have fallen to their re-order level, together with supplier details and recommended re-order quantities;
- *Stock list* - a full or limited (for example, within a certain stock code range) list of stock items, giving details of quantities held and their value. The value may be calculated using the cost or sale price, depending on the costing method used by the business;
- *Outstanding order report* - a list of all purchase orders not yet fulfilled and the dates ordered. This may be used to `chase up' orders when stocks are falling dangerously low.

This is not an exhaustive list and some packages offer many other analytical reports which can help a business to maintain an efficient customer service and plan future production and purchasing more effectively.

A DIY Store Example

The Astex Homecare chain of DIY stores has branches all over the country and each branch maintains stocks of thousands of items used in the home. These items range from building materials such as sand and cement to bedroom furniture, fitted kitchens, bathroom suites, ceramic wall and floor tiles, lights and light fittings, garden materials such as plants, plant pots and garden furniture, nails, screws, paint, wallpaper and numerous other common household goods.

Each branch has its own small computer system dedicated to dealing with the *point of sale* (POS) terminals located at the customer tills. The POS terminals are used to record purchases and provide customer bills by scanning the bar code on each purchase using a hand-held scanner. The stock number contained in the bar code is fed by the POS terminal to the local computer which returns the description and price to be printed on the customers' receipts as well as the bill totals.

Each branch maintains its own stock file on the local computer but ordering stock is controlled by a mainframe computer at the Astex head office. Each Astex branch is laid out according to a *merchandise layout plan* (MLP) in which the store is organised into a large number of four foot sections, each having its own MLP code. Each item of stock is allocated to one MLP section and its computer record contains the MLP code together with the minimum and maximum stock level for that particular section of the store. When an item has been sold, the relevant information is transmitted automatically by the local computer to the mainframe at head office. The head office computer determines from the MLP data whether the item needs to be re-ordered from a supplier. It uses the MLP information regarding minimum and maximum stock levels in order to determine how many of a particular item to order.

Overnight, while the stores are closed, the head office computer transmits suggested ordering information back to the individual branches where order sheets are printed out on local laser printers, so that they can be checked manually by the appropriate personnel before stock is ordered. This manual monitoring of computer-generated information allows the information system to cope with unexpected situations and prevents the occurrence of gross errors. About ninety percent of all orders can be made electronically using communication links to the computers used by suppliers. Other suppliers not linked to the central Astex computer are contacted manually by telephone.

The security of the Astex information systems are ensured in two major ways. Firstly, because of the importance of the local computer system for producing customer bills, a backup processor is always available for use in the event of the primary processor failing. Secondly, access to the various users of the computer systems is provided on several different levels. Each person who uses the computer system has his or her own access code which provides access to only those areas he or she is authorised to use. These measures are essential to maintain the security and reliable operation of such large-scale systems.

Sales Order Processing and Invoicing

Sales Order Processing

Sales order processing is concerned with the handling of customers' sales orders. It has three main functions:

- validation of orders. This means checking, for example, that the goods ordered are supplied by the business or that the customer's credit status warrants the order's completion;
- to identify quantities of individual items ordered. A customer may request several different items on the same order form. An item will probably appear on many different order forms and the quantities for each need to be totalled to provide lists (picking lists) for warehouse staff to retrieve the goods;
- to monitor back orders. If an order cannot be fulfilled it may be held in abeyance until new stocks arrive. The system should be able to report all outstanding back orders on request.

The efficient processing of customer orders is of obvious importance to the success of a business and in whatever form an order is received, the details should be immediately recorded. Preferably, the details should be recorded on a pre-designed order form which ensures that all relevant details are taken. The order details should include:

- the date the order is received;
- the customer's order number;
- a description of each item required including any necessary stock references or codes;
- the quantity of each item ordered;
- the price per item excluding VAT;
- the total order value excluding VAT;
- any discount which is offered to the customer;
- the VAT amount which is to be added to the total price;
- the total order value including VAT;
- the delivery date required.

Invoicing

The invoice is the bill to the customer, requesting payment for goods or services supplied by the business. The following section describes typical package facilities which allow the integration of the sales order processing and invoicing systems.

Package Requirements and Facilities

To be effective, the sales order processing system needs to have access to the customer file (sales ledger) for customer details and to the stock file, so that prices can be extracted according to stock item codes entered with the order. This latter facility means that the system may also be integrated with invoicing.

Files

Customer file - when a customer account number or name is keyed in with an order, the package usually accesses the customer file and displays the address details, so that the operator can confirm the delivery address or type in an alternative address if this is required. The process also ensures that all orders are processed for registered customers;

- *Stock file* - as stock item codes are entered from an order form, the system accesses the price and displays it on the screen for confirmation by the operator. Access to the stock file also ensures that only valid stock codes are used;
- *Completed order file* - this is used for the generation of invoices after an order's completion;
- *Back order file* - this is needed to ensure that orders which cannot be fulfilled immediately are kept on file and processed as soon as goods become available.

Transactions

- Sales Order - details concerning an individual order, including customer number, items required (by item code), quantity of each item, delivery date, discount allowed and the date of the order.

Outputs

- *Invoice* - an invoice can be generated by using the details of customer number, stock codes and quantities from the order, together with information retrieved from the customer and stock files;
- *Back order report* - a report can be requested detailing all unsatisfied orders. This is useful for planning production schedules or generating special purchase orders;
- *Picking list* - a summary of the quantities required of each item ordered. These are used by warehouse staff to extract the goods needed to make up orders for delivery;
- *Sales data* - details of each customer's order need to be extended to include the financial ledgers (sales, purchase and nominal ledger). Such integration should not usually be attempted all at once but full integration does reduce the number of inputs necessary and automates many of the updating procedures described in this chapter.

Payroll

The task of calculating wages for a large company having hundreds or even thousands of employees is an enormous task. It involves taking into account some or all of the following factors:

- number of hours worked;
- amount of overtime;
- bonus payment;
- sickness leave;

- type of employee (for example, weekly or monthly paid, shop floor or management);
- deductions (for example, national insurance contributions and union fees);
- holidays;
- tax code;
- tax rate;
- cash analysis.

The gross pay is calculated from the hours worked and hourly pay rate for weekly paid employees, and is a standard sum for salaried employees. Added to this gross payment are any allowances from overtime or bonuses, for example. Tax is calculated and subtracted from the total earnings and other deductions such as national insurance, union fees and pension contribution are also taken from it. Thus the total calculation is quite complicated, and it will probably be different for each employee.

Producing payslips manually is therefore very time consuming and prone to error, so computers are particularly well suited to the task. Most computerised payroll systems use batch processing in which long-term employee information held on a master file is used in conjunction with a transaction file containing recent information such as hours worked and overtime details. The transaction file changes from week to week or month to month but most of the information on the master file either doesn't change at all or it changes only occasionally.

ACME COMPUTERS LTD					
Name:	J. Winns	**Empl no:**	725012	**Date:**	15/1/94
Hours:	45	**Rate:**	£6.80		
Gross pay:	£306.00				
Allowances:	£ 21.50				
Total:	£327.50				
Tax:		£ 65.50		**Tax to date:**	£420.27
National Insurance:		£ 32.24			
Other deductions:		£ 6.50			
Total deductions:		£104.24			
Net pay:	£223.26				

Figure 10. 1.*Example payslip*

A payslip produced as output from a payroll system might look like the example shown in Figure 10.1. If employees are paid weekly, at the end of each week details of hours worked, bonus payments, overtime payments and deductions are recorded on a payroll transaction file which contains a record for every employee. This sequential transaction file is then sorted into employee number order so that it is in the same order as the payroll master file. The two files are then used by the computer to calculate and print the payslips, and to update the master file which must keep track of such things as tax paid to date, total national insurance contributions and holiday and sickness leave for each employee for the current tax year. A *systems flowchart*, as illustrated in Figure 10.2, is often used to describe business data processing systems such as this.

The systems flowchart shows the computer operations involved in a payroll run. Payroll systems normally use batch processing when the majority of the employees need to be paid. This lends itself to the use of magnetic tape devices (the flowchart does not specify the medium) which are restricted to sequential access. The payroll data is first stored on the payroll transaction file using keyboards as the input devices. Each employee's pay information is stored in a separate record identified by employee number. Because the master file records are stored on tape in order of employee number, the transaction file must also be sorted into the same order. This is to avoid having to search for matching master file and transaction file records for each employee - because both files are in the same order, the next record in each file should be for the same employee. The sorted transaction file must be validated by the computer before processing the payroll data to produce payslips. This process performs various checks on the transaction file to ensure that only correct data will be processed. Any errors detected at this stage must be corrected before the payslips are generated.

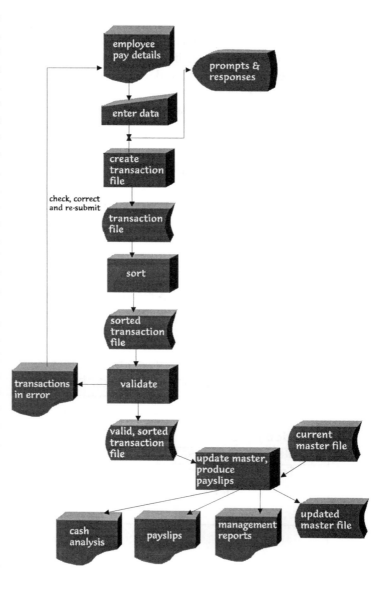

Figure 10.2. *System flowchart for payroll system*

Finally, the validated and sorted transaction file is processed against the payroll master file in order to produce the payslips. In addition to updating the master file, the payroll system might also produce summary reports for the management personnel of the company, and, if employees are paid by cash rather than by cheque or transfer to a bank account, a cash analysis might be produced. The cash analysis calculates exactly how many of each currency denomination will be required for all the pay packets, so that the correct money can be obtained from a bank. The cash analysis might produce a table of the form shown below.

Denom	Number	Amount
£20	1492	£29,840.00
£10	213	£2,130.00
£5	102	£510.00
£1	622	£622.00
50p	97	£48.50
20p	81	£16.20
10p	127	£12.70
5p	102	£5.10
2p	100	£2.00
1p	534	£4.34
Total Cash Required		£33,189.84

Each payslip would also have a corresponding breakdown for a single pay packet to make it easier for the cashiers to make up the pay packets.

A large company will probably use a mainframe computer for the task of processing the payroll information. Data entry will often be carried out using key-to-tape systems by a number of data entry clerks, and the output of the payslips will probably be by means of pre-printed stationery used on a line printer for speed. Backing storage will normally be in the form of magnetic tape or magnetic disk, but sequential *batch processing* will almost invariably be used. Of course, small companies having only a few employees might use a microcomputer system for the payroll, or even produce the payslips manually without the use of a computer at all.

Booking Systems

Travel Agents

If you go to a travel agent to book a seat on a major international airline, the travel agent will need to check the airline for the availability of the flight that you require. This normally involves communicating with the airline's computer to obtain up-to-date flight information. Remember that the same thing can be happening from all over the world: numerous travel agents could be accessing the same airline's computer at the same time, several of them even trying to book seats on the same flight that you want.

To cope with this type of demand, the airline will use a mainframe computer allowing on-line communication with each travel agent via the public telephone network. Each travel agency will have one or more terminals connected by modem to the airline's computer. Flight reservations will be performed in *real-time*, that is, the mainframe's flight and passenger information will be updated immediately to prevent the possibility of double-booking a seat on a particular flight. This ensures that the information that the travel agent obtains will be completely accurate and reliable. This form of processing, where a master file is updated immediately, is called *transaction processing* (see Processing Methods).

The process of reserving a seat on a flight is further complicated by the fact that several airlines might have scheduled flights to your destination, each offering different flight times, facilities and costs. Rather than contacting each one separately, a process that could take a considerable amount of time, the travel agent links into a wide area network(WAN) which connects the main computers of the different airlines. This allows the agent to choose the most appropriate flight for you and book it immediately. Though each airline in the system might have a different passenger reservation information system, the network software presents the same information format to the travel agents and takes care of transferring data in the correct format to the individual computer systems of the airlines.

When you have decided on your choice of airline and flight, your details are entered at the travel agent's terminal. While this is happening, other travel agents are prevented from accessing that particular flight record. On completion of the reservation, the flight record becomes available again. Booking cancellations and changes are handled in the same way. Your ticket, which will have been produced by the airline's computer, is usually sent out to you a few days prior to the departure date. Individual airlines' computers also produce passenger lists automatically for use at the departure airports.

An airline's master passenger reservation and flight information file will be held on a high-capacity magnetic disk drive. For backup purposes, in case the master file is in some way lost or partly erased, or the disk drive fails, a separate disk drive will be used to hold an exact duplicate of the master file, and this duplicate file will be updated at the same time as the other master file. This duplication is necessary because the master file will be in constant use, night and day, and there will be no opportunity to stop updating it in order to make a backup on magnetic tape. For the same reasons of security, there will also be a duplicate main computer immediately ready to be used if the other one fails for some reason. Because of the importance of the fast response time required of the system, it will almost certainly be used exclusively for passenger booking purposes, and it will have been designed to operate without break, 24 hours a day, every day of the year.

Similar real-time systems are used by holiday firms, some of which are able to offer thousands of holidays all over the world. Travel agents must have access to accurate information regarding the availability of all the holidays on offer. Again it is important to ensure that exactly the same holiday is not sold to more than one customer, so the booking file held on the holiday company's main computer must be completely up-to-date.

Hotel booking

Hotels frequently use booking systems for keeping track of room reservations made by guests. These systems generally provide additional facilities relating to hotel management, typically keeping track of guests' accounts and producing hotel room usage information.

When someone reserves a room in the hotel, a record is created in the guest file. The file contains three types of data:

- Details of the guest, such as name, address, telephone number.
- Room details, such as type (single, double etc.), number, period of occupancy.
- Charges incurred by the guest during the stay at the hotel. For each charge, the item code, cost and date will be recorded.

The first two types of data are entered at the time the reservation is made; items and services bought by the guest during his or her stay, such as telephone calls, drinks, newspapers and extra meals, are recorded as and when they occur. When the guest leaves, the hotel system calculates the total bill and prints out an itemised list that the guest can check.

A hotel management system such as this can easily be implemented with a microcomputer system, though large hotel chains might also have a large central computer at their headquarters for general accounting purposes (such as producing financial reports covering the whole chain of hotels, and for payroll calculations).

Library Systems

Dotherstaff College is a split site college of further and higher education. Each site has a large library which has recently been supplied with a microcomputer network for a library automation system called "Alice", produced by a software company called Softlink. The software has a number of interlinked modules covering all aspects of typical library operation. Only the first three of the modules listed below are currently used by Dotherstaff College but there are plans to increase the scope of the system in the near future:

- Catalogue and Classification - managing the book database;
- Circulation - managing borrowers;
- Enquiries - information retrieval;

- Acquisition - ordering books;
- Reports and utilities- producing reports of publishers details, author details and library usage figures;
- Periodicals- managing the ordering of magazines.

Catalogue and Classification

This module is mainly used for the addition of new titles to the book database. Figure 10.3 shows the data entry screen as the details of a book are being entered.

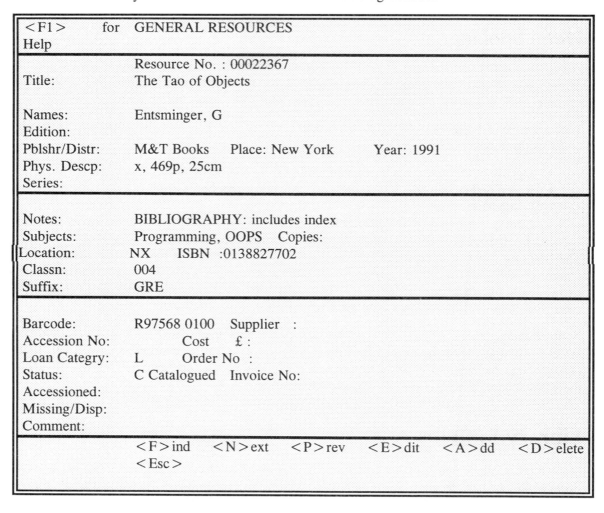

Figure 10.3. *Data entry screen for book details*

Cursor keys are used to move around the screen and the control key in combination with the letters in angle brackets shown on the bottom line of the screen provide access to the functions indicated. You can see from this bottom line of the screen that book details can be created, edited and deleted, as well as allowing the file to be browsed through using *<P>rev* and

<N>ext, or searched using *<F>ind*. The software automatically extracts from the title of the book keywords which can be used in the *Enquiry* module which is described later.

Circulation

The circulation module is used for managing borrowers' details. Figure 10.4 shows the data entry screen for this module. Again the bottom line of the screen shows what functions are available and how to access them.

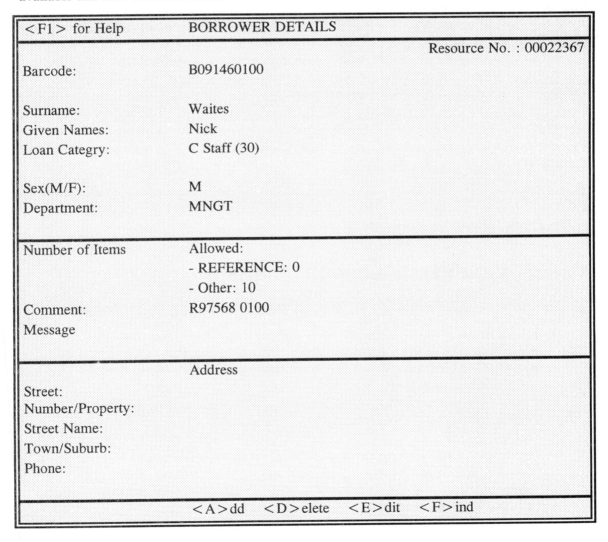

<F1> for Help	BORROWER DETAILS	
		Resource No. : 00022367
Barcode:	B091460100	
Surname:	Waites	
Given Names:	Nick	
Loan Categry:	C Staff (30)	
Sex(M/F):	M	
Department:	MNGT	
Number of Items	Allowed:	
	- REFERENCE: 0	
	- Other: 10	
Comment:	R97568 0100	
Message		
	Address	
Street:		
Number/Property:		
Street Name:		
Town/Suburb:		
Phone:		
	<A>dd <D>elete <E>dit <F>ind	

Figure 10.4 *Data entry screen for borrowers*

To borrow a book from the library a borrower must produce his or her ticket on which there is a unique bar code. This bar code is scanned by a librarian and the borrower's record then appears on the screen. When the bar code of the book is scanned, the code is stored in the borrower's record. To return a book, the bar code of the book is scanned or typed in and the book is automatically removed from the borrower's record. The system also allows the display of all books currently borrowed by any person. Periodically, about every two weeks, the borrower file is searched for overdue items so that reminders can be generated automatically.

Enquiry

The enquiry module is used by staff and students to search the book database for books satisfying certain criteria. For example, a user can type in the name of an author and obtain a list of all books in the library written by that person. The title of a book, or part of the title can be entered and a list of books closely matching the title will be displayed. Alternatively, one or more keywords can be used to produce a list of books which contain the keywords in the title. The book information retrieved by an enquiry is summarised on the screen in several sections containing such things as the book titles, subjects covered and author(s). Any book selected from the list can have its full details displayed on screen or printed. This type of enquiry facility can save a great deal of time searching shelves or catalogues for specific information.

The network used for the library information system currently supports about 20 terminals, but it is also linked to the main college networks which provide access to other software such as word processors and spreadsheets.

Objectives of Data-handling Systems

A number of general objectives can be identified as being of relevance to most organisations.

- Improved *operational efficiency*. *Speed* and *accuracy* of operations should be radically improved. This is not automatic as the computer-based system may be badly designed and the staff may be ill-trained, but given proper design and implementation administrative systems will normally be more efficient;
- Better *control of resources*. Administrative systems such as those for financial control and the control of resources such as staff and raw materials benefit particularly from the rapid production of up-to-date information by computer;
- Improved *productivity*. Redundancy is not always follow from computerisation, particularly if the organisation is an expanding business. Computer-based systems should permit large increases in the volumes of business which can be handled without the need for extra staff;
- Improved *security of information*. With proper physical security, clear operational procedures to restrict access to computer facilities to those properly authorised and sophisticated use of software control mechanisms such as passwords, information can be made more secure than equivalent manual systems;
- Opportunities to *share data*. This is most likely where database systems and networked computer systems are employed;

- Improved *quality of information* for *decision taking* at the operational, strategic and corporate levels in an organisation. Operational decisions concern day-to-day operations, such as handling of customer orders or delivery of new stocks. At the strategic level, decisions may relate to issues such as production planning and the selection of suppliers. Corporate decision examples include the setting of prices, targeting of markets and the production of new products. Most systems generate a range of management information reports, generated from the routine processing of transactions and these are primarily of use at the strategic level, but may also help with corporate decisions. Accounts software, for example, produces reports on outstanding debts, potential bad debtors, dates when payments to suppliers are due and analysis of sales patterns.
- Improved *external image*. An organisation can improve its external image by the improved presentation of correspondence and by an improved service to its customers or clients, but badly designed procedures can also make life more difficult for them.
- Improved *working conditions*. This is highly debatable in respect of an office environment, but computer-based manufacturing systems usually provide a less dirty and dangerous environment for employees as much of the work is done by robots and other computer-controlled machinery.

Choosing a System Type

Whether batch processing, one of the on-line types, or distributed processing is appropriate depends on a number of factors:

- the type and size of organisation. Large organisations generally have larger volumes of data to handle, than do small ones. Batch processing is efficient in the sense that it is a concentrated activity and if transactions can be accumulated and handled together, then it may be more efficient than dealing with each transaction as it arises. On the other hand, delay may prevent achievement of an important objective, such as the provision of up-to-date management information. Distributed processing through computer networks is an increasingly popular option for a medium or large organisation, because it gives local control to branches and allows data to be shared and communicated across the whole organisation.
- the activity (for example, financial accounts, hotel booking);
- the objectives of the activity (see previous section)

As explained in Chapter 14, a batch processing system provides numerous opportunities to ensure the accuracy of data, as it passes through the system. In this way, the type satisfies one of the main objectives of many systems and if this were the only criterion for selection, all systems would use batch processing. Of course, there are other criteria which must be applied to the selection process, including: system purpose(s); size and type of organisation; other objectives, such as security, speed, or the provision of extra management information. For example, an airline's passenger reservation system cannot be effective unless files are updated at the time each reservation is made and transaction processing is found to be appropriate. An organisation's stock control system may need to reflect stock changes on the same basis as the airline reservation system, particularly if delivery has to be immediate. Discount stores, such as Argos, sell a huge range of consumer items and some are expensive; it is not desirable to hold high stock levels, because this ties up large amounts of cash, so the stock records need to be updated as goods are delivered and sold. In some organisations, stock movements (stock received and stock issued) do not have to be instantly reflected in stock records, because delivery times to customers can be longer, perhaps up to several weeks. If the goods are not of high value, then it may be convenient to hold larger stocks, which ensure the satisfaction of customer demand. For example, if the stock record for an item shows 1000 units and 50 units is the maximum customer requirement, then a physical stock level which is only 800 units, is not an immediate problem.

The size of the organisation is also a significant factor in determining the most appropriate type of data handling system. A small plumbing firm, perhaps consisting of two partners and a couple of employees is unlikely to include anyone to keep the accounts; this will probably be the job of one of the partners, who will only have time to do the work at weekends. Thus, customer invoices and payments are dealt with in a batch, perhaps every week. As a small firm, a major objective will be to collect customer debts as quickly as possible and the computerised system can help to do this, in the limited time that the partner has to deal with such matters.

Chapter 11

System Development

The System Life Cycle

In business, *systems analysis and design* is the process of investigating a business, existing or new, with a view to determining how best to manage the various procedures and information processing tasks that it involves. Though it frequently means considering the use of a computer system to replace some manual operations, this need not always be the case. The *systems analyst,* whose job it is to perform the investigation, might recommend the use of a computer to improve the efficiency of the information system under consideration, but he/she might equally well decide that a manual system is adequate, or even preferable. Thus, the intention in systems analysis is to determine how well a business copes with its current information processing needs, and whether it is possible to improve the procedures involved in order to make it more efficient, or more profitable, or both. Systems design involves planning the structure of the information system to be implemented. In other words, analysis determines what the system should do, and design determines how it should be done.

The job of the systems analyst starts with studying the current, or proposed, system; this involves collecting facts which will help the analyst to determine whether a computer would improve the information system, and if so, in what areas it would be most beneficial. Once the decision has been made to go ahead with a new or improved system, the analyst must develop a plan for putting the proposed system into practice. This includes specifying all the procedures involved, computerised or otherwise, how data is to be captured, what software will be required to process the data, what equipment will be necessary, what staff will be needed and how they will be trained, and so on. In other words, the analyst must provide a complete plan of every detail of the proposed system. A key feature of this complex task is communicating with staff, whether they are ordinary employees or managers. The people who work in the business are most likely to know what works and what does not, what causes problems and how they can be avoided, and where improvements to the current system are most necessary.

Figure 11.1. *The systems development life cycle*

This chapter describes the *systems development life cycle*, the sequence of activities involved in analysing, designing and implementing an information system. As well as systems analysts, who play key roles in the process, other personnel such as computer programmers and computer managers are also involved to a large degree. Though the steps are described separately, in practice they may be performed in a different order, or even be difficult to distinguish one from another; sometimes one part of the system will be in the process of being implemented while another is still being analysed. The cyclic nature of system development is illustrated in Figure 11.1. The system development stages illustrated in the diagram may be repeated a number of times during the life of a system. Each time a significant change or improvement is required, the cycle is repeated.

Preliminary study

Before an organisation embarks on a costly project involving the development of a new information system, it is necessary to determine whether the system is possible to achieve and, if so, whether there will be sufficient benefits in doing so. The main part of this investigation is called a *feasibility study*. However, even before the feasibility study commences, it will be necessary to fully clarify what is being proposed. The systems analyst dealing with the proposal will talk with the people who have suggested the project in order to determine exactly what they have in mind and their reasons.

Once the proposal has been fully clarifed, the feasibility study can be undertaken. The feasibility study is usually carried out by a team of people with experience in information systems techniques, with a knowledge of the type of system being proposed and who are skilled in systems analysis and design. The team will be responsible for determining whether the potential benefits of the proposed system can justify the costs involved in developing it. It may be that the consequences of not adopting the new system make the change essential. For example, if a company is unable, through volume of work, to deal with customers effectively, the latter may take their business to more efficient competitors. It then becomes essential to the company's survival to improve its information system.

The feasibility study must also establish whether the new system can operate with available technology, software and personnel. In most instances, for example where a currently manual system is to be replaced or improved by using a computer system, the existing technology will most probably exist, but a new, innovative idea might require hardware or software that don't exist. If this is the case, the feasibility study team will attempt to determine whether the new items can be developed within a reasonable time.

Finally, the team will consider how well the system will be received by the people who will have to use it. This must have been a prime concern, for instance, of the first analysts who considered the use of cash points such as those now commonly provided by banks and building societies: would customers trust them and would they be sufficiently easy to use?

Investigation and Fact Finding

If the feasibility study produces a favourable report, the next stage, that of making a detailed analysis of the current system, will commence. The systems analyst will investigate all aspects of the current system:

- what services are being offered;
- what tasks are being performed;
- how they are being performed;
- how frequently they are done;
- how well they are done;
- what staff are involved and the nature of their involvement
- what is lacking in the system;
- any faults with the system;
- how the system can be improved.

Finding the answers to these questions requires the analyst to talk to all the people involved in operating the current system, from ordinary employees to managers and directors. This will frequently involve the use of questionnaires as well as personal interviews with employees, the study of manuals and reports, the observation of current working practices, and the collection and study of forms and other documents currently used. As this process is going on, the analyst will be starting to form views on how the new system should work in order to overcome the problems with the current system. At the end of this stage, the systems analyst will thoroughly understand how the current system works and be in a position to begin to design and produce a specification for the new system.

System Design

This stage produces the details of how the system will meet the requirements identified in the previous analysis stage. A major part of this stage involves identifying the inputs to the system (what they are and how they are to be captured), and the outputs from the system, such as reports, invoices, bills and statements. The designers will also specify in detail what files will be needed, their structures and what devices and media will be used to store them. All this information will be written down in the form of reports, tables and digrams. Such diagrams as system flow charts and data flow diagrams (Chapter 17) will be used to show how the overall system is integrated. The system designers will also provide detailed specifications on what the software is required to do so that programmers in the next stage will have a clear idea of what they are expected to produce.

Software Development

Depending on the system requirements, existing software may be purchased or it may be necessary to have software written specially. Software that is already available will usually be much cheaper than software that has to be custom-designed, but in many instances suitable software will not be available. Large organisations frequently employ their own systems analysts and programmers, but smaller firms may have to resort to using a software house for the necessary programs. Software development has its own sequence of procedures as described in Chapter 18.

System Testing

Before the system is put fully into operation, all aspects of it must be tested, not just the software that has been developed, but also the manual procedures involved. Personnel who have not been directly involved in developing the system will often be used to test the system after they have been given some appropriate training; such people may do things that were not anticipated by the system designers. In fact, the people testing the system will often deliberately attempt to make it fail in some way. It is vitally important to discover any serious shortcomings in the new information system before it is fully operational.

System Documentation

System documentation serves much the same purposes as program documentation described briefly in the earlier section on software development. All aspects of the system's operation will need to be described in detail. The documentation will include:

- user manuals describing the operation of the system;

- technical manuals for the computer hardware;

- program documentation;

This documentation serves a number of purposes:

- To provide reference material for training purposes. This will be of value to all employees using the new system. Each task and procedure will be clearly detailed and explained in terms appropriate to the staff involved.

- To explain in detail how the system is intended to work so that the people using the system can cope with problems and unfamiliar situations. This will be of particular value to managers and supervisors responsible for organising the work.

- To specify how to test the system to ensure that it is working correctly.

- To make it easier to modify or improve the system in future.

Implementing the System

In this stage the system designers will actually install the new system, putting new equipment into operation, installing and setting up software, creating data files and training people to use the system. A common practice is to run the new system in parallel with the old one to ensure that if anything does go wrong, the business will not come to a grinding halt.

When the system has become fully operational, there will still be the possibility of unforseen events causing problems. The system developers will therefore need to be available to deal with any problems that do arise, as well as making modifications as circumstances change. If the system has been developed by an outside firm, this *system maintenance,* normally will be subject to a separate financial arrangement such as an annual charge.

Monitoring and review

The final phase of the system development process is the assessment of the completed system. In this *review*, or *evaluation*, a number of factors are examined, including:

- How well the system is performing with reference to the needs that were initially identified.

- The final cost of the system compared to how much was originally budgeted.

- The time taken to complete the work.

Even after the system is fully operational its performance will of course be continually *monitored* throughout its life. At some stage, monitoring will identify needs that are no longer satisfied by the current system, and the system development process will begin once more with a preliminary study.

Chapter 12

The Feasibility Study

Introduction

The purpose of a feasibility study is to determine whether the potential benefits of a proposed system can justify the costs involved in developing it. There are many and various pressures which can 'trigger' the thought of using a computer, either for the first time or, where a computer is already installed, for other applications still operated manually. Some examples are as follows:

    (i)   the business is expanding and to cope with the increased workload it appears that the only alternative to computerisation is increased staffing;

    (ii) the business is expanding at such a rate that more information is needed to manage it properly. To obtain the information manually is too time consuming and by the time it has been gathered is probably out-of-date;

    (iii) staff are being asked to work regular and increasing amounts of overtime and backlogs of work are building up;

    (iv) customers are complaining about the speed and quality of the service provided;

    (v) where stock is involved, it is difficult to keep track of stock levels and while some customer orders cannot be filled because of stock shortages, other stock is 'gathering dust' on the shelves;

    (vi) a great deal of advertising literature is constantly reminding business management that they are out-of-date and at a disadvantage with their competitors;

    (vii) other businesses providing a similar service use a computerised system.

Examples (i), (ii) and (iii) suggest that the business is operating successfully and needs to take on extra staff or streamline its systems. Examples (iv) and (v) may be symptomatic of generally poor business management. In such cases, computerisation alone may not solve the problems. Examples (vi) and (vii) may tempt the management to computerise simply "to keep up with the Jones's". Although a computerisation programme resulting directly from one or more such pressures may be completely successful and worthwhile, the pressure itself should not be the reason for computerisation. Instead, management should establish the business objectives they wish to achieve.

Establishing Objectives for Computerisation

It is important for management to establish what overall objectives they are trying to achieve, before identifying systems which contribute to their achievement. For example, two major business objectives may be to improve the delivery of customers' orders and to minimise stock levels (which tie up valuable cash resources). The achievement of these objectives may involve contributions from several different information systems. The list may include:

- stock control - records stock movements and controls stock levels;
- purchasing - responsible for the ordering of new supplies from suppliers;
- sales order processing - receives customers' orders and initiates the process of order fulfilment;
- purchase ledger - the accounting record of amounts owed and paid to suppliers of stock;
- invoicing - the production of invoices requesting payment from customers for goods supplied;
- sales ledger - the accounting record of amounts owing by and received from customers for goods supplied.

These and other applications within a business are interconnected by the information which flows between them. Such connections can be illustrated with the use of data flow diagrams (DFD - see Chapter 17).

Establishing Priorities for Computerisation

Although a data flow diagram may indicate the mutual involvement of several separate applications, it is not generally advisable or even practicable to attempt the computerisation of more than one or two applications at the same time. In any case, it is likely that some applications make a greater contribution to the achievement of the required business objectives than do the others. Thus, the applications which are going to bring greatest benefit to the business should be computerised first.

Establishing Individual System Objectives

Before any single application can be computerised, it is necessary to establish its objectives clearly because users may have become so used to its procedures that they no longer question their purpose. It is self-evident that, before any informed judgements can be made on the design of a system, the objectives of the relevant application must first be clearly understood. The following example for stock control serves to illustrate the definition of such objectives.

Example: objectives of a typical stock control system
- to maintain levels of stock which will be sufficient to meet customer orders promptly;

- to provide a mechanism which removes the need for excessively high safety margins of stock to cover customer orders. This is usually effected by setting minimum stock levels which the computer can use to report variations below these levels;
- to provide automatic re-ordering of stock items which fall below minimum levels;
- to provide management with up-to-date information on stock levels and values of stocks held.

The Feasibility Report

The Feasibility Report should contain the following sections:

Terms of Reference

These should set out the original purpose of the study, as agreed by management and detail the business objectives to be achieved, for example:

- improvement of customer service, so that orders are delivered in 24 hours;
- the provision of more up-to-date management information on current stock levels and projected customer demand;
- a tighter control of the business's cash resources, primarily through better stock management.

Applications Considered for Computerisation

The applications which may assist the achievement of the business objectives set out in the Terms of Reference are listed, for example:

- stock control;
- purchasing;
- sales order processing;
- invoicing;
- accounts.

System Investigations

For each application under consideration there should be:

- a description of the existing system;
- an assessment of its good and bad points. For example, the sales order processing system may be slow to process customer orders and this results in poor delivery times, which in turn causes customers to take away their business;
- the costs of the existing system. For example, apart from the cost of staffing, an estimate has to be made of the cost of lost business, which could be avoided with an improved system.

Envisaged System Requirements

This section should detail, in general terms, those aspects of each application which need to be improved and a broad outline of how each system may operate following computerisation. Of course, it is still possible that not all applications will benefit from computerisation and can be improved by other methods.

Costs of Development and Implementation

These will include both *capital* costs and *revenue* or running costs. Capital costs are likely to be incurred for the following:

- computer hardware;
- systems software and software packages ('off-the-shelf' or 'tailor-made');
- installation charges for hardware and software;
- staff training.

Revenue costs include those for the maintenance and insurance of the system. In addition, computer specialists may need to be employed.

Time Scale for Implementation

This will depend on the scale of the operation, the type of application and whether packaged software is to be used.

Expected Benefits

These are more difficult to quantify than the costs but may include, for example:

- estimated savings in capital expenditure on typewriters and photocopiers;
- more efficient stock management, allowing customer service to be maintained whilst keeping stock levels lower. This releases valuable cash resources and reduces possible interest charges on borrowed capital;
- expansion in business turnover, without the need for extra staff. Overtime requirements may also be reduced.

Other Considerations

The staff have to support any development for it to be successful and this usually means consultation at an early stage in the feasibility study and the provision of a proper staff training programme. Customers must also be considered. For example, when a customer receives a computer-produced invoice it should be as easy to understand as the type it replaced. If the feasibility study concludes that computerisation is worthwhile (according to the criteria set out in the report) then more detailed investigation and design can be carried out.

Chapter 13
Systems Analysis and Design

Introduction

If the feasibility report supports a computerisation project, then a more detailed investigation of each candidate system begins. The facts gathered about each system will be analysed for their bearing on the design and implementation of a computerised version. The objectives of the analysis are to gain a thorough knowledge of the current way of working and to establish, in a fair amount of detail, the way in which a new system will operate. It is extremely important that the replacement system does not simply duplicate existing procedures. The design should, as far as possible, ignore existing departmental structures, which may inhibit the introduction of different and improved procedures. For example, it may be that customer credit limits are fixed by the Accounts Department and that Sales staff have to refer to the Accounts Department before accepting a customer order. A new system may allow Sales staff to access credit limits directly without reference to the Accounts Department. This method could be used in most cases and the computer could indicate any customer accounts which needed to be specially referred to the Accounts staff.

The aim of the investigation and design process is to produce a *system specification*.

Fact-finding Methods

There are five main methods which can be used to gather facts about a system:

- interviewing;
- questionnaires;
- examination of records and procedure manuals;
- examination of documents;
- observation.

Each method has its own particular advantages and disadvantages. The method(s) chosen will depend on the specific circumstances surrounding the investigation. These may concern, for example, the size of the business, the number of staff employed, their location and distribution.

Interviewing

This method has much to recommend it, in that the facts can be gathered directly from the person or persons who have experience of the system under investigation. On the other hand, a business with a number of geographically distributed branches makes the process of extensive interviewing expensive and time-consuming. Further, interviewing skills need to be acquired if the process is to be effective. The interviewer needs to know how to gain the confidence of the interviewee and ensure that the information which is given is of value in the design of the new system. Questions need to be phrased unambiguously so that the interviewee supplies the required information . A checklist of points can help to ensure that all relevant questions are asked. Of course, the interview may need to 'stray' from the points in the checklist, if it becomes apparent that the interviewee is able to provide relevant information not previously considered. For example, clerical procedures may be designed quite satisfactorily but may be made less effective because of personality conflicts between staff. Such tensions may be revealed only through personal interview.

The interviewer also needs to detect any unsatisfactory responses to questions and possibly use alternative methods to glean the required information. Some possible unsatisfactory responses are given below:

- refusal to answer. Such refusal may indicate, for example, that set procedures are not being followed and that the member of staff does not wish to be 'incriminated';
- answer with irrelevant information. It may be that the question is ambiguous and has to be re-phrased in order to elicit the required information;
- answer with insufficient information. If a system is to be designed which covers all foreseeable user requirements and operational circumstances, it is important that the analyst has all relevant information;
- inaccurate answer. The interviewer may or may not be aware that an inaccurate answer has been given but it is important that other sources of information are used to cross-check answers.

Questionnaires

Questionnaires are useful when only a small amount of information is required from a large number of people. To provide accurate responses, questions need to be unambiguous and precise. The questionnaire has a number of advantages over the interview:

- each respondent is asked exactly the same questions, so responses can be analysed according to the pre-defined categories of information;
- the lack of personal contact allows the respondent to feel completely at ease when providing information, particularly if responses are to be anonymous;
- questionnaires are particularly suited to the gathering of factual information, for example, the number of customer orders received in one week;
- it is cheap, particularly if users are scattered over a wide geographical area.

A number of potential disadvantages attach to the use of questionnaires.

- Questions have to be simple and their meaning completely unambiguous to the respondents;
- If the responses indicate that the wrong questions were asked, or that they were phrased badly, it may be difficult to clarify the information, particularly if the respondents were anonymous;
- Without direct observation it is difficult to obtain a realistic view of a system's operation. The questionnaire often provides only statistical information on, for example, volumes of sales transactions or customer enquiries.

Examination of Records and Procedure Manuals

If existing procedures are already well documented, then the procedure manuals can provide a ready-made source of information on the way procedures should be carried out. It is less likely, however, that procedures will be documented in the smaller organisation. In any event, it is important to realise that procedures detailed in manuals may not accord entirely with what happens. The examination of current records and the tracing of particular transactions can be a useful method of discovering what procedures are carried out.

Special purpose records which may involve, for example, the ticking of a box when an activity has been completed, can be used to analyse procedures which are causing delays or are not functioning efficiently. The use of *special purpose* records imposes extra burdens on staff who have to record procedures as they happen and the technique should be used only when strictly necessary.

Examination of Documents

It is important that the analyst examines all documents used in a system, to ensure that each:

- fulfils some purpose, that is, it records or transmits information which is used at some stage. Systems are subject to some inertia, for example, there may have been a 'one-off requirement to record and analyse the geographical distribution of customers over a single month and yet the summary document is still completed because no-one told the staff it was no longer necessary;
- is clear and satisfies its purpose. For example, a form may not indicate clearly the type of data to be entered under each heading. In any case, it may well require re-designing for any new system.

The documents, which should include, for example, source documents, report summaries, customer invoices and delivery notes, help to build a picture of the information flows which take place from input to output.

Observation

It is most important to observe a procedure in action, so that irregularities and exceptional procedures are noticed. Observation should always be carried out with tact and staff under observation should be made fully aware of its purpose, to avoid suspicions of 'snooping'.

The following list details some of the features of office procedures and conditions which may usefully be observed during the investigation:

- office layout. This may determine whether the positioning of desks, filing cabinets and other office equipment is convenient for staff and conducive to efficient working;
- work load. This should indicate whether the volume of documents awaiting processing is fairly constant or if there are peak periods of activity;
- delays. These could show that there are some procedures which are constantly behind schedule;
- methods of working. A trained observer can, through experience, recognise a slow, reasonable or quick pace of working and decide whether the method of working is efficient. It is important that such observations should be followed up by an interview to obtain the co-operation of the person under observation;
- office conditions. These should be examined. Poor ventilation, inadequate or excessive temperatures or poor lighting can adversely affect staff efficiency.

Often the observation will be carried out in an informal way. It may be useful, sometimes, to work at a user's desk and observe directly the way that, for example, customer orders are processed. It is important to realise that a user may 'put on a performance' while under observation and that this reduces the value of the information gathered.

Documenting the Results of Analysis

A number of standard approaches, apart from narrative description, can be used to document the results of the system analysis, including:

- information and data flow diagrams (Chapters 9 and 17, respectively);
- decision tables;
- organisation charts;
- system flowcharts.

It is beyond the scope of this text to make a detailed examination of these standards but their use is illustrated in the following section which examines the categories of information needed to be gathered and recorded during the investigation.

Categories of System Information

The major categories of information which need to be gathered involve:

- functional relationships and data flows;
- personnel and jobs;
- inputs;
- processes;
- outputs;
- storage.

The following sections examine each of these categories, which are relevant to both the analysis and design stages. The analysis of the present system naturally involves some of the design stages. In other words, while the analyst is investigating the current system, he or she is considering the design of the new system. The results of the investigation and design processes are recorded in specifications regarding, primarily, input, output and process.

Functional Relationships and Information Flows

An organisation has a number of functional areas; typical business functions inlcude Sales, Accounts, Stock Control and Purchasing. However, the computerisation of a system in one functional area cannot be carried out without considering its effects on the rest of the business. Information systems within a business interact with and affect one another. A business, as an entity, also interacts with and is influenced by individuals and organisations in the surrounding 'environment' and the organisation's individual information systems should be co-ordinated to allow the achievement of overall objectives.

The relationships between individual functional areas can be illustrated with the use of an information flow diagram (see Chapter 9)

Personnel and Jobs

It is possible to design a computerised system without involving staff, but such a system is likely to be less successful, partly because users can provide valuable insights into the practical aspects of system operation and partly because they will feel less motivated if they have had little or no influence on the final design. A formal organisation chart can be used to gain an overall picture of staff relationships and responsibilities (an example is shown in Figure 13.1), but it should be remembered that designated and actual job responsibilities can differ radically. For example, it may turn out that a junior sales clerk is carrying out the checking of orders, which should be the responsibility of the sales supervisor.

Thus, it may be necessary for the analyst to draw an alternative informal organisation chart to show the actual working relationships of staff. Apart from identifying working relationships between staff, it is useful to draw up brief job descriptions so that consultation on individual system procedures can take place with the appropriate staff. For example, a job description for a sales clerk may include the following activities:

- completion of standard order forms;
- checking stock availability;
- notification of orders to Accounts.

Therefore, although the sales departmental manager may have knowledge of such procedures, the sales clerk will have practical experience of their operation and should be consulted.

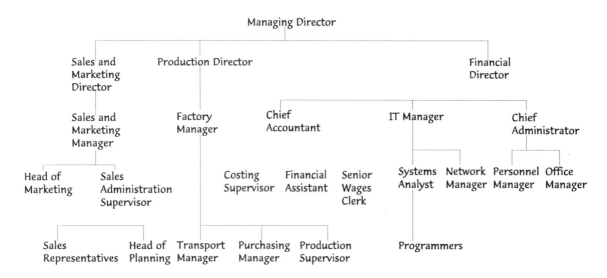

Figure 13.1. *Organisation chart*

System Inputs

A number of details concerning the data inputs to a system need to be established, including the:

- *source* of the data. It may, for example, originate from a customer, a supplier, or another department in the organisation;
- *form* of the data. The data may arrive, for example, by telephone, letter, electronically (e-mail or fax) or a standard form such as an order form or supplier's invoice;
- *volume* of data and its *frequency*. For example, the number of orders received each day or week;
- *contents* of the data. For example, the individual items of data which appear on a supplier's invoice.

Such information allows the analyst to make recommendations on the most appropriate methods of computer input. The design of appropriate input methods also has to take account of several tasks involved with the collection and entry of data to a system:

- recording of data. For example, the completion of a customer order form following receipt of a customer order by telephone;
- transmission of the data for processing. For example, the order details may need to be transferred to another department or branch of the business for encoding and computer processing or they may be keyed in directly at the point of collection;
- checking of data for obvious errors and omissions. It may be, for example, that a customer order has no quantities entered;

- encoding of data into machine-readable form. Verification procedures need to be designed to prevent transcription errors when data is encoded onto a computer storage medium for processing;
- validation of data by computer. Data is checked by a data validation program against set limits of validity. For example, account numbers may have to fall between a particular range of values.

Thus, decisions need to be made concerning:

- data collection procedures;
- methods for the transmission of data to the place of processing;
- data entry, data verification and data validation procedures.

Data Collection

The designer needs to be aware of the available input technologies. These can be divided into two categories, keyboard entry, and data capture technologies such as bar code reading, document scanning and optical mark reading (OMR), which allow direct input to the computer.

- Keyboard entry. This is the most common method of input and requires the transcription of data from source documents. These can be designed to minimise the possibility of transcription errors at the data collection stage.
- Direct input. Bar codes are pre-encoded and are thus immune from errors of transcription (if the bar code is correct in the first place). Optical mark reading requires that pencil marks are used to indicate particular values from a limited set on a pre-designed form. Although no keyboard entry is required, mistakes may be made by the originator of the document and good design is therefore important. Using an optical scanner (Chapter 5) and character recognition software, text can be entered into a word processor, without the need for keyboard entry (except to make corrections to the document). Voice input is also a practical option where a limited range of values needs to be entered.

Data Transmission

It may be that no data transmission is necessary because the data is processed at the point of collection. For example, customer orders may be recorded on order forms at the sales desk and then taken into the next room for keying into the computer. Alternatively, the data may have to be transmitted some distance, perhaps to another floor of the building or to another building some miles away. A fundamental decision has to be made, whether to localise processing at the points of collection, or to use a central facility with data communications links from each location.

Data Entry

The data entry method chosen will depend on the data collection methods used and may involve keyboard transcription from source documents or data may be captured directly (see Data Collection). Where keyboard transcription is used, verification and validation procedures

(Chapter 14) are likely to be *interactive*; data entry operators have to respond to prompts on screen and make corrections whenever the system requires them. Most computer systems will be used for on-line processing, where transactions are processed immediately with master files at the data entry stage. Consequently, validation and verification have to be carried out immediately before the processing of each transaction.

On-screen Verification

At the end of each transaction entry, the operator is given the opportunity to scan the data on the screen and to re-enter any incorrect entries detected. This usually takes the form of a message at the bottom of the screen which is phrased in a way such as "Verify (yes or no)".

On-screen Validation

Character, data item and record checks, such as range and mode checks, can be made each time the < enter > key is pressed during data entry. For example, the screen may prompt for the entry of an account number, which must be 6 digits long and be within the range 000001 to 500000. Any entry which does not conform to these parameters is erased and the prompt re-displayed for another attempt. Appropriate screen dialogue to allow the data entry operator to enter into a 'conversation' with the computer is a crucial part of the interface design process.

Batch Data Entry

The type of keyboard transcription used will be affected by the type of input data. Where, for example, files need to be updated weekly, transaction data may be batched and entered onto magnetic disk. Processing is carried out later in one update run.

System Processes

All the clerical and machine-assisted processes, which are necessary to achieve the desired output from the given inputs, need to be identified. This will allow the systems analyst to determine the role of the computer in the new system, the programs necessary to take over the processing stages and the changes needed to clerical procedures, before and after computer processing. There are many instances when the processing requires not only the input data but also data retrieved from files. For example, to generate a customer invoice requires:

- input data concerning commodity codes and quantities ordered;
- data from the stock master file concerning prices of items ordered by reference to the input commodity codes;
- customer details from the customer master file.

The above processes can be completely computerised but other processes may require human intervention. For example, before a customer order is processed, the customer's credit status may need to be checked and referred to a supervisor before authorisation.

Non-Standard Procedures

Most processes will follow standards suitable for their particular circumstances. For example, before an order is processed, stock items ordered are checked for availability. It is important, however, that the investigation identifies and notes any non-standard procedures. For example, what procedure is followed when there is an insufficient quantity of an ordered item to fulfil completely a customer order? It may be that some customers will take part-orders, whilst others require the full quantity of an item or none at all. If non-standard procedures are needed, it is important to know their complexity, how often they are used and what extra information is required. Ideally, a system should be designed to cope with all possible circumstances, but cost sometimes forces a compromise. If cost prohibits the inclusion of certain system features, for example, the ability to deal with part-orders, then it is important that the business is aware of such limitations so that it can modify its business objectives.

Document Flow

Most processes involve the use of documents to allow the transmission of information from one stage to another. *System flowcharts* can be used to model the movement and interaction of documents and the data they record, as well as the processes involved, as they pass from one functional area or department of the business to another. So that the involvement of each section, department or personnel grouping in the processes can be identified, the system flowchart is divided into columns representing these divisions of responsibility.

A system flowchart may use a range of standard symbols which are illustrated in Figure 13.2.

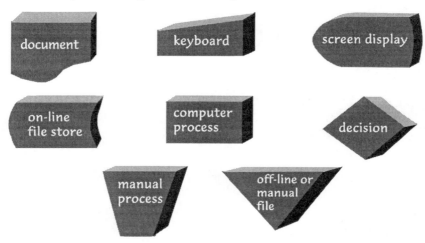

Figure 13.2. *System flowchart symbols*

A number of standards exist for the drawing of system flowcharts. The range of symbols used depends on which stage of the investigation and design process has been reached. For example, in the early stages of investigation of an existing manual system, there will be no representation of computer methods of input, processing, output or storage. At a later stage, when computer methods are being considered, it will be necessary to use suitable symbols in the flowchart. Figures 13.3, 13.4 and 13.5 show example system flowcharts. Figure 13.3

illustrates a manually operated order processing and invoicing system. Figure 13.5 represents the computerised aspects of a similar system; it does not detail procedures needed to prepare, for example, the data for input or the distribution of output. A computerised system must have the necessary clerical procedures to support it. Figure 13.4 represents a batch processing update of a stock master file. Notice the sorting and validation stages which are essential to this type of system (see Chapter 14).

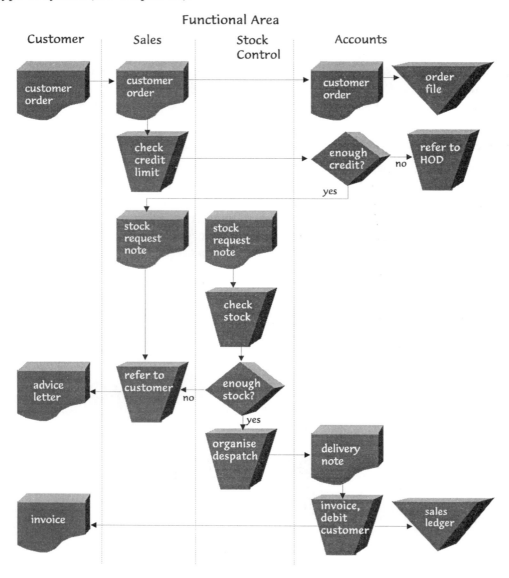

Figure 13.3. *Flowchart of manual order processing and invoicing system*

Decisions

Most business systems require alternative actions to be taken dependent upon some variable condition or circumstance. For example, 15 per cent customer discount may be allowed if the invoiced amount is paid within, say, 14 days of the invoice date, after which time all discount is lost. Figure 13.3 includes two decision symbols, one which poses the question "enough credit?" and the other "enough stock?"; the system must be able to handle the situations which arise when, for example, there is not enough stock to fulfil an order. Note that the decision box only allows two paths, one for "yes" and the other for "no". So that computerised and non-computerised processes can be properly designed, the investigation must identify all: *decisions* made during system operation; *conditions* and circumstances which lead to alternative decisions; *actions* to be taken following a decision. Some decisions and consequent actions will need to be documented for clerical procedure guidelines. Others, which involve computer processing, will form part of program specifications used in program writing or as bases for choosing packaged software.

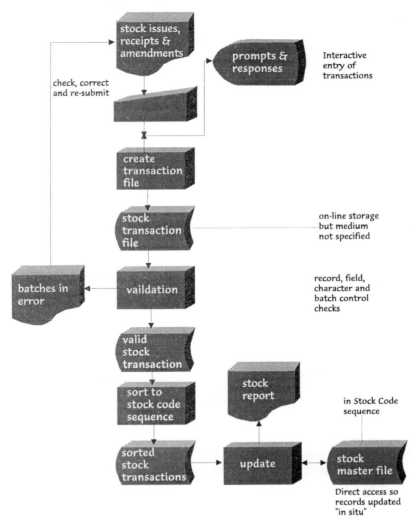

Figure 13.4. *System flowchart - batch processing, stock file update*

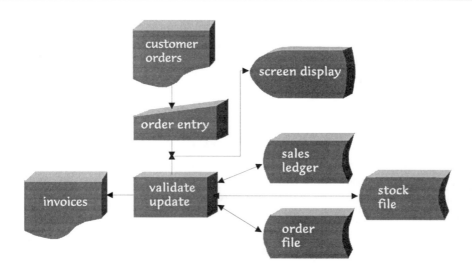

Figure 13.5. *System flowchart - on-line order processing and invoicing*

System Outputs

Output design requires identification of the:

- data items required as output. Some may be revealed in the existing system, whilst others may be requested by users as being desirable in any new system;
- form of the output, for example, whether or not printed copy is required;
- volume of data with each output and the frequency of the output. This information assists decisions on the type and number of output devices required.

Using the above information, the following tasks can be carried out:

- selection of an appropriate output device to display or communicate the outputs. Available technologies are described in Chapter 5.
- designing screen and document layouts.

System Storage (Files)

The storage of historical and current information is a vital part of any business system. For example, to produce a payslip requires not only transient input data, concerning hours worked and sickness days. Also needed are the relevant figures for rate of pay, tax code, deduction of tax and superannuation to date. These are held in the payroll *master file* (Chapter 3) stored on magnetic disk or tape. Information on the contents of files is gathered from existing manual files. Users should be consulted about their output requirements. If packaged software is to be used then the contents of files will be dictated by the package, in which case some data item types may be surplus to requirements, whilst others which are required may not be available.

File Contents

Each file consists of a number of logical records, each of which has a number of associated data items. For example, each stock record in a stock master file may include:

- stock code
- description
- unit price
- minimum stock level
- re-order quantity
- quantity in stock

File Sequence or Organisation

This concerns the logical ordering of records within a file. Organisation methods are described in Chapter 3, but a number of possibilities and considerations are given below:

- The file can be organised in a particular sequence so that the output is readily available in that order. For example, it may be convenient for a file of clients paying annual subscriptions for a magazine to be stored in date order rather than client number order;
- The input may be presented in a particular order and sequencing the file in the same order will save re-sorting the input data;
- File access requirements may be entirely random so no particular sequence is needed.

File Access Methods

The output requirements of users and the data requirements of processes will determine the choice of access method, of which there are three:

- *serial*. The complete file is accessed according to its physical sequence. This is of use only when a transaction file is created immediately before it is sorted and processed against the relevant master file.
- *sequential*. The complete file is processed according to its logical sequence. Magnetic disk allows direct access to individual records, even if they are not physically next to one another. Thus, for example, a stock file organised in stock number order may be accessed in that sequence, even though records may be physically distributed all over the disk.
- *random*. Records are accessed in no particular sequence. Both indexed sequential and randomly organised files allow random access. Random access is appropriate where access requirements are rarely in any sequence and rapid system response is needed.

Relational Database Management Systems (DBMS)

An increasingly popular alternative to traditional file processing systems is to construct databases controlled by a relational DBMS. The design process requires that data is analysed according to subject area, for example, raw materials or staffing, rather than by department or functional area. Relational database systems are described in Chapter 17.

Choice of Storage Device

All computer systems provide direct access storage, generally in the form of magnetic disk. Even where random access files are not needed, there is little choice to be made, except in terms of capacity and speed of access. A full description of the various storage technologies is given in Chapters 5 and 6.

Chapter 14

Data Control and Security

Introduction

Computerised systems present particular problems for the control of data entering the system, because for much of the time, it is not in human-readable form. Even when it is stored, the data remains invisible until it is printed out or displayed on a screen. If proper system controls are not used, inaccurate data may reach master files, or unauthorised changes to data may be made, resulting in decision-making based on incorrect information. System controls can be divided into three main categories, according to the purposes they serve:

- data control;
- auditing;
- data security.

To appreciate the significance of the various controls, you need to be familiar with the *data processing cycle*, which is described in the chapter of that title.

Data Control

Controls should be exerted over:

- input;
- file processing;
- output.

Controls can be implemented by:

- clerical procedures;
- software procedures.

It is only through the combined application of both clerical and software controls that errors can be minimised. Their entire exclusion can never be guaranteed.

Input Controls

Before describing the types of control, it is necessary to outline the activities which may be involved in the collection and input of data. Depending on the application, these may include the following.

- Source document preparation. To ensure standardisation of practice and to facilitate checking, data collected for input, for example, customer orders, are clerically transcribed onto specially designed source documents.

- Data transmission. If the computer centre is geographically remote from the collection point, data is transmitted through a telecommunications link.

- Data encoding and verification (see Verification). This involves the transcription, usually through a keyboard device, of the data onto a storage medium such as magnetic tape or disk. A process of machine verification, accompanied by a repeated keying operation, assists the checking of keying accuracy.

- Data input and validation. Data validation is a computer controlled process which checks data for its validity, according to certain pre-defined parameters, so it must first be input to the computer. The topic of validation is examined in more detail later.

- Sorting. In order to improve the efficiency of processing, input data is sorted into a sequence determined by the primary key of each record in the relevant master file (see Computer Files). This is always necessary for efficient sequential processing, but direct access files allow records to be processed by transactions "as they come".

Transcription of data from one medium to another, for example, from telephone notepad to customer order form, or from *source document* (for example, an order form or requisition) to magnetic disk, provides the greatest opportunity for error. A number of strategies can be adopted to minimise input errors, including:

- minimising transcription. This may involve the use of automated input methods, such as bar code reading and *turnaround* documents. These are forms which the information system produces as output and which can at a later date be returned to the system as input. For instance, a mail order book club might periodically produce a combined invoice and statement for its customers and, at the same time, attach an order form as shown in Figure 14.1. The customer completes the order form by entering the catalogue codes in the boxes provided and then returns the document together with the amount due in an addressed envelope provided by the club. Notice that the club member needs only to enter the catalogue code numbers for his or her book selections; even the membership number has been printed on the order form to prevent members from either forgetting about it or getting it wrong.

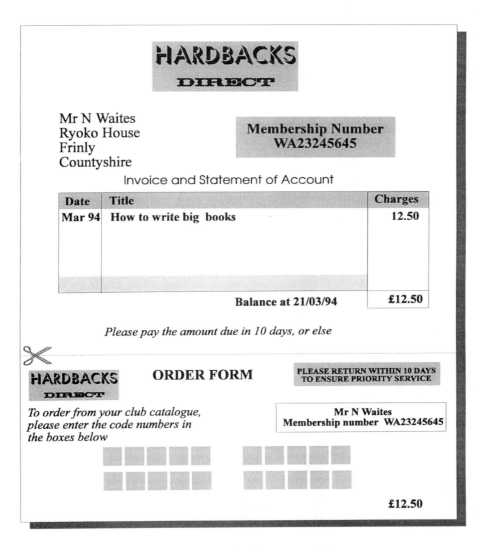

Figure 14.1. *An example of a turnaround document*

- designing data collection and input documents in ways which encourage accurate completion. The turnaround document in Figure 14.1 is a good example.

- using clerical checking procedures such as the re-calculation of totals or the visual comparison of document entries with the original sources of information;

- using codes of a restricted format, for example, customer account numbers consisting of two alphabetic characters, followed by six digits. Such formatted codes can easily be checked for validity;

- employing batch methods of input which allow the accumulation and checking of batch control totals, both by clerical and computerised methods (see Data Control in Batch Processing;

- using screen *verification* (visual checking of input on screen) before input data is processed and applied to computer files.

- checking input data with the use of batch or interactive screen validation (see Validation) techniques;

- ensuring that staff are well trained and that clerical procedure manuals are available for newly trained staff;

- controlling access to input documents. This is particularly important where documents are used for sensitive applications such as payroll. For example, input documents for changing pay rates may be available only to the Personnel Manager.

Verification

Figure 14.2 illustrates the verification process. When information is gathered using source documents such as forms which cannot be read directly by the computer, it needs to be converted into a form which can be processed. A common method of performing this task is by means of *key-to-storage* devices such as *key-to tape* or *key-to-disk*.

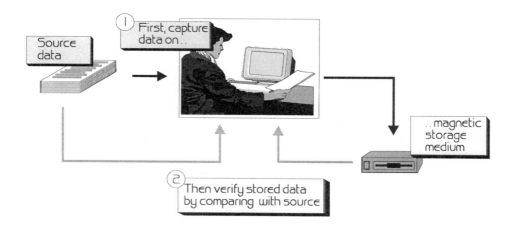

Figure 14.2. *Verifying source data*

The data are entered using a workstation consisting of a keyboard and monitor. As data are typed in they are displayed on the screen and stored on the magnetic storage medium (tape or disk). This process is error prone - it is a very easy matter for workstation operators to omit characters or type them in the wrong order - so, before the data are processed by the computer, it is usual to verify them by re-typing the data using the same source documents but with the key-to-storage device in *verify mode*. In this mode, the data is typed in a second time and compared with that typed in originally, and any differences are signalled to the operator who is then able to make the appropriate corrections.

Validation

This process is carried out after the data has been encoded onto an input medium and involves a *data vet* or *validation program*. Its purpose is to check that data falls within certain parameters defined by the systems analyst. A judgement as to whether data is valid is made possible by the validation program, but it cannot ensure complete accuracy. This can only be achieved through the use of all the clerical and computer controls built into the system at the design stage. The difference between validity and accuracy can be illustrated with a simple example. A company has established a Personnel file and each record contains a field for the Job Grade. The permitted values are A, B, C, or D. An entry in a record may be *valid* and accepted by the system if it is one of these characters, but it may not be the *correct* grade for the individual worker concerned. Whether a grade is correct can only be established by clerical checks or by reference to other files. During systems design, therefore, *data definitions* should be established which place limits on what constitutes valid data. Using these data definitions, a range of software validation checks can be carried out. Some typical validation checks are outlined below.

- Size. The number of characters in a data item value is checked; for example, a stock code may consist of 8 characters only;

- Range. Data must lie within maximum and minimum values. For example, customer account numbers may be restricted within the values 00001 to 10000;

- Format checks. Data must conform to a specified format. Thus, a stock code designated as having 2 alphabetic characters, followed by 4 numeric digits must always be entered this way. Any other arrangement is rejected;

- Consistency. Data items which are related in some way can be checked for the consistency of their relationship. For example, in a personnel file, any employee aged 25 years or over must be contributing to the company superannuation scheme. Conversely, employees under the age of 25 years cannot be members of the superannuation scheme. Any record which does not show such consistency indicates that either the age or the superannuation entry is incorrect;

- Check digit. An extra digit calculated on, for example, an account number, can be used as a self-checking device. When the number is input to the computer, the validation program carries out a calculation similar to that used to generate the check digit originally and thus checks its validity. This kind of check will highlight transcription errors where two or more digits have been transposed or put in the wrong order. One of the commonest methods of producing a check digit is the modulus 11 algorithm. The following example serves to illustrate its operation.

Consider a stock code consisting of six digits, for example 462137.

The check digit is calculated as follows:

1. Each digit of the stock code is multiplied by its own *weight*. Each digit has a weight relative to its position, assuming the presence of a check digit in the rightmost position. Beginning from the check digit (x) position the digits are weighted 1, 2, 3, 4, 5, 6 and 7 respectively as shown in Table 14.1.

Stock Code	4	6	2	1	3	7	(x)
Multiplied by Weight	7	6	5	4	3	2	(1)
Product	28	36	10	4	9	14	

Table 14.1

2. The products are totalled. In this example, the sum produces 101.
3. Divide the sum by modulus 11. This produces 9, remainder 2.
4. The check digit is produced by subtracting the remainder 2 from 11, giving 9.

Whenever, a code is entered with the relevant check digit, the validation software carries out the same algorithm, including the check digit in the calculation. Provided that the third stage produces a remainder of zero the code is accepted as valid. This is proved in Table 14.2, using the same example as above.

Stock Code	4	6	2	1	3	7	9
Multiplied by Weight	7	6	5	4	3	2	1
Product	28	36	10	4	9	14	9

Table 14.2

The sum of the products in Table 14.2 is 110, which when divided by 11, gives 10, remainder 0. Therefore, the number is valid.

If some of the digits are *transposed* (swapped around) the check digit is no longer applicable to the code and is rejected by the validation program because the results of the algorithm will not leave a remainder of zero. This is shown in Table 14.3.

The sum of the products in Table 14.3 equals 111, which when divided by 11, gives 10, remainder 0. The number is, therefore, invalid.

Stock Code	6	4	1	2	3	7	9
Multiplied by Weight	7	6	5	4	3	2	1
Product	42	24	5	8	9	14	9

Table 14.3

File Processing Controls

Once validated data has entered the computer system, checks have to be made to ensure that it is:

- applied to the correct files;
- consistent with the filed data.

Header Records

Files can have header records which contain function, for example, Sales Ledger, version number and *purge date*. The purge date indicates the date after which the file is no longer required and can be overwritten. Thus, a file with a purge date after the current date should not be overwritten. Such details can be checked by the application program, to ensure that the correct file is used and that a current file is not accidentally overwritten.

File Validation Checks

Some validation checks can be made only after data input when reference can be made to the relevant master file data. Such checks include:

- new records. When a new record is to be added to a master file, a check can be made to ensure that a record does not already use the record key entered;
- deleted records. It may be that a transaction is entered, for which there is no longer a matching master record. For example, a customer may order a product which is no longer supplied;
- data consistency checks. A check is made that the transaction values are consistent with the values held on the master record which is to be updated. For instance, an entry to indicate maternity leave would obviously be inconsistent with a record for a male employee.

Data Integrity

The printing of all master file changes allows the user department and auditors to check that all such changes are authorised and consistent with transaction documents. All data used by applications for *reference* purposes should be printed periodically. Price lists, for example, may be held as permanent data on master files, or in table form within computer programs.

Output Controls

It might reasonably be supposed that input and file processing controls are sufficient to ensure accurate output. Nevertheless, a number of simple controls at the output stage can help to ensure that it is complete and is distributed to the relevant users on time. They include:

- the comparison of filed control totals with run control totals. For example, when an entire sequential file is processed, the computer counts all records processed and compares the total with a stored record total held in a *trailer record* at the end of the file;

- the reconciliation of control totals specific to the application with totals obtained from a related application. For example, the total sales transactions posted to the Sales Ledger in one day should agree with the total sales transactions recorded in the Sales Day book for that day;

- the following of set procedures for the treatment of error reports;

- the proper checking and re-submission of rejected transactions.

Data Control in Batch Processing

Batch processing involves the processing of batches of input data at regular intervals. The data is generally of identical type. Examples include customer orders or payroll details. Although generally associated with large organisations using mainframe or minicomputer systems, the technique is equally applicable to microcomputer-based systems. The controls used combine both clerical and software methods and are briefly as described below.

Batch Totals - Clerical Preparation

Batch totals allow the conciliation of clerically-prepared totals for a batch of transactions, with comparable computer-produced totals. Following the arrangement of source documents into batches, totals are calculated on add-listing machines for each value it is required to control. On an order form, for example, quantities and prices may be separately totalled to provide separate control totals. Totals may also be produced for each account number or item code, simply for purposes of control, although otherwise they are meaningless. For this reason, such totals are called "hash" or "nonsense" totals.

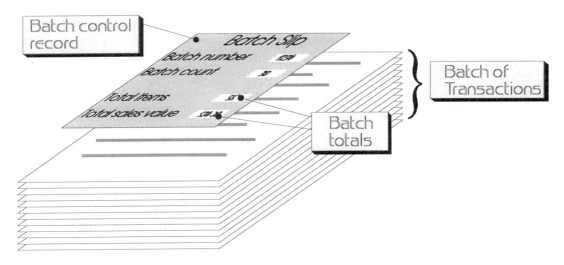

Figure 14.3. *A batch of transactions with a batch control record*

The totals are recorded on a *batch control record* (see Figure 14.3) attached to the batch, together with a value for the number of documents in the batch and a batch serial number. The batch serial number is kept in a register held by the originating department so that missing or delayed batches can be traced.

Batch Totals - Software Checking

The details from each batch control record are encoded, with each batch of transactions, onto the storage medium. The resulting *transaction file* thus consists of a series of transactions, with each batch being preceded by the relevant batch totals. A *validation program* then reads the transaction file from beginning to end, accumulating its own comparable batch totals for each batch as it proceeds. At the end of each batch, the validation program checks its accumulated totals with the clerically-prepared totals and reports any which are in error. Rejected batches and associated batch totals must be re-checked and corrected where necessary, before re-submission. The corrections should be carried out by the originating user department. Where volumes of input are not particularly large, involving say, two staff for an hour each day, a modified version of the full scale batch processing method may be used. Thus, when batch totals do not agree, only erroneous transactions are re-submitted. A validation program should also check individual data items against pre-defined limits. Such validation can be carried out as part of the batch processing system described above, or *interactively* (through screen/keyboard dialogue between the computer and the data entry operator) as data is entered.

Auditing

There are two types of auditing, *external* and *internal*. In its narrowest sense, the purpose of internal auditing is to minimise the incidence of accidental or fraudulent errors in financial accounting systems. A wider definition may extend internal auditing beyond the checking of financial accounting systems to include the monitoring of non-financial operations, such as production control, for operational efficiency. For the purposes of simplicity, this text will assume use of the first definition. Whereas data controls are concerned with the checking of entries as they occur, internal auditing makes additional, physical checks on the entries after they have been made. It is "internal" in the sense that it is performed under the direction of the business itself. There is no legal requirement for internal auditing but many businesses without specialist auditing staff make use of external auditors to ensure that no fraudulent or accidental errors have entered the system. The duty of auditors is to see that all transactions are entered, that there are no duplicate entries, that arithmetic is correct (either manual or computerised), and that proper documents for all recorded transactions exist. Such auditing is application-based, so it is advisable that appropriate mechanisms to facilitate the process are built into each system at the design stage.

External auditing involves an examination of accounting records only, by an independent party, who is usually a professional auditor. The process is not concerned with the efficiency of a system, only the completeness and accuracy of its operation. External audits are a legal requirement to ensure that a business's accounting statements provide a true picture of its financial operations.

There are two main techniques available for computer system auditing. One technique involves the use of test data and the other of audit enquiry programs.

The Test Data Method

With this method, the auditor runs the target application with test data, the expected processing results of which are already known. In this way, the computation of, for example, payroll figures can be tested for accuracy in a variety of circumstances. The logical outputs of the program can also be verified. In fact, the method is similar to that used by systems designers prior to a system's implementation. The test data may be recorded on a batch of source documents, in which case, the input will test not only the application's computerised processing and controls, but also the suitability of the source document design for input purposes. The auditing process may also include the testing of batch preparation and input data verification procedures. Software validation checks should be subjected to testing with *normal* and *exceptional* data. Normal data includes the most general data which the software is designed to handle. Exceptional data includes any which the software is not designed to accept. The software should demonstrate that it can reject all such data and continue its normal operation. Test data runs may take one of the following forms.

Live Data Testing

The auditor selects examples of live data from the system which fulfil the conditions to be tested. The results are calculated manually and checked against the computer-produced outputs. It is essential that manual calculations are made, as a casual assessment of the accuracy of processing can often lead to errors being overlooked. A severe disadvantage of this approach is that the auditor may be unable to find examples of all conditions to be tested in the available live data. It is also quite possible that examples of exceptional or nonsensical data will not be found at the time of the audit and it is important that such conditions are tested. "Murphy's law" will probably ensure that such exceptional data appears the day after the audit. The testing can give only a "snapshot" of the system's performance which may be radically different on other occasions.

Historical Data Testing

Sampling of transactions which have already passed through the system is an important part of internal auditing. It is important that the original transaction documents are made available for inspection to allow the auditor to check their validity, authorisation and consistency with associated results. Results can be calculated manually and then compared with any printed results. If results were not printed at the time, then use may be made of a file dump utility to access the appropriate historic file.

Dummy Data Testing

With this method, the auditor constructs fictitious or dummy data which contains the conditions to be tested. To ensure that such test data is not applied to the application's operational files, it is also usual to set up dummy files, for example, customer or supplier files, specifically for audit purposes. If such data is used in an actual processing run, and the entries are not reversed out in time, there is a danger that the results will be taken as real by users. There are a number of apocryphal stories concerning lorries which delivered goods to non-existent addresses as a result of such fictitious entries. For this reason, it is always advisable to make use of specially created audit files or copies of the master files.

In summary, the test data method is useful for the audit of:

- data preparation procedures, such as the completion of batch controls;

- data verification and validation controls;

- an application's computational and logical processes.

A number of drawbacks and limitations of the test data method of auditing can also be identified.

- It provides only a snapshot view of the system at the time of the audit. On the other hand, it may be used repeatedly in order to cover a more extended period of assessment;

- It may involve the setting up of dummy files if fictitious data is to be used;

- If fictitious data is used, source documents and batch totals have to be prepared for data which is not of operational use to the business;

- The computer system has to be made available to the auditor for the period of the test. During this time it is not available for operational use.

Audit Enquiry Programs

These programs overcome many of the disadvantages inherent in the test data method and are an essential audit tool, particularly for external auditing which requires the examination of live data already processed. Audit enquiry programs vary in sophistication but generally provide facilities to:

- examine the contents of computer files;

- retrieve data from computer files;

- compare the contents of files. Thus, for example, two versions of identical files may be compared, to ensure that the structure has not been altered (perhaps to include an extra field or record type);

- produce formatted reports according to the auditor's requirements.

A major benefit to the auditor is that any data stored on computer file can be retrieved. Of course, many financial packages for small business systems update files "in situ", so that each updating transaction causes the overwriting of the relevant master record with new values. Thus, there may be circumstances when the results of processing individual transactions can be established only in terms of the cumulative effect of a group of transactions on a particular record. For example, during one day, a stock record may be updated by several transactions but the values held in the stock record at the end will not show their individual effects. However, provided that the source documents are retained or the transactions are logged onto a separate file, the auditor can still reconcile their expected effect on the master file with the actual values held there.

Audit Trails

An audit trail should allow the tracing of a transaction's history as it progresses from input through to output. Computerised systems present particular difficulties in that the trail disappears as it enters the computer system. The auditor may ignore the computer system and pick up the trail at the output stage (auditing around the computer). This has obvious limitations in that the auditor cannot trace a transaction which does not result in printed output. Although audit enquiry programs allow the auditor to examine the contents of files, not every transaction effect is recorded permanently on computer file. Audit trails have to be designed into the system such that intermediate stages of a transaction's progress are recorded for audit purposes.

Security

The controls used for data security have several main functions, which are the:

- prevention of data loss caused by software or procedural errors, or by physical hazards;

- protection of data from accidental or deliberate disclosure to unauthorised individuals or groups;

- protection of data from accidental or deliberate corruption or modification. This is known as the maintenance of *data integrity*;

- to protect the rights of individuals and organisations to restrict access to information which relates to them and is of a private nature, to those entitled or authorised to receive it. This is known as data privacy.

Security Against Data Loss

The loss of master files can bring extremely serious consequences for a business, so properly organised security procedures need to be employed. Evidence indicates that, among business organisations that have lost the major part of their information store, a large percentage subsequently fails. The main causes of data loss are as follows.

- Environmental hazards, such as fire, flood and other natural accidents.

- Mechanical problems. For example, a magnetic disk can be damaged by a faulty drive unit.

- Software errors resulting from program "bugs".

- Human error. For example, a wrong file may be loaded, or a disk mislaid or damaged.

- Malicious damage. It is not unknown for disgruntled staff to intentionally damage storage media, or to misuse programs at a terminal.

The standard solution to such problems is to take regular copies of master files and to store them in a separate, secure location. It is also necessary to maintain a record of transactions affecting a file since the last copy was taken, so that if necessary, they can be used to reconstruct the latest version of the file.

Magnetic Tape File Security

When a tape master file is updated by a tape transaction file the physical nature of the medium makes it necessary for a new tape file to be produced. As Figure 14.4 illustrates, the updating procedure provides a built-in security system referred to as the Grandparent, Parent and Son (generation) System.

In the first run, Master 1 is updated by the transactions file to produce Master File 2 as its son. Master File 1 is the parent. Should the son file be damaged and the data lost, it can be re-created from the parent master file and the relevant transactions. At the end of the second run, Master File 1 becomes the grandparent. Master File 2 becomes the parent and Master File 3, the child.

Each generation provides security for subsequent files. The number of generations used will depend on the policy of the organisation. Three generations are usually regarded as providing sufficient security and the oldest files are re-used by being overwritten as each cycle of generations is completed.

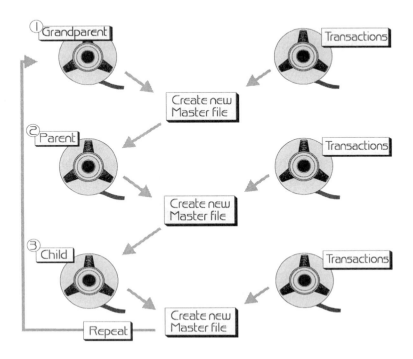

Figure 14.4. *Generation back-up system for sequential tape files*

Internal Header Labels

Internal header labels are designed to deal with two major areas of concern:

- It is important that the correct file is used in a file processing operation to ensure correct results. Thus, the subject of the file and the version must be identifiable. For example, it is no good producing monthly payslips using information from a payroll master file which is three months out of date.

- A tape file must be protected against accidental erasure. This may occur because tapes are re-usable and when a file is no longer required it can be overwritten by new information.

To ensure that the correct file is used for any particular job, a tape file usually has an internal header label. The label appears at the beginning of the tape and identifies it. The identifying information in the label is usually recorded under program control or by a data encoding device.

A tape header label usually contains the following items of information:

- File name, for example, "Payroll", "Stock", "Sales";

- Date created;

- Purge date - the date from which the tape is no longer required and may be re-used.

The label is checked by the program, before the file is processed, to ensure that the correct tape is being used.

File Protection Ring

A device called a file protection ring can be used to prevent accidental erasure. When tapes are stored off-line, the rings are not fitted. To write to a tape, the ring must first be fitted to the centre of the reel. A tape can be read by the computer whether or not a ring is fitted. The simple rule to remember is "no ring, no write".

Disk File Security

Security Backups

Disk files can be treated in the same way as tape files in that the updating procedure may produce a new master file leaving the original file intact. On the other hand, if the file is updated "in situ" (which in so doing overwrites the existing data), then it will be necessary to take regular back-up copies as processing proceeds. The frequency with which copies are taken will depend on the volume of transactions affecting the master file. If the latest version of the master file is corrupted or lost, then it can be re-created using the previous back-up together with the transaction data received since the back-up.

Transaction Logging

In an on-line system, transactions may enter the system from a number of terminals in different locations, thus making it difficult to re-enter transactions for the re-creation of a damaged master file. One solution is to log all the transactions onto a transaction file at the same time as the master file is updated. Thus, the re-creation process can be carried out without the need for keying in the transactions again.

The systems flowchart in Figure 14.5 illustrates this procedure.

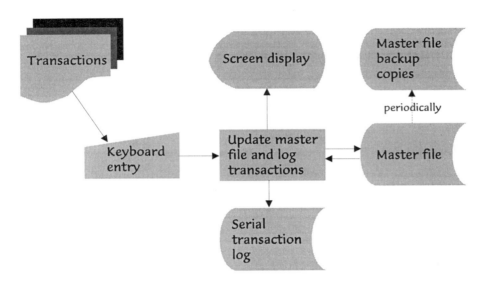

Figure 14.5. *Transaction logging and security back-up system*

Access Controls

Unauthorised access to a system may:

- provide vital information to competitors;

- result in the deliberate or accidental corruption of data; allow fraudulent changes to be made to data;

- result in loss of privacy for individuals or organisations.

To avoid such hazards an information system should be protected physically, by administrative procedures and software. To detect any unauthorised access or changes to the information system:

- users should require authorisation (with different levels of authority depending on the purpose of access);

- the computer should log all successful and attempted accesses;

- users should be identifiable and their identity authenticated;

- the files should be capable of being audited;

- the actions of programmers should be carefully controlled to prevent fraud through changes to software.

Physical Protection

These include the use of security staff, mechanical devices, such as locks and keys and electronic alarm/identification systems. Computer systems with terminals at remote sites present a weak link in any system and they must be properly protected and software plays an important protection role. Disk and tape libraries also need to be protected, otherwise it would be possible for a thief to take file media to another centre with compatible hardware and software.

A variety of methods may be used to identify and possibly authenticate a system user. They include the following.

- Identity Cards. Provided that they cannot be copied and have a photograph, they can be effective and cheap. The addition of a magnetic strip which contains encoded personal details including a personal identification number (PIN), which the holder has to key in, allows the user to be checked by machine. This method is used to allow access to service tills outside banks. Of course, the user of the card may not be the authorised holder, possession of the PIN being the only additional requirement; the following methods allow authentication as well as identification;

- Personal Physical Characteristics. Voice recognition or fingerprint comparison provide effective, if expensive, methods of identification and authentication.

Such methods are only effective if the supporting administrative procedures are properly adhered to.

Software Protection

Ideally, before a user is given access to a system, the log-in procedures should check for:

- authorisation;
- identification;
- authentication.

Authorisation is usually provided by an account code, which must be keyed in response to a computer prompt. Similar prompts may appear for a *user name* (identification) and a *password* (authentication).

Further control can be exerted with fixed terminal identifiers. whereby each terminal and its location is physically identifiable by the controlling computer, thus preventing access from additional unauthorised locations. Such controls can also be used to restrict particular terminals to particular forms and levels of access.

Password Controls

Access to files can be controlled at different levels by a series of passwords, which have to be keyed into the terminal in response to a series of questions displayed on the screen. For example, a clerk in a Personnel Department may be given authority to display information regarding an employee's career record but only the Personnel Manager is authorised to change the information held on file. Passwords should be carefully chosen, kept secure (memorised and not divulged) and changed frequently. Using people's names, for example, may allow entry by trial and error. Characters should not be echoed on screen as the password is entered.

Handshaking

This technique requires more than a simple password and may be used between two computers or a computer and a user, as a means of access control. In the latter case, the user would be given a pseudo-random number by the computer and the expected response would be a transform, of that random number. The transform may be to multiply the first and last digits of the number and add the product to a value equal to the day of the month plus 1. Provided the transform is kept secret, handshaking provides more security than simple passwords.

One-time passwords

With this method, the computer will only accept a password for one access occasion; subsequently, it will expect the user to provide a different password for each additional access, in a pre-defined sequence. Provided the password list and their expected sequence list are kept separate, then possession of one list only will not be of any assistance.

The number of attempts at logging-on should be controlled, so, for example, after three unsuccessful attempts, the user should be locked out and a record kept of the time and nature of the attempt.

Data Encryption

If data signals being transmitted along the telecommunication links are not properly protected, hackers can pick up the signals and display them on their own machines. To prevent such intrusion, data encryption methods are used to protect important financial, legal and other confidential information during transmission from one centre to another. Encryption scrambles the data to make it unintelligible during transmission. As the power and speed of computers has increased, so the breaking of codes has been made easier.

Code designers have produced methods of encryption which are currently unbreakable in any reasonable time period, even by the largest and most powerful computers available. An example of such an elaborate coding system is illustrated by the operation of the Electronic Funds Transfer (EFT) system. This is used by banks and other financial institutions to transfer vast sums of money so these transmissions are protected by the latest data encryption techniques. The Data Encryption Standard (DES) was approved by the American National Bureau of Standards in 1977, but as costs of powerful computers have fallen and come within the reach of criminal organisation, EFT makes use of the DES standard, plus additional encryption techniques.

Security to Maintain Data Integrity

Data integrity refers to the accuracy and consistency of the information stored and is thus covered by the security methods outlined above.

Security to Maintain Privacy of Data

The rights of individuals and organisations concerning their confidential records are similarly protected by the security controls outlined earlier. In addition, legislation by parliament (the Data Protection Act 1984) attempts to exert some control by requiring persons or organisations holding personal information on computer files to register with the Data Protection Registrar.

Computer Viruses

A computer virus is program code designed to create nuisance for users, or more seriously, to effect varying degrees of damage to files stored on magnetic media. Generally, the code:

- is introduced via portable media, such as floppy disks, particularly those storing "pirated" or "shareware" programs;

- transfers itself from the *infected* medium into the computer's main memory as soon as the medium is accessed;

- transfers from memory onto any integral storage device, such as a hard disk and commonly conceals itself in the boot sector (and sometimes in the partition sector where it is less likely to be traced), from where it can readily infect any other media placed on line in that computer system, whether it be stand-alone or networked. Naturally, any write-protected media cannot be infected.

Some virus codes are merely a nuisance, whilst others are developed specifically to destroy, or make inaccessible, whole filing systems. They pose a serious threat to any computer-based information system, but a number of measures can be taken to minimise the risk:

- only use proprietary software from a reliable source;

- write-protect disks being used for reading purposes only;

- use virus detection software, although this is only effective in respect of viruses using known storage and proliferation techniques;

- use diskless workstations on networks;

- control access to portable media and forbid employees to use their own media on the organisation's computer system.

Chapter 15

Privacy, Fraud and Copyright

Personal Privacy

Since the 1960s, there has been growing public concern about the threat that computers pose to personal privacy. Most countries, including the UK, have introduced legislation to safeguard the privacy of the individual. The Data Protection Act of 1984 was passed after a number of Government commissioned reports on the subject. The Younger Report of 1972 identified ten principles which were intended as guidelines to computer users in the private sector. A Government White Paper was published in 1975 in response to the Younger Report, but no legislation followed. The Lindop Report of 1978 was followed by a White Paper in 1982 and this resulted in the 1984 Data Protection Act. Apart from public pressure concerning the protection of personal privacy, a major incentive for the Government to introduce the Act stemmed from the need to ratify the Council of Europe Data Protection Convention. In the absence of this ratification, firms within the UK could have been considerably disadvantaged in trading terms through the Convention's provision to allow participating countries to refuse the transfer of personal information to non-participating countries. The principles detailed in the Younger Report formed the foundation for future reports and the Data Protection Act. They are listed below.

- Information should be regarded as being held for a specific purpose and should not be used, without appropriate authorisation, for other purposes.

- Access to information should be confined to those authorised to have it for the purpose for which it was supplied.

- The amount of information collected and held should be the minimum necessary for the achievement of a specified purpose.

- In computerised systems handling information for statistical purposes, adequate provision should be made in their design and programs for separating identities from the rest of the data.

- There should be arrangements whereby a subject could be told about the information held concerning him or her.

- The level of security to be achieved by a system should be specified in advance by the user and should include precautions against the deliberate abuse or misuse of information.

- A monitoring system should be provided to facilitate the detection of any violation of the security system.

- In the design of information systems, periods should be specified beyond which information should not be retained.

- Data held should be accurate. There should be machinery for the correction of inaccuracy and updating of information.

- Care should be taken in coding value judgements.

The White Paper which followed the Younger Report identified certain features of computerised information systems which could be a threat to personal privacy:

- The facility for storing vast quantities of data;

- The speed and power of computers make it possible for data to be retrieved quickly and easily from many access points;

- Data can be rapidly transferred between interconnected systems;

- Computers make it possible for data to be combined in ways which might otherwise not be practicable;

- Data is often transferred in a form not directly intelligible.

The 1984 Data Protection Act sets boundaries for the gathering and use of personal data. It requires all holders of computerised personal files to register with a Registrar appointed by the Home Secretary. The holder of personal data is required to keep to both the general terms of the Act, and to the specific purposes declared in the application for registration.

Terminology

The Act uses a number of terms that require some explanation:

data. Information held in a form which can be processed automatically. By this definition, manual information systems are not covered by the Act;

- *personal data.* That which relates to a living individual who is identifiable from the information, including any which is based on fact or opinion;

- *data subject.* The living individual who is the subject of the data;

- *data user.* A person who processes or intends to process the data concerning a data subject.

These requirements may result in an organisation having to pay more attention to the question of security against unauthorised access than would otherwise be the case; appropriate education and training of employees are also needed to ensure that they are aware of their responsibilities and fully conversant with their roles in the security systems. The Act also provides that right of a data subject (with some exceptions) to obtain access to information concerning him or her; normally, a data user must provide such information free or for a nominal charge of around £10.

Computer Fraud

Computer fraud is invariably committed for financial gain, but unlike some forms of fraud, the perpetrator(s) will make considerable efforts to prevent discovery of any loss by the victim. The rewards for such efforts may be complete freedom from prosecution, or at least a delay in discovery of the fraud and a consequent chance of escape. Unless proper controls and checks are implemented, computer systems are particularly vulnerable to fraudulent activity, because much of the time processing and its results are hidden. The following section examines some methods for committing fraud and the measures which can be taken to foil them.

To extract money from a financial accounting system requires its diversion into fictitious, but accessible accounts. To avoid detection, appropriate adjustments must be made to ensure that the accounts still balance. Sometimes, fraudulent activity may involve the misappropriation of goods rather than cash. Frequently, the collusion of several people is necessary to effect a fraud, because responsibility for different stages of the processing cycle is likely to be shared. Some common methods of fraud are given below.

- bogus data entry. This may involve entering additional, unauthorised data, modifying valid data or preventing its entry altogether. Such activity may take place during the data preparation or data entry stages.

- bogus output. Output may be destroyed or altered to prevent discovery of fraudulent data entry or processing.

- alteration of files. For example, an employee may alter his salary grading in the payroll file or adjust the amount owing in a colluding customer's account.

- program patching. This method requires access to program coding and a detailed knowledge of the functioning of the program in question, as well as the necessary programming skill. By introducing additional code, in the form of a conditional subroutine, certain circumstances determined by the perpetrator can trigger entry to the subroutine, which may, for example, channel funds to a fictitious account.

- suspense accounts. Rejected and unreconciled transactions tend to be allocated to suspense accounts until they can be dealt with; fraud may be effected by directing such transactions to the account of someone colluding in the crime. Transactions can be tampered with at the input stage to ensure their rejection and allocation to the suspense/personal account.

Fraud Prevention and Detection

An organisation can minimise the risk of computer fraud by:

- controlling access to computer hardware; in centralised systems with a limited number of specialist staff access can be readily controlled (Chapter 14). On the other hand, if power is concentrated in the hands of few staff, then the opportunities for undetected fraud are increased. Distributed systems or centralised systems with remote access may increase the number of locations where fraud can be perpetrated;

- auditing of data and procedures; until hard copy is produced the contents of files remain invisible and a number of auditing techniques can be used to detect fraudulent entries or changes. The topic of auditing is dealt with in the chapter on System Controls.

- careful monitoring of the programming function; program patching can be controlled by division of the programming task, so that an individual programmer does not have complete responsibility for one application program. Unauthorised alterations to existing software can be detected by auditing utilities which compare the object code of an operational program with an original and authorised copy.

Computer Copyright

A computer program can now obtain the status of literary work and as such, retains protection for 50 years from the first publishing date. Computer software is now covered by the Copyright Designs and Patents Act 1988 and infringements include:

- the pirating of copyright protected software;

- the running of pirated software, in that a copy is created in memory;

- transmitting software over telecommunications links, thereby producing a copy.

The major software producers have funded an organisation called FAST (Federation Against Software Theft) which successfully lobbied for the inclusion of computer software into the above-mentioned Act.

Chapter 16

Health and Safety

Introduction

Although a computer is not inherently dangerous, users should be aware of a number of potential risks to their safety and general health. Most employers have obligations (under Section 2 of the Health and Safety at Work Act, 1974) to protect the health, safety and welfare of their employees, by ensuring safe equipment, work systems and working environment. This legislative protection applies to work with a computer *workstation* (a visual display unit and its associated equipment and furniture), as it does to other work. In 1993, specific legislation was introduced to implement European Directive 90/270/EEC, "on the minimum safety and health requirements for work with display screen equipment".

This section examines the potential hazards of using a computer workstation and the steps that can be taken to avoid them. The 1993 legislation recognises that good work organisation and job design, and the application of established *ergonomic* principles, can largely avoid the hazards to health and safety.

Ergonomics

Ergonomics is the "study of efficiency of workers and working arrangements" (Oxford English Dictionary). Although a separate science in its own right, certain aspects of ergonomics are being applied increasingly to the design of:

- furniture associated with office computer systems;
- computer equipment for person/machine interfacing, for example, screen displays and keyboards;
- office and workstation layout.

It is generally recognised that, if workstation facilities and the working environment are inadequate, computer users will tend to be inefficient and may suffer from general fatigue and boredom. The increased emphasis on ergonomic design has come about because of the large increase in the number of computer users. The term *user* includes, not only computer specialists, but also non-specialist users, such as data entry operators, clerks, accountants and managers.

Hazards to Operator Health and Efficiency

In designing a suitable workstation, the designer needs to be aware of a number of potential hazards, which are described in the following paragraphs.

Visual Fatigue

Various symptoms may indicate the onset of visual fatigue: sore eyes; hazy vision; difficulty in focusing when switching vision between near and distant objects; aching behind the eyes.

Certain workstation features and user behaviour can contribute to visual fatigue. The screen display and the positioning of documents that are being transcribed, typically contribute to this fatigue. More specifically, the fatigue may be caused by one or more of the following.

- screen glare;

- poor character-definition on screen;

- excessive periods of screen viewing and consequent short distance focusing;

- screen flicker;

- screen reflection;

- insufficient or excessive ambient (surrounding) lighting;

- frequent, excessive eye movement when switching between screen and document.

Bodily Fatigue

Tense and aching muscles, generally in the shoulders, neck and back, may result from:

- adopting a poor seating posture;

- bending frequently to reach various parts of the workstation;

- using a keyboard which is not at a comfortable height. *Repetitive strain injury* (RSI) is now recognised as a disabling condition, which can result from intensive keyboard work. Products are available to support wrists and help users to avoid the injury.

- holding the head at an awkward angle to view the screen or a document.

Other Hazards to Health and Safety

The proper design and positioning of a workstation can help prevent a number of potential hazards, generally relating to the use of equipment. The hazards may include:

- *electric shock*. A person may receive a live electric shock, from faulty equipment (such as incorrect earthing of the power supply), and from incorrect use of equipment (such as the removal of the machine's casing, without first isolating the machine from mains power). This form of electric shock will persist until the person breaks contact with the machine, or else the power is cut. Clearly, this hazard is life threatening, and although this is the primary concern, it will probably also cause damage to the machine.

- *static electric shock*. This is caused by the sudden discharge through any conducting material of static electricity, which may have built up in the body. The equipment earths the static electricity which the person has accumulated. A person may build up static electricity by walking on a nylon carpet. Sometimes, static electricity accumulates on the computer screen and a shock may be received when it is touched (the person acts as the earth). If the screen is cleaned with special anti-static wipes, this problem should be avoided. Static electric shock is momentary and, whilst in exceptional circumstances it may injure someone, it is more likely to damage the equipment and, possibly, the stored data.

- *injury from impact*. For example, someone may bump against the sharp corner of a desk, be injured by dropping equipment when attempting to move it or be cut by sharp edges on equipment;

- *muscular or spinal strain*. Lifting heavy equipment may cause strained or torn muscles, or spinal injuries such as a 'slipped' disc;

- *burns, cuts or poisoning caused by equipment breakdown*. These injuries may result from fire or overheating of equipment.

Analysis of Workstation Requirements

There is no single standard for workstation design. The type of equipment and its layout will depend on, amongst other things, who is going to use it and how it is going to be used. Therefore, before choosing an appropriate workstation design, information should be gathered on the following topics.

Users

The physical characteristics and abilities of potential users should, if possible, be identified. User features may include: gender; physical or mental handicap; age range; height; build.

Obviously, it may not be possible to identify personally all members of a user group, in which case, information may be more generalised. Questions to ask may be as follow:

- does the user group include males only, females only or both?

- what is the age range?

- are there any handicapped users and if so, what are the handicaps?

- are the physical characteristics of users similar or highly varied?

In addition to identifying the features of current users, it is important to allow for possible changes. For example, there may be no wheelchair users at present, but business policy may result in their inclusion in the future.

Existing Workstations

If there are workstations already in use within the organisation, then it is useful to determine if there are any good features to include, or bad features to avoid, in any new workstations. The general physical state of the old workstations should be determined. Questions to pose may include:

- have screen displays lost some clarity or steadiness?

- is the seating still clean and serviceable?

- are keyboards still fully operable?

The opinions of users should also yield useful information on the suitability of the existing workstations concerning, for example, seating comfort, positioning of equipment and reliability of hardware.

The Location of the Workstation

The size of the room in which the workstation is to be located and the layout of existing furniture may place constraints on any design features.

Workstation Usage

The various kinds of work to be carried out at a workstation may involve:

- data entry involving transcription from source documents;

- use of large reference manuals;

- storage of file media;

- customer enquiries which involve customers viewing the screen display;

- side-by-side working with another member of staff;

- use of a mouse which requires a flat surface area for its movement;

- some activities which do not involve the use of a computer. There may be no other available work areas in the office, so sufficient space should be available at each workstation.

It is also important to know how often particular activities are likely to be carried out and how long they will last.

Designing an Appropriate Workstation

A number of workstation features are considered in the overall design and together can contribute to a good working environment.

Work Surface

Height. A user should have thigh clearance amounting to at least 180mm, measured from the front surface of the seat, to the underside of the work surface. Obviously, this measurement can be obtained if the chair is adjustable in height and the work surface height does not require seat adjustment below its minimum height. The minimum clearance may be insufficient for someone to sit cross-legged, a position which he or she may wish to adopt for short periods, so some extra thigh clearance may be desirable.

Typical heights of manufactured workstations are either 710mm for fixed or between 520mm and 750mm when adjustable. The standard 710mm which manufacturers use for a fixed height desk is based on the ideal writing height for an average male and does not take account of keyboard thickness.

Area. The work surface area required obviously depends on the nature of the work being carried out at the workstation. If transcription work is to be carried out, a *document holder* can be attached to one corner of the mobile workstation. Where more space is available, users may prefer that the document holder is positioned between the keyboard and the screen to reduce the amount of eye movement when alternately viewing the screen and the document. As with all computer equipment, a *matt surface* is desirable to avoid screen reflection and possible eye strain.

Chair

Where a fixed height desk of, say, 710mm is bought, then it is particularly important that the chair's height is *adjustable* and that a footrest is available for persons of small stature. This is obviously necessary for a comfortable keying height. At the same time, support is provided for the feet (if they are not supported, blood circulation in the legs may be impaired as pressure is exerted by the edge of the seat on the back lower thighs). The footrest should allow the thighs to be slightly raised above the front edge of the chair, thus avoiding 'pins and needles' in the legs and feet. An adjustable chair should be variable in height from 340mm to 520mm.

Invariably, manufacturers produce computer workstation chairs which are adjustable for height and back, particularly lower back, support.

Screen Display

In workstation design, the screen display has to be judged for its *quality* and its *position* in relation to the operator.

Screen quality is measured for the clarity and steadiness of the images it displays. A high *resolution* screen is generally desirable, even for word processing work, but is of paramount importance if it is used for detailed design work. Several precautions can be taken to minimise eye strain if a poorer quality display is being used:

- appropriate lighting; this is examined in the next subsection;

- comparisons can be made with other screen displays (the clarity may deteriorate with age) and any deterioration reported;

- the use of a higher resolution screen, appropriate to the application and colour where graphical work is involved;

- the correct adjustment of contrast and brightness controls. Filters can cut glare and improve character definition by preventing screen reflection from inappropriate lighting. However, their quality is highly variable and a good quality screen should avoid the problem of glare.

There are two major concerns regarding the *positioning* of the screen. First, there is an optimum viewing range. Second, its location should be aimed at minimising excessive head and eye movement. The distance between the user's eyes and the screen should, ideally, fall somewhere between 450mm and 500mm and the design should try to achieve a viewing distance within this range. However, eye strain is more likely to result from repeated re-focusing for lengthy periods, whilst attention is switched from the screen to a document on the desk top. This can be avoided by attempting to position documents approximately the same distance away as the screen. A document holder can be useful in achieving this aim, even if it is positioned to one side and thus requires some head movement to view the document. Some head movement helps to keep the neck and shoulder muscle loosened and avoids stiffness and aching in those areas. A user should try to look away from the screen occasionally, perhaps to the other side of the office, to avoid eye strain which stems from constant focusing at one distance.

Lighting

Natural light falling through office windows may, at times, be adequate for healthy and efficient working but there will be many occasions when it is either too dark or too bright. It is generally necessary to supplement the natural light with artificial lighting and control the entry of bright sunshine with window blinds. The detailed study of lighting is beyond the scope of this text but the following points provide some basic guidelines as to the artificial lighting requirements for a workstation;

- attempt to avoid glare. This can result if there is insufficient lighting and the screen's brightness contrasts sharply with the ambient level of brightness;

- reflection on screen can make it difficult to see the displayed characters and cause eye strain. The use of window blinds and non-reflective work surfaces and equipment can help.

Cabling

Cabling is needed to power individual systems, connect the component parts of system unit, printer, keyboard and screen and for communications purposes when separate systems are networked. Loose cable trailing beneath desks or across the floor can result in injury to staff who trip over it. If, in the process, hardware is pulled from a desk onto the floor, it is likely to be damaged and may result in loss of data and temporary loss of system use. Cabling should be channelled through conduit or specially designed channels in the workstation. Cable 'bridge' conduit is specially designed to channel cable safely across floor areas.

Floor Covering

It is important to choose the right type of floor covering and a number of considerations concerning choice are given below.

Noise

Staff generally prefer an office floor to be carpeted because it makes the room feel more 'comfortable'. Carpet also serves to absorb some office noise and results in a quieter environment than would prevail with a tiled floor.

Chair Movement

If operator chairs are on casters then the carpet should be sufficiently firm and smooth to allow the operator to move easily while still seated. Movement should not be so easy that the operator has difficulty in maintaining position. A chair with casters is difficult to control on a tiled floor.

Static Electricity

Carpets made with a large percentage of man-made fibre tend to cause rapid build-up in body static. The static is caused through friction as a person walks across the carpet. Woollen carpets produce less static electricity but are more expensive than the synthetic variety. An alternative is to use anti-static mats to cover carpet areas around workstations. An anti-static mat is earthed and designed to drain away body static when a person stands on it. Another way of preventing static is to spray a special chemical solution onto the carpet every six months.

Office Layout

If the designer has the luxury of starting from 'scratch', then the simplest approach to designing the layout is to make a scale drawing of the office on which the location of equipment and furniture can then be marked. Designated work positions should also be indicated. Numerous drawing and computer aided design packages make experimentation easy. Libraries of standard symbols (representing office equipment, and furniture) are available, which the designer can select and locate on screen. The designer has to take into account a number of constraints which will dictate the location of some furniture and equipment. Fixed items should be placed on the drawing first so that those with fewer constraints can be tried in different locations until an optimum layout is achieved. Ideally, the designer should present two or three alternatives for consideration by management and office staff, whose opinions ought to be paramount. A number of factors should be taken into account when choosing the location of workstations:

- staff should not be obliged to work in areas which are subject to extremes of temperature, for example, next to radiators or near a frequently used door which creates a draught each time it is opened;

- computer equipment should not be placed next to a radiator as overheating may cause the system to malfunction;

- computer screens should be protected from direct sun-light which causes screen reflection and glare;

- there should be sufficient space for staff to move around the office without moving equipment or furniture;

- workstations should have sufficient space to allow routine maintenance and cleaning to be carried out;

- there should always be easy access to fire fighting equipment and fire exits should be kept clear.

Chapter 17

Relational Database Management Systems

Introduction

Databases are based on the idea that a common 'pool' of data, with a minimum of duplication, can be organised in such a way that all user requirements can be satisfied. Therefore, instead of each department or functional area keeping and maintaining its own files, where there are topics of common interest, they are grouped together to form a 'subject' database. DBMS (Database Management Systems are available for mainframe, mini and microcomputer systems. Although a database is normally used for a variety of applications, they should have some common interests concerning the data they use. For example, sales, purchasing, stock control and production control applications are likely to have some common data requirements, concerning raw materials or finished products.

The first part of this chapter examines the principles of database design and definition, as well as the role of a *relational database management system* (RDBMS) package. The final part of the chapter looks at some *data modelling tools and techniques,* which can be used in database design and development. RDBMS software packages are designed for the construction and control of *databases*. Packages, such as dBase, Paradox and Access, are often loosely referred to as 'databases'. Strictly and to avoid confusion, they are database management systems (DBMS). There are other types of DBMS (*hierarchical* and *network*), designed for use with mainframe computer systems, but they are not of concern here. All DBMS packages for microcomputer systems, including the examples given above, fall into the *relational* category, and the rest of this chapter refers to RDBMS only.

A fair amount of jargon is associated with database theory but the ideas represented are straightforward and simple to understand. A relational DBMS is designed to handle data in two-dimensional, *table* form and a single database is likely to contain a number of separate, but related, tables. This tabular view of data is easy to understand; everyday examples include telephone directories, train timetables and product price lists. Numerous examples of tables are provided in Database Construction and Operation.

Database Design

Design is an important prerequisite for database construction. For example, a common mistake is to create one table, containing all the data items required by the applications programs. Consider the Product table in Figure 17.1. Additional fields could be included for suppliers' names and addresses, but, on the assumption that many products come from one supplier, much data would be needlessly duplicated. It is more useful to create a separate table for the suppliers' names and addresses, as shown in Figure 17.2. Note that the Supplier table also contains a Supplier Code field; this allows a *relationship* to be established with the Product table. Similarly, a database for the maintenance of student records, may contain a single table consisting of twenty or thirty data items ranging from student name, address, and date of entry, to all assignment and exam grades for all subjects studied within a given course. Clearly, such a database is unwieldy when, for example, a list of student names and addresses is all that is required by a particular user. The following sections describe some of the more important concepts and techniques relating to proper database design.

PartCode	Description	Price	Quantity	SupplierCode
A123	Table (Cottage)	£23.50	15	KSU518
A124	Chair (Cottage)	£42.23	36	KIT518
A125	Stool (Cottage)	£28.15	6	KIT518
A133	Bar Stool	£33.55	4	KSU518
A136	Bread Bin (wood)	£14.25	4	KIT518
A139	Bread Bin (metal)	£10.25	6	KSU518
B122	Spanner (adjustable)	£8.25	4	BCS436
B126	Step Ladder (small)	£19.50	6	PAR116
B129	Screw Driver (ratchet)	£15.55	13	BCS436
B133	Ladders (aluminium)	£85.66	2	STA436
B136	Spirit Level	£13.55	6	STA436
B145	Step Ladder (medium)	£31.25	4	PAR116
B181	Hammer (medium claw)	£6.75	12	STA436

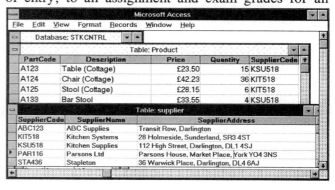

Figure 17.1. *Product table*

PartCode	Description	Price	Quantity	SupplierCode
A123	Table (Cottage)	£23.50	15	KSU518
A124	Chair (Cottage)	£42.23	36	KIT518
A125	Stool (Cottage)	£28.15	6	KIT518
A133	Bar Stool	£33.55	4	KSU518

SupplierCode	SupplierName	SupplierAddress
ABC123	ABC Supplies	Transit Row, Darlington
KIT518	Kitchen Systems	28 Holmeside, Sunderland, SR3 4ST
KSU518	Kitchen Supplies	112 High Street, Darlington, DL1 4SJ
PAR116	Parsons Ltd	Parsons House, Market Place, York YO4 3NS
STA436	Stapleton	36 Warwick Place, Darlington, DL4 6AJ

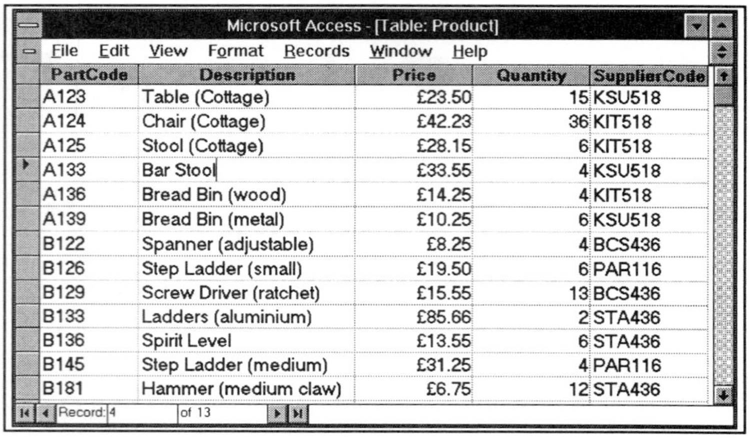

Figure 17.2. *Product and Supplier tables*

Entities

A database should contain a number of logically separate tables, each corresponding to a given subject or part-subject (an *entity*). In the example of the product database (Figure 17.2), two logically separate tables (one for the Product entity and the other for the Supplier entity) are constructed. *Entities* are the objects of the real world, which are relevant to a particular information system.

Attributes

An entity has a number of related *attributes*, which are of interest to users. Consider, as an example, a Personnel database (see also *Personnel* case study in Database Construction and Operation). An entity, StaffMember, may have the attributes of StaffCode, Name, JobCode, JobTitle, DeptCode, DepartmentName. These attributes determine the *fields* which are associated with the StaffMember *table*. Some attributes may be kept in a separate table. For example, JobTitle and DepartmentName are likely to contain the same values in numerous records in the StaffMember table. In other words, some employees work in the same department and some have the same job title. With an RDBMS, it is more efficient to separate these attributes, through the creation of separate tables (one for Department and the other for Job). Although an employee has a given job title and works in a particular department, these attributes are also of separate interest; each is a separate *entity*. For example, a new job title may be identified before an employee has been assigned to it. Figure 17.3 shows the tables which represent these entities.

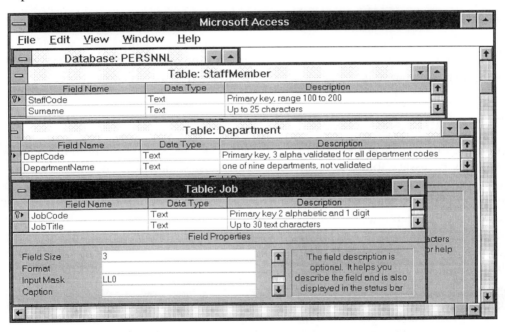

Figure 17.3. *Tables for StaffMember, Department and Job entities*

Identifying and Non-identifying Attributes

Some attributes, for example, Name and JobTitle, are descriptive. Another (StaffCode) may serve as a unique identifier. Attributes can be classified, therefore, as being either *identifying* or *non-identifying*. In Figure 17.3, StaffCode acts as the unique identifier (or *primary key field*) for a StaffMember record; Department and Job records use DeptCode and JobCode, respectively.

These entity and attribute structures can be expressed in the form shown in Figure 17.4. Unique identifiers are underlined.

StaffMember (<u>StaffCode</u>, Name, JobCode, DeptCode)

Job(<u>JobCode</u>, JobTitle)

Department(<u>DeptCode</u>, DepartmentName)

Figure 17.4. *Entity structures*

Sometimes, more than one attribute is needed to uniquely identify an individual record; such attributes form a *composite identifier* or *key*. An example of such a key is given below.

Order Line (<u>OrderNo</u>, <u>ItemNo</u>, Description, Price, Quantity)

Figure 17.5. *Entity structure using composite primary key*

An order form usually has several lines, each relating to a separate item which a customer wants. The same item may be ordered by other customers, so the OrderNo and ItemNo are needed to identify a particular order line, relating to a particular customer order.

Relationships and Link Fields

Notice that, in Figure 17.4, the JobCode and DeptCode fields also remain in the StaffMember table. This is necessary to allow relationships, or links, to be established between the tables. Suppose, for example, that a user wishes to view a list of employee details, which includes Name, DepartmentName and JobTitle. The list is obtained by *querying* (see Database Construction and Operation) the database. To process the query, the RDBMS needs to extract information from more than one table. An examination of the entity structures in Figure 17.4 reveals that all three are needed (StaffMember, Job and Department). The user must specify which fields are used to link the tables to one another. Figure 6 illustrates these links.

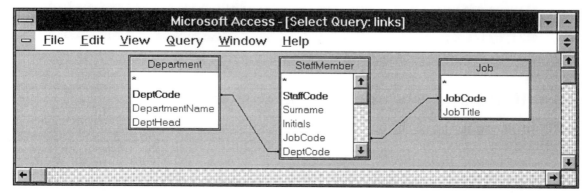

Figure 17.6. *Link fields to establish relationships between tables*

DeptCode is the primary key for the Department table, but the same attribute also appears in the StaffMember table. When the two are linked, DeptCode in the StaffMember table is acting as a *foreign key*. JobCode in the StaffMember table also serves as a foreign key when it is used to link with the Job table.

Data Analysis

This process (see Database Modelling Tools and Techniques, later) is concerned with establishing what the entities, attributes and links (*relationships*), for any given database, should be. To make such an analysis, it is obviously necessary to have knowledge of the organisation to which the information relates, because there will be certain items of information which only have significance to that particular organisation. For example, in an Academic database, the following entities may be identified and a table established for each.

```
Student; Course; Tutor; EducationHistory; ExamGrade
```

Normalisation

Normalisation is a technique established by E.F. Codd to simplify the structure of data as it is *logically viewed* by the programmer or user. The data requirements for a database are systematically analysed to establish whether a particular attribute should be an entity in its own right, or simply an attribute of some other entity. When an attribute is identified as a separate entity, the link or relationship must be maintained with the original entity. Normalisation is a step-by-step process for analysing data into its constituent entities and attributes. Its main aim is to improve database efficiency. There are three stages of normalisation described here, though there are others which are beyond the scope of this text. To illustrate the process of normalisation, the example of an *Academic* database is used. When a student enrols for one or more courses, a registration form is completed. An example is shown in Figure 17.7.

Dotherstaff College, Shaftsbury, Dunshire	Principal: M. Squeers, PhD, MEd, MBA, MBIM, FIB, FOB, BEM		
Student Registration Form			
Student Number	G234563		
Surname	Harrison		
Forename	Pauline		
Address	123 Newcastle Rd, Sunderland SR3 2RJ		
Sex	Female		
Course Code	**Course Title**	**Tutor Code**	**Tutor**
4PDCS1	Computing	124	Watkin
4PDNE1	Electronics	133	Parks
4PDFR1	French	118	Teneur
4PDGE1	German	166	Roberts

Figure 17.7. *Extract from student registration form*

First Normal Form (1NF)

Treated as a single entity, the structure could be described, initially, as shown in Figure 17.8.

```
Student  (StudNo,  Surname,  Forename,  Address,  Sex,  [CrseCode,
CrseTitle, TutNo, TutName])
```

Figure 17.8. *Structure of Student entity*

The unique identifier (primary key), StudNo, is underlined. Each student registration form (see Figure 17.7) may show enrolments on several courses. Thus, the attributes [CrseCode, CrseTitle, TutNo and TutName] can be identified as a *repeating group*.

The first stage of normalisation demands the removal of any repeating groups. This is achieved by creating a new entity. The attributes in question relate to the activity of enrolment, which is of separate interest and an entity in its own right. The new entity is called Enrolment-1 and is used to store details of individual enrolments; each enrolment will be a separate record in the Enrolment table. Neither StudNo nor CrseCode, on its own, uniquely identifies an individual enrolment. A *composite key*, using both attributes, is used to uniquely identify a single enrolment. The two entity descriptions are shown in Figure 17.9.

```
Student-1(StudNo, Surname, Forename, Address, Sex)

Enrolment-1(StudNo, CrseCode, CrseTitle, TutNo, TutName)
```

Figure 17.9. Entity structures after conversion to first normal form (1NF)

The entities are now in first normal form (1NF) and this is indicated by suffixing each entity name with a 1. The unique identifier is underlined in each entity description. Note the *composite key* in the Enrolment entity.

To relate the Enrolment records to the relevant Student records requires that StudNo (as the link field) appears in both the Student and Enrolment tables in the Academic database. Thus, to ensure that entities and attributes are in first normal form requires the removal of repeating groups of attributes, rewriting them as new entities. The identifier of the original entity is always included as an attribute of any such new entity, although it is not essential for it to form part of the identifier of the new entity (it could be a non-identifying attribute).

Some necessary *data redundancy* is created by including StudNo in both entities, to allow a given student to be connected with a particular enrolment. Such duplication of data does not necessarily mean an increased use of storage because normalisation is concerned with the *logical structure* of the data and not with the ways in which the data is physically organised.

Second Normal Form (2NF)

The second stage of normalisation ensures that all non-identifying attributes are *functionally dependent* on the unique identifier (the primary key); if the identifier is composite (comprising more that one attribute), then non-identifying attributes must be functionally dependent on the whole of the identifier. This rule is best explained by example. Consider the 1NF entity descriptions, produced from the first stage of normalisation (Figure 17.9). Referring to the Enrolment entity, it can be seen that TutNo and TutName each depend on both parts of the composite identifier. For example, if a student enrols on more than one course, he or she has a different tutor for each course. To identify a tutor in an enrolment record, requires specification of both values (StudNo and CrseCode). However, CrseTitle is not functionally

dependent on the whole of the composite identifier, only on CrseCode; the title of a course could be found through entry of the CrseCode value alone. Figure 17.10 illustrates both these points with a diagram. An arrowed line connects the box, which surrounds the composite identifier, to TutNo and TutName. CrseTitle is connected only to CrseCode.

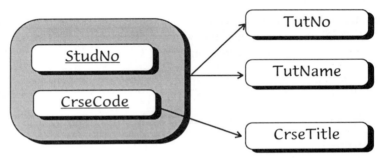

Figure 17.10. *Functional dependency*

The second stage of normalisation is achieved by the creation of a new entity, Course-2, with the attributes CrseCode (the identifier) and CrseTitle. The entity descriptions now appear as in Figure 17.11. The suffix 2 indicates that all entities and attributes are now in second normal form.

```
Student-2(StudNo, Surname, Forename, Address, Sex)

Enrolment-2(StudNo, CrseCode, TutNo, TutName)

Course-2(CrseCode, CrseTitle)
```

Figure 17.11. *Entity structures in second normal form (2NF)*

Benefits of 2NF

Conversion of entities and attributes to second normal form brings advantages apart from the avoidance of some data duplication. The entry of new data into the database is also facilitated. Suppose, for example, that a new course is to be added to the database and that the data is stored as arranged after the first stage of normalisation. The new course entry could not be made until the first enrolment for that particular course. Also, if a particular course has no enrolments, then information concerning the course is not held in the database.

Third Normal Form (3NF)

At this stage we are concerned with finding any *functional dependencies* between non-identifying attributes. These can be identified from Figure 17.11 as TutNo and TutName and are illustrated in Figure 17.12. Again, the problem is solved by the creation of a new entity, Tutor-3. The entity contains TutNo as the identifier

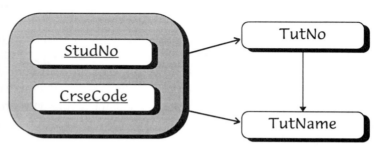

Figure 17.12

and TutName as a non-identifying attribute. The entities in third normal form (indicated by the suffix, 3), as shown in Figure 17.13.

```
Student-3(StudNo, Surname, Forename, Address, Sex)

Enrolment-3(StudNo, CrseCode, TutNo)

Course-3(CrseCode, CrseTitle)

Tutor-3(TutNo, TutName)
```

Figure 17.13. *Entity structures in third normal form (3NF)*

Defining a Database Structure

Each entity structure, shown in Figure 13, must be defined as a table in the *Academic* database. In the case of Student-3, it would be beneficial to sub-divide Address into separate attributes of, say, Street, Town and PostCode. Each definition includes reference to *primary keys*, *field names*, *data types* and *field lengths*. All these terms are explained, through examples, in Database Construction and Operation, but are briefly defined below.

Primary Keys

In the Academic database, for example, StudentNo, CrseCode and TutorNo, act as primary keys for the Student, Course and Tutor tables, respectively. Although an Enrolment record can be identified through the combined use of StudNo and CrseCode, you could add an additional field, such as EnrolmentNo, to act as the primary key.

Data Types

A typical RDBMS provides the following data types:

Character, text or alphanumeric

This is for a field which may contain text, or a mixture of text, symbols and numbers. Sometimes a field may only contain numeric digits, perhaps an account number or telephone number. If it is not treated numerically, but as text, character type is normally used.

Numeric

This type must be used for fields containing numerical values (such as money amounts or quantities) to be used in calculations;

Logical (Yes/No)

This type allows the entry of two possible values, indicated by *true* or *false*. Sometimes, *yes* and *no*, respectively, may be used instead. For example, the Student table in the academic database contains a field to record the sex of a student. Use of the field name 'Male' means that 'Yes' is entered for a male student and 'No' for a female. If the field name 'Female' is used, 'No' is entered for a male and 'Yes' for a female student. The name of the field determines whether an affirmative or a negative (Yes or No) is entered.

Date Type

Although character type may be used for the storage of dates, the *date* type allows the correct sorting of dates. Also, in defining queries, date type fields enable the database to compare dates held in records, with a specified date. This is not practical with a character type field.

Field Lengths

Logical and *date* type fields invariably have a pre-determined length, typically, 1 and 8 respectively. For a character field, a maximum length must be specified (allowing for the number of digits, letters or symbols to be accommodated within it). Numeric fields are defined according to the number range which needs to be accommodated and the number of decimal places.

Abbreviating and Coding Data

There are a number of benefits to be gained if data can be abbreviated or coded, without obscuring its meaning. Some are described below.

- *Saving space*. Codes and abbreviations take up less space, but must be of sufficient length to allow the entry of unique values. The minimum length of such a field is determined by the number of different values which need to be represented.

- *Query expressions* can be shorter. As long as users are aware of what the codes mean and are happy with using them, much time and keying effort can be saved.
- *Data entry*. If there are a large number of records to be keyed in, the procedure is extremely time-consuming and tedious. Coding and abbreviating data may reduce the time and labour requirements considerably.

Querying a Database - Query by Example (QBE) and SQL

A query is a request for information from a database. Queries can include *criteria* for the selection of information. For example, the Academic database could be queried for details of all male students, or students on a particular course. If the query requires that the RDBMS takes data from more than one table, appropriate link fields must be indicated. Suppose, for example, that a report is required listing the names of all students, together with the name(s) of the course(s) on which they are enrolled. It is assumed that no criteria are specified. Student names are held in the Student table, the course code is in the Enrolment table, and the name of the course is in the Course table. Therefore, to process the query requires that these three tables are used. The QBE form of the query is shown in Figure 17.14.

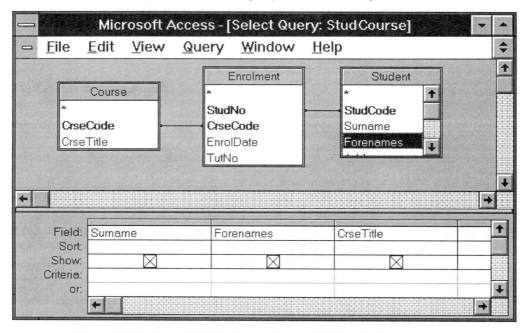

Figure 17.14. *Query (QBE form) using three tables from Academic database*

The query can also be expressed in Structured Query Language (SQL), as shown in Figure 17.15.

```
SELECT DISTINCTROW Student.Surname, Student.Forenames,
Course.CrseTitle

FROM Student INNER JOIN (Course INNER JOIN Enrolment ON
Course.CrseCode = Enrolment.CrseCode) ON Student.StudCode =
Enrolment.StudNo;
```

Figure 17.15. *Structured Query Language (SQL) form of query in Figure 14*

The use of SQL and QBE is dealt with in Database Construction and Operation. The query produces more than one record per student, but this is because a student may be enrolled on more than one course. The output appears in Figure 17.16.

Surname	Forenames	CrseTitle
Pallister	Robert	Electronics - Foundation
Atkinson	Fiona	French - Foundation
Wilson	John	German - Foundation
Cancello	Carla	German - Foundation
Williamson	Peter	Art - Foundation
Adamson	Rachel	Art - Foundation
Erikson	Karl	Art - Foundation
Pallister	Robert	German - Intermediate
Laing	Alan	Electronics - Advanced
Pompelmo	Paolo	Electronics - Advanced

Microsoft Access - [Select Query: StudCourse]
File Edit View Format Records Window Help
Record: 6 of 10

Figure 17.16. *Output from query in Figure 17.14*

Secondary Keys

Apart from the primary keys, which are used to identify records uniquely, an important function of an RDBMS is to allow the querying of the database, by reference to *secondary key* values. Thus, in the Academic database, useful secondary keys could be CrseTitle, and TutName (if neither code was available). Secondary keys can also be used as foreign keys (see Relationships and Link Fields), when joining tables in a query.

Data Dictionary

An essential part of the database design process is to maintain a data dictionary. Its main function is to store details of all the data items in a database. Such details can be wide ranging, but should include, as a minimum:

(i) field names and the table(s) in which they occur;

(ii) field definitions, including field types and lengths;

(iii) additional properties, concerning, for example, data formats and validation controls;

(iv) synonyms. Sometimes, the same field occurs in more than one table, but using different names. Generally it is better not to use synonyms.

The *database administrator* (the person who controls development of a database) has to ensure the consistent use of data across the whole database. For example, a functional area may request new data to be added to a database, when it already exists. This can happen when different departments in an organisation refer to a field by different names. For example, a Sales department may refer to the name 'Product Code', whilst the Warehouse staff may use the term 'Stock Code', when referring to the same field. During database development, it is easy to forget the precise definitions given to a field and when adding the field to another table, introduce inconsistencies.

Database Modelling Tools and Techniques

Data Analysis - Entity Relationship Modelling (ERM)

Data analysis is a technique primarily concerned with determining the *logical structure* of the data, its *properties* and the *processes* needed to make use of it. Its objective is to produce a model which represents the information needs of a particular information system or sub-system and it should be understandable by users as well as analysts, in order to provide a basis for discussion and agreement. The main tool used within data analysis is the Entity-Relationship Model (ERM), which classifies information into:

- entities;
- attributes;
- relationships.

Entities are objects which are of interest or relevance to the organisation, for example, Supplier, Customer, Stock. An entity will normally equate with a database table; an *entity occurrence* is normally synonymous with a *record* within that table.

Attributes comprise those properties of an entity which are identified as being of interest to users. It may be helpful to equate attributes with fields in a conventional record, but it is important to note that in database systems (where the term 'data item type' is sometimes used), it is not always necessary to have all the attributes for an entity stored in the relevant record in the database; it is necessary, however, to ensure that all attributes relevant to a particular entity can be associated with it. This point is explained earlier in this chapter.

Relationships exist between entities. For example, an Employee works for a particular Department and a Purchase Order is sent to one particular Supplier. The degree of the relationship may be:

- one-to-one;
- one-to-many;

- many-to-many.

One-to-one relationship

Figure 17.17 provides an example of a one-to-one relationship. Each hospital patient develops a unique medical history and each medical history can only relate to one hospital patient.

Figure 17.17. *One-to-one relationship*

One-to-many relationship

Figure 17.18 illustrates that an order may comprise one or many order lines, but each order line will be unique to a particular order. Note the double arrow head to indicate the *many* side of the relationship. By 'many', we mean one or more, whereas 'one' means one only.

Figure 17.18. *One-to-many relationship*

Many-to-many relationship

A stock item may be ordered in a number of purchase orders and a single purchase order may include a number of stock items. This is symbolised in Figure 17.19.

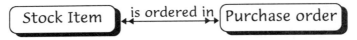

Figure 17.19. *Many-to-many relationship*

Some of the practical implications of these relationship types are explained in the *Stock Control* case study in Database Construction and Operation (Editing Tables through Query Dynasets).

An ERM for a given information system or sub-system may consist of a number of entities, the attributes associated with each and the relationships between those entities. The modelling process requires that any given model is continually refined until its efficiency in satisfying users' needs is optimised and its structure is in a form dictated by the requirements of the RDBMS in use.

An ERM for the Academic Database

Figure 17.20 shows a normalised (3NF) entity relationship model (ERM) for the Academic database already outlined in the Database Design section, earlier in this chapter. The diagram can be interpreted as follows. You should find it helpful to refer to Figure 17.13, which shows the Academic database model in third normal form (3NF).

- Each student registers for one or more enrolments, but each enrolment relates to only one student. This is a one-to-many relationship, the enrolments being the many side. The single arrow head indicates the 'one' side and the double headed arrow, the 'many side'.

- Each tutor is named in many enrolments, but each enrolment only names one tutor; this is also a one-to-many relationship. Although tutors are assigned students, the process is carried out through the enrolment entity, so there is no direct relationship between the Student and Tutor entities; instead the connection is through the Enrolment entity. This structure is arrived at through the normalisation process.
- Each course has many enrolments, but each enrolment only concerns one course. Therefore, there is a one-to-many relationship between the Course and Enrolment entities.

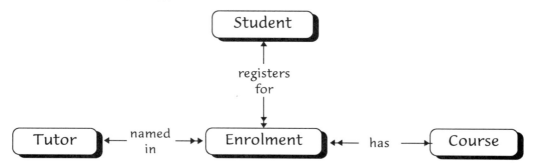

Figure 17.20. *Normalised Entity Relationship Model for Academic database*

An ERM for a Personnel Database

Figure 17.21 is an ERM for the *Personnel* database, used as a case study in Database Construction and Operation.

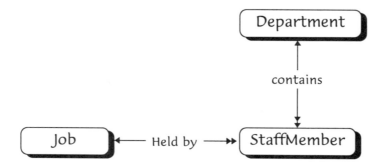

Figure 17.21. *Normalised Entity Relationship Model for Personnel Database*

The diagram shows the following relationships between the three entities.

- Each department contains many staff, but each member of staff is based in a single department. There is a one-to-many relationship between Department and StaffMember.

- Each job (job title or grade) is held by one or more members of staff, but each member of staff has only one job title. The relationship between Job and StaffMember is also one-to-many.

The ERMs shown in Figures 17.20 and 17.21 illustrate database structures after data normalisation. They can be drawn at various stages of the modelling process, to help clarify the entities which are needed and the relationships which arise between them. Thus, an ERM drawn for the Academic database after the first stage of normalisation (1NF), would only show the Student and Enrolment entities (see Figure 17.9). The second and third stages of normalisation are 'fine-tuning' the structure, but it must be in first normal form (no repeating groups) before you can attempt to construct a database. Entity relationship modelling can be a complex process, which requires much training and experience, so at this stage, you are likely to be constructing databases from fully normalised ERMs.

Data Flow Diagrams (DFDs)

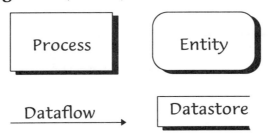

Figure 17.22. *DFD symbols*

Figure 17.22 shows some typical, standard symbols for the drawing of data flow diagrams. DFDs are used to illustrate, in a diagrammatic form, the logical data flows between entities, accompanying processes and any file storage or data stores. DFDs can be used at various stages in the analysis and design process. In the early stages, they will be at a high level and may, for example, show little detail except for a department's general function, such as sales accounting or stock control; later, DFDs may

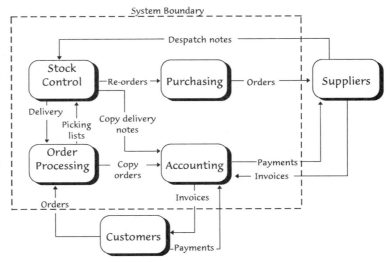

Figure 17.23. *High level DFD for trading business*

be drawn at a lower, more detailed level, to show for example, the checking of a customer's account before sending an invoice reminder or statement of account. Figure 17.23 shows a *high level* DFD for a typical trading organisation. More details on the data flows in its Sales Order Processing system are shown in the low level DFD in Figure 17.24.

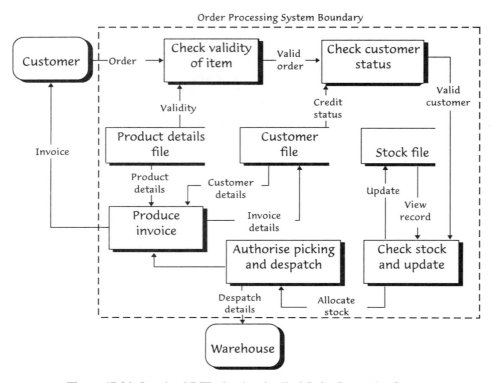

Figure 17.24. *Low level DFD showing detail of Order Processing System*

Normalisation

Normalisation (see Database Design) is a technique which is particularly useful in the design of relational database models. It is used to determine the validity of the logical data model produced in the data analysis stage and is particularly concerned with:

- minimising data redundancy or duplication;
- establishing dependencies between data items and grouping them in the most efficient way;
- obtaining a measure of data independence, such that a database can be supplemented with new data without changing the existing logical structure and thus the applications programs.

Structured Query Language (SQL)

Many new RDBMS packages provide a Structured Query Language (SQL). Developed by IBM, SQL is a *non-procedural* language and as such belongs to the group of programming languages known as 4th Generation Languages (4GLs); this means that programmers and trained users can specify what they want from a database without having to specify how to do it. Procedural languages such as COBOL, Pascal and C, require the programmer to detail, explicitly, how a program must 'navigate' through a file or database to obtain the necessary output. The programmer must, for example, code procedures such as 'read the first master record, process it, read the next, process it and so on until the end of the file is reached'.

As explained below, SQL is an attempt to provide a language which includes the facilities normally provided separately by a *data description language*, a *data manipulation language* and a *query language* (to allow 'on-demand' queries by users).

Features of SQL

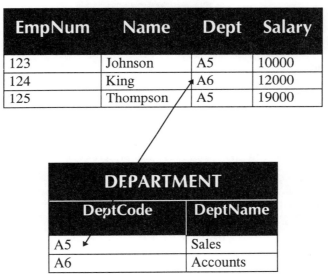

Figure 17.25. *Extract from Company Database*

The example database extract in Figure 17.25 is used here to illustrate some of the main features of SQL by showing how a programmer or trained user could use SQL to access a database without specifying procedures. Practical examples of SQL are given in Database Construction and Operation.

Selection by Criteria

Referring to Figure 17.25, if the Name and Salary of EMPLOYEE 124 is required, the SQL statements may take a form similar to the example in Figure 17.26).

```
SELECT Name, Salary

FROM EMPLOYEE

WHERE EmpNum = 124
```

Figure 17.26. *SQL statement to extract details of Employee* **124**

The output would be as in Figure 17.27.

Name	Salary
King	12000

Figure 17.27. *Output from SQL query in Figure 26*

SQL supports all the functions expected of a *relational* language including, for example, the operators, JOIN and PROJECT.

Updating the Database

SQL can also change values in a database; for example, to give all employees in the A5 (Sales) department a 6 per cent pay increase, the statements shown in Figure 17.28 may be used:

```
UPDATE EMPLOYEE

SET Salary = Salary * 1.06

WHERE Dept-Code = A5
```

Figure 17.28 *SQL update query*

SQL has built-in functions and arithmetic operators to allow the grouping or sorting of data and the calculation of, for example, average, minimum and maximum values in a particular field.

Defining the Database

As a multi-purpose database language, SQL can be used to define, as well as manipulate and retrieve data. This definition function is traditionally carried out using a separate data description language (DDL) but SQL incorporates this facility for implementing the logical structure (*schema*) for a database. For example, to create a new table called QUALIFICATIONS the statements in Figure 17.29 may be entered:

```
CREATE TABLE QUALIFICATION

(EmpNum CHAR (3)

Qual VARCHAR (20));
```

Figure 17.29. *SQL statement to create a table*

The table would contain two fields, namely, EmpNum with a fixed length of three characters and Qual with a variable number of characters up to twenty. Following creation of the table, data can be entered immediately if required.

Modifying the Database Definition

Tables can be modified to allow for the removal or addition of fields, according to changes in user requirements. Existing data does not have to be re-organised and applications programs unaffected by data changes do not have to be re-written. The independence of the logical database from the applications programs is known as *logical data independence* and constitutes one of the main features of a relational database.

Two major aims are inherent in the design of SQL:

(i)   As a non-procedural language it is expected to increase programmer productivity and reduce the time and costs involved in application development.

(ii) SQL allows easier access to data for the purposes of on-demand or ad hoc queries.

Chapter 18
High-level Languages

This chapter explores high-level languages (HLLs) from a number of different viewpoints. We first look at their common features before going on to summarise the individual characteristics of a range of well-known languages. Other aspects that we explore are the different ways that high-level languages are translated into a machine-usable forms and how their use is supported by software-based programming environments.

Features of High-level Languages

Though all HLLs can be applied to a wide variety of programming tasks, and are in that sense general-purpose languages, most high-level languages have been designed specifically for particular application areas. For example, Fortran is particularly good for mathematical problems, COBOL allows data processing and file handling applications to be coded in a convenient manner, and Logo was written to encourage children to approach problem solving logically and to explore mathematical concepts.

The table below summarizes the characteristics of a number of well-known languages. All of the languages below are to a greater or lesser extent general-purpose, so only special application areas are mentioned. The code *c* means 'Compiled' and *i* means 'Interpreted'.

Language	Date	Type	Application areas
Ada	1979	c	Real-time systems programming; embedded systems or military vehicles.
Algol	1960	c	General-purpose.
APL	1966	i	Scientific/mathematical problems involving vectors and matrices.
BASIC	1963	i,c	Teaching programming; for casual users rather than serious professional programmers.
C	1972	c	Systems programming.
COBOL	1960	c	Data processing.
Forth	1969	i/c	Control of servo-driven devices.
Fortran	1954	c	Mathematical/scientific problems.
Lisp	1960	i	Artificial intelligence.

Logo	1967	i	Helping children with problem solving; artificial intelligence.
Modula-2	1979	c	Systems programming.
Pascal	1970	c	Teaching program/algorithm design.
PL/1	1965	c	General-purpose.
Prolog	1972	i	Artificial intelligence.
Smalltalk	1972	c	Object oriented programming.
SNOBOL	1966	i	Text processing

All of these languages, and many others not mentioned here, have a considerable number of similarities: most programming problems require data to be stored, calculations to be performed, values to be read from some external source or displayed in some form, alternative sets of operations to be executed depending on some condition arising, sections of programs to be repeated a specified number of times, and so on. For convenience, we can group these similarities under a number of headings:

- Reserved words
- Identifiers
- Data structures
- Operations on data
- Input/output operations
- Control structures
- File handling
- Functions and procedures

Reserved Words

All high-level languages contain a number of words having special meanings. For example, in Pascal begin, end and while are such words. These are called *reserved words* because the programmer is not allowed to use them as identifiers; they are used only in specific contexts and their meanings are recognised by the language compiler. In languages such as COBOL, having over 300 reserved words, this constitutes something of a problem for programmers.

Identifiers

In addition to reserved words or keywords, programs contain names created by the programmer. Names are given to program variables or constants; names are assigned to subprograms or program modules; names are given to user-defined data structures. These names are collectively called *identifiers*. They comprise groups of alphanumeric characters, typically beginning with a letter, which allow programmers to give convenient names to program items.

Data items whose values are allowed to change during the execution of a program are called *variables*; *constant* data items retain their values throughout the execution of the program. In some HLLs, variables, constants, procedures and functions have to be declared before they can be used, usually at the start of the program or subprogram in which they appear. Declarations are used to define the form or type of identifiers.

Data Structures

The commonest data types are:

- Integer - a whole number such as 255 or 12 or -10)
- Real - a number which may have a fractional part, such as 1.45, 0.343, -34.65)
- Character - a single character such as 'a' or 'G' or '*' or '6'
- String - a number of characters treated as a unit, such as 'Freddy'
- Boolean - a value representing a logical state of TRUE or FALSE
- Array - a set of data items of one specific type, with individual elements referenced by means of one or more subscripts
- Record - a collective name assigned to a group of variables of different types
- File - collection of identically structured records

A number of HLLs, notably Pascal and C, allow new user-defined data types to be constructed from primitives or other (previously declared) user-defined data types, in order to create data structures of almost any complexity.

Operations on Data

The operations available in a HLL normally include:

- Arithmetic operations involving addition, subtraction, multiplication and division,
- Logical operations, usually the operations AND, OR, NOT and EOR (exclusive OR).

Results of such operations may be stored in variables by means of assignment statements taking the form of mathematical identities. For example, an assignment statement in Fortran looks like this:

```
Sum = A + B
```

The variable Sum would be assigned the value corresponding to the sum of the values of the variables A and B. The normal rules of precedence normally apply, and brackets may be used freely as in ordinary algebra.

Input and Output Operations

Most HLLs provide special input statements for capturing data from a standard input device such as a keyboard for allocation to a specified variable, and special output statements for displaying data on a standard output device such as a VDU.

Control Structures

Control structures are the means by which the normal top to bottom execution order of statements may be modified. The basic control constructs are:

- *Selections*, such as `IF..THEN..ELSE` and `CASE` allowing the current states of specified variables to determine the next action to be taken by the program; in other words, the means by which alternative courses of action may be taken.
- *Iterations*, such as `FOR..NEXT`, `REPEAT..UNTIL`, `WHILE..DO`, allowing blocks of instructions to be repeated.

File Handling

High-level languages invariably provide a set of instructions for manipulating files held on backing storage devices such as magnetic disks. By means of these types of instructions, blocks of data may be transferred to and from backing storage. A typical set of file-handling instructions might include instructions for:

- opening files ready for use;
- closing files;
- reading records from a sequential file;
- writing records to a sequential file;
- reading records from a random file;
- writing records to a random file.

Other languages, COBOL for example, provide facilities for processing indexed-sequential files. Sometimes a language will provide low-level file-handling instructions for reading/writing single bytes, single numbers or strings from backing-storage. C is such a language.

Scope of Variables

The term *scope* refers to the degree of accessibility of a variable. Variables which are defined in the main program have *global scope*, that is they are accessible to the whole program, including its subprograms. Such variables are called *global variables*. When such declarations are made in *subprograms* (see the next section), the declared variables are usually termed *local variables*. This means that their values are defined only when the subprogram is being executed, and otherwise, as far as the main program is concerned, they do not exist. The scope of these variables, depends on the language. In C, the scope of such variables, that is the area of the program able to recognise them, is restricted to the subprogram only; in Pascal it is restricted to that subprogram and any other subprograms defined within it.

Functions and Procedures

Languages such as Pascal and C allow the programmer to create *subprograms* (also called *subroutines* or program *modules*) which may be referenced by name in the main program. Broadly speaking, a subprogram is a self-contained section of program code which performs some identifiable task. This facility is invaluable when designing large programs because it allows the programmer to split a large, complex task into a collection of smaller, simpler tasks.

Subprograms are usually allowed to contain local variables, which are declared within the subprogram, and whose scopes are restricted to the extent of the subprogram. These variables are usually dynamically created when the subprogram is invoked and are destroyed, that is, their memory areas are released, on completion of the subprogram.

Subprograms, are frequently called *procedures* or *functions*. Simply speaking, a procedure is a subprogram which when invoked, or *called*, from the main program (or another subprogram) performs some task and then returns control to the place where it was called; a function does much the same thing but, in addition, it returns a value to the calling program or subprogram.

The difference between procedures and functions is best illustrated by means of an example. Suppose, as part of a large program which has been produced as an aid in the design of buildings, a subprogram is required to display a rectangle, of given dimensions, on the VDU. Then this would probably be written as a procedure invoked by a statement such as

```
call draw_rectangle(10, 5)
```

where the numbers in the brackets are *parameters* specifying the dimensions of the rectangle to be drawn. The code for the procedure `draw_rectangle` would exist either within the program or on some backing storage medium, such as a magnetic disk, accessible to the language compiler. The code would be executed, causing a rectangle of the required dimensions to be drawn, and the program would continue with the next instruction following the call.

Suppose now that another subprogram is required to calculate the area of building material required to produce a rectangular shape of the same dimensions. This task would most probably be implemented as a function of the form

```
area = call calc_area(10, 5)
```

Again two parameters are passed to the function, but this time it is expected to calculate and, on completion, return a value which is to be stored in the variable `area`.

This is a rather simplistic view of procedures and functions; in practice there are many variations and enhancements of these basic ideas. Pascal and C both make extensive use of subprograms assuming a variety of different forms.

Parameters

An important characteristic of procedures and functions is the ability to pass parameters to and from them. Parameters are frequently shown as variables enclosed within brackets after the name of the procedure/function, as illustrated in an earlier section. Parameters allow the programmer to use the same subprogram to process different values, without the necessity of repeating the code for the subprogram wherever it is needed. Two types of parameters are in common use: *value parameters* and *variable parameters*.

With value parameters, the transfer of data is one way only - from the calling program to the subprogram. A copy of the value to be passed to the subprogram is made before transfer takes place, and therefore the original is unchanged by whatever processing occurs within the subprogram. This is often termed a call by value.

In the case of variable parameters, the subprogram uses an alias (ie a different name) for the variable passed as a parameter; this means that the subprogram can alter the value of the variable even though it may use a different name for the variable. This is often termed a *call by value-result*.

Pascal supports both of these systems of parameter passing.

Language processors

The general function of translators (or language processors) is to convert program statements written in one programming language into another, most commonly into machine code. This section briefly examines the function and operational characteristics of the three main types of translators, namely *assemblers*, *compilers* and *interpreters*.

Assemblers

In the history of programming languages, one of the first significant innovations was the development of assembly languages. Assembly languages make use of alphabetic *operation codes* and *symbolic addresses* to represent machine code instructions. For example, an instruction to add two numbers together might be represented in assembly language by

```
ADD N1, N2
```

where ADD is the operation code for the addition of two values and N1 and N2 are symbolic addresses, that is, names representing memory locations which contain the two values to be added.

The problem arises, however, that because a program written in assembly language is no longer directly executable by the computer, it needs an *assembler* to carry out the necessary translation to machine code. The assembler accepts an assembly language program as data, converts operation codes (op-codes) to their numeric equivalents, assigns symbolic addresses to memory locations and produces as output the required machine code program. The original assembly language program is termed the *source program* and the final machine code program is the *object program*. This is illustrated in Figure 18.1.

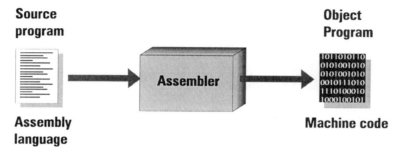

Figure 18.1.*The function of an assembler*

Though it is true that by far the majority of computer programming today is in high-level languages such as Pascal, C or COBOL, programming in assembly languages is still essential for certain tasks. The reason for this, despite continual improvements in compiler design, is simply that the programmer, having total control over the structure of the machine code generated by the assembler, is able to write much faster and more efficient code than that produced by a compiler. The very nature of high-level languages, allowing us to deal with a greatly simplified, virtual machine, often prevents the programmer from being able to optimise code according to particular circumstances.

A consequence of the one-to-one correspondence between an assembly language instruction and its equivalent machine-code instruction is that assemblers are machine dependent, producing machine code for a specific type of processor. For instance, the machine code generated by an Intel 486 assembler could not be used directly by a computer with a Motorola 68000 processor. For this reason, there is no single, univeral assembler; rather, each assembler is related to the architecture of the processor for which it has been designed.

Compilers and Interpreters

There are two main types of high-level language *translators* (or *language processors* as they are often known), namely *compilers* and *interpreters*. Since the choice of translator has implications regarding program development time, debugging and testing, memory requirements, execution speed and program security, it is important from a programming point of view to be quite clear about the difference between the two types.

A compiler accepts a source program, that is, a program written in some high-level language, Pascal for instance, checks that it is correctly formed and, if so, generates the equivalent object program in a low-level language. The translated program may be in the form of an assembly language, in which case it must first be assembled before it is executed, or it may be in machine code, allowing it to be executed directly without further modification. If any errors are detected during compilation, they will be reported and, if serious enough, may prevent the compiler from completing the translation process. Figure 18.2 illustrates the operation of a compiler.

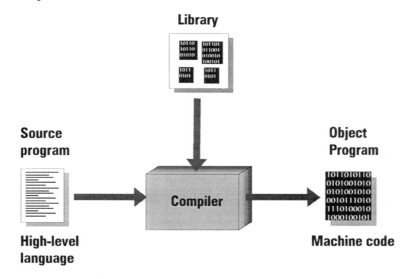

Figure 18.2. *The function of a compiler*

A compiler will often have access to a library of standard routines and special routines appropriate to the application area for which the source language was designed; this collection of subprograms is usually called a *library*. Included in this library of machine code subprograms will be routines for performing arithmetic operations, input/output operations, backing storage data transfers and other commonly used functions. Whenever the source code refers to one of these routines specifically, or needs one to perform the operation specified, the compiler will ensure that the routine is added to the object program.

Note that the final object code is usually completely independent of both the source code and the compiler itself. That is, neither of these two programs needs to be resident in main store when the object code is being executed. However, if the source program is later modified, it must again go through the compilation process before the modifications can have any effect.

An interpreter uses a different method to translate a source program into a machine-sensible form. An object program is not generated in this form of translation - instead, the source program or an intermediate form of it, is scanned statement by statement, each in turn immediately being converted into the actions specified. Figure 18.3 illustrates the operation of an interpreter.

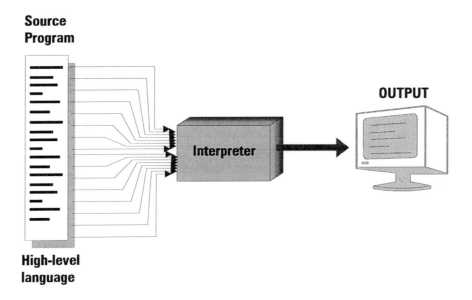

Figure 18.3. *The function of an interpreter*

The source code statements are translated and executed separately, as they are encountered, while the source code is being processed by the interpreter. The object code actually executed is held within the interpreter; the latter merely identifies from the source statement which piece of machine code is relevant and causes it to be performed. On completion of a statement, control returns to the interpreter which then processes the next logical statement in the program sequence. Thus the output from the program is produced directly from the source program without the need to convert the source program into machine code.

It might seem, therefore, that an interpreter has a big advantage over a compiler. In terms of the amount of effort required in obtaining an executable program, this is certainly true, but there are a number of other factors which favour the use of a compiler. For example, an interpreter must do a considerable amount of work before it can even begin to cause a source statement to be executed (error checking, for instance); on the other hand, a compiler has already done this work during compilation. Moreover, should a section of source code be repeated one or more times, an interpreter must re-interpret the section each time. Consequently, interpreted programs tend to run significantly slower than equivalent compiled programs, and for time-critical applications this might be a major concern. Furthermore, because the translation and execution phases are interwoven, the interpreter must be resident in memory at the same time as the source code. If memory space is at a premium, this can be a severe limitation of an interpreted language.

Languages designed for use by children or for teaching purposes are often interpreted. Logo, for example, originally designed as a language for children, is interpreted to facilitate its interactive nature. Similarly, BASIC is interpreted in order to simplify its use for novices.

Programming Environments

Developing a computer program involves a number of stages which can be aided by software. For instance, preparation of the source code requires a text editor or word processor and testing the program can be greatly speeded up with the aid of debugging aids. Many language processors now are sold as part of an integrated set of support programs together providing a program development environment. A typical programming environment might include the following facilities:

- Filing - such as allowing program files to be stored on disk and retrieved from disk, and source code to be printed
- Text editing - such as allowing source code to be produced, formatted and modified, with functions such as cut, copy and paste, and search and replace being easy to perform
- Compilation options - such as allowing syntax and other errors to be displayed when programs are being compiled and linking subprograms in library modules to object code
- Debugging aids- such as allowing users to single step through a program and observe the effect on variables and output, or to insert breakpoints which halt the program at key points
- Help - containing on-line information about the programming language, examples of its use and instructions on using the complete environment

Turbo Pascal has all of these facilities plus many more

Summary of High-Level Languages

In the following sections we give a brief introduction to a number of well-known high-level languages.

BASIC (*Beginners All-purpose Symbolic Instruction Code*)

BASIC was developed at Dartmouth College, in the USA, in 1963 and was intended to be easy to learn and appropriate for a wide variety of applications. Its popularity has been largely the result of its ease of implementation on microcomputers, and it is frequently supplied with them. There is a standard for BASIC, just as there are standards for Fortran and COBOL, and most versions of BASIC adhere to this standard, but each version usually has additional features, many of which are specific to the particular version. Fortunately, however, having learnt one version makes it easy to adapt to a different one.

In the past, BASIC has been heavily criticised for its tendency to encourage bad programming habits. Initially, few versions of BASIC had control structures to encourage or facilitate the use of structured programming techniques, and consequently large programs tended to be difficult to understand and modify. Some recent versions, however, have rectified this deficiency to greater or lesser extents by incorporating Pascal-like facilities.

Originally BASIC was an interpreted language, a feature which contributed to its suitability for novices, but over the past few years, such has been its popularity, that a significant number of software houses have produced BASIC compilers which allow programs to be run independently of an interpreter and with the usual speed and security benefits provided by compiled languages.

C

C is a programming language developed by Bell Laboratories of the USA around 1972. It was designed and written by Dennis Ritchie who was at the time working on the development of the UNIX operating system. UNIX was designed to be particularly useful to the software engineer by providing a wide variety of software tools. In fact, the UNIX operating system was written in C, and even the C compiler is now written in C.

It was designed to be easy to learn and use, powerful and reliable and it has many characteristics of structured languages such as Pascal. Its roots are based in the language Algol, and C retains many of its features, but C's strength lies in its simplicity, the facility with which complex programs may be built from simple building blocks.

Because Dennis Ritchie worked in the field of systems software, C is orientated to such applications as operating systems, computer language development and text processing. Its suitability for these areas is largely attributable to the fact that it is a relatively low-level language which facilitates very efficient programming, yet at the same time it retains the advantage of high-level languages to hide the details of the computer's architecture.

COBOL (*CO*mmon *B*usiness *O*rientated *L*angauge)

On the whole, data processing applications involve a great deal of input and output operations with a relatively minor amount of calculation in between. The data operated upon generally consists of files comprising a large number of records. For example, a computerized stock control system for a wholefood warehouse would contain details of each item held: description of item, sale price, unit size, number currently in stock etc. This collection of data is termed a record, and together all these records form the stock file. Each time an item of stock is sold, the record for that item would need to be changed by reducing the stock level for that item. In terms of the data processing requirements of this type of operation, it would be necessary for the computer to read the details of the sales, find the appropriate stock records, subtract the appropriate amounts from the current stock levels and store the modified records. This sequence would be necessary for each sale recorded on a sales file.

COBOL is ideally suited to this type of application; it was designed to facilitate the manipulation of large amounts of data requiring fairly simple processing operations. Programs written in COBOL tend to be lengthy compared to other languages capable of performing similar processing tasks, the reason being that it requires the programmer to identify the purpose of the program, the computing equipment to be used, and the format of the files to be processed, as well as the procedure to be adopted for processing the files. All this information must be contained within the program itself. Subsequently, COBOL is often criticised for being very cumbersome, but on the credit side, all this detail helps to make a COBOL program easy to read and understand.

A COBOL program is divided into four areas termed `DIVISIONS` which appear in the order `IDENTIFICATION DIVISION`, `ENVIRONMENT DIVISION`, `DATA DIVISION` and `PROCEDURE DIVISION`. Each division comprises a number of `SECTIONS` and these are further divided into `SENTENCES`.

The `IDENTIFICATION DIVISION` allows the programmer to describe the whole program in general terms by supplying, under appropriate headings, such information as the name of the program, its author, when it was written and what it does. Some of this information is optional and none of it has a direct effect on the program's operation.

In the `CONFIGURATION SECTION` of the `ENVIRONMENT DIVISION` are details of the computers on which the program was developed and is intended to be run, and the `INPUT-OUTPUT SECTION` specifies the peripheral devices to be used for reading or writing the files which will be defined later in the program.

The `DATA DIVISION` contains a `FILE SECTION` in which each file named in the `INPUT-OUTPUT SECTION` is given a File Description (`FD`). The `FD` contains the file name and one or more record names. The structure of a record is defined hierarchically using level numbers starting at 01 and getting progressively bigger for finer definitions. The `WORKING-STORAGE SECTION` of the `DATA DIVISION` contains definitions of other data items specifically referenced in the `PROCEDURE DIVISION` of the program but which are not part of any file.

Finally, the `PROCEDURE DIVISION` defines precisely how the processing is to be performed. The programmer may give *paragraph* names to groups of *sentences* to which reference may be made from other parts of the program, and these paragraphs may be grouped together into `SECTIONS`.

Each sentence defines one or more basic operations to be performed on data; in keeping with the general philosophy of making a COBOL program easily readable, the instructions often read like ordinary English sentences as, for example, the sentence

```
add Vat to Cost giving Total-Cost
```

Forth

Forth was developed around 1969 by Charles H. Moore who, dissatisfied with the traditional languages available to him, designed Forth as an interface between himself and the computers he was programming at the time. He developed the final version of the language while working on an IBM 1130 regarded, at the time of its introduction, to be an advanced third generation computer. The resulting language seemed to him to be so powerful that he regarded it as a fourth generation language. He therefore would have liked to call it 'Fourth' but the 1130 would only allow five-character identifiers, so he settled for 'Forth'.

Forth offers a combination of fast execution time and interactive program development. Forth is an extensible language in the sense that the programmer is allowed to add new facilities to the language by defining them in terms of the basic operations that are originally supplied. These new facilities may be temporary or permanent features depending on how they are defined by the programmer.

The language makes extensive use of a data structure called a *stack* and arithmetic operations are defined in *reverse Polish notation*. (In this form of notation an expression such as A×(B+C) would be written as ABC+×, where the arithmetic operators +,-,× and / follow their arguments rather than separate them).

A program is defined in a modular fashion in which sections, called *words*, of a program are defined in terms of basic operations; further words can make reference to words defined previously in a hierarchical structure.

Fortran (*For*mula *tran*slator)

Fortran was designed by John Backus of IBM in 1953 for the science and engineering field. A compiler for the language first appeared in 1955 for an IBM machine, and since that time it has enjoyed widespread popularity as a powerful software tool. Since its introduction, Fortran has steadily evolved, giving rise to such versions as WATFOR (developed at the university of WATerloo, Canada) and WATFIV as well as Fortran IV.

Mainly orientated towards scientific / mathematical / engineering applications, many of its statements resemble and provide for numerical calculations. A Fortran program may be defined as a subroutine (subprogram) which may be referred to (called) by other programs in order to perform some standard or common operation. By forming libraries of these subroutines a programmer is able to reduce the amount of work required to write a new program; where possible, his program will make reference to these prewritten modules which will be combined with his code when the program is compiled. The language has many standard mathematical functions, such as SIN, COS, and SQRT, built in.

Lisp (*Lis*t *p*rocessing)

Though Lisp is one of the oldest computer languages (nearly as old as Fortran) it is used extensively in one of the most innovative of today's research areas: artificial intelligence. As its popularity increases it is becoming available on more and more machines; most mainframes and an increasing number of microcomputer systems support a version of the language.

Lisp was designed as a purely functional language. By this we mean that statements in Lisp look like functions. For instance, the function which adds numbers in Lisp is called PLUS and is written

```
(PLUS 2 3)
```

The function PLUS operates on the arguments 2 and 3. All statements are written in this way.

However, Lisp is primarily a language for manipulating symbols rather than performing complex numeric calculations. It treats all forms of data as being elements of lists and has facilities for conveniently manipulating these lists in various ways. Moreover, the language is extensible in that the user is able to create his own functions to be used like any of those supplied.

Programs in Lisp are developed interactively. Typing the name of a function, followed by its arguments, causes the function to be performed and the result displayed. In the addition example above, Lisp would return the number 5 as soon as the function had been entered. This characteristic is one of the strengths of the language in that programs are written in small, easily testable steps, the effects of which can be seen immediately.

Logo

Designed as a language to provide a very early and easy route into programming, Logo is probably best known as the first language to use 'turtle graphics'. When running Logo, the turtle appears as a graphics cursor which can be instructed to move across the screen using commands such as FORWARD 20 or RIGHT 30. Remotely controllable devices can also be connected to the computer and controlled by the same commands.

The `turtle' commands have been designed to be appealing and to motivate children to write programs to make the turtle perform visually pleasing manoeuvres. Seymour Papert, the American mathematician who designed the language, was largely influenced by Piaget's well-known ideas on intellectual development in children. Consequently Logo is emerging as an important educational tool. Unlike much educational software currently available in which the computer is the teacher, and the child reacts to it, Logo offers a completely different approach to computer assisted learning. With Logo the roles are reversed, the child teaching the computer what to do.

In his book,'Mindstorms', Seymour Papert explains the philosophy of Logo, how it was developed and how it works.

Logo, however, is more than a language just for children. It is based on Lisp and shares many of its features. Like Lisp it is extensible, based on list processing, and allows recursion. Because it is interpreted, it is easy to use and allows programs to be edited without difficulty. In fact it is a surprisingly powerful language, as well as being easy to learn. It is by no means a `toy' language and is attracting much interest in all kinds of areas, including artificial intelligence applications.

Here are two simple subprograms in Logo to enable the turtle to draw a box of side L screen units:

```
TO SIDE :L
FORWARD :L
RIGHT 90
END
```

```
TO SQUARE :L
REPEAT 4 [SIDE :L]
END
```

The first subprogram, `SIDE`, instructs the turtle to move forward L units and then turn right by 90 degrees.

The second subprogram, `SQUARE`, draws a square of side L by repeatedly calling `SIDE`.

The turtle would be instructed to draw a square of side 100 units with the command

```
SQUARE 100
```

The functional nature of the language is illustrated by the manner in which arithmetic is performed. For example, to add two numbers and store them in the variable, S, we would write:

```
MAKE S SUM :A :B
```

where `SUM` is the function taking two arguments, in this case the values of variables A and B.

Pascal

Devised by Professor Niklaus Wirth in 1970 and named after the gifted 17th century mathematician and philosopher Blaise Pascal, Pascal is a general-purpose language based on Algol-60.

Because Pascal, like BASIC, was designed as a teaching language, it is a very easy language to learn. Moreover, being orientated towards structured programming, it encourages the clear expression of the logical structure of the program. This makes Pascal a very easy language to write programs in, and is particularly suitable for the development of large programs. For these reasons it is widely used in teaching, and is being adopted by more and more establishments of further and higher education as the main programming language for computing courses. Many people believe Pascal to be superior to any other general-purpose programming language in use today, and its expanding use in all sectors of industry is evidence in support of this claim.

Each Pascal program consists of a declarations section in which the structure of the data to be processed and produced is defined, a section for the definition of functions and procedures which are referenced in the program body section. The program body defines the operation of the program in a precise series of steps. Functions and procedures may be called from the program body whenever required. Chapter 30 deals with programming in Pascal in more detail.

Prolog (*Programming in Logic*)

The languages discussed so far are often classified as *imperative* or *procedural languages*. These terms are used to describe high-level languages which require the programmer to show explicitly the order in which program statements are to be executed, and precisely how the programming solution is to be reached. The sequence of commands in a program is a key feature of imperative languages such as Pascal, Fortran and COBOL, since they are based on a computer model in which a stored program is executed by sequentially stepping through instructions stored in the immediate access store of a computer. Store locations are modified as a direct result of the action of the program. Similarly, imperative languages achieve their objectives by modifying program variables using assignment statements, and by causing sequential execution of program statements. Because imperative languages are so closely related to the operation of conventional computers, they are relatively efficient.

However, other computer architectures, such as those using parallel processing, give rise to different types of programming languages. *Declarative languages* rely on a different mechanism for solving programming problems. In these languages the emphasis is on defining the problem to be solved, not on the detailed sequence of instructions that are required in order to achieve the desired solution. It can be argued that a language such as Pascal is less procedural, and therefore more declarative, than an assembly language because there is less need for the programmer to define precisely how to do standard processing tasks such as input/output or arithmetic operations. For example, in an assembly language, it would require quite a complex sequence of instructions to perform the Pascal floating point calculation

```
x := (-b + sqrt(det))/(2.0*a);
```

Yet in Pascal it is merely a matter of specifying the calculation to be performed and allowing the compiler to determine how to organize the instructions required to do it. Thus languages that are predominantly procedural have elements of non-procedural characteristics. Declarative languages take this a stage further, allowing the language translator to do much more of the work, so that the programmer can concentrate on specifying what the problem is rather than how to solve it.

Because declarative languages do not rely on the programmer specifying precisely in which order instructions are to be executed, it is often possible to process a number of instructions in parallel if the mechanism exists to allow this. The logic programming language Prolog is generally regarded as a good example of a predominantly declarative, or non-procedural, language which allows it to take advantage of alternative computer architectures.

Invented by Alain Colmerauer in the early 1970's, Prolog was first implemented in Marseilles in 1972. It provided a means of allowing the programmer to specify a problem in terms related to formal logic rather than procedures. It has been used extensively in the development of expert systems and other programs involving artificial intelligence because it includes facilities ideal for this type of application.

Prolog is said to be goal oriented, that is to say the programmer specifies the problem to be solved in terms of a goal, and is not expected to provide detailed instructions regarding the achievement of the goal. A goal is defined in terms of subgoals, the achievement of which will lead to the final solution. A subgoal may be a simple statement which evaluates to logical true or false, or may depend on its own subgoals which Prolog will try to evaluate. Since there may be alternative sets of subgoals for a particular goal, Prolog may, having failed to successfully resolve one combination, backtrack and try another combination. It will continue to try different combinations until either a solution is reached or there are no further combinations of subgoals to try. The power of Prolog lies in its built-in ability to select goal combinations and to backtrack; in other languages this would have to be programmed explicitly.

Programming in Prolog involves defining objects to be manipulated and relationships between them. A program consists of facts and rules (or clauses): facts are taken to be true statements about objects and rules declare that statements about objects are true if certain conditions (subgoals) are true. Executing a Prolog program involves stating a goal to be achieved and allowing Prolog to determine whether the goal can be achieved with the current facts and rules.

Fourth Generation Languages(4GLs)

In order to put fourth generation language into context, it is perhaps appropriate here to define in broad terms the first three generations of languages. First generation languages were just machine code, the most basic form of programming language. Evolving from this original form, assembly languages, the second generation, eased the programming task by making the computer take care of a number of functions that were not directly related to the processing problems being addressed. High-level languages such as Pascal and COBOL represent the third generation of programming languages and are characterised by the concise way they allow a problem to be defined; consequently, these languages are relatively easy to learn and use.

Fourth generation languages represent the latest innovation in the evolution of programming languages, allowing a programmer to specify the problem to be solved in relatively general terms and leaving the computer to fill in the programming details. Such languages continue the tradition of reducing the work of the user and increasing the load on the computer. The terms Fourth Generation Language, and its contraction, 4GL, are subject to a wide variety of interpretations and definitions, but they all have a number of characteristics in common:

- easier to use than existing high-level languages, particularly by non-specialists;
- more concise than existing high-level languages;
- the language is closer to natural language;
- user-friendly;
- non-procedural.

With the possible exception of the last one, these points are self-explanatory. The terms *non-procedural* and *declarative* refer to languages which allow the user to define a goal and leave the computer to determine (within bounds) how to achieve it.

To illustrate the difference, compare the following two sets of instructions for making a cup of tea:

(1)

1. Put water into the kettle
2. Turn the kettle on
3. Put tea in the teapot
4. When the kettle has boiled, pour the boiling water into the teapot
5. Wait for the tea to infuse
6. Put small amount of milk in a teacup
7. Pour tea into the cup

(2)

    Make a cup of tea

The first list defines the procedure, step by step, for making a cup of tea. The instructions imply that the procedure is not familiar to the tea maker; this is not the case in (2) where the implication is that the tea maker already has the required knowledge and merely needs to be told to get started on the task. The person issuing the command in (2) is not interested in the precise way that the task is accomplished as long as the tea that arrives tastes good and does not take an unreasonable length of time. (1) represents *procedural programming* and (2) the *declarative* approach.

Two examples of current software systems which fit this loose definition of a 4GL are *Structured Query Languages* (SQL's) and *Program Generators*.

Structured Query Languages(SQLs)

Developed by IBM, SQL's operate on relational databases and are becoming the recognised standard for this type of application. Briefly, a relational database is one in which the database is considered to be a table(relation) of rows, which are equivalent to records, and columns, which are related to fields within records. New relations can be created in response to user queries. An SQL simplifies the task of specifying queries by allowing the user to use a series of key-words. The resulting query, while not being in natural language, is easily understandable to the non specialist and certainly more user friendly than many other query languages. SQLs are dealt with in more detail in the chapter on relational databases.

Program Generators

One such system accepts a type of pseudocode as the source/specification language and uses it to generate the appropriate COBOL program. Pseudocode allows expression of processing requirements in very high-level, well structured terms which are not specific to a particular programming language. This is comparable to the way a compiler operates, accepting a high-level language as source code to generate a machine code program. In this case the output from the 4GL is the source code for a high-level language (ie COBOL). The specification language may be related to a system design technique such as Jackson Structured Design.

Chapter 19

Modelling and Simulation

Introduction

The term *modelling* is used in information technology for computer applications which, for example, are used to investigate, analyse or plan a complex activity, or to *simulate* a complex process. Some models are concerned with investigating financial systems using a software tool such as a *spreadsheet* program. For example, a manufacturing company might use a spreadsheet-based model to determine the minimum number of items the company must produce in order to make a profit.

Other computer models are concerned with representing physical systems. For example, before a new chemical plant is built, its designers often will first model the complex arrangement of pipes and other equipment using a 3-D computer graphics program, and also simulate its operation with other types of software. In this way many potential problems can be identified and solved before construction work is started.

This chapter begins by describing the nature and purpose of mathematical models and simulations. Some of the areas that have benefited from modelling and simulation are discussed in the next section. We then give some spreadsheet-based examples of simulations and conclude by investigating the application of 3-D computer graphics programs to modelling.

Mathematical Models

Physical models are usually simplified versions of actual objects or objects that may be constructed at some later date. Thus, a car manufacturer might produce a scaled-down model of a new car to investigate its wind-resistance characteristics. Though the model accurately represents the shape of the car, it is much easier to construct than a full-sized working version. Producing a model therefore provides a convenient and cheap method of investigating certain aspects of the final product.

A *mathematical model* takes modelling a stage further: it provides a means of investigating something without the need to make a physical model. Mathematical models are symbolic representations of things that we want to know more about. For example, a mathematical model of the distance travelled by a body accelerating from rest is

$$s = \tfrac{1}{2}at^2$$

where s is the distance travelled, a is the acceleration of the body and t is the time period. This mathematical model now allows us to investigate the effects of different accelerations and different time periods on the distance travelled by the body, without having to build a working model. Using this model we can predict that a body uniformly accelerating at 5 meters/sec^2 for ten seconds will have travelled $\frac{1}{2} \times 5 \times 10^2$ metres, that is 250 metres.

Of course not all mathematical models are as simple as this. Some mathemetical models attempt to describe much more complex things such as human behaviour or weather patterns. Such complex models involve defining the relationships between the many variables of the system being modelled, and they almost invariably require the use of very powerful computers to investigate them.

Simulation

In computer science, *simulation* refers to the use of computers to model and investigate systems which involve some changing process. Thus a computer simulation will generally incorporate a mathematical model of the system of interest. The purpose of a computer simulation often is to enable experimental measurements to be made or to predict behaviour. Simulation can provide an experimental system for designers to investigate behaviour under a variety of different circumstances, or it may be used to provide a teaching aid for the system being simulated.

The prime reason for developing a simulation is that the cost of experimenting with the actual system is prohibitive, and since simulations are themselves expensive, there must be very sound economical reasons for justifying their use. For example, it is much cheaper and quicker to test a large number of design variations of a nuclear reactor by using a simulation rather than by building prototypes. Here are more possible reasons for simulating a complex system:

- *Testing* - it is necessary to test the system to destruction, that is, identify the factors that will cause it to fail and a complex device might be too expensive to use for the investigation.
- *Safety* - it is too dangerous or expensive to use the actual equipment. An example is teaching an aircraft pilot to respond to a range of emergency situations.
- *Prediction* - an accurate model is needed of an existing system so that its future behaviour can be predicted accurately. A good example of this is weather forecasting.
- *Speed and flexibility* - the system might require frequent modification and development. For example, in control systems electronically-based instruments can be simulated by a computer. These so-called virtual instruments allow devices, such as meters and indicators, and other electronic components, to be represented by software which is cheaper and easier to modify or replace than physical devices (see the chapter on computer-based control systems in the skills part of this book).

Simulation Parameters

A mathematical model of a system usually consists of a linked set of formulas in which the result of one formula may affect one or more others. These formulas will generally use one or more key factors, or *parameters*; altering the value of a parameter will generally alter the overall behaviour of the system. A number of different types of parameters can be identified:

Controllable inputs. These are factors, or *variables*, which are under the direct control of the system designers. For example, in a stock control simulation where items of stock are continually being sold to customers and received from suppliers, two of the controllable inputs are likely to be the re-order quantity and re-order level. In a traffic lights simulation, the timing of the red/green cycle is also under the control of the system designers.

Non-controllable inputs. These are factors which are not under the direct control of the system designers. For example, in a simulation of a supermarket checkout queue, the arrival rate of customers is an input variable which cannot be controlled, but there will be some statistical information regarding its characteristics. Similarly in a traffic lights simulation, the arrival and departure rates of vehicles at the junction are not directly under the control of the designers. These types of variables frequently have characteristics which can be described using probability.

Seasonal variations. Some factors, again not under the control of the system designers, can vary significantly according to the time of day, the day of the week, or the season of the year. For instance, traffic density is usually heavier in the morning when people are travelling to work and in the evening when people are returning home than at other times of the day. Supermarkets often attract more customers at the weekend and just before bank holidays than on other days.

Monte Carlo Simulation

One common technique used in simulation is called the *Monte Carlo* method which uses random numbers to solve problems. The method is particularly suitable for problems which involve statistical uncertainty. For example, when you throw a die, you are never certain which number is going to show: there is an equal probability of each of the number 1 to 6 appearing. A computer program could be used to generate a random number in the range 1 to 6 in order to simulate a die being thrown. This is a simple application of the Monte Carlo method.

Most high-level programming languages and spreadsheet programs provide random number generators. However, the random number function usually will return a fraction between 0 and 1, but this can be converted into the required range quite simply. For instance, if we multiply the random number by 6, add one and ignore the fractional part of the number, we will have a random number between 1 and 6. Thus if the random number was 0.3245 then when multiplied by 6 it gives 1.9470. Adding 1 gives 2.9470, and ignoring the fractional part gives us our random number 2. The queue simulation example later in this chapter uses random numbers produced by a spreadsheet to simulate traffic arriving at traffic lights.

Applications

Mathematical models and simulation are used in many areas including:

Marketing. This involves activities related to getting goods from the producer to the consumer. Marketing research involves the use of surveys, tests, and statistical studies to analyse consumer trends, to identify profitable markets for products or services and to produce sales predictions. Such research and forecasts require mathematical models of social behaviour and consumers' needs for various products. The cost implications of predicted demands for goods can also be modelled so that a company can be fully prepared to cope with the production, distribution and sale of the products.

Sociology is a social science that deals with the study of human social relations or group life. Quantitative sociology, which attempts to analyse sociological phenomena using mathematics, ranges from the presentation of large amounts of descriptive statistical data to the use of advanced mathematical models and computer simulations of social processes. One popular area of investigation is identification of the factors that are mainly responsible for people succeeding or failing in their chosen occupations.

Social Psychology is a branch of psychology concerned with the scientific study of the behavior of individuals as influenced, directly or indirectly, by social factors. Social psychologists are interested in the thinking, emotions, desires, and judgments of individuals, as well as in their outward behavior. Numerous kinds of research methods and techniques are being used in social psychology. In recent years accurate mathematical models of social behavior have been used increasingly in psychological studies. Such models allow predictions of social behaviour to be made, given a system of social relationships.

Educational Psychology involves the application of scientific method to the study of the behavior of people in instructional settings. Different theories of learning help educational psychologists understand, predict, and control human behavior. For example, educational psychologists have worked out mathematical models of learning that predict the probability of a student making a correct response to a multiple-choice question; these mathematical theories are used to design computerized instruction in reading, mathematics, and second-language learning.

Weather forecasting involves reporting, predicting, and studying the weather, including temperature, moisture, barometric pressure, and wind speed and direction. In addition to their regular and special services to the public, weather services conduct research projects. In their meteorological investigations, primarily concerned with forecasting techniques and storm behavior, these agencies make use of the findings from studies of mathematical modelling of the general circulation of the atmosphere, advances in radar meteorology, high-speed computer methods, and earth-orbiting artificial satellites.

Fluid Mechanics is a physical science dealing with the action of fluids at rest or in motion, and with applications and devices in engineering using fluids. Fluid mechanics is basic to such diverse fields as aeronautics, chemical, civil, and mechanical engineering, meteorology, naval architecture, and oceanography. Turbulent flows cannot be analysed solely from computed predictions and depend on a mixture of experimental data and mathematical models for their analysis, with much of modern fluid-mechanics research still being devoted to better models of turbulence. The nature and complexity of turbulent flow can be observed as cigarette smoke rises into very still air. At first it rises in a stable streamline motion but after some distance it becomes unstable and breaks up into an intertwining eddy pattern.

Population Biology is the study of populations of animals and plants. A population is a group of interbreeding organisms in a specific region - for example, the members of a species of fish in a lake. Populations are analysed in terms of their variability, density, and stability, and of the environmental and other processes and circumstances that affect these characteristics. Among such key features of a given population are birth and death rates; the distribution of ages and sexes; behavioral patterns of competition and cooperation; predator-prey, host-parasite, and other relationships with different species; food supplies and other environmental considerations; and migration patterns. To analyse populations biologists try to develop mathematical models of the group under study that incorporate as many of these variables as possible. Such models enable scientists to predict what effect a change in any one factor may have on a population as a whole.

Catastrophe Theory is the term for an attempt to develop a mathematical modelling system for dealing with abruptly changing natural events. One such physical 'catastrophe', for example, could be an avalanche resulting from a gradual build-up of snow. In the area of human relations, a 'catastrophe' could be someone suddenly losing his or her temper after being patient for a long period. Catastrophe theory was primarily intended to be useful for describing events in the biological and social sciences.

Science Education. Laboratory experiments to determine the characteristics of falling bodies, colliding balls, pendulums and projectiles can all be simulated quite easily by a computer; students can investigate the effects of chaging various parameters such as the weight of the pendulum, or the speed of colliding objects, or the angle at which an object is projected, or any one of a number of other factors that affect the experiment of interest.

Medical Education. Medical diagnosis is a very complex activity and very difficult to learn. Though the typical symptoms of most ailments are well-known, the manner in which a given illness manifests itself varies from patient to patient. This means that physicians must acquire the ability to assign the correct level of importance to each recognisable symptom in order to make a correct diagnosis.

Computers can help with this task by simulating illnesses and associated symptoms. The computer model of the illness can be set up so that the symptoms vary each time the same illness is simulated. The computer might present a case study of a patient, supplying the student with the type of information gained from tests and by questioning the patient; the student is then required to arrive at a diagnosis of the ailment and suggest appropriate treatment. The student's diagnosis and suggested treatment can then be compared with the correct ones stored in the computer in order to provide feedback concerning the accuracy of the student's analysis. In this way, students can very quickly "experience" many different manifestations of a particular illness, a situation which could be very difficult to organise using actual patients.

Computers can also be used to show the effects of drugs on the human body. How long a drug remains active in the bloodstream and the concentration of the drug after repeated doses are very important factors. However, because of the complexity of the human body and the great number of factors which contribute to the effects of a particular drug, predicting the effects of a drug is very difficult. Computer simulations which use complex theoretical models of the human body can allow students to experiment with typical drug dosages and observe the resulting effects. A common approach is to present the student with a number of screens of text and/or graphical information. After this information has been assimilated, the student is then in a position to understand the purpose of the simulation and what information must be supplied. By providing typical drug characteristics and dosages, the student can observe the predicted affect of the drug as simulated by the computer. Finally, the student completes a multiple-choice test which is marked by the computer. Any weaknesses in the student's understanding of the material can thus be identified and remedied by suggesting that the student repeats certain parts of the simulation program.

With the enormous increase in desk top computing power over recent years, it is now feasible to produce computer programs which use graphics to allow students to explore the human body in great detail. Software simulates the structure and function of the nervous, circulatory, immune and other systems of the body using multimedia. Though they are not used as replacements for actually dissecting cadavers, these products can give students a useful grounding in physiology and anatomy.

Queuing theory. This deals with the analysis of the waiting lines that occur in many areas of modern life. Whenever something is in demand, there is the possibilty of a queue of some description forming, resulting in restricted access to resources, or losses in time, money and patience. Efforts to avoid and control congestion are therefore of great interest to providers of services which can cause queues, and this has led to the study of waiting lines using mathematical models and simulation. An area which has benefited greatly from queuing theory is that of time-shared computer systems in which each user is given a small amount of processing time and users waiting their turn are put in a queue; the computer decides which job will be serviced next and for how long using a scheduling algorithm based on queuing theory.

Instrumentation. Computer measurement systems frequently involve monitoring a physical system, analysing the data gathered and displaying the results. Traditionally, many such systems have used hardware components, such as filters, frequency analysers, meters and LED displays, but computers can be used to replace many of these devices. *Virtual instruments* allow many physical devices to be simulated using a computer. A virtual instrument uses software components to process the data measured externally to the computer, and to present results of processing using realistic representations of instrument panels containing meters, switches, digital and other types of displays. (See Figure 19.1). Graphically based programming languages allow complex processing tasks to be programmed by connecting together symbols which represent electronic devices.

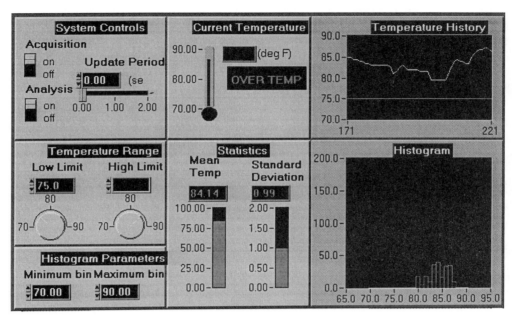

Figure 19.1. *An example of a virtual instrument*

The advantage of this approach is that new devices can be constructed, tested and modified without the need to produce costly, purpose-built hardware devices. Virtual instruments used to construct simple computer control systems are discussed in Chapter 32.

Three-dimensional models. Many software products are available for simulating the structure of solid objects. These programs allow designers to create three-dimensional drawings of objects which can be viewed from any angle, rotated, and modified using a wide variety of software tools. Many 3D drawing programs also allow objects to be animated. For example, detailed computer models of buildings are used as the basis of *fly-throughs* in which a simulated camera navigates through the building, going from room to room, zooming in and out. Simulations

Figure 19.2. *An example of a 3D model of a building*

such as this, animated or otherwise, allow complex objects to be visualised prior to production, thus speeding up and reducing the design process.

Modelling and Simulation using Spreadsheets

In this section we look at the use of spreadsheet for performing a break-even analysis to investigate a manufacturing business, to simulate a stock control system and to simulate traffic arriving at traffic lights. The skills part of this book explains in detail the operation and use of spreadsheet programs. Here we limit expanations to special functions that are required for simulation purposes and to the formulas that are required for the various calcuations involved.

Financial Planning - Break-even Analysis

The prime objective of most organisations is the achievement of profit. In order to make a profit the organisation must earn sufficient revenue from the sale of its products to exceed the costs that it has incurred in operating and producing. It is usually a relatively simple task to calculate revenue:simply determine the number of goods which have been sold and multiply this quantity by the price per item. The calculation of cost is slightly more complicated owing to the fact that the organisation incurs a variety of different costs in producing its products. *Fixed costs* remain constant irrespective of the number of items produced. Examples include rent on the premises or local council rates. Therefore, as production rises the fixed cost per item reduces. Other costs, however, increase with production. These are called *variable costs*. Raw materials are an example of variable costs since as more items are produced, more raw materials are required.

Combining fixed and variable costs gives the organisation its total costs and it is these which must exceed its total revenue before it can make a profit. Clearly then, an organisation may make a loss if its output is low, but as it produces and sells more it will eventually move through a *break-even point* into profit. As the name suggests, the break-even point is where the organisation neither makes a loss nor a profit- it simply breaks even. Management are obviously very interested to know the level of production required to exceed the break-even point and make a profit. Combining the revenue and cost figures in order to determine the break-even point is called *break-even analysis*, and a graphical representation of the figures is termed a *break-even chart*. An example of a break-even analysis and equivalent chart are shown in Figure 19.3.

The UNITS PRODUCED and VARIABLE COSTS columns of the spreadsheet are constant values. FIXED COSTS are copied from the Fixed Costs(FC) parameter cell. The TOTAL COSTS column is the sum of FIXED COSTS and VARIABLE COSTS. The REVENUE is calculated by multiplying the units produced by the Unit Cost(UC) parameter. Finally, the profit is found by subtracting the TOTAL COSTS from the REVENUE.

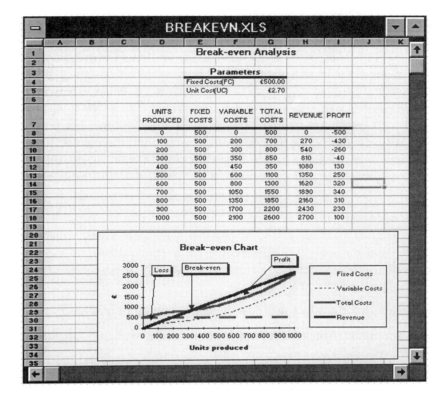

Figure 19.3. *A break-even analysis*

The break-even chart shown below the spreadsheet graphs the three costs and the revenue figures; the break-even point is where the TOTAL COSTS curve crosses the REVENUE line. Profit occurs to the right of the break-even point, and you can see that in this case, when the fixed costs are at £500 and the selling price is £2.70, the break-eeven point occurs when just over 300 items are produced. Interestingly, the graph also shows that maximum profit occurs when between 600 and 700 items are produced and that at about 1000 items the company again breaks even.

Stock Control Simulation

Suppose that Agros is a large retail outlet which sells a wide range of household materials. It has a computerised stock control, or *inventory*, system which deals with obtaining, storing and supplying the goods it offers to the general public. Agros provides free catalogues containing descriptions of items which customers can obtain by visiting one of their outlets. The items shown in the catalogue are kept in a warehouse attached to the outlet. It is of vital importance to Argos to ensure that it has a full range of items in stock so that customers can immediately obtain those that they require.

If an item is out of stock, the potential customer might decide to shop elsewhere thus causing Agros to lose the sale, and possibly future sales too. Agros attempts to prevent this situation by ordering quantities of those items that are in danger of being sold out. However, the time taken for the items to arrive from the suppliers may be several days, by which time the goods still could have sold out. Moreover, if the demand for an item is overestimated, and there are a large number of the item in the warehouse, Argos again loses money because each item incurs a warehouse storage cost. Argos must try to achieve a balance between over-ordering and under-ordering goods. This would be an easy problem to solve if Argos knew exactly what the demand for a particular item is likely to be at any one time, but unfortunately this is never the case. Possibly the best prediction of demand will still involve a large amount of uncertainty. For example, past experience might provide an estimate of the average demand per day for an item, but the actual demand on a particular day will probably fluctuate fairly randomly.

A possible means of investigating this type of system is therefore a Monte Carlo simulation in which demand is simulated using a random number generator such as that described in the previous example. Before we go on to show how a spreadsheet can be used for such a simulation, we will define a number of terms commonly used to describe stock control systems.

Demand - the quantity of a product that customers are willing to purchase.

Opening stock - the number of items of stock immediately available for purchase at the start of trading on any day.

Closing stock - the number of items of stock that remain in the outlet at the close of trading on any particular day.

Re-order quantity - the number of items of stock ordered from a supplier at any one time.

Re-order level - the minimum number of items held in stock before the item is re-ordered. As soon as the level of stock reaches this level, or drops below it, the re-order quantity is ordered from the supplier.

Carrying costs - the cost of storing an item waiting to be sold.

Stock out costs - the financial loss incurred when the demand for an item exceeds the stock level. In other words, a company loses money when it cannot supply an item to a customer because that item is out of stock. The term *Loss of Goodwill* also applies to this type of loss, because the disappointed customer might not use the outlet in the future.

Order costs - the cost to the company of making an order a re-order quantity of a product. This in addition to the actual cost of buying the items from the supplier. Each time an order is generated, there is an order cost.

Lead time - this is the time it takes to receive an item from the supplier once the order has been generated.

The simulation shown in Figure 19.4 illustrates the effects of the stock control parameters, shown at the top of the spreadsheet, over a period of fourteen days. The columns in the table have been calculated as follows:

OPENING STOCK - On the first day of the simulation period this is the value OS which appears in the parameter table. On the second day it is the closing stock value for the first day, that is, the number of stock items left after close of business the previous day. On the third and subsequent days its is the closing value for the previous day plus any stock that was ordered two days previously. Thus, for day four, the opening stock (10) is the sum of the third day's closing stock (2) and the quantity ordered on the second day (8).

DEMAND - This is produced using a random number generator which produces a random number between half the average demand and one and a half times the average demand. For example, if the average demand is 6 items per day, a random number between 3 and 9 is generated. This represents the actual demand for the item on a particular day, and this is where the uncertainty factor is introduced.

CLOSING STOCK - the number of items remaining in the warehouse/storeroom at close of trading on that day.

NUM ORDERED - the number of items ordered that day. This will be either the re-order quantity, if the closing stock level is equal to or below the re-order level, or zero if the CLOSING STOCK level is greater than the re-order level.

ORDER COSTS - each time the item is re-ordered, there is an order cost incurred.

CARRYING COSTS - there is a charge for each item in stock at the close of trading on each day. Thus, on day 5, CLOSING STOCK was 9 and the order costs at £2 per item means that the CARRYING COSTS amount to £18.

STOCK OUT COSTS - a fixed cost is incurred for each item out of stock that a customer was willing to buy. This is calculated by subtracting OPENING STOCK from DEMAND and multiplying the result by the LOSS OF GOODWILL cost shown in the parameter table.

TOTAL COSTS - calculated by summing ORDER COSTS, CARRYING COSTS and STOCK OUT COSTS.

The column totals for the four costs calculated are shown below the appropriate columns.

Examples of the spreadsheet formulas used for these calculations are shown in the shadowed formula boxes on the spreadsheet.

Note that the OPENING STOCK parameter is a constant value that can be changed in this particular simulation only by changing the formulas in the OPEN STOCK column.

Each time the spreadsheet is recalculated (by pressing F9 in Excel) new DEMAND random numbers are generated for each day, and the resulting costs are displayed. This allows you to investigate the effects of changing the various parameters. You could, for example, investigate the effect on the total costs of increasing the re-order level, or of reducing the re-order quantity, or the effect of changing both of these parameters together.

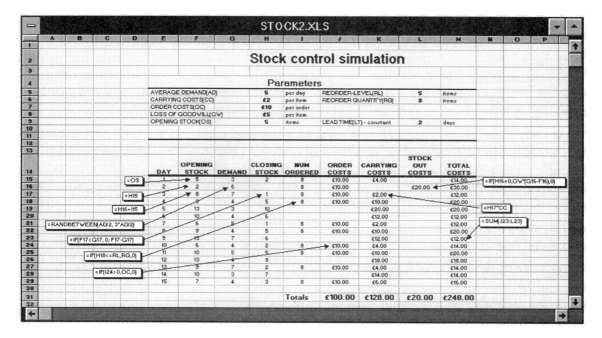

Figure 19.4. *A stock control simulation*

Simulating Vehicles Arriving at Traffic Lights

At a road junction controlled by traffic lights, vehicles arriving at the junction form a queue when the lights are on red. The size of the queue depends on two factors: the length of time the lights remain on red and the rate at which vehicles arrive at the junction. When the lights turn to green, the queue reduces as vehicles pass through the junction. At the same time, however, vehicles are still arriving at the junction while the lights are on green.

In this simple simulation, we use four *parameters*, that is factors which affect the size of the queue:

1. The average rate of arrival of vehicles at the lights. We assume that if the average rate is say, A, then during any stop period the actual rate is modelled by generating a random number between A/2 and 3A/2. For example, if the average arrival rate is 4 vehicles per minute, then we generate a random number between 2 and 6 and use this as the actual arrival rate for one instance of the lights being on red. We generate a new value for the actual arrival rate the next time the (simulated) lights turn to red.

2. The average rate of departure from the lights. We use the same scheme as for the arrival rate: if the average departure rate is L vehicles per minute, then we generate a random number between L/2 and 3L/2 to represent the actual departure rate for one instance of the lights being on green. We generate a new value for the actual departure rate the next time the lights turn to green.

3. The length of time (in minutes) the lights are on red. This affects the build-up of the vehicle queue, since the longer the lights are on red, the more vehicles that will arrive at the junction and join the end of the queue.

4. The length of time (in minutes) the lights are on green. This controls how many vehicles can leave the queue.

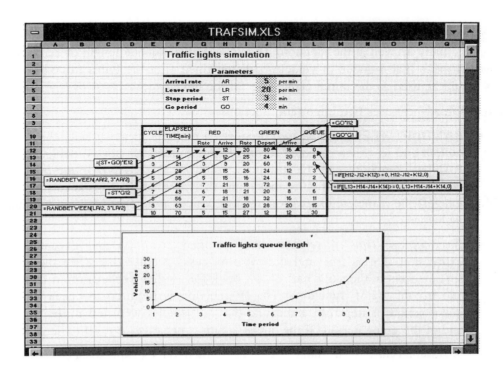

Figure 19.5. *A traffic lights queue simulation*

A complete cycle of the lights is one stop (ie red) period followed by one go (ie green) period. The simulation calculates the size of the queue after each of these cycles. As an example, suppose that the average arrival rate at the lights (called *AR* on the spreadsheet) is 5 vehicles per minute, the average departure rate (*LR*) is 20 vehicles per minute, the lights are on red for 3 minutes (*ST*) and green for 4 minutes (*GO*), then for the first cycle, assuming that there were no vehicles waiting, the calculation might go as follows:

1. Vehicles arriving when lights are on red : 3×R1 = 3x2 = **6** to the nearest whole number (assuming R1 was 2), where R1 represents a random number between 1.5 and 4.5

2. Vehicles leaving the junction when lights are on green : 4×R2= 4×5 = **20** to the nearest whole number (assuming R2 was 5), where R2 represents a random number between 2 and 6.

3. Vehicles arriving at the junction while the lights are on green : $4 \times R1 = 4 \times 2 = 8$ to the nearest whole number.

Therefore, the queue length after one cycle of the lights is given by

4. Vehicles arriving(red) - Vehicles departing(green) + Vehicles arriving(green)

$$=6 - 20 + 8 = -6.$$

The negative number indicates that it was possible for six more vehicles to go through the lights than actually arrived at the junction. This would give a queue length of zero. A positive value would mean that a queue of vehicles still remained after the lights turned back to red, and this would be used as the initial queue size for the next cycle.

The Excel spreadsheet uses two important functions:

- RANDBETWEEN(*bottom*, *top*) produces a random integer greater than or equal to *bottom* and less than or equal to *top*. If this function is not available, the standard RAND() function can be used as follows: INT(RAND()*(*top-bottom*+1) + *bottom*). The INT function rounds down the value inside the brackets to the nearest integer; the complete expression again produces an integer between *top* and *bottom* inclusively.

- IF(*condition*, *true*, *false*) tests the specified *condition* and executes the *true* expression if it is true and the *false* expression otherwise. (See the section on spreadsheets in the skills part of this book for a fuller explanation of the operation and use of the IF function). The IF function is required to check whether the queue length is negative, indicating that no vehicles were left in the queue at the end of the green period. If the queue length is negative, it is set to zero.

All of the different types of formulas used are shown on the spreadsheet. Note that the simulation parameters have been given names (AR, LR, ST and GO) in order to clarify their use in the formulas. The spreadsheet recalculation facility has been set to manual so that function key F9 must be pressed in order to generate a new set of random numbers and for their effects to be shown. The graph automatically reflects the change in the queue after each recalculation.

Once the simulation spreadsheet has been created, the effects of changing the parameters can be investigated. This allows the parameters to be set to values which reduce the probability of a large queue of vehicles forming. The parameter that is least likely to change frequently is the departure rate of vehicles, and the arrival rate is not under the direct control of the system designer; however, the timing of the signals is under the control of the designer and this type of simulation provides the opportunity of doing detailed analysis of how crucial the timing is likely to be in the reduction of large traffic jams. The principles used in this study could equally be used to investigate other types of queues, for example, supermarket checkouts or entrances and exits to football stadiums. Finally, note that this simulation could be improved in a number of ways. For instance, more accurate models could be devised for the arrival and departure rates, or perhaps another parameter representing the number of available lanes could be introduced, or the time of day could be taken into account since this would affect the volume of traffic.

Chapter 20
Control Systems

Introduction

As the name suggests, a **control system** controls the operation of some process. The human body, for example, contains a temperature control system which maintains it at a constant temperature. If your body becomes too hot, it produces perspiration which cools it down, and if you become too cold you warm yourself by shivering. A muscle control system operates whenever to try to catch a ball: your senses provide constant data regarding the position of the ball and the position of your body so that you can adjust the position of your hands to coincide with the trajectory of the ball. A domestic central heating system is a control system in which the temperature of the air in a house is regulated, for example, by means of a boiler pumping hot water through radiators. The output of the boiler is controlled by thermostats which sense the temperature of the air in their vicinities, switching the boiler on when the temperature drops below a required level, and switching it off when that level has been attained. In computer control systems, a computer is the component of the control system which uses data from sensors in order to maintain the outputs of the system at certain levels.

Many control systems involve the use of *measurement systems* to provide data concerning the current output of the system, so that the output can be increased or reduced to maintain it at a certain level. In engineering, measurement systems are used in many different ways and for many different purposes. Sometimes a measurement system is simply required to monitor some process by obtaining data about it. For example, a rotating vane anemometer might be used to provide wind speed data for an athletics meeting. Some measurement systems are used to ensure that a device is operating according to specification for safety or quality reasons. An example is a microwave leakage tester, which measures microwave emissions from commercial microwave appliances and displays the strength of the emissions on the integral meter. Other measurement systems provide data for control systems. For example, in a computer-controlled car engine management system, a measurement system provides information regarding the composition of exhaust gases for the microprocessor which automatically adjusts the engine settings to keep emissions within required limits.

Control Systems

Control systems are used to monitor and control physical systems automatically. Such systems almost invariably use devices called *transducers* to convert from one form of energy into another. Most transducers used in computer control systems convert some form of energy into electrical signals that can processed by a computer, or they convert signals from a computer into a form that can be displayed or converted into mechanical movement. Here are some examples of such transducers:

- *Thermistor* - the electrical resistance of the material used in a thermistor varies according to the temperature of the material.

- *Strain gauge* - the electrical resistance of the material used in a strain gauge varies according to the mechanical strain applied to the material.

- *Seven-segment display* - this converts digital information into characters that can be read.

- *Stepper-motor* - this converts electrical pulses into small, controlled angular movements of the shaft of an electric motor.

- *Loudspeaker* - this converts electrical energy into sound.

The first two are examples of input transducers, and the other three are output devices.

Another important feature of control systems is *feedback*. Feedback is the process of regulating the system by using output information to control the input, thereby keeping the output within certain limits. This usually involves using the computer to compare the input signal, or signals, with some critical values. If the input signals show that the quantities being measured need to be adjusted, output signals are used to activate devices which affect the quantities. For example, a control system for maintaining the temperature of a vat of liquid at a constant 20 degrees Centigrade will use a sensor to monitor the temperature of the vat and a heater to increase its temperature if it cools below the required value. A computer program could be used to compare the actual temperature of the vat, as supplied by the sensor, with the desired temperature; a temperature lower than that required will result in the computer issuing an output control signal to activate the heating element.

Figure 20.1 illustrates the main features of a control system.

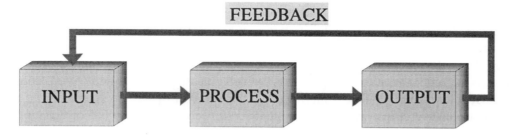

Figure 20.1. *The components of a control system*

A Control System for Heating Water

An example of a control system which illustrates the concepts discussed above is the domestic water heater. (See Figure 20.2).

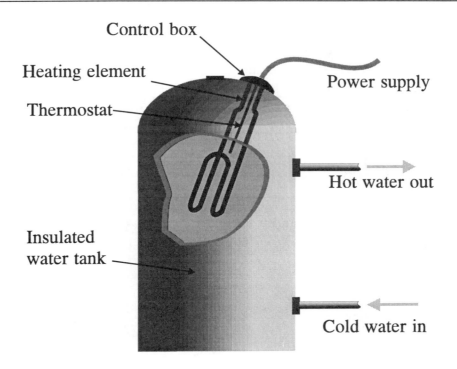

Figure 20.2. *An immersion heater control system*

The insulated water tank contains a combined *heating element* and *thermostat*. The thermostat is simply a heat activated switch which is off when the temperature of the water reaches a certain level, and is on when the water temperature is below that level. The heating element is connected to the electricity supply via the thermostat so that while the temperature of the water is below a certain level, the heating element is on, otherwise it is off. The control box contains the connections between the heater, the thermostat and the power supply.

In this simple control system for regulating the temperature of the water in the tank, the thermostat is the transducer, heat generated by the heating element is the output and *feedback* is provided by the resulting temperature of the water. The thermostat switches the heater off when the water reaches the required temperature. When hot water is drawn from the tank, cold water enters and reduces the temperature of the water. This reduction in temperature is detected by the thermostat which activates the heater, thus heating the water until it again reaches the required temperature. Thus the output (heat) provides feedback to the transducer so that the water temperature can be regulated.

Of course, this simple control system does not require a computer to control it but, if there were such a requirement, a computer could easily be used. The mechanical thermostat could be replaced by a different transducer providing a voltage proportional to the temperature of the water. This signal could be monitored by a computer and compared with the required temperature of the water. The computer could easily control a relay to switch the heater on when the temperature falls below a predetermined minimum value and switch it off when the temperature exceeds a predetermined maximum value. The computer controlled version is shown in Figure 20.3.

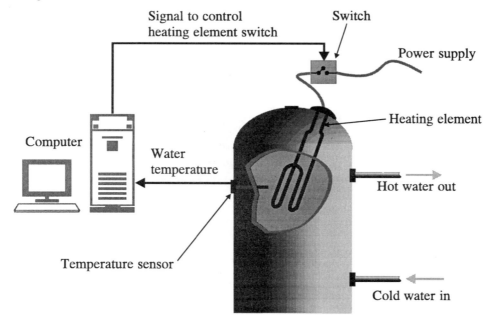

Figure 20.3. *A computer-controlled water heating system*

In this version the water temperature is detected by a sensor immersed in the water. A voltage proportional to the water temperature is transmitted to the computer which determines whether it is necessary to turn on an electronic switch to activate the heating element.

Computer Control System Components

Because PCs are so popular and now provide powerful, cost-effective solutions to many processing problems, more PCs are being used in both process monitoring and control applications. Consequently, many plug-in devices have been developed to simplify these tasks, and software has also kept pace with development needs. The components of a typical PC-based control system are:

- Sensor(s) to monitor the process.

- Signal conditioning module to convert sensor signals to meet input/output specifications. As well as being the front end for a DAQ board, these also isolate the computer from the environment.

- Data acquisition board (DAQ) which plugs directly into the PC. Input and output transducers can be connected directly to them (depending on the type) or through signal conditioning modules. These boards often can perform a variety of functions, including analog to digital conversion, digital to analog conversion and digital input/output.

- Interface software which facilitates control and communication through the DAQ board.

The heat regulating system described in the next section illustrates how these components combine to form a computer control system.

A Heat Regulating System

Since the signal from any temperature sensing device, whatever the type of transducer employed, is a continuously varying (that is, *analogue*) signal, it must be amplified using a signal conditioning unit and then converted into a *binary* signal using an *analogue-to-digital converter* (ADC) before it can be used directly by a computer.

The analogue signal from the sensor unit is converted to binary signals by the ADC. ADCs take as input a voltage in a certain range and produce a number of parallel binary outputs which represent the current input voltage. A typical ADC will provide eight binary outputs corresponding to the input voltage. So, if the input range is -5V to +5V , a binary output of 0 corresponds to -5V, an output of binary 127 corresponds to 0V and +5V is represented by 255 in binary. Figure 20.4 illustrates an ADC producing a binary output of 240 corresponding approximately to an input of 4V.

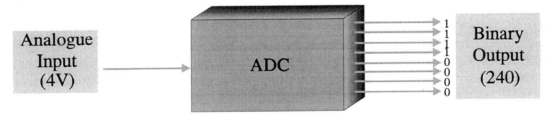

Figure 20.4. *The operation of a typical ADC*

Let us suppose, for example, that a certain microprocessor-controlled washing machine allows the selection of a large range of water temperature settings. Such an appliance might use a system similar to that just described to convert water temperatures between 0°C and 100°C to a binary signal. If the ADC produces an 8 bit binary output corresponding to an input voltage in the range 0V to 5V, the temperature range 0°C to 100°C will be represented by a binary signal in the range 0 to 255 (that is, 00000000 to 11111111 in binary) such that binary 0 represents 0°C and binary 255 represents 100°C. Since a temperature transducer is unlikely to generate the voltage range required by the ADC, namely 0V to 5V, it must first be conditioned. Thus after the transducer signal had been conditioned, a temperature of 25°C would produce about 1.25V and this would translate to binary 63 (00111111).

Figure 20.5 illustrates the use of an ADC contained within a PC data acquisition (DAQ) board in a simple system intended to maintain a tank of liquid at a certain temperature. The DAQ board also allows the PC to output a digital control signal to operate a power switch which activates the tank's heating element.

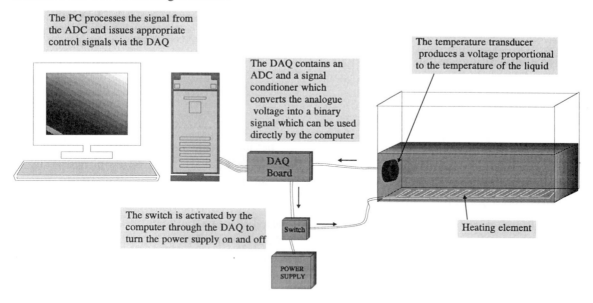

Figure 20.5. *A PC control system using a DAQ board*

The figure shows a temperature sensor immersed in a tank of warm liquid. The sensor contains a thermal transducer and an electronic circuit that produces as output an analogue signal in the form of a voltage proportional to the temperature of the liquid in the tank. The output from the sensor unit is converted to binary by the ADC. A computer program then compares the temperature of the liquid, as represented by the binary signal, with the required temperature of the liquid and activates the heating element switch accordingly. Note that the temperature sensor unit, switch and ADC all require a power supply to function.

Control Systems Applications

Computer control systems are used in a wide variety of application areas, including:

- Process monitoring and control - see the *Process Control Systems* later in this section

- Data logging - gathering and recording data.

- Quality control - testing products to ensure that they fulfil specific standards of quality.

- Machine control - for example, controlling the machines used in manufacturing processes. Includes the use of robots (see later)

In the following sections we describe the application of computer control in motor vehicles, chemical processes and manufacturing. To simplify the illustrations, the signal conditioning and converting components of the systems are not shown.

Control systems used in cars

Some modern cars, particularly in the USA, have a "cruise control" that allows a driver to set the speed of the car to be maintained automatically by pressing a button. A microprocessor is used to monitor the speed of the car, from data provided by a sensor, and continuously compare it with the required speed. If the car starts to slow down while going up a hill or speeds up going down a hill, the microprocessor activates a control that changes the car's speed. Figure 20.6 illustrates this idea.

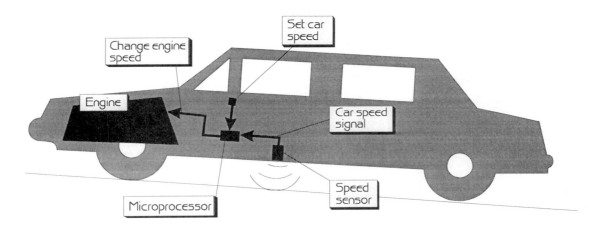

Figure 20.6. *Cruise control for a car*

The microprocessor uses *feedback* provided by the speed sensor to determine whether the car is travelling at the required speed. Some systems have sensors which use the rotation rate of the wheel drive shafts to determine the speed of the car, while others use microwave technology to measure the Doppler shift of a signal bounced off the road. If the microprocessor detects that the car is travelling slower than the required speed, it increases the delivery of fuel to the engine. This speeds the car up so that the difference between the actual speed and the required speed is reduced. The microprocessor continuously reacts to speed changes as they occur and adjusts the fuel delivery to keep the car travelling at a nearly constant speed. The driver, by braking or accelerating, can override the cruise control and assume normal control of the car at any instant.

Early versions of this type of control were achieved using complicated electromechanical devices, but the advent of cheap microprocessors rapidly caused them to be replaced with computer-based machines. The great advantage of using a microprocessor in this type of application is that its function can be duplicated by a more powerful computer system used for the purpose of designing and evaluating the final system before putting it into production. This reduces the time taken to produce a workable system and allows its performance to be thoroughly investigated and modified easily before testing it in a car.

Another application of control systems in cars is the *anti-locking brake system,* usually known as *ABS.* These devices prevent locking of the wheels during braking so that:

- The vehicle does not tend to swerve during braking;
- The vehicle can still be steered during braking;
- Stopping distances are reduced;
- Tyre damage during emergency braking is eliminated;
- Less physical effort is required of the driver in emergency situations.

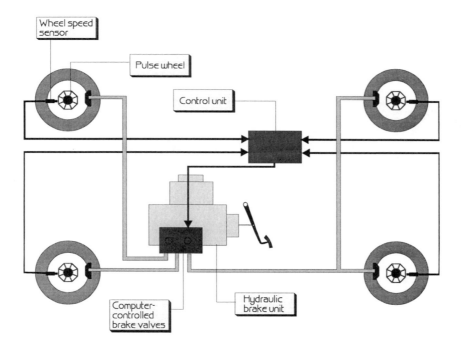

Figure 20.7. *Anti-locking brake system (ABS) on a car*

Cars with an ABS fitted are therefore considerably safer in hazardous conditions than those having ordinary braking systems. Figure 20.7 illustrates the components of one type of ABS system. The rotational speed of the wheels, continuously measured by the wheel speed sensors, are transmitted to the ABS control unit. The control unit processes the rotation data for each wheel separately and if a wheel is in danger of locking, it sends a signal to the brake valves to reduce the braking effect for that wheel. If the braking effect on a wheel is too weak, the control unit increases the braking effect, still ensuring that the wheel does not lock.

The wheel sensors measure the rotational speed of the wheels from the pulse-generating wheels which revolve at the same speed as the road wheels. The pulse-generating wheels and generate a voltage in the sensor proportional to the speed at which they are revolving.

The ABS control unit contains two microprocessors which perform exactly the same functions of using the wheel rotation information to control braking. Two microprocessors are used for safety: they continuously monitor and test each other to ensure that the ABS system is operating correctly. If a fault in the ABS system is detected by one of the microprocessors, the system shuts itself down and normal manual braking is made available.

Engine management systems

Engine management systems use a microprocessor to monitor and control the operation of a car's engine. Though devices to control such things as exhaust emissions, fuel supply and ignition timing have been available for years, recent regulations regarding pollution control have resulted in new computer-controlled systems which integrate a number of functions and use feedback to continuously regulate the operation of the engine. These systems sample exhaust gases to provide feedback to the computer system which modifies the engine settings to keep emissions within required limits. A modern engine management system can provide system support for such things as:

- ignition timing
- fuel injection
- exhaust gas recirculation
- engine idle speed

Process control systems

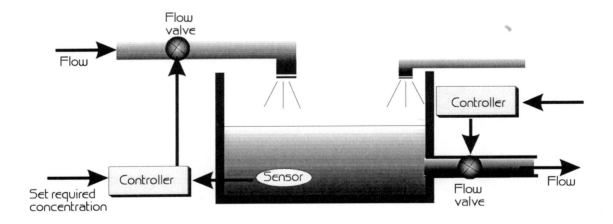

Figure 20.8 *Chemical process control*

The term *process control* is applied to systems which involve the automatic control of manufacturing, material handling, or treatment handling of processes. Such processes were controlled mechanically or manually in the past, but the advent of microprocessors allowed digital control systems to take over. Microprocessor-based control systems allowed process control to become more efficient and profitable by providing a means of responding to changes much more rapidly than was previously possible. Process control systems are typically found in industries that produce chemicals, steel, aluminium, food, beverages, petroleum products etc. For example, suppose that a certain chemical process requires that a concentration of a particular chemical is maintained in a tank from which fluid is being drained at the same time as other chemicals are being added. A sensor in the tank provides continuous information to a microprocessor regarding the concentration of the chemical concerned (see Figure 20.8). The output to be controlled here is the concentration of the chemical in the tank. The difference between the required concentration and the concentration as measured by the sensor is compared by the controller. If the difference between the two becomes too large, the controller opens the flow valve until the difference is reduced to an acceptable level. The process has been controlled when the concentration of the chemical is maintained at the required level. Note that there may be several processes interacting with each other, with each separate controller keeping its particular process under control.

Robotics

Since 1962, when General Motors of the USA first used one commercially on one of its production lines, robots have been used profitably for a wide range of tasks. The word "robot" was first coined by a Czechoslovakian playwright called Karel Capek who in 1921 used the Czech word "robota", meaning worker, to describe a human-like machine which served humanity in one of his plays. Later, Isaac Asimov, a very popular science fiction writer, was the first person to use the word "robotics" to refer to the science of robots. Though as yet robots are not advanced enough to need them, Asimov's well-known "Laws of Robotics" may be required in the not too distant future. His three laws state

>   1. *A robot must not harm a human being or, through inaction, allow one to come to harm.*
>   2. *A robot must always obey human beings unless that is in conflict with the First Law.*
>   3. *A robot must protect itself from harm unless that is in conflict with the first or second laws.*

Asimov's fictional robots had very advanced "positronic brains" which gave them the power to reason like humans, but the robots in use today are much more rudimentary machines usually used for fairly simple and repetitive tasks. It will be some time before intelligent, humanoid robots are more than just an interesting themes for novels.

According to the Robot Institute of America, a robot is a "*reprogrammable, multifunctional manipulator designed to move material parts, tools or specialised devices through variable programmed motions for the performance of a variety of tasks*". However, there are many very different types of machines that are covered by this definition. Most robots have an "arm" with a number of joints linking the sections. Joints rotate or slide or combine the two movements, as illustrated in Figure 20.9. Until recently, nearly all robots were mounted on a stationary base and were therefore fixed in one position. However, with the availability of low-cost computers able to cope with the added problems caused by providing mobility, manufacturers now provide robots which can move in a number of different ways. Most mobile robots are restricted to moving on a track either on the ground or on an overhead gantry, but there are some robots with wheels used as household "assistants". Some robots have been equipped with legs so that they are able to walk over uneven terrain, but there are many problems associated with making such machines, and they are still in the very early stages of development.

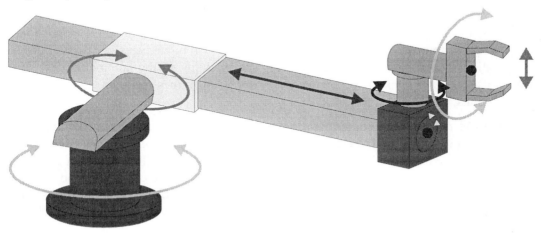

Figure 20.9. *An example of a robot arm*

The advantages of using robots

Here are some of the reasons for using robots in industry:

- Although robots are very expensive, when the cost is averaged over several years, it turns out that the cost per hour of using a robot is much less than using human labour. One of the main reasons for this is that robots, unlike people, do not need such things as holidays, sick leave (except when they break down), medical benefits or pensions.

- Robots work nearly 100% of the time at their tasks, whereas people have to be given tea breaks and lunch breaks and time off for other reasons.
- Robots do not make mistakes resulting from tiredness or lack of attention because they repeat the same operations in exactly the same way every time almost without fail.
- Robots can work much faster and with more accuracy at some tasks than human workers can. This results in the production of more and better quality articles.

- Certain manufacturing operations take place in conditions hazardous to humans but harmless to robots. For example, robots are not affected by red hot flying sparks in a steel forge, or by toxic fumes given off by certain types of paint.

- Because robots can be programmed to perform many different sequences of movements, a single robot can be used to perform a wide variety of tasks, whereas a machine made to perform a specific task is limited to doing that one thing.

Uses of robots

Robots have been used for many years to do simple tasks in factories, such as picking up items at one location and feeding them to a machine at another fixed location.. Another common use of robots is spray painting. Here, a spray paint nozzle is attached to the robot arm which is programmed to move through a sequence of movements to carry out the painting operation. Many robots are also used for spot welding in the automobile industry. These robots use welding guns to weld car chassis and body frames together at a number of programmed points.

More sophisticated robots, called *adaptive robots*, which are able to sense their environment and use this data to modify their behaviour, are used for more complex tasks such as the assembly of small products, the inspection of automobile bodies travelling along an assembly line so that faulty assembly of components can be recorded and later corrected, and welding metal along seams which cannot be precisely aligned beforehand. These applications have resulted from the development of computer controlled vision systems which allow the robot to "recognise" simple shapes.

Measurement Systems

In general, measurement systems have three component parts:

1. A sensor, or *transducer* it is frequently termed, responds in some measurable way to the quantity of interest. For example, in a hot wire anemometer, the transducer is a thermistor (see later) whose electrical resistance changes according to air movement.

INPUT
Change in wind speed

OUTPUT
Change in resistance

Figure 20.10. *Input and output signals for a hot wire anemometer*

2. A *signal conditioning* device which converts the physical response of the transducer into a form suitable for operating a display device. In the hot wire anemometer example mentioned previously, the signal conditioner is an independently powered electrical circuit which converts the resistance changes of the thermistor into an electrical signal suitable for driving a digital or

analogue wind-speed display. Some conditioning circuits are *amplifiers* which convert small electrical signals into signals which can drive a display. In computer control systems, the output from the measuring device must be converted into a form suitable for input to a computer. Since a computer processes binary data, an *analogue-to-digital converter* will often form an additional signal conditioning stage. Figure 20.11 illustrates these types of conditioning devices. Signal conditioning circuits are also called *Signal converters* and *signal processors*.

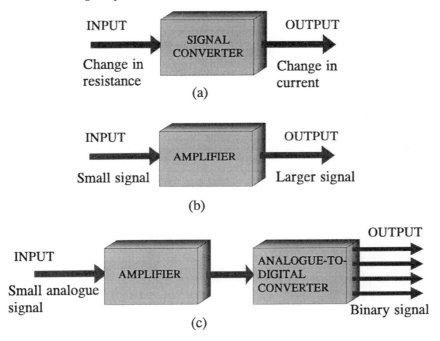

Figure 20.11 *Three types of signal conditioning devices. (a) a signal converter (b) an amplifier (c) an analogue-to-digital converter*

3. A *display* which takes the signal from the conditioning element and presents it in a form which can be interpreted by an observer. For example, the output from an amplifier could be used to deflect the needle of a meter or it could be converted into a digital signal to be displayed as figures on a computer screen or another type of digital display.

Figure 20.12 illustrates a complete measurement system consisting of a transducer, a signal conditioner and a display element.

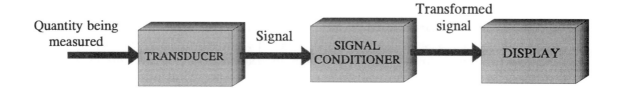

Figure 20.12. *The three components of a measurement system*

Transducers

As mentioned earlier, transducers convert one form of energy into another but, because of the ease with which electrical energy may be transmitted and amplified, the most useful transducers are often those that convert forms of energy, such as heat, light or pressure, into electrical energy. If a computer is to be used to process the information provided by a transducer, then it is essential that the quantity measured by the transducer is translated into a proportionally scaled electrical signal. Some transducers are simply switches which turn an electrical signal on and off. For example, domestic thermostats used in electric kettles and heaters turn the electricity supply on and off, but many transducers used in computer control systems are measuring devices, rather than just switches. These devices are used, for example, to supply the computer with the temperature of some substance or the rate of flow of a liquid.

Transducers can be readily obtained from suppliers of electronic components and devices. Many of these companies also provide technical advice and technical data sheets which show how the devices can be incorporated into measurement and control systems and suggest typical uses.

Input Transducers

Input transducers, or sensors, supply data to the computer system by converting such things as heat, light or sound energy into electrical signals which can be used in a computer. Once in the computer, these electrical signals have numeric values which can be processed. A number of different types of input transducers are described in the following sections.

Proximity switches

Proximity switches are used to turn an electrical signal on or off depending on the near presence of objects. The type of object that can be detected, its distance from the detector and the speed of response are dependent on the physical effect that the transducer utilises.

- *Inductive* proximity switches sense the presence of ferrous and non-ferrous metals using *inductance*. Typically these sensors can only detect very close objects, that is up to a distance of about 15mm. Uses include alarm systems to detect windows and doors opening, for detecting the depression of a button where button wear is a problem, and for counting objects.

- *Capacitive* proximity switches sense the presence of non-metallic materials such as liquids or wood as well as metallic materials. These transducers have a slightly greater range - up to about 25mm for non-metallic objects and about 65mm for metallic objects. Applications are similar to those for the inductive proximity switches.

- *Ultrasonic* proximity switches emit an utrasonic beam which reflects off any objects in the immediate path of the beam. The reflected beam is detected by the sensor which outputs a voltage proportional to the distance of any object within the angle of the beam. The range of these sensors is limited to about one metre.

- *Optical* proximity switches are of two types: *passive* and *active*. The passive infrared detector (PIR) monitors the heat radiation emitted from any object which enters its detection zone. If the object is hotter than the ambient temperature, the detector activates a switch. These devices have a range of several metres. Active optical proximity switches generate a beam of infrared or visible red light and use the strength of the reflected beam to detect the presence of objects. Some of theses devices are called retro-reflective sensors because they use a special disc of reflective material to "bounce" the light beam off. These devices also have ranges of several metres.

Thermal Transducers

There are several types of transducers which utilise heat in their operation. An example is a temperature gauge in which a spiral metallic spring converts thermal energy into a mechanical deflection of a dial pointer. The small movements and limited forces generated by many thermostatic devices often require electrical amplification via relay switches to activate the system controls. Thus, the bimetallic element of the usual home-heating thermostat can be made to trip a mercury-contact switch that permits the flow of a current sufficiently high to operate the controls of, say, a furnace.

Other devices, such as resistance-temperature detectors (RTDs), thermistors and thermocouples, can also be used as the temperature-sensing elements for systems involving the regulation of temperature, when the small variation in the electrical properties of the transducer is amplified to operate the system controls or the display element.

Thermostats

A thermostat is a device that is used to automatically regulate the temperature of a system by maintaining it at a constant level or varying it over a specific range. Thermostats are widely used in industrial furnaces, in heating systems, and in other engineering applications in which a process must take place at controlled temperatures. Thermostats are also frequently used to control the cooling water flow through the radiator of automobile engines.

Most thermostats depend on the expansion of a substance corresponding to an increase in temperature. A *bimetal thermostat* is illustrated in Figure 20.13. Bimetal thermostats are essentially switches that are normally used to turn a system on and off, that is, when there is no need for a continuous form of control and, because they are relatively inexpensive, they are frequently used for domestic applications.

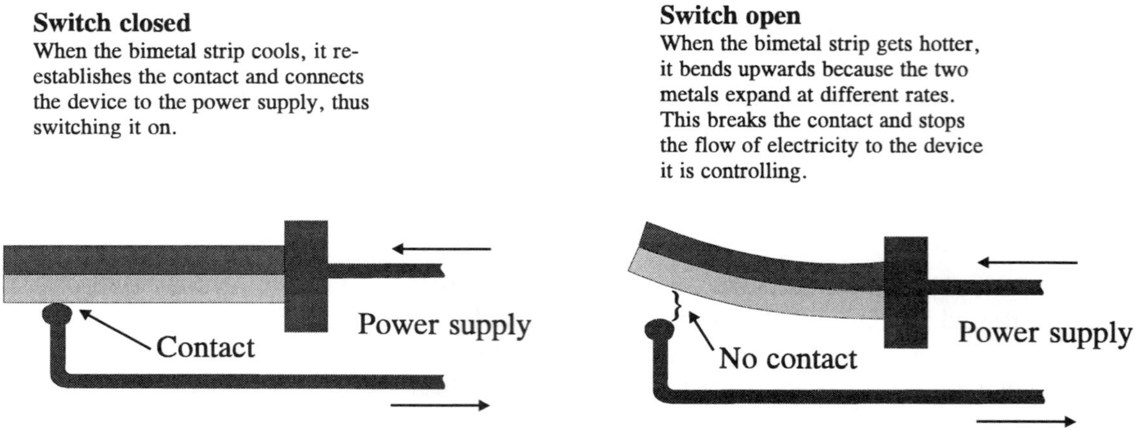

Switch closed
When the bimetal strip cools, it re-establishes the contact and connects the device to the power supply, thus switching it on.

Switch open
When the bimetal strip gets hotter, it bends upwards because the two metals expand at different rates. This breaks the contact and stops the flow of electricity to the device it is controlling.

Power supply

Contact

Power supply

No contact

Figure 20.13. *A bimetal thermostat*

A bimetal thermostat uses a special strip of metal to open and close a circuit as temperature fluctuates. Two metals with different expansion rates are bonded to make the strip. The thermostat is arranged so that when the metals are hot, the strip bends upward (toward the metal with the lower expansion rate) and disconnects the circuit. In our example, the thermostat allowed electricity to flow through an immersion heater when the circuit was closed, and disconnected the immersion heater when the circuit was open.

Resistance-temperature detectors (RTDs)

The electrical conductivity of many materials varies according to the temperature of the material. Resistance-temperature detectors(RTDs) use the fact that the a of certain metals increase almost linearly with temperature. So, for example, to measure the temperature of a liquid, we can immerse an RTD in the liquid and then measure its resistance; we can then calculate the liquid's temperature from a formula that uses the resistance of the metal from which the RTD is made. Figure 20.14 is a typical resistance vs temperature graph for a metal showing that over a certain range of temperatures (that is between T1 and T2) the graph is approximately a straight line; this means that a simple linear equation can be used to determine the temperature of the metal. Generally, the resistance of an RTD changes by a small amount (in the order of 0.5Ω) per $^{\circ}$ C change in temperature.

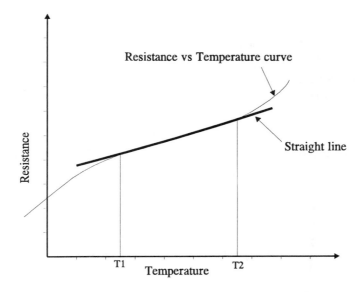

Figure 20.14 *A resistance-temperature graph for an RTD metal*

One type of *platinum film* RTD is constructed by depositing a track of platinum ink on an alumina base and then coating it with a ceramic material (see Figure 20.15). This assembly may optionally be sheathed in stainless steel or plastic, depending on the environment in which it is to be used. The typical effective temperature range of a platinum-based RTD is -100 °C to 650 °C. An RTD, like a bimetal thermostat, is known as a *passive* device because it does not by itself generate an output. Thus to use an RTD for measuring temperature in a computer control system it is necessary to incorporate it in an electronic circuit which will convert its resistance to an electrical signal whose magnitude is proportional to the surrounding temperature.

Platinum film track

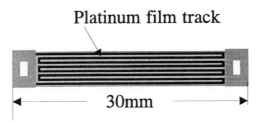

Figure 20.15. *A resistance-temperature detector (RTD)*

Thermistors

The thermistor is another type of passive temperature transducer that uses the changes in resistance of materials to measure temperature. However, the thermistor uses a semiconductor rather than a metal in its fabrication. The semiconductors used in thermistors exhibit large changes in resistance with temperature. For example, a thermistor with a resistance of, say,

10kΩ may change by 1kΩ for a 1°C change in temperature. The type of semiconductor used in its construction determines the range of temperatures over which the thermistor will operate effectively, but a typical range might be -50°C to 250°C. The disadvantage of thermistors over resistance-temperature detectors is that the relationship between temperature and resistance is not as simple: Figure 20.16 illustrates the highly non-linear relationship between temperature and resistance. The curve shows that at the temperature range extremes its usefulness is very limited, but in the middle of the temperature range it is very responsive.

There are a number of types of thermistors, including *rod*, *disc* and *bead* thermistors, each having their own operational characteristics and special uses.

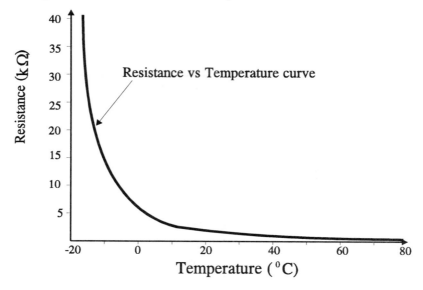

Figure 20.16. *The resistance-temperature curve for a thermistor*

Thermocouples

Thermocouples are classed as active transducers because they produce a measurable electrical current as a direct result of a temperature differential. When the ends of a piece of metal are kept at different temperatures, that is, there is a *temperature differential* between the two ends, there is a drift of electrons from the hotter end to the cooler end. If the two ends are connected by means of another electrical conductor, a current is found to flow through the closed loop. This is illustrated in Figure 20.17. The output voltage from a thermocouple is very small, typically less than 50mV, and this necessitates the use of a high gain amplifier.

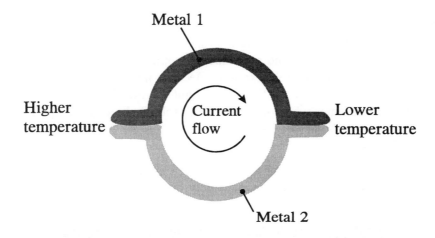

Figure 20.17. *A thermocouple*

Integrated temperature sensors

Many transducer manufacturers now provide fully integrated transducers and appropriate electronic circuits to simplify use in computer control systems. For example, there are temperature sensors which generate voltage outputs proportional to temperature (over a typical range of -50 °C to +150 °C) and also provide control signals when the device is either above or below specific temperature ranges. The devices are fabricated as tiny integrated circuits. Applications include temperature controllers, electronic thermostats and process control systems which use computers.

Light-activated Devices

Just as the electrical properties of some materials are affected by heat, so other materials are affected by visible light. Transducers which use such properties are often called *photodetectors*, three of which are described here.

Light-dependent Resistor (LDR)

This is a small passive electrical component incorporating a semiconductor material. The conductivity of the semiconductor material used in the LDR changes with the intensity of the light striking it, and so such devices are also called *photoresistive* cells. A typical device might have a minimum resistance in bright light of a few hundred ohms and a maximum resistance in complete darkness of several mega (million) ohms.

Photovoltaic Detector

This is an active transducer which converts electromagnetic energy such as light into electrical energy. Some photovoltaic devices use solar energy to provide a source of electrical power while others are used for instrumentation and measurement purposes.

Photodiode Detector

The *pn* junction of a diode is sensitive to light striking it. Light striking the junction affects its current and voltage characteristics, and consequently some diodes are manufactured in such a way that the pn junction is deliberately exposed. Because the junction is very small, a lens is usually incorporated in the device to focus any light on the junction. These are very fast transducers with response times which make them suitable for high speed applications.

Coded Plate Transducers

This device uses a plate or disc, such as that shown in Figure 20.18, which contains a number of binary coded concentric tracks. The most widely used code is called *Gray code*, which is shown in Table 20.1 in 3-bit form.

Value	Gray Code	Binary	Angle
0	000	000	0 (360)
1	001	001	45
2	011	010	90
3	010	011	135
4	110	100	180
5	111	101	225
6	101	110	270
7	100	111	315

Table 20.1. *3-bit Gray code*

Gray code is used in preference to standard binary code because it has the property that each successive value in the sequence of codes changes by only a single bit. In pure binary, also shown in Table 20.1, this is not the case: you can see that, for example, going from 011 to 100, all three bits change, whereas in Gray code the transition is from 010 to 110 in which only the most significant digit changes from 0 to 1. The significance of this can be seen if we consider what might happen if the disc shown in Figure 20.18 were to be 3-bit binary coded rather than 3-bit Gray coded.

The angular position of the disc is determined by the light detectors. They are able to detect the presence of light in the three positions corresponding to the disc's three concentric tracks. However, the disc can stop at any angular position, including the boundaries between two adjacent codes. For example, because of the limited sensitivity of the light detectors, if the disc is at the boundary of 001 and 010, it is possible that two adjacent transparent and opaque areas will be read incorrectly. This means that the position of the disc could be mistakenly read as 000 or 011 just as easily as one of the two correct values. However, using Gray code the equivalent codes to 001 and 010 are 011 and 010 respectively, in which only the least significant bit changes value. Thus the position of the disc cannot be misinterpreted. This is illustrated in Figure 20.19. In (a) the Gray coded disc is at the boundary of 001 and 011. The only possible ambiguity is with sensor *b*, but the three sensors will still only detect either 001 or 011 as required. However, with the binary coded disc shown in (b), sensors *a* and *b* could read a zero or a one, possibly providing an erroneous value for the angle of rotation of the disk.

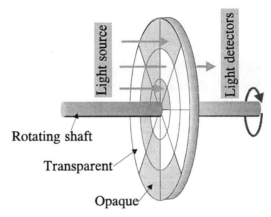

Figure 20.18. *A coded plate transducer for measuring angular rotation*

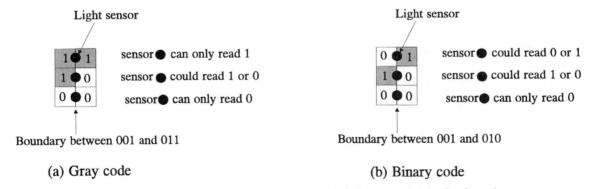

(a) Gray code   (b) Binary code

Figure 20.19. *Comparing binary code and Gray code for measuring angle of rotation*

In order to be able to relate the Gray code output signals from the light sensors to an angular position, the code must be converted into binary. This may be accomplished in two ways:

1. Using a logic circuit (Figure 20.20) - the outputs from the sensors are fed into a logic circuit which produces the correct binary outputs which can then be related to an angular rotation (see Table 20.1).

Figure 20.20. *A logic circuit to convert from Gray code to binary*

2. Using a look-up table - after appropriate conditioning, the outputs from the light sensors are used to access a small amount of ROM or RAM containing a table such as that shown in Table 20.2 for a 3-bit code. The memory locations in the first column contain the appropriate binary code allowing any Gray code to be quickly looked up.

Address	Contents
000	000
001	001
011	010
010	011
110	100
111	101
101	110
100	111

Table 20.2 *A look-up table to convert from Gray code to binary*

Shaft Encoders

This type of transducer also uses a rotating disc but this time it has a set of equally spaced radial lines on its surface. A special track on the disk has a zero reference mark on it. An optical sensor is used to detect the radial lines, incrementing a counter each time a mark is detected. This allows the angular position of a shaft to be accurately determined. A typical shaft encoder might have over a thousand radial lines giving a resolution of less than a third of a degree. Some shaft encoders also provide outputs allowing the direction of rotation of the shaft to be determined as well as its current position and rotational speed. By linking the spindle of a shaft encoder to the spindle of another rotating shaft, speed position and directional data can be accurately obtained.

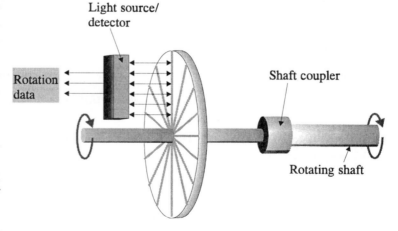

Figure 20.21. *A shaft encoder*

Figure 20.21 illustrates the operation of a shaft encoder. The rotating shaft of the spindle to be monitored is linked to the shaft of the encoder by means of a suitable shaft coupler. The rotation of the shaft thus causes the shaft of the encoder to rotate at the same rate. An optical sensor uses reflected light to detect the radial lines on the encoder's disc.

Strain Gauges

A typical strain gauge consists of a wafer of polyester containing an element made from a copper-nickel alloy foil (see Figure 20.22).

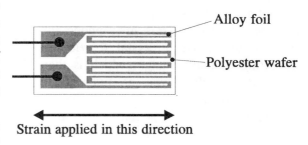

The wafer is attached to the surface that is to be monitored. The resistance of the metal foil changes according to the strain applied along its length. This change of resistance can then be converted into an electrical signal whose strength is proportional to the strain being applied. Some strain gauges use wire or a semiconductor material rather than an alloy foil. Strain gauges, as well as being used as strain transducers, are often used to measure pressure when attached to a flexible diaphragm, or to measure weight when attached to a *load cell*. A load cell is simply a rectangular block or a cylinder which is compressed by the weight to be measured. Strain gauges are often used in arrangements called *rosettes* when strain is be measured in more than one direction.

Figure 20.22 *A strain gauge*

Piezoelectric transducers.

Piezoelectric transducers use the property possessed by certain crystalline substances that an electric potential across certain faces of a crystal is produced when it is subjected to mechanical pressure. Conversely, when an electric field is applied on certain faces of the crystal, the crystal undergoes mechanical distortion. Because of their capacity to convert mechanical pressure into voltages, and voltages into mechanical motion, piezoelectric crystals are used in such devices as the transducer, record-playing pickup elements, and the microphone. Piezoelectric crystals are also used as resonators in electronic oscillators and high-frequency amplifiers, because the mechanical resonance frequency of adequately cut crystals is stable and well defined.

Microphones

A *microphone* is a device used to transform sound energy into electrical energy. Microphones are important in many kinds of communications systems and in instruments for measuring sound and noise. The simplest type of modern microphone is the carbon microphone, used in telephone apparatus. This microphone consists of a metallic cup filled with carbon granules with a movable metallic diaphragm mounted in contact with the granules at the open end. Wires attached to the cup and diaphragm are connected to an electrical circuit and carry a current. When sound waves make contact with the diaphragm, it vibrates, varying the pressure on the carbon granules and thus causing a variation in the electrical resistance of the granules.

The current in the circuit varies with the resistance, and the changes can be used to actuate a remote loudspeaker.

Another common type, the crystal microphone, utilizes the piezoelectric effect described earlier. In this microphone the sound waves cause a crystal to vibrate, generating a small voltage, which is then amplified. Another type of microphone used occasionally is the condenser microphone, in which sound waves alter the spacing between two thin metallic plates and hence change the electrical capacity between them. By placing such a microphone in a suitable circuit, these variations may be amplified, producing a varying electrical signal.

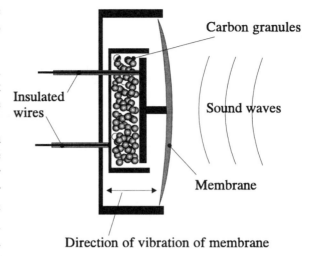

Figure 20.23. *A carbon granule microphone*

Output transducers and display devices

The transducers described so far are used as input devices, but there are also a number of transducers which are used for output purposes. The output transducers described in the following sections convert electrical signals into other forms of energy. For example, a loudspeaker converts electrcal signals into sound waves, a solenoid converts electrical energy into mechanical movement, and a light-emitting diode converts electrical energy into light. Even computer displays can be considered to be transducers in that they allow electrical representations of binary data to be converted into their equivalent visual forms.

Other obvious forms of output devices used in control systems include heaters for increasing temperature, fans for reducing temperature, light sources and valves for contolling the flow of liquids and gases.

Solenoids

An electromagnet is a coil of wire which produces a strong magnetic field when an electrical current flows through it. A *solenoid* is an electromagnet used in conjunction with moving iron or steel central core, or *armature*, which is attracted by the magnetic field generated by the electromagnet. A solenoid is illustrated in Figure 20.24

Solenoids are used in such things as

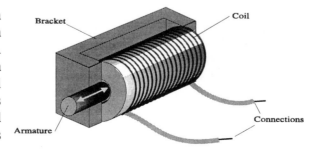

Figure 20.24 *A solenoid*

remote-controlled locks, food-dispensing machines and car starter motors; such applications require powerful magnetic fields produced by quite high electrical currents, and so solenoids are not usually operated directly by an electronic circuit. Under the direct control of an electronic circuit, a type of solenoid called a *relay*, is usually employed to switch in the appropriate power supply required to activate the solenoid.

Relays

Figure 20.25 shows the construction of a typical relay.

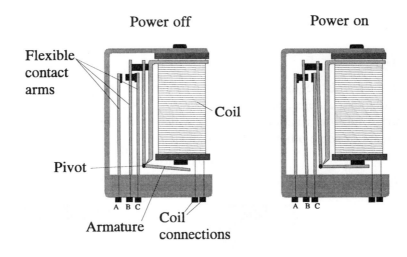

Figure 20.25. *The operation of a relay*

When there is no power to the relay's electromagnet, the switch formed by contacts B and C is closed, and the switch formed by contacts A and B is open. When power is applied to the coil connections of the relay, the magnetic field induced by the electromagnet attracts the metal armature thus opening the contacts B and C and closing the contacts A and B. The two pairs of contacts can thus be used as electronically operated switches which can close and open circuits containing devices requiring relatively high currents. The circuit diagram shown in Figure 20.26 shows a relay being used to operate a solenoid.

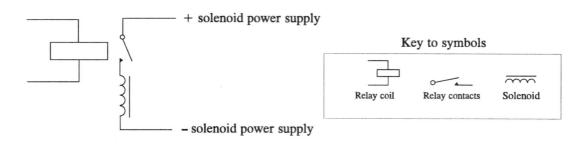

Figure 20.26. *A relay used as a switch for a solenoid*

Electric Motors

When electrical energy is required to be used for more complex movements than those possible from a solenoid, an electric motor may be employed. In an electric motor, an electric current is converted into the rotation of an axle which could be connected to a pulley, some arrangement of gears or some other mechanical device.

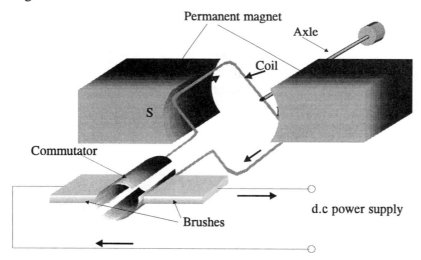

Figure 20.27. A d.c. electric motor

An electric motor uses the principle that if a current is passed through a conductor located in a magnetic field, the field exerts a mechanical force on it, and Figure 20.27 illustrates the way that this principle is utilised in the construction of a direct current (d.c.) electric motor. When a current flows through the coil of wire (for simplicity shown as a single loop in the diagram), a magnetic field of opposite polarity to that of the permanent magnet is induced, causing the coil to be repelled by the magnet. This rotation causes the split commutator to rotate and reverse the direction of the current in the coil so that the magnetic field in the coil is always the same polarity as the magnet. Thus the coil, always repelled by the magnet, continues to rotate while a current flows through it. By using a number of coils attached to a commutator having the same number of segments, the power of the motor can be increased considerably.

The magnetic field of a permanent magnet is strong enough to operate only a small practical motor. As a result, for large machines, electromagnets are used. Motors thus consist of two basic units: the *field*, which is the electromagnet with its coils, and the *armature*, which usually comprises a multi-segment commutator and a number of wound coils.

Stepper Motors

A stepper motor is a type of electric motor that can be controlled by a computer. Instead of having a single field coil, a stepper motor has several field coils which can be activated sequentially under control of a computer. The coils are arranged so that each one in turn causes the armature to turn a set amount, perhaps $10°$. Each time a control pulse is sent to the stepper motor, the next coil in the sequence is activated; this means that the shaft of the motor can be rotated forwards or backwards, quickly or slowly, all under precise control.

Applications of stepper motors include controlling valves to regulate the flow of gas, water and other liquids in pipes, for precise positioning of robot arms and for computer peripherals such as plotters and printers.

Loudspeakers

A loudspeaker is an output transducer which converts small electrical signals into sound waves. Most loudspeakers depend on electromagnetism for their operation. The construction of a typical loudspeaker is illustrated in Figure 20.28. A light paper cone is attached to a cylindrical former around which there is a coil of wire. This coil of wire fits exactly inside a cylindrical magnet. When a current flows in the coil, the magnetic field generated causes it to be attracted or repelled by the magnetic field produced by the magnet, and the resulting movement of the paper cone generates sound waves.

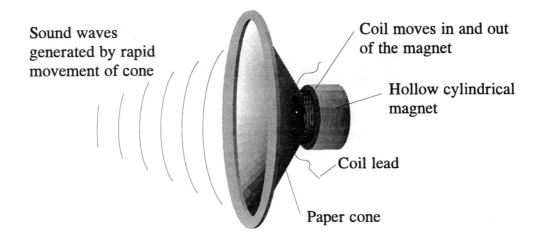

Figure 20.28. *The operation of a loudspeaker*

Light-emitting diodes (LEDs)

Light-emitting diodes are very small light bulbs which produce light as a result of the movement of electrons in a semiconductor. LEDs can be made to emit different colours and also infra-red radiation. They use very little electrical current and have very long lifetimes. They have the further advantage that they can be switched on and off very quickly.

Seven-segment displays

Seven-segment displays are the familiar digital displays used in many domestic devices such as watches, calculators, stereos and cameras. Each character is composed form up to seven tiny LEDs organised in the shape of a number eight as shown in Figure 20.29(a). The seven segments, labelled *a* to *g* in Figure 20.29(b), can be activated separately so that characters are formed from appropriate combinations of characters. Figure 20.29(c). shows the combinations of segments which are required in order to display the digits 0 to 9. Another device commonly used for seven-segment displays is based on liquid crystal materials whose optical properties can be modified by passing an electric current through them. Unlike devices which use LEDs, LCD-based displays need to be separately illuminated, but they require much less power for their operation than LEDs. Complete computer display screens, particularly for use with portable computers such as 'notebooks', are manufactured using large arrays of LCDs because of their very low power consumption characteristic.

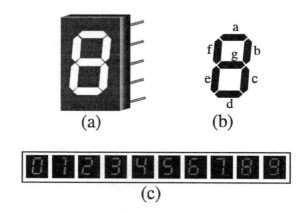

(a)   (b)

(c)

Figure 20.29. *Seven-segment displays*

Chapter 21

Word Processing

Introduction

Word processing describes the activity of writing with the aid of a computer. The term 'writing' is used in its widest sense and includes, for example, the production of personal or business documentation, such as letters, reports and memoranda, legal documents, articles, books and even the addressing of envelopes. Most word processors include tools for the production of columns and tables, as well as the inclusion of graphics; these tools play an important role in document production and they are examined in some detail. Any situation that requires communication by the *printed* word (including graphical images) may be appropriate for word processing. The word 'printed' normally means that the products of word processing activity are printed onto paper (*hard copy*), which is then sent or given to the intended recipient for him or her to read. Although this is usually what happens, *electronic mail* users can send word processed communications to one another without the need for hard copy. The person or persons (a single document can be addressed and sent to more than one user at the same time) receiving the electronic document can choose to read it on screen and if they wish, print it.

Creating a Document

Page Set-up

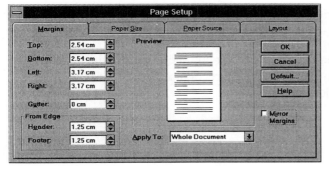

Figure 21.1. *Page set-up dialogue box*

Before you start entering text, or at some point before you print the final document, you may need to work through a *page set-up* procedure. This allows specification of the margin sizes, paper size and orientation that the printer will use when it prints the document. Even though the package has a *default* (already set) page specification, you should check that it conforms to your requirements and if necessary, adjust the appropriate settings. Figure 21.1 shows a dialogue box for the setting of margins and Figures 21.2 and 21.3 point out the location of each setting on the page.

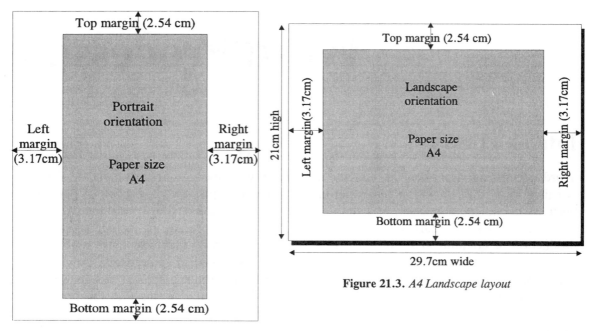

Figure 21.2. *A4 Portrait layout*

Figure 21.3. *A4 Landscape layout*

Top margin. This sets the amount of space the printer leaves at the top of the page before printing text.

Bottom margin. The value you give here determines the amount of space that the printer will leave at the end of a full page.

Left margin and *right margin*. These are the offsets from the left and right sides of the paper and determine the limits of the print line. Printer margins are usually measured in inches or centimetres.

Figure 21.2 shows the page in *portrait* orientation. To take advantage of *landscape* orientation (Figure 21.3), both the word processor and printer must support the facility.

You should also be able to specify the *paper size*, to determine the point at which the printer throws a new page in a multi-page document. Commonly recognised paper sizes include A5, which is half of A4, and A3, which is twice A4.

Entering Text

The Word Processor Screen

A basic word processor will accommodate up to 80 characters on each line and up to 25 lines of text is visible at any one time. However, all modern word processors can display a wide range of characters in different *fonts* and sizes (measured in *points*) which permit the display of many more than 80 characters on a single line. In any event, the useful length of the line is constrained by the printer's maximum line length and the paper size and orientation (either landscape or portrait) you use. When viewing a document on screen, a word processor allows you to 'zoom' (magnify or reduce the view of) a page and even display, albeit with very small characters on a 14" screen, a complete page at one time. Larger screens (such as A4 size) are used in publishing so that a complete page can be viewed, and yet be large enough for editing.

Although word processor screen layouts vary widely and cannot, therefore, be described in detail here, you should be aware of a number of functional elements that are common to most. An example is shown in Figure 21.4.

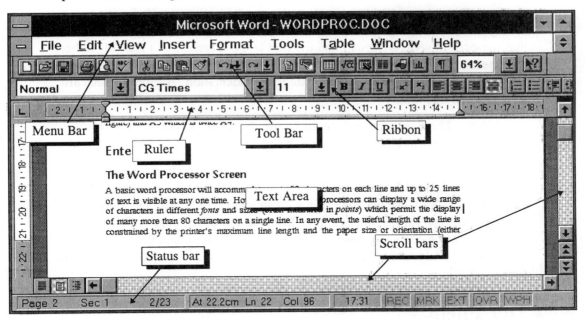

Figure 21.4. *Word processor screen features*

- *Ruler*. This allows you to change left and right margin settings and apply them to a complete document or to individual paragraphs. In Figure 4 the ruler markings are shown in centimetres and the white strip indicates the margin settings for the current paragraph. In respect of existing text, moving the margin settings on the ruler alters the margins for the paragraph where the *insertion point* (see New Document) is located. To apply changes to other paragraphs requires that they are first highlighted. If the margins are set before commencing the document, they apply to text as it is entered. Note that the margins on screen can be set to produce a shorter line within the boundaries of the printer margins defined in the Page Set-up procedure (see previous section). You should avoid adjusting the screen margins beyond the limits of the printer margins (these can, of course be changed up to the maximum permitted by the paper width), as the lines will be truncated or be wrapped onto the next line. The ruler also allows the setting of *tab* positions which allow you to indent the insertion point from the left margin by pressing the TAB key.

- *Text area*. This is simply the area of screen in which you can enter text or place graphical images.

- *Menu area*. Menu options relating to document handling and editing may be displayed at the top or bottom of the screen; clicking on a word on the menu bar pulls down other related options. Many options may also be executed directly through buttons on the *toolbar*, as an alternative to the menu system.

- *Ribbon*. The ribbon provides *switches* (they are either on or off) for the setting of certain text enhancements and styles. In Figure 21.4, you can see that the current style is normal and the font is CG Times, point size 11. Other switches can be seen relating to: emboldening, italicising and underscoring of text; paragraph alignment; bullets; paragraph indentation. All these topics are dealt with in detail later.

- *Scroll bars*. These are common to all mouse driven packages and allow vertical and horizontal scrolling through the document.

- *Status bar*. This displays the current position of the insertion point. For example, the status bar in Figure 21.4 shows the current position to be Page 2, Section 1; '2/23' means Page 2 in a document of 23 pages. The position on the page is shown in centimetres (cm) from the top of the page, or as line 22. 'Col 96' is not a character position on the line, because characters are of variable size and spacing between characters and words also varies. '17:31' is the current time.

New Document

When you start the word processor, an empty document may be automatically presented to you, or there may be a range of commands or menu options from which you can choose to create a *new* document file.

The cursor is positioned at the top left of the text entry area; the position occupied by the cursor at any point is often referred to as the *insertion point*. If your keyboard has keys that can function either as numbers or as *navigational arrow* keys, make sure that NUM LOCK is off. This is because you may need the arrow keys to move around the document.

Alternatively, you may use the mouse and scroll bars to navigate through a document. You cannot move the insertion point past the end of a document. If you want some blank space before entering text, press the ENTER key (this acts as a carriage return and moves the insertion point onto the next line) for each blank line you require.

Text entry is simple, but note the following important guidelines.

- **Do not** press the ENTER key at the end of each line because this will destroy the word processor's ability to adjust or *reformat* line endings to take account of newly inserted or deleted text. During text entry, you should only use the ENTER key after a paragraph or heading, or to insert a blank line.

- **Do** rely on the word processor's *word wrap* facility, which automatically adjusts text between the left and right margins and starts a new line as necessary.

- **Do not** use the SPACEBAR to move the insertion point within an existing line of text or to indent new text. Only use it to insert a space between words or after a punctuation mark. Spaces are characters, not just blank areas on the page. The word processor treats them as such when formatting text. Instead, use arrow keys or the mouse to re-position the insertion point and use the TAB key or margin settings to indent text.

- **Do not** use the SPACEBAR to delete other character (you would have to be in *overtype* mode - see below- to do this anyway). Use the BACKSPACE rubout or the DELETE key (see Navigational and Editing Keys).

Existing Document

If you have an existing document file on which you want to work further, then you will have to retrieve it from disk. Typically, this is referred to as *opening* a document. The guidelines given in the previous paragraph apply, except that you will be able to use the arrow keys or mouse to move the insertion point to the required position in the document (which may be at the end or anywhere before it).

Insert and Overtype Mode

Insert mode is normally the default and ensures that any text which follows the insertion point is moved to accommodate any new text which is entered. *Overtype* mode means that text following the insertion point will be deleted by any new text entered. Generally, you should use insert mode, unless you do not wish to keep text that follows the insertion point. *Toggling* (switching from one to the other and back again) between these modes is usually achieved with the *insert* key.

Navigational and Editing Keys

There are four navigational or arrow keys used for moving around your document, one each for up, down, left and right. In addition, there are keys for moving up or down a complete screen page (the amount of text visible on screen at one time) at a time. If you are using a mouse and a 'Windows type' word processor, you will be able to 'click' to indicate an editing position and use the scroll bars to view different parts of the document.

There are two keys for rubbing out or deleting text, the *destructive backspace* or *rubout*, often labelled ◀━━ and the *delete*, usually marked accordingly, or abbreviated to *del*. The destructive backspace moves the cursor to the left rubbing out characters as it goes; any characters to the right of the cursor move left to replace the vacant space. The delete key is used to remove the character immediately to the right of, or with some word processors, in the same position as, the cursor. As with the backspace, it can be pressed repeatedly or held down to remove a series of characters. If you wish to delete more than a few characters it may be better to use your word processor's highlighting facility and then delete the text as a block. With the *cut* and paste *facility* (see Copying, Cutting and Pasting), you can delete text and *move* it elsewhere in the document.

Editing Guidelines

If you are to use a word processor effectively, you must be aware of the features and facilities it provides for modifying or *editing* a document on screen, before printing the final version. In addition you should develop the skill of *proofing* or searching for errors in a document. You are likely to miss errors if you limit the exercise to a quick read of the document on screen. Proofing requires concentration and systematic searching for several types of error which commonly occur. They are detailed below, together with examples.

Spelling

You may have little trouble with spelling, but most people have a 'blind spot' with certain words and some common errors are listed below.

Correct	Common misspelling
sep*a*rate	seperate
station*e*ry	stationary (if referring to paper)
station*a*ry	stationery (if you mean stopped/not moving)
sincer*e*ly	sincerly
lia*i*son	liason
person*n*el	personel
revers*i*ble	reversable
com*m*ittee	comittee

Table 21.1. *Common spelling mistakes*

Apart from checking for misspellings, you should try to be consistent where a word has more than one acceptable spelling. Frequently, for example, you will find that the letter '*s*' can sometimes be used in place of '*z*'. The Oxford English Dictionary will give you the word 'organization', but you will frequently see it spelt as 'organisation'. Similar examples include, 'specialize' or 'specialise', 'emphasize' or 'emphasise'. These are only examples and not demonstration of a rule. For example, 'advertise' is correct, 'advertize' is wrong and 'advize' is *not* an alternative to 'advise'.

Typographical or Keying Errors

Categories of typographical errors include, words or individual characters out of order (*transposed*), missing or surplus words or characters and inappropriate or inconsistent use of lower case and capital letters. Look carefully at the two sentences which follow and you should be able to identify at least one example of each category of typographical error.

"Apart from being late, he was also poorly dressed."

"apart form being late, HE was was aslo dressd poorly ."

Punctuation Errors

You need to look for incorrect and missing punctuation. Some rules, such as the use of a full stop at the end of a sentence, are absolute. Rules on the use of, for example, commas are less clear. Generally, they are used to improve the readability of a document and are often a matter of personal judgement. For example, the sentence

'Apart from being late he was also poorly dressed."

would not be incorrect but would be more readable if a comma was used as follows.

"Apart from being late, he was also poorly dressed."

Spacing Errors

This relates to the incorrect omission of space or the inclusion of surplus space between words, sentences, lines or paragraphs. Generally, you should leave a single space between words and one space, possibly two, between a full stop and the beginning of the next sentence. You should also leave a blank line between paragraphs (note the exception to this, under Paragraph Formatting). Your word processor may provide the option to display characters which are normally *hidden*. These include spaces, tabs and carriage returns, and can make proofing for spacing errors easier.

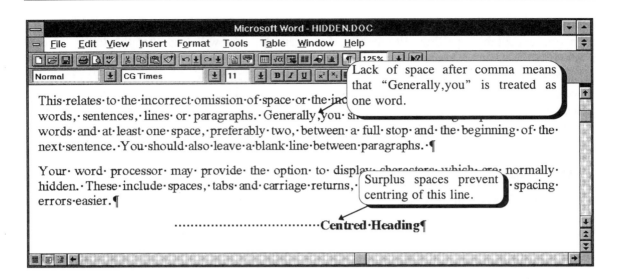

Figure 21.5. *Spacing errors*

Figure 21.5 shows some hidden characters, with a space represented by a · and a carriage return by a ¶. Two possible consequences of erroneous spacing can be identified in the Figure.

- 'Centred Heading' is off centre because the preceding spaces are taken as characters and included as part of the heading.

- The lack of a space after a comma means that the word before and after it, and the comma itself, are taken as one word; this would mean, for example, that the word processor's spell checker would highlight 'Generally,you', in Figure 21.5, as a misspelling. To correct it you would have to insert the required space.

Grammatical Errors

Clearly, your grammar and spelling need particularly careful attention if you are to give the recipient, not only the right professional image, but also the right message. Errors in either area can make the message difficult to understand and may even convey the wrong meaning.

General Proofing Guidelines

You should try to be systematic and look for all types of error. Generally, except for very short documents, it is very difficult to carry out proofing on screen and you will probably find that you need to print a draft copy to read. 'Hard copy' allows you to view the complete document and to use a ruler to guide your eyes as you scan each line.

Editing Facilities

Spell Checker

If your word processor includes a *spell checking* facility, you may find that, for example, it throws up words like 'organization' as being incorrectly spelled and indicates that only 'organisation' is correct. This does not mean that you cannot use the 'z' form. It simply means that the spellchecker's rules have not allowed for it. Spell checkers will identify as misspelled any word that does not appear in its *dictionary* (stored on disk). Thus, you may find that proper names, such as 'Wilkinson', or abbreviations like 'GNVQ', as well as

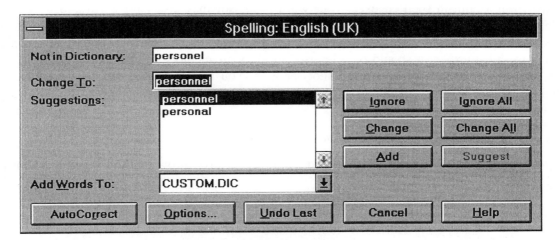

Figure 21.6. *Spellchecker dialogue*

many specialist technical terms, are highlighted as being incorrect. Most spell checkers allow you to add words to the dictionary, so that they are not identified as misspellings. If you misspell a word and it happens to be the correct spelling for another word, then the computer will not detect it. For example, 'stationery' and 'stationary' are both correctly spelled but have entirely different meanings. Such errors can only be found by careful proofing. Figure 21.6 shows the dialogue box of a typical spell checker; it has identified 'personel' as being incorrect and offers two possible alternatives, both of which are correctly spelled words, but with entirely different meanings. If the word you want is 'personal', rather than 'personnel', you need to highlight it before clicking on the 'Change' button. The other options are explained in Table 21.2.

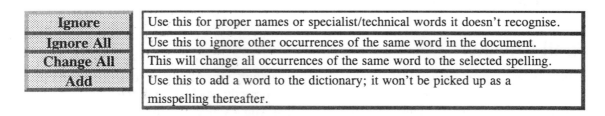

Ignore	Use this for proper names or specialist/technical words it doesn't recognise.
Ignore All	Use this to ignore other occurrences of the same word in the document.
Change All	This will change all occurrences of the same word to the selected spelling.
Add	Use this to add a word to the dictionary; it won't be picked up as a misspelling thereafter.

Table 21.2. *Spellchecker options*

Thesaurus

Apart from a built-in spell checker, your word processor may also have a *Thesaurus*, which allows you to check the meanings of words and suggests alternatives. This facility should be used with great care, to avoid the use of unusual words which may obscure what you are trying to say. Further, it should only be used to jog your memory for an alternative word. If you use a word with which you are not familiar, you may discover that the word has a similar, but not identical, meaning to the original. For example, the meaning of the following sentence is quite clear.

> *"She was studious and passed all her examinations."*

If you checked the Thesaurus for the word 'studious', it may throw up the suggestions shown in Figure 21.7.

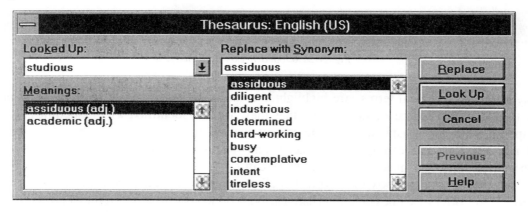

Figure 21.7. Thesaurus dialogue box

These include 'assiduous', 'diligent', 'hard-working' and 'industrious', none of which has exactly the same meaning. The adjectives do not necessarily relate to the activity of studying. To keep the meaning similar, you could change both adjectives to adverbs and keep the verb 'to study'. Possible alternatives of this form are shown below.

"She studied industriously and passed all her examinations."

"She studied diligently and passed all her examinations."

"She studied assiduously and passed all her examinations."

Even with these forms, the meaning is changed slightly. In the original, it is inferred that she was studious by nature, whereas the others suggest that she was studious for a limited period. The original is probably the easiest to read and best expresses the intended meaning.

However, provided you clearly understand the meanings of the words suggested by the Thesaurus and that they are not simply 'wordy' alternatives, then the facility can make your language more varied and lively.

Grammar Checker

The rules of grammar are too numerous to mention here, but your word processor may have a grammar checking facility which should accurately identify obvious errors and point out any grammatical constructions which it considers you should check. Use the facility with care and ensure that any suggestions it gives are valid before you accept them.

Search or Find

This facility allows you to search a document, or a selected part of it, for occurrences of a particular character, string (group) of characters, word, phrase or sentence.

Suppose that you have prepared a report on 'Information Technology at Work' and wish to look up references you have made to the use of spreadsheets. You would simply select the 'search' or 'find' option and key in the character string 'spreadsheet'. An example dialogue is shown in Figure 21.8.

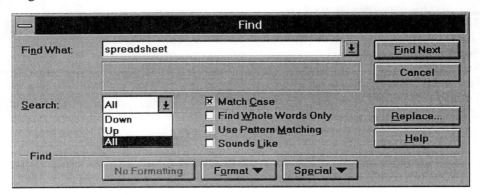

Figure 21.8. *Search or find dialogue*

The process may operate as follows. The word processor scans the document, highlights the first occurrence of 'spreadsheet' and after an appropriate command, moves to the next and so on, until all occurrences have been examined. The 'Down' and 'Up' options take the search from the current insertion point to the end and the beginning of the document, respectively. 'All' ensures that the whole document is searched regardless of the position of the insertion point. You can, of course, conclude the process once you have found a particular point in the document. A number of settings can be selected ('Match Case' is selected in Figure 21.8) to control the find process, including the following, which also appear in Figure 21.8.

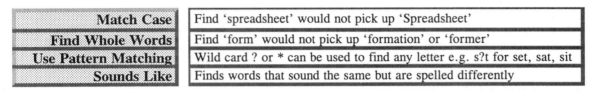

Match Case	Find 'spreadsheet' would not pick up 'Spreadsheet'
Find Whole Words	Find 'form' would not pick up 'formation' or 'former'
Use Pattern Matching	Wild card ? or * can be used to find any letter e.g. s?t for set, sat, sit
Sounds Like	Finds words that sound the same but are spelled differently

Table 21.3. *Text search settings*

Finding a Page

Page numbering (see Headers and Footers) is useful if, following the printing of a document, you spot an error on one of the pages in the middle of the document. You can immediately identify the page number from the header or footer on the page and instruct the word processor to *find* that page. Figure 21.9 shows a dialogue box which includes options to select a particular page, section or line number, as well as a range of other document locations.

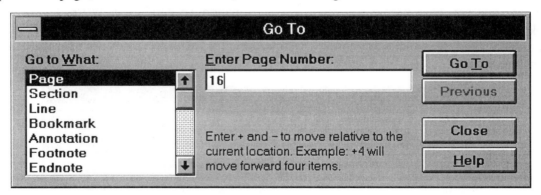

Figure 21. 9. *'Go to' dialogue box*

If, having made the correction, the *pagination* (where each new page begins) is not affected, you can simply re-print the single page. Alternatively, you can use the text *find* facility to locate the required page. Clearly, you should try to use a search string which is unique to that page, or at least, does not occur more than two or three times.

Search and Replace

This facility allows you to

- replace occurrences of a particular character, string of characters, word, phrase or sentence, with your chosen alternative.

The facility is the same as for 'find', except that you are prompted for a character string which is to replace the occurrences found. For example, if you decide that you are going to change 'specialise' to 'specialize', then you key in the first word as the search string and the second as the replacement string (see Figure 21.10).

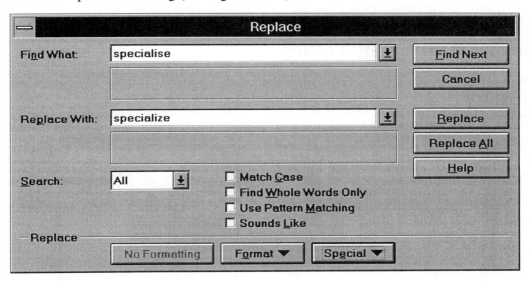

Figure 21.10. *Search and replace dialogue*

Table 21.4 explains some of the search and replace settings shown in Figure 21.10.

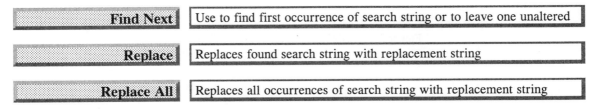

Find Next	Use to find first occurrence of search string or to leave one unaltered
Replace	Replaces found search string with replacement string
Replace All	Replaces all occurrences of search string with replacement string

Table 21.4. *Search and replace settings*

If the string may be part of other words (if 'Find whole words only' is not selected), then be careful not to choose the 'replace all ' option and examine each one as it is found, before confirming a replacement.

Undo and Redo Options

Your word processor may provide a facility to 'undo' a particular operation, such as the reformatting of a paragraph or the deletion of some text. You would use this to reverse a mistake or, perhaps, to view the effect of a particular change before making it permanent. Despite the usefulness of the undo feature, not all operations can be reversed; for example, it is not possible to reverse a 'file save' operation. Some packages will only allow you to reverse the last operation. For example, if you change the format of a complete paragraph and then delete a space, you may only be able to recover the space character, not the original format of the paragraph. Increasingly, however, packages allow numerous undo levels, so you can reverse operations out of their original sequence. Redo reverses an undo.

Copying, Cutting and Pasting

To save re-typing a block of text which you wish to use in other parts of a document, you can copy the original, by highlighting the required text and executing a *copy* command (see Figure 21.11). If you want to remove it from its original location, you can *cut* the text.

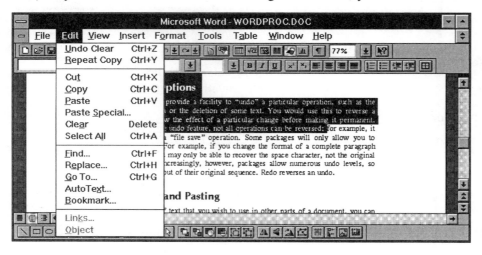

Figure 21.11. *Highlighted text and Copy Command*

The cutting and copying processes have the effect of storing the text in an area of *buffer* (temporary storage) memory, from where it can be retrieved as often as required for insertion at selected points in the document. Sometimes the buffer is referred to as the *clipboard* (Figure 21.12). Note that the text on the clipboard is *unformatted* (words are split at the end of lines). When you paste it from the clipboard to your document, it is formatted according to the settings for that document. To insert a copied or cut block of text, you would move the insertion point to the position you require and execute the *paste* command, also shown in Figure 21.11. If the text is not being added to the end of the document, any text which follows will be shuffled forward to accommodate the new text.

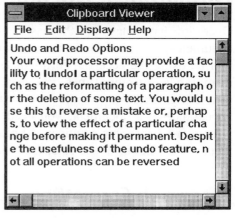

Figure 21.12. *Copied text on clipboard*

In cutting and copying operations, the text remains in the buffer or on the clipboard until you replace it with something else or leave the package. If you are using a *multi-tasking* system, such as Windows, then you can copy or cut text (or graphical images) to the clipboard and insert the contents into another application. You can, of course, paste copied or cut text (or graphical images) into other documents within the word processor.

Moving Text by Dragging

Mouse-driven packages usually allow text to be moved by highlighting and dragging with the mouse. Figure 21.13 shows the operation in progress, with the mouse pointer indicating the insertion point of the text when it is removed from its current position.

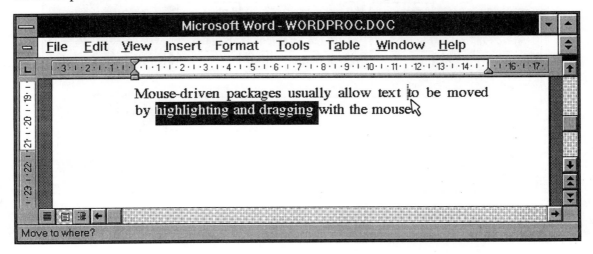

Figure 21.13. *Highlighting and dragging*

Formatting a Document

Once you have mastered the basics of entering text, saving, retrieving, editing and printing documents, you will be concerned with improving layout and presentation. Sometimes you will be using the accepted forms of layout commonly applied to business letters, reports and memoranda. At other times, you may be typing continuous prose for an essay, or using your own design skills to prepare, for example, a notice, advertisement or menu. To change the appearance of a document, you need to be know how to use the various *formatting* facilities your word processor provides. Typically, the facilities will be provided through command menus, the ribbon, or the ruler (see section on Entering Text).

Paragraph Formatting

Any line or group of lines, with only one carriage return at the end of the last line, is treated by a word processor as a paragraph. By using the word processor's automatic *word wrap* (see Entering Text) facility, you only need to press ENTER when you are ready to start a new paragraph. Following standard practice, even when typing continuous prose, you should insert a blank line by pressing the ENTER key a second time, after each paragraph. Alternatively, you can specify that spacing, measured in *point* (pt) size, is left after a paragraph, once you press the ENTER key. Figure 21.14 shows a dialogue box indicating selection of an 8 pt space after a paragraph.

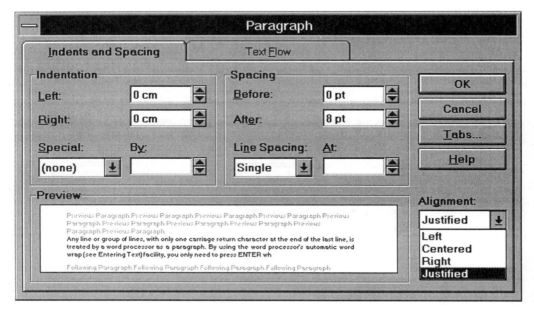

Figure 21.14. *Paragraph format dialogue*

Paragraph formatting allows you to determine the alignment, either of a complete document or of individual paragraphs, in relation to the left and right margins.

Thus, a single document may have a number of paragraphs, each with a different alignment. Spacing between lines can also be varied. Figure 21.14 also shows a line space selection box. The following paragraphs describe commonly used formatting facilities.

Paragraph Alignment

Paragraph formatting allows you to determine the alignment, either of a complete document or of paragraphs, in relation to the left and right margins. A single document may have a number of paragraphs, with a different alignment. Line spacing can be varied.

Figure 21.15. *Left aligned*

Global Corporation plc
Hargrave House
London WC2
30th August 1995

Figure 21.16. *Right aligned*

Paragraph formatting allows you to determine the alignment, either of a complete document or of paragraphs, in relation to the left and right margins. A single document may have a number of paragraphs, with a different alignment. Line spacing can be varied.

Figure 21.17. *Justified*

Ambridge Garden Club

Annual Show

30th September 1995

in the

Village Hall

Figure 21.18. *Centred*

Left alignment ensures that each line of text begins in the left margin, as Figure 21.15 illustrates. Note that the right margin is ragged. Your word processor will normally be set to this format by default, and the word wrap facility will always begin the next line at the selected left margin. Pressing the ENTER key will also return the cursor or insertion point to the left margin. Figure 21.18 shows a notice where each line of text is centred on the page.

Right alignment ensures that the right margin remains straight and that the left margin is ragged, as shown in Figure 21.16. You may wish to use this facility for the return address and date in a letter.

Figure 21.17 shows a *justified* paragraph, where both the right and left margins are straight. There may be occasions when you need to split a word at the end of a line, to prevent words being too widely spaced. This is more likely to happen if you have set wide margins, or are using multiple columns, and the line length is particularly short. Figure 21.19 illustrates the problem and Figure 21.20, the appearance of the text after hyphenation.

I am incapable of viewing transmogrification or transubstantiation with equanimity. The strangeness of the concept is such that I am uncertain whether I wish to pursue the enterprise.

Figure 21.19. *Justified text with excessive spacing*

> I am incapable of viewing transmogrification or transubstan-
> tiation with equanimity. The strangeness of the concept is such
> that I am uncertain whether I wish to pursue the enterprise.

Figure 21.20. *Hyphenation to remove excessive spacing*

You may have to carry out such hyphenation manually, but the word processor may provide a facility similar to that shown in Figure 21.21. Suggested hyphenation points are given for you to select; alternatively, hyphenation can be carried out automatically.

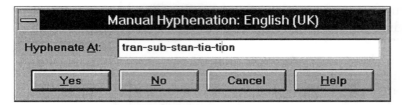

Figure 21.21. *Hyphenation dialogue*

Hidden Characters and Alignment Problems

You may find that when you try, for example, to centre a paragraph of text, that it does not do so. The problem may be caused by the presence of *hidden characters*. It is most important that there are no surplus hidden characters, such as spaces or tabs, on a line, as this will prevent proper alignment. Figure 21.5, earlier in this chapter illustrates this problem.

Indents and Hanging Indents

An *indent* is a starting point for text which is not in line with the left (or occasionally, the right) margin. You can choose to indent the first line only in a paragraph, a complete paragraph, or all but the first line of a paragraph. This last form is known as a *hanging indent*. The three forms are shown in Figure 21.22. To set up an indent may involve the use of menu options and/or the ruler. Figure 21.22 shows the ruler set for the hanging indent.

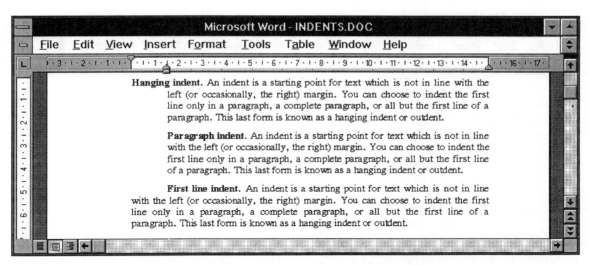

Figure 21.22. *Hanging, Paragraph and First line indents*

Line Spacing

By default, your word processor should leave a single line space between each line of text, as part of automatic *word wrap* (see Entering Text). Most word processors provide an option which automatically inserts two and sometimes one-and-a-half blank lines between each line in a paragraph. This option may be helpful in the preparation of a notice or advertisement, in combination with a larger font (see Character Formatting). Sometimes, your tutor may ask for work to be double line spaced to make marking and the insertion of comments easier. Figure 21.14 shows a dialogue box for the selection of line spacing preferences.

Tabulation

Tabulation is particularly useful for typing lists in columns, or text and figures in table form. If you wish to begin text entry to the right of the existing left margin, you can change the margin setting, but this will mean that word wrap or pressing the ENTER key will always place the insertion point at the new margin setting. To move the insertion point for a single line of text, use the TAB key. The screen ruler probably has some default TAB settings, possibly set every 0·5 inch or 1.27 centimetres. Each time you press the TAB key the insertion point is moved to the next TAB point. You can either begin typing at that point or press the TAB key to move to the next position. Once you reach the right margin, the insertion point may be moved to the first TAB position on the next line or to the preceding one on the same line. If you have chosen the exact tabulation settings, then it is better to clear the default settings and insert tabulation points as required. This may be achieved through a menu option if they are to be regularly spaced. If the spacing is irregular, your word processor will probably allow you to set and move them on the ruler. Figure 21.23 shows a tabulated document with the normally hidden TAB characters displayed.

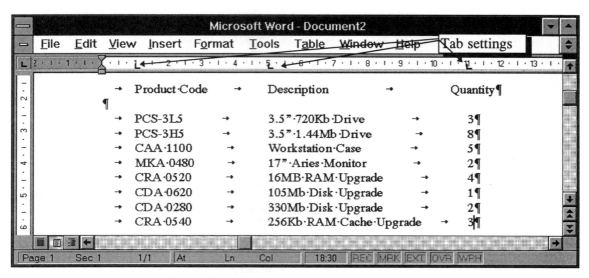

Figure 21.23. *Tabulated document and TAB settings*

Character Formatting

Apart from the daisy wheel printer, which only allows the use of one character set at a time, all dot matrix (impact, ink jet and thermographic) and laser printers allow the printing of a wide range of character styles. Some common examples are given below.

    this is bold   *this is italic*   ~~this is strike through~~   <u>this is underline</u>

    this is bold italic

For some word processing work, these variations are quite sufficient and your printer may well have a control panel to select a different *font*, but any such selection will be applied to the whole document. Typically, your printer may offer

    `courier`, roman, condensed

Variable sizing of character *fonts* is a facility which, until recently, was associated with desktop publishing (DTP) software. Some examples are given below (size is measured in *points*).

This is Phyllis ATT 16

This is Lucida Casual 14

Using Character Formatting

You should use character formatting facilities sparingly. A business document can look very unprofessional, as well as a little silly, if you use too many different character formats. Thus, to emphasise, you may use bold or underlined characters. A quotation may be in italic print and headings in a report may be improved by using a larger font.

WYSIWYG Packages

WYSIWYG stands for What You See Is What You Get, which means that the results of paragraph and character formatting commands are seen on screen. Thus, lines can be seen as centred, characters can be viewed as **bold**, *italic*, underlined, or even in

different sizes and fonts.

Apart from the package's WYSIWYG facilities, your screen must have the necessary graphics capability and *resolution* (see Computer Hardware).

Bullets and Numbered Lists

Bullets and numbers can be used to emphasise or sequence items in a list. Two examples are given below.

This pack includes the following items:

- assembly instructions
- colour illustrations
- components for assembly

The tasks should be carried out in the following order:

   (i) initial investigation;

   (ii) analysis;

   (iii) design;

   (iv) implementation.

In the second example, the numbering sequence is carried out automatically and a variety of number styles may be available, using Arabic or Roman numerals, or letters of the alphabet. Figure 21.24 shows a dialogue box for the selection of various bullet formats.

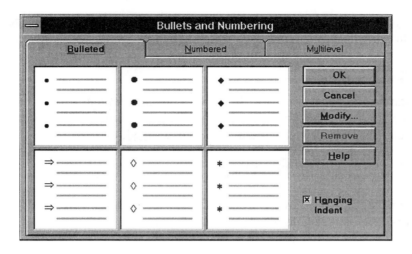

Figure 21.24. *Bullet format dialogue*

Styles

In preparing a more lengthy document, such as a booklet, or magazine article, it is advisable to make use of styles, which may be pre-defined, or which you have defined yourself. A style defines a number of features concerning text; some of them, including, paragraph alignment, line spacing, character font and size have already been described. As explained later, styles can be applied, not only to headings and paragraph text, but also to *tables* and *frames*. An example style definition is detailed in Table 21.5. Figure 21.25 shows the style itself.

Style	Heading 2
font	CG Omega
font size	16 pt
format	bold
paragraph alignment	flush left
spacing before	10 pt
spacing after	6 pt

Table 21.5. *Example Defined Style*

In preparing a more lengthy document, such as a booklet, or magazine article, it is advisable to make use of styles, which may pre-defined, or which you have defined yourself. A style defines a number of features concerning text; some of them, including, paragraph alignment, line spacing, character font and size have already been described.

10 pt space before

Heading Style CG Omega 16 Bold Flush Left

6 pt space after

As explained later, styles can be applied, not only to headings and paragraph text, but also to *tables* and *frames*.

Figure 21.25. *Example Style*

You should make use of different text styles to emphasise, for example, titles, chapter headings, sub-headings or body text. The word processor will normally have a set of named styles, which you can use immediately. You can modify any of these styles and keep the same names or you can create new styles and name them yourself. The ready-made styles are held in what is often referred to as the *style palette*. Figure 21.26 shows a variety of user-defined styles with some of the style names displayed in the pull down palette.

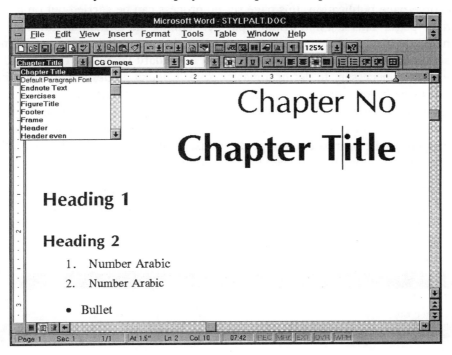

Figure 21.26. Example styles and style palette

To apply a style, you would need to place the insertion point within the relevant paragraph and then use the pointer tool to select the appropriate style from the palette. Styles which you create can be added to the palette, but they will only be available for the current document, unless you make them part of a *document template* (known as a *style sheet* in desktop publishing programs). The topic of templates is examined later.

Of course, character styles can also be applied to selected areas of text. Instead of applying a style to a complete paragraph, for example, you can alter the *character* style (bold, underline, italic) and font of a block of text which you have *highlighted*.

Columns

Although you can use tabulation for column work, the technique is only suitable for lists of, for example, product descriptions or prices on an order form. For continuous prose, such as appears in a newspaper, you need a column facility. Typically, when you start your word processor you will be presented with a default page with a single column, spanning the width available between the left and right margins. The arrangements for setting columns vary from package to package, but there are two main approaches. The first is commonly used in *desktop publishing* (DTP) programs and the second in recent versions of word processors.

- To obtain multiple columns you may need to mark their positions before you place any text or graphics into the publication. If you are producing a multiple-page publication, this page set-up process can be carried out on a *master page*. This is a non-printing page containing the formatting guides which you want repeated on every page in a publication. If you are producing a single page publication or you don't want a standard layout for each page, then it is unnecessary to define a master page. *Column guides* are non-printing guides which you can use to position your columns. Typically, there is an option of the form 'snap to column guides'. When you set this option, they behave rather like a magnet, so that each column edge becomes attached or 'snapped' to the nearest column guide. Thus, if you wish to set column widths and positions yourself, you need to set the option to 'off'.

- A word processor may allow columns to be created before or after the entry of text and be altered at will. You can choose to have the columns the same width and equally spaced, or vary the column widths and spacing according to preference. Figures 21.27 and 21.28 show two and three column text, respectively.

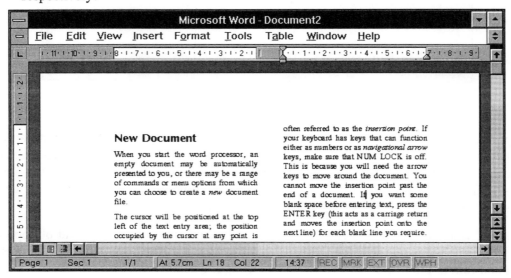

Figure 21.27. *Two column layout*

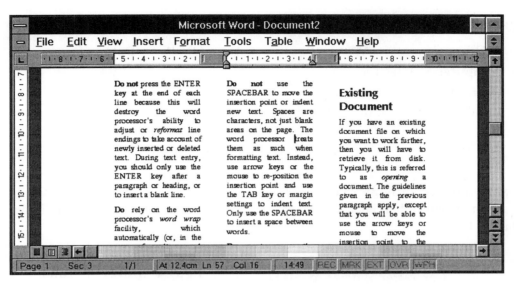

Figure 21.28. *Three column layout*

Note that the rulers in Figures 21.27 and 21.28 reflect the relevant number of columns. Figure 21.28 shows that three (or more) columns can present a problem if the paragraphs are justified (straight right and left margins), in that large gaps may be left between some words (you can use hyphenation to solve the problem). Clearly, the problem would be less obvious if landscape orientation were used, as the overall width of the document could be greater.

Tables

If you need to present text in a tabular way, you can use tabulation, but a *table* tool allows much greater control over layout. It may also provide extra features to enhance presentation and even allow simple calculations on numeric items. To define a basic table, you need to specify the number of *rows* and *columns*.

Table 21.6 has 4 rows and 3 columns. Each box in the grid is known as a *cell*.

Title	Authors(s)	Date
Computer Studies for BTEC	Knott, Waites	1994
GCSE Information Systems	Waites	1994
Small Business Computer Systems	Knott	1994

Table 21.6. *Example table with borders*

Additional rows, columns or cells can be added, inserted or deleted. The insertion point can be moved from cell to cell with the arrow keys or by clicking on an individual cell with the mouse. The cells in Table 21.6 have *borders*, but Table 21.7 shows the same data before borders were assigned.

Title	Authors(s)	Date
Computer Studies for BTEC	Knott, Waites	1994
GCSE Information Systems	Waites	1994
Small Business Computer Systems	Knott	1994

Table 21.7. *Example table without borders*

The word processor may provide a number of table formats, which you can apply, or you may assign your own borders and *shading*. A number of examples are given in Tables 21.8, 21.9 and 21.10.

Title	Author(s)	Date
Computer Studies for BTEC	Knott, Waites	1994
GCSE Information Systems	Waites	1994
Small Business Computer Systems	Knott	1994

Table 21.8. *Example built-in format*

Title	Author(s)	Date
Computer Studies for BTEC	Knott, Waites	1994
GCSE Information Systems	Waites	1994
Small Business Computer Systems	Knott	1994

Table 21.9. *Example built-in format*

Title	Author(s)	Date
Computer Studies for BTEC	Knott, Waites	1994
GCSE Information Systems	Waites	1994
Small Business Computer Systems	Knott	1994

Table 21.10. *User-developed format*

Figures 21.29 and 21.30 are examples of dialogue boxes for the placing of borders and shading within the table.

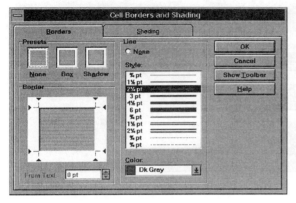

Figure 21.29. *Borders dialogue box*

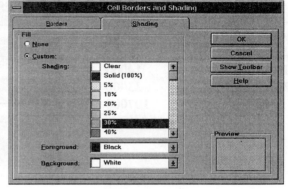

Figure 21.30. *Shading dialogue box*

Formulae in Tables

If you have used a spreadsheet package, you should be familiar with the idea of carrying out calculations automatically, with the use of formulae. Word processor tables provide a number of simple functions, such as SUM, to add the contents of a range of cells and PRODUCT, to multiply the contents of cells. Table 21.11 shows a list of sales details for individual salespersons; the SUM function has been used to total the shaded cells, as shown. Figure 21.31 shows the dialogue box used to enter the formula.

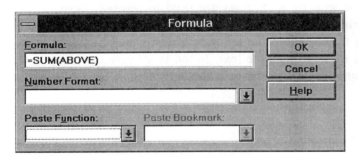

Figure 21.31. Dialogue for entry of SUM function

Name	Units Sold
Jones	15000
Avia	22000
Wiemann	33000
Anderson	23000
Ricci	14000
Total	**107000**

Table 21.11. Formula in table

Table Sorting

Your word processor may also allow you to treat the table as a simple database and sort rows, as if they were records. Table 21.12 repeats the data previously shown in Table 21.11, but with the names and associated sales figures in ascending alphabetical order; the first column is used as the *sort key*. Figure 21.32 shows the dialogue box for executing the sorting process; the names and sales figures are highlighted, before the sort is executed. It is important that you do not highlight any rows which you do not wish to be included in the sort; thus, the headings and the total row in Table 21.12 would not be highlighted.

Name	Unit Sold
Anderson	23000
Avia	22000
Jones	15000
Ricci	14000
Wiemann	33000
Total	107000

Table 21.12. *Sorted Table*

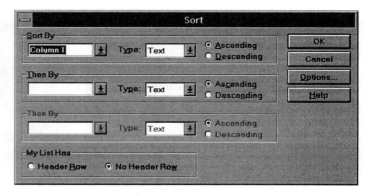

Figure 21.32. *Table sort dialogue*

Figure 21.32 shows that the sort key is selected by identifying a column in the table. In this case, it is column 1 (the leftmost column).

Frames

A frame can be used to position an item on a page, independently of any accompanying text. An item can consist of text or graphics (see Graphics). The text or graphics items may be produced within the package or they may be obtained from other sources, such as a drawing package or a 'clip art' file and then pasted into the frame. Normal paragraph text can be made to flow around the frame, or it can be split by it. Frames are used to position most of the diagrams and tables in this book. Figure 21.33 shows a dialogue box for setting frame formats. Once you have positioned a frame within the paragraph text, you can assign it an exact position on the page, or allow it to move with the text. In the latter case, inserting new text above the frame will move the frame forward as the new text is entered.

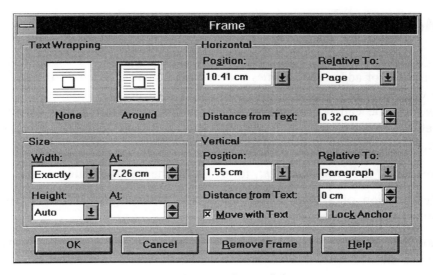

Figure 21.33. *Frame format dialogue*

Templates and Wizards

A template can be used to create publications or documents of the same type. It is similar to a

style sheet, except that a package will normally include several templates, each designed for a particular kind of publication or document. A special template (often referred to as *normal.dot*), is used to set the default layout and formats, for a new document. Typically, templates of various forms may be available for immediate use (you can modify a template if it does not fit your need exactly).

Annual General Meeting
23rd August 1995
13:15 to 14:25, Lipman Building

Meeting called by:	Chief Executive	

----- Agenda Topics -----		
1. Meeting Overview	Chief Executive	13:15-13:25
2. Financial Report	Financial Director	13:25-13:45
3. Marketing	Marketing Manager	14:00-14:10
4. Profitability	Financial Director	14:10-14:25

Figure 21.34. *Agenda produced with a wizard*

They may include, for example, memorandum, invitation, bulletin, report, dissertation and invoice templates. Apart from simple templates, the word processor may provide a number of document *wizards*; a wizard takes you through a number of dialogue boxes, taking information on the data to be included in the document. Typical examples include wizards for the production of calendars, agendas and faxes. An agenda produced with a wizard is shown in Figure 21.34; the design and main headings are provided by the wizard, so all you have to provide is the *variable* data, such as meeting title, location, times, topics and so on.

Mail Merge and Address Labels

A *mail merge* facility allows the printing of multiple copies of a standard letter, with the automatic insertion of addressees' names and addresses and other personal details. It requires access to a database file containing the relevant personal details of the intended addressees; alternatively, the file can be created within the word processor. Using the same data, an address labelling facility allows you to print labels of your own design or address envelopes of a given size. The process involves several stages:

(i)   creation of the *main document*, for example, the standard letter;

(ii) identification of a *data source* containing the merge data, for example, names and addresses;

(iii) labelling of *merge data fields* as, for example, 'Title', 'Initials', 'Surname' and so on

(iv) insertion of *field labels* at the appropriate points in the main document.

Example field «labels» are shown in Figure 21.35.

«Title» «Initials» «Surname»
«Address1»
«Address2»
«County»
«PostCode»

Dear «Title» «Surname»,

main body of letter goes here

Yours faithfully,

Figure 21.35. *Mail merge document showing field labels*

When the merge is executed, a copy of the letter is produced for each record in the merge data file. The merge can be restricted to addressees living, for example, within a particular county, or those whose surnames begin with a particular letter.

More Advanced Topics for Complex Documents

This section looks at the facilities which you would find useful, if not essential, for the preparation of longer and more complex documents. Such documents may include chapters or sections.

Outlining

Figure 21.36 shows an example of the *outline* view of a document. The indentation represents the hierarchy of the topics. The full document is concerned with the topic of word processing and the main divisions of the topic are 'Introduction', 'Creating a Document' and Editing a Document'. Sub topics are identified by their level of indentation from the main list. The title 'Creating a Document' has two sub-topics, identified as 'Page Set-up' and 'Entering Text'. This latter heading has one sub-topic, 'The Word Processor Screen'.

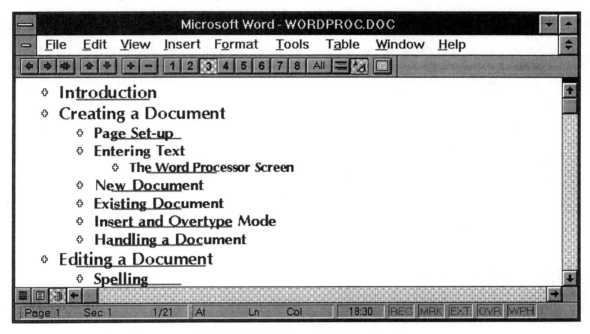

Figure 21.36. Outline view of document

Thus, if you are planning the contents and structure of a report, you should find an outlining facility extremely useful. Even if your word processor does not provide such a facility, you would be wise to plan an outline on paper before starting on the report. The outlining facility in Word for Windows relies on the use of heading styles (Heading1, Heading 2 ...), defined and stored in a style palette (see Styles).

An outline facility goes far beyond the typing of a hierarchical list. By moving the cursor to a particular point in the outline, you can switch to normal text entry mode and begin typing under the chosen section or sub-section. At any point, you can switch back to the outline view, perhaps to begin on another part of the document, or to insert an additional section or sub-section. Each heading in the outline serves as an entry point into a particular part of the document, enabling you to 'home into' a section without scrolling through the whole of the preceding text.

The outline facility can also be used to move or copy complete sections. Instead of highlighting a complete block of text, you can highlight the section heading in the outline and move or copy it to a new position in the outline. All text and headings subordinate to the selected heading are moved or copied with the heading. In this way, you can re-arrange the sections of your document.

Pagination

As you develop a document, the word processor automatically inserts a *soft* page break each time you add another page. The word processor usually displays such breaks on screen, or you may only find out where they occur when the document is printed. The point at which a soft page break is inserted depends on the length of the page as defined in *page set-up* (see Page Set-up). Normally, you will select one of a number of standard sizes, such as A4 or A5. If you return to edit an earlier part of a document, perhaps to add or remove text, then the pagination process recalculates the amount of text on the page and adjusts subsequent soft page breaks accordingly.

A soft page break may occur at an inconvenient point, perhaps immediately after a heading or in the middle of a table and in such an event you can force a *hard* page break at a more suitable point. Subsequent soft page breaks are again adjusted accordingly. Generally, you should leave the insertion of hard page breaks until you are satisfied that your document is complete and does not require any further revision. This is because hard page breaks are not moved in the automatic pagination process and after further editing you may have to remove certain hard page breaks or relocate them.

Page View and Print Preview

These two facilities allow you to view a document as individual pages. *Page view* shows you the edges of the page, if the 'zoom' is set to 'page width'. You can see the bottom and top edges as you scroll from one page to another. You can edit and format the text while in page view and see the effects of re-pagination as you work. *Print preview* shows you each page of the document (either one, two or more pages at a time) in miniaturised form as they will appear on the printer. These are true WYSIWYG (What You See Is What You Get) features. If your word processor has these facilities, the results of pagination are easy to see and the points at which hard page breaks are needed are clear.

Headers and Footers

A *header* is descriptive text which appears above the top margin on every page. For example, a header may include the page number, date, report title and the author's name. A *footer* serves a similar function except that it is located beneath the bottom margin on each page. You only have to enter a header or footer once and the word processor automatically places it on each page when the document is printed. Creating a header or footer is a separate operation from normal text entry and you can only create, edit or remove one through the relevant package commands. If you do not wish to place a header or footer on every page, there is normally a facility, for example, to exempt the first page or assign a different header or footer to the odd or even pages. Figure 21.37 shows a document in print preview, with a header 'Pagination' and a footer, used in this example, for page numbering.

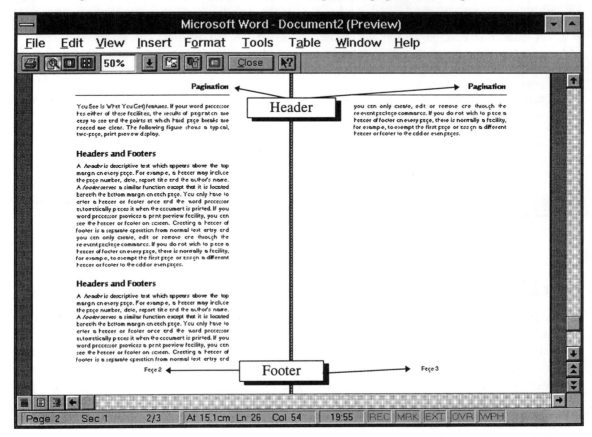

Figure 21.37. *Print preview showing headers and footers*

Footnotes

Footnotes are useful if you want to briefly explain a word or phrase, without including the explanation within the main body of the text. Instead, a reference number is placed next to the relevant word or phrase and the explanation is put at the foot of the page, identified by the same reference number. Figure 21.38 provides an example, where the footnote reference[1] points to an explanation of 'top margin' at the foot of the page.

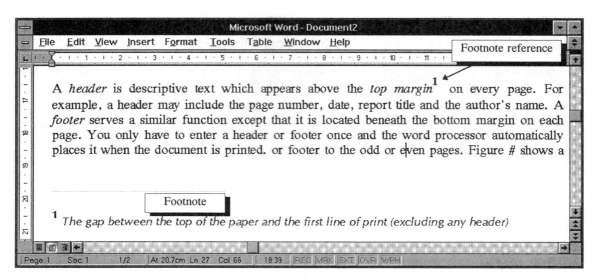

Figure 21.38. *Footnote*

Combining Documents

If you are preparing a lengthy document, such as a report, you may manage it more easily if you tackle it, chapter by chapter, or section by section. Your computer's memory limits may necessitate this anyway. Thus, you will create and save each section or chapter as a separate document file. You will want to ensure that each part of the complete document is of a consistent format. This will mean that, when you print each document file (which forms part of the complete document), the

- margin widths,
- heading sizes,
- section and page numbering,
- paragraph indents,
- paragraph alignment,
- tabulation and column settings,
- and bullet styles,

and so on, are consistent with the rest.

Graphics

Although you may use a specialist graphic design or drawing package to produce illustrations and diagrams, word processors provide drawing tools, which are adequate for most purposes.

Figure 21.39 shows part of a typical drawing toolbar. The use of these tools is explained in detail, in Graphic Design.

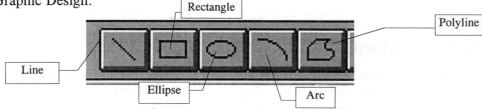

Figure 21.39. *Drawing tools*

Figure 21.40 shows more tools concerned with text annotation (text and call out boxes are used in this and other Figures), colour fill and line styles. Drawing tools produce drawing objects, which are manipulated separately from any surrounding text. Unlike imported graphics objects, they do not have to be in a frame to allow free positioning on the page. The pointer tool is used for selecting drawing objects.

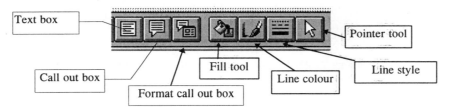

Figure 21.40. *Text, fill, line and pointer tools.*

Figure 21.41 illustrates various drawing objects and identifies the tool(s) with which each is drawn.

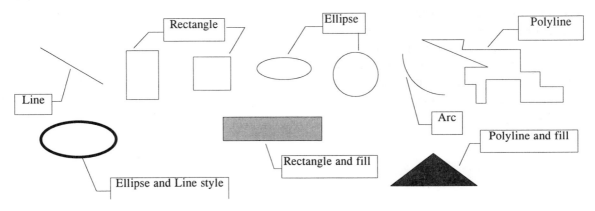

Figure 21.41. *Drawing Objects*

All the annotations are call out boxes. For more detail on using these and other tools, see Graphic Design.

Sizing and Manipulating Graphics

When a graphic is selected with the pointer tool, it can be manipulated in a variety of ways, some of which are illustrated in Figure 21.42 (all operations were carried out on the original). The re-size operation makes use of *handles* (see Graphic Design) which appear around the drawing object when it is selected.

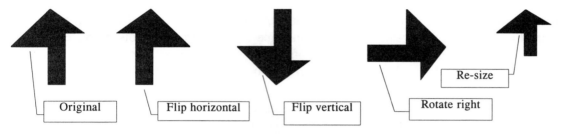

Figure 21.42. *Flipped, rotated and re-sized graphic object.*

Importing Text and Graphics

Although modern word processors include facilities normally associated with desktop publishing, graphic design and drawing packages, it is sometimes necessary and desirable to import images from a specialist package. Similarly, although a word processor may include facilities for simple spreadsheet-type calculations (see Tables) and simple database sorting, you are likely to use specialist spreadsheet and database packages for such work. It is important that data can be transferred from one package to another, to avoid any re-entry or editing of data. For example, if you are preparing a report on personnel issues in an organization and need to include some actual data from a personnel database, you should be able to import that data into your document. Commonly, imported images are either *objects* or *pictures* (depending on their format); imported text items are known as objects. Figure 21.43 illustrates these ideas.

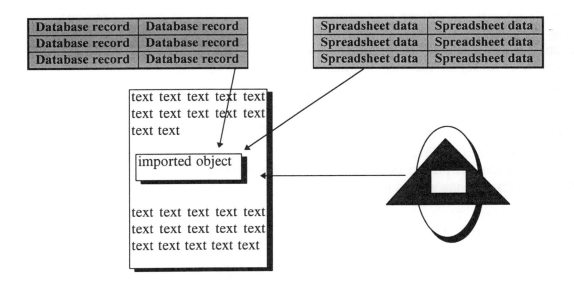

Figure 21.43. *Importing data from other packages*

The following paragraphs provide examples of imported objects.

Clip Art Images

Figure 21.44. *Clip art image and sizing handles*

Figure 21.44 shows an imported clip art picture. The image is a 'tif' file, which means that it uses the file extension .tif. There are numerous formats which may be used to store images, including .bmp or bitmap image format, which are commonly acceptable for importing by most word processing packages. The ways in which the image can be manipulated are limited to re-sizing and *cropping*; any imported object or picture will be placed at the current position of the insertion point and can only be moved freely on the page if it is placed in a frame (see Frames). Figure 21.45 shows the same clip art picture in a frame, with this paragraph text flowing around it.

Figure 21.45. *Clip art picture inside frame*

Figure 21.46 shows the image after cropping, which means that part of it is obscured.

The format of the image means that it cannot be rotated or flipped (see Sizing and Manipulating Graphics). Graphics produced with the word processor's own drawing tools can be manipulated in these ways.

Figure 21.46. *Cropped image*

Importing Drawing Objects and Object Linking

Figure 21.47 shows a drawing produced with CorelDraw and then imported into this

Figure 21.48. *Re-sized object*

Figure 21.47. *CorelDraw object*

document. Figure 21.48 shows the same drawing after re-sizing. If you are using Windows, or a similar operating environment, you can edit the imported object without quitting the word processor, or separately loading the drawing package. Double clicking on the drawing automatically opens the drawing application and the drawing can be edited; when editing is finished and you return to the document, the image is automatically updated (you can choose that this does not happen). This *object linking*, as it is known, can be carried out with any package which supports this type of operation.

Word Art

Text can be entered as an artistic image, rather than as normal paragraph text. It is treated as an object, in the same way as other imported images, even though the program which produces it (Microsoft WordArt 2.0™) is accessed from within the word processor itself. Figure 21.49 shows some examples of this 'word art'.

Figure 21.49. *Artistic Text objects*

Importing Spreadsheet and Database Files

The simplest way to import spreadsheet and database data into a document is to use the *clipboard* (see Cutting, Copying and Pasting). The relevant data is highlighted within the relevant package, before the copy command is executed. The data is then pasted into the document within the word processor; you will need to switch between applications using a multi-tasking facility. Table 21.13 shows imported data from the Excel spreadsheet. If the data can been pasted into the document as an *object of the source application*

Holiday Destination	Country Code	Country	Currency	Currency Cost	Current Exchange Rate	Sterling Cost
New York	US	USA	US Dollar	2000	1.42	£1,408.45
Vienna	AU	Austria	Schilling	4000	17.5	£228.57
Heidelberg	GE	Germany	Mark	3600	2.5	£1,440.00
Los Angeles	US	USA	US Dollar	1750	1.42	£1,232.39
Vancouver	CA	Canada	Can. Dollar	2750	1.9	£1,447.37
Strasbourg	FR	France	Fr. Franc	5175	8.46	£611.70
Florence	IT	Italy	Lire	1600000	2425	£659.79
Marseilles	FR	France	Fr. Franc	6275	8.46	£741.73
Milan	IT	Italy	Lire	1850000	2425	£762.89
Frieberg	GE	Germany	Mark	1245	2.5	£498.00

Table 21.13. *Imported (linked object) Excel spreadsheet*

(the spreadsheet or database), it can be edited by double clicking on the object. Depending on the package you are using, the editing may be *embedded* (see Figure 21.50) within the word processor, or the application may be opened in a separate window.

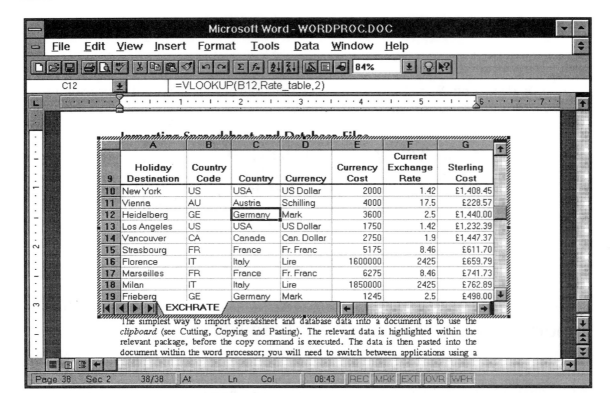

Figure 21.50. *Spreadsheet object being edited within the word processor*

If you paste the data simply as text, the spreadsheet cells are converted to a word processor table and the contents can be edited within the word processor. However, no link is established with the source package. Table 21.14 shows data pasted from the Access database package. The data within this table can be also be edited as a word processor table.

StudNo	StudName	StudAddress	Male	DOB	Fees	Paid
3126	Williamson, James Arthur	32 Wellington Square	Yes	17-Jul-48	£352.00	Yes
3128	Wilson, Kenneth	23 Smith Street	Yes	23-Jun-82	£167.20	Yes
3129	Parkinson, Helen	14 Parry Street	No	13-Apr-66	£356.40	No
3138	Atkinson, Harold	The Towers	Yes	14-May-71	£390.50	No
3152	Adamson, Peter	14 Wallsend Way	Yes	23-Jun-79	£563.57	No
3166	Laing, Marita	14 Longfellow Heights	No	15-Dec-77	£354.79	Yes
3170	Pompelmo, Roberto	23 Via Tortellini	Yes	14-Jun-74	£1,479.01	Yes
3178	Cancello, Carla	Villa Romatica, Via Stretta	No	12-Mar-65	£1,723.08	Yes
3418	Pallister, Raymond	43 Baliol Square, Happy Oaks	Yes	16-Jun-75	£356.40	Yes
3426	Erikson, Anna	14 Adams Way	No	12-Jun-72	£1,345.81	No

Table 21.14. *Imported (pasted from cliboard) Access database records*

Chapter 22
Spreadsheets

Introduction

Spreadsheet packages are designed, primarily, for the manipulation of numerical information. The term *spreadsheet* is not new and has long been used to describe the computerised system's manual equivalent, commonly used by accountants to prepare, for example, budgets and financial forecasts. A manual spreadsheet is a large sheet of paper with a grid of intersecting rows and columns; a computerised spreadsheet adopts the same layout. Apart from financial applications, spreadsheets are used for statistical analysis and data modelling. Spreadsheet packages provide a graphics facility for the construction of graphs and charts (see Spreadsheet Graphics).

Worksheet Features

When you load your spreadsheet program, the screen displays a *worksheet*; a number of functional features can be identified. The features labelled in Figure 22.1 are described below.

Cells. These are formed in a *grid*, each one being identified by a *column letter* (sometimes, columns may be numbered) and a *row number*. A worksheet provides hundreds of columns and thousands of rows, typically 256 and 16,384 (2^7) respectively, so more than the 26 letters of the alphabet are needed to uniquely identify each column. The problem is overcome by using two letters (AA, AB, AC ... AZ and then BA, BB, BC ... BZ and so on), from column Z onwards. The grid of cells is marked out by *gridlines* and your package may allow you to hide or display them. Each cell is a separate data entry point. The types of entry you can make are described later in the section titled Entering Data.

Active cell. The spreadsheet's cursor is the cell highlight (in Figure 22.1, it is D6 and contains the text 'sample entry'), which, like the insertion point in a word processor, indicates where the next entry will be made. So, if you want to make an entry into a particular cell, you first have to move the highlight to it. This can be done, either with the arrow keys or by clicking on the relevant cell with the mouse.

Active cell reference. This provides visual confirmation of the current location of the cell highlight. It is a more reliable method of identification than scanning the column and the row to identify the relevant letter and number.

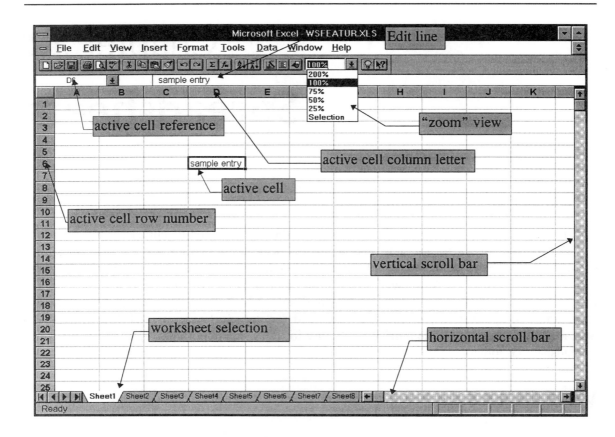

Figure 22.1. *Main features of a worksheet*

Edit line. The contents of the active cell are displayed here. Through an appropriate operation (such as clicking the mouse on the edit line) the contents can be altered and then confirmed.

'Zoom' view. The grid of cells which you can see is only a small part of the complete worksheet. The vertical and horizontal *scroll bars* or arrow keys allow you to view other parts of the worksheet as necessary. As with other types of package, you can 'zoom' to see more rows and columns, in a condensed form, or magnify the image at the cost of seeing a smaller section of the worksheet. Figure 22.1 shows that the current selection of 100% can be magnified to 200% or condensed to 75%, 50% or 25%. If variations, such as 15% or 70% are required, then you can simply type in the value. It is important to mention that, although you may not be able to see all the cells and their contents at one time, the computer is holding them all in its main memory or RAM.

Worksheet selection. You may be able to store (under one filename), several worksheets and be able to switch attention between them without further reference to backing storage.

Entering Data

When a new worksheet is displayed, you will find that cell highlight is in the top left cell and that the active cell reference (*A1* or *R1C1* for Row1 Column1) is displayed in a corner of the screen; this changes to reflect the current position of the cell highlight. Having decided on the cell you want to use, you need to make it the active cell, before you enter any data. While you are entering data into a cell, the characters will be displayed on the edit line and may also appear in the cell itself. Until you confirm the entry with the ENTER key (the cell highlight remains over the cell), a navigational arrow key (the entry is confirmed and the highlight is moved to the next cell) or the mouse, you can use the BACKSPACE rubout key and make corrections or even cancel the entry altogether. This may be important if you accidentally start to enter data into an occupied cell (if you complete and confirm it you will destroy the previous contents).

Types of Data

Figure 22.2 identifies three main types of cell entry.

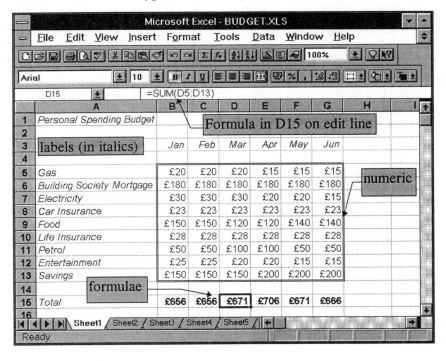

Figure 22.2. *Types of cell entry*

- a *label* or *text* entry consisting of alphanumeric characters. This sort of entry is used for headings which identify numeric contents of another cell or group of cells. The italicised entries in Figure 22.2 are all textual. Text entries cannot be used in any numerical calculation;

- a *numeric value*, used in calculations and sometimes, for other special types of entry, such as dates.

- a *formula*, which normally makes reference to and performs calculations on other cells. A formula can comprise a single cell reference (this point is explained later, in the Cash Flow example) or refer to several, interspersed by arithmetic operators. Thus, for example, to multiply the contents of cell B6 by those of B7 and B8 and place the result in B9, you would enter the formula =B6*B7*B8 into cell B9 (the active cell). Figure 22.2 shows a formula, on the edit line, which makes use of a *function*. The formula in the active cell, D15 (shown on the edit line) uses the SUM function to add together the contents of cells D5 to D13, inclusive. The same function is used to total the adjacent columns, B, C, E, F and G.

Determining the Type of Entry

Spreadsheet packages use various methods to determine the type of entry you are making. Some establish the type of entry as soon as the first key is pressed. Thus, if you press a numeric key (typically any digit from 0 to 9, or an arithmetic symbol, such as + or -) the package assumes that you are entering a *number*. If the first key is a non-numeric character, the entry is assumed to be *text*. If you are entering a formula, you usually have to signal the fact by the prior entry of a special character, such as the = sign. Otherwise, the entry of a formula C6+F5 would be taken as text (the first character is a letter 'C').

Numbers as Text

Suppose that you want to enter a telephone number, for example, '0181 376 3562'. Although the entry contains digits, it also contains spaces and you do not want to subject it to any calculations. Alternatively, you may be entering an address, such as '14 Sloan Street', which begins with a number but also includes spaces and letters. In both cases, you want to treat the entries as text. A spreadsheet package may use one of the following methods to deal with the problem.

(i) Some packages assume, that if the first character is numeric, then you are entering a numeric value and the inclusion of spaces, or other non-numeric characters, results in an error message and non-acceptance of the entry. In these circumstances, wherever a text entry begins with a numeric character you need to indicate that the entry is text before you begin it. This may be signalled with a ' mark or a space.

(ii) Most modern packages will not be so restrictive and the inclusion of any spaces or other non-numeric characters ensures that the entry is accepted as text. If the entry consists of spaces followed by an otherwise numeric entry, the package may strip out the leading spaces. This avoids the error, commonly made by novice users, of attempting to centre or right align the entry, by inserting leading spaces.

Entering Dates

If you enter a date in the form dd/mm/yy, for example, 23/6/75, then you need to be sure how the spreadsheet will treat it. There are two main possibilities:

(i) the package assumes that you intend to carry out a division calculation, that is 23 divided by 6, divided by 75 and gives you an appropriate answer;

(ii) the package requires a prefix, such as =, to indicate that a formula or calculation is being entered and, in the absence of this prefix, accepts the data as a date. If you intended it as a calculation, you would have to give it the appropriate prefix: =23/6/75.

Date entries are explained in more detail, under Formatting.

Formulae

When you enter a formula, it may well begin with a *function*, such as SUM (see Using Functions) or a cell reference. For example, you may want to multiply cell A3 by cell A5. The first character is a letter and unless you signal that you are entering a formula, it will be accepted as text and appear in the cell as A3*A5. The indication that you are entering a formula is often an = sign (otherwise it's a +), in which case you would enter =A3*A5. You would then see the result of the calculation in the cell. Usually, entry of a function also requires a prefix, such as = or @. An example of a formula using the =SUM function is given in Figure 22.2. Typically, a spreadsheet provides numerous functions for arithmetic, statistical and financial calculations. These are detailed in the section, Using Functions.

Editing

You can alter a cell entry before you have confirmed it and the cursor is still on the edit line. If you wish to alter an existing entry you can make the appropriate cell active and

- select the appropriate edit option (after which the process is the same as for an unconfirmed entry), or

- simply type the new entry (this will erase the existing cell contents), or

- *blank* the cell (not with the space bar, but using the appropriate package function) and then type the new entry.

If you have made a number of incorrect entries in adjacent cells within a column or row, you can *highlight* the relevant cells (see Highlighting a Range of Cells) and use the appropriate package function to delete the entries. The section on Formatting describes circumstances when you need to do more to fully clear an entry, perhaps to remove various cell attributes or formats (such as shading)

Using Formulae

The main power of the spreadsheet lies in its ability to use formulae which cause values contained in individual cells to be made dependent on values held in other cells. Any changes in cells referred to in a formula are reflected in the cell containing the formula. For example, if you look at the worksheet in Figure 22.2, you should see that any changes in the contents of cells within the range *D5* to *D13* would result in a change to the value displayed in cell *D15*, which contains the formula =*SUM(D5:D13)*. This formula automatically totals the contents of cells *D5* to *D13* and displays the result in cell *D15* where the formula is located. Similar formulae are contained in the adjacent cells, A15, B15, C15, E15, F15 and G15.

Whenever changes are made to *numeric* values (which may themselves be generated by formulae) in the worksheet, any dependent formulae reflect these changes in the values they display. This automatic calculation is usually referred to as the spreadsheet's '*what if*' facility. It is possible to set up complex combinations of inter-dependent factors and see 'what' happens to the final results 'if' one or more of the factors is changed. More complex examples are provided later, to illustrate the power of the spreadsheet for the solution of *predictive modelling* problems (see Data Modelling).

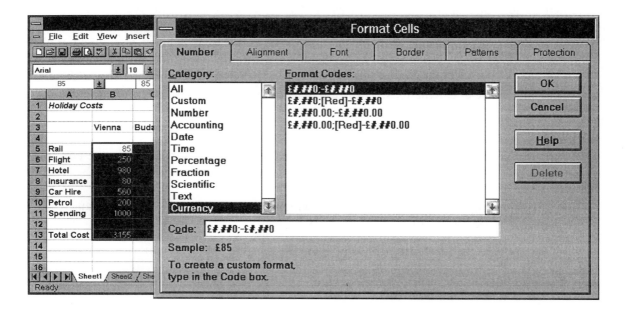

Figure 22.3. *Highlighted cells and format dialogue*

Typical Spreadsheet Facilities

Highlighting a Range of Cells

If you wish to process a number of cells at once, you can highlight them, so that they can be treated as a single unit. However, the cells must be adjacent and the range must be a rectangle. This is illustrated in Figure 22.3. In terms of cell references, a range is identified by the extreme top left and bottom right cells which border it. Typically, you will highlight cells for special treatment, such as deleting the contents, moving them elsewhere, altering the font, or perhaps adding shading or borders. Figure 22.3 shows a highlighted range of cells, containing costs of various expenditure items, for a holiday; a dialogue box shows selection of a currency format, which will prefix all the amounts with the £ sign. The dialogue shows how the first cell in the range will look (£85), as a sample.

Pointing

A formula often includes reference to another cell and, frequently, to a range of cells. For example, you may enter the formula =SQRT(B12) into cell A4. This has the effect of displaying in cell A4 the square root of the value held in cell B12. Similarly, you may wish to display the result of adding a range of cells by entering a formula, such as =SUM(F5:F14). Typically, you may be able to enter a formula by:

- typing the complete formula, including any cell references;

- *pointing*. This facility allows you to point (using the arrow keys or the mouse) at the cells as you want them to appear in your formula. When the highlight is moved to the relevant cell, its reference appears on the edit line as if you had keyed it in. If you need to refer to a range of cells, as with the formula =SUM(F5:F14), you can use the mouse to click on the first cell in the range and then drag down to the last cell in the range. Figure 22.4 shows this process, as a SUM formula is entered to add cells ranging from B5 to B11. The first part of the formula is keyed in as =SUM and then the appropriate range of cells is selected by pointing and dragging (Figure 22.4 shows a broken line surrounding the range of cells and the mouse pointer (a white cross, in this case) indicating the last cell in the range.

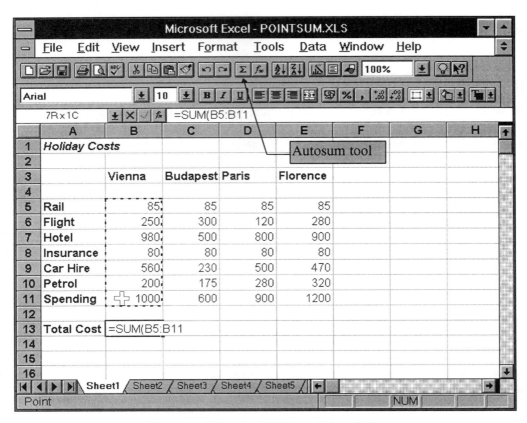

Figure 22.4. *Entering SUM formula by pointing*

Figure 22.4 also indicates the Autosum tool, which automatically enters the =SUM function and also selects the range of contiguous (no blanks or non-numeric entries in between) numeric entries above it or along side it. All you have to do is ensure the selection range is correct, before confirming the entry.

Pointing has two particular benefits. First, it reduces the likelihood that you will make a mistake in entering cell references. Second, pointing is helpful if you wish to refer to cells that are not within view; in other words, you cannot scroll the worksheet to see them and check their references, without losing sight of the cell where you are entering the formula.

Naming Cells

You can make a spreadsheet formulae more readable by *naming* a cell or range of cells. Naming may be used for another purpose, which is to make reference to a cell or cells *absolute*, before copying a formula to other cells. The circumstances when this is necessary are explained below, but in more detail in the section on Copying Data.

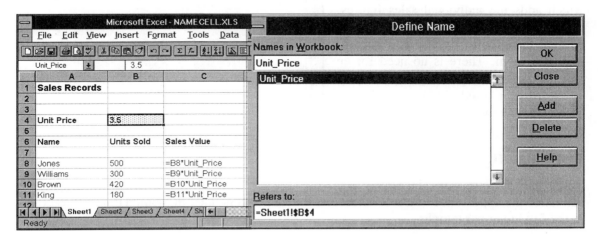

Figure 22.5. *Naming a cell*

In Figure 22.5, cell B4 (the shaded cell) contains the unit price of a product sold by the four salespersons. The formula =B8*Unit_Price, in cell C8 (the result of the calculation would normally be displayed) calculates the value of sales made by Jones. Instead of referring to the unit price by its cell reference, it has been *named*, in this case, as 'Unit_Price'. Figure 22.5 also shows the dialogue used to define this cell's name. As it happens, the package has picked up the label in cell A4 and suggested its use as the cell name for B4. If you wanted to name it differently, you would simply type in another name. The name is then used in the formula, making its meaning more obvious. The formula can then be copied to the other cells in the 'Sales Value' column. The cell reference B8 is automatically changed to B9, B10, B11, as the formula is copied to rows 9, 10 and 11, respectively. This is known as *relative* copying. Because cell B4 has been named as Unit_Price, it remains absolute in each copy of the original formula (it does not change). It is important to note that you must use the appropriate package facility to name the cell. You cannot use a name in a formula without telling the package that you wish the name to refer to a particular cell (or range of cells).

Figure 22.6 shows the use of a *named range* of cells. The cells (C8, C9, C10 and C11), outlined with a broken line and showing their displayed values, have been named as 'Total_Sales' and this name has been used in the SUM formula which adds the individual sales figures, to produce a total sales value. Before naming the group of cells, you need to highlight them. There is no need for an absolute reference to this group of cells, so the name is used simply to make the SUM formula more meaningful.

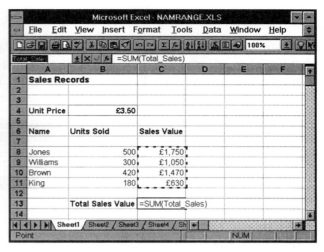

Figure 22.6. *A named range of cells*

Formatting

There are various ways in which you can tailor the appearance of a worksheet and the values contained in them. They are described in the following paragraphs.

Currency and Percentage Formats

You can format the way that a number is displayed, although its internal representation does not alter. So, for example, money amounts can be displayed with a £ sign prefix, in other words, in *currency* format. Similarly, if the amounts included pence, they could be displayed with two decimal places. Altering the displayed precision (the number of decimal places) of a number does not affect its internal precision.

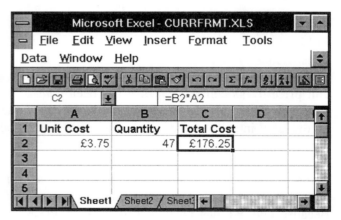

Figure 22.7. *Currency format*

Consider the cell entries in Figure 22.7. Cell C2 contains a formula =B2*A2 (shown on the edit line) and the stored result, accurate to 2 decimal places, is as shown. If, however, you formatted cell C2 as integer, you would only see £176, which would appear to be wrong. The internal value would be correct, but you could not see it.

The VAT amount, shown in Figure 22.8, is formatted as currency, with two decimal places and is thus displayed as £30.84. Its internal value, accurate to 5 decimal places, is 30.84375, but that degree of accuracy is not necessary here. Displayed as an integer, however, it would appear as £31 (rounded to the nearest £); this would be unacceptable if the £31 Figure 22.is used to draw up a customer invoice.

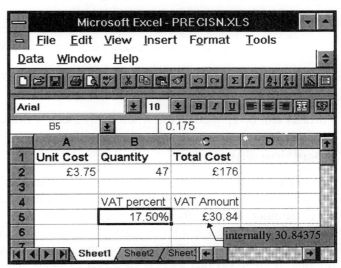

Figure 22.8. *Precision of values*

When you create a formula which uses values stored elsewhere on the worksheet, you should use the appropriate cell references and not their displayed contents (this will also mean that if the contents of cells referred to in a formula alter, the formula can reflect those changes). The displayed precision required depends on the application. When quoting the attendance figures at a football match, the nearest thousand or five hundred would suffice, but displaying product prices (ranging from, say, £1.00 to £95.00), rounded to the nearest £10, is certain to be unsatisfactory. Figure 22.8 also shows cell B5 displaying a value of 17.50%, but the edit line shows a decimal fraction of 0.175. This is because the value is stored as a decimal fraction but formatted as a percentage; the formatting process multiplies the contents by 100 to produce a percentage figure.

Date and Scientific Formats

- *date*. Typical example display formats are:

day-month-year	month-day-year	day-month-year	month-day-year	month-year
23-Jun-1993	Jun-23-1993	23-06-93	06-23-93	Jun-1993

  Each date has an internal value which equates with the number of days since 1st January 1900 (value 1). This allows dates to be compared, sorted, or used in formulae and calculations.

- *scientific*. Numbers output from computers are frequently presented in scientific or *standard index form*, but using the letter 'E' to separate the decimal part of the number (usually called the *mantissa*) from the *index* (usually called the *exponent*). The following are examples of numbers represented in this form.

$-4.365982E+07$ which means $-4.365982 \times 10^7 = -43659820$

$7.025E\text{-}3$ which means $7.025 \times 10^{-3} = 0.007025$

The format is useful for the display of either very large integers or fractional numbers to great precision.

Formats can be applied to the whole worksheet, a single cell, or a range of cells.

Resetting Formats

The earlier section on Editing explains the various methods of erasing or altering the contents of cells. If formats have also been applied, you may have to reset them to the default format, or to another format, through a separate operation. For example, if you assign currency format to a cell, any numeric value which you place in there will use the currency display. Deleting the contents will not remove the format. Figure 22.9 shows a menu command with options to clear various aspects of a cell or cells, namely: contents; formats; notes (see Cell Notes); all three. Tapping the delete key normally only clears the contents.

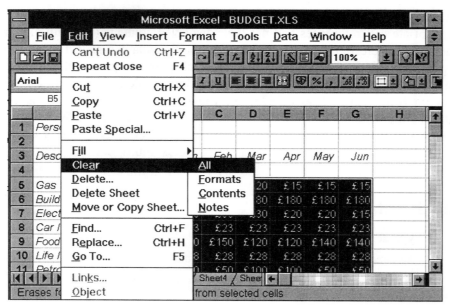

Figure 22.9. *Clearing cell contents, formats and notes*

The menu option 'Clear/Formats', in Figure 22.9, would also include shades and borders around cells. Many packages allow the format to be changed by the form of any new entry. Thus, for example, keying 20% into a cell automatically applies a percentage format, but stores it as a decimal fraction; this means that the internal value is 0.02 and for display purposes, this figure is multiplied by 100.

Column Widths and Alignment

A column has a default width, but you can change it if the displayed entry requires more space. Remember, however, that even if the full entry is not displayed, it is stored in RAM in its complete internal format. Figure 22.10 is a worksheet extract which illustrates some of the different circumstances when you need to change the width of individual columns and align (left or right) or centre labels.

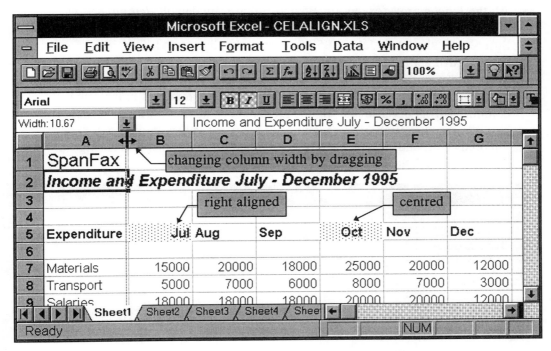

Figure 22.10. *Alignment and changing column width*

Note from the Figure 22.10 that:

- The title 'Income and Expenditure July - December 1995' spans several columns. The entry is in stored in cell A2, but is displayed as spilling over into other cells. If you want to edit the entry, you would have to make A2 the active cell by moving the highlight to it. Figure 22.10 shows A2 as the active cell and so the text appears on the edit line. Because there are *no entries in the cells to the right* you do not need to change the column width to the length of the label entry. If there were an entry in cell B2, it would obscure the overspill from A2 (in which case, you would increase the width of A2 accordingly, or use a text wrap facility).

- The heading 'Expenditure' in A5 has more characters than any of the entries beneath it, so it dictates the width of the column. It is necessary to change the column width, because unlike the entry in A2, the cells to the right are occupied and the entry in B5 would obscure any A5 characters in excess of the column width. Figure 22.10 shows the column width being altered by dragging, although it can also be altered through a menu and dialogue, for entry of a precise measurement.

- The month headings are shorter than the numbers beneath, and it is the longest entry in a column which dictates its width. Therefore, you would need to use a column width to suit the maximum value to be stored in the column.

- All the *label* entries (except for B5 and E5) are, by default, *left aligned* in their cells, but *numeric* values are *right aligned*. So that you can see the differences, the label 'Jul' in B5 has been right aligned and 'Oct' in E5, centred, using a formatting command. Either of these alterations improves the alignment with the numbers beneath. As a general rule, it is advisable to change the alignment of labels to suit the position of numbers in the same column. This is because altering the alignment of numbers with a fractional part can result in vertical 'zigzagging' of the place values (units, tens, hundreds etc.) and, if they have fractional parts, the decimal points. Figure 22.11 illustrates the problem.

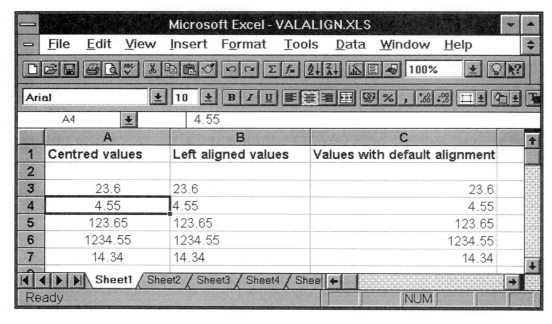

Figure 22.11. *Misalignment of place values by left alignment and centring*

Using Functions

Functions provide you with in-built facilities, which allow you to execute a range of processes. A function requires one or more *arguments*, normally bracketed after the function name. For example, the =SUM function requires a cell range to be specified. Thus, to add the contents of cells F23 to F36, requires the function =SUM(F23:F36). The function =AVERAGE (A3:K3) calculates the average of the values stored in cells A3 to K3.

Other functions require different arguments. The function =PMT requires three arguments, *principal*, *interest* and *term* and calculates the periodic payment required to pay off a loan, given a particular periodic interest rate and number of payment periods. For example, the function =PMT(30000, 15%, 25) relates to a loan (the principal) of £30000, with interest charged at 15% per annum, repayable over a 25 year term.

Typically, a spreadsheet package will provide *statistical, mathematical, financial, lookup* and *logical* functions. The function names used here are not necessarily the same as you may find in the package you use, but you should be able to identify related functions from the examples which follow.

Statistical Functions

- =AVERAGE(*range*) which averages the values in a range of cells.

- =MAX(*range*) which finds the largest value in a range of cells.

- =MIN(*range*) which finds the smallest value in a range of cells.

- =STDEV(*range*) calculates the population standard deviation of the values in a range of cells.

- =SUM(*range*) sums the values in a range of cells.

Mathematical Functions

The arguments symbolised by x, y and n may be cell references or fixed values.

- =SQRT(x) calculates the square root of x.

- =SIN(x) calculates the sine of angle x.

- =TAN(x) calculates the tangent of angle x.

- =ROUND(x,n) rounds the number x to n places.

- =MOD(x,y) calculates the remainder (*modulus*) of x divided by y.

Financial Functions

- =NPV(*interest, range*) gives the net present value of a series of future cash flows, discounted at a fixed interest rate.

- =FV(*payments, interest, term*) computes the future value of money invested in equal periodic payments, at a given interest rate, over a given term.

Lookup and Reference

- =HLOOKUP(*lookup_value, array, row_index)* Looks up a search value in a table (array) and returns an associated value from another row in the array. The function is described in detail later, with examples.

- =VLOOKUP(*lookup_value, array, column_index)*. This is the same as HLOOKUP, except that the array is organised in columns (vertically as opposed to horizontally).

- =CHOOSE(*index_no, value1, value2,...)*, uses an index number to choose a value from a list of values.

Logical

- =IF(*logical_test, value_if_true, value_if_false*). Alternative values are returnable depending on whether the result of a logical test is true or false. Examples of logical tests are: B3>25; Salary<15000 ('Salary' would be a *named* cell - see Naming Cells). The function is described in detail later.

- =AND(*logical_test1, logical_test2,...*). Returns logical *true*, if all logical tests are true. It can be used in combination with IF. The function is used as part of examples illustrating the IF function, later.

- =OR(*logical_test1, logical_test2,...*). Returns logical *true*, if any of the logical tests are true. Forms part of the group of logical functions, commonly used in combination with the IF function, which include, AND, OR, NOT.

Copying Data

You can copy numbers or labels to other cells. The contents are copied without change. You can also copy a formula, *relatively*, to another cell or range of cells. This is necessary if you want the same calculation to be carried out in a different row or column, by referencing a different group of cells. Thus, for example, the formula in Figure 22.12, =SUM(B4:B7), which totals a group of values for the month of January can be copied to succeeding columns to the right for February as =SUM(C4:C7), for March as =SUM(D4:D7), for April as =SUM(E4:E7) and so on. The formula is logically the same but the column references change according to the position of the formula. If you wish part of a formula to remain unchanged, you must make the relevant cell reference *absolute*. Typically, the software prefixes the row and column reference with a $ sign when you make it absolute. Thus, for example, the formula =(B3+C3)*A6 would add the contents of B3 and C3 (because the brackets give the expression precedence) and then multiply the resulting sum by the contents of A6. The $ prefixes will ensure that when the formula is copied, the reference to A6 remains constant. Thus when copied to, for example, rows 4 and 5 the formula becomes =(B4+C4)*A6 and =(B5+C5)*A6 respectively. If you *name* a cell or range of cells (see Naming Cells) the reference is normally made absolute automatically, but you may have to make it so by a separate operation. Figure 22.5, earlier, provides an example which uses an absolute cell reference (by naming) to refer to a price, which is multiplied by a series of sales figures. Absolute cell referencing is also used in later examples, to fix reference to a table (an array of cells) used with the HLOOKUP and VLOOKUP functions (see Using Functions). The copying process may require a series of operations which identify what is being copied (which may be a single cell or range of cells), and the cell or range of cells to which the copy is directed; this is similar to the *copy* and *paste* operation in a word processor. The process may be simplified and allow you simply to drag a 'handle' on the cell (or highlighted group of cells) being copied, over the group of adjacent cells, where you wish the copy to be directed. An example of the process is illustrated in Figure 22.12.

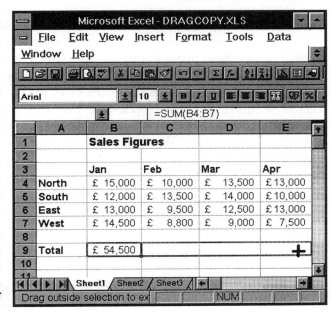

Figure 22.12. *Copying by dragging*

Moving Data

The process of moving the contents of a cell or cells elsewhere in the worksheet is similar to that for copying, except that the original location is left empty. You need to be careful that any move operation does not destroy the contents of cells that you wish to keep. The operation is similar to the *cut* and *paste* operation described in Word Processing, although you may also be able to drag cell contents to a new position. As with the copy command, cell references used in a formula are altered to take account of their new position, unless they have been made absolute. If by moving or copying a formula, you destroy the contents of a cell referenced in the formula, an error message is displayed.

Find and Replace

More sophisticated spreadsheets provide a *cell find* option, similar in operation to the *text find* facility in a word processor. A particular cell or set of cells can be found by quoting, either specific data contents (*wild cards* can be used if you are unsure of the precise contents) or specific types of data (for example, all formula cells). The range of search can be the whole worksheet or a highlighted group of cells. A *find and replace* facility may also be available, to allow the contents of particular cells to be replaced with new data.

Protecting Cells

If you are developing a worksheet to be used by someone else, then it may be useful to protect the contents of certain cells from being overwritten or erased. For example, you may develop a cashflow forecast model, into which the user has only to enter the anticipated amounts of monthly payments and receipts. Clearly, the cells used for the storage of these figures must remain accessible, but the cells which contain text headings and your formulae need to be protected. Many spreadsheet packages allow you to specify ranges of cells (or the whole worksheet) as *protected* or 'read only'. It must be emphasised that if the user of your cashflow model knows the commands to unprotect cells, then, unless you can assign a password to this operation, there is little that you can do if he or she chooses to change the settings and alter the contents of the related cells. To allow recovery of your work in such an event, you should be maintaining backup copies. Proper staff training and adherence to standard procedures should prevent corruption of data accidentally or through tampering.

Inserting and Deleting Rows, Columns and Cells

You may find that, having constructed part or all of a worksheet, you need to insert one or more rows or columns. Rows are moved down to make room for inserted rows. Columns are moved to the right to make way for inserted columns. When you delete rows or columns, the space is closed up. Before removing rows or columns, you should make sure that the process will not destroy the contents of cells currently out of view. If you simply wish to remove the entries in a row or

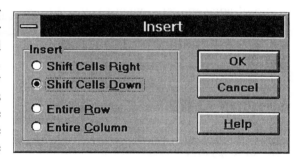

Figure 22.13. *Insert cell dialogue*

column, you should use the clear contents facility, rather than removing the entire row or column. Individual cells can be inserted or deleted, adjacent cells being moved as necessary. Figure 22.13 shows a 'cell insert' dialogue to specify where adjacent cells are to be moved.

Freezing Titles

You may wish to keep one area of the worksheet in view whilst scrolling to another part. For example, you may have titles which you want to keep in view while you enter associated values along the same rows. You can freeze the column(s) or row(s) containing these headings so that they remain in view, while adjacent rows or columns are scrolled. Figure 22.14 illustrates a column of frozen titles (Column A); you can see that columns B, C, D and E are missing and that column F is now adjacent to A. This is because, as the worksheet is scrolled right, successive columns appear to pass underneath the frozen column. When the sheet is scrolled left, they will reappear, one at a time. You can do the same with any row or column.

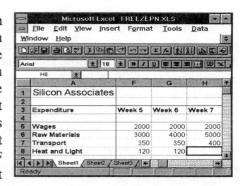

Figure 22.14. *Freezing titles*

Documenting a Worksheet

Even if a spreadsheet application is only to be used by the person who developed it, the worksheet should be fully documented. Documentation is particularly important if others are to use it or if it needs to be modified at some future date. The volume of documentation should depend on the complexity of the model; a few brief notes is probably sufficient for a simple personal cash budget model. As a general guide, the documentation should include the following elements:

- full print-out of the worksheet, including sample data;

- print-out of worksheet, showing formulae displayed, or a list of cell references with associated cell formulae;

- user notes on the operation of the model, including data entry requirements and expected forms of output;

- where explanation is needed, annotation of cells containing formulae;

Cell Notes

Sophisticated spreadsheet packages allow you to attach a comment to a cell (explaining the contents) as a text *note*. Facilities may also be provided to display text notes in a box with an arrow pointing to the relevant cell. If your package doesn't do this, you can write the comments on after printing the worksheet. The most important point is that you should annotate the worksheet where explanation is needed.

A Cashflow Model

Although you should find that some applications, such as a simple spending budget, are relatively simple to develop, the main problem for the spreadsheet user lies in the development of more useful and often more complex models. Learning the basic skills of worksheet construction will not, in itself, help you to see its applications. Model building to allow 'what if' projections on, for example, a *cash flow forecast*, requires an understanding of the concepts behind the application, not simply an understanding of spreadsheet package operation. Figure 22.15 shows a model, which can assist a business in predicting its *cash flow* over a number of months.

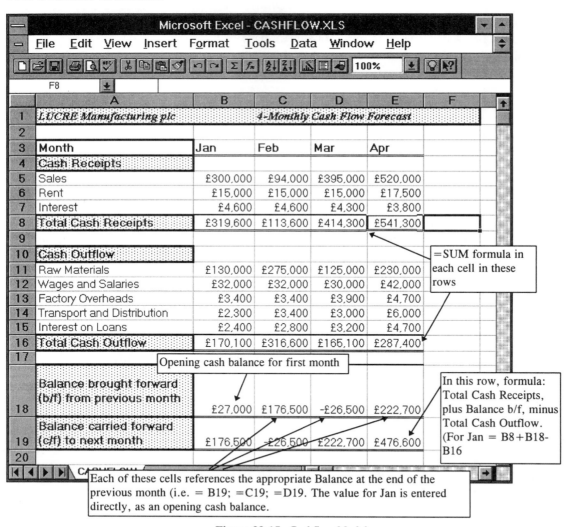

Figure 22.15. *Cashflow Model*

By cash flow, we mean the cash surplus or deficit the business has at the end of each sub-period (in this case each month). Once developed, the only entries which need to be made are those concerning anticipated income and expenditure under a variety of itemised headings. The formulae built into the model automatically calculate new cash balances at the end of each month. The balance at the end of any particular month is carried forward to be taken into account in the calculation of the next month's balance. This means that changes in anticipated income or expenditure, at any point before the end of the cycle, are reflected in the figures which follow. In other words, the model will allow 'what if' predictions to be made on what happens to the cash flow, when certain income or spending alternatives are placed into it.

Explanation of Model Entries

It is assumed that the model is being used at the beginning of January and that apart from the opening cash balance (which is known), all other figures are estimated. The accuracy of such figures depends on the stability of the company's business and their future sales orders. The model can be used to cover any period, for which future income and expenditure figures can be estimated. The various model entries are detailed in Table 1.

Cell	Explanation
B5 to E5	sales income
B6 to E6	rent income
B7 to E7	interest on investments
B8 to E8	total cash receipts
B11 to E11	raw materials costs
B12 to E12	wages and salaries costs
B13 to E13	factory overheads
B14 to E14	transport (sales distribution) costs
B15 to E15	interest payable on a loans
B16 to E16	total cash outflows
C18 to E18	previous month's closing cash balance brought forward
B18	opening cash balance
B19 to E19	balance carried forward to next month

Table 22.1. *Cashflow model entries*

Figure 22.16 shows the worksheet with all the formulae displayed. The only formula that may need explanation appears first in cell C18. Note that it consists of a single cell reference, B19. This ensures that the 'balance c/f' figure is displayed in the next month's 'balance b/f' cell. Like all formulae in the worksheet example, this formula has been copied to the other relevant cells. Note from Figure 22.16, the spreadsheet's ability to copy formulae *relatively* (the same formula, but changing any cell references used to take account of a formula's new position).

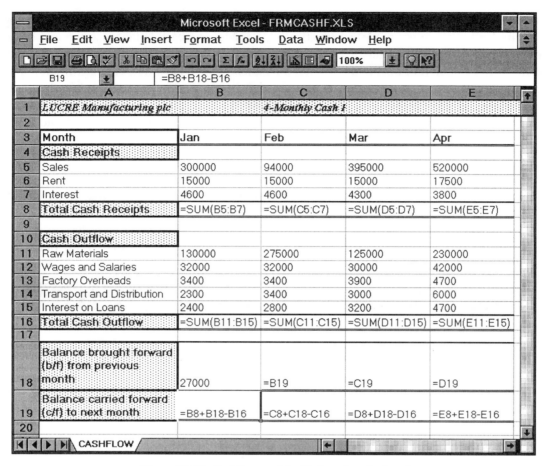

Figure 22.16. *Cashflow model with formulae displayed*

Worksheet Layout

The finished layout of the cashflow model is shown in Figure 22.15. Although, you will sometimes need to make use of the spreadsheet's facilities, to insert and delete rows and columns, or to move the contents of cells elsewhere, you will save a great deal of time and effort if you plan the layout before you start. For a simple model, you probably don't need to write it down. For more complex models, you need to work out fairly precisely where everything should go. Most importantly, you need to decide what formulae you are going to use. Remember, if you need to use the same value (that is with the same purpose, such as a product price) more than once, only enter it once in the worksheet. If you need to use it elsewhere, reference it by formula. If the value needs to be changed, you only need to make one cell alteration and any formula which uses that cell then uses the new value.

The Logical IF Function

Your spreadsheet package provides a set of *logical* functions, which allow you to test the contents of cells against defined *logical tests*. The result of the test is either *true* or *false*. The idea can be illustrated without reference to a spreadsheet. Suppose, for example, that you are asked if you are over 25 years of age; your answer will be 'yes' or 'no'. If you answer 'yes', this equates to 'true'; you are over 25. A 'no' will confirm that you are 25 or less. The same question can be put to anyone, the answer being true (yes) or false (no), in each case. If you receive a 'no' answer, there is no need then to ask if a person is 25 or less, because the negative answer to the original question provides the information you want. Similarly, if you wish to know if someone subscribes to a superannuation scheme, you only need to ask one question, which can be phrased positively or negatively, thus: 'Do you subscribe to the superannuation scheme?' or 'Do you *not* subscribe to the superannuation scheme?'. Concerning your spreadsheet's logical functions, you should view such questions as logical tests.

The IF function has the following format. It has three arguments, separated by commas.

> =IF(*logical_test, value_if_true, value_if_false*).

A Simple Example

Now consider the simple example in Figure 22.17. Column D is used to display a status message, indicating acceptance or rejection of each applicant for 'The Over 25 Club'. Only those aged over 25 are accepted.

The IF formula in cell D5 (shown on the edit line) tests the value in cell C5 (the applicant's age), to determine if it is greater than 25. The first argument is, therefore, $C5 > 25$. The value in cell C5 is 22, which means that the logical test returns *false* and that the word 'reject' is displayed. Cells D6, D7 and D8 contain the same formula, but testing the contents of cells C6, C7, and C8, respectively. The tests on C6 and C8 are found to be *true*, so the word 'accept' is displayed in the adjacent cells. The applicant Kerr, P is 25, so the logical test

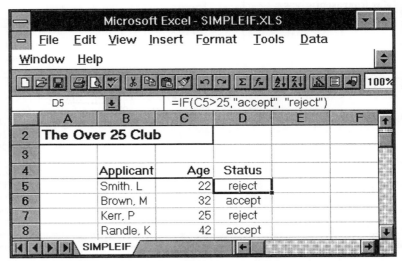

Figure 22.17. *Simple example using logical IF function*

returns *false* and 'reject' is shown in the relevant Status cell.

A Sales Target Model

Suppose that you are Sales Manager for The Target Corporation and wish to monitor the sales performance of the sales representatives for whom you are responsible. You set up the worksheet model shown in Figure 22.18 to record, in respect of each representative:

1. the monthly sales figures (columns B, C and D) and total sales for the quarter (column E);

2. the quarter's sales target (column F);

3. a bonus of 15% of the quarter's sales total, if the target has been beaten. Otherwise, the bonus is £0 (column G).

4. the amount by which the target has been exceeded (column H);

5. the target excess, as a percentage of the target (column I);

6. a new target for the next quarter (column J). If the 1st quarter's target has been exceeded by more than 20%, the new target should be set at 10% more than the 1st quarter's target. Otherwise, the new target is to remain the same as that of the 1st quarter.

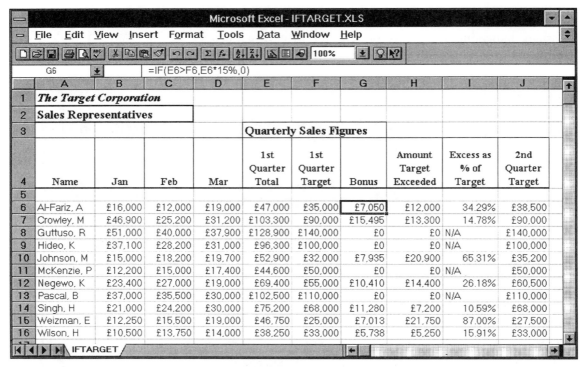

Figure 22.18. *Sales Target model*

Columns G, H, I and J are shown in Figure 22.19, with the formulae displayed.

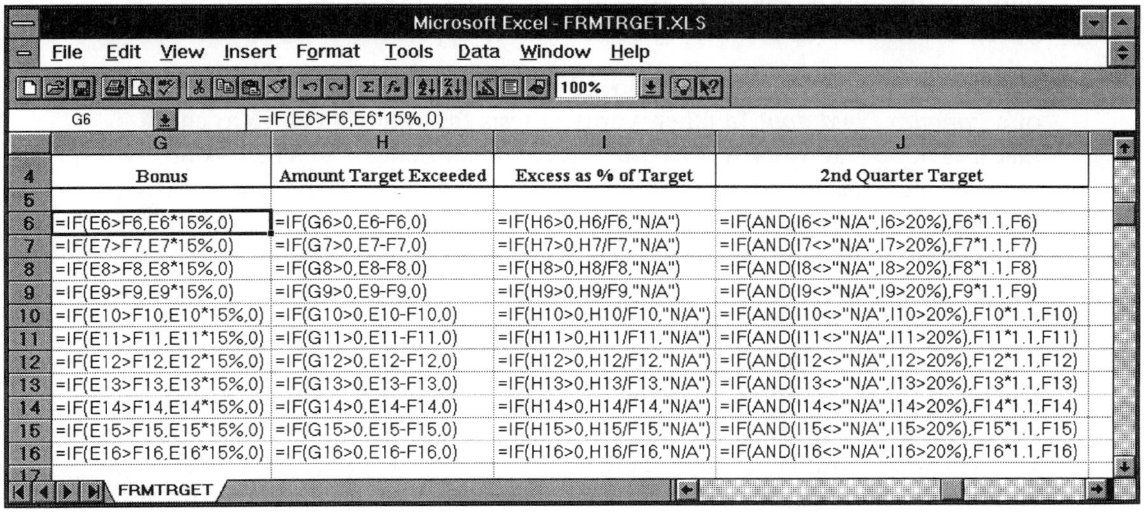

	Microsoft Excel - FRMTRGET.XLS			
	File Edit View Insert Format Tools Data Window Help			
G6		=IF(E6>F6,E6*15%,0)		

	G	H	I	J
4	Bonus	Amount Target Exceeded	Excess as % of Target	2nd Quarter Target
5				
6	=IF(E6>F6,E6*15%,0)	=IF(G6>0,E6-F6,0)	=IF(H6>0,H6/F6,"N/A")	=IF(AND(I6<>"N/A",I6>20%),F6*1.1,F6)
7	=IF(E7>F7,E7*15%,0)	=IF(G7>0,E7-F7,0)	=IF(H7>0,H7/F7,"N/A")	=IF(AND(I7<>"N/A",I7>20%),F7*1.1,F7)
8	=IF(E8>F8,E8*15%,0)	=IF(G8>0,E8-F8,0)	=IF(H8>0,H8/F8,"N/A")	=IF(AND(I8<>"N/A",I8>20%),F8*1.1,F8)
9	=IF(E9>F9,E9*15%,0)	=IF(G9>0,E9-F9,0)	=IF(H9>0,H9/F9,"N/A")	=IF(AND(I9<>"N/A",I9>20%),F9*1.1,F9)
10	=IF(E10>F10,E10*15%,0)	=IF(G10>0,E10-F10,0)	=IF(H10>0,H10/F10,"N/A")	=IF(AND(I10<>"N/A",I10>20%),F10*1.1,F10)
11	=IF(E11>F11,E11*15%,0)	=IF(G11>0,E11-F11,0)	=IF(H11>0,H11/F11,"N/A")	=IF(AND(I11<>"N/A",I11>20%),F11*1.1,F11)
12	=IF(E12>F12,E12*15%,0)	=IF(G12>0,E12-F12,0)	=IF(H12>0,H12/F12,"N/A")	=IF(AND(I12<>"N/A",I12>20%),F12*1.1,F12)
13	=IF(E13>F13,E13*15%,0)	=IF(G13>0,E13-F13,0)	=IF(H13>0,H13/F13,"N/A")	=IF(AND(I13<>"N/A",I13>20%),F13*1.1,F13)
14	=IF(E14>F14,E14*15%,0)	=IF(G14>0,E14-F14,0)	=IF(H14>0,H14/F14,"N/A")	=IF(AND(I14<>"N/A",I14>20%),F14*1.1,F14)
15	=IF(E15>F15,E15*15%,0)	=IF(G15>0,E15-F15,0)	=IF(H15>0,H15/F15,"N/A")	=IF(AND(I15<>"N/A",I15>20%),F15*1.1,F15)
16	=IF(E16>F16,E16*15%,0)	=IF(G16>0,E16-F16,0)	=IF(H16>0,H16/F16,"N/A")	=IF(AND(I16<>"N/A",I16>20%),F16*1.1,F16)
17				

FRMTRGET

Figure 22.19. *Sales target example with formulae displayed*

Using the sales representative, Al-Fariz (row 6) as the example, the formula in each column can be explained as follows. You need to refer to Figures 22.18 and 22.19 when reading the explanations.

- Cell E6. =SUM(B6..D6). This formula is not shown in the second figure, but you should be familiar with it. The SUM function adds the contents of the *range* (in this case, B6, C6 and D6) of cells identified as the function's *argument*.

- Cell G6. =IF(E6>F6,E6*15%,0). The logical test is a comparison of cells E6 and F6. If the first quarter's total (E6) is greater than the target (F6) a bonus of 15% of the first quarter's total (E6) is displayed. Otherwise a Figure 22.of zero is shown. In the case of Al-Fariz, the logical test returns *true* and a bonus of £7050 is displayed.

- Cell H6. =IF(G6>0,E6-F6,0). Testing the bonus cell (G6) for a value greater than zero, tells us whether the target has been exceeded. Alternatively, you could use the logical test (E6>F6), from the previous formula, which calculated the bonus. If the logical test returns true, the excess is calculated by subtracting the target (F6) from the first quarter's total (E6). If false, a figure of zero is shown. For Al-Fariz, the test is true and the excess of £12000 is displayed accordingly.

- Cell I6. =IF(H6>0,H6/F6,'N/A'). This formula tests the value in the target excess (H6) cell to see if it is greater than zero. If true, the excess is calculated as a fraction of the target figure. The displayed percentage value is achieved with the *formatting* facility, which multiplies the fraction by 100. If false, the N/A (meaning 'not applicable') message is displayed. Note that you must enclose this non-numeric data in quotation marks. In the case of Al-Fariz, the test is true and the figure of 34.29% appears.

- Cell J6. =IF(AND(I6< >'N/A',I6>20%),F6*1.1,F6). This is an example of a *complex condition*. In other words, it tests the value in cell I6 to check that it is not equal to 'N/A' AND that it is greater than 20%. There is no point in checking for a percentage value if the cell contains the letters 'N/A', so both conditions must be satisfied before the value for true is returned. This is the case for Al-Fariz and the target is increased by 10% (F6*1.1) from £35000 to £38500. There is another reason for testing for both conditions. It so happens that, for the computer, 'N/A' is greater than the value 20%. If you did not test for the 'N/A' value, you would find that the target is still increased for those cells containing the 'N/A' value. If either test returns false, the new target remains the same as the old (it displays the same value as F6). Crowley (row 7) has beaten the target, but not by 20%, so the new target remains the same as the old. The excess percentage cell for Guttoso (row 8) shows 'N/A', so the new target is not increased.

The LOOKUP Function

This function is used to extract a value from a table by reference to another value. It is likely that you already use *lookup tables*, but not necessarily in the context of a spreadsheet package. For example, when you want the price of an item in a catalogue, you scan the product list for the relevant item and thereby find the price. Thus the product name or code is the *lookup value* and the associated price is the *extracted value*. Similarly, banks often display a table of currency exchange rates. By scanning the list of countries, you can find the appropriate exchange rate, from one of the adjacent columns. Usually, there are four rate columns, to separately identify the rates at which the bank buys and sells notes and travellers' cheques. Once you have found the right country, you have to scan across to the appropriate column to extract the rate you want.

Country	Currency	We buy notes at	We sell notes at	We buy cheques at	We sell cheques at
Austria	Schilling	18.0	17.50	17.95	18.22
Belgium	Bel. Franc	52.1	51.40	51.95	51.55
Canada	Can. Dollar	1.95	1.90	1.93	1.92
France	Fr. Franc	8.95	8.46	8.80	8.57
Germany	Mark	2.65	2.50	2.60	2.55
Italy	Lire	2500	2425	2485	2475
Spain	Peseta	208	202	206	204
Switzerland	Sw. Franc	2.20	2.10	2.15	2.12
USA	US Dollar	1.47	1.42	1.46	1.44

Table 22.2. *Exchange rates vertical table*

A spreadsheet's LOOKUP function works in a similar fashion to that described above. There are two types: VLOOKUP, for tables organised vertically, or in column form and HLOOKUP for tables which are set out horizontally or in rows. Table 22.2 illustrates the vertical format, with an exchange rate example; Table 22.3 shows the horizontal format, using rates of pay as an example.

Job Grade	A	B	C	D
Hourly Rate of Pay	£5.00	£7.50	£8.50	£12.00

Table 22.3. *Pay rates horizontal table*

To identify a particular rate of pay, you need to identify the Job Grade (the lookup value is a letter in this case) from the top row and then look at the second row for the Hourly Rate, which appears beneath the letter.

Format of the LOOKUP Function

The arguments for the two LOOKUP forms are shown below.

=VLOOKUP(*lookup value, table array, column index*)

=HLOOKUP(*lookup value, table array, row index*)

Note that they only differ in respect of the third argument; one refers to column and the other to row. The purposes of these arguments are given below.

1. *lookup value*. This will normally be a cell reference, which contains the value to be used to search the table. It may contain, for example, a product code to search a price table.

2. *table array*. This identifies the location of the table in the worksheet. The range of cells will be identified by the top left and bottom right cell references.

3. *column/row index*. This identifies the column or row in the table array, from which the value is to be taken. In the earlier exchange rate example, you would use this argument to specify which exchange rate column was to be used. The Excel spreadsheet refers to the leftmost column in a table as 1 and columns to the right are identified as 2, 3 and so on. For a horizontal table, the top row is 1 and rows beneath are similarly incremented. The Lotus 123 package refers to the leftmost column as 0 and adjacent columns are referred to as *offset* column 1, 2 and so on. An equivalent pattern is used in horizontal tables. It is important to note that column and row indexes, or offsets, refer to the table array and not to the worksheet as a whole.

Note that the values in the leftmost column (for a vertical table) or the top row (for a horizontal table) must be in *ascending* sequence. Thus, alphabetic values must be in ascending alphabetical order and numeric values in ascending numerical order. Remember that the lookup value (the first argument) is compared with these values and if they are not in ascending sequence, the formula will not work properly.

An Exchange Rate Example

Suppose that you wish to calculate holiday costs by reference to the currency table (Table 22.2). For the sake of simplicity, it is assumed that only one set of exchange rates is required. You may design the worksheet as shown in Figure 22.20.

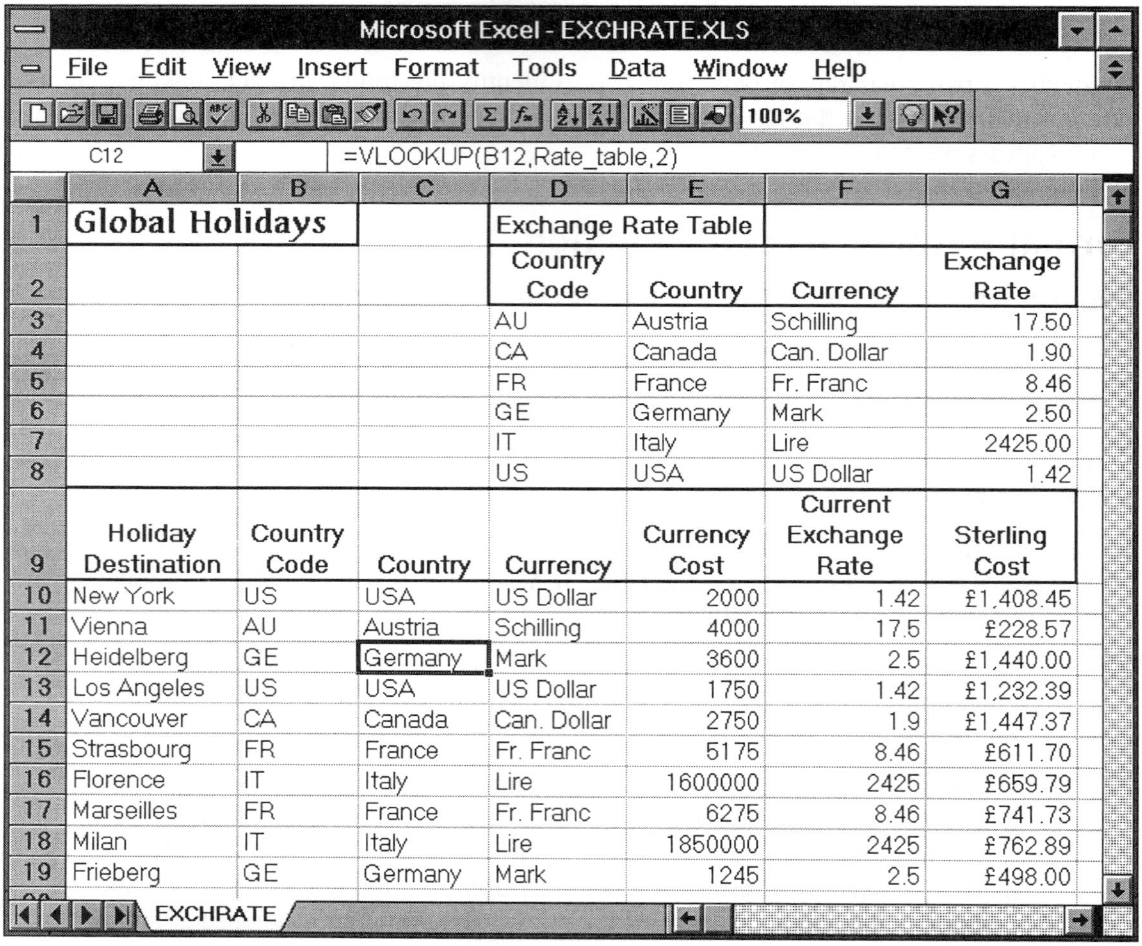

Figure 22.20. *Using VLOOKUP with an exchange rate table*

In designing the worksheet, your main aims are to minimise data entry and ensure selection of the correct exchange rate, for the calculation of individual holiday costs. To create the worksheet, you:

1. set up the Exchange Rate Table. Figure 22.20 shows that the table range extends from D3 to G8. To make your lookup formulae more meaningful, you decide to call the table 'RateTable' (see earlier section on Naming a Cell or Range of Cells). You put suitable headings at the top of each column in the table, but they do not form part of the table which is to be referenced in the lookup formulae. Placing the table above the main data entry area ensures that numerous holidays can be costed without interfering with the lookup table range. You remember to ensure that the country code values in the first column of the table are in ascending alphabetical order.

2. set up the data entry area which is to display the holiday details and costs. You place suitable headings at the top of each column;

3. enter the necessary formulae.

Figure 22.21 shows these formulae in columns C, D, F and G. Referring again to Figure 22.20, this means that, once your worksheet is set up, data entry is restricted to three items for each holiday. They are: Holiday Destination (column A); Country Code (column B); Currency Cost (column E). The information in columns C, D, F and G is generated automatically. Of course, you would need to amend the table values when exchange rates alter.

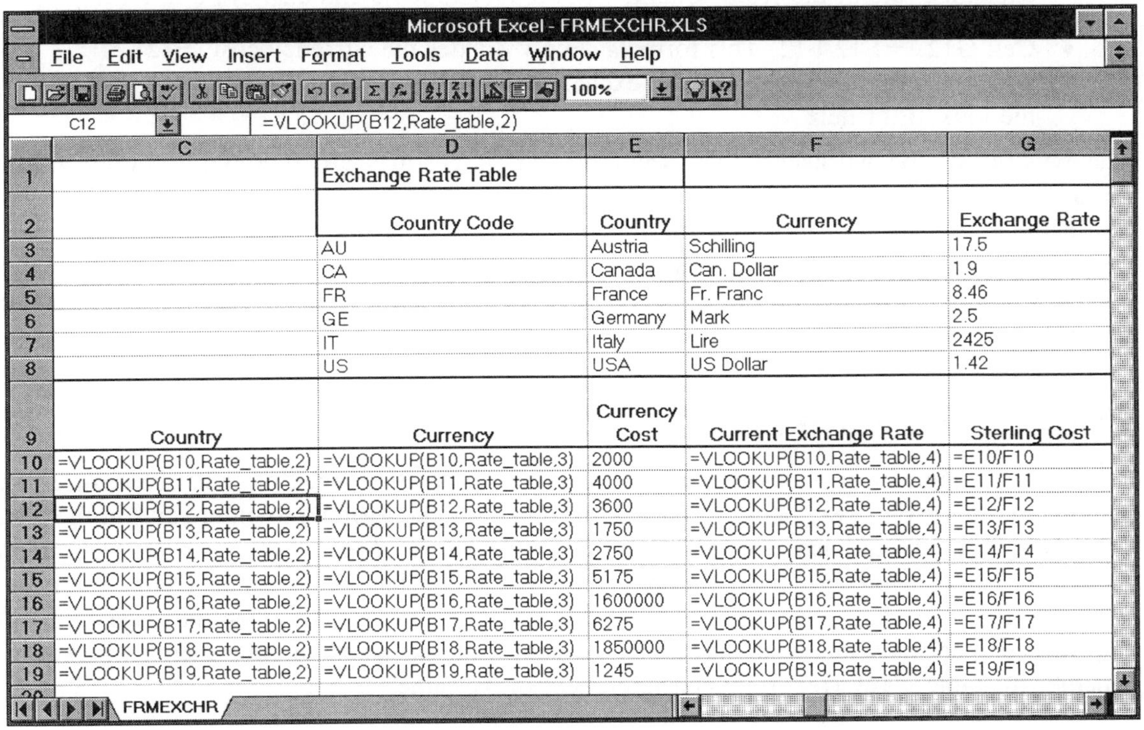

	Microsoft Excel - FRMEXCHR.XLS				
File Edit View Insert Format Tools Data Window Help					

C12   =VLOOKUP(B12,Rate_table,2)

	C	D	E	F	G
1		Exchange Rate Table			
2		Country Code	Country	Currency	Exchange Rate
3		AU	Austria	Schilling	17.5
4		CA	Canada	Can. Dollar	1.9
5		FR	France	Fr. Franc	8.46
6		GE	Germany	Mark	2.5
7		IT	Italy	Lire	2425
8		US	USA	US Dollar	1.42
9	Country	Currency	Currency Cost	Current Exchange Rate	Sterling Cost
10	=VLOOKUP(B10,Rate_table,2)	=VLOOKUP(B10,Rate_table,3)	2000	=VLOOKUP(B10,Rate_table,4)	=E10/F10
11	=VLOOKUP(B11,Rate_table,2)	=VLOOKUP(B11,Rate_table,3)	4000	=VLOOKUP(B11,Rate_table,4)	=E11/F11
12	=VLOOKUP(B12,Rate_table,2)	=VLOOKUP(B12,Rate_table,3)	3600	=VLOOKUP(B12,Rate_table,4)	=E12/F12
13	=VLOOKUP(B13,Rate_table,2)	=VLOOKUP(B13,Rate_table,3)	1750	=VLOOKUP(B13,Rate_table,4)	=E13/F13
14	=VLOOKUP(B14,Rate_table,2)	=VLOOKUP(B14,Rate_table,3)	2750	=VLOOKUP(B14,Rate_table,4)	=E14/F14
15	=VLOOKUP(B15,Rate_table,2)	=VLOOKUP(B15,Rate_table,3)	5175	=VLOOKUP(B15,Rate_table,4)	=E15/F15
16	=VLOOKUP(B16,Rate_table,2)	=VLOOKUP(B16,Rate_table,3)	1600000	=VLOOKUP(B16,Rate_table,4)	=E16/F16
17	=VLOOKUP(B17,Rate_table,2)	=VLOOKUP(B17,Rate_table,3)	6275	=VLOOKUP(B17,Rate_table,4)	=E17/F17
18	=VLOOKUP(B18,Rate_table,2)	=VLOOKUP(B18,Rate_table,3)	1850000	=VLOOKUP(B18,Rate_table,4)	=E18/F18
19	=VLOOKUP(B19,Rate_table,2)	=VLOOKUP(B19,Rate_table,3)	1245	=VLOOKUP(B19,Rate_table,4)	=E19/F19

FRMEXCHR

Figure 22.21. *Exchange rate example with formulae displayed*

Using the holiday destination, Heidelberg (row 12), as the example, the formula in each cell can be explained as follows.

- Cell C12. =VLOOKUP(B12,RateTable,2). The first argument, B12, contains the lookup value, which in this case is 'GE' (country code). The second argument identifies the location of the lookup table. You have instructed the spreadsheet that 'RateTable' refers to the array of cells bounded on the top left by D3 and the bottom right by G8. If you did not name the range, you would use the cell references (D3:G8) as the second argument. The third argument indicates that the extracted value is to be taken from column 2 of the lookup table. Thus, for the Heidelberg example, the word 'Germany' appears in cell C12 (see Figure 22.20).

- Cell D12. =VLOOKUP(B12,RateTable,3). The first argument again refers to B12, which contains the country code. The second argument remains the same in all three lookup formulae. The third argument results in the value being extracted from column 3 of the lookup table. Thus, the currency is identified as the Mark.

- Cell F12. =VLOOKUP(B12,RateTable,4). The third argument extracts the exchange rate of 2.5 from column 4 of the lookup table and displays it in F12.

- Cell G12. =E12/F12. This formula simply divides the currency cost (E12), which has been keyed in, by the exchange rate (F12), which is generated by the lookup formula.

The benefits of the worksheet may seem limited, if costings are required for only a few holiday destinations. However, without the lookup table, the entry of more numerous holiday destinations, would probably require frequent repetition of the same details, concerning country, currency and exchange rate. In addition, if the exchange rate for a particular currency changes, the lookup table ensures that the costings for all relevant holidays can be amended by a single alteration to the table.

Copying the Formulae

The second argument in a lookup formula refers to a particular range of cells. To ensure that reference to the table array does not alter when you copy the formula to other rows in the data entry area, you would need to make the cell references *absolute* (see earlier section on Copying Data). In the previous example, the table range has been named (RateTable) and with the Excel package, this makes the reference absolute. This is not the case with all spreadsheet packages and you may have to carry out the absolute referencing procedure, whether the table is referred to by cell references or by name.

A Pay Calculation Example

This example uses a table of pay rates, referenced by job grade, to calculate some simplified payroll details. Figure 22.22 shows some example output for this worksheet.

	A	B	C	D	E
1	*The Target Corporation*				
2	Rates of Pay				
3	Job Grade	A	B	C	D
4	Hourly Rate	£5.00	£7.50	£8.50	£12.00
5					
6	Employee	Hours Worked	Job Grade	Basic Rate	Gross Pay
7					
8	Al-Fariz, A	42	C	£8.50	£357.00
9	Crowley, M	38	D	£12.00	£456.00
10	Guttuso, R	30	A	£5.00	£150.00
11	Hideo, K	45	B	£7.50	£337.50
12	Johnson, M	42	B	£7.50	£315.00
13	McKenzie, P	40	D	£12.00	£480.00
14	Negewo, K	28	A	£5.00	£140.00

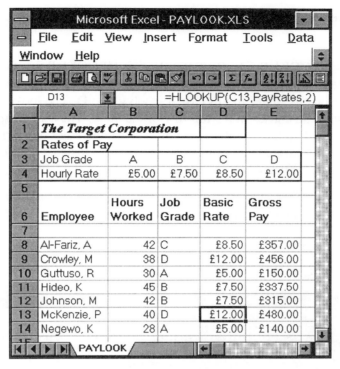

Figure 22.22. *Pay calculation using HLOOKUP*

The worksheet is repeated in Figure 22.23, with the formulae displayed.

	A	B	C	D	E
1	*The Target (*				
2	Rates of Pay				
3	Job Grade	A	B	C	D
4	Hourly Rate	5	7.5	8.5	12
5					
6	Employee	Hours Work	Job Grade	Basic Rate	Gross Pay
7					
8	Al-Fariz, A	42	C	=HLOOKUP(C8,PayRates,2)	=B8*D8
9	Crowley, M	38	D	=HLOOKUP(C9,PayRates,2)	=B9*D9
10	Guttuso, R	30	A	=HLOOKUP(C10,PayRates,2)	=B10*D10
11	Hideo, K	45	B	=HLOOKUP(C11,PayRates,2)	=B11*D11
12	Johnson, M	42	B	=HLOOKUP(C12,PayRates,2)	=B12*D12
13	McKenzie, P	40	D	=HLOOKUP(C13,PayRates,2)	=B13*D13
14	Negewo, K	28	A	=HLOOKUP(C14,PayRates,2)	=B14*D14

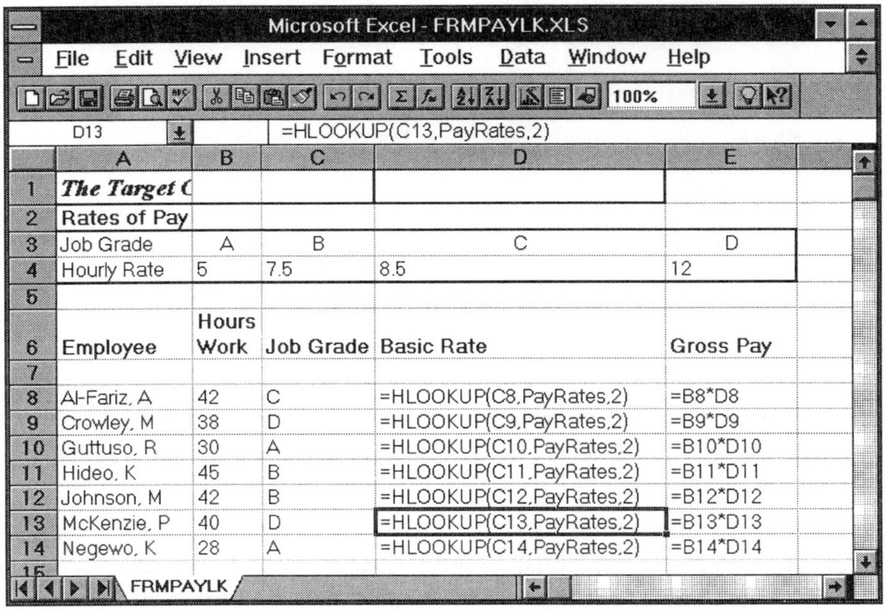

Figure 22.23. *Pay calculation example with formulae displayed*

Using the Employee McKenzie (row 13) as the example, the formulae can be explained as follows.

- Cell D13. =HLOOKUP(C13,PayRates,2). The HLOOKUP function ensures that the table is referenced horizontally, by row. The first argument, C13, contains the lookup value. In this case it is job grade D. The lookup value is compared with the entries in the top row of the table. The second argument identifies the lookup table as the range of cells named PayRates (array B3:E4). The third argument ensures that the value associated with this grade (in this case, £12.00) is taken from the second row of the table.
- Cell E13. =B13*D13. This simply multiplies the hours worked Figure 22.(in B13) by the rate of pay extracted from the lookup table, to give the gross pay for McKenzie.

Lookup Tables Using Value Ranges

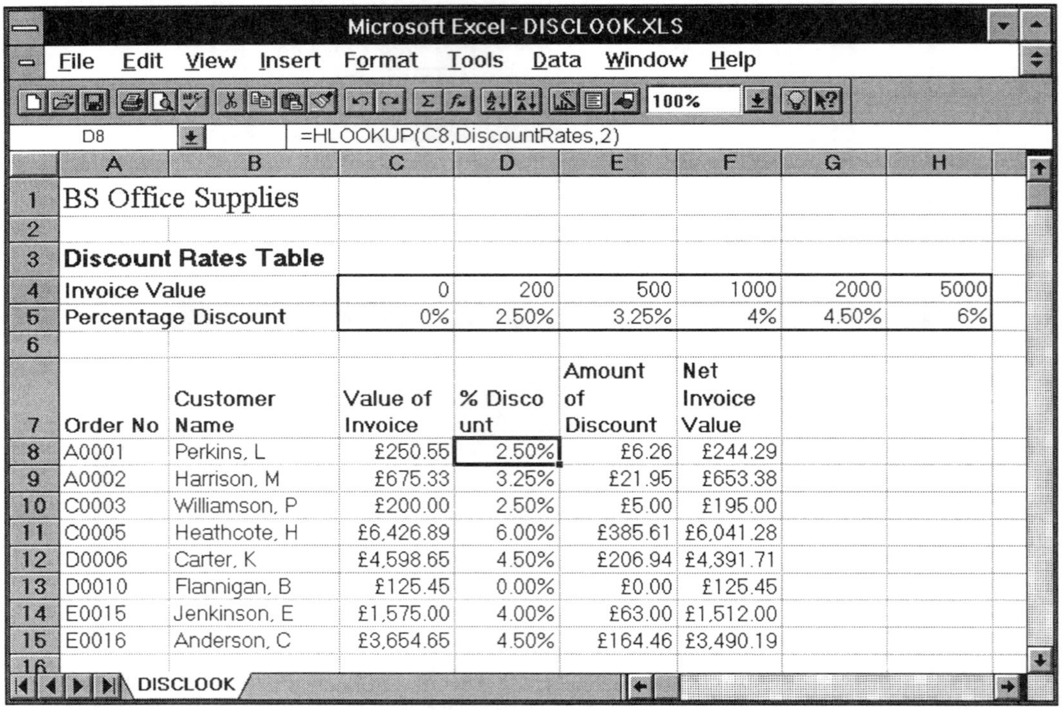

	A	B	C	D	E	F	G	H
1	BS Office Supplies							
2								
3	**Discount Rates Table**							
4	Invoice Value		0	200	500	1000	2000	5000
5	Percentage Discount		0%	2.50%	3.25%	4%	4.50%	6%
6								
7	Order No	Customer Name	Value of Invoice	% Disco unt	Amount of Discount	Net Invoice Value		
8	A0001	Perkins, L	£250.55	2.50%	£6.26	£244.29		
9	A0002	Harrison, M	£675.33	3.25%	£21.95	£653.38		
10	C0003	Williamson, P	£200.00	2.50%	£5.00	£195.00		
11	C0005	Heathcote, H	£6,426.89	6.00%	£385.61	£6,041.28		
12	D0006	Carter, K	£4,598.65	4.50%	£206.94	£4,391.71		
13	D0010	Flannigan, B	£125.45	0.00%	£0.00	£125.45		
14	E0015	Jenkinson, E	£1,575.00	4.00%	£63.00	£1,512.00		
15	E0016	Anderson, C	£3,654.65	4.50%	£164.46	£3,490.19		

Figure 22.24. *Discount rates lookup table*

The examples provided so far assume that every possible lookup value (the first argument) has a precise match in a lookup table. Thus, in the first example, all Country Codes appear, and each has a set of related values. Similarly, in the payroll example, each Job Grade letter can be found in the table. Figure 22.24 shows how you can use *value ranges* in a lookup table. Suppose that you wish to calculate discounts by reference to a table of percentage rates and according to the value of each customer invoice. You allocate discount rates on the following basis:

- invoice values up to £199.99 attract no discount;
- discount of 2.5% is given for amounts between £200 and £499.99;
- invoices for amounts between £500 and £999.99 are discounted at 3.25%;
- for amounts between £1000 and £1999.99, 4% discount is allowed;
- invoices valued at between £2000 and £4999.99 are given a discount of 4.5%;
- invoices for £5000 or more attract a discount of 6%.

These sample invoice and discount details are shown in Figure 22.24.

Figure 22.25 shows the same worksheet, with the formulae displayed.

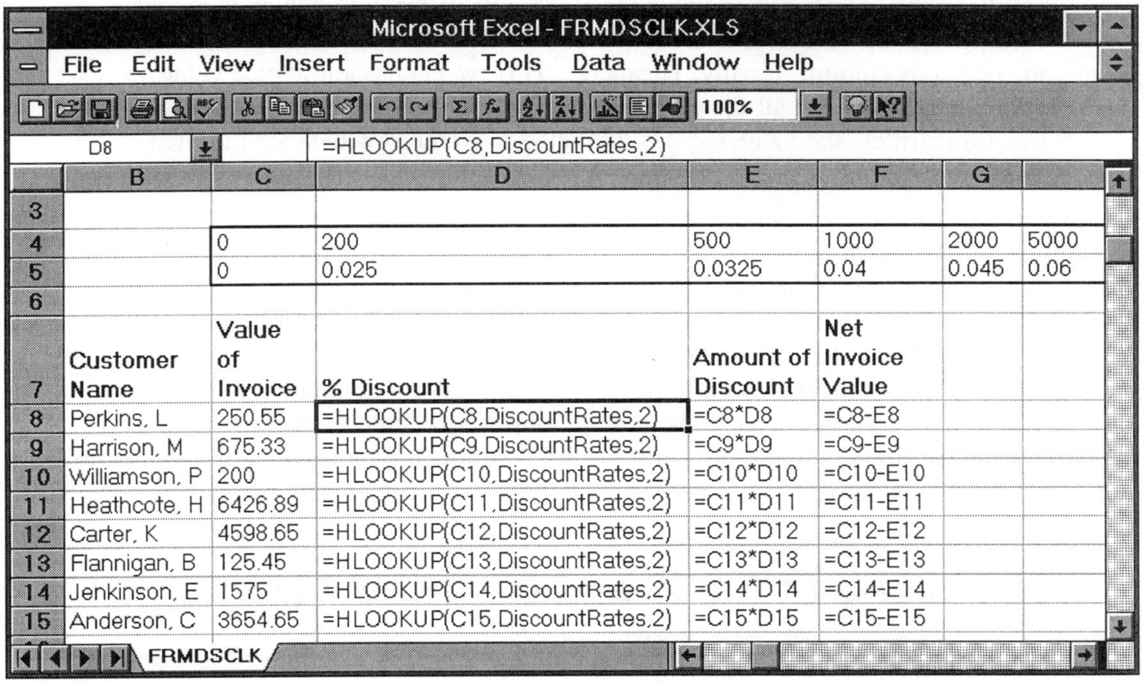

	B	C	D	E	F	G	
3							
4		0	200	500	1000	2000	5000
5		0	0.025	0.0325	0.04	0.045	0.06
6							
7	Customer Name	Value of Invoice	% Discount	Amount of Discount	Net Invoice Value		
8	Perkins, L	250.55	=HLOOKUP(C8,DiscountRates,2)	=C8*D8	=C8-E8		
9	Harrison, M	675.33	=HLOOKUP(C9,DiscountRates,2)	=C9*D9	=C9-E9		
10	Williamson, P	200	=HLOOKUP(C10,DiscountRates,2)	=C10*D10	=C10-E10		
11	Heathcote, H	6426.89	=HLOOKUP(C11,DiscountRates,2)	=C11*D11	=C11-E11		
12	Carter, K	4598.65	=HLOOKUP(C12,DiscountRates,2)	=C12*D12	=C12-E12		
13	Flannigan, B	125.45	=HLOOKUP(C13,DiscountRates,2)	=C13*D13	=C13-E13		
14	Jenkinson, E	1575	=HLOOKUP(C14,DiscountRates,2)	=C14*D14	=C14-E14		
15	Anderson, C	3654.65	=HLOOKUP(C15,DiscountRates,2)	=C15*D15	=C15-E15		

Figure 22.25. *Discount rates example, with formulae displayed*

How the LOOKUP Function Operates

The HLOOKUP function uses the same format as that described in the earlier examples, so is not further described here. However, it is useful to understand how the function operates when used with value ranges. As with all lookup tables, you must ensure that the values in the top row (or leftmost column, in a vertical table) are in ascending sequence.

Using the customer Perkins, L (row 8 in Figures 22.24 and 22.25) as the example, the operation of the lookup function can be described as follows.

- Cell D8 =HLOOKUP(C8,DiscountRates,2). The first argument (C8) contains the lookup value, which for Perkins is an invoice value of £250.55. The function compares the lookup value with each entry in the top row of the table (or leftmost column for VLOOKUP), until it finds a value which is greater than or equal to the lookup value. Thus, the first entry (0) is less than the lookup value, as is the next entry of 200. Comparison with the third entry (500) brings the scan to an end. The lookup function then 'knows', according to the rules already described, that the extract value is to be taken from the second column in the table. The third argument indicates that the value is to be extracted from the second row. This results in the display of 2.50% in D8, which contains the lookup formula. Using Carter, K (row 12) as a second example, comparing the invoice total of £4,598.65 with the table entries results in the search ending when the 5000 entry is reached, which is greater than the lookup value. The extract value of 4.50% is taken, therefore, from the previous column. Finally, Heathcote, H (row 11) has an invoice value which is greater than all the entries in the top row of the table. Using the function's rules, the value (6%) is extracted from the row beneath the final entry in the table.

It is apparent from this explanation that you must understand how the VLOOKUP and HLOOKUP functions deal with value ranges, before you can properly set up the table. It should also be clear to you that the values in the top row of a horizontal table and the leftmost column of a vertical table, must be in ascending sequence. As explained earlier, this rule applies to all lookup tables, whether they contain every value that is required or (as in the above example) value ranges. You also need to ensure that the minimum value (the first in the top row or leftmost column) in the lookup table must not be greater than the minimum lookup value. Thus, if the minimum lookup value is −50, then the minimum value in the lookup table must be −50 or less (that is a larger negative number).

Combined Use of the IF and LOOKUP Functions

In the introduction to the LOOKUP function (see earlier), the example of an exchange rate table is used. The worked example in that section only allows for one exchange rate column in the lookup table. In reality, the exchange rate for any particular currency varies according to whether you are buying or selling and whether you are dealing in notes or travel cheques. Thus, a typical exchange rate table (see Table 22.2), displayed in a bank or travel agency window, has six columns. The first two columns contain the names of the countries and currencies. The other four are used for the bank or travel agency 'buy' and 'sell' rates, for notes and travel cheques. The IF function is used to allow the LOOKUP function to select from the appropriate column. A worked example is shown in the following section.

A Further Exchange Rate Example

Figure 22.26 illustrates a worksheet which includes an exchange rate table, used as a lookup table and several example transactions which refer to it.

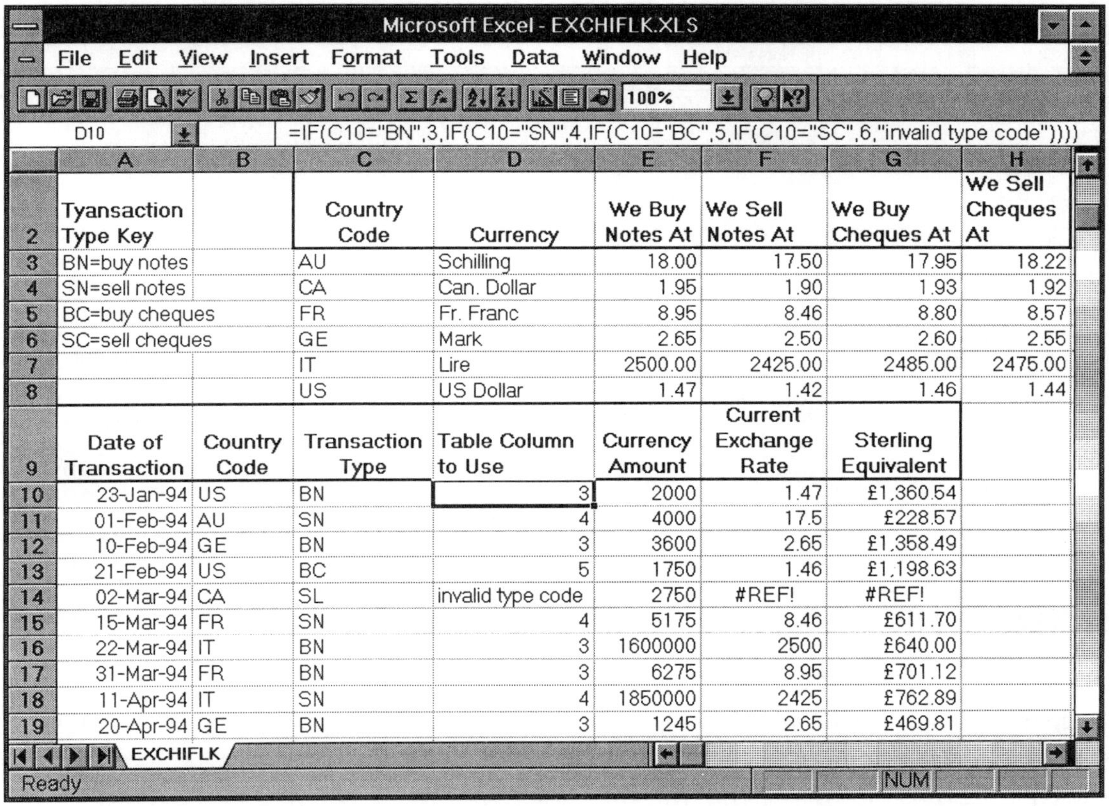
Microsoft Excel - EXCHIFLK.XLS

File Edit View Insert Format Tools Data Window Help

D10 =IF(C10="BN",3,IF(C10="SN",4,IF(C10="BC",5,IF(C10="SC",6,"invalid type code"))))

	A	B	C	D	E	F	G	H
2	Tyansaction Type Key		Country Code	Currency	We Buy Notes At	We Sell Notes At	We Buy Cheques At	We Sell Cheques At
3	BN=buy notes		AU	Schilling	18.00	17.50	17.95	18.22
4	SN=sell notes		CA	Can. Dollar	1.95	1.90	1.93	1.92
5	BC=buy cheques		FR	Fr. Franc	8.95	8.46	8.80	8.57
6	SC=sell cheques		GE	Mark	2.65	2.50	2.60	2.55
7			IT	Lire	2500.00	2425.00	2485.00	2475.00
8			US	US Dollar	1.47	1.42	1.46	1.44
9	Date of Transaction	Country Code	Transaction Type	Table Column to Use	Currency Amount	Current Exchange Rate	Sterling Equivalent	
10	23-Jan-94	US	BN	3	2000	1.47	£1,360.54	
11	01-Feb-94	AU	SN	4	4000	17.5	£228.57	
12	10-Feb-94	GE	BN	3	3600	2.65	£1,358.49	
13	21-Feb-94	US	BC	5	1750	1.46	£1,198.63	
14	02-Mar-94	CA	SL	invalid type code	2750	#REF!	#REF!	
15	15-Mar-94	FR	SN	4	5175	8.46	£611.70	
16	22-Mar-94	IT	BN	3	1600000	2500	£640.00	
17	31-Mar-94	FR	BN	3	6275	8.95	£701.12	
18	11-Apr-94	IT	SN	4	1850000	2425	£762.89	
19	20-Apr-94	GE	BN	3	1245	2.65	£469.81	

EXCHIFLK

Ready NUM

Figure 22.26. *Combined use of IF and LOOKUP*

The operation of the worksheet can be explained as follows:

1. The user enters the date of the transaction (column A), the country code (column B), the currency amount (column E) and the transaction type (column C). The transaction type consists of four codes, the meanings of which are shown in Figure 22.26.

2. Column D contains a formula to identify, from the transaction type in column C, which exchange rate column to use in the lookup table. This is done by converting the transaction type to an appropriate column number. The error messages in row 14 are explained after Figure 22.27.

3. Column F contains the lookup formula to extract the rate from the table.

4. The value of the transaction is calculated in column G, with a formula which divides the currency amount (column E) by the exchange rate (column F).

Part of the worksheet, with the IF and LOOKUP formulae displayed, is shown in Figure 22.27.

	D	E	F
2	Currency	We Buy	We Sell Notes At
3	Schilling	18	17.5
4	Can. Dollar	1.95	1.9
5	Fr. Franc	8.95	8.46
6	Mark	2.65	2.5
7	Lire	2500	2425
8	US Dollar	1.47	1.42
9	Table Column to Use	Currency	Current Exchange Rate
10	=IF(C10="BN",3,IF(C10="SN",4,IF(C10="BC",5,IF(C10="SC",6,"invalid type code"))))	2000	=VLOOKUP(B10,RateTable,D10)
11	=IF(C11="BN",3,IF(C11="SN",4,IF(C11="BC",5,IF(C11="SC",6,"invalid type code"))))	4000	=VLOOKUP(B11,RateTable,D11)
12	=IF(C12="BN",3,IF(C12="SN",4,IF(C12="BC",5,IF(C12="SC",6,"invalid type code"))))	3600	=VLOOKUP(B12,RateTable,D12)
13	=IF(C13="BN",3,IF(C13="SN",4,IF(C13="BC",5,IF(C13="SC",6,"invalid type code"))))	1750	=VLOOKUP(B13,RateTable,D13)
14	=IF(C14="BN",3,IF(C14="SN",4,IF(C14="BC",5,IF(C14="SC",6,"invalid type code"))))	2750	=VLOOKUP(B14,RateTable,D14)
15	=IF(C15="BN",3,IF(C15="SN",4,IF(C15="BC",5,IF(C15="SC",6,"invalid type code"))))	5175	=VLOOKUP(B15,RateTable,D15)
16	=IF(C16="BN",3,IF(C16="SN",4,IF(C16="BC",5,IF(C16="SC",6,"invalid type code"))))	1600000	=VLOOKUP(B16,RateTable,D16)
17	=IF(C17="BN",3,IF(C17="SN",4,IF(C17="BC",5,IF(C17="SC",6,"invalid type code"))))	6275	=VLOOKUP(B17,RateTable,D17)
18	=IF(C18="BN",3,IF(C18="SN",4,IF(C18="BC",5,IF(C18="SC",6,"invalid type code"))))	1850000	=VLOOKUP(B18,RateTable,D18)
19	=IF(C19="BN",3,IF(C19="SN",4,IF(C19="BC",5,IF(C19="SC",6,"invalid type code"))))	1245	=VLOOKUP(B19,RateTable,D19)

Figure 22.27. *Combined use of IF and LOOKUP with formulae displayed*

Using row 10 as an example, the formulae displayed in Figure 22.27 can be explained as follows.

CellD10.   =IF(C10='BN',3,IF(C10='SN',4,if(C10='BC',5,if(C10='SC',6,'invalid   type code')))). Note that, instead of the third argument (the value if logical test is false) referring to a value or another cell reference, it comprises another IF condition. Expressed in ordinary English, it is equivalent to saying, 'If the transaction type code is 'BN', store and display the value 3; if the code is 'SN', store and display 4 and so on'; otherwise display 'N/A'. You can see that there are four separate conditions, each with a different second argument (value if logical test is true). Finally, the single third argument (value if test is false) is an error message, to allow for none of the logical tests being satisfied. You can see that the first of the two previous figures, includes the message 'invalid type code' in cell D14. This results from the entry of 'SL' (which is not one of the four transaction type codes) in cell C14. You should notice the four closing brackets at the end of the formula. These accord with the four opening brackets used in the formula.

The lookup formula in column F should not need any further explanation, as it is used in earlier examples. The #REF error messages in Figure 22.27 arise because, in column F, the lookup formula has no valid first argument and in column G, the exchange rate needed in the formula is missing. These error messages can be suppressed with the use of another function, which is not dealt with in this text.

Chapter 23

Spreadsheet Graphics

Introduction

The communication of information through pictures is something with which we are all familiar. For example, a pictorial advertisement in a magazine can often convey information that, without a picture, would take a few hundred words of text. The meaning of numeric data is often made clearer and more concise, if they are represented pictorially, as *graphs* or *charts* (the terms are interchangeable, but we will use the term 'chart'). The annual financial reports of companies often include charts depicting, for example, sales performance over the year, or profits over a number of years. All modern spreadsheet packages allow you to represent numeric data in a worksheet, as a chart.

Although spreadsheet packages allow you to produce a large variety of charts, in either two or three-dimensional form, there are four basic types, which are common to most:

- bar chart;
- line chart;
- pie chart;
- xy chart.

This section concentrates on the mechanics of constructing charts with a spreadsheet program. It is assumed that you know the general application of each chart type and its significance for the representation of numerical information. It is important that you are able to select the right kind of chart (sometimes more than one may be suitable) for any particular type of numeric data. Although a package may allow you to produce, for example, a pie chart from a given set of data, it may be completely meaningless. For this reason, you should make sure that you understand the function of any particular chart, and how to construct one manually, before you attempt spreadsheet graphics. Some of the latest spreadsheet packages include many automated functions which you can use to make chart production simpler. It is common to provide a utility (Excel refers to it as a 'Chart Wizard') to take you, step by step, through the chart production process. It even displays the current state of the chart at each stage. This is particularly useful if you are required to make a selection, perhaps of the type of chart you want, and are unsure which to choose. You can simply try one, and if it is not what you want, select another. In any event, the principles of spreadsheet chart construction are described below.

Linking Data to a Chart

A set of numeric values which you want to use in a chart, is commonly known as a *data range* or *data series*. Various examples of such data series are shown in the figures which follow. Before you start the charting process, you should have decided (although you can change your mind later) on the type of chart you want. If you decide to produce a bar chart, then the data series you choose can also be used for a line graph (and vice versa). The following sections describe the component parts of each chart type listed in the introductory paragraph, and the procedures used to produce them.

Bar Charts

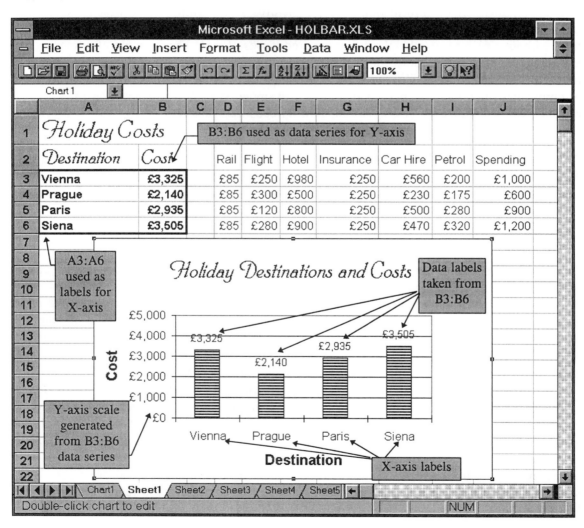

Figure 23.1. *Bar chart of holiday destinations and costs*

Figure 23.1 shows an example *bar* chart, embedded in a worksheet which calculates the costs of various holidays. The chart's *axes* are generated from the shaded cells A3:B6. The Y-axis uses the costs in cells B3, B4, B5 and B6. The maximum value on the *Y-axis scale* has been set at £5000; the default maximum would be £4000, because the largest value in the data series is £3,505 and the scale is in divisions of £1000. The *X-axis labels* are taken from the holiday destinations of Vienna, Prague, Paris and Siena, in cells A3 to A6. *Data labels* can be used to show the precise figure represented by each bar, although the main purpose of the bar chart is to compare costs, as measured against the Y-axis scale. If data labels are not used and more precise comparison is wanted, then the Y-axis scale can be divided into £500 intervals. To generate the chart in Figure 23.1, the adjacent cells containing the X-axis labels and the Y-axis data series are highlighted. From this highlighted information, the spreadsheet can generate the basic chart, showing an X-axis with labels, a Y-axis suitably scaled to cover the range of values in the data series and bars representing each value. Other detail, such as chart title, axes titles and data labels can then be added. In Figure 23.1, the Y-axis title is 'Costs' and the X-axis title is 'Destination'.

Bar Chart with Multiple Data Series

The chart in Figure 23.1 has only one data series. In other words, each bar relates to the cost of holidays. Figure 23.2 shows a worksheet and chart, which represent the sales figures (units sold) of three products, namely dishwashers, washing machines and cookers. This means that there are three sets of values, or data series, to represent. The process of chart construction is the same as that for the chart in Figure 23.1. The range of cells from D2 to G6 is highlighted and used by the program to generate the chart. One feature of the chart in Figure 23.2, which is not present in Figure 23.1, is a *data legend*. This identifies each bar with the relevant product. If there is only one data series, then a legend is not necessary. You will also note that Figure 23.2 shows a bar chart, with a vertical X-axis and a horizontal Y-axis. The basic form of chart is, however, the same as that represented in Figure 23.1.

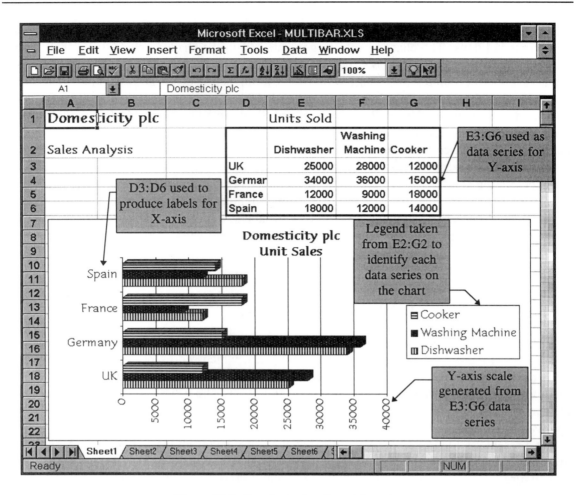

Figure 23.2. *Bar chart using three data series*

Line Chart

A *line* chart is useful for showing trends, or changes over time. Figure 23.3 illustrates the movement in sales of two models of computer, by Microfile, a computer supplier. Although a bar chart could have been used, the comparison of these two sets of sales figures (the data series) is more clearly illustrated with a line chart.

The procedures for constructing a line chart are very similar to those for the bar graph. Note that each of the two lines has a different symbol at the *data point*. This serves the same purpose as the cross-hatching and colour in the bar chart. The legend is used to label each symbol.

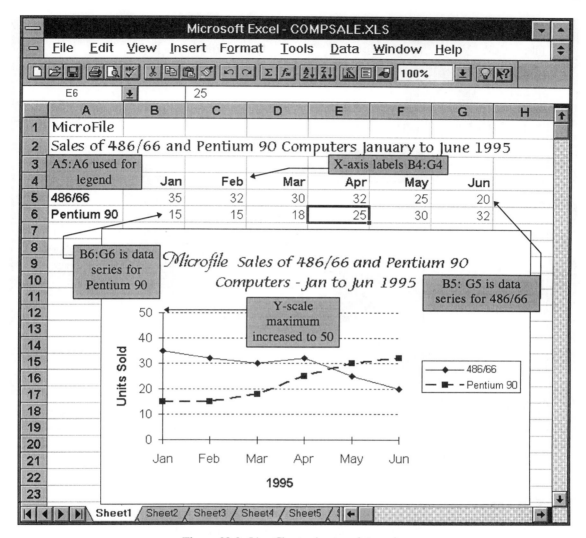

Figure 23.3. *Line Chart using two data series*

Pie Chart

Figure 23.4 shows a typical *pie* chart, together with the data series represented in the chart. A pie chart always contains just one data series and shows each value as a percentage of the total for the series. Each 'slice' or 'wedge' represents one value. Colour or cross hatching is used to differentiate one slice from another.

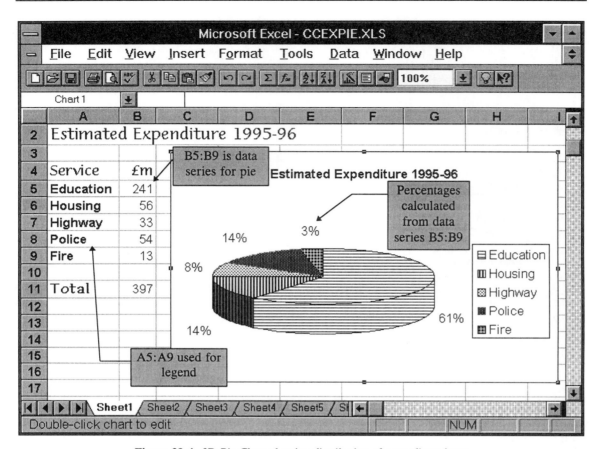

Figure 23.4. *3D Pie Chart showing distribution of expenditure items*

XY Chart

Figure 23.5 shows an XY chart, which plots various costs and revenues against different levels of output; there are four lines on the chart, representing four Y-axis data series. These Y-axis series are plotted against one X-axis data series. The chart is illustrating the *break-even point* for a computer manufacturing company; it does this by plotting *total costs* and *total revenue* on the Y-axis against different levels of *output* on the X-axis. *Variable* and *fixed costs*, which together form total costs, are also plotted on the chart. The topic of *break-even analysis* is dealt with in Data Modelling.

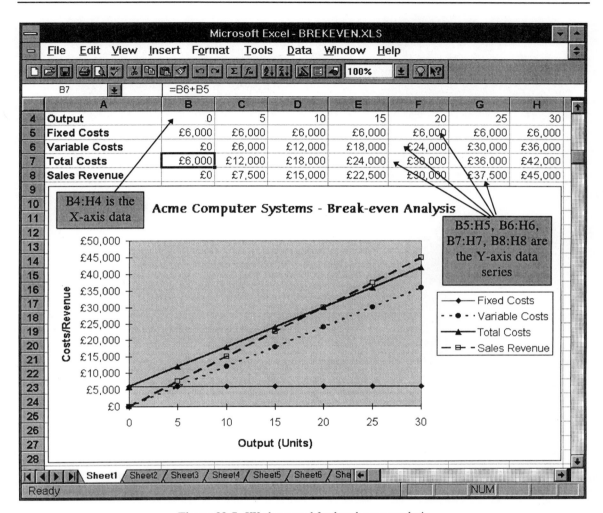

Figure 23.5. *XY chart used for break-even analysis*

Chapter 24

Graphics

Introduction

This chapter looks at three types of software, all designed for graphical work:

(i) 'paint' packages for bit mapped images;

(ii) computer-aided drawing packages for vector graphics;

(iii) slide show presentation packages, for assembling images from other sources, including (i) and (ii).

Although drawing packages are designed primarily for vector graphics, they also make use of bit maps. CorelDRAW is a good example of an illustrator's package, with sophisticated facilities for the manipulation of all types of image. Before you use a graphics package, you need to be clear about what is meant by 'bit map' and 'vector' graphics.

Bit Maps

The topic of bit mapping, in the context of screen displays, is dealt with in detail in Chapter 5. Examples of bit maps include clip art and files produced from a scanning process (Chapter 5). A bit map comprises a fixed number of *pixels* (the dots which form the image) and as such has a particular *resolution*. When you enlarge a bit map image, the pixels become more widely separated and the image becomes 'grainy', although this is only apparent when it is output to a high resolution device. Although you can manipulate the image, by re-sizing and perhaps rotating or cropping it (concealing part), alterations in the detail of the image can only be achieved at the pixel level. Figure 24.1 shows the Paintbrush screen, with a 'zoomed in' view of the car image. At this magnification the

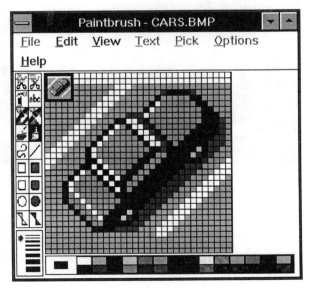

Figure 24.1

individual pixels can be edited, that is altered in colour. The normal view of the image is shown in the top left corner of the screen. Figure 24.2 shows the same image with some of the pixels altered to create a circle on the bonnet and a cross on the roof; the image to the left of the car is meant to give the impression of a cyclist.

Although the image at the pixel level is very jagged, its 'zoomed out' appearance is quite satisfactory. There are numerous types of bit map files, identified by different file extensions. Common examples include *.pcx* (Paintbrush), *.cmx*, *.tif, .wmf* (Windows metafile) and *.bmp*. Images created with the Paintbrush package, for example, are saved as *.pcx* files. CorelDRAW's Photo-paint, for example, saves images with the file extension *.cpt*. Packages vary widely in their ability to handle various bit map formats. Paintbrush is a very simple package and can only

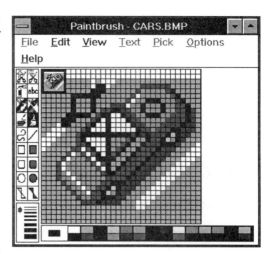

Figure 24.2

handle three or four formats, including *.bmp* and *.cmx* and its own *.pcx*. The very powerful Photo-paint package, designed primarily for the processing of photographic images, can handle all the most important formats, including Kodak Photo-CD images. To import images of different formats, a package must have the necessary graphics filters (programs which

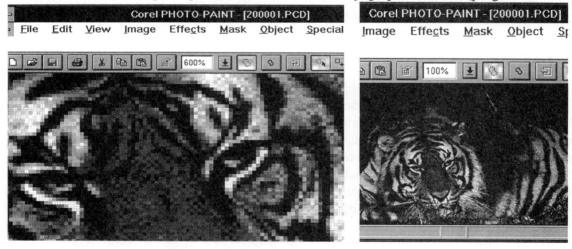

Figure 24.3   Figure 24.4

convert from one format to another. A photographic image is shown in Figure 24.4 and part of the same image, magnified 600% is displayed in Figure 24.3. You can see the individual pixels which make up the magnified image, although its high resolution still makes it fairly clear, in marked contrast to the 'building block' appearance of the magnified Paintbrush picture. Of course, the bit maps produced by Paintbrush and similar packages are perfectly adequate for the resolution provided by most screen and printers.

Vector Graphics

A vector, in mathematical terms, is a quantity which represents both magnitude and direction. Vectored images, therefore, are recorded in these terms and unlike bit maps, do not have a fixed resolution. This means that when a vector image is re-scaled, there is no loss of definition. For example, if you draw a 2cm square and fill it with a colour, there will be a particular number of pixels forming the image; the number will depend on the software used and the resolution capability of the screen. If you then re-scale the image to a 4cm square, it will be formed with proportionally more pixels, thus giving the same density and clarity to the enlarged image.

Paint Software

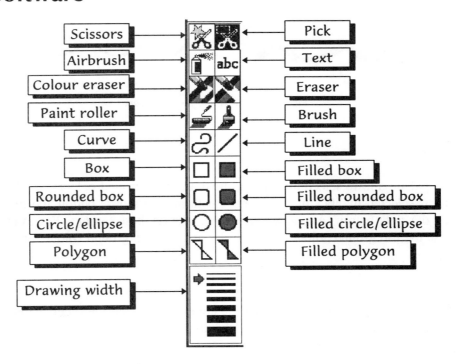

Figure 24.5. *Tool box in Paintbrush package*

A number of tools are briefly described in the following sections. You should note that, in a 'paint' package, you cannot create *objects*. Thus, for example, if you draw a rectangle, there is no pointer tool to select it as an object. You can, however, use the copy or cut tools to indicate the *area of the screen* to be cut or copied, and this can include the rectangle (or part of it). In other words, paint packages are for sketching or painting, not for geometric design.

Free Form Painting

There are usually two painting tools for this type of operation, symbolised by a *brush* and an *air brush* (or spray can). The spray produces a round spot of varying diameter, depending on the width selected and the density of the spray is achieved by repeated application or by dragging the spray more slowly. Typical effects are shown below.

Figure 24.6. *Airbrush effects*

The brush can be varied in width and is used for applying brush strokes or free drawn lines.

Figure 24.7. *Brush for freehand work*

Colour

The colour palette allows selection of foreground and background colours. In Paintbrush, the foreground is selected by clicking on a colour with the left mouse button and the background by clicking the right button. Any new images will take on these settings. For example, a filled box will use the foreground colour for its border and the background colour for the fill.

Erasers

Figure 24.5 shows two erasers, one being the colour eraser and the other the eraser. As you would expect the latter tool simply rubs out the area over which you drag the tool and like all the tools, the size of the eraser can be altered. Note that the erased area takes on the currently selected background colour. Figure 24.8 shows an image with erased sections each effected with different eraser widths.

Figure 24.8. *Eraser tool effects*

Not surprisingly, the symbol for this tool is often an eraser on the end of a pencil. The pointer takes the form of a square (it can be varied in size), which rubs out any image over which it passes. The colour eraser can be used either to replace the current foreground colour to a selected background colour or to replace every occurrence of a colour with another.

Area Fill

The tool for this operation is symbolised by a paint roller. The operation is similar to 'object fill' in a drawing package, except that the 'roller' will fill any *enclosed area* with the chosen colour. If there is not an enclosed area, the colour will fill the whole screen.

Text

Text can be typed onto the screen, using a variety of styles and fonts. Text manipulation facilities are restricted compared with those in CAD programs. The rubout tool can be used on text in the same way as images produced with other tools.

Pick and Scissors tools

Figure 24.9. *Sections cut from image with pick and scissors tools*

The pick tool is used to select a rectangular area to be cut or copied (the selection can then be pasted into another area or picture or application). The scissors allow freehand drawing of a selection, rather like using a pair of scissors.

The other tools, for drawing rectangles, ellipses and polygons are similar to those available in drawing packages, which are the subject of the next section.

Computer Aided Drawing

Line Drawings

A graphics program provides a range of tools which you can use to draw geometric figures, as well as freeform shapes. The next figure shows a simple line drawing.

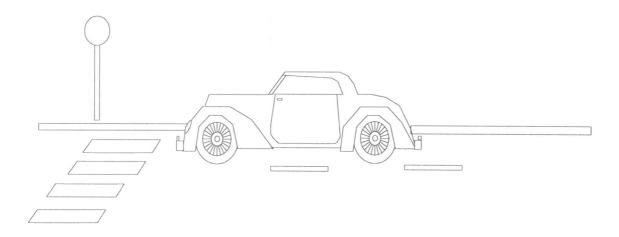

Figure 24.10. *Simple line drawing*

Freeform

Freeform drawing is the most difficult, because it requires a very steady and confident hand to produce smooth, flowing lines. If, as is likely, you are using a mouse (rather than a light pen or graphics tablet), you need to use the drag function to draw freeform lines. This means positioning the *pencil tool* pointer (typically, a cross) at your chosen starting point and then holding the appropriate mouse button down, while *dragging* the tool pointer through the required outline. To signal the end of the line, may simply require that you release, or *double click*, the mouse button.

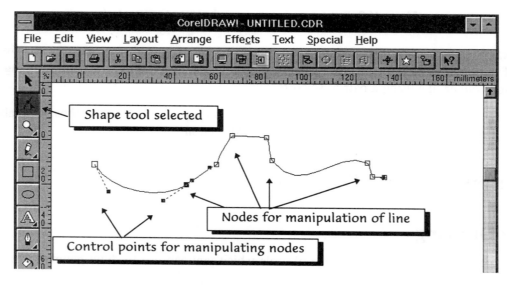

Figure 24.11. *Node manipulation on freeform line*

Some, more sophisticated packages, allow you to smooth out any curves that are a little ragged, by using control points to manipulate selected nodes on the line. Figure 24.11 shows a line being manipulated in this way.

Regular Shapes

The tools for drawing rectangles, circles, ellipses and polylines are described in Word Processing, so are not dealt with further here.

Line Styles

The *default line style* is a solid, with a thickness approximating to that drawn with a sharp pencil. You may wish to vary the thickness of a line, make it dotted, or dashed, or place an arrow head on either, or both ends (some packages do not include arrow head symbols). A small sample of line styles is shown in Figure 24.12

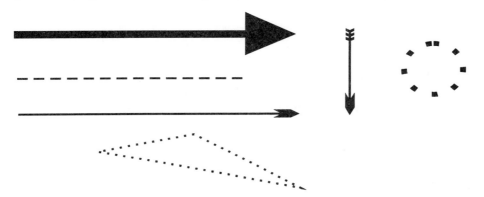

Figure 24.12. *Various line styles*

Colour and Shade

If you are not using a colour printer, then you need to make use of shading to differentiate between various aspects of an image. The symbol of a file server, on the right, makes use of such shading to produce a three-dimensional appearance. Five shades are shown in Figure 24,13, as percentages of black.

FS1 Server

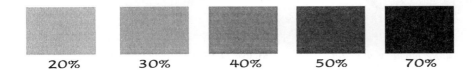

Figue 24.13. *Shades of black*

Handling Objects

An object is any graphical figure that can be handled as a unit. Thus, when you use any drawing tool, or key in some text (in one completed operation) you are creating an object. Some tools always produce an easily defined object. These include the ellipse (or circle), the rectangle (or square), the curve and single straight line tools, which all produce precise geometric forms. The freeform and polygon tools can be use to produce graphics that may be simple or complex. The completion of such a graphic as an object is determined by the point at which you indicate its completion (usually by double clicking the mouse button).

Selecting and re-sizing

Once you complete an object, *control handles* (see Graphics in Word Processing) appear around it, or you may have to *select* the object with the pointer tool. These handles can be used to alter the size and proportions (by varying its overall length or height.

Editing

The facilities for editing vary considerably. Some packages do not allow editing beyond, for example, changing the length of a line or re-sizing a geometric shape, but others allow precise manipulation of various control points on the object. Thus, for example, the edit facility may place a number of control handles on polygonal shapes, line series or freeform lines, which can be separately manipulated (See Figure 24.11, earlier).

Object Fill

Figure 24.14 shows two objects, a rectangle with no fill and, behind it an ellipse filled with 70% black. In other words, the rectangle is transparent, allowing the ellipse behind it to be seen (apart from the areas covered by the rectangle border. If the rectangle is filled, for example with white, then the result is as in Figure 24.15

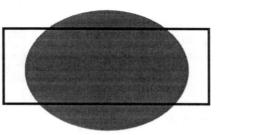

Figure 24.14. *Rectangle with no fill*   **Figure 24.15.** *Rectangle with white fill*

Magnifying

Generally known as a 'zoom' facility, it is usually represented in the toolbox by a magnifying glass symbol. You can use the tool to alter the amount of detail you have in view at any one time. If you want to see the whole page, you can reduce the magnification. To view a small part of an object in detail (for precise working), you can select the area to be magnified and then, a level of magnification. Often, these magnification levels are measured in percentages.

Grouping

As explained earlier, each separate drawing operation produces a separate object. As you build up a drawing, you may want to treat several objects as a group, for separate manipulation. For example, having completed a drawing consisting of, say, 25 objects, you may want to alter its size. By selecting all the objects and then using the *group objects* option, a rectangular control box will appear around the complete image, each time it is selected. The control handles can then be used for re-sizing or re-proportioning the image as a whole. Typically, you may select multiple objects by:

- using the pointer tool to drag a rectangle around the relevant objects;
- clicking on each object separately, whilst holding down the shift key.

If you wish to edit a grouped object, you must first *ungroup* (separate into the original discrete objects) it. This may be an iterative (repeated an unspecified number of times) process, since you might have built up a group as a series of hierarchical sub-groups.

Stacking

There will be many occasions when you want to superimpose one image onto another. In fact, you may end up with several objects stacked one on top of another. In such cases, you may need to alter the order of the objects in the pile. Figure 24.14 shows an ellipse with a rectangle on top of it. If, for example, you want to place some text inside a filled ellipse, you need to make sure that the text is on top, or it will be hidden by the ellipse. Clearly, you want to leave the text visible. Depending on which you do first, you may have to place the ellipse at the back, or the text at the front.

Packages vary widely in the amount of flexibility they provide for changing the stacked order of objects. The simplest packages provide only two options - 'bring to the front' and 'take to the back'. If you are working with several stacked objects, you need to plan their stacking order carefully, or you will forget where a particular object is in the stack. Also complex reshuffling is impossible without separating all the objects and starting the stacking procedure again. More sophisticated packages allow more flexibility, by including additional options to bring an object 'one forward' or take it 'one back', and to reverse the stacking order.

Selecting Hidden Objects

If you cannot see an object because it is hidden amongst others, you may be able to find it by working through the stack. You may also be able to select it by using the pointer tool to drag over the area that you suspect contains the object. If you are successful, the control handles will appear and you can than drag it to where it is visible.

Rotation

This facility can be used to alter the angle at which an object lies. Typically, an object (or several if they have been grouped) can be *rotated* 90 degrees to the left or to the right. The operation may be repeated if rotations of 180 or 270 degrees are required. *Flipping* an object allows you to turn it through 180 degrees about a vertical or horizontal axis. Examples of rotation and flipping are shown in the Graphics section of Word Processing. Some packages allow more precise rotations, using single degrees, or even tenths of degrees.

Duplicating

By selecting an object or group of object you can duplicate an image. This is useful if you want exactly the same image, or to modify it slightly, leaving the original intact. If for example, you want a series of squares, all the same size, duplication is the only sensible option to use.

Aligning

To align objects, you can use the *grid* (an arrangement of intersecting vertical and horizontal lines), which (if switched on) *snaps* any new or moved object to it. The density of the grid (the number of lines per inch) dictates the precision with which you can position objects. The grid is very useful if you need to arrange groups of objects in rows or columns. If the grid is switched on, any object you create, or one that you move, will snap to the nearest pair of intersecting grid lines (horizontal and vertical). With a density of, say, 8 lines per inch, you will notice a slight jerkiness of movement as you move an object around and it snaps to various points on the grid.

To position objects precisely, without the constraints of the grid, you may be able to use *guidelines* or some other alignment facility. Two guidelines are normally available, one for vertical alignment and the other for horizontal. The difference from the grid is that you can move the guideline to any desired position. An object brought near to a guideline automatically attaches to it. Objects can be attached to either side of either guideline (aligned left, right, top or bottom) or be centred on it. By using the intersection of both guidelines, you can, for example, align a group of circles (of various sizes) concentrically (all have the same centre).

Copying, Cutting and Pasting

You have probably come across these facilities in your word processor or desktop publishing package. In a graphics package, however, the facilities are used more for the transfer of images to other applications (see Using Multiple Applications). Both the *copy* and *cut* operations create a copy of the selected object(s) in a memory buffer (*clipboard*). As the terms suggest, 'copy' leaves the original intact, whilst 'cut' removes it. You may need to use the copy facility to duplicate objects, although there may be a separate 'duplicate' option.

Deleting or Clearing

This option has the same effect as the cutting operation, except that no clipboard copy is created. This may be useful if you want to preserve the existing contents of the clipboard (another cut operation would destroy its existing contents).

Setting Dimensions

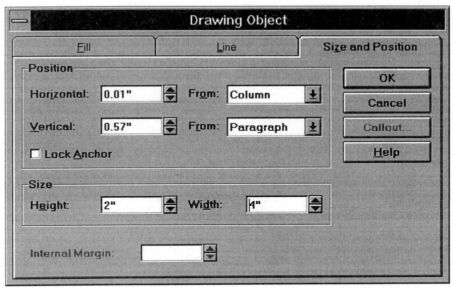

Figure 24.15. *Setting the dimensions of a drawing object*

If you are producing a technical drawing, you will probably want to draw images to scale, so you need to be able to set precise dimensions. For example, of you are using a scale of 1:50, to draw a room layout, this means that your drawing's dimensions are one fiftieth of the real layout. There are a variety of facilities you can use to set dimensions, the most common being:

(i) a grid of horizontal and vertical lines (perhaps invisible), a set distance apart, to which you can 'snap' the limits of an object;

(ii) rulers along the top and down the side of the drawing area, which you can use to size an image.

(iii) specify the dimensions of each object through a dialogue.

Figure 24.16 shows a dialogue box from Word 6.0, which shows dimension settings of 2 inches high by 4 inches wide. The units of measurement could also be in centimetres. Room layout and product design are examples of technical drawing. Figure 24.17 shows a washroom layout.

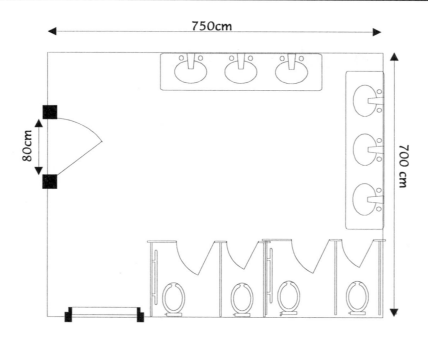

Figure 24.16. *Layout for public washroom*

Text

The text tool is usually represented by a letter 'A' and the pointer is a short, vertical line, similar to the insertion point cursor in a word processor. Like sophisticated word processors, CAD packages provide you with a wide variety of fonts, which can be varied in size and style. Entry of a text string produces an object, which like other graphics objects, can be selected for moving, copying, cutting or deleting. Although some sophisticated CAD packages allow you to use the control handles (see earlier section on Handling Objects) to vary the size of the text, most require that you select the appropriate menu option. You may also be able to rotate text objects, which is useful if you want to label a drawing.

Slide Show

Slide show packages, such as Microsoft Powerpoint and CorelSHOW enable the assembly of multi-page presentations, formed from images and text. Slides may be stand-alone and used, for example as overhead projector display, or there may be several which follow one another on screen, in a slide show presentation. Facilities also include various screen 'wipes', 'zooms' and 'dissolves' (commonly available with camcorders). Images can be produced or taken from a library within the package, or they may be produced in another application and then imported. Figures 24.18, 19 and 20 show some of the features of a sample slide show.

Figure 24.17. *CorelSHOW screen with opening slide*

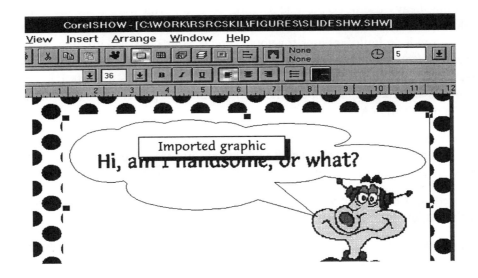

Figure 24.18. *Second slide*

Figure 24.19. *Final slide*

The main facilities you need are:

- *Backgrounds*. You can select a background from a library provided with the package, or create your own. Most of the backgrounds in the library are only suitable for screen presentation, because, that is the way they are meant to be used. If you do want to print them, you should probably design one of your own, using only limited shading; heavy use of colour and shading does not print well in monochrome. A colour printer, on the other hand, should produce satisfactory results. The package may provide in-built facilities for you to create your own backgrounds, or you may have to create them in another graphics package and then import them. CorelSHOW uses OLE (Object Linking and Embedding), to allow access to CorelDRAW such graphics work and then embeds the image within the presentation automatically when you quit CorelDRAW.

- *Graphics objects from other packages*. This includes clip art (see Word Processing), and other graphics images created with other software. The appropriate import filters must be available to convert one form of image to another.

- *Text entered within the package*. The usual text formatting facilities are available, including the facility to add bullets to listed items.

- *Sound and animation*. The package may allow the inclusion of sound objects and animation sequences created with a package, such as CorelMOVE.

- *Slide sorter*. This facility allows you to insert or delete slides and change their sequence.

- *Run screen show*. This starts the display, one after another, of the slides you have included in your show. You can set a standard time for the display of each slide or use a *timeline* to set individual timings for each slide.

- *Transition effects*. These are commonly available with camcorders and provide various screen 'wipe' or 'dissolve' modes to smooth the transition between slides.

Chapter 25

Database Construction and Operation

Introduction

A *database* can be broadly defined as "a collection of data, related to some subject or topic area and of use in a variety of applications". Although a database can be used for various applications, they should have some common interests concerning the data they use. For example, sales, purchasing, stock control and production control applications are likely to have some common data requirements relating to raw materials and finished products. Thus, a database containing information on raw materials and products can be structured and organised to allow each of these applications to use it. Database theory, design methods and tools are examined in the section on Relational Database Management Systems within the Knowledge Resource. This section guides you through the practicalities of constructing and operating a *database*, with the use of a *relational database package*, such as Access, dBase or Paradox. These software packages are examples of relational database management systems (RDBMS) and in this text, we will use the abbreviation 'RDBMS'. When we use the word 'database', we mean the structures used to store the data and the data itself. The Overview section takes you through the main facilities provided by an RDBMS, using a simple database example. Then there are three database case studies to provide varied illustrations of RDBMS usage. They are: *EuroTent*, holding information on European campsites; *Personnel*, which stores staff details for Pilcon Electronics; *Stock Control*, which records details of products and suppliers. In the Knowledge Resource, another case study, *Academic*, is used to illustrate the design process of a relational database.

Overview of RDBMS Operation

Database Components

When you use an RDBMS, you need to be familiar with the purpose and functioning of a number of components, which are described in the following paragraphs. A simple Products database is used to illustrate the descriptions.

Tables

An RDBMS is designed to handle data structured in two-dimensional *table* (the term 'relation' is also used) form. A single database may contain one or more tables. The *EuroTent* database has only one table, which holds all the information on the European campsites it has in its brochure. The *Personnel* database separates the data into three separate tables, each being concerned with a different aspect of staff information. Thus, there is a table holding staff names, department codes, job codes and salaries; the other two tables contain further information on jobs and departments. *Stock Control* is a database comprising two tables, one for product and the other for supplier details. The *Academic* database (see Knowledge Resource) places information on enrolments, students, courses and tutors into four separate tables. The idea of dividing information into separate tables is fundamental to the operation of an RDBMS and is explained fully, in the Knowledge Resource. Although the information may be in more than one table, it is related and can be brought together as and when you require, by linking or joining the tables. It is anticipated that you will work through the EuroTent example first, as this will allow you to develop your skill in the practical operation of the RDBMS package, without concern for relational database theory. To fully understand the Personnel and Stock Control examples you should have studied the relevant section in the Knowledge Resource. You will use tables in two ways:

(i) to *define the structure* of the data which is to be held within it; you need to do this before you can enter any data into the database;

(ii) to *enter* and subsequently *view* and *edit* the data within a table.

Figure 25.1 shows data held in a Product table.

Microsoft Access - [Table: Product]

File   Edit   View   Format   Records   Window   Help

PartCode	Description	Price	Quantity	SupplierCode
A123	Table (Cottage)	£23.50	15	STA436
A124	Chair (Cottage)	£42.23	36	KIT518
A125	Stool (Cottage)	£28.15	6	KIT518
B126	Step Ladder (small)	£19.50	6	PAR116
B145	Step Ladder (medium)	£31.25	4	PAR116
B181	Hammer (medium claw)	£6.75	12	STA436

Record: 6   of 6

Figure 25.1. *A Product table showing some sample records*

Each column in Figure 25.1 corresponds to a particular type of data and is referred to as a *field*. A name which identifies a particular field is know as a *field name*. There are five fields in the Product table, called PartCode, Description, Price, Quantity and SupplierCode, respectively. Each row in the table is a *record* occurrence. The PartCode field is used to uniquely identify an individual product and is know as the *primary key* field. For example,

PartCode 'A125' allows unique identification of the 'Stool(Cottage)' record and the information contained within it. The Product table will contain a record for each product.

Figure 25.2 displays the definition of the Product table shown in Figure 25.1.

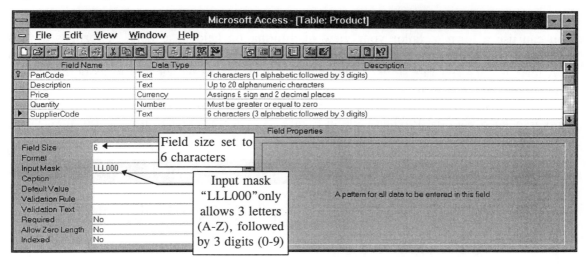

Figure 25.2. *Definition of Product table*

A number of table features can be identified from Figure 25.2. There are three columns in the upper part of the window. From left to right, the columns are used for:

- *field names*. You enter a field name for each item of data you are going to store concerning the table topic. In Figure 25.2, the table defines a product *record* which comprises five fields: PartCode; Description; Price; Quantity and SupplierCode;

- *data types*. You can define the kind of data which is to be stored in a field. For example, in Figure 25.2, you can see that the Description field allows the entry of *text*; this means any characters, alphabetic or numeric. Obviously, the Quantity field is defined as *number*, because it will contain numeric quantities only. The definition of the Price field as *currency* ensures that a £ sign and 2 decimal places are automatically assigned to each price entered. Thus, for example, if you enter the value 3.5, it will be altered to £3.50. Other data types include date and logical, but these will be described in more detail later.

- *field descriptions*. These are not used by the RDBMS and are simply there to allow you to document some aspect of the field.

Field Properties

The lower half of the window is for the specification of *field properties*. Figure 25.2 displays the additional properties set for the SupplierCode field:

- *field size* has been restricted to 6 characters;

- an *input mask* ensures that each supplier code is entered as 3 letters followed by 3 digits. You should also note that *validation* parameters can also be set. For example, the Quantity field prevents entry of values less than zero.

Forms

You can use a form to tailor your view of information held in a table. A form is always associated with a particular table and allows you to enter, edit and view the data held within it. A form is not a separate store of data, but simply an alternative view of its associated table. A major benefit of a form is that it allows you to view or edit one record at a time; a table displays as many records as can be accommodated within its window. Figure 25.3 shows a form associated with the Product table in Figure 25.1. It was created using a 'Form Wizard', in the Access RDBMS.

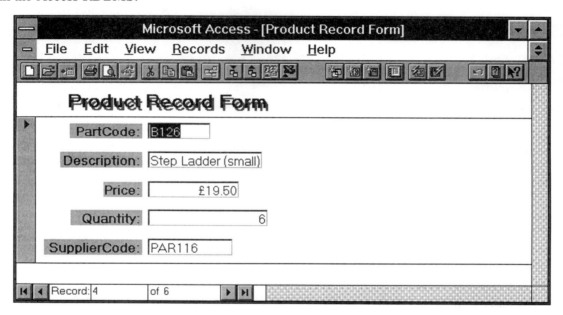

Figure 25.3. *A form for the entry viewing and editing of Product records*

You can begin with a blank form and design your layout, or more easily, you can produce one with a 'wizard' and then modify it to your requirements. Figure 25.4 shows the Product Record Form in design mode, with the 'Description' field label selected. You can see from Figure 25.4 that a form consists of a number of objects, including field labels and data entry points. Each data entry point uses the field name defined in the table definition and ensures that each entry point on the form is associated with the correct field in a record. As a consequence, field names should not be altered on the form (unless they are also altered in the table definition). Field labels, on the other hand can be altered; the field names are used by default, unless you specify otherwise. The form design is divided into sections: *header* (for titles); *detail* (for the field names and data entry points); *footer* (for additional comments, perhaps to guide the data entry process).

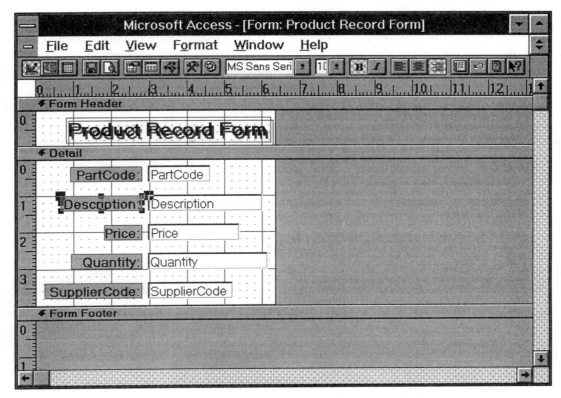

Figure 25.4. *Product Record Form in design mode*

Queries and Dynasets

A query is a request for information from a database. You can use a query to:

    (i)   display all the records in a table;

    (ii) display information from several tables by *joining* them (see Personnel Stock Control and Academic Case Studies);

    (iii) display limited information by specifying that only certain fields are displayed;

    (iv) use *criteria* to *filter* records from one table or from several joined together.

The data extracted by a query is known as a *dynaset*. Referring to (iv), you may want to query, for example, a Product database for all products supplied by a particular supplier; alternatively, you may wish to identify products within a particular category. Each of these is an example of a *criterion*. If you specify more than one requirement, such as products from a particular supplier, under a particular price, then you are using two *criteria*. When criteria are used in a query, a filter is being applied; only those records which satisfy the criteria pass through the filter. If you want to identify an individual record, you will normally use the primary key; in the case of the Product table, this would be the PartCode. To retrieve groups of records, such as products from a particular supplier, you can use the SupplierCode, which is an example of a *secondary key*. You can only identify products within a particular category if there is a field in the table which allows for it. In the Product table in Figure 25.1, you can see that the PartCodes beginning with 'A' are connected with items of furniture, whereas, the 'B' items are do-it-yourself or DIY items. Assuming this is the intended categorisation, you could use the first letter of the PartCode for such a query. In this case, the PartCode field will be serving as a secondary key; this is because only part of it (the first character) is being used. A query can be made on a single table or, as demonstrated in the Personnel, Stock Control and Academic examples, on more than one. Queries can be expressed in one of two forms:

(i) *query by example (QBE)*. With this method, queries are carried out according to the criteria you provide, in the form of examples. The query in Figure 25.5 uses the Product table from Figure 25.1. By entering the expression ' < 10', which means 'less than 10', under the Quantity field, you are effectively applying a filter; only records which satisfy the criterion pass through the filter and are selected by the query.

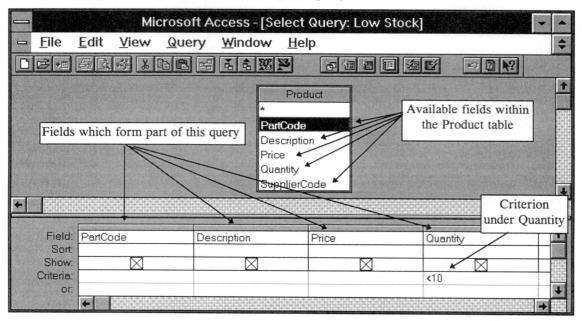

Figure 25.5. *Query by example QBE to retrieve products with a quantity less than 10*

Figure 25.6 shows the result of running the query. Compare it with Figure 25.1 to see the effect.

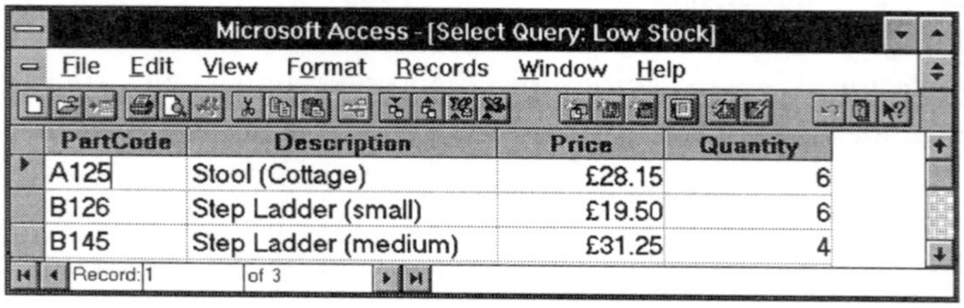

Figure 25.6. *Dynaset from query shown in Figure 25.5*

- *Structured Query Language (SQL)*. This method requires that you know the form of the language, in order to write the query expressions. However, if you create a query using the QBE method (which is the simplest), you can request the RDBMS to show you the SQL equivalent. For most queries you will use QBE, but SQL is needed if the query you want to make is not possible with QBE. Figure 25.7 displays the SQL equivalent of the QBE example in Figure 25.5.

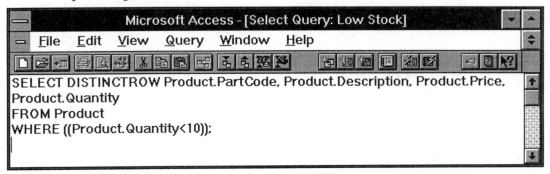

Figure 25.7. *SQL statement for query shown in Figure 25.5*

A number of component parts can be identified in the SQL statement in Figure 25.7. The lower case words are table and field names. The upper case words: SELECT; DISTINCTROW; FROM; WHERE, are all SQL *reserved words*. Like any programming language, they have a particular meaning to the language processor and can only be used for a specified purpose. Briefly, each has the following use:

- SELECT. This is used to select individual or groups of records from named table(s); it is followed by the fieldnames (each prefixed by its table name) to be displayed when the query is executed;

- DISTINCTROW. This prevents the selection of duplicate (values are the same in the fields selected for the query) records;

- FROM is used to identify the table(s) to which the query is directed; in Figure 25.7, the named table is Product.

- WHERE is followed by the criterion which, in Figure 25.7, is that the Quantity is less than 10. The field name is prefixed by the name of the table (Product). This is because a criterion can be directed at a different table from the one identified in the FROM clause.

Sorting

Although a table or query output may have a particular sequence, perhaps in the order of the primary key, there will be occasions when you want to change the sequence. If for example, you are viewing a list of personnel, you may wish the list to be in alphabetical order by surname. Alternatively, you may prefer to see them first grouped into departments (which you also want in alphabetical order) and then, within each department, ordered alphabetically by surname. Before executing a sort, you need to indicate which column or field is to dictate the sequence; apart from this, you can choose ascending or descending order. Indexing (see below) can be used to speed the sorting process.

Indexes

Indexes are used to speed the sorting and retrieval of records. If you index (see Table definition in Figure 25.1) a field, this speeds the sorting and retrieval of records, using that field as a key. The effect will only be noticeable with databases containing hundreds of records. The RDBMS creates an index file for each field you index and has to update it every time you modify the contents of the table to which it relates. Indexes take up space and because of the need for their updating, may have the effect of slowing data entry and editing. For this reason, you should avoid using them indiscriminately. An index file contains all the values taken from the indexed field. For example, if you indexed the SupplierCode field in the Product table in Figure 25.1, each value in that column would be in the index file. Each value would then have a pointer which indicated the physical location of the record containing that value. Referring to Figure 25.1, you can see that some supplier code values are duplicated; this is necessary because numerous products may be supplied by a single supplier. You can choose that the index allows for duplicates. The primary key in the Product table in Figure 25.1 is indexed and duplicates are not permitted; this is obvious, because the purpose of the primary key is to uniquely identify a record.

Reports

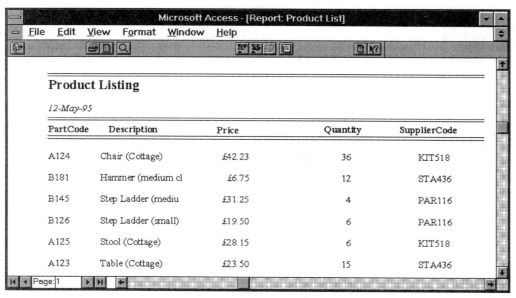

Figure 25.8. *Column report on contents of Product table*

Report facilities allow you to decide what information from a table or query is visible when you view it or print it. Reports are usually categorised as:

- *single column*. Records are displayed in full down the side of the page or screen, rather than across the page in columns.

- *multiple column*; a column is provided for each field you specify and records are placed one after another. You can allow the field names to be used as column headings, or design your own;

- *grouped*. If the information can be grouped into different levels. Then the report can be presented in this way, with sub-totals or other calculations on numeric or currency fields, at the end of each group or subgroup.

Figure 25.8 shows a report on screen, generated with a 'report wizard', using the Product table from Figure 25.1. The sequence is by Description and this was specified as part of the report construction process. Like *forms*, you can design reports from 'scratch' or use a 'wizard' and then modify the design (see Figure 25.4 for Form design) as necessary.

EuroTent Database Case Study

EuroTent is a small holiday agency, specialising in a range of French campsites, details of which are published in its brochure. It also provides a ferry and site reservation service. Some clients have no clear idea about the sites they wish to use and sometimes are not even sure which region they want to visit. For these clients, the main criteria for selection are price and campsite rating. Campsites charge on a nightly basis, but the price varies according to the season. There are two charging periods: Low Season (from March to May and September to October) and High Season (from June to August). Most campsites are closed outside those periods. A computer database would allow flexible retrieval of information, using criteria, such as price range or region. Also, amendments, perhaps to site ratings or prices, could be recorded. This would allow checks to be made on the current situation, where the printed brochure may be out of date. EuroTent decide to create a single table database to manage the campsite information. A database named EuroTent is created and the task for defining the campsite table begins.

Defining the Campsite table

Figure 25.9 shows the table definition, including field names, data types and field descriptions. The lower half of the figure, shows the field properties chosen for the Pitches field. A number of points may need clarification:

(i) You can see that the selected data type is number and that the field size is *integer* (whole number only). Other optional field sizes allow for the storage of *real* numbers (they can have a fractional element) at different levels of precision (more or fewer significant digits);

(ii) A validation rule has been set, using the expression ' < =30 And > =500'. This ensures that only values between 30 and 500 are accepted; the validation text is the message which appears when an attempt is made to enter a value outside this range.

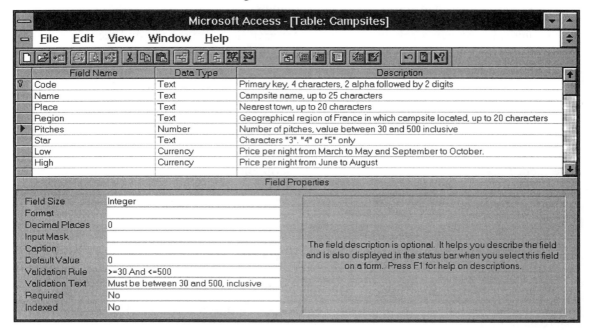

Figure 25.9. *Definition of Campsites table in EuroTent database*

The properties for three of the other fields are shown in Figure 25.10.

	Code	Star	Low
Field Size	4	1	Currency
Format			
Input Mask	LL00	0	
Validation Rule		= '3' Or '4' Or '5'	> =7 And < =25
Validation Text		Characters '3', '4' or '5'	Must be between £7 and £25
Required	Yes	No	No
Indexed	Yes (no duplicates)	No	No

Figure 25.10. *Field properties for Code, Star and Low fields*

The entries in Figure 25.10 are explained below. The Name, Place and Region fields are all text fields or varying lengths, with no other properties specified.

(i) Code field. As you can see from Figure 25.9, this is a text field. Figure 25.10 shows that the size has been set to 4. If no other controls are exerted, any four characters can be entered. However, an *input mask* ensures that the data must have a particular pattern of entry. 'LL00', in the Access RDBMS, ensures that the first two characters are letters (A-Z) and that the last characters are digits (0-9). You can only use an input mask to set patterns for a *text*, *date* or *time* field. The field is indexed, but as the primary key for the table, it allows no duplicates (each campsite has a unique code).

(ii) Star field. This stores a 'star' rating for a site. You can see from Figure 25.9 that this is a text field, even though the input is apparently numeric (sites are rated as '3', '4' or '5' Star). This enables an input mask to be used (0) which ensures entry of a single digit between 0 and 9. You cannot do this with a numeric field. A byte field, for example, which allows storage of values between 0 and 255 (an integer field allows -32,768 to 32,767) will not prevent the entry of real numbers, but will simply round them to the nearest whole number. The validation control for the Star field is completed by the expression = '3' Or '4' Or '5'. A suitable error message is set to display if any other characters are entered.

(iii) Low field. This stores the price of a pitch (per night) during the less popular seasons. The High field stores the high season price. It will hold prices in sterling and the currency format ensures that if values are entered without a £ sign or without 2 decimal places, it is altered to this format. A validation rule is included to restrict values to the range 7 to 25 (you don't enter the £ sign in the expression, but it is shown in the validation text message). The High season price field has similar settings except that the prices are from £10 to £28.

Form data entry

Figure 25.11 shows some sample records in the Campsite table.

Code	Name	Place	Region	Pitches	Star	Low	High
DR13	Camping De Roffy	Sarlat	Dordogne	200	3	£10.00	£14.00
DR14	La Palombiere	Sarlat	Dordogne	150	4	£15.00	£19.00
DR19	St. Avit Loisirs	Le Bugue	Dordogne	180	4	£10.00	£14.50
DR22	Les Hauts De Ratebout	St. Foy	Dordogne	180	5	£17.00	£24.50
DR23	Camping Limeuil	Limieul	Dordogne	80	3	£9.00	£14.50
HP11	Camp Du Verdon	Castellane	Haute Provence	300	5	£16.50	£19.50
HP12	Les Lacs Du Verdon	Regusse	Haute Provence	150	3	£16.00	£22.00
MC11	Camping L'Ardechois	Vallon	Massif Central	120	4	£11.00	£14.50
MC16	Val De Cantobre	Cantobre	Massif Central	200	3	£9.50	£12.00
MC19	Les Tours	St Amans	Massif Central	130	3	£7.00	£10.50
MC21	Camping L'Europe	Murol	Massif Central	175	4	£13.00	£17.50
RV13	Camping De La Baie	Cavalaire	French Riveria	350	4	£14.00	£19.00
RV14	Domaine Des Naiades	Port Grimaud	French Riviera	200	4	£13.00	£16.00
RV15	Camping Des Pecheurs	Roquebrune	French Riviera	100	3	£10.00	£14.50
RV16	L'Etoile D'Argens	St. Aygulf	French Riviera	300	5	£16.50	£22.00
RV17	Residence Du Campeur	St. Aygulf	French Riviera	300	4	£13.00	£18.50
RV19	Camping De La Baume	Frejus	French Riviera	400	4	£13.50	£17.00
RV22	Les Pins Parasols	Frejus	French Riviera	80	4	£10.00	£14.50

Record: 1   of 18

Figure 25.11. *Sample contents of Campsite table*

As explained in the Overview section, you can use a *form* to enter, view and edit records. You can do the same in the table's 'data view', but you have no control over the layout or the fields which are displayed. Figure 25.12 shows a form generated with a 'form wizard'; it has then been modified, in design mode, to include different entry labels. Unless you specify otherwise, the field names from the table definition are used.

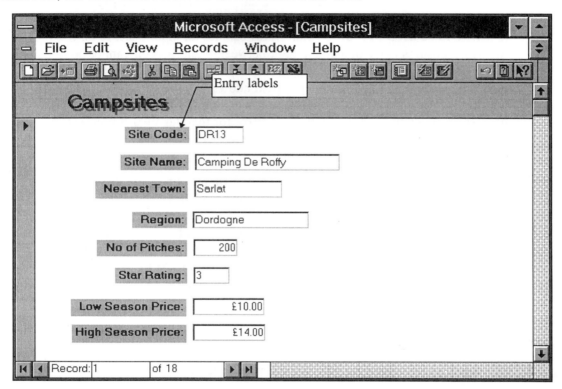

Figure 25.12. *Form with entry labels modified*

Querying the EuroTent database

EuroTent Query 1 - Low Season Prices

The design of the first query, 'Low Season Prices', is shown in Figure 25.13. A customer is visiting France during March, which is part of the low season and is willing to consider any area at the moment. Therefore, a list of all sites is appropriate, but only showing the prices for the relevant season. As Figure 25.13 shows, the Campsites table is selected for the query (as it happens, the database only has one table at present). Then the fields to be included in the query (Name, Place, Region, Star and Low) are placed in the relevant row in the QBE grid. If the query is to be used in a report, you can alter the order of the fields then.

This query does not filter records with criteria, because a list is required of all sites in the database. However, not all details are needed and as Figure 25.13 reveals, only five field names have been placed in the QBE grid. The query is also sorting the records into ascending alphabetical order, by region.

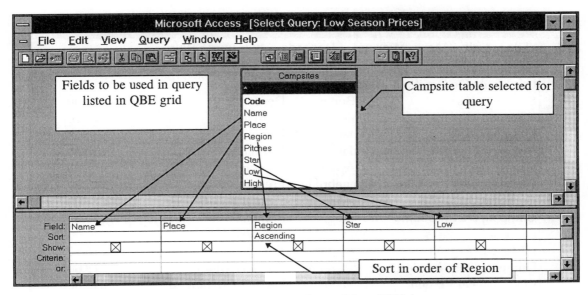

Figure 25.13. *Design of Low Season Prices (QBE) query*

The query, expressed in SQL, is shown in Figure 25.14.

```
SELECT DISTINCTROW Campsites.Name, Campsites.Place, Campsites.Region,
Campsites.Star, Campsites.Low

FROM Campsites

ORDER BY Campsites.Region;
```

Figure 25.14. *SQL form of Query 1 to display low season prices of sites*

The SQL reserved words 'SELECT', 'DISTINCTROW' and 'FROM' have already been used and defined in the Overview. The phrase 'ORDER BY' means sequence, or sort, using the named field; in this case it is 'Region' and is prefixed by the name of the table. Every time you use a field name in an SQL statement, you need to prefix it with its table name. This is despite the fact that the EuroTent database has only one! Note from Figure 25.13 that the table used in the QBE query has to be selected first. The table must always be named, because you can use the same field name repeatedly, provided each occurrence is in a different table.

The output from the Low Season Prices query is shown in Figure 25.15.

Name	Place	Region	Star	Low
Les Hauts De Ratebout	St. Foy	Dordogne	5	£17.00
St. Avit Loisirs	Le Bugue	Dordogne	4	£10.00
Camping Limeuil	Limieul	Dordogne	3	£9.00
La Palombiere	Sarlat	Dordogne	4	£15.00
Camping De Roffy	Sarlat	Dordogne	3	£10.00
Residence Du Campeur	St. Aygulf	French Riviera	4	£13.00
Camping Des Pecheurs	Roquebrune	French Riviera	3	£10.00
Camping De La Baie	Cavalaire	French Riviera	4	£14.00
Camping De La Baume	Frejus	French Riviera	4	£13.50
Les Pins Parasols	Frejus	French Riviera	4	£10.00
L'Etoile D'Argens	St. Aygulf	French Riviera	5	£16.50
Domaine Des Naiades	Port Grimaud	French Riviera	4	£13.00
Les Lacs Du Verdon	Regusse	Haute Provence	3	£16.00
Camp Du Verdon	Castellane	Haute Provence	5	£16.50
Les Tours	St Amans	Massif Central	3	£7.00
Camping L'Europe	Murol	Massif Central	4	£13.00
Val De Cantobre	Cantobre	Massif Central	3	£9.50
Camping L'Ardechois	Vallon	Massif Central	4	£11.00

Record: 2   of 18

Figure 25.15. *Dynaset from Low Season Prices query*

EuroTent Query 2 - Pitches 150 or less, Low Season, 4 to 5 Star

Customers visiting France when campsite prices are lower can afford to be more selective and frequently choose small, but good quality sites. This query (Figure 25.16) is designed to produce the kind of information they require.

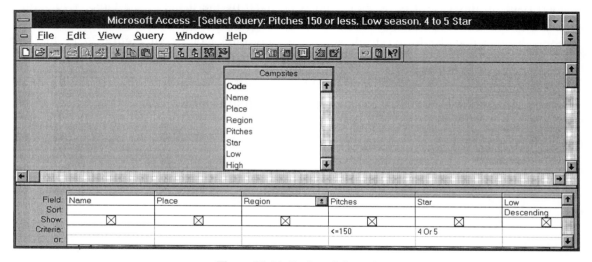

Figure 25.16. *Design of Query 2*

The SQL form of Query 2 is shown in Figure 25.17.

```
SELECT DISTINCTROW Campsites.Name, Campsites.Place,
Campsites.Region, Campsites.Pitches, Campsites.Star,
Campsites.Low

FROM Campsites

WHERE ((Campsites.Pitches<=150) AND (Campsites.Star="4" OR
Campsites.Star="5"))

ORDER BY Campsites.Low DESC;
```

Figure 25.17. *SQL form of Query 2*

The meaning of the SQL statement, shown in bold, should be quite clear when you compare it with the criteria used in the QBE form in Figure 25.16. The reserved word 'WHERE' is followed by two criteria; the first is that the Pitches field must contain a value of 150 or less; the second criterion is that the Star field must contain either '4' OR (used as a *logical operator*) '5'. The 'AND' logical operator means that both criteria must be satisfied, before a record is selected. The final statement in this SQL query contains the reserved word DESC, which means *descending* (order).

The output from Query 2, showing the smaller, better quality sites, with low season prices, is shown in Figure 25.18.

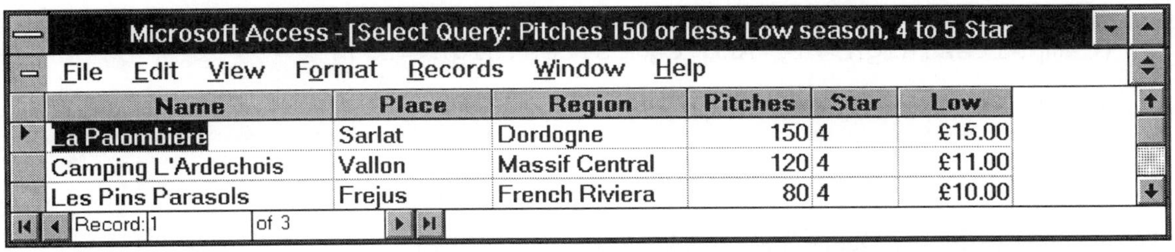

Name	Place	Region	Pitches	Star	Low
La Palombiere	Sarlat	Dordogne	150	4	£15.00
Camping L'Ardechois	Vallon	Massif Central	120	4	£11.00
Les Pins Parasols	Frejus	French Riviera	80	4	£10.00

Record: 1 of 3

Figure 25.18. *Dynaset from Query 2*

EuroTent Query 3 - French Riviera £14 to £19

This query is in response to a more precise request for information. A family wish to stay in the Riviera region during the High season and are willing to pay between £14 and £19 a night. The query design is displayed in Figure 25.19. The main point to note is that there are two criteria, one concerning the Region and the other, the High season price. The latter is similar to the criterion used in Query 2. The criterion that the Region should be the French Riviera could have been expressed fully, in the form ='French Riviera'. QBE does not require the use of an '=' sign, so you could simply type 'French Riviera' as the criterion. In Figure 25.19, a wild card (*) is used, thus: *Riviera. The RDBMS takes this as being a request for any string of characters which ends with 'Riviera' and prefixes it with 'Like', which is the proper form of the expression. If there were other occurrences of the string 'Riviera' in the Region column, such as 'Italian Riviera', you would have to be more specific.

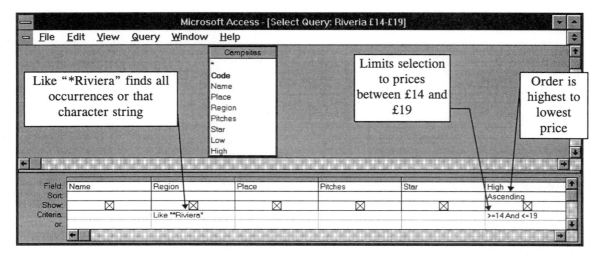

Figure 25.19. *Design of query for Riviera sites between £14 and £19*

The SQL form of Query 3 is displayed in Figure 25.20.

```
SELECT DISTINCTROW Campsites.Name, Campsites.Region,
Campsites.Place, Campsites.Pitches, Campsites.Star,
Campsites.High

FROM Campsites

WHERE ((Campsites.Region Like "*Riviera") AND
(Campsites.High>=14 And Campsites.High<=19))

ORDER BY Campsites.High;
```

Figure 25.20. *SQL for of Query 3*

The results of running Query 2 are displayed in Figure 25.21.

Name	Region	Place	Pitches	Star	High
Les Pins Parasols	French Riviera	Frejus	80	4	£14.50
Camping Des Pecheurs	French Riviera	Roquebrune	100	3	£14.50
Domaine Des Naiades	French Riviera	Port Grimaud	200	4	£16.00
Camping De La Baume	French Riviera	Frejus	400	4	£17.00
Residence Du Campeur	French Riviera	St. Aygulf	300	4	£18.50
Camping De La Baie	French Riviera	Cavalaire	350	4	£19.00

Record: 1 of 6

Figure 25.21. *Dynaset from query for Riviera sites at £14 to £19 a night*

A Grouped Column Report

Query 1 produces the full list of campsites, ordered alphabetically by Region. Since there are several sites in each region, each region's name is repeated. A grouped column report only displays each group name once. Figure 25.22 shows a grouped report on the output from EuroTent's Query 1.

EuroTent		Low Season Prices		
14-May-95				
Region	**Name**	**Place**	**Star**	**Low**
Dordogne				
	Camping Limeuil	Limieul	3	Ł9.00
	St. Avit Loisirs	Le Bugue	4	Ł10.00
	Camping De Roffy	Sarlat	3	Ł10.00
	La Palombiere	Sarlat	4	Ł15.00
	Les Hauts De Ratebout	St. Foy	5	Ł17.00
French Riviera				
	Camping Des Pecheurs	Roquebrune	3	Ł10.00
	Les Pins Parasols	Frejus	4	Ł10.00
	Residence Du Campeur	St. Aygulf	4	Ł13.00
	Domaine Des Naiades	Port Grimaud	4	Ł13.00
	Camping De La Baume	Frejus	4	Ł13.50
	Camping De La Baie	Cavalaire	4	Ł14.00
	L'Etoile D'Argens	St. Aygulf	5	Ł16.50
Haute Provence				
	Les Lacs Du Verdon	Regusse	3	Ł16.00
	Camp Du Verdon	Castellane	5	Ł16.50
Massif Central				
	Les Tours	St Amans	3	Ł7.00
	Val De Cantobre	Cantobre	3	Ł9.50
	Camping L'Ardechois	Vallon	4	Ł11.00
	Camping L'Europe	Murol	4	Ł13.00

Figure 25.22. *Grouped Report on output for Query 1*

Personnel Database Case Study

This case study demonstrates the use of a relational database by using multiple tables to store the information. Pilcon Electronics is organised into the following departments (the abbreviation in brackets is used in the database as the DeptCode):

- Accounting and Finance (ACC);
- General Office Services (GOS);
- Management Information Services (MIS);
- Personnel (PER);
- Production (PRO);
- Purchasing (PUR);
- Research and Development (RAD);
- Sales and Marketing (SAL);
- Warehousing (WAR).

The Personnel database holds basic information on individual staff, departments and job grades; the database has three tables, one for each of these categories of information. They are named: StaffMember; Department; Job. The database allows the staffing in the departments to be monitored, in terms of salary costs and the individuals who are employed in them. It is also useful to be able to monitor the structure of staffing by grouping staff according to job titles; this analysis can be carried out across Pilcon Electronics, as a whole, or it can be specific to one department.

Each table has to be separately defined, in the same manner as the Campsites table in the EuroTent case study. The definition of the StaffMember table is displayed in Figure 25.23.

StaffMember Definition

Field Name	Data Type	Description
StaffCode	Text	Primary key, range 100 to 200
Surname	Text	Up to 25 characters
Initials	Text	2 Initials (full stop after each)
JobCode	Text	2 alphabetic plus 1 digit
DeptCode	Text	3 alpha validated for all department codes
Salary	Currency	Values must be in range 8000 to 45000
StartDate	Date/Time	Validation prevents entry of future dates
Superann	Yes/No	Yes, if paying into superannuation scheme

Field Properties

Format	Medium Date
Input Mask	
Caption	
Default Value	
Validation Rule	<=Now()
Validation Text	Date must be today or earlier
Required	No
Indexed	No

A field name can be up to 64 characters long, including spaces. Press F1 for help on field names.

Figure 25.23. *Definition of StaffMember table*

The field properties of the StaffMember table are shown in Figure 25.24

	StaffCode	**Surname**	**Initials**	**JobCode**
Field Size	3	25	4	3
Input Mask	000			LL0
Validation Rule	> =100 And < =200			
Validation Text	Range 100 to 200			
Required	No	No	No	No
Indexed	Yes(no Duplicates)	No	No	No
	DeptCode	**Salary**	**StartDate**	**Superann**
Field Size	3	Currency		
Format			Medium	Yes/No
Input Mask	LLL			
Validation Rule		> =8000 And < =45000	< =Now()	
Validation Text		Range 8000 to 45000	Invalid date	
Required	No	No	No	No
Indexed	No	No	No	No

Figure 25.24. *Field Properties in Staff Member table*

The lower half of Figure 25.23 shows the field properties chosen for the StartDate (the date a member of staff's employment with Pilcon began) field and you should note the following:

(i) The data type is *date/time* and the format is *medium date*. This means that data can be entered as, for example 1/4/95 and it will be displayed as 01-Apr-95, or similar. Formatted as long date, it would appear as 1 April 1995.

(ii) A validation rule is used to ensure that the starting date for an employee must not be in the future. A *function* 'Now()' returns the system date (the current date and time is stored in the computer) and the expression '< =Now()' means 'less than or equal to today's date'.

Most of the other field properties, shown in Figure 25.24, have already been introduced in Figure 25.10 and are explained thereafter. One detail not given in Figure 25.24 is the validation rule for DeptCode. It is as follows.

```
=ACC Or GOS Or MIS Or PER Or PRO Or PUR Or RAD Or SAL Or WAR
```

The expression checks that the DeptCode is one of the three character strings listed; these are the abbreviations for each of the departments (see earlier). The Superann (Superannuation Scheme Member) field is a *logical* or *yes/no* field. It is used as a true/false indicator. Thus, with a field name Superann, 'yes' indicates that the person is a member of the company superannuation scheme; 'no' obviously means he or she is not a member.

Department Definition

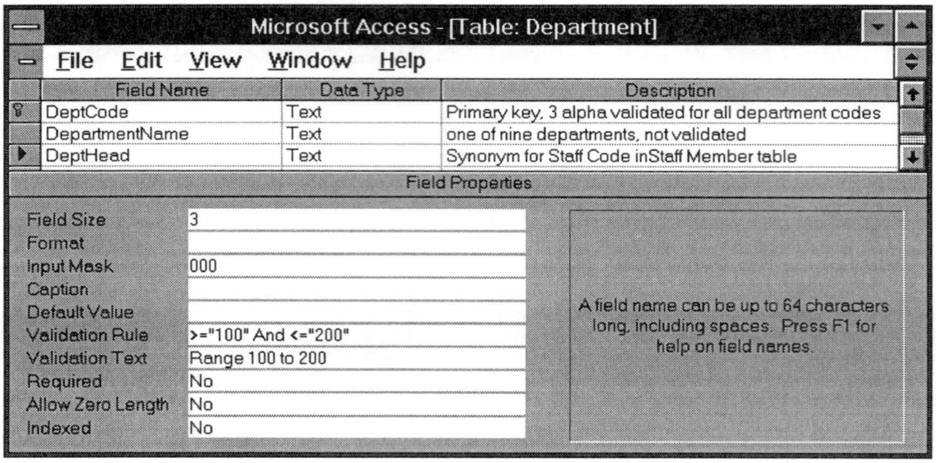

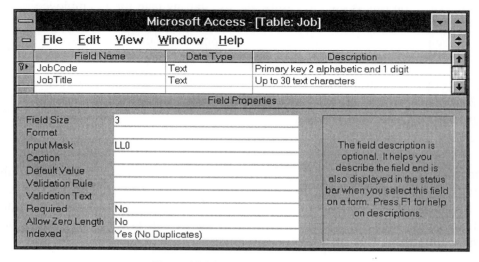

Figure 25.25. *Department table definition showing properties for DeptHead field*

Synonyms

The DeptCode and DepartmentName fields in Figure 25.25 need little explanation. You should notice that the DeptHead field has the same format as StaffCode in the StaffMember table definition; the same input mask is used. DeptHead and StaffCode are *synonyms*; they are different names, but they have the same meaning. You could make the DeptHead field size, say 25, and store the names of heads of departments in the Department table. There is no point however, because as members of staff, their names are already held in the StaffMember table. As shown later, information can be drawn from several tables in a database, provided there are *link fields* to establish *relationships* between them.

Job Definition

Figure 25.26. *Definition of Job table*

In Figure 25.26, you can see that JobCode is the primary key for the Job table. You should recognise that the field of the same name in the StaffMember table enables access to the job titles in the Job table. The fields have exactly the same pattern, so the same input mask is used (LL0 - two alphabetic and one digit) to control input to the JobCode field.

Contents of Personnel Database

Figures 25.27, 25.28 and 25.29 show sample contents for the StaffMember, Department and Job Tables, respectively.

StaffCode	Surname	Initials	JobCode	DeptCode	Salary	StartDate	Superann
100	Picket	W.	CL2	ACC	£15,000	23-Jan-77	Yes
101	Ringwood	K.	HD1	PRO	£33,000	14-May-95	Yes
103	Clacket	D.	CL0	GOS	£13,500	01-Jan-86	No
106	Boreham	L.	SS1	ACC	£23,000	23-Sep-72	Yes
108	Winkle	R.V.	SU1	WAR	£18,000	01-Sep-88	Yes
110	Dickens	C.	OP1	PRO	£8,000	14-May-95	No
115	Cratchit	B.	CL2	ACC	£8,500	01-May-94	No
118	Boffin	C.	HD1	RAD	£38,000	01-Sep-66	Yes
123	Heap	U.	HD1	SAL	£37,500	31-Oct-93	Yes
124	Miggins	M.	SU1	GOS	£14,500	31-Oct-93	Yes
126	Squeers	W.	SS1	PER	£17,500	13-Jun-88	Yes
128	Chiseller	M.	HD2	ACC	£43,000	01-Apr-83	Yes
131	Marley	J.	OP1	PRO	£8,600	16-Jun-91	No
133	Server	I.	HD1	WAR	£32,000	01-Sep-60	Yes
136	Grabbit	U.	HD2	PUR	£45,000	12-Apr-66	Yes
138	Stackit	I.	OP1	WAR	£9,200	03-Apr-68	No
139	Broaket	H.E.	OP2	PRO	£13,000	17-Apr-76	Yes
145	Ramidos	Z.	SU1	MIS	£17,900	12-Jun-88	Yes
149	Machem	I.	HD2	PRO	£40,000	01-Apr-90	Yes
155	Pusher	P.	HD2	GOS	£44,000	01-Feb-60	Yes
159	Nervey	M.	OP1	WAR	£10,000	01-Apr-95	No
160	Surcoat	I.	HD2	MIS	£40,000	02-May-66	Yes
168	Sached	U.R.	HD2	PER	£38,000	01-May-82	Yes
172	Tefal	B.	HD2	RAD	£37,000	02-Mar-66	Yes
180	Leavmey	B.	HD2	SAL	£42,000	01-Oct-72	Yes
187	Lostem	I.	HD2	WAR	£32,500	31-Oct-88	Yes

Record: 11 of 26

Figure 25.27. *StaffMember records*

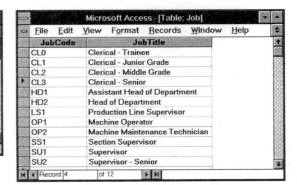

DeptCode	DepartmentName	DeptHead
ACC	Accounting and Finance	128
GOS	General Office Services	155
MIS	Management Information Services	160
PER	Personnel	168
PRO	Production	149
PUR	Purchasing	136
RAD	Research and Development	172
SAL	Sales and Marketing	180
WAR	Warehousing	187

Record: 3 of 9

Figure 25.28. *Department records*

JobCode	JobTitle
CL0	Clerical - Trainee
CL1	Clerical - Junior Grade
CL2	Clerical - Middle Grade
CL3	Clerical - Senior
HD1	Assistant Head of Department
HD2	Head of Department
LS1	Production Line Supervisor
OP1	Machine Operator
OP2	Machine Maintenance Technician
SS1	Section Supervisor
SU1	Supervisor
SU2	Supervisor - Senior

Record: 4 of 12

Figure 25.29. *Job records*

Querying the Personnel Database

Queries can be applied to single tables or to more than one. Multiple tables can be queried because *relationships* exist between the tables. For example, the relationship between the Department table and the StaffMember table is through the DeptCode field, which exists for that purpose in both tables. The relationship is *one-to-many*; this means that each StaffMember record relates to only one Department, but each Department record relates to many StaffMember records. Similarly, the relationship between Job and StaffMember is one-to-many. There is no direct relationship between Job and Department; this is only possible through the StaffMember table, which relates to both. For this and other types of relationship, refer to the Database section in the Knowledge Resource.

Personnel Query 1 - Department Heads and Salaries

In preparation for a meeting of Pilcon's Board of Directors, details of the salaries earned by the Heads of Department are required. The information should comprise, each Head's surname, salary and their Department's name; the output is to be in descending numerical order, by Salary. The names and salaries of Heads of Department are held, with those of the rest of the staff, in the StaffMember table and the Department names are in the Department table. This means that the query has to join these two tables. The full details of the query design (using QBE) are shown in Figure 25.30.

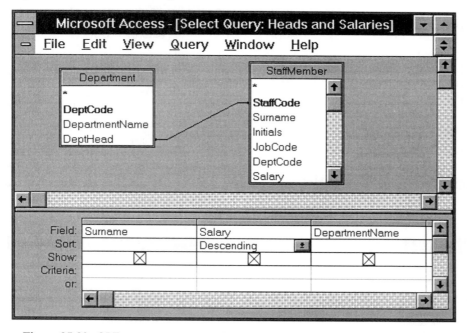

Figure 25.30. *QBE to extract names, salaries and department of Heads of Department*

You might be surprised that no criterion is necessary to select the JobCode 'HD2', which identifies Heads of Department. This can be explained as follows. You can see from Figure 25.30 that a *relationship* is established between DeptHead in the Department table and StaffCode in the StaffMember table (remember these field names are synonyms). This ensures that, when the tables are *joined* in the query, data is only used from those records where the value in StaffCode matches with the value in its synonym, DeptHead. The latter field is an example of a *secondary foreign key*. A link could also be established between the DeptCode fields in each table, but it is unnecessary; having linked the tables through StaffCode and DeptHead, the DepartmentName details are made accessible.

The query, expressed in SQL is displayed in Figure 25.31.

```
SELECT DISTINCTROW StaffMember.Surname, StaffMember.Salary,
Department.DepartmentName

FROM Department INNER JOIN StaffMember ON Department.DeptHead =
StaffMember.StaffCode

ORDER BY StaffMember.Salary DESC;
```

Figure 25.31. *SQL form of Query 1 to display Heads of Department details*

Much of the SQL in Figure 25.31 is used in earlier examples. The new points to note relate to the second statement. Joining tables establishes relationships or links between them. Figure 25.31 shows two such relationships. 'INNER JOIN' is the most commonly used operation which merges information from two tables where values in the link fields are common to both tables. The SQL word 'ON' is followed by the table names and fields to be joined. As can be seen from the QBE form of the query in Figure 25.30 and the SQL statement in Figure 25.31, records are combined when the DeptHead (Department table) value equals the StaffCode (StaffMember table) value.

The dynaset from Query 1 is shown as a report in Figure 25.32.

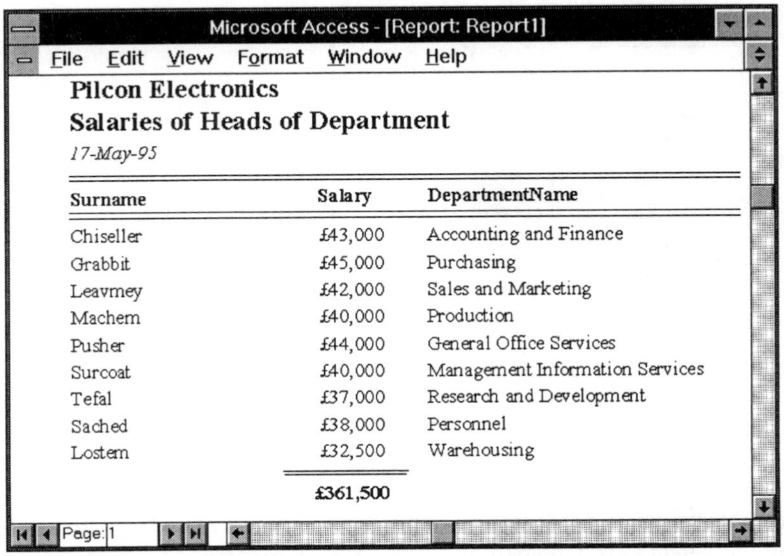

Pilcon Electronics
Salaries of Heads of Department
17-May-95

Surname	Salary	DepartmentName
Chiseller	£43,000	Accounting and Finance
Grabbit	£45,000	Purchasing
Leavmey	£42,000	Sales and Marketing
Machem	£40,000	Production
Pusher	£44,000	General Office Services
Surcoat	£40,000	Management Information Services
Tefal	£37,000	Research and Development
Sached	£38,000	Personnel
Lostem	£32,500	Warehousing
	£361,500	

Figure 25.32. *Column report on Heads of Department query*

Note that the report design process automatically inserts a SUM formula (see Spreadsheets) to calculate and display the total for the Salary column (see Figure 25.33 for report design screen). Note also the use of the *Now()* function to display the current date.

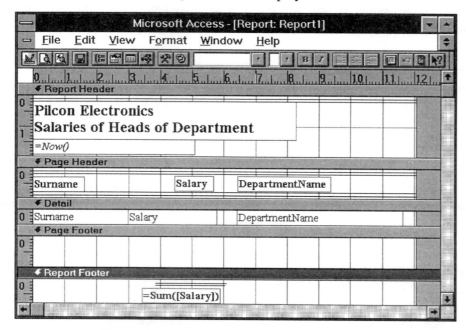

Figure 25.33. *Design screen for report in Figure 25.32*

Personnel Query 2 - Non-HODs in Superannuation scheme

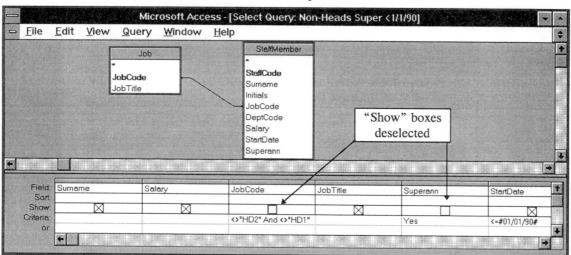

Figure 25.34. *QBE form of Personnel Query 2*

This query uses the criterion < > 'HD1' And < > 'HD2', which means 'staff who are not Heads or Assistant Heads of Department', to extract records of other staff. There are two other criteria: member of Superannuation scheme; appointed on or before 1st January 1990.

To produce this information requires the joining of the StaffMember and Department tables. Figure 25.34 shows the QBE form of this query.

Note that the JobCode and Superann fields are needed in the QBE grid to allow entry of the appropriate filter criteria. However, they do not need to displayed, so the 'Show' check boxes are deselected. The SQL form of the query is shown in Figure 25.35. All the SQL features in this query have already been met, so it should be self-explanatory. Note that the deselected fields are not included in the first statement.

```
SELECT DISTINCTROW StaffMember.Surname, StaffMember.Salary,
Job.JobTitle, StaffMember.StartDate

FROM Job INNER JOIN StaffMember ON Job.JobCode =
StaffMember.JobCode

WHERE ((Job.JobCode<>"HD2" And Job.JobCode<>"HD1") AND
(StaffMember.Superann=Yes) AND
(StaffMember.StartDate<=#01/1/90#));
```

Figure 25.35. *SQL form of Personnel Query 2*

The simple table form of output for this query is shown in Figure 25.36.

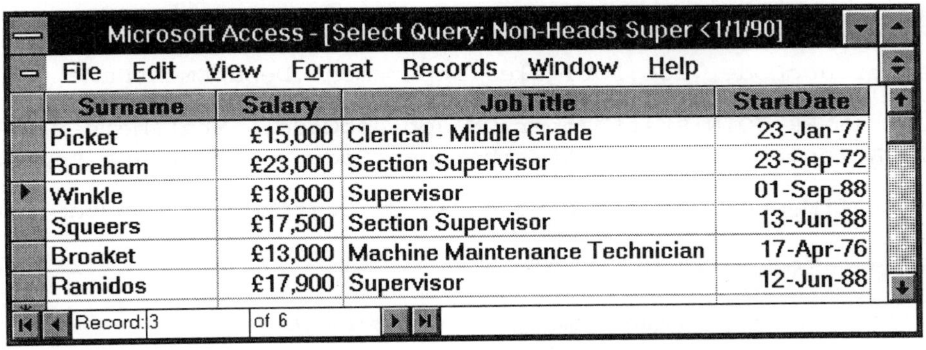

Surname	Salary	JobTitle	StartDate
Picket	£15,000	Clerical - Middle Grade	23-Jan-77
Boreham	£23,000	Section Supervisor	23-Sep-72
Winkle	£18,000	Supervisor	01-Sep-88
Squeers	£17,500	Section Supervisor	13-Jun-88
Broaket	£13,000	Machine Maintenance Technician	17-Apr-76
Ramidos	£17,900	Supervisor	12-Jun-88

Record: 3   of 6

Figure 25.36. *Dynaset for Personnel Query 2*

Personnel Query 3 - Operator and Clerical Staff

This query (see Figure 25.37) involves the use of all three tables. To enable selection of operators and clerical staff, the JobCode is needed. Note that a wild card is used to pick up the various grades in each group. Thus, *Like 'CL*'*, will find CL0, CL1 and CL2. Similarly, *Like 'OP*'* picks out OP1 and OP2

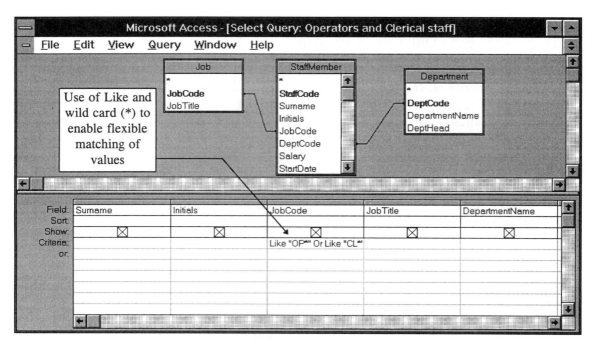

Figure 25.37. *QBE for of query to identify operator and clerical staff*

The SQL form of the query is shown in Figure 25.38.

```
SELECT DISTINCTROW StaffMember.Surname, StaffMember.Initials,
StaffMember.JobCode, Job.JobTitle, Department.DepartmentName

FROM (Job INNER JOIN StaffMember ON Job.JobCode = StaffMember.JobCode)
INNER JOIN Department ON StaffMember.DeptCode = Department.DeptCode

WHERE ((StaffMember.JobCode Like "OP*" Or StaffMember.JobCode Like
"CL*"));
```

Figure 25.38. *SQL form of Personnel Query 3*

The output is displayed in Figure 25.39.

Surname	Initials	JobCode	JobTitle	DepartmentName
Picket	W.	CL2	Clerical - Middle Grade	Accounting and Finance
Clacket	D.	CL0	Clerical - Trainee	General Office Services
Dickens	C.	OP1	Machine Operator	Production
Cratchit	B.	CL2	Clerical - Middle Grade	Accounting and Finance
Marley	J.	OP1	Machine Operator	Production
Stackit	I.	OP1	Machine Operator	Warehousing
Broaket	H.E.	OP2	Machine Maintenance Technician	Production
Nervey	M.	OP1	Machine Operator	Warehousing

Figure 25.39. *Dynaset for Query on Operator and Clerical staff*

Personnel Query 4 - Updating Salaries

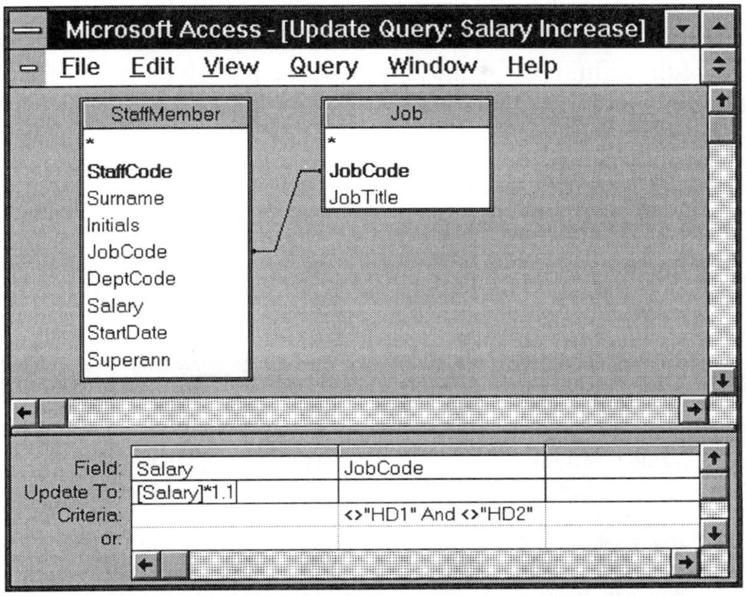

Figure 25.40. *Update query to increase salaries by 10%*

Figure 25.40 is an example of an *update query*. Using this type of query you can update groups of records with a single operation. Of course, the update has to be of a form which allows group updating, such as a percentage increase in salaries. The salary increase of 10% is effected with the expression *[Salary]*1.1*. On performance, Pilcon have decided not to increase the salaries of Heads and Assistant Heads of Department (see criteria in Figure 25.40). If you did increase their salaries, you would first have to alter the validation rule for the Salary field, which restricts values to the range 8000 to 45000.

The SQL form of this update query is displayed in Figure 25.41.

```
UPDATE DISTINCTROW StaffMember INNER JOIN Job ON StaffMember.JobCode =
Job.JobCode SET StaffMember.Salary = [Salary]*1.1

WHERE ((StaffMember.JobCode<>"HD1" And StaffMember.JobCode<>"HD2"));
```

Figure 25.41. *SQL form of update query*

The main points to observe from Figure 25.41 are:

   (i)   Instead of SELECT, the first SQL word is UPDATE.

   (ii)   The INNER JOIN is carried out ON a SET of records, WHERE JobCode is not equal to 'HD1' and not equal to 'HD2'.

Viewing the StaffMember table would reveal that all salary figures (except those of Heads and Assistant Heads) are increased by 10%.

Stock Control Database Case Study

This example makes use of the Product table, used for illustration in the Overview, plus a Supplier table. The full definitions of the database are not given here. The main purpose of the Stock Control case study is to illustrate editing tables through a query dynaset and further aspects of *forms*.

Editing Tables through Query Dynasets

The contents of the Product and Supplier tables are shown in Figures 25.42 and 25.43, respectively.

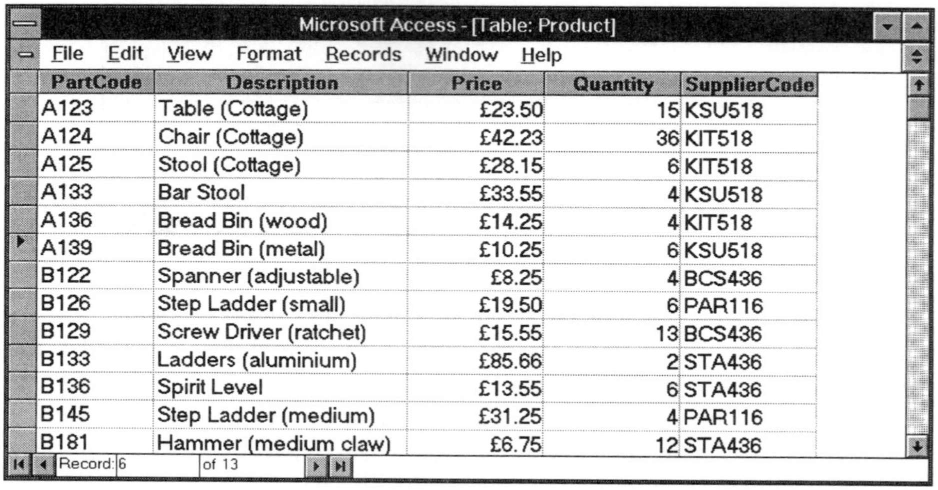

Microsoft Access - [Table: Product]

File Edit View Format Records Window Help

PartCode	Description	Price	Quantity	SupplierCode
A123	Table (Cottage)	£23.50	15	KSU518
A124	Chair (Cottage)	£42.23	36	KIT518
A125	Stool (Cottage)	£28.15	6	KIT518
A133	Bar Stool	£33.55	4	KSU518
A136	Bread Bin (wood)	£14.25	4	KIT518
A139	Bread Bin (metal)	£10.25	6	KSU518
B122	Spanner (adjustable)	£8.25	4	BCS436
B126	Step Ladder (small)	£19.50	6	PAR116
B129	Screw Driver (ratchet)	£15.55	13	BCS436
B133	Ladders (aluminium)	£85.66	2	STA436
B136	Spirit Level	£13.55	6	STA436
B145	Step Ladder (medium)	£31.25	4	PAR116
B181	Hammer (medium claw)	£6.75	12	STA436

Record: 6 of 13

Figure 25.42. *Sample contents of Product table*

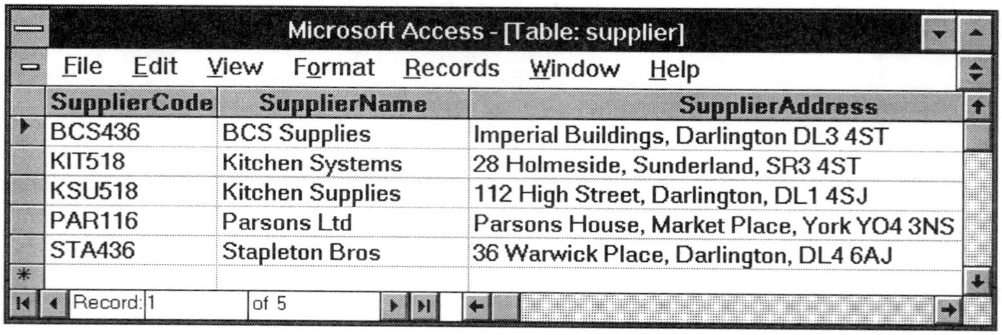

Microsoft Access - [Table: supplier]

File Edit View Format Records Window Help

SupplierCode	SupplierName	SupplierAddress
BCS436	BCS Supplies	Imperial Buildings, Darlington DL3 4ST
KIT518	Kitchen Systems	28 Holmeside, Sunderland, SR3 4ST
KSU518	Kitchen Supplies	112 High Street, Darlington, DL1 4SJ
PAR116	Parsons Ltd	Parsons House, Market Place, York YO4 3NS
STA436	Stapleton Bros	36 Warwick Place, Darlington, DL4 6AJ

Record: 1 of 5

Figure 25.43. *Sample contents of Supplier Table*

Suppose, for example, that you wish to view and edit the combined information from both tables. You could join the tables in a query, the design of which is shown in Figure 25.44.

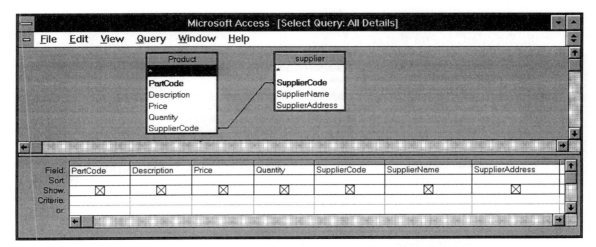

Figure 25.44. *Query to join information from Product and Supplier tables*

The simple datasheet view of the resulting dynaset is shown in Figure 25.45.

PartCode	Description	Price	Quantity	SupplierCode	SupplierName	Su
B181	Hammer (medium claw)	£6.75	12	STA436	Stapleton Bros	36 Warwick Place, Dai
B133	Ladders (aluminium)	£85.66	2	STA436	Stapleton Bros	36 Warwick Place, Dai
B136	Spirit Level	£13.55	6	STA436	Stapleton Bros	36 Warwick Place, Dai
A124	Chair (Cottage)	£42.23	36	KIT518	Kitchen Systems	28 Holmeside, Sunder
A125	Stool (Cottage)	£28.15	6	KIT518	Kitchen Systems	28 Holmeside, Sunder
A136	Bread Bin (wood)	£14.25	4	KIT518	Kitchen Systems	28 Holmeside, Sunder
B126	Step Ladder (small)	£19.50	6	PAR116	Parsons Ltd	Parsons House, Marke
B145	Step Ladder (medium)	£31.25	4	PAR116	Parsons Ltd	Parsons House, Marke
A123	Table (Cottage)	£23.50	15	KSU518	Kitchen Supplies	112 High Street, Darlir
A133	Bar Stool	£33.55	4	KSU518	Kitchen Supplies	112 High Street, Darlir
A139	Bread Bin (metal)	£10.25	6	KSU518	Kitchen Supplies	112 High Street, Darlir
B129	Screw Driver (ratchet)	£15.55	13	BCS436	BCS Supplies	Imperial Buildings, Dai
B!45	Spanner (adjustable)	£8.25	4	BCS436	BCS Supplies	Imperial Buildings, Dai

Record: 2   of 13

Figure 25.45. *Dynaset from Query joining Product and Supplier tables*

You should notice that each supplier name and address is repeated several times. The relationship between the Supplier and Product tables is one-to-many, which means that many products are bought from a single supplier, but each product is ordered from a single supplier. Although the information from both tables can be viewed, only certain fields can be edited to update the tables, upon which the query is based. In the case of a one-to-many relationship, changes can only be made to dynaset fields which come from the *many* side of the relationship. Two important points need to be understood.

- Referring to Figure 25.44, if the query uses the SupplierCode from the Product table, you will be able to alter the Supplier codes in the dynaset shown in Figure 25.45. The name and address will then change accordingly (by using the relationship established with the Supplier table). The changes to the supplier details will be applied to the underlying Product table. The changes are made to the many side of the relationship, only. Figure 25.46 shows that the supplier of the 'Hammer (medium, claw)' is now Parsons Ltd, instead of Stapleton, as shown in Figure 25.45. This is achieved by altering the SupplierCode for that record.

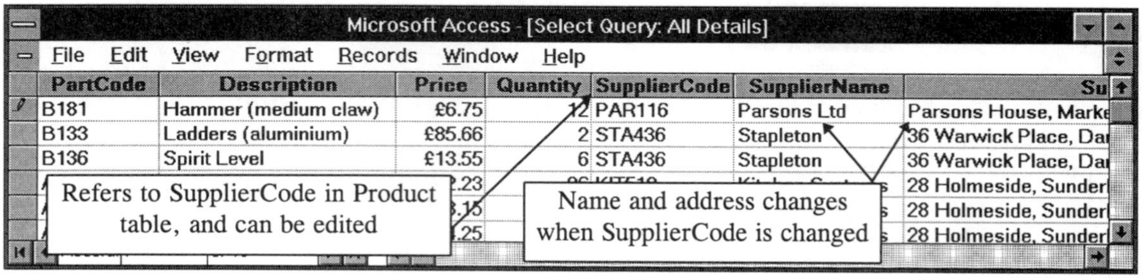

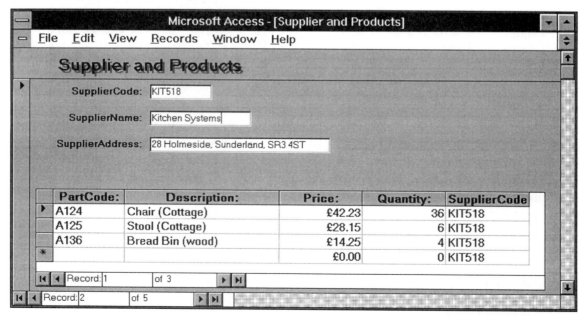

Figure 25.46. *Change of Supplier for Hammer (medium, claw) record*

- If, in designing the query in Figure 25.44, you use the SupplierCode from the Supplier table, the RDBMS would not let you edit it through the dynaset. In this example, this means that you can edit the Product table (the *many* side), but not the Supplier table (the *one* side), through the query dynaset.

If the underlying tables have a one-to-one relationship there are no editing restrictions through the dynaset. If you want to prevent any editing through a dynaset, the RDBMS provides an option to disable the facility. There are other circumstances when dynaset editing is restricted, but they are beyond the scope of this text. This topic is explained in more detail in the Database section in the Knowledge Resource.

Viewing and Editing with Main/Sub Forms

Figure 25.47. *Main/sub Form showing one Supplier record and the associated Products*

Figure 25.45 shows a dynaset which provides a view of all the information in both the Product and Supplier tables. The main drawback is that the suppliers' names and addresses are repeated several times. In addition, as a dynaset, the Supplier table (the *one* side of the one to many relationship) cannot be edited through it. Editing could be carried out using a separate form for each table, or more effectively, with the main/sub form shown in Figure 25.47. The form can be created using a 'form wizard', but you can start with separate forms and then combine them, making the Product form the sub. As you scroll through each Supplier record (you can see from Figure 25.47, that there is a scroll bar for each part of the form), all the associated (through the SupplierCode relationship) Product records appear in the lower, sub form. You can edit or add new Supplier Records, by using the upper, main form.

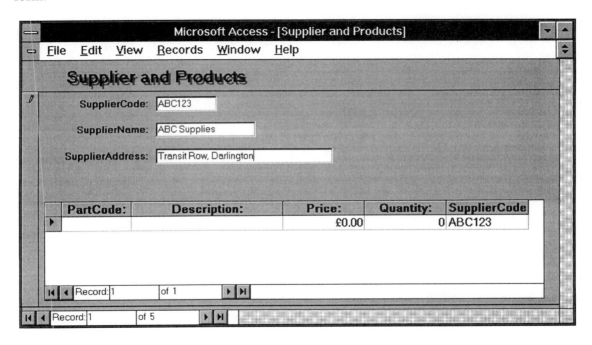

Figure 25.48. *Entry of new Supplier, but before entry of products*

Figure 25.48 shows a new supplier record entered within the main form, but before entry of any product records for that supplier. Entry of a new supplier code would mean that there would be no Product records in the sub form; you could then enter any details of products supplied by the new supplier. Similarly, you can edit or add new Product records in the sub form, for an existing supplier. Remember, changing a SupplierCode in the Product section of the form (the *many* side) will not affect records in the Supplier table (the *one* side).

Forms for Dynasets

The rules which apply to dynaset editing and detailed already, also apply to editing through a form. Thus, creating a form for the dynaset shown in Figure 25.45, does not alter the restrictions concerning the editing of any underlying table on the 'one' side of a one-to-many relationship.

Chapter 26

Local Area Network Operation

Introduction

A network is a shared resource and should be used responsibly and according to standards. The precise standards will depend on the nature of the organisation and the purposes for which the network is used. Users have responsibilities towards one another and to the organisation which owns the network. This applies to a college network used exclusively by students, but it is even more important in a commercial or governmental organisation which could not function without its computer facilities.

If users are properly trained and are aware of the general operation and function of a network and its shared resources, much annoyance, frustration and even disaster, may be avoided. For example, a poorly trained user may request the printing of work and when the work is not immediately printed, request it a second or even third time; the delay may be as a result of heavy network use, or there may be a fault. Of course, all the user is doing is placing several copies of the same job into a *printer queue*; if there is no fault, all copies will be printed. The same user may decide not to wait and simply switch off their workstation and leave it; the work will still be printed, possibly delaying another user who wants to send work to the same printer. The network supervisor or administrator can use network commands to remove unwanted jobs from the printer queue. Because a printer server is a shared resource and handles the work of numerous users, they are not normally able to remove jobs from a printer queue. Access rights to certain network commands, including those for managing printer queues are not normally assigned to users. This section touches on some issues which are the responsibility of a network administrator, but concentrates mainly on user operation.

Login and Network Attachment

Workstations are often computer systems in their own right (diskless workstations cannot be used independently) and are only 'attached' to a network after the *login* procedure. Although the computer systems remain physically connected to the network cable, you *attach* to a file server (a network may have more than one) by 'telling it' that you are there and want to use its resources. This is the function of the login process. The section on Local Area Networks, in the Knowledge Resource, describes the various components which form a network, but they are repeated below, to remind you.

- *Workstation*, usually a stand-alone computer which may be operated independently of the network when not logged in. In a *client-server* network (see Local Area Networks in Knowledge Resource), it uses shared file storage, printing and communication facilities and retrieves software from the file server. On the other hand, once software is retrieved, the workstation does its own processing and manages the running of software and processing of data files. The login process is controlled by the network operating system, from the file server.
- *Server*, a computer assigned to the control of a shared resource on the network; in the case of printing resources, it may be a dedicated device, rather than a microcomputer. A network has one or more file servers, printer servers and communications servers.
- *Cable*, the network medium used to connect all the network devices and *connectors*, which connect the devices to the medium.

The Workstation

As a stand-alone computer, a workstation will run under a particular operating system 'platform', for example, MS-DOS, UNIX, OS/2 or Macintosh. MS-DOS machines may also be using the popular MS Windows operating environment. Usually, a network will be set up with workstations which use the same operating system, but the development of *open* systems enables the attachment of 'foreign' devices. So, for example, Macintosh machines can be attached to a network designed for MS-DOS systems. Primarily, because of their importance in the LAN market, examples in this text assume the use of MS-DOS machines and a *client-server* network (as opposed to a *peer-to-peer* system -

Figure 26.1. *Workstation components*

Knowledge Resource). However the fundamental principles are the same for all types.

To operate as a workstation, a microcomputer must be installed with:

- a *network card* or *board*;
- *network connection software*.

These components are in addition to the microcomputer's own 'local' operating system. The network card is installed in an expansion slot inside the system casing. These components are illustrated in Figure 26.1. The local operating system and network connection software are stored on the workstation's integral hard disk. The process of connecting the workstation to the network is started from the integral hard disk. With *diskless* workstations, the booting process has to be carried out from the network's file server and workstations cannot be operated as stand-alone machines. Otherwise, the principles of network connection are the same.

The Network Connection

The connection process can be separated into the following stages:

1. The microcomputer's initial self-test;
2. Booting the local operating system;
3. Executing the *autoexec.bat* file;
4. Loading network connection software;

Initial Self-test

When a computer system is switched on it uses instructions held on a ROM (read only memory) chip to run a number of self-test routines. These routines check the system's components for normal operation. Thus, it will detect and signal any failure in, for example, the operation of main memory (RAM) or a faulty keyboard connection. Using values stored in CMOS RAM (a low power memory chip, the contents of which are maintained by battery), the defined configuration is checked against the actual hardware installed; this includes the hard disk, floppy drives, CD-ROM drive and any additional RAM.

Booting the Operating System

The initial configuration check will also identify the location of the operating system. This will be the integral hard drive, known on MS-DOS machines as the C:\ drive.

Executing the *Autoexec.bat* File

This file is held in the *root* directory of the C:\ drive and is executed when MS-DOS is first loaded. Certain commands must be included in the file, but others can be used to customise the machine for a particular type of use. Thus, for example, it can be used to automatically load the Windows operating environment. In the case of a workstation, it includes commands to load the network connection software.

Loading Network Connection Software

The components of this software are identified and explained in the Knowledge Resource (Local Area Networks) under Network Connection Software, so are not further described in detail here. It is sufficient to say that it includes software which:

- drives the network card;
- · is the *protocol* for the workstation to communicate across the network and with other devices.

The software will probably be held in a special directory on the workstation's hard drive. If the network connection is to be automated, the command to load the network connection software will be included in the autoexec.bat file (see previous paragraph). Once the software is loaded the login stage can be initiated. Figure 26.2 shows a simplified autoexec.bat file, including the commands to load the network connection software; the comments would not form part of the file.

Command	Comments
`C:`	{Directs MS-DOS to integral C: drive
`CD\CLIENT`	{Directory CLIENT containing network connection software
`LSL.COM`	{Software to enable use of different protocols over same network
`NE2000`	{Software to drive network card
`IPXODI`	{Protocol for Novell networks
`VLM`	{Enables workstation to use network services
`F:`	{Switches to file server's main file storage
`LOGIN {username}`	{Executes login software and prompts for a username

Figure 26.2. *Sample Autoexec.bat file to automate connection of workstation to network*

Note that the file includes a command to switch the attention of the operating system to drive F:, rather than the C:, which is the identifier for the workstation's integral hard drive. Typically, the letter F: is assigned to the main network drive (held in the file server), because letters A to E may be reserved for identification of hard, floppy and CD-ROM drives within the workstation itself. Attention has to be directed to the network drive, because it holds the program which is used to execute the login procedure. Assume for the moment that this program is called *login.exe*, the letters 'exe' meaning *executable*. If this program is not executed from within the autoexec.bat file, you will have to issue the command before you can enter your user name and password (if required).

Logging In to the Network

Once the network connection software has been loaded, you can login to the network. Three stages of login can be identified (Figure 26.3)

1. Execution of *login.exe* This program prompts you to enter your *user name* (this is an identification name assigned to you when the network supervisor sets up your *user account*).

2. Entry of your user name;

3. Entry of a password (if required); again, this is determined by settings in your user account.

```
C:\>F:
F:\>login
Login name:
Password:
```

Figure 26.3. *Login procedure*

If you are given access to more than one file server, you have to prefix your user name with the name of the server you require. *Logging out* detaches you from the network's resources; it does not remove the network connection, as this is only done when the connection software is removed from the workstation's memory (when the machine is switched off).

Functions of Login Procedure

The login procedure is one aspect of *network security* and is used to:

*   *identify* you. When the network supervisor creates your user account, it is given a *user name*. If you enter a name for which there is no account, you will not be able to log into the network. Before access is denied, you will still be asked for a password; this is to ensure that an unauthorised user does not know whether the user name or the password is invalid.
*   Check your account restrictions. When you login with your user name, it references your account to determine any restrictions. For example, you may only be able to login on certain days of the week, or within restricted times. Your account will also specify if there is a limit on the number of unsuccessful login attempts you can have before you are 'locked out'. Such locking out requires that reference is made to the network supervisor before a further attempt can be made. This is a further barrier to protect against someone trying to 'hack' into the network.
*   set up your particular network environment; for example, you may be restricted to a particular group of applications and be allocated workspace (a *user directory*) on the network drive. Similarly, your printing requirements are likely to be assigned to a particular printer.

A Network Filing System - Novell Netware

The file server contains the shared file storage system and handles requests for access to it. Like any filing system, it has to be organised to allow efficient access to and management of the resource. Commonly, such organisation is *hierarchical* and the Novell Netware system provides a typical example. Figure 26.4 shows how a Novell Netware file system might be structured.

Volumes

Referring to Figure 26.4, the server (FS1) disk storage may be divided into *volumes*; a volume is a physical amount of storage, which can be a section of one storage device or it may incorporate several devices. Volumes can be used to divide the network's filing system according to separate organisational requirements. For example, separate volumes may be assigned to Accounts, Manufacturing and Personnel. One reason for such separation is security; security backups can be carried out separately on each volume and allocation of users to the separate organisational functions is made easier. However, these volumes are still part of the same network filing system and a user can be allowed to access more than one, when necessary. For simplicity, Figure 26.4 shows that the server has only one volume (SYS:, which is automatically created when Netware is set up). A workstation accesses a volume by a drive letter (F:\> for example).

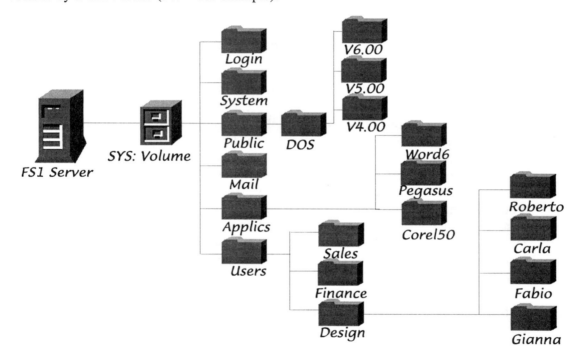

Figure 26.4. *An example Novell Netware file system*

Directories and Sub-directories

Directories are subdivisions of a volume's space. Referring to Figure 26.4 and volume SYS:, a number of different types of directory can be identified:

- *system*; there are four (Login, System, Public and Mail), created when the file server's network software is installed;
- *DOS* (a sub-directory of Public). Each version of the MS-DOS operating system, used by workstations attached to the network, has a sub-directory; one workstation may be using version 6.0, whilst others may be using version

5.0 or 4.0 and if applications are to run correctly, they must have access to the appropriate operating system commands.

- *applics*; these contain the executable files of applications software. There are three sub-directories within this directory: Word6 (word processor); Pegasus (accounting); Corel50 (graphics).
- *users*; the workspace allocated to user data files. Figure 26.4 shows three main sub-divisions of users: Sales; Finance; Design. The Design group has four separate user areas allocated to it: Roberto; Carla; Fabio; Gianna. The other user groups of Sales and Finance may well be similarly sub-divided, but this is not shown in Figure 26.4.

The highest level (the top row) in this *tree* structure contains a number of *system* directories. Figure 26.4 shows four:

- *login*; this directory contains programs concerning the login procedure;
- *public*; this holds Novell network (as opposed to MS-DOS) operating system commands and utilities which can be accessed by users;
- *system*; files and programs used by the network operating system and the network supervisor are held in here;
- *mail*; this contains a sub-directory relating to each network user and containing their *login script*. A *user login script* can be used to tailor the network environment for a particular user, such as the display of a special applications menu or greeting. More usually, the *system login script* is used for all users; programming statements, such as IF ...THEN ...ELSE can be used to determine the network environment for different users or groups of users. Thus, for example, the Sales, Finance and Design groups may each have a different menu, giving access to a different set of applications.

The network supervisor needs to create other directories, for the applications and data areas. Figure 26.4 shows an *applics* (applications) directory, which is divided into three sub-directories, one each for word processing, accounting and graphic design packages. The *users* directory is divided into a series of sub-directories, one data or work area for each user; each of these, usually identified by the user name, is the allocated workspace for a user. A data directory may be shared by a number of individual users, belonging to the same group, such as Finance. Alternatively, as in the case of the four design users in Figure 26.4, each may have their own data directory. As a student user, you are likely to have an individual data directory. When you login, your user name is used to *map* your workstation to your own data directory; this is done through the login script, an example of which is given later.

Accessing Network Applications

Displaying Applications

Typically, network applications are presented through a *menu* system or a graphical user interface (GUI), such as Windows. As explained earlier, it is desirable to limit access to network resources, including applications, to those users who properly need them. Thus, different groups of users may well be presented with different applications menus, when they login.

Network applications are executable files or programs and as such, your *access rights* (see later) to the directories containing them are restricted. This means that you will only be able to see the applications and execute them. You will not be able, for example, to copy a program, delete it or rename it. The reasons for this are obvious: applications are a shared resource and must be protected from tampering, unauthorised copying or removal. You can only execute programs to which you have been given the necessary access rights.

If, for any reason, an application is not displayed you can scan the applications directories for the relevant executable files (for example *winword.exe*). Provided that you have the necessary access rights, a program can be executed by using the mouse to point at the relevant file and 'double clicking' the mouse button.

Executing Applications

When you access a network application, a copy is transferred into the memory (RAM) of your workstation, which then uses its own processor to run the application. This is illustrated in Figure 26.5.

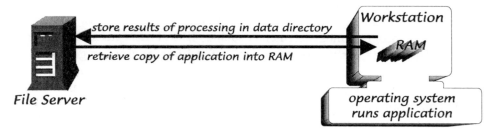

Figure 26.5. *Running an application*

Printing from Applications

Shared printers are managed by *printer servers* and work is allocated to servers through *print queues*. When you login, your user name is used to assign your jobs to a particular print queue and thus, to a particular printer; you may be assigned to a particular printer by virtue of being a member of a particular group. Thus, members of the Publishing (PUB) group may be assigned to a laser printer, whilst members of the Accounts (ACCT) group are assigned to a queue for an ink jet. Assignment to print queues is normally carried out through the system login script. The following statements could be used to this effect.

```
if member of 'ACCT' then #capture q=act_laser

if member of 'PUB' then #capture q=pub_ink
```

Figure 26.6. *Example print queue assignment statements*

You may be a member of more than one user group and, thus be given access to different printers, depending on the work you are doing. So, for example, logged in as a member of the 'PUB' group, you have access to a laser printer. With the Novell Netware system, every user is a member of the group 'EVERYONE', even if they are members of another group or groups. Logged on as one of these users gives you access to the printer shared by that group.

User Directory and File Management

When you login, your workstation is *mapped* to your *user directory*. Thus, at the MS-DOS prompt, you may see something similar to the following ('ST001' is your user name).

```
F:\USERS\ST001
```

Figure 26.7. *Workstation mapped to user directory 'ST001'*

Within that directory you have full directory and file rights, which means that you can:

- create a structure of sub-directories, within your user directory, to suit the division of your own work. You can also modify that structure as your needs change;
- read, write, copy, delete or rename any files you store within that structure.

Creating a Directory Structure

Directories and sub-directories can be used to divide your network user space into separate areas, so that files can be grouped logically. For example, you may decide to allocate one area to work produced with the word processor and another to spreadsheet files; further, you may decide to subdivide these into different areas of work, perhaps relating to different Units wihtin your course. Alternatively, you may ignore the type of application and simply create a subdirectory for each aspect of your course work. To identify it, you give each directory or folder a *name*. There is no single structure which is right; just try to keep the divisions simple and logical. A secretary in a commercial organisation may decide to use separate directories for documents relating to internal and external communications. Referring to Figure 26.4, the Design user, Roberto, may create a structure as shown in Figure 26.8.

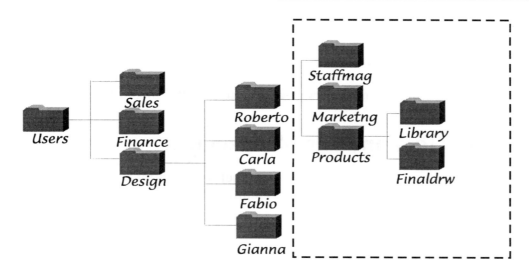

Figure 26.8. *Example, user-created, directory structure*

The broken line box in Figure 26.8, indicates the directory space used by Roberto. He cannot create directories in other user areas, unless he is given rights to do so. He allocates his design work for the staff magazine, marketing publications and products to separate data directories. He decides to divide Products into Library, to hold standard drawing objects which he produces, and Finaldrw, for completed drawings.

Directory Commands

Directory creation and handling can be effected through commands given at the operating system prompt, or they can be executed through an interface, such as Windows File Manager. First, a brief summary is provided of commands which can be used with the Novell Netware and MS-DOS operating systems.

Creating Directories - MD

MD stands for 'make directory' and is used for the creation of directories. Referring to Roberto's data directory structure in Figure 26.8, the commands to create it are shown in Figure 26.9. It is assumed that the commands are given at the 'F:\ROBERTO>' prompt (when Roberto logs in, his workstation is mapped to that directory).

Directories can be removed using the command **RD** (Remove Directory) and the working directory (the directory to which data files will be directed from applications) can be changed with the **CD** (Change Directory) command.

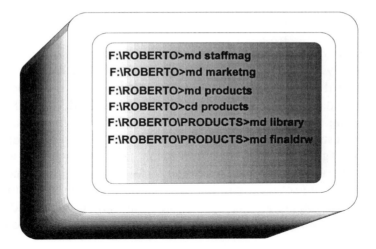

Figure 26.9. *Commands to create a user's data directory structure*

The commands in Figure 26.9 should be easy to understand, although you should note that the 'cd products' command directs the operating system's attention to the 'products' directory, before executing the commands to create the two sub-directories beneath it ('library' and 'finaldrw'). Roberto could have created these sub-directories without changing directories, but would have had to specify a *path*. Thus, to create the sub-directory 'library' from the 'ROBERTO>' prompt, he could have entered 'md\products\library'. The back slashes (\) indicate the path. A similar command could have been used to create 'finaldrw'.

File Manager, one of the components of the Windows graphical user interface, can be used to carry out the same tasks outlined above. Directories are represented graphically, as the next figure shows. Using the mouse, and pull down menus, directories can be created, renamed and removed. In addition they can be easily moved from one part of the structure to another. Figure 26.10 shows the File Manager view of the structure (created on floppy disk, but the principles are the same).

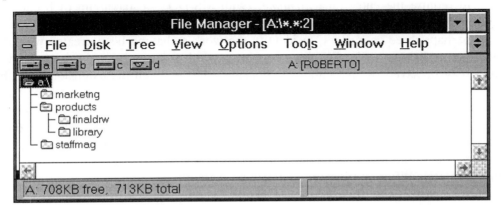

Figure 26.10. *File Manager view of a directory structure*

Working with Data Files

Once you have created your user directory structure on the network drive, you should aim to use the space effectively. The processes described here apply, whether you are using network storage, an integral hard disk in the workstation, or a floppy drive. In respect of the network drive, you are restricted to using your allocated data directory and you will be prevented, by the network operating system, from using others. Hard or floppy drives within the workstation are not restricted in this way. For this reason, the responsibility of using the workstation's own storage rests with you. Irresponsible tampering with the workstation's own hard drive may corrupt the settings which allow it to use the network. Although the network supervisor can restore those settings, you are likely to be extremely unpopular if you are the cause of the problem. If you are an employee in an organization, you would be reprimanded, at the very least. Some workstations are *diskless*, so the only storage you have is on the network drive.

Saving and Retrieving

A computer cannot hold software (apart from a small core of basic instructions which are held on a special ROM - *read only memory* device) or data, once power has been removed and a file storage system is fundamental to its operation. The computer uses RAM (*random access memory)* to store the software and data currently in use, but its contents are lost when electrical power is removed. Your data directory space on the network drive is your permanent storage area. When you are using an application, you command it to *save* the results of your computer work for future use. So, for example, if you are word processing a report, you can save it, not only when it is completed, but at various intervals during its preparation. This helps to ensure that part-completed work is not lost because of computer failure or an error by yourself. At any time, you can command the computer software to *retrieve* the most recently saved copy of your work.

When you command any particular piece of work to be *saved* for the first time, the software package will require the entry of a *filename*, (with MS-DOS, a maximum of 8 characters), which you will use when you want to retrieve it. The software package will add a *file extension*, perhaps three characters, to identify the work as having been created with its use, and save it onto disk as a *file*. So, for example, a word processed document about housing legislation may be saved by the author as 'housing' and be given the extension 'doc' by the package. A listing of the relevant directory will show a suitable entry, perhaps of the form 'housing.doc'. Unless you wish to preserve the contents of an existing file then subsequent save commands will not require the entry of a filename, but will use the one already given and overwrite the existing file with the *amended* version. Some packages may ask you to confirm that you want this to happen and, if you give a negative response, will give you the opportunity to use a different filename to create a separate file.

Targeting Directories

'Save As' Command

Once you have created directories, any data file can be directed to its relevant directory, either directly with the use of MS-DOS commands or (more usually) through the applications software. When Roberto (Figures 26.8 and 26.9) wishes to save a drawing from within the CorelDraw package, he uses the 'Save As' command to direct the operating system's attention to the required sub-directory in his structure. Figure 26.11 shows a dialogue box, through which this operation can be carried out (the structure is on floppy disk).

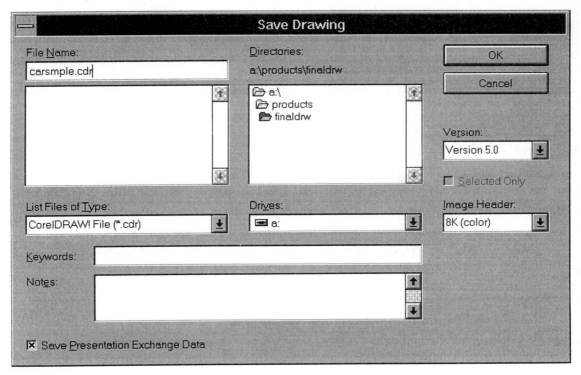

Figure 26.11. *'Save As' dialogue to direct file to 'finaldrw' directory*

Each file stored within a single directory or sub-directory must have a unique filename, or if the filename is the same, the extension must differ. However, you can use the same name for files held in different directories.

'Open File' Command

In the same way that you can direct an application to save a file to a particular directory, you can *open* a file from a selected directory. Figure 26.12 shows an application dialogue box to open the file featured in Figure 26.11. Typically, in Windows-type packages, changing directories is achieved by double clicking *folders* (the Windows name for 'directory') until the required one is reached.

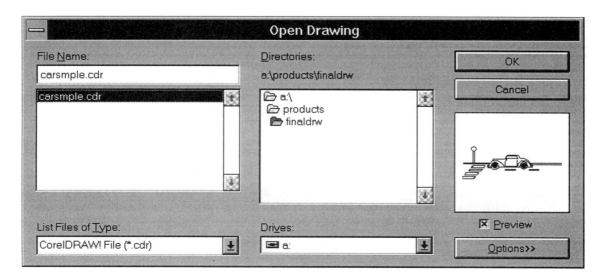

Figure 26.12. *Opening file from "finaldrw" directory*

Viewing Directory Contents

As explained earlier, it is essential to organise file storage space and to allocate files relating to a given application or subject to a separate sub-directory. To view the contents of a particular directory may require the entry of commands to:

- select the *drive letter*. If the main network drive is F:\>, there will be other logical drives (G, H and so on); Novell Netware assigns a drive letter to each *volume*- see Volumes. When you login, your workstation is mapped to your data directory, so that you see the drive letter and, possibly your username (as the directory name). Drive letters are used because MS-DOS applications cannot recognise volume names, only logical drives.
- switch to the relevant *data directory*, using the *CD* (change directory) command, or by mouse pointer selection, if you are using a Windows application.

The contents of the working directory can be viewed using the DIR (directory) command at the directory prompt. The Novell Netware equivalent is NDIR, which can display more information than DIR, including the access rights (see later) you have within the current directory (the one in which you execute the command). Network commands can only be used if you are logged in (they are held in the Public directory - see Figure 26.4).

Using a Wild Card

```
F:\ROBERTO\PRODUCTS\FINALDRW>dir *.cdr
```

Figure 26.13. *Using a wild card to list directory contents*

A wild card allows the user to broaden the scope of a command. For example, to display details of files created with CoreDraw (file extension *.cdr*) could be entered as shown in Figure 26.13. The current directory is shown and the command is entered after the > prompt. A wild card can also be used with the NDIR command.

File Housekeeping

File Manager

A file manager is a software *utility* that forms part of the *operating system.* It provides facilities associated with the management of the disk file storage system and allows you to:

- keep backup copies of important files;
- remove files and create space for new ones;
- list the details of files in a given directory;
- sort files into particular sequences.

These housekeeping operations can sometimes be carried out from within the software package you are using, but are more efficiently dealt with through the file manager utility or the command line (such as the MS-DOS prompt).

Copying Files

It is advisable to keep at least one additional copy of work on a separate floppy disk, particularly if the work has taken a long time to prepare. It is almost inevitable that at some point, whether you are using the network drive or floppy disk storage, that a fault will occur or that you will accidentally erase work and the computer will be unable to retrieve it. Taking regular and frequent backup copies of your work is an important habit to develop if you are to use a computer effectively. This can be done in one of three ways:

- by copying the individual file or a group of files that you wish to secure to a
  separate disk;
- by copying the complete contents of one disk to another disk;
- by copying the files to another directory.

The first method is appropriate for individual working, because you tend to work on only one file at a time. The second method makes a replica of the disk contents, even blank areas and is suited to situations where a number of files have changed, as would occur in a business operation. The huge storage capacity of a network drive means that it is not practical to use floppy disks to secure its contents; instead special devices called *tape streamers* or other high capacity disk storage devices are used as backup systems. The backing up of the network drive is the responsibility of the network supervisor, but you should take responsibility for the security of files within your directory. You should, know how to carry out both the file and disk copying (for a second backup) procedures to secure your own files on floppy disk.

Erasing Files

To ensure that your disk space is efficiently used, you will need to erase files which are no longer needed. Apart from creating space for new files, you will find that the presence of numerous unwanted files makes it more difficult to find those you do want. Erasing an individual file involves linking the appropriate command to its *filename* and *extension*, either by keying it in or selecting it with the mouse. Most operating systems will prompt you to confirm the operation before executing it, thus allowing you to cancel an accidental file selection. The operating system should also allow you to erase groups of files with the use of a *wild card* symbol. Thus, for example, giving MS/DOS the command shown in Figure 26.14

```
F:\ROBERTO\STAFFMAG>erase a:*.doc
```

Figure 26.14. *MS-DOS command to erase a group of files with the same file extension*

removes all files in the working directory (STAFFMAG), with the file extension 'doc'. Clearly you must be particularly careful in the use of this facility. The Windows graphical user interface allows you to select a group of files to be deleted (see Figure 26.15).

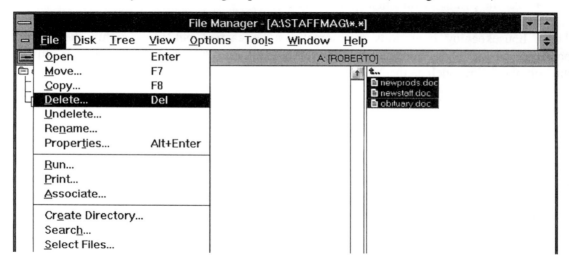

Figure 26.15. *File Manager used to a erase group of files*

Finding Files

This facility may be available within an application package. A *file search* or *find* option is often provided with the *file manager* utility. Clearly, such a facility is useful if you have forgotten the precise file name and possibly the name of the directory in which it is stored. If the file is stored on floppy disk, there shouldn't be too much difficulty in finding a particular file; the task may be more difficult if you have numerous subdirectories in your network user directory. You may lose track of, for example, a *document file* (word processed file) because you have not saved it to the usual directory for that category of work. You can target the search to particular directories, to a group of directories or to an entire disk. The following list provides some examples of file search criteria.

• complete filename, plus extension; for example, 'staffing.doc'.

- partial filename, plus wild card symbol and file extension; for example, st*.doc, which would search for all filenames beginning with 'st' and ending with the file extension 'doc'.
- no filename, plus extension; for example, '*.doc', which would limit the search to files with the extension 'doc'.
- filename, plus wild card for extension; for example, staffing.*, which would search for files with the filename 'staffing' and any extension.

Access Rights

Network storage is shared, so access to it needs to be carefully controlled. Thus, users should only be able to gain access to those directories and files which they need and are authorised to use.

There are a number of different rights, each of which permits a certain operation to be carried out in respect of a file or directory. The rights for files and directories are the same. The directory and file operations available to a user are determined by their rights. Rights only relate to the use of network storage and are not relevant to the integral drives of a workstation. The examples given here relate to the Novell Netware operating system. As explained in the section 'Logging in to the Network', when you are assigned user status, you are given particular rights concerning:

- network applications (*executables*), which you can only access and run;
- access to your default user directory and data files within it. These are broadly unrestricted, although the physical space allocation is likely to be set. You can create and modify a directory structure to suit your work requirements and you have full housekeeping rights concerning the files within that structure.

	Right	Meaning
S	Supervisory	Unrestricted in the directory. Can grant rights to other users.
R	Read	Can open files, read contents and run programs in the directory.
W	Write	Can open and alter the contents of files in the directory.
C	Create	Can create new files and subdirectories in the directory.
E	Erase	Can erase directory, sub-directories and files contained in them
M	Modify	Can alter file attributes or names
F	File Scan	Can see files and directories covered by this right.
A	Access Control	Can alter trustee assignments in a given directory.

Table 26.1. *Novell Netware directory and file access rights*

Table 26.1 lists the directory and file rights, which can be assigned with the Novell Netware 3.12 operating system. Following the table are brief explanations on the significance of each type for network operation and security. You need to be familiar with the various directory and file rights when you set up a new user on the network and give other users access to your files. The 8 rights shown in Table 26.1 can be granted in respect of a given *directory* and will thus be restricted to that directory (except in the case of *inherited rights* - not dealt with in this text). Rights can also be related to specific *files*. Table 26.2 gives typical circumstances when a user needs some of the rights in Table 26.1.

Operation	Rights Needed
Create a new directory	Create
Execute a program (an *executable* file)	Read, File Scan
Erase a file	Erase
See a filename	File Scan
Look through a directory for files	File Scan
Copy files to another directory	Write, Create, File Scan
Rename a directory or file	Modify
Create a file and write to it.	Create.

Table 26.2. *Rights needed for example directory and file operations*

Default Rights

When a Novell server is set up, a SUPERVISOR user is created, with S(upervisory) rights in all directories. A user group called EVERYONE is also created, to which all new users are assigned, unless the supervisor creates other groups in which to place them. The EVERYONE group members are given the following default rights.

(i)   *C(reate)* in the SYS: MAIL directory, which contains a sub-directory for every user (not their data directory). Each sub-directory contains the relevant user's *login script* (see Directories and Sub-directories).

(ii)   R(ead) and F(ile Scan) in the SYS:PUBLIC, which holds the executable network operating system commands for users (for example: NDIR and NCOPY).

Additional rights need to be assigned to allow users to run applications software. From Table 26.2, you can see that a user would need R(ead) and F(ile Scan) rights to the directory containing the required applications. The methods by which users can be assigned rights are dealt with in the next section on User Administration.

User Administration

Four categories of *Novell user* need to be identified:

(i).   *SUPERVISOR.* This user has unrestricted access and operational power in any part of the network server for which he or she is responsible. The network administrator will be the only SUPERVISOR user.

(ii) *Console Operator. Security equivalence* enables a user to be given the same rights as another, so although there is only one SUPERVISOR user for a Novell file server, another person can be given the same rights by being given supervisor equivalence. *Console Operator* is the term given to a person given supervisor equivalence.

(iii) *Workgroup Manager.* The network administrator can create this category of user if it is necessary to give another person *supervisory* rights over a particular volume or directory. This is useful if another person is to be given responsibility for their own users and data.

(iv) *User.* This is the ordinary user, who has no supervisory rights and whose access to any part of the network is controlled by user *account restrictions.* Accounts also exist for the special users in (i), (ii) and (iii). When a new user is installed, he or she becomes part of the group EVERYONE, every member of which is assigned R(ead) and F(ileScan) rights (Tables 1 and 2) to the SYS:PUBLIC directory and SYS:MAIL (see earlier - Directories and Sub-directories). Additional rights can be assigned directly to the user, or by making him or her a member of a group, which has additional rights. Alternatively, additional rights can be given to all users by altering the rights of the group EVERYONE.

Groups

Network administration can become very complex if file and directory rights are separately assigned to each user. A much better method is to create groups. By making a user a member of a particular group, the rights of that group are automatically assigned to that user. Most users can be dealt with in this way. Figure 26.4 shows a network server's directory structure, which reflects some of the functional activities in a business. The figure shows that there are directories for Sales, Finance and Design. Clearly, the staff in the Accounts department are going to need access to the same files (customer Sales Ledger, for example), which are held in the Finance directory. Equally, they are likely to need access to the same accounts applications and will need R(ead) and F(ile Scan) rights in the Pegasus directory (this contains executable files for the accounts software). By creating a group called 'ACCOUNT', and assigning the appropriate rights to it, staff in the Accounts Department can be added to the group and gain the necessary rights automatically. If a member of the Accounts department moves to another job within the business, they can be transferred to another group (with rights to access other directories and files) and their rights will be modified accordingly.

How Rights Can Be Assigned

The ways in which a network administrator can assign rights are illustrated in Figures 26.16, 26.17 and 26.18.

Figure 26.16. *Individual rights assigned directly to user*

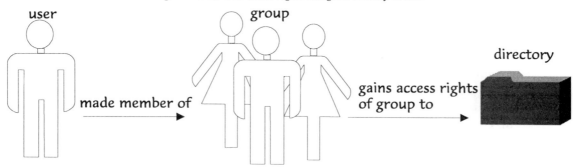

Figure 26.17. *Assigned rights through group membership*

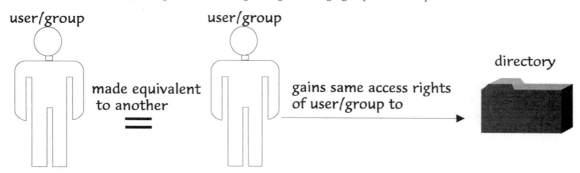

Figure 26.18. *Assigned rights by user/group equivalence.*

Unless a user has very particular requirements, then the most appropriate method (Figure 26.17) of giving rights is to assign users to a group which has the assigned rights he or she needs. Another useful method of giving a user or group the same rights as another is to use *security equivalence* (Figure 26.18). This is the method used by the network administrator to give a console operator the same rights as the SUPERVISOR user (the network administrator).

Directory and File Trustees

Each directory and file on a file server has a *trustee list*, which specifies the users who can use that storage area. The rights granted to a trustee, by whatever method (Figures 26.16,

26.17 and 26.18) dictate the kind of access the trustee is allowed to have. Thus, a user or group of users can be trustees of multiple directories and files, but the rights they have in each may be different. Thus, for example, SALES user group may be a trustee of the Accounts directory, but their access rights may be limited to R(ead) and F(ile Scan). This would allow members of that group to view, for example, customer details and amounts owing, but not modify them or erase them. The SALES group may also be trustee of the Orders directory, with the additional rights of C(reate), W(rite) and E(rase). Each member of the user group, would also be a member in his or her own right, and have full rights, within their default data directory.

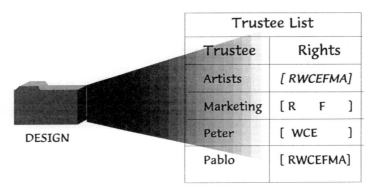

Trustee List	
Trustee	Rights
Artists	[RWCEFMA]
Marketing	[R F]
Peter	[WCE]
Pablo	[RWCEFMA]

DESIGN

Figure 26.19. *A directory trustee list, showing access rights of trustees*

Figure 26.19 shows a directory's trustee list, together with the access rights of each trustee. The letters in the 'Rights' column are the initial letters of the access rights detailed in Table 26.1.

Creating Users with SYSCON (System Console)

The Novell Netware operating system provides a utility called SYSCON (System Configuration), primarily for use by the network administrator. The opening screen appears as shown in Figure 26.20.

SUPERVISOR User and Workgroup Managers

SYSCON and other utilities, such as FILER (for network storage management) are held in a Private directory, which is not visible to users generally. The network administrator is a special user, referred to in Novell Netware as SUPERVISOR, who has access to all the network utilities. The network administrator can make the SYSCON utility available to a Workgroup Manager, who is another special type of Novell user. A Workgroup Manager can create users or groups and manage their accounts, but does not replace the SUPERVISOR user, who still has full rights to manage all user accounts. Existing users and groups cannot be controlled by a Workgroup Manager, unless he or she has been given User Account Manager status by the SUPERVISOR user. The User Account Manager status will only apply to the users and groups assigned by the SUPERVISOR user. For security reasons, a Workgroup Manager is only given S(upervisory) rights in a specific volume or directory, enabling him or her to assign trustee rights to the users in that area only. For example, a Workgroup Manager may have control over the Design directory shown in Figure 26.4.

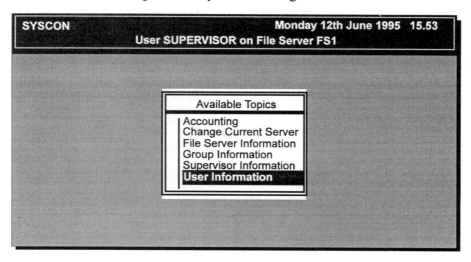

Figure 26.20. *SYSCON utility main menu*

Creating a New User

The steps described here assume use of a Novell Netware system, although the principles are applicable to client/server network operating systems generally. You are assumed to have the status of Workgroup Manager, with responsibility for the directory, called 'Design', which is a sub-directory of the 'Users' directory and is shown in the file structure in Figure 26.4. The SUPERVISOR user has given you S(upervisory) rights in the Design directory. You can create and delete users with trustee rights in that directory. For obvious reasons, you cannot make yourself, or any other user, a SUPERVISOR equivalent. No existing users have been assigned to you. The following list summarises the steps you can follow, with the SYSCON utility, to create a new user and assign initial rights.

1. Login as the Workgroup Manager (you have been assigned the user name 'Artist', which is separate from your regular user name, and a password);

2. Run the SYSCON utility (see Figure 26.20);

3. Create a new user, Fabio and make his default directory a sub-directory of the Design directory (see Figure 26.4). Ensure that he has all rights, except S(upervisory) in his own directory. Make Fabio a trustee of the Design Directory with R(ead), F(ile Scan), W(rite), C(reate) and E(rase);

4. Set Fabio's user account restrictions, including password requirements.

5. Create Fabio's User Login Script to map the network drive (F:) to his home directory. This means that when he logs in this will be the active directory.

6. Exit SYSCON and logout;

7. Login as Fabio and check his trustee rights in the Design and his home directory.

Creating User 'Fabio'

To create this new user you carry out the following steps.

1. Select 'User Information' from the SYSCON main menu. A list of users appears.

2. Press the <Insert> key and a text box appears for you to enter a new name. Enter ' Fabio' and then the path to his directory. This is shown in Figure 26.4, as SYS:Users\Design\Fabio. You are then asked to confirm creation of the directory.

Assigning Fabio's Home Directory Trustee Rights

1. From the SYSCON opening menu, choose the 'User Information' option. When the user list appears, select Fabio and press the <Enter> key. The resulting list of options is shown in Figure 26.21.

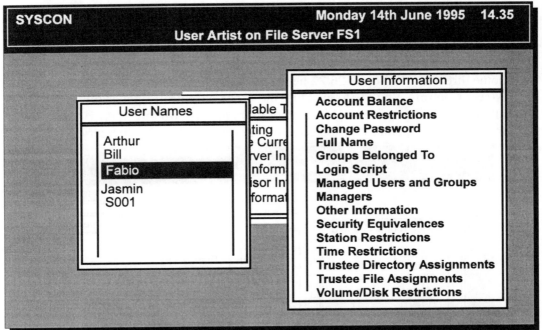

Figure 26.21. *User Information Options*

2. Select the 'Trustee Directory Assignments' option from the User Information options. A list of the directories in which Fabio has trustee rights is then listed, as shown in Figure 26.22.

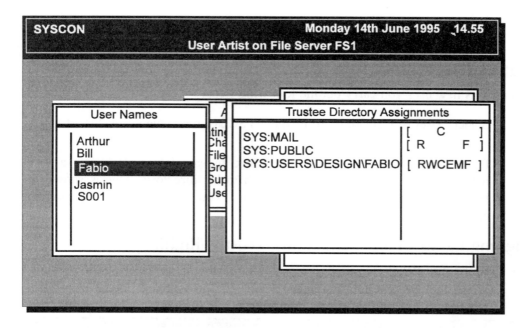

Figure 26.22. *Trustee Directory Assignments for Fabio*

Fabio is automatically a member of the group EVERYBODY and gains the trustee rights which the SUPERVISOR user has set as the default for a user's home directory. In Figure 26.22 he has all rights but S(upervisory) and A(cess Control). You are to give him the A(ccess Control) right as this will allow him to give trustee rights to other users for his own directory. He can then designate another user to access the files in his (Fabio's) directory.

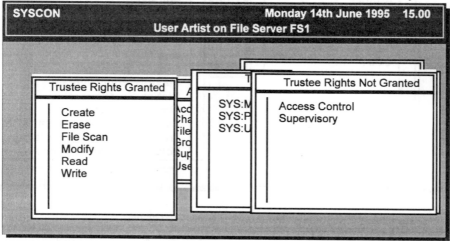

Figure 26.23. *Trustee rights not granted list for Fabio*

3. Referring to Figure 26.23, we can give Fabio the A(ccess Control) right in his home directory, by: choosing the SYS:USERS\DESIGN\FABIO directory;

pressing the <Enter> key and then <Insert> and the 'Trustee Rights Not Granted' list appears.

4. Select the A(ccess Control) right and press <Enter> to add this to Fabio's list of rights granted. Press <Escape> to apply the changes.

Making Fabio a Trustee of the Design Directory

You need to ensure that Fabio's existing Trustee Directory Assignments are displayed (see previous stage).

In the Trustee Directory Assignments window, press the <Insert> key and you will be prompted for the directory path for the new assignment. Make it SYS:USERS\DESIGN. You can then assign the R(ead), F(ile Scan), C(reate), W(rite) and E(rase), by following the same procedure used for his home directory assignments.

Mapping the Network Drive to Fabio's Home Directory

Choose Login Script from the User Information window in SYSCON (see Figure 26.20). The *user* login script is executed (unless the *system* login script is used as a default) as part of the login process and ensures that initially, a user is in his or her home directory. Enter the mapping statement shown in Figure 26.24.

```
MAP F:\USERS\DESIGN\FABIO
```

Figure 26.24. *Mapping command in User Login Script for Fabio*

If you don't want the user to be presented with the full path, namely 'F:\users\design\fabio', you can use the ROOT command to hide the path and just present the user with the network drive letter (F:\>). This presents a less complicated view of the network drive to the user, having the same appearance as the root directories on the C: and A: drives in the workstation. The full command is shown in Figure 26.25.

```
MAP ROOT F:\USERS\DESIGN\FABIO
```

Figure 26.25. *Mapping command to hide path and simply display F:\>*

Setting Account Restrictions

Figure 26.21 shows the User Information list. Two options are of particular importance in controlling a user's access to the network: 'Account Restrictions'; 'Change Password'. Each user account includes properties which place limits on the user's initial access to the network (during login). Login security is supported by Account Restrictions on:

• the allocation of a user name;

- requiring a password of minimum length; the settings may also require, for example, periodic password change. A user can be allowed or prevented from making their own password changes.
- limiting the times during which a user can login.

The Change Password option allows the Supervisor to initially set and subsequently alter a user's password. By setting default account restrictions, from the Supervisor options menu, all users can be controlled by basic settings. If special controls are required for individual users, then this can be done separately. You can practise these procedures on Fabio's account.

Enabling Other Users to Access Your Files

There may be occasions when a user wishes to make their own files available to another user or user group. This can be achieved by making the user or user group a *trustee* of the relevant directory. We will assume that the directory is your default, which is assigned to you and identified by your user name. Normally, you will have all rights in your own directory. To make another user or group a trustee, you must have the A(ccess Control) right (see Table 26.1). For this procedure, you do not need to be a Workgroup Manager. Although SYSCON can be used, you can also make use of the GRANT command (at the command line prompt). The format of the command is as shown in Figure 26.26.

```
GRANT rightslist . . . [FOR path] TO [USER | GROUP] name
```

Figure 26.26. *Format of GRANT command*

You can use ALL after GRANT, if you want to assign all rights to the trustee user or group. Figure 26.27 shows an example, where user Fabio (see Figure 26.4 for the directory structure) makes user Gianna a trustee of his own default directory (users\design\fabio), with all rights except S(upervisory) and A(ccessControl). As the command is being issued from the user's default directory, no *path* needs to be specified.

```
GRANT r w c e m TO USER gianna
```

Figure 26.27. *Example use of GRANT command*

Use the REVOKE command to remove Gianna's trustee rights, as shown in Figure 26.28 (you can list specific rights if you want some to remain).

```
REVOKE ALL FROM USER gianna
```

Figure 26.28. *Removing trustee rights with the REVOKE command*

Communicating Across the Network

Electronic mail (e-mail) or messaging, as it is sometimes called when referring to a LAN, is an increasingly important function for many organisations. In the same way that you have to have a user account to login to the network, e-mail systems allow the creation of user accounts and the allocation of password requirements. Like all network resources, it needs to be controlled and protected from misuse. Your user name is used to allocate an 'in tray' where messages addressed to you are stored. If you wish to send a message to another user or group of users, you assign addressing instructions before the message is despatched. Messages are held on the network drive until cleared, so a user does not have to be logged into the network when the message is received in his or her in tray. For more details on electronic mail systems, please refer to Computer Networks in the Knowledge Resource.

In-house Standards

In-house standards, adopted by an organisation for network use, can be crucial to the security, reliability and effiency of their networked computer systems. For example, the logging in procedure identifies the requirement for a user name and, if required, a password. In-house standards would apply to the allocation of user names and passwords. Thus, users' names may have to follow a particular format, perhaps starting with a code identifying the user's department. Passwords may have to be a minimum of, say, 6 characters and may have to be changed every two weeks.

User Identification

Before allowing login, the network operating system requires identification of the user, through entry of the user name and a password. An organisation can set standards concerning both. These standards will be implemented through *user account restrictions*; typically they allow setting of:

- user name formats; standards could determine a strict format for the assignment of user names. For example, each user name may have to begin with a 3 character code, which identifies their department;
- a minimum password length. The organisation may set a standard minimum length and this can be enforced through the network user's account. The longer the password, the less likely it is that others will guess it, or identify it from watching the keys that the user presses.
- requirement for a periodic password change or a unique password (can only be used once). The organisation may require each user to renew his or her password every week. Infrequent changes increase the likelihood that passwords will not remain secret. Unique (once only) passwords are appropriate for users who only have occasional need to access the network. Each occasion is specially authorised though the assignment of a unique password.

- login restricted to certain days or times of day; if the network remains active after normal office hours, for a restricted group of users, other users can be excluded by placing time limits on their accounts.
- number of 'grace' logins after expiry of the user's password; a user may be allowed, say, three logins after password expiry and if the password is not renewed within that period, the user is locked out. Reference then has to be made to the network supervisor to regain entry. The organisation's standards may require that such circumstances are reported to, for example, the relevant Head of Department, before the user account is unlocked.

Intruder Lockout

After a certain number of unsuccessful attempts, a user will be locked out and will have to ask the supervisor to allow further attempts. The network software may record such attempts and these may form part of the organisation's security system; standards could require that intruder lockouts are reported to a senior member of staff, for further investigation.

Security Conventions

The section on Security in the Knowledge Resource identifies four aspects of network security:

- the control of *access to resources* (hardware, software and data);
- the prevention of *unauthorised access*;
- the *protection of resources* from damage, loss, or corruption;
- the maintenance of *data privacy*.

Clearly, the standards set by an organisation for user identification and intruder lockout contribute to all these aspects of network security. Control of initial entry to the network is important, but once users are logged into the network, their activities need to be controlled. File security is an important feature of this control.

File Security

When a network is set up, a single *volume* may be used for all network storage needs, or for greater security, it may be divided into two or more volumes according to, for example, the functional areas of the organisation. One volume may be for Sales, another for Accounts and another for Manufacturing. Within each volume, directories are created to separate executable files (application programs and utilities) from data files. Further divisions are often needed to separate groups of applications, according to the needs of different groups of users. Finally, user directories have to be created in a way which allows them to be secured from one another. The hierarchical tree structure, typically used to achieve these divisions is illustrated in Figure 26.4, earlier in this chapter.

An organisation's in-house standards will determine what form the structure takes and the way that it arrives at the structure. It may, for example, rely on the network specialists within the organisation or it may require full involvement by users.

The organisation must set standards to ensure that directory and file rights (see Access Rights):

- are assigned in such a way that users only have access to the network resources they need for the fulfilment of their duties.

The network supervisor has unlimited rights and has responsibility for assigning directory and file rights to users and user groups. Although the network supervisor is probably the technical expert, with regard to this work, he or she would probably be responsible to a senior person in the organisation. Before rights are assigned, for example, to a directory containing payroll data, written permission may be needed by the Head of Department, or the Financial Director.

Copyright Requirements

In-house standards concerning copyright must accord with legal requirements. A computer program can now obtain the status of literary work and as such, retains protection for 50 years from the first publishing date. Computer software is now covered by the Copyright Designs and Patents Act 1988 and infringements include:

- the pirating of copyright protected software;
- the running of pirated software, in that a copy is created in memory;
- transmitting software over telecommunications links, thereby producing a copy.

The major software producers have funded an organisation called FAST (Federation Against Software Theft) which successfully lobbied for the inclusion of computer software in the above-mentioned Act. Network applications software is generally sold on a licence basis for a specified number of users. Thus, if a package is licensed to be used by 20 users, the licensee must ensure that this number is not exceeded; if further workstations are added and they have access to that same package, the licence must be extended accordingly.

Procedural Requirements

The procedures which various users are to follow when using the network must be clearly defined. There are general procedures which all users should follow, such as logging off when they have finished using a workstation, reporting faults to the network supervisor and ensuring that printing operations do not waste paper. There are other rules which apply to different categories of user. For example, a junior member of staff may require permission to use the network. Whatever the procedures, they should all have the aim of ensuring the security and efficient operation of the network. Its efficiency should be measured against its fulfilment or otherwise of the organisation's purposes for it. Thus, a network which is very secure, may be so restrictive that users cannot make appropriate use of its resources. This does not need to be the case; a network can be secure and still give a good service to its users.

Allocated Workspace

The capacity of a network's file server has to allow for the storage of network software, applications, and user data. To conserve space, the organisation should set standards on the amount of disk space allowed to each user. Clearly, some users will require much more space than others. A user with requirement to store a few items of correspondence may be allocated a megabyte, but 100 megabytes may be required for the Sales group to store customer records.

Chapter 27

Data Communications System Operation

Introduction

This chapter takes you through the practical aspects of using data communications hardware and software. The theoretical background to this subject is dealt with, in detail, in the Knowledge Resource, although one or two new concepts, particularly related to the use of modems are introduced here. The following sections explain how to:

- set up and use an interactive (conversational) data communications link between a microcomputer and a remote computer system;

- effect the transfer complete files between computers, either remotely, through the public switched telephone network (pstn) or through a *null modem* cable (see later).

Hardware Components

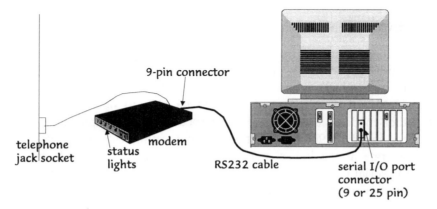

Figure 27.1. *Computer, RS232 cable, modem and telephone jack components*

Figure 27.1 shows the main hardware items (power cables are not shown) you need to link into a data communications network, through the pstn. Chapter 7 explains the need for a modem when a link is made to the analogue sections of the telecommunications network. Note from Figure 27.1 that the RS232 cable is a *serial* cable, which connects one of the computer's serial I/O ports (RS232 ports) to the modem. The connector at the modem end of the cable is usually a 9-pin D-connector, whilst the computer connector could be either a 9-pin or 25-pin D-connector.

Null Modem Cable

To set up communication between two computers in the same room (without modems), you need a *null modem* cable, which is an RS232 cable, with modified pin functions. Each machine must have the terminal software (see later) already described. The null modem cable is connected to a serial port in each machine and, effectively, each computer treats the other as a modem. The two machines must be fully compatible, although null modem devices allow the connection of incompatible devices.

Modem Features

Internal and External Modems

Figure 27.1 shows an external modem. An internal modem is a circuit board which plugs into one of the expansion slots inside the system casing (Chapter 6). An external modem requires a separate power supply and a spare serial port for connection to the computer, whereas an internal modem uses the computer's power supply and incorporates its own serial port. The main disadvantage of an internal modem (apart from the fact that it uses an expansion slot and has to be installed) is that there are no status lights to allow monitoring of the modem's activity. Communications software (see later) may include a program to show a bit map image (Chapter 5) of a modem's status panel, with which to monitor its operation. More is said about status lights later.

Modem Speeds

The speed with which a modem transmits data over a telephone line (its *connect* speed) is measured in bits per second (bps). A modem's quoted speed is generally its maximum and commonly available products quote 1200, 2400, 9600, 14400 or 28800bps. Although a modem has a maximum connect speed, it must be able to operate at lower speeds, for connection to other modems operating at those speeds. For example, if your modem has a maximum connect speed of 9600bps, but is communicating with a 2400bps modem, your modem has to operate at the lower speed. However, the rate at which data is sent to, or received from, the serial port does not have to be the same as the modem's connect speed and it can be higher if your modem uses *data compression* (see later).

CCITT Standards

The speeds quoted in the previous paragraph are associated with particular standards set by the CCITT standards body (Chapter 7). Table 27.1 shows maximum connect speeds and the relevant CCITT standards (*bis* means an improvement on the previous standard). Although some modem manufacturers quote other speeds, such as 16800 or 19200bps, they are not CCITT standards and can only communicate at those speeds, with other modems of the same type.

Speed (bps)	CCITT Standard
1200	V22
2400	V22bis
9600	V32
14400	V32bis
28800	V34

Table 27.1. *CCITT speed standards*

Data Compression

This feature enables a modem to transmit data at a quicker rate than its connect speed. The number of bits per second does not alter, but by using fewer bits to represent the data, the effective transmission rate is increased. Like connect speed, a modem can only make use of its data compression facility if the modem to which it is connected can use the same compression method. Data compression relies on a range of techniques, too complex to examine here, but involves the removal of surplus characters and the use of a 'shorthand', where a single character can represent a whole 'word' or 'phrase'. CCITT's data compression standard is V42bis and is built into most modems. Not all types of data will compress to the same degree. V42bis compresses ordinary text to 25 per cent of its uncompressed size, but program (executable) files will only reduce to around 50 or 75 per cent. This means that, for example, a 2400bps can transmit text at an effective rate of 9600bps (4 x 2400); this is provided the receiving modem uses the same compression standard. Data compression is often to save space on computer storage; if a file is already compressed or 'zipped', it will only be transmitted at the modem's connect speed (the modem cannot compress it any further). Obviously, higher speed transmission can bring major cost savings if large files are being transferred over long distances.

Error Correction

A range of error detection and correction techniques is described in Chapter 7. They are needed because ordinary telephone lines are subject to interference, such as static, and can corrupt the data. The CCITT standard is V42, but a manufacturer standard called MNP 1-4 is also widely used.

Status Lights and Speaker

Audible output from a modem can be used to monitor its operation, for example, when it is dialling and making the connection with the remote modem. Status lights on the front of the modem (see Figure 27.1) also give such indications, plus clear identification of other states, including *carrier detect* (CD - connection is made), *transmitting data* (TD) and *receiving data* (RD).

FAX/data Modem

A fax/data modem enables a computer to send or receive data in the encoded form used by fax machines. A document you create with your word processor can be faxed directly from your hard drive to another machine with a fax/data modem, or to a conventional fax machine. Incoming faxes can be saved to disk and printed if required. A fax document is in bit map form (Chapter 5) so cannot be edited without first converting it to text with the use of *optical character recognition* (OCR) software. A problem with an incoming fax is that it cannot be paused, so the machine needs to be able to multi-task (Chapter 2); Microsoft Windows and the OS/2 operating systems operate in this way. Even so an incoming fax can use a great deal of memory and slow down the machine's operation considerably during the process.

Terminal Software

Figure 27.2 shows the *settings* menu for Terminal in Windows. The various options are explained in the following paragraphs. The word 'terminal' does not mean that the software is 'on its last legs'! The primary function of terminal software is to enable the whole communication process, in both directions. Although the sophistication of different products varies widely (and Terminal in Windows is rather basic), all terminal software includes certain essential facilities to select:

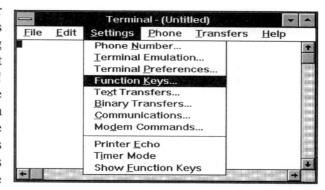

Figure 27.2. *Settings options*

- the serial (COM) port address;
- baud rate (see Modem Speed earlier);
- the type of terminal *emulation* to be used;
- terminal *preferences*.

COM Port Address

The Communications option in Figure 27.2 allows the setting of a COM port address (see Figure 27.4) for the attached modem. A microcomputer usually has, at least, two serial ports, which on MS-DOS machines, are *addressed* as COM1, COM2, COM 3 and so forth. These are names for locations in the computer's main memory, which are used for the storage of data which is to be output to the modem or, as incoming data to be received from it. In other words, it is the point of exchange for data passing between the serial port (and thereby the attached modem device) and the computer's memory. Figure 27.3 illustrates this idea.

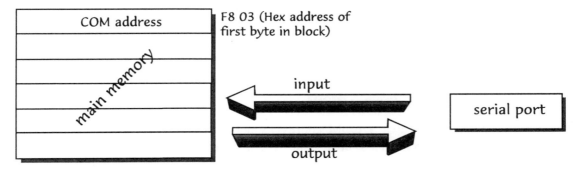

F8 03 (Hex address of first byte in block)

Figure 27.3. *Memory block allocated to a COM address and used for serial I/O*

Part of the modem installation process requires that you set the COM (1, 2, etc.) address used by the serial port, to which the modem is connected; the setting is carried out through the terminal software. Figure 27.4 shows the dialogue box presented by Terminal (Windows 3.1) for the various Communication settings.

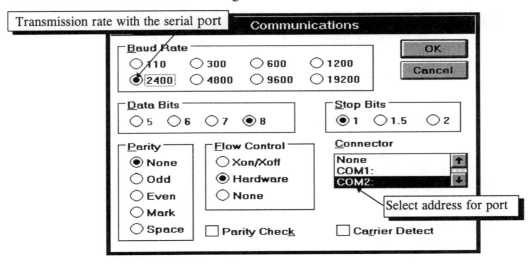

Figure 27.4. *Communications settings in Terminal (Windows 3.1)*

Before assigning a COM address to the required serial port, you need to discover which ones are already being used by other port(s). If there are only two serial ports on the machine, one will use COM1 and the other COM2. Sometimes, the ports may be labelled on the system casing. Thus, for example, if the mouse is plugged into a port marked 'COM1', this means that the COM1 address is in use. If there is no labelling, then you need to use software to determine which COM address is assigned to the serial port for the modem. There are a number of ways of doing this, the simplest probably being to use Terminal (Figure 27.4) to select a COM address through the Communications option. If, for example, you select COM1 and it responds with the message, "The selected COM port is either not supported or is being used by another device", then try COM2 (if the machine only has two serial ports, then the free port for the modem will be using COM2). If there are three or four serial ports, you will have to try selecting each COM address in turn until one is accepted. The phrase "not supported" means that there is no serial port with this address (the port does not exist).

Although MS-DOS refers to the port addresses as COM1, 2, 3 and 4, the actual memory address used by a port is referred to by its *hexadecimal* (base 16) representation. The hexadecimal addresses may be as follows.

```
F803    F802    0000    0000

COM1    COM2    COM3    COM4
```

The address 0000 indicates that a COM address is not allocated to a serial port; in other words the port does not exist. The above table would indicate that the machine in question only has two serial ports. This list of COM addresses can be found by loading the DEBUG utility at the MS-DOS prompt, then typing D40:00. The first row of the table which appears provides the COM addresses. Figure 27.6 shows that these addresses can be found through the Ports option in the Control Panel of Microsoft Windows.

IRQ Address

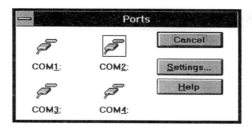

Figure 27.5. *Ports settings dialogue*

A port also needs an *interrupt request* (IRQ) address (labelled IRQ3 and IRQ4) in memory, to receive an interrupt from the attached modem that there is incoming data. When the processor receives an interrupt, it determines

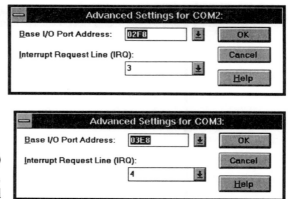

Figure 27.6. *COM and IRQ settings*

its source and then accesses the appropriate IRQ address in memory. The processor then 'knows' that incoming data has been received into the associated COM address, for example, COM1 (F803$_{hex}$). The IRQ address in memory is used by the port to draw the processor's attention to the fact that data, received through the port, is in memory and waiting to be read, in this example, from COM1. Figure 27.5 shows the Ports option in Microsoft Windows' Control Panel, which is used to set the default COM and IRQ addresses, and Figure 27.6 the settings for COM2 and COM3. Every COM port needs an exclusive IRQ address, if it is used at the same time as another port. If, for example, you assign a serial mouse port to COM3 and a modem to COM1, and both are allocated IRQ4, to use the modem, you would first have to unload the mouse driver software. The settings in Control Panel are initial settings and can be altered as required through the terminal software (see Figure 27.4).

Terminal Emulation

A terminal emulation program makes your microcomputer operate as a dedicated computer terminal. The need for such programs stems from the continued practice of using *dumb* terminals (see Chapter 8) which can only be used with their associated mainframe computer. Having said that, most mainframes now support a range of terminal types. If you want to use your microcomputer to communicate with a

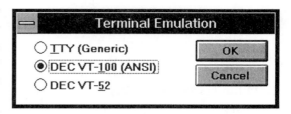

Figure 27.7. *Terminal emulation types*

remote IBM mainframe you have to use a terminal emulation type which it understands. Otherwise, the keys you press may mean something entirely different to the remote mainframe. Figure 27.7 shows the terminal emulation types available in Terminal; these are the most commonly used by mainframe computers which provide database services. If you want to be absolutely certain that the remote mainframe can understand your terminal, you can use *TTY generic*. The drawback is that TTY (Teletype) only provides plain text and will not display any colours or provide any cursor control (which makes normal editing impossible). DEC VT-100(ANSI - American National Standards Institute) terminal emulation is the most suitable choice, as it is widely supported and includes colour and cursor control, as well as a range of special functions. Of course to operate your keyboard as a particular terminal type, you need to know what changes are made to key functions. The Microsoft Windows User's Guides provides a conversion table for each terminal type it supports.

Baud Rate - the Port Speed

When your modem establishes a communication link, part of the *handshaking* (Chapter 7) process is to establish the *connect speed* (see Modem Speeds). If the modem's have different maximum speeds, then the lower speed must be used.

In Figure 27.4, the *port speed setting* is 2400 baud (or bits per second), which means that the terminal software communicates with the serial port at that rate. This setting does not dictate the speed that the modem uses when it makes a connection over the telephone line (some modems are capable of dropping their own speed to that of the remote modem and indicate to the terminal software that the baud rate is dropped). The serial port is, therefore, able to communicate with the terminal software at one speed and with the modem at a different speed. If you set the port speed at a lower speed than the modem's speed, the communication will take place at the lower rate.

Data compression (see earlier) means that your port speed (baud rate - see Figure 27.4) can be greater than the modem's connect speed. For example, if the connect speed is 2400bps and the data can be compressed to a quarter of its original size, then you should use the terminal software (see later) to set the port's baud rate to 4 times 2400, which is 9600 baud. If the modem uses data compression and has the facility to automatically drop the port's baud rate to its own connect speed, you should disable this facility; otherwise the data compression advantage is lost. If the modem does not incorporate data compression, the port speed should be limited to the modem's maximum connect speed. Figure 27.8 illustrates the difference between port speed and connect speed.

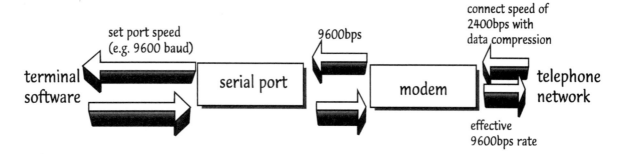

Figure 27.8. *Port and modem speeds (with data compression)*

Handshaking Protocols

A protocol is a set of rules, which in this context, is agreed (by handshaking) between communicating devices. They comprise:

- number of data bits;

- parity setting;

- number of stop bits.

The meanings and purposes of parity and stop bits are given in Chapter 7. Figure 27.4, earlier, shows the Terminal dialogue for Communications settings, which include these three protocol elements. The figure shows that the current settings are 8 data bits, no parity and 1 stop bit per character (sometimes written as 8-N-1). This protocol is the norm for communicating PCs.

Connection to a mainframe usually requires 7-E-1, or 7 data bits, even parity and 1 stop bit. Occasionally, a protocol may use one-and-a-half or two stop bits.

Flow Control - XON/XOFF and RTS/CTS

The meaning of term *flow control* is explained in Chapter 7, but the settings in Figure 27.4 display the option of XON/XOFF. If this setting is enabled, then flow control is monitored by the terminal software. When the modem's buffer is nearly full, it signals the terminal software, which responds with an XOFF (stop data flow) character. When the modem is ready to receive more data, it signals the terminal software, which then restarts the data flow by sending an XON character to the modem.

If a modem incorporates hardware flow control, then XON/XOFF should be disabled and RTS/CTS enabled. RTS (*ready to send*) and CTS (*clear to send*) are control lines within the RS232 cable and are used for hardware flow control. The terminal software needs to know which is being used. RTS/CTS operates as follows.

The terminal software signals the modem to keep receiving data as long as RTS is on (high); thus RTS is for flow control from modem to computer. When the terminal software switches RTS off (low), the attached modem signals the remote sending modem to pause transmission, until RTS is switched on again. CTS has the reverse function. The modem uses CTS to signal the terminal software to stop or start sending data to the modem. Thus, RTS gives the computer the ability to start and stop data flow and CTS enables the modem to do the same, depending on whether the data is incoming or outgoing.

Carrier Detect

When your modem dials a connection number (having first waited for a dialling tone), it looks for a *carrier wave* from the remote modem. This is, effectively, waiting for the modem to answer. When the handshaking is complete, the CD (*carrier detect*) status light (Figure 27.1) is illuminated. The carrier wave is the remote modem's response to your modem's handshake signals. If the carrier wave is not detected then connection has not been made. This is a bit like ringing a person and getting no answer.

Terminal Preferences

Figure 27.9 shows Terminal's preference options, the significance of which can be briefly explained as follows.

- Line length obviously determines the number of characters which are displayed across the screen before wrapping onto the next line; usually, the setting can remain at 80.

- Line wrap. In word processing this is referred to as *word wrap*, but it means the same thing; enabled, it ensures that characters are wrapped onto a new line once the number of characters on a line reaches the specified line length. When line wrap is not enabled and incoming data exceeds the line length (for example, a 132 character line), you have to scroll horizontally to see complete lines.

- CR->CR/LF. A carriage return (CR) takes the cursor to the beginning of the line, whereas a carriage return plus line feed (CR->LF) also takes the cursor onto the next line. In the case of inbound data, enabling this option would add a line feed for every carriage return character. If the remote computer is also sending line feed characters, you would see a blank line between each line, so you only use this option if you see that lines are being printed on top of one another (that no line feeds are being received). The outbound selection adds a line feed for every carriage return character which is transmitted.

- Translation. Unfortunately, this does not mean that your English can be translated into another language! It simply means that you can specify another country's character set for transmission or receipt of text in that language.

- Local echo. Enabling this option causes every keystroke you make to be echoed on screen, which is only necessary if the link to the remote system is half duplex (Chapter 7). A full duplex link allows the remote computer to echo your key presses back to your screen. So, enabling this option when communicating over a full duplex link results in tthhiiss hhaappeenniinngg!!

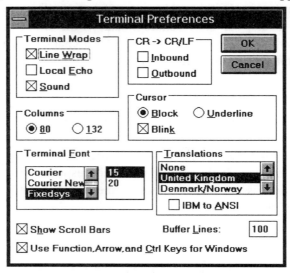

Figure 27.9. *Terminal preferences*

File Transfer

This topic and that of file transfer protocols are examined in Chapter 7, but more of the practical aspects are dealt with here. Terminal in Windows only offers two, Xmodem and Kermit. The latter is slower, but has the benefit of being suitable for file transfers between computers of every type and over any form of serial transmission link. Xmodem is the most widely

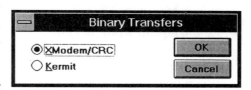

Figure 27.10. *File transfer protocols*

used protocol and ensures that files arrive uncorrupted, which is vitally important for executable files. Ymodem and Zmodem are more sophisticated transfer files much more rapidly than Xmodem or Kermit and are available with many terminal software products. Terminal Plus (the producers of Terminal in Windows) provides these additional protocols.

Downloading Files

Internet (Chapter 8) makes 'the world your oyster', providing access to a seemingly limitless supply of information and software. Text, graphics and program files may be downloaded (retrieved) from, for example, remote mainframe databases and bulletin board systems (BBSs). Owing to the large number of files which may be found on an individual bulletin board, you need to have some idea of what you are looking for (call costs can be very high while you are browsing). Fortunately, a BBS will maintain an up-to-date catalogue of files, which you can download first and look at after you have disconnected the link. Further, many files are compressed. You can recognise compressed files by their file extension, common ones being: *.ZIP (PKZIP/UNZIP packs and unpacks); *.ARJ. To use them you need the appropriate utility to 'unpack' them.

Setting up Text and Binary File Transfers

The requirements for setting up a link with a remote computer have already been described and the following relates to the requirements for sending or receiving two types of files. *Text*, or *ASCII* files, are produced with a text editor or word processor and stored without any formatting. Your word processor may have a facility to save word processed documents as plain text files and thereby remove any formatting you have included. *Binary* files can be of any kind, including program or executable files, word processed document (with formatting) or ASCII text files. As explained in Chapter 7, using the ASCII protocol option is only appropriate for plain, unadorned text files. A transmission error may terminate the transfer and not error correction facility is available. Therefore, for most purposes, you should use binary file transfer, with one of the protocols (such as Xmodem) already mentioned.

Text File Transfer

Figure 27.11 shows Terminal's settings, all of which have already been explained, for ASCII file transfers and Figure 27.12 the selection of a file to send.

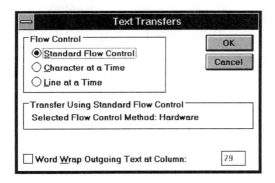

Figure 27.11. *Text file settings*

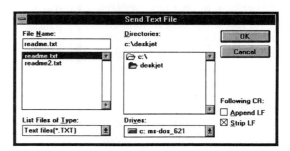

Figure 27.12. *Selecting text file to send*

When the file is transmitted, Terminal scrolls the text on screen. Receiving a file is a similar process, the text being scrolled onto the screen.

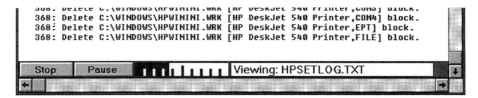

Figure 27.13. *Terminal during receipt of a text file*

Binary File Transfer

To send or receive a binary file you need to specify the type of protocol to be used (see Figure 27.10). If a file is corrupted because of a communications error, the transmitting system tries again. The Xmodem protocol permits 20 retries, but Kermit only allows 5. Figure 27.13, showing the receipt of a text file, includes a pause button, but this is not present when a binary file is being transferred. The transmission of a binary file must be uninterrupted if it is to be completed successfully.

Hanging Up

When you have completed a communications session, it is important that you:

1. execute the exit command required by the remote system, typically 'bye';

2. 'hangup' the phone, that is disconnect the modem. In Terminal, choose the Hangup option from the Phone menu.

If you hangup before you sign off from the remote system, its connection remains open and you may continue to be charged for the connect time (until the remote computer detects that the connection has been severed).

Modem Commands

Your terminal software needs to use the command set applicable to the attached modem. Figure 27.14 shows the command sets supported by Terminal. Your modem manual will tell you which command sets are supported. For example, many modems are Hayes-compatible, which means that Hayes commands are recognised. If your modem does not recognise

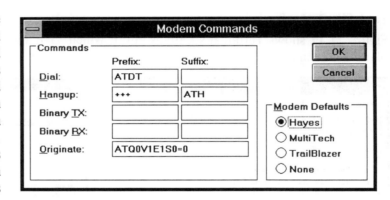

Figure 27.14. *Modem command sets*

any of the command sets, you can choose None and enter them by reference to the manufacturer's manual. The Hayes commands in Figure 27.14 can be explained as follows.

*   ATDT. 'AT' - gain the modem's attention; 'D' - tell modem get ready to dial; 'T' use touch tone dialling (as opposed to 'P' - pulse dial);

*   ATH is the command for 'hangup'.

Chapter 28

Automated Procedures

Introduction

The motivation for the development of high-level programming languages, and the production of software generally, has been the need to automate important information processing tasks. Programming languages allow complex tasks to be translated into forms that can be handled automatically by computers. Such *automated procedures* have two important advantages over manual methods, namely increasing the speed at which tasks can be performed and reducing the likelihood of errors being made. Because of the importance of high-level languages in computing, the whole of Chapter 18 is devoted to a discussion of their characteristics and uses.

However, the foregoing comments regarding the purpose of programming languages also apply to the many software systems that provide higher-level facilities for automating tasks. Three of these are described in the following sections. Note that the examples regarding the creation of templates and macros are based on Microsoft's Word for Windows; detailed, step by step instructions are not provided because they are immediately available from the on-line help provided with the word processor. Other programs which provide for the creation of templates and macros are likely to differ in the precise manner that they are handled, but they most probabaly will be identical in concept. The creation of batch files is related to MSDOS, and the comments made above regarding differences between similar items of software apply equally well to operating systems. A further, commonly used typed of automated procedure, is the mail merge facility frequently found in word processing packages. This procedure is described in Chapter 21.

Batch files

Operating systems allow you to create text files which contain sequences of operating system commands so that they can be executed one after the other automatically. (See Chapter 2). For example, you could create a batch file to display a menu of your favourite programs when you switch on your computer:

```
                  System Menu

      1.MS Windows

      2.Turbo Pascal

      3.Doom

      4.LBA

      5.Quit to DOS


  Type a number between 1 and 5:
```

Batch files also allow you to create directories, display lists of files, move files and delete files - in fact you can include sequences of any commands that the operating system provides. Batch files usually can be created with a word processor or any text editor that will allow you to save the file as plain text.

Templates

A *template* is a document to use as the basic pattern for other similar documents. When you create a new document from a template, you get an exact copy. You can save time and effort when creating new documents by basing them on templates designed for a specific type of document you create frequently. Many word processing, spreadsheet and graphics programs allow you to create templates. For example, in Word for Windows you could create a document template for your letters so that you do not have to put your address and the date at the top every time you writeto someone. The template contains everything that always appears on the document; you just add the extra information that is required, such as the text of your letter. A template for a company memo might look as follows:

M E M O R A N D U M

DATE: July 12, 1995

TO: [*Names*]

FROM: [*Names*]

RE: [*Subject*]

CC: [*Names*]

[*Type your memo text here*]

To create a template such as this (in Word for Windows) you simply save it as a document template. Later, when you want to use the template to produce an actual memo, you simply choose **New** from the **File** menu and then select the appropriate template from the list that you are presented with (see Figure 28.1).

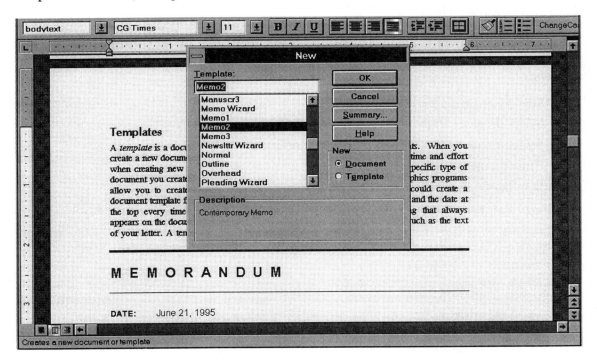

Figure 28.1. *Creating a document based on a template*

A document template in Word for Windows is a blueprint for the text, graphics, and formatting that are the same in every document of a particular type. Templates also store styles, macros, toolbar buttons, and customized menu and shortcut key settings that can simplify your work. Word provides templates for several common types of documents, such as memos, reports, and business letters. You can use these templates just as they are, you can modify them, or you can create your own templates. Word automatically bases new documents on the Normal template unless you specify another template. The Normal template is a general, all-purpose template for any document.

The same principal applies to spreadsheet programs such as Microsoft's Excel. For instance, you could create a tax form, a quarterly report, or an annual budget, save it as a template, and then use the template to insert data that varies every month, quarter, or year.

Macros

A *macro* is a custom-made command to allow users to perform complicated or frequently used operations with a single command. In Word for Windows macros can be created in two ways: by 'recording' a sequence of actions or by using the macro language, WordBasic. When a macro is recorded by instructing Word to 'remember' your sequence of keystrokes, a WordBasic macro is automatically generated. To repeat the sequence of recorded actions you simply run the macro. For example, you might want to create a macro to save a file in a certain directory automatically. Suppose you have a directory on drive C called \GNVQIT (see the section on using MSDOS in Chapter 2). To record a macro to save the current document in C:\GNVQIT, you start the macro recorder, give the new macro a name, and then proceed as normal to save the file in the required directory. Finally you stop the recorder:

1. Start macro recorder
2. Select drive C: in the drive panel
3. Select directory GNVQIT from the directories panel
4. Click on the OK button
5. Stop macro recorder

The macro that was created by the recorder is a sequence of two WordBasic commands:

```
Sub MAIN
ChDefaultDir "C:\GNVQIT\", 0
FileSaveAs .Name = "AUTOPROC.DOC", .Format = 0, .LockAnnot = 0,
.Password = "", .AddToMru = 1, .WritePassword = "", .RecommendReadOnly
= 0, .EmbedFonts = 0, .NativePictureFormat = 0, .FormsData = 0
End Sub
```

Now you can automatically save a document by simply running the macro. Word also allows you to assign a keystroke, menu item or toolbar icon to the macro to make it even easier to run. It is necessary to understand the WordBasic commands thoroughly only if you need to write a macro rather than simply to record one, but you should be able to see that the macro contains two commands: ChDefaultDir to change the default directory and FileSaveAs to save the current document. The commands are placed between Sub MAIN which is the start of the macro and End Sub which indicates the end of the macro.

As a second and final example, Listing 28.1 shows a WordBasic macro which produces a menu within Word to allow non-windows programs to be run. It displays a menu of programs (mostly games) and allows the user to click on the desired program name (or press the underlined key) and the appropriate program is run. This Menu macro can be used as a model for making any menu of executable programs, whether or not they are windows applications.

```
Sub MAIN
REM Sets up a dialog box Menu for starting DOS applications from
REM within Word
REM First set up and display dialog box
REM ------------------Dialog Box------------------------------------
Begin Dialog UserDialog 363, 131, "Run DOS App"
   GroupBox 16, 13, 204, 86, "Run DOS application" 'Group box around
                                                    option buttons
      OptionGroup  .Run
         OptionButton 26, 25, 70, 16, "&Doom", .Option2
      OptionButton 26, 42, 57, 16, "&LBA", .Option3
      OptionButton 26, 59, 121, 16, "&Magic Carpet", .Option4
      OptionButton 26, 76, 150, 16, "&3D Modelling Lab", .Option5
      OKButton 251, 18, 88, 21
      CancelButton 251, 42, 88, 21
End Dialog
Dim DosDlg As UserDialog        'Declare dialog box
Dialog DosDlg                   'Display dialog box
REM--------------------------------------------------------------
REM Detect the DOS application to be run by using the variable
REM DosDlg. Run and start the application
Select Case DosDlg.Run
      Case 0
            Shell "c:\Games\Doom\Doom.exe", 1
      Case 1
            Shell "c:\Games\LBA\LBA.exe", 1
      Case 2
            Shell "c:\Games\Magic\MC.exe", 1
      Case 3
            Shell "c:\Models\ModLab\ML.exe", 1
End Select
End Sub
```

Listing 28.1. *A Word Basic macro*

The macro is in two parts: the first part is to define the form of a dialog box conataining the menu. A dialog box allows the user to communicate with the macro. In this case the communication takes the form of a mouse click on the required program. The dialog box produced is shown in Figure 28.2. The definition of the dialog box includes the types of buttons to be shown, where they are to be positioned relative to the top left-hand corner of the box, the text that accompanies the button and a variable name assigned to the button.

The second part of the Menu macro is concerned with running the option that was selected by the user as soon as the OK button is clicked. The `Select` statement uses the variable `DosDlg.Run` to determine which of the `Shell` commands to execute. If the user clicked the first option (Doom), `DosDlg.Run` will contain 0; the second option will give it the value 1, and so on. The `Shell` command causes the program named within the quotes to be run. When the selected program terminates, control returns to Word and the Menu macro finishes.

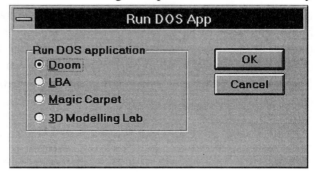

Figure 28.2. *A Word dialog box*

Chapter 29

Program Design

Introduction

The single most important requirement of a computer program is that it runs without error at all times, since a program that either produces erroneous results or 'hangs up' under certain circumstances is almost useless. Because of this stringent requirement, computer program design and production is a very skilled activity demanding meticulous attention to detail. It is not sufficient to address only the relatively easy problem of designing and implementing a program which produces the correct output when provided with ideal data. Rather, the program must be able to cope with non-ideal data such as that provided by a user who may be unfamiliar with its operation or data input requirements. Such a user might supply inappropriate input by, for example, entering alphabetic instead of numeric characters, and even experienced operators of the program might accidentally enter invalid data on occasions.

In fact there are many ways that a program could be presented with exceptional - that is, invalid or unreasonable - data and it is the responsibility of the program designer to allow for such. Consequently, the program design stage of program production, in which possible problems - and their solutions - are identified, is of vital importance. As a result, there are now a number of established program design methodologies to aid the program designer to produce well-crafted, error-free programs. The design method described here is a form of *structured programming* using *top-down, stepwise refinement*. Two forms of notation that we will use to express solutions to design problems are *pseudocode* and *structure charts*; these are called *program design languages* (PDLs). Structure charts provide a graphical representation of a program, allowing its logical structure to be easily appreciated, whereas pseudocode, having a form similar to program instructions, aids program writing and testing.

A number of the programs designed later in this chapter have been converted to Pascal and are described in the chapter 'Programming in Pascal'. Many of the ideas presented here are also covered in the Pascal chapter so we recommend that you refer to the appropriate sections in the latter while studying this chapter.

Problem solving

Whether a problem is computer-related or otherwise, the strategy for solving it has essentially the same three main stages: (1) *understand the problem*, (2) *devise a solution*, and (3) *test the solution.* In addition, for program design tasks there is a further stage which is to (4) *document the solution.*

1. Understand the problem

This first stage requires a *thorough* understanding of the problem being addressed so that you can identify what assumptions can be made and what can't in order to test your solution in the correct context.

Some problems are apparently straightforward but, when analysed with a view to producing a program design, become much more complex. As an example, consider the following outline program specification:

> *Write a program to read in a date and convert it to the number of days from the start of the calendar year.*

It sounds simple enough until you start to consider what the problem implies. For example, what format is to be used for the date? - 15th January, 1995 or 15 Jan 95, or 15/1/95, or 15-01-95 or 150195, or 950115, and so on. Is a particular format to be adopted and incorrectly formatted dates to be rejected, or is the program to attempt to interpret different formats? Are leap years to be considered when calculating the day number? Do you assume that the date is for the current year or can the date be for a different year? You may be able to think of more problems that could arise. We will return to this example later in the chapter and provide a possible solution.

2. Design a solution

The method adopted here to design the solution involves tackling the problem in a number of steps. An outline program is designed first, showing the main modules of the program, and the order in which they are to be executed. Each main module is then reduced to a number of smaller, simpler, and more manageable components, and this process of refinement continues until the program designer judges that there is sufficient detail in the design for a programmer to be able to convert the design directly into a programming language. The process of reducing components into sequences of smaller components in stages is often termed *stepwise refinement*. Top-down, stepwise refinement encourages program design to be tackled methodically in a number of stages of increasing detail.

Although structure charts and pseudocode are both suitable program design languages, we recommend that you adopt our approach of first using structure charts to produce your program designs in outline form and then translating them into detailed pseudocode prior to testing and subsequent conversion to program code.

An example of a simple structure chart and the equivalent pseudocode for the addition of two real numbers are shown below. (Note that a *real* number is a number with a fractional part such as 23.456, whereas an *integer* is a whole number such as 32).

Structure chart   Pseudocode

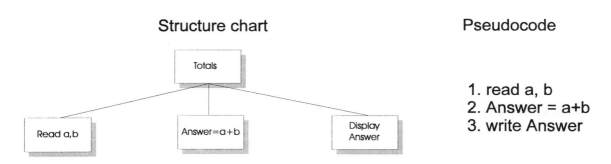

1. read a, b
2. Answer = a+b
3. write Answer

Figure 29.1. A simple program design for the addition of two real numbers

`Answer`, `a` and `b` are called *variables* which serve a similar function to the symbols used in algebra - they are general, symbolic representations of data that is to be processed. Thus statement 1 above means 'read two values from the input device (such as a keyboard) and call them `a` and `b` respectively'. Statement 2 adds the two values and calls the result `Answer`. Statement 3 displays `Answer` on the output device (such as a display screen). By using variables rather than actual numbers, this sequence of statements defines how a computer is to deal with the addition of *any* two numbers.

In addition to the problem solution itself, another part of the design is a *data table* which defines the purpose and type of the variables used in the solution. The data table would identify whether these variables were integers or real numbers and their purpose:

Name	Description	Type
Answer	Holds the sum of the two numbers	real variable
a	First number entered	real variable
b	Second number entered	real variable

3. Test the solution

This involves using test data to manually step through the solution statements so that the computed output can be compared with the expected output. For instance, the date example mentioned above should give an answer of 69 for 10th March 1995, assuming that the days are calculated from 1st January, 1995. This value would be compared with that provided by the design - if the answer was different then the apparent design fault would need to be investigated and corrected before continuing with further testing.

4. Document the Solution

The documentation contains the following:

1. The problem statement.
2. The top-level program design
3. The final detailed program design
4. The data table

These are produced during the course of the first three stages of program design. The examples in later sections show the form of this documentation.

Structured programming

Most current program design methodologies are based on *structured programming* concepts. Structured programming is generally associated with certain basic principles:

1. **Restricted use of control structures**. These are limited to three types: *sequence* consisting of instructions which are performed one after the other in the order that they appear in the program; *selection* of one set of instructions from several possible sets of instructions so that the program is able to deal with a number of different circumstances; *repetition*, or *iteration,* of a set of instructions using some kind of program loop. Restricting design to using only these three constructs does not necessarily produce error-free code, but it does help to produce a program which is clear and relatively easy to test.

2. **Modularity**. This is the subdivision of a program into easily identifiable and manageable segments, or *modules*. Each module should require no more than about one page of code. A module may be realised in the final program as one or more small subprograms (see functions and procedures later in this chapter). Using modules helps to clarify the logical structure of a program for human readers and, by incorporating subprograms, aids its construction.

3. **Top-down, stepwise refinement**. This program design method was described in the earlier section *Problem Solving*.

4. **Clear program format**. This is concerned with the layout of the program instructions. Each page of coding should contain clearly identifiable control structures and blocks of code. One main method of achieving this clarity of structure is by the consistent use of indentation showing the limits of loops, selections and blocks of instructions. Formatting standards apply both to pseudocode and actual program code.

5. **Comments**. The thorough use of comments within the pseudocode design and the actual program in order to explain the purpose of each variable and each few lines of logically related code.

6. **Simplicity**. Where there is a choice between a simple solution to a problem and a slightly more efficient solution which perhaps uses less code, then the simple solution is to be preferred. Straightforward, simple code is easier to test, modify and understand than obscure, 'clever' code.

Basic control structures

As explained earlier, structured programs are constructed using the three control structures sequence, selection and iteration. In order to illustrate how each of these is expressed and used in program design, consider the following programming problem:

Read a set of ten positive and negative numbers entered from a keyboard and find the separate totals of the positive numbers and the negative numbers. Print the two totals.

It is assumed that only valid real numbers such as 1.2, -7.3, 25, -6 will be entered. The program can be considered to be a *sequence* of three simple modules:

1. **Initialise variables**. Two variables will be required: one for the total of the positive numbers and the other for the total of the negative numbers.

2. **Process the numbers**. This involves a loop to read numbers typed in from the keyboard until ten values have been entered. A count will be incremented every time a number is read in.

3. **Display the results**. This will involve writing out the two totals.

This top-level design is illustrated by the structure chart shown in Figure 29.2

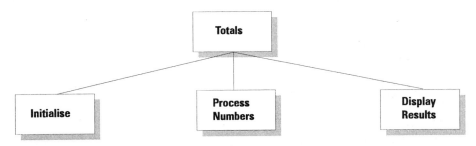

Figure 29.2 *Top-level design as a **sequence** of three modules*

The equivalent pseudocode for the top-level design is as follows:

```
{Totals}
1     Initialise
2     Process numbers
3     Display results
```

The first refinement of the design results in the structure chart shown in Figure 29.3.

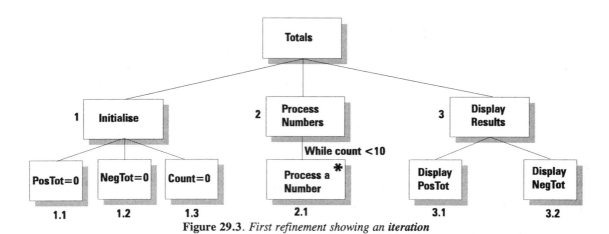

Figure 29.3. *First refinement showing an **iteration***

The loop that reads the ten numbers, in other words the *iteration*, is indicated in the structure chart by an asterisk in the top right-hand corner of the component that is to be repeated. The condition governing the loop is written above this component; in this case the loop continues while the count variable has a value less than ten.

The equivalent pseudocode is shown below:

```
{Totals}
1.1    PosTot=0
1.2    NegTot=0
1.3    Count=0
2      while Count < 10
2.1       Process Number
2      endwhile
3.1    write PosTot
3.2    write NegTot
```

Each of the original statements numbered 1, 2 and 3 have all been refined; statement 1 (initialise) has been replaced by three detailed instruction, 1.1, 1.2 and 1.3. Similarly, statements 2 and 3 have also been refined. (These statement level numbers reflect the depth of the structure diagram; a single statement level such as 1 indicates a top-level module, a statement number such as 1.2 indicate the second step of a refinement of level 1, 2.3.1 indicates the first step of a refinement of statement 2.3, and so on. A refinement of a statement is denoted by adding another level to the statement number.)

Notice that the end of the loop is indicated by endwhile and the instruction inside the loop, Process Number, is indented. A loop thus translates into **three** pseudocode statements: one statement for the type of loop and the condition that governs it, another for the item that is to be repeated, and the third for the end of the loop.

The final refinement is to expand Process Number since this is the only statement that has not yet been fully defined: we need to show *how* a number is to be processed. The full design is shown in Figure 29.4.

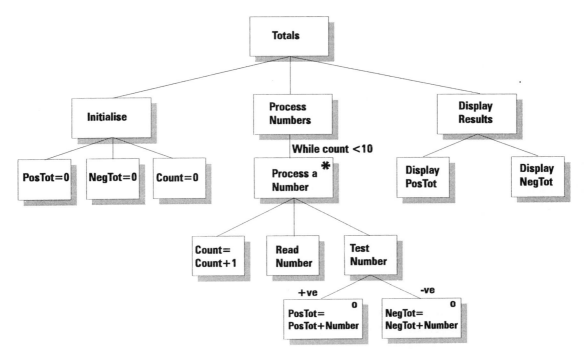

Figure 29.4. *The Final refinement showing a selection*

The structure chart shows that the repeated component Process Number involves three steps: increment the count, read a number, and test the number to determine its sign. Positive numbers are to be accumulated in PosTot and negative numbers are to be accumulated in NegTot. The test involves a *selection*, each independent choice being indicated by a small circle in the top right-hand corner of the box. The condition governing each choice is written above the appropriate box as shown.

This version of the design needs no further refinement since it is now in a suitable form for conversion to pseudocode and subsequently to a programming language such as Pascal.

The pseudocode below uses a select statement for the selection. If the condition following the first select is true, the statement or statements following are obeyed, otherwise the next select is considered. The endselect statement must be used to terminate the select statement. Note that the number of alternative sets of statements is not limited to two - as many as necessary can be chained together in this way. If some action is necessary when none of the select statements are true then the select when otherwise statement can be included before endselect.

```
        {Totals}
1.1         PosTot = 0
1.2         NegTot = 0
1.3         Count  = 0
2           while Count < 10
2.1             Count = Count + 1
2.2             Read Number
```

```
2.3          select
2.3.1a         when Number > 0
2.3.1b            PosTot = PosTot + Number
2.3.2a         when Number < 0
2.3.2b            NegTot = NegTot + Number
2.3          endselect
2         endwhile
3.1       write PosTot
3.2       write NegTot
```

The numbering follows the refinement levels of the structure charts. Thus if the first module is refined as a sequence of two statements, these statements are labelled `1.1` and `1.2`. In the case of an iteration, the start and end statements are given the same number. Thus in the example above, the `while` and `endwhile` both are labelled `2` showing that the iteration is the second top-level module in the program. The start and end statements of a selection are similarly labelled, but each option, which might involve a number of steps has a small letter added to indicate that it is a step within the option. (For example, `2.3.1a` and `2.3.1b` above). In addition, in the examples that follow, where a structure chart step has been expanded in the pseudocode, each part of the expansion is also designated with a lower case letter. This frequently occurs when the structure chart shows that a value is to be entered by a user via a keyboard; the pseudocode might be expanded thus:

```
5.1     read Number        becomes

5.1a    write 'Enter a number'
5.1b    read Number
```

This helps to prevent the structure chart from becoming too detailed and thus unclear.

To complete the design the three variables used must be defined in a data table:

Name	Description	Type
Count	Counts how many numbers have been entered	integer variable
PosTot	The sum of the positive value numbers	real variable
NegTot	The sum of the negative value numbers	real variable

Summary

Figure 29.5 summarises the structure chart and pseudocode notation used for the three basic control structures, sequence, selection and iteration. Iteration is shown in a commonly used alternative form in which the condition is expressed as `repeat until <condition>`. In this form the condition is tested at the end of the loop rather than at the beginning; this means that the statements within the loop will be repeated at least once. The `repeat until` loop is illustrated in the worked examples.

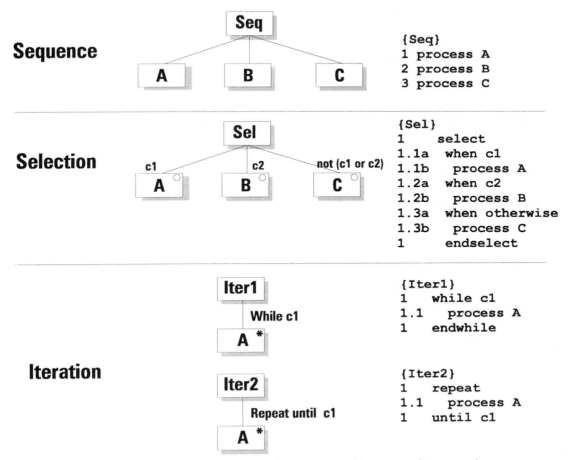

Figure 29.5. *The three basic control structures used in structured programming*

Worked examples

The worked examples presented in the next sections use a combination of structure charts and pseudocode to arrive at the final program design. Structure charts are used for the design refinements in order to express the overall logic in a clear, easily understandable form. The design is then presented in pseudocode in order to present it in a form more suitable for testing and subsequent conversion to a programming language. At this stage some fine detail may also be added to the design. We will indicate which designs have been converted into Pascal code in the chapter on programming in Pascal by means of an asterisk. Note, however, that the program design technique presented here, rather than being targeted at a particular programming language such as Pascal, is in a form suitable for conversion to any one of a number of quite different high-level languages.

Each of the following worked examples is in the format:

(i)   the problem statement;

(ii) any assumptions that have been made;

(iii) structure charts showing the top-level design and any further refinement stages;
(iv) pseudocode for the final design;
(v) the data table for the complete design;
(vi) comments

1. Reading and displaying information *

Problem statement

Design a program which will accept from the keyboard a value representing a number of inches and display the equivalent number of centimetres.

Assumptions

1. The input is a valid real number.
2. There is no preferred format for the output.

Top-level design

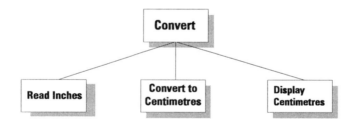

The top-level design now requires only minor refinements concerned with the precise form that the output is to take. This can be accomplished conveniently in pseudocode without the need to draw another structure chart.

Pseudocode

```
{Convert}
1a      write 'Enter the length in inches: ', <newline>
1b      read Inches
2       Centimetres = Inches*2.54
3a      write <newline>.
3b      write 'A length of ', Inches, ' inches is equivalent to ',
                        centimetres, ' centimetres', <newline>
```

This represents the final program design.

Data Table

Name	Description	Type
Inches	The value to be entered at the keyboard and converted to centimetres	real variable
Centimetres	The value to be output	real variable

Comments

`<newline>` indicates that the cursor is to move to the beginning of the next line.

2. Loops - Running totals *

One very frequent programming task is to keep a running total when a number of values are read within an iteration (that is, *loop*). This next example illustrates the technique usually adopted to accumulate a total in a variable.

Problem statement

Design a program to read ten numbers from a keyboard and display their sum.

Assumptions

1. Exactly ten valid real numbers will be entered using a keyboard.
2. The sum of the numbers is to be accumulated as the numbers are entered, and thus there is no requirement to store them.

Top-level design

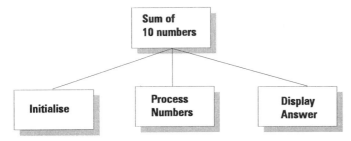

The top-level design is a simple sequence of three modules. The second module, Process Numbers, involves a loop which is to repeat a known number of times (namely 10). It can therefore be implemented using a count variable as shown in refinement #1.

Refinement #1

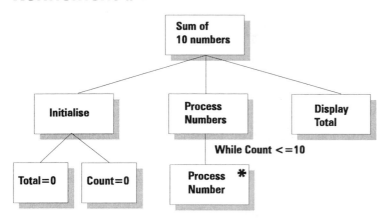

The variable `Total` is to be used to accumulate the sum of the ten numbers and therefore must start with an initial value of zero. Similarly `Count` is to start at zero because it must be increased by one each time a new number is read. Each time through the loop a new number is read into the variable `Number` and then added to `Total` which accumulates the numbers. When `Count` reaches 10, the loop terminates.

Refinement #2

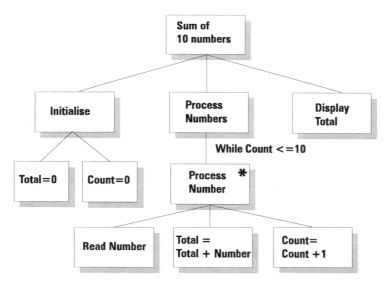

The statements required for processing a number and incrementing the loop control variable have been added; this represents the final structure chart form of the design.

Pseudocode

```
{Sum of 10 numbers}
1.1     Total = 0
1.2     Count = 0
2       while Count <= 10
2.1a       write <newline>, 'Enter number #', Count
2.1b       read Number
2.2        Total = Total + Number
2.3        Count = Count + 1
2       endwhile
3       write <newline>, 'The sum of the 10 numbers is: ', Total
```

This pseudocode form of the final refinement is to make the program a little more user friendly by adding some text to prompt the user to enter a number - this is much better than presenting the user with a blank screen and expecting him/her to know exactly what to do. The final instruction adds some text to announce the answer.

Data table

Name	Description	Type
Total	Accumulates the ten numbers	real variable
Number	Stores the latest number input	real variable
Count	The control variable for the loop	integer variable

Comments

1. Variables that are used as running totals and counts must always be initialised before a loop commences.
2. Control variables for loops are always of type integer.
3. A count variable is used to control the duration of a loop when the number of repetitions is known before the loop commences.

3. Loops - Rogue values *

There are many occasions when the exact number of repetitions of a loop are not known in advance. Frequently loops are terminated when a special value is entered by the user. Such special values are often called 'rogue values'.

Problem statement

Design a program to read a set of numbers representing the cost of some purchased items. The end of the list is to be indicated by entering 0 for the cost. Display how many items were purchased and the total cost of the items.

Assumptions

1. The values entered will be valid real numbers
2. No negative numbers will be entered

Top-level design

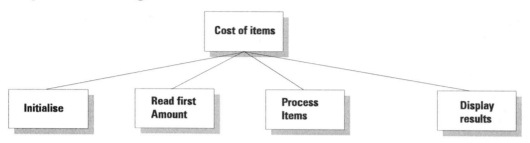

The strategy used in this instance is to read a value before the loop represented by the module, `Process Items`, is commenced. The condition governing the continuation of the loop will be `While Amount > 0` and this means that `Amount` needs to have been assigned a value before the loop starts. (This is called *reading ahead* and is a common method used for reading files, as we will see later in this chapter).

Refinement #1

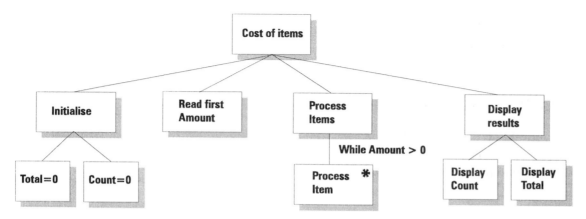

This refinement now shows that if the user initially enters zero for the amount, the loop is not executed at all because the condition, Amount > 0, is false. This is a very important characteristic of the `while` loop and a reason for not using the `repeat   until` loop construct in this instance.

Refinement #2

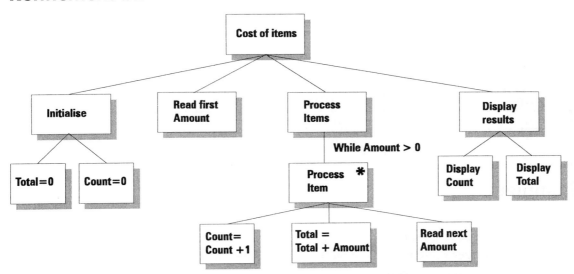

Processing an item requires a sequence comprising incrementing the item count, adding the current item's cost to the running total and finally obtaining another amount. Again, if this latter amount is zero, the condition for continuing the loop becomes false and the loop is terminated. The results are then displayed. Notice that the last statement executed in the loop is a read statement which obtains the data to be processed next.

Since no further detail is required for the structure chart, this is the final refinement before writing the pseudocode.

Pseudocode

```
{Cost of items}
1.1     Total = 0
1.2     Count = 0
2a      write 'Enter the cost of the first item, or 0 to end'
2b      read Amount
3       while Amount > 0
3.1        Count = Count + 1
3.2        Total = Total + Amount
3.3a       write <newline>, 'Enter the cost of the next item, or
                                                  zero to end'
3.3b       read Amount
3       endwhile
4.1a    write <newline>,
4.1b    write <newline>, Count, 'items were purchase'
```

```
4.2a     write <newline>
4.2b     write 'The total cost was: £', Total
```

The detail added to the pseudocode is again to improve communication with the user by displaying prompts such as that in statement 2.1 and by using blank lines (that is, `write <newline>`) to improve the clarity of the output.

Data table

Name	Description	Type
Total	Accumulates the cost of the items	real variable
Amount	Stores the current item's cost	real variable
Count	Counts the number of items	integer variable

Comments

Try to avoid using a `while` condition such as `Amount <> 0` (not equal to zero) instead of `Amount > 0` because real numbers may not be represented exactly within a computer; the representation of zero might not be **exactly** zero and the condition `Amount <> 0` may still be true even when zero is entered for `Amount`.

4. Making decisions - the `select` statement *

This example introduces the idea of taking one of several courses of action depending on the value of a variable read in from the keyboard. A loop is again terminated by testing for a rogue value, this time a negative value.

Problem statement

Design a program to accept a number of values representing student examination marks. Each mark is to be displayed as a grade as follows:

Mark	Grade
80 or over	Distinction
60 or over	Merit
40 or over	Pass
less than 40	Fail

A negative value is to be used to indicate the end of the set of marks.

Assumptions

The marks are entered as valid integers.

Top-level design

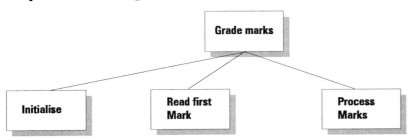

The third module in this sequence is an iteration which repeatedly reads and grades a mark until a negative mark is entered.

Refinement #1

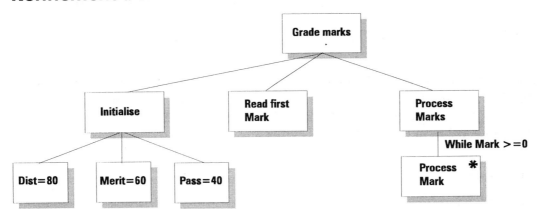

The threshold values for the grades are assigned to integer constants. Any negative value entered will be regarded as the signal to terminate the program.

Refinement #2

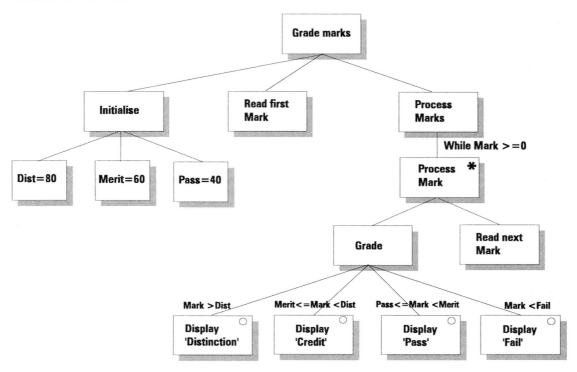

The four actions comprising the selection statement, Grade, which determine the message to be displayed should not be considered as a sequence of tests; the selection notation simply shows which action is to be taken depending on the one condition which is true, and as such the four actions could have been drawn in any order.

Pseudocode

```
{Grade marks}
1.1       Dist = 80
1.2       Merit = 60
1.3       Pass = 40
2.1a      write 'Enter the first mark(-1 to end):'
2.1b      read Mark
3         while Mark >= 0
3.1          select
3.1.1a          when Mark >= Dist
3.1.1b              write 'Distinction', <newline>
3.1.2a          when  Mark >= Merit and Mark < Dist
3.1.2b              write 'Merit', <newline>
3.1.3a          when Mark >= Pass and Mark < Merit
3.1.3b              write 'Pass', <newline>
3.1.4a          when Mark < Fail
3.1.4b              write 'Fail', <newline>
```

```
3.1          endselect
3.2a         write 'Enter the next mark(-1 to end):'
3.2b         read Mark
3          endwhile
```

The three thresholds for the grades are stored in the integer constants `Dist`, `Merit` and `Pass`. The advantage of doing this rather than using the actual values 80, 60 and 40 respectively is that if any of these values need to be modified, they need only be changed in the initialisation module and nowhere else.

Data table

Name	Description	Type
Dist	The distinction mark	integer constant = 80
Merit	The merit mark	integer constant = 60
Pass	The pass mark	integer constant = 40
Mark	The student's exam mark	integer variable

Comments

The precise form of a selection statement in a programming language can vary considerably; it is the responsibility of the programmer to choose the most appropriate form available in the target language that exactly represents the required logic.

5. Decisions - A menu program

Where a program offers a user a number of different options, a menu-based program structure is often employed. The options are displayed and the user is invited to choose one of them by, for example entering its first letter. The program then performs the requested operation and re-displays the menu after it is completed. One of the options always allows the user to exit the program. This example illustrates the structure of a program which presents the user with four options concerned with currency conversion.

Problem statement

Design a menu-based program to allow a user to choose between converting pounds sterling to German marks, American dollars or French francs. The program will ask the user to enter the number of pounds and it will display the equivalent amount in the chosen currency before returning to the menu.

The menu is to appear at the top of a blank screen and have the following appearance:

```
Currency conversion program


(M)arks

(D)ollars

(F)rancs

e(X)it



Which currency do you want to convert to Pounds?
```

Assumptions

1. Invalid choices (that is entering a letter other than M, D, F or X) will produce an error message and an invitation to try again.
2. Upper and lower case letters will be allowed.
3. The amount in pounds entered by the user will be a valid real number.
4. A single statement, ClearScreen, is available to blank the display screen.

Top-level design

The top-level design in this instance is very simple: the initialisation module sets the values for the three currency conversion factors and the remaining module, Main, repeatedly displays the user options and executes the one chosen.

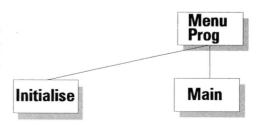

Refinement #1

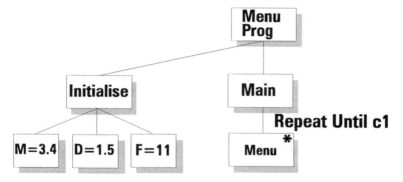

Three constants used for the currency conversion calculations are defined at this point (don't rely on these figures for holiday plans!). In addition, the iteration is defined as a repeat `until` loop with condition c_1. Logical conditions governing loops and selections can be coded in this way so that defining their precise form can deferred until the design has been completed. We will see later in refinement #3 that c_1 is the condition that the user has chosen the exit option.

Remember that the `repeat` loop causes the statments within the loop to be repeated at least once, and that the test for continuing to repeat the statements is made at the end of the loop.

Refinement #2

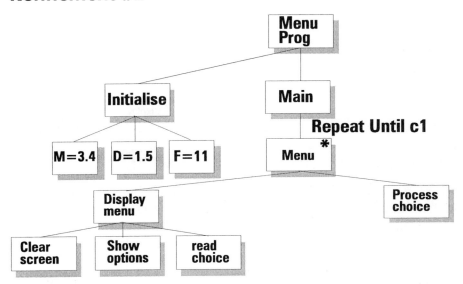

This refinement now shows that the loop controls a sequence of two modules. The first, `Display menu`, repeatedly clears the display screen, shows the menu of options and then reads the user's choice. The second module is a selection statement which processes the option chosen. The final refinement defines the operation each of the options and under what circumstances each is chosen

Refinement #3

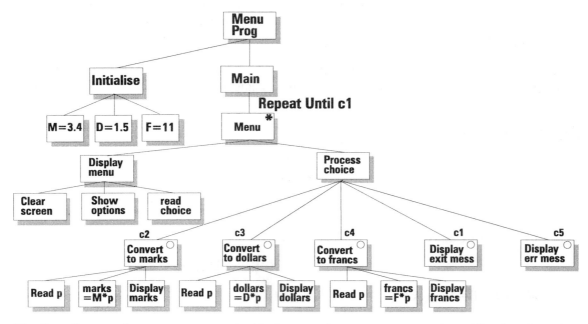

The firat three options are concerned with the actual currency conversions. The fourth option displays a message to confirm that the user has chosen to exit the program. The final select statement is only invoked if the user has entered an invalid choice, that is, the letter entered is not 'M', 'D', 'F' or 'X'. The condition codes c_1 - c_5 are defined in the table below:

c1	choice = ('X' or 'x')
c2	choice = ('M' or 'm')
c3	choice = ('D' or 'd')
c4	choice = ('F' or 'f')
c5	choice <> ('X' or 'x') or ('M' or 'm') or ('D' or 'd') or ('F' or 'f')

Pseudocode

```
{Menu program}
1.1     M = 3.4
1.2     D = 1.5
1.3     F = 11
2       repeat
2.1.1   ClearScreen
2.1.2a  write 'Currency conversion program', <newline>
2.1.2b  write <newline>
2.1.2c  write '(M)arks'
```

```
2.1.2d     write '(D)ollars'
2.1.2e     write '(F)rancs'
2.1.2f     write <newline>
2.1.2g     write 'Which currency do you want to convert to pounds?'
2.1.3      read Choice
2.2        select
2.2.1a       when Choice = ('M' or 'm')
2.2.1b         write <newline>, 'Enter amount'
2.2.1c         read p
2.2.1d         Currency = M*p
2.2.1e         write ' = ', Currency, ' Marks'
2.2.1f         write <newline> 'Press <Enter> to return to the menu'
2.2.1g         read key
2.2.2a       when Choice = ('D' or 'd')
2.2.2b         write <newline>, 'Enter amount'
2.2.2c         read p
2.2.2d         Currency = D*p
2.2.2e         write ' = ', Currency, ' Dollars'
2.2.2f         write <newline> 'Press <Enter> to return to the menu'
2.2.2g         read key
2.2.2a       when Choice = ('F' or 'f')
2.2.3b         write <newline>, 'Enter amount'
2.2.3c         read p
2.2.3d         Currency = F*p
2.2.3e         write ' = ', Currency, ' Francs'
2.2.3f         write <newline> 'Press <Enter> to return to the menu'
2.2.3g         read key
2.2.4a       when Choice = ('X' or 'x')
2.2.4b         write 'Exiting program..'
2.2.5a       when otherwise
2.2.5b         write 'Invalid option. Please try again'
2.2.5c         write <newline> 'Press <Enter> to return to the menu'
2.2.5d         read key
2.2        endselect
2.3        until Choice = ('X' or 'x')
```

Data table

Name	Description	Type
M	Conversion factor for pounds to marks	real constant = 3.4
D	Conversion factor for pounds to dollars	real constant = 1.5
F	Conversion factor for pounds to francs	real constant = 11
p	The number of pounds to convert	real variable
Choice	The user's menu choice	character variable
Currency	The equivalent value in the currency chosen	real variable
key	Dummy variable to accept the <Enter> key	character variable

Comments

1. This is a good model for constructing menu-driven programs.

2. The manner of implementing the `select` statement can vary considerably with the target programming language. Pascal provides `if` and `case` statements which each have their particular advantages and disadvantages. The programmer will be responsible for choosing the most appropriate selection construct from those available.

File handling

The term *file* can be used to describe a number of different forms of storing data on backing storage. Here are some examples of different types of files:

- *Program source file* - the source code for a program written in a high-level language such as C or Pascal. This is usually a text file such as that produced by an editor or word processor.

- *Executable, or binary, file* - a file, containing compiled program code, which is in a form suitable for running. It could be a word processor or spreadsheet program or a scientific program, for example.

- *Picture file* - a collection of data representing a coloured or black and white picture which can be displayed on a computer screen with the aid of suitable software. It probably would have been created with the aid of a graphic design program.

- *Data file* - a file organised as a collection of *records*, each record comprising a number of fields. Such files are commonly used in data processing applications such as payroll, stock control and accounting.

We will be concerned with this last type of file. Most general-purpose high-level programming languages are able to create, read and modify files organised as collections of records; they provide single program instructions to transfer a complete record as a unit from backing storage into memory, at the same time splitting the record into separate data items called *fields*. The data in the fields are automatically allocated to variables declared for this purpose. This is the process of *reading a record* from a file. Another instruction allows the programmer to transfer a single, complete record as a unit from memory to a backing storage medium. This is the process of *writing a record*. Two other important file-handling operations are (1) *opening a file* in an appropriate mode and (2) *closing a file* that previously has been opened. The open file statement usually involves naming the file to be opened and specifying whether it is to be opened for input (that is, for reading records) or output (that is, for writing records).

The program designs that follow are concerned only with reading and writing sequential files, that is, where the records can be read only in a fixed sequence. Simple examples illustrate the logic required to create, read, search and update sequential files.

6. Creating a sequential file *

Problem statement

Design a program to create a sequential file of car details. Each car record will contain the following data:

Make	*: maximum of 10 characters*
Model	*: maximum of 10 characters*
Insurance group	*: an integer value*
Cost	*: a real value*

Assumptions

1. The data will be stored in the form that it is entered - no validation checks will be performed.
2. A backing storage device such as a hard disk drive or a floppy disk drive is available to store the records of the file.

Top-level design

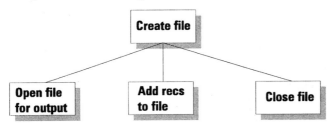

The top-level design is a sequence of a statement to prepare the file for output, followed by an iteration which allows the user to keep adding records to the file, and finally a statement which closes the file.

Refinement #1

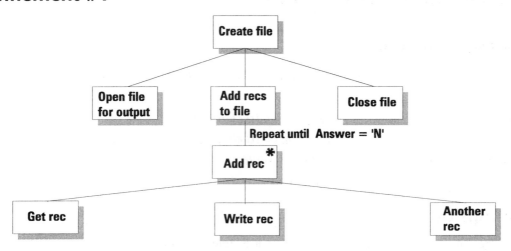

The iteration is implemented as a `repeat` loop which terminates when the user answers 'no' to the opportunity to add another record to the file. The loop repeatedly (1) requests the user to enter a set of car details (that is, a car record), (2) stores the record if the user consents to it, and (3) then asks if another record is to be entered. The character variable, `Answer`, will contain 'N' if the user wishes to discontinue adding records to the file and this will cause the `repeat` loop to terminate.

Refinement #2

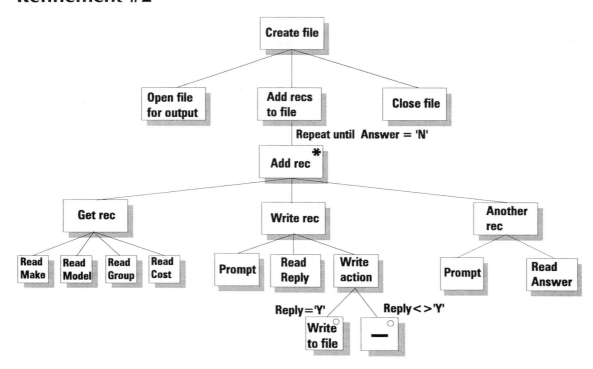

In this final refinement, the detail of the `Add rec` module is added. The selection statement, `Write action`, shows that we are interested only in `Reply` containing the character `'Y'` indicating that the car record is to be stored; any other character simply results in no action being taken, which is indicated by the dash in the box.

Pseudocode

```
{Create file}
1               fopen output, Carfile
2               repeat
2.1.1a            write <newline>, 'Make (eg Ford):'
2.1.1b            read Car.Make
2.1.2a            write <newline>, 'Model (eg Escort):'
2.1.2b            read Car.Model
2.2.3a            write <newline>, 'Insurance group (eg 7):'
2.1.3b            read Car.InsGp
2.1.4a            write <newline>, 'Cost (eg 8450.50):'
2.1.4b            read Car.Cost
2.2.1             write <newline>, 'OK to save this record(Y/N) '
2.2.2             read Reply
2.2.3             select
2.2.3.1a            when Reply = ('Y' or 'y')
2.2.3.1b               fwrite CarFile, Car
2.2.3.2a            when otherwise
2.2.3.2b               next statement
2.2.3             endselect
2.3.1             write <newline>, 'Add another record to the file?(Y/N)'
2.3.2             read Answer
2               until Answer = ('Y' or 'y')
3               fclose CarFile
```

The data table in the next section shows that `Car` is a record data structure with fields `Make`, `Model`, `InsGp` and `Cost`. The *dot notation* is used to specify a field within a record, so that, for example, the insurance group variable is designated `Car.InsGp`. This same notation is used in the pseudocode above. This allows a complete record to be treated as a unit for the purposes of reading and writing records. Thus the file write statement ,

```
2.2.3.1b            fwrite CarFile, Car
```

specifies that the current `Car` record is to be written to `CarFile`.

The complete list of file-related commands used in this chapter have the following general formats:

```
fopen    output, FileName          Opens the named file for writing
fopen    input, FileName           Opens the named file for reading
fwrite   FileName, RecordName       Writes the named record to the named file
fread    FileName, RecordName       Reads the named record from the named file
fclose   FileName                   Closes the named file
```

Finally, note that statement

```
2.2.3.2b          next statement
```

means, in effect, that no action is to take place at this point and control passes to the next available statement. It is included to make the logic of the selection statement clear and consistent with the structure chart component that it represents.

Data table

Name	Description	Type
Car	A car record	record
Car.Make	The manufacturer of the car	string field
Car.Model	The model of the car	string field
Car.InsGp	The insurance group of the car	integer field
Car.Cost	The price of the car	real field
CarFile	Sequential file of car records	file of Car record
Reply	Holds the user's answer (Y or N) regarding whether a record is to be written to the file	character variable
Answer	Holds the user's answer (Y or N) regarding whether another record is to be entered	character variable

Comments

This program is designed to initially create the car file; each time that it is used, the car file would be re-created. A technique for extending a sequential file is presented in a later example.

7. Reading sequential files

Two variations of reading the records in a sequential file are presented here. The first design is the most general form which assumes that a programming language will detect the end of a file when an attempt is made to read a record after the last one in the file. The read file statement in this instance has an at end clause which allows some action (in our case setting an flag called EOF to boolean true) if an end-of-file condition has arisen. Languages such as C and COBOL handle sequential files in this way.

The second design assumes that EOF is a built-in system function which checks the file and returns a value of true if there are no more records in the file remaining to be read. This is how Pascal handles sequential files.

Problem statement

Print in tabular form the contents of the car file created in the previous progam.

Assumptions

1. The file is to be printed in the same order in which it was created.
2. Version #1 assumes that the variable EOF is set to true when an attempt is made to read past the last record in the file.
3. Version #2 assumes that the function EOF becomes true when there are no records in the file remaining to be read.

Top-level design

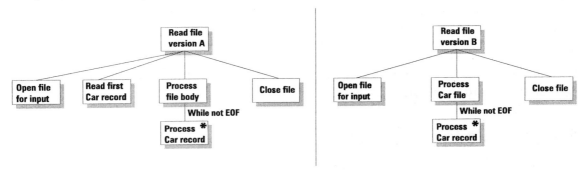

This shows that in version A the first record is read outside the loop, and the final operation within the loop is to read the next record (see refinement #1). In version B, this first read is not necessary.

Refinement #1

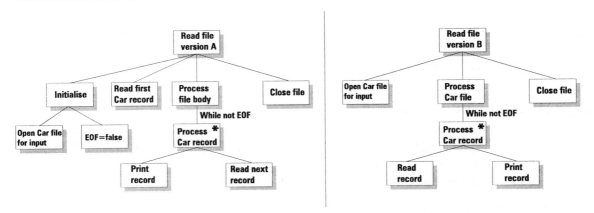

Processing a record in version A requires the current record to be printed before an attempt is made to read the next record. If there are no more records remaining to be read, EOF becomes true and the loop is terminated. With version B, a record is read and then printed. If it is the last record, EOF becomes true and the loop exits.

Pseudocode for version A

```
{Read file version A}
1.1          fopen input, Carfile
1.2          EOF = false
2a           fread CarFile, Car
2b             at end set EOF = true
3            while not EOF
3.1            write <newline>, Car.Make, Car.Model, Car.InsGp, Car.Cost
3.2a           fread CarFile, Car
3.2b               at end set EOF = true
3            endwhile
4            fclose CarFile
```

Note the at end option used with the read file statements - if an attempt is made to read past the last record in the file, EOF is set to true.

Pseudocode for version B *

```
{Read file version B}
1            fopen input, Carfile
3            while not EOF(CarFile)
3.1              fread CarFile, Car
3.2              write <newline>, Car.Make, Car.Model, Car.InsGp, Car.Cost
3            endwhile
4            fclose CarFile
```

Here, EOF(CarFile) checks CarFile and if there are no more records remaining to be read, it returns boolean true, otherwise it returns boolean false. When available, this facility simplifies sequential file processing.

Data table for version A

Name	Description	Type
Car	A car record	record
Car.Make	The manufacturer of the car	string field
Car.Model	The model of the car	string field
Car.InsGp	The insurance group of the car	integer field
Car.Cost	The price of the car	real field
CarFile	Sequential file of car records	file of Car record
EOF	Boolean variable used to detect the end of the file	boolean variable

Data table for version B

This is the same as for version A except that the variable `EOF` is not used - instead `EOF(CarFile)` is a system function which returns `true` if there are no more records to be read in `CarFile`, otherwise it returns `false`.

Comments

These two versions should be sufficient to describe the logic of sequential file processing for the majority of commonly used high-level languages.

8. Searching sequential files

The next example illustrates the logic of extracting details from all the records in a file that satisfy some criterium. In this instance we want to find all the cars that are under a certain price, but the logic would be the same if we were searching for any other characteristic of the data held in the car records. The sturcture of the design is very similar to that for reading a sequential file, and the structure diagrams should be self-explanatory.

Problem statement

Produce a report of all cars which are within £1000 of a price which the user enters.

Assumptions

1. The `EOF(FileName)` function described in version B of the previous example is available. Follow the guidelines given for version A if the target programming language does not offer this facility.
2. The complete record of cars matching the criterium will be printed.

Top-level design

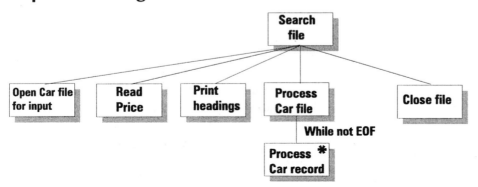

Refinement #1

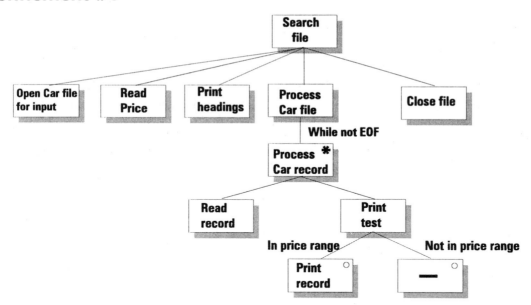

Pseudocode

```
{Search file}
1        fopen input, Carfile
2a       write <newline>, 'Enter the approximate price of cars to be
         listed'
2b       read Price
3        write <newline>,'Cars which are within £1000 of £', Price,':'

4        while not EOF(CarFile)
```

```
4.1          fread CarFile, Car
4.2          select
4.2.1a         when Price-1000 <= Car.Cost <= Price+1000
4.2.1b           write <newline>, Car.Make, Car.Model, Car.InsGp,
                   Car.Cost
4.2.2a         when otherwise
4.2.2b             next statement
4.2          endselect
4          endwhile
5          fclose CarFile
```

Data table

Name	Description	Type
Car	A car record	record
Car.Make	The manufacturer of the car	string field
Car.Model	The model of the car	string field
Car.InsGp	The insurance group of the car	integer filed
Car.Cost	The price of the car	real field
CarFile	Sequential file of car records	file of Car record
Price	Approximate car price entered by the user	real variable

Comments

If the target programming language does not deal with sequential files in the same way as Pascal, remember that you must use a variable in the `while` condition to register the end of the file and terminate the iteration.

Subprograms

One of the characteristics of programming in high-level languages is the use of *subprograms* such as *procedures* or *functions* to allow a large program to be separated into a number of independent units. These subprograms are connected together by means of a main program. A subprogram usually communicates with the main program with the aid of *parameters* which allow data to be passed to and from the main program. Subprograms and parameters are discussed in more detail in Chapter 18. Here we show how subprograms can be represented by structure charts and pseudocode.

Structure chart symbols and pseudocode

Figure 29.6 shows the symbols used for subprograms in structure charts and the equivalent pseudocode statement. Diagram (a) shows the simplest case in which component Sub 1 is a

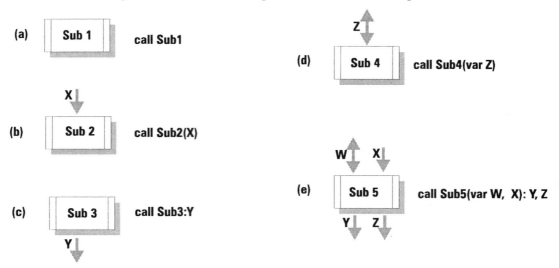

Figure 29.6. *Symbols for subprograms*

procedure which has no parameters. The subprogram has its own structure chart which is drawn separately from the main program. The pseudocode statement which invokes the subprogram is call Sub1. Again, the contents of the subprogram is defined as a separate piece of pseudocode.

In diagram (b), Sub 2 has a single value parameter to which the variable X is passed. In pseudocode, brackets indicate that the variables inside are parameters. Sub 3 returns a value to the main program variable Y; in pseudocode this is indicated by putting the variable after the colon, as in call Sub3:Y. Diagram (d) shows how a subprogram which has a variable parameter Z is depicted; the double arrow indicates that Z is passed to the subprogram and that it is also returned to the main program. In pseudocode, a variable parameter is indicated by preceding it with var, as in call sub4(var Z). Finally, diagram (d) shows how a subprogram with more than one parameter and more than a single return value is represented. Notice that in the pseudocode statement call Sub5(var W, X):Y,Z, var only refers to W; X is a value parameter because it is not immediately preceded by var.

In a structure diagram these new symbols appear as illustrated in Figure 29.7

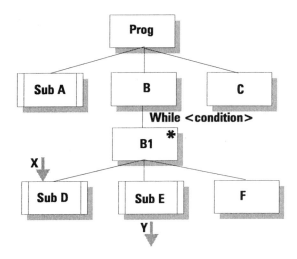

Figure 29.7. *Use of subprogram symbols in structure charts*

The diagram shows that component A is a simple subprogram with no parameters, subprogram D has a value parameter and accepts a variable X from the main program, and subprogram E returns a value to variable Y. Here is the equivalent pseudocode:

```
{Prog}
1      call SubA
2      while <condition>
2.1      call SubD(X)
2.2      Y = call SubE
2.3      F
2      endwhile
```

Notice line 2.2 in which the call to subprogram E results in a value being returned to the main program variable, Y.

The data table for the main program needs to contain entries defining each subprogram:

Name	Description	Type
SubA	Procedure to ….	proc
SubD	Procedure to ….	proc(string)
SubE	Function to ….	func:integer

This shows that SubA is a procedure which has no parameters; SubD is a procedure which requires a string type to be passed as a parameter; SubE is a function which has no parameters but which returns an integer type.

Defining subprogram structures

Figure 29.8 shows the structure chart for a subprogram called Sub 2. It shows that a value is passed into value parameter P from the main program and that it returns a value in variable R to the main program (or subprogram) that called it. Notice that a subprogram can itself also contain further subprograms (component D).

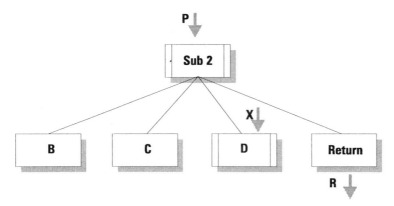

Figure 29.8. *A subprogram*

The pseudocode equivalent to this subprogram is shown below.

```
Function Sub2(P)
1    process B
2    process C
3    call D(X)
4    return R
```

The parameters to which values are passed are shown inside the brackets after the name of the subprogram. The value that is returned is named after the word return at the end of the subprogram.

Each subprogram must also have its own data table which must define all of the parameters of the subprogram and any other variables used. For example, the previous subprogram would require that P and R have entries such as those shown below:

Function Sub2(P):R		
Name	**Description**	**Type**
P	Parameter used for ...	integer value parameter
R	Returns ..... to main program	real value parameter
etc.		

The following worked example shows the complete design of a program which uses subprograms to extend a sequential file.

9. Extending a sequential file - putting it all together

We mentioned earlier that when a sequential file is opened for output it must be re-created. In the next example we examine a general method of extending a sequential file without using a special extend-file command. (Some languages, notably COBOL, allow you to open a sequential file in a mode especially for extending it, but this is not generally the case).

The method uses a temporary file to which the sequential file is copied. While this temporary file is still open for output, the additional records are added and then the complete temporary file is copied back to the original file.

Problem statement

Design a program to enable car records to be added to the car file.

Assumptions

1. Any number of extra records can be added to the car file.
2. The EOF (FileName) function described in previous examples is again available.

Main program

Top-level design

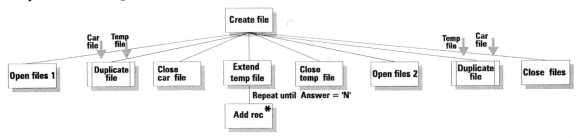

The procedure `Duplicate file` copies the first-named file to the second file. Thus it appears twice here: the first time to copy the current car file to a temporary file to which the extra records are to be added; the second time to copy the temporary file, now containing the extra records, back to the original file.

Refinement #1

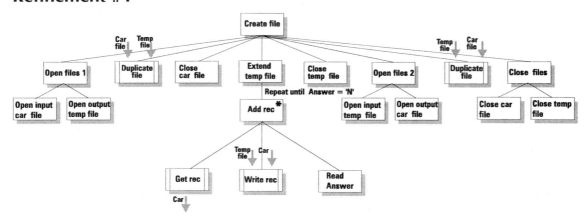

The further detail shows the order in which the two files need to be opened and closed, and also that two further subprograms are used. Get rec is used to get the details of a new car and return this record to the main program. Write rec writes the record to the temporary file. Both the record and the name of the file to which it is to be written are passed as parameters to this procedure.

Pseudocode

```
{Extend file}
1.1     open input CarFile
1.2     open output TempFile
2       call DuplicateFile(CarFile, TempFile)
3       close CarFile
4       repeat until Answer = 'N'
4.1        Car = call GetRec
4.2        call WriteRec(TempFile, Car)
4.3a       write <newline>, 'Add another record to the file(Y/N):'
4.3b       read Answer
4       until Answer = ('N' or 'n')
5       close TempFile
6.1     open output CarFile
6.2     open input TempFile
7       call DuplicateFile(TempFile, CarFile)
8.1     close CarFile
8.2     close TempFile
```

Data table

Name	Description	Type
DuplicateFile	Procedure to copy one sequential file to another	proc(file of Car record, file of Car record)
GetRec	Function which gets and returns a car record	func:Car
WriteRec	Procedure to write a car record to a car file	proc(file of Car, Car)

Car	A car record	record
Car.Make	The manufacturer of the car	string field
Car.Model	The model of the car	string field
Car.InsGp	The insurance group of the car	integer field
Car.Cost	The price of the car	real field
CarFile	Sequential file of car records	file of Car record
Answer	Used to ask the user if another record is to be added to the car file	character variable

Comments

The data table includes entries for the three subprograms that are called in the main program. These subprograms must also be fully defined using structure charts, pseudocode and data tables.

Procedure - Duplicate file

Top-level design

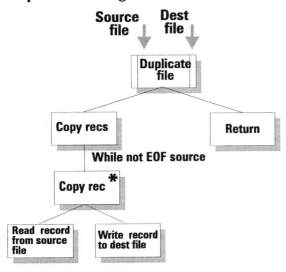

Pseudocode

```
Procedure DuplicateFile(SourceFile, DestFile)
1       while not EOF(SourceFile)
1.1        fread SourceFile, Rec
1.2        fwrite DestFile, Rec
1       endwhile
2       return
```

Data table

Procedure DuplicateFile(Sourcefile, DestFile)		
Name	Description	Type
SourceFile	The file to be copied	file of Car records
DestFile	The copy file	file of Car records
Rec	A single car record from the file	Car record

Procedure - Get rec

Top-level design

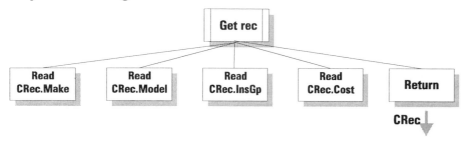

Pseudocode

```
Function GetRec:Crec
1a      write <newline>, 'Make:'
1b      read Crec.Make
2a      write <newline>, 'Model:'
2b      read Crec.Model
3a      write <newline>, 'Insurance Group:'
3b      read Crec.InsGp
4a      write <newline>, 'Cost:'
4b      read Crec.Cost
5       return Crec
```

Data table

Function GetRec:Crec		
Name	Description	Type
CRec	A car record	record
CRec.Make	The manufacturer of the car	string field
CRec.Model	The model of the car	string field
CRec.InsGp	The insurance group of the car	integer field
CRec.Cost	The price of the car	real field

Procedure - Get rec

Top-level design

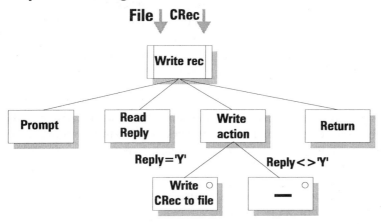

Pseudocode

```
Procedure WriteRec(File, CarRec)
1a      write <newline>, 'OK to save this record?(Y/N) '
1b      read Reply
2       select
2.1a    when Reply = ('Y' or 'y')
2.1b      fwrite File, CRec
2.2a    when otherwise
2.2b      next statement
2       endselect
3       return
```

Data table

Procedure WriteRec(File, CRec)		
Name	Description	Type
File	The file to be written to	value parameter file of Car records
CRec	A single car record from the file	value parameter Car record
Reply	User reply	character variable

Program Testing, Debugging and Documenting

Once the program has been written, it must go through two stages in order to remove errors which almost inevitably will be present. No matter how much care has been taken in the design and coding of a program, it is very likely to contain errors in syntax, that is incorrectly formed statements, and almost as likely to contain errors in logic as well. *Debugging* is the term given to the process of detecting and correcting these errors or *bugs*.

The first stage in the removal of errors is the correction of syntax errors. Fortunately for the programmer, modern interpreters and compilers will provide a large amount of assistance in the detection of syntax errors in the source code. Badly formed statements will be reported by a compiler after it has attempted to compile the source code; an interpreter will report illegal statements as it attempts to execute them.

Logic errors, however, are largely undetectable by the translating program. These are errors which cause the program to behave in a manner contrary to expectations. The individual statements in the program are correctly formed and it runs, but the program as a whole does not work as it should; it may give incorrect answers, or terminate prematurely, or not terminate at all.

Hopefully, even the most puzzling logic errors, having been detected, eventually can be removed. But how can the programmer be confident that the program will continue to behave properly when it is in use? The answer is that the programmer never can be absolutely certain that the program will not fail, but by the careful choice of test data in the second stage of the debugging process, the programmer can test the program under the sort of conditions that are most likely to occur in practice. Test data is designed to determine the robustness of the program: how well it can cope with unexpected or spurious inputs as well as those for which it has been designed specifically to process.

The purpose of *documentation* is to provide the user with all the information necessary to fully understand the purpose of the program and how that purpose has been achieved. The precise form that the documentation takes will be determined by a number of factors:

- The type of program.
- Who is likely to use the program.
- Whether it will be necessary to modify the program coding after it has been finally tested and accepted.

General guidelines for the contents of program documentation are given at the end of this chapter.

Detecting logic errors

If, after examining a program listing for a reasonable amount of time, the cause of an error remains a mystery, there are a number of courses of action which will probably be much more productive than continuing to pore over the listing:

1. Ask a fellow programmer to listen while you explain the operation of the program and the way it is behaving. Quite often you will see the cause of the error as you are making the explanation. Alternatively, your helper might recognise the type of error and its probable cause from his/her own experience, or might ask a question which makes you reconsider some aspect of the program which you have assumed to be correct or had no direct bearing on the problem. It is surprising how often this simple approach works.

2. Examine the values of key variables while the program is running by installing temporary lines of code throughout the program to display the values of key variables. Comparison of the values actually displayed with expected values will normally indicate the likely source of the error.

3. Use debugging utilities provided in the language itself or separately in the system software. Several versions of BASIC have a trace facility which, when turned on, displays the line number of statements prior to their execution. Sometimes a particular implementation of a language will provide more sophisticated debugging facilities which will display the values of particular variables as they are encountered during program execution. Some Pascal compilers have similar facilities for tracing a program as it is running. Minicomputer systems and mainframes usually have special debugging software which can be used with any of the languages supported by the system. It is up to the programmer to investigate the debugging aids available and make good use of them.

Test data

When the programmer feels that the gross program errors have been detected and removed, the next stage is to test the program using carefully selected data. The nature of the test data should be such that:

- every statement in the program is executed at least once;
- the effectiveness of every section of coding devoted to detecting invalid input is verified;
- every route through the program is tried at least once;
- the accuracy of the processing is verified;
- the program operates according to its original design specification.

In order to achieve these aims, the programmer must be inventive in the design of the test data. Each test case must check something not tested by previous runs; there is no point in proving that a program which can add successfully a certain set of numbers can also add another similar set of numbers. The goal is to strain the program to its limit, and this is particularly important when the program is to be used frequently by a number of different people.

There are three general categories of test data:

1. *Normal data*. This includes the most general data for which the program was designed to handle.

2. *Extreme values*. These test the behaviour of the program when valid data at the upper and lower limits of acceptability are used. The process of using extreme values is called 'boundary testing' and is often a fruitful place to look for errors. For numeric data this could be the use of very large or very small values. Text could be the shortest or longest sequence of characters permitted. A program for file processing could be tested with a file containing no records, or just a single record. The cases where zero or null values are used are very important test cases, frequently highlighting programming oversights.

3. *Exceptional data*. Programs are usually designed to accept a certain range or class of inputs. If 'illegal' data is used, that is data which the program is not designed to handle, the program should be capable of rejecting it rather than attempting to process it. This is particularly important when the program is to be used by people other than the programmer, since they may be unaware of what constitutes illegal data. A programmer should from the outset assume that incorrect data will be used with the program; this may save a great deal of time looking for program errors which may actually be data errors.

Validation

At some point the programmer must decide that the program has had sufficient testing. He or she will be confident that the program will operate according to specification and without 'crashing' or 'hanging up' under extreme or unexpected circumstances; the reputation of a professional programmer relies on this. Prior to release, the final testing is then performed by the user for whom the program was developed. The programmer may have overlooked areas of difficulty because it is often difficult to view a program objectively or entirely from the point of view of the user. If this is the case then the program will be modified and re-tested until all user requirements are met.

Program Documentation Requirements

A program which validates a temporary file prior to creating it permanently will probably require a minimum of user interaction and only a small number of instructions for the benefit of the person who will run the program. However, at some later date, it might be necessary for the author of the program, or a different programmer, to modify it. This possibility means that the structure of the program will have to be explained in great detail, and test procedures to ensure its correct operation will have to be provided.

A general purpose program such as a spreadsheet, designed for people who just want to use the computer as a tool, will require extremely detailed instructions regarding its function and use. Such programs are generally accompanied by extremely detailed user manuals and tutorials. On the other hand, users would not be expected (and definitely not encouraged) to modify the program coding; thus no details would be provided regarding the way the program has been written. This latter type of documentation would only be required for the people responsible for producing the program.

In addition to the documentation requirements of users and programmers, there is a third category of person to be catered for. These are people such as managers who are neither likely to use programs extensively nor want to attempt to modify them. They merely need to have an overview of the program - its function, capabilities, hardware requirements etc.

Thus there are many factors governing the coverage of documentation, and for this reason, in the next section, it is only possible to provide a checklist of items which might reasonably be included.

Documentation checklist

The documentation for a simple program generally falls into four sections:

- Identification
- General specification
- User information
- Program specification.

Most users will need access to the first three sections; in general the fourth section will only be needed if the program is to be modified. The amount of detail in each section will depend entirely on the particular application and, to some extent, the implementation language. COBOL, for example, is largely self-documenting: it contains an Identification Division containing all the information listed in the first section below; the Data Division of a COBOL program contains precise details regarding all of the files used by the program and which devices are required; the Procedure Division is written in 'English-like' sentences which are generally easy to understand, even by a non-programmer. Consequently, a program written in COBOL will generally require less documentation than one written in BASIC, a language which is not self-documenting.

The following checklist is a guide to what might reasonably be included in the documentation for a program.

1. Identification.

- title of program;
- short statement of its function;
- author;
- date written;
- language used and version if relevant;
- hardware requirements.

2. General specification.

- description of the main action(s) of the program under normal circumstances;
- file specifications;
- restrictions and/or limitations of the program;
- equations used or references to texts explaining any complex procedures/techniques involved.

3. User information.

- format of input required, e.g. source document or screen mask;
- output produced, e.g. typical printout or screen display;
- detailed instructions for initially running the program;
- medium on which program located, e.g. floppy disk(s).

4. Program specification.

- structure charts/flowcharts/decision tables;
- annotated listing;
- testing procedure including test data and expected output.

Chapter 30

Programming in Pascal

Introduction

This unit addresses the task of developing a piece of software using the programming language Pascal. Here we look at Pascal in enough depth for you to be able to develop your own simple programs, provided of course that you have access to a Pascal compiler. The programs presented in this unit were written and tested using Borland's Turbo Pascal. However, apart from a small number of possible exceptions, the programs should work with any standard version of Pascal. Any special features of Turbo Pascal used in example programs are noted and explained; if you are not using Turbo Pascal, your version will most likely have very similar features that you can substitute, but you will need to refer to the appropriate language reference manual for the precise instruction format required.

Turbo Pascal was chosen because it provides an ideal, easy to use environment for developing programs since it combines in one package all the tools required for the task. For example, it has

- an editor for creating and editing source programs;
- a compiler to check the syntax of a program, to report and identify errors and to produce object code;
- a linker to produce executable code;
- a debugger to help with locating runtime errors;
- a file manager to allow you to quickly save, retrieve and print source programs.

Before going on to look at the language itself, we outline all the stages involved in producing a working program to put the process of actually using a Pascal compiler in its correct context.

Program development

The stages in developing a program in Pascal are essentially the same as those for any programming language:

1. *Understand the problem* - the problem being addressed must be fully understood in terms of what data the program is expected to process, what

the processing task actually involves and what form the output from the program is expected to take.

2. ***Design the solution to the problem*** - identify the precise sequence and form of processing steps that must be performed in order to produce the desired output. This is termed an *algorithm*.

3. ***Convert the algorithm into Pascal instructions*** - this is the production of the program's *source code*. Each step of the algorithm is converted into one or more suitable Pascal instructions using a suitable text editor or word processor. The source program is written according to specific rules of syntax which define how instructions in Pascal are to be formed. These syntax rules specify, for example, that every Pascal program must have a name, that the main program instructions must appear between the words *begin* and *end*, and that the final line of the program must be the word *end* followed by a full stop. The complete set of syntax rules define precisely the only ways that the individual instructions of a Pascal program may be formed. The reason for this precision in the definition of the language is that Pascal, in common with many other high-level language, uses a translating program called a *compiler* to convert the source code into a form that a computer can process directly. Because a compiler is itself simply a computer program which has been designed to recognise Pascal instructions, it is capable only of processing well-formed Pascal programs. Instructions which do not conform exactly with Pascal syntax rules are rejected by the compiler and only a program which has been written in accordance with the rules of syntax can be converted into a form which can be executed by a computer.

4. ***Remove any syntax errors from the program*** - this involves a cycle of compiling the program and correcting any errors reported by the compiler repeatedly until the program compiles successfully and produces *object code*. Compilers will normally indicate the position and probable cause of syntax errors, but it is up to the programmer to make the necessary corrections. Thus a programmer must understand the rules governing the language and apply them accurately.

5. ***Link the program*** - this part of the process involves using a *linker* program to collect together pre-compiled subprograms which have been referenced in the source code. For example, a mathematical program might use special mathematical functions such as sine and cosine which are available in a special mathematical library of pre-written, tested and compiled functions. Pascal allows the programmer to use such functions by simply referencing them in the source code, but the linker must integrate them within the object code in order to produce an independent, executable program.

6. ***Test the program*** - in order to be confident that a program performs as expected, it must be tested with data that, as a minimum, causes all the instructions in the program to be executed at least once. Important programs

are subjected to much more rigorous testing using a variety of testing techniques.

The structure of a Pascal program

A Pascal program consists of two main parts: a declarations section and a procedural section arranged in that order. The first section requires the programmer to define the *identifiers* that will appear in the second section. These identifiers are programmer-defined *constants* and *variables* which are used to represent numbers, text and other types of data which are to be processed or produced by the program. The procedural section of the program specifies the operations that are to be performed by the program using the identifiers previously declared.

Listing 30.1. shows the general structure of a Pascal program.

```
program Name(input, output);
  {Declarations of variables, constants and other items
      go here}
begin
  {The main body of the program containing the procedures
      to be performed go here}
end.
```

Listing 30.1. *The general structure of a Pascal program*

As a simple example to illustrate these ideas, Listing 30.2 shows a program which calculates the total cost of a purchased item by calculating VAT and adding it to the price of the item. The algorithm on which the program is based is as follows:

1. *Ask the user to enter the price of the item*
2. *Store the price*
3. *Calculate the VAT at 17.5% (i.e. multiply the price by 0.175)*
4. *Calculate the total price by adding the VAT to the price*
5. *Display the total cost on the screen.*

Note that the line numbers preceding each line in the program, being enclosed between '{' and '}', are regarded as comments and are ignored by the compiler - they are included in the example programs presented in this chapter simply for ease of reference to specific lines when describing them.

The operation of program `Example1`

Line 1 declares that this program is called 'Example1' and `(input, output)` indicates that the program uses the keyboard for the input of data and the screen for the display of data.

Lines 2 and 3 declare that VAT is a *constant* value.

```
{1}     program Example1(input, output);
{2}     const
{3}       VAT = 0.175;
{4}     var
{5}       Price        :real;
{6}       Tax          :real;
{7}       TotalCost :real;
{8}     begin
{9}       write('Enter price of the item');
{10}      readln(Price);
{11}      Tax:= Price*VAT;
{12}      TotalCost:= Price + Tax;
{13}      writeln('The total cost is:' , TotalCost:8:2);
{14}    end.
```

Listing 30.2. *A simple program to calculate the total cost of a purchase*

Lines 4 - 7 declare three *variables* Price, Tax and TotalCost (hence the word var on line 4) each as being of type real. Variables are used to store data, which in this case are in the form of real numbers, that is, numbers which are not whole numbers. Every variable used in a Pascal program must be declared in this way.

Up to this point the programmer has defined a number of *identifiers* that will be used in the procedural part of the program which follows.

Line 8 indicates the beginning of the procedural part of the program, that is, the section of the program which states what operations are to be performed. This is the part of the program in which the tasks identified by the algorithm are coded.

Line 9 causes the message 'Enter price of the item' to be displayed on the screen.

Line 10 stores causes the computer to pause and accept numeric data typed in to be stored in the variable Price before continuing.

Line 11 stores the result of Price multiplied by VAT in the variable Tax.

Line 12 stores the result of adding Price and Tax in TotalCost.

Line 13 then displays the text, 'The total cost is: ' followed by the value stored in TotalCost. The total cost is shown as a total of eight characters with two figures after the decimal point.

Finally in **Line 14**, the word end followed by a full stop indicates the end of the program.

Some general remarks

Before going on to explore Pascal in more depth, it is worth mentioning a few general points at this stage:

1. Pascal does not distinguish between the use of capitals and lower-case letters. Thus it regards BEGIN, begin and Begin as being exactly the same.

2. Pascal uses the semicolon to indicate the end of an instruction, which is why you will see a semicolon at the end of most of the lines in a program. (You will quickly learn where a semicolon is not necessary). If you forget to terminate a complete instruction with a semicolon, the compiler will 'think' that the instruction is continued on the next line and, more often than not, it will say that there is an error in the next line.

3. It is a good idea to include comment lines (that is, text enclosed between '{' and '}') to describe the purpose of lines or sections of your program. Particularly for large, complex programs, this is very helpful if it is necessary to change the program at some later date.

4. Using spaces, blank lines and indentation can greatly improve the appearance and the clarity of a program, thus making the program easier to read and understand if it has to be modified later for any reason.

5. Programming involves meticulous attention to detail; omitting punctuation marks, including them in the wrong place or making spelling mistakes will usually lead to the compiler reporting syntax errors, but sometimes such slips might cause serious errors which are more difficult to detect, so be very careful to form instructions precisely.

Identifiers and data types

The term *identifier* is a general term used for *variables*, *constants* and other programmer-defined names such as *procedures* and *functions*. Variables and constants are always associated with a data *type*. Pascal requires that variables are given a type such as integer or real so that the necessary amount of memory can be reserved for their use.

Variables

A variable, which represents an item of data such as a single number, has a name and a current value. Variables are given names such as Amount, Total or Numb3 and are assigned values by program instructions. These values are stored in the memory of the computer and they are accessed whenever a variable is referenced in a program instruction. So, for example, in the instruction

```
Total := Price + Tax;
```

the value associated with the variable Price is added to the value of the variable Tax and the sum is then assigned to the variable Total. If in a previous instruction total had already been assigned a value, that value would be replaced by the new one.

Constants

Constants too are assigned values but only once after the word const preceding the main program. The constant VAT in Listing #.2 is an example. Constants retain their values throughout the execution of a program; Pascal does not allow you to use a constant in an instruction which tries to change the value of the constant. Thus, if in Listing #.2, you included an instruction such as

```
VAT := 0.2;
```

in the main program, the Pascal compiler would report an error.

Notice that a constant is assigned a value using only the "=" sign without the ":".

Special identifiers and reserved words

Certain words in Pascal are classed as *special,* or *standard, identifiers* because they perform the same function as programmer-defined identifiers but they are recognised by the compiler as being pre-defined and they are therefore to be used only in a certain context. Examples of special identifiers are the words write, writeln, read, readln, input and output. If you use any of these words for identifiers, for example by declaring

```
var
    Read   :integer;
```

then Pascal will not necessarily regard this as a mistake, but you will have overridden the standard definition of read as an input instruction, and you will have to use it as an integer variable; you will not be able then to use read as an input instruction since, in effect, you will have redefined its function. The moral is to avoid using these special identifier names for your own, programmer-defined identifiers.

Reserved words such as begin, end, real and program are words which are actually part of the Pascal language and are unavailable for use as identifiers.

Pascal's reserved words and special identifiers are shown below.

Reserved words:

and	array	begin	case	const
div	do	downto	else	end
file	for	function	goto	if
in	label	mod	nil	not
of	or	packed	procedure	program
record	repeat	set	then	to
type	until	var	while	with

Special identifiers:

abs	arctan	boolean	char	chr
cos	dispose	eof	eoln	exp
false	get	input	integer	ln
maxint	new	odd	ord	output
pack	page	pred	put	read
readln	real	reset	rewrite	round
sin	sqr	sqrt	succ	text
true	trunc	unpack	write	writeln

Rules for naming identifiers

Pascal imposes a number of restrictions concerning the formation of names for identifiers:

1. The name must consist only of alphabetic and numeric characters.
2. The name must start with an alphabetic character.
3. The name must not be a special identifier or a reserved word.

Examples of valid identifiers:

```
firstNum   NUMBER1 abc31    Counter    x
```

Examples of invalid identifiers

```
12abc           (starts with a numeric character)

first-number (contains a non-alphabetic/numeric character)

var 1           (contains a space)

End             (a reserved word)

READ            (a special identifier)
```

Data types

As well as having a names and values, variables are also given a *type*. Three commonly used types are integer, real and char (character). Data types are declared before the main program. For variables, the type must be shown after the name of the variable, as illustrated on lines 5-7 of Listing 30.2. More examples of type declarations are shown below:

```
     var
Amount          :real;
CodeLetter      :char;
NumberOfItems  :integer;
```

The type `real` means that these variables can be used for numbers such as 123.456, 0.22 or -9.93, that is, signed numbers that are not whole numbers. The computer holds `real` numbers in floating-point form so that very large, and very small numbers can be stored.

Signed whole numbers, that is, `integer` values are stored as two's complement binary values in the computer. Some examples of integers are 23, 0, -1, 32767 and -559.

`char` means that the named variable (`CodeLetter` in the example above) stores a single character such as 'a', 'D', '6' or '?'.

Turbo Pascal provides a further data type to handle *strings*. A string is simply a number of characters which are collected together and used as a unit. For example, a person's name is a string of alphabetic characters, and a stock number such as 100-234/ABC in a mail order catalogue is a string containing a mixture of alphabetic, numeric and special characters. String variable declarations are illustrated in the examples below:

```
Surname         :string[20];
StockNumber     :string[12];
Address1        :string[30];
```

The number inside the brackets specifies the maximum number of single characters to be handled by the named variable.

A further standard data type is the type `boolean`. This type of variable has only one of two possible values, namely `true` or `false`. A boolean variable declaration is made as follows:

```
Morevalues     :boolean;
```

Pascal provides the two reserved words `true` and `false` which can be used to assign a value to a boolean variable, as in:

```
Morevalues:= true;
```

The use of boolean variables will be explored in a later section.

Performing calculations

Probably every program that you will ever write will contain at least one calculation, and this is true of the majority of programs. It is not surprising therefore that Pascal and other high-level languages make calculations easy to perform. Arithmetic instructions simply involve defining what arithmetic operations are to be performed on numeric identifiers and constants. The four common arithmetic operations - add, subtract, multiply and divide - use the symbols +, -, * and /, respectively. The examples of arithmetic operations provided in Table 30.1 assume that the following data declarations have been made :

```
const
  PI      =3.14;
var
  Length, Width, Perimeter           :integer;
```

```
Area, Radius, Gallons, Miles, Mpg  :real;
a, b, c, x, y                          :real;
```

Expression	Pascal statement
Area = length × width	`Area:= Length*Width;`
$Area = \pi r^2$	`Area:= PI*Radius*Radius;`
$perimeter = 2 \times (length + width$	`Perimeter:= 2*(Length + Width);`
mpg = gallons ÷ miles	`Mpg:= Gallons/Miles;`
x=0	`x:= 0;`
$x = \dfrac{-b + \sqrt{b^2 - 4ac}}{2a}$	`x:= (-b + sqrt(b*b - 4*a*c))/(2*a);`

Table 30.1. *Examples of arithmetic operations with real variables*

All of the statements in Table 30.1 involve calculating a value using `real` or `integer` variables or a combination of `reals` and `integers`. Pascal's rules concerning how such calculations may be expressed are called *assignment compatibility* rules. They state that:

1. A calculation which involves a mixture of integers and `reals` must be assigned to a real variable.

2. A calculation which involves only integers may be assigned to either an integer variable or a real variable.

Another point to note is that Pascal provides two divide operators. The '/' divide operator may be used with any values, `real` or `integer`, but if both values are integers, the result is a `real` value and must be assigned to a `real` variable. The second divide operator, `div`, is only allowed to be used with integers. If the result of a division does not produce a whole number, the fractional part is ignored. In other words, the result is rounded down to the nearest integer. The remainder when one integer is divided by another is produced by the `mod` operator. Some examples should help to clarify these points:

Operands	Example	Answer	Answer type
`real/real`	`7.3/0.2`	`36.5`	`real`
	`0.5/0.25`	`2.0`	`real`
`real/integer`	`13.9/5`	`2.78`	`real`
`integer/real`	`1116/7.2`	`155.0`	`real`
`integer/integer`	`33/11`	`3.0`	`real`
	`33/10`	`3.0`	`real`
	`3/5`	`0.6`	`real`
`integer div integer`	`33/11`	`3`	`integer`
	`33/10`	`3`	`integer`
	`10/33`	`0`	`integer`

integer div real real div integer real div real	Not allowed		
integer mod integer	33/10 10/33	3 10	integer integer
integer mod real real mod integer real mod real	Not allowed		

Table 30.2. *Examples of divide operations*

Listing 30.3 is an example of the use of integer division. The program converts a number of seconds into hours, minutes and seconds.

```
{1}     program ModAndDiv(input, output);
{2}         {Program to convert a time given in seconds
{3}          to hours, minutes and seconds}
{4}
{5}     const
{6}         SECONDSPERMINUTE    =60;
{7}         MINUTESPERHOUR      =60;
{8}     var
{9}         Hours               :integer;
{10}        Minutes             :integer;
{11}        Seconds             :integer;
{12}        Duration            :integer;
{13}        Temp                :integer;
{14}
{15}    begin
{16}        writeln;
{17}        write('Enter the time in seconds: ');
{18}        readln(Duration);
{19}
{20}        Seconds := Duration mod SECONDSPERMINUTE;
{21}        Temp    := Duration div SECONDSPERMINUTE;
{22}        Minutes := Temp mod MINUTESPERHOUR;
{23}        Hours   := Temp div MINUTESPERHOUR;
{24}
{25}        writeln;
{26}        writeln(Duration, ' seconds is: ');
{27}        writeln;
{28}
{29}        write(Hours, ' hours ');
{30}        write(Minutes, ' minutes ');
{31}        writeln(Seconds, ' seconds.');
{32}    end.
```

Listing 30.3. *The* div *and* mod *integer division operators*

On line {17} the user is requested to enter the time to be converted from seconds to hours, minutes and seconds. The number of seconds is stored in the variable Duration. The first stage in the calculation is to calculate the remainder when Duration is divided by the number of seconds per minute stored in the constant SECONDSPERMINUTE which has the value 60. Suppose, for example, the user entered the number 6573 when asked for the time in seconds. Line {20} would produce the value 6573 mod 60, that is, 33. This is assigned to the variable, Seconds. Next, the temporary variable Temp is given the value 6573 div 60, that is, 109. The remainder when this last number is divided by the number of minutes per hour, that is 60, gives the value for Minutes: 109 mod 60 = 49. The number of hours is calculated using 109 div 60 = 1. Thus, when the program is run, it produces the following output:

```
Enter the time in seconds: 6573⏎

6573 seconds is: 1 hours 49 minutes 33 seconds.
```

Operator precedence

The term operator precedence applies to the order in which the operators in an arithmetic expression are used. For example, to evaluate the expression

$$x = y + z \times 3,$$

z is multiplied by 3 before the result is added to y; the multiply operator thus has precedence over the addition operator. If y had a value of 2 and z had a value of 4, x would be calculated as

$$x = 2 + 4 \times 3 = 2 + 12 = 14$$

The higher the precedence of an operator, the sooner it is used in the evaluation of an expression. The use of parentheses within an expression can alter the way a calculation is performed. So, in the above expression, to force the addition to be performed before the multiplication, we would write $x = (y + z) \times 3$. This would result in y being added to z before multiplying by 3. Thus,

$$x = (2 + 4) \times 3 = 6 \times 3 = 18$$

In Pascal, the operators *, /, div and mod have equal precedence; this means that in an expression involving two or more of them, they are simply used in the order that they appear in the expression. These four operators all have higher precedence than + and -. Again, + and - have the same precedence. As a further example, consider the program in Listing 30.4.

```
{1}    program Example2(input, output);
{2}    var
{3}       x1    :real;
{4}       y1    :real;
{5}       n     :integer;
{6}    begin
{7}       n:= 11;
{8}       y1:= 5;
{9}       x1:= 1.0/2.0*(y1 + n div y1);
{10}      writeln(x1:8:2);
{11}   end.
```

Listing 30.4. *An example to illustrate operator precedence*

The order of evaluation of line { 9} is as follows:

1. `1.0/2.0`   i.e.   0.5

2. `n div y1`   i.e.   11 div 5 = 2

3. `y1 + n div y1`   i.e.   5 + 2   = 7

4. `1.0/2.0*(y1 + n div y1)` i.e. 0.5*7   = 3.5

Reading and Displaying information

Practically every program requires that data are provided by some input device such as a keyboard and that results are produced on an output device such as a monitor. Pascal provides a number of instructions to simplify these operations. The example program in Listing 30.4 used three input-output instructions, namely `readln`, `writeln` and `write`. In this section we examine these instructions in a little more detail.

The `readln` instruction uses data provided by a standard input device such as a keyboard to assign values to variables . The word `input` inside the brackets after the program name at the beginning of a Turbo Pascal program tells the Pascal compiler that a keyboard is to be used to enter character-based data (see Listing 30.4 for an example). You use the `readln` instruction to read real numbers, integers, single characters or strings into appropriately declared variables. For example, the statement

```
readln(Price);
```

would cause the program to wait for the user to enter a number to be stored in the real variable `price`. The user presses the ENTER key (⏎) to signify the end of data entry. It is good practice to include a `write` instruction to precede `readln` to inform the user what information is required. So, for example, the statements

```
write('Please enter the price of the item: ');
readln(Price);
```

would cause the computer to display

```
Please enter the price of the item:
```

on the display screen and then, with the text cursor remaining on the same line, wait for the user to type in a value and press the ENTER key. The `writeln` instruction is almost identical to `write`, except that the text cursor is automatically moved to the beginning of the line immediately following the line on which the message is displayed. Which one of the instructions `write` and `writeln` you use depends on how you want your output to appear.

Listing 30.5 illustrates the use of `write`, `writeln` and `readln`.

```
{1}    program convert1(input, output);
{2}       {Program to convert inches to centimetres }
{3}    const
{4}       CENTIMETRESPERINCH =2.54;
{5}    var
{6}       Centimetres :real;
{7}       Inches         :real;
{8}    begin
{9}       write('Enter the length in inches: ');
{10}      readln(Inches);
{11}      Centimetres := Inches*CENTIMETRESPERINCH;
{12}      writeln;
{13}      write('A length of ', Inches:5:2,' inches');
{14}      write(' is equivalent to ');
{15}      writeln(Centimetres:5:2, ' centimetres');
{16}   end.
```

Listing 30.5. *Using* `write`, `writeln` *and* `readln` *instructions*

The program would produce the following output when run:

```
Enter the length in inches: 12 ⏎


A length of 12.00 inches is equivalent to 30.48 centimetres
```

Notice the different form of the `writeln` instruction on line {12} : it simply produces a single blank line when the round brackets are not used. This is useful for making your output clear and easy to read. The output shows that the user entered the number *12* followed by ENTER when prompted to type in the length in inches.

In line {13} `write('A length of ', Inches:5:2,' inches');`, the purpose of the numbers after the variable `Inches` is to control the number of characters printed, that is, the *field width* and the number of decimal places of the displayed variable. In this instance the field width, including the decimal point, is to be restricted to five, with two figures after the decimal point. When the variable is of type `integer`, only one figure representing the total number of digits to be displayed is provided. If the field width is larger than the item to be displayed, the output is padded with blanks. Using a field width of zero, as in Inches:0, or less than the number of digits in the number, causes the minimum number of digits to be displayed. Table 30.3 contains a number of examples using various output formats.

Value	Type	Format	Output	Remarks
15.234	real	:10:1	∇∇∇∇∇∇15.2	Six leading spaces are added
6.6666	real	:10:1	∇∇∇∇∇∇∇6.7	The figure after the decimal point is rounded up
6.6666	real	:0:2	6.67	The minimum number of digits is displayed
-8.3124	real	:0:3	-8.312	As above
234.56	real	:1	2.3E+02	Number is displayed in floating-point form
234.56	real	none	2.3456000000E+02	The maximum number of decimal places is displayed
123	integer	:5	∇∇123	Two leading spaces included in the field
123	integer	:2	123	Minimum number of figures displayed and no leading spaces
'hello'	string	:10	∇∇∇∇∇hello	Strings are treated like integers
'hello'	string	:0	hello	As above

Table 30.3. *Examples of various output formats and their effects*

Note that the instructions that we have covered in this section, namely `readln`, `write` and `writeln`, are actually implemented as *standard procedures* which are explored later in this chapter.

Loops

A very frequent programming requirement is to perform a set of instructions several times. Rather than writing the set of instructions several times (which is impractical for all but a small number of repetitions), they are controlled by a special instruction which causes them to be repeated as many times as desired. Such program constructs are called *loops*, and each repetition of a set of statements is often called an *iteration*. For example, suppose a program is required to read 10 numbers, add each one to a running total and then display the final total. The program in Listing 30.6 accomplishes this task without using a loop.

```
{1}   program RunningTotal1(input, output);
{2}      {Program to add ten numbers }
{3}   var
{4}      Number          :real;
{5}      Total           :real;
{6}   begin
{7}      Total:= 0;
{8}      writeln('Enter ten numbers: ');
{9}      readln(Number);              {1st number}
{10}     Total:= Total + Number;
{11}     readln(Number);              {2nd number}
{12}     Total:= Total + Number;
{13}     readln(Number);              {3rd number}
{14}     Total:= Total + Number;
{15}     readln(Number);              {4th number}
{16}     Total:= Total + Number;
{17}     readln(Number);              {5th number}
{18}     Total:= Total + Number;
{19}     readln(Number);              {6th number}
{20}     Total:= Total + Number;
{21}     readln(Number);              {7th number}
{22}     Total:= Total + Number;
{23}     readln(Number);              {8th number}
{24}     Total:= Total + Number;
{25}     readln(Number);              {9th number}
{26}     Total:= Total + Number;
{27}     readln(Number);              {10th number}
{28}     Total:= Total + Number;
{29}     Writeln('The total is ', Total:10:2);
{30}  end.
```

Listing 30.6. *Adding ten numbers*

The instruction on line {10}, Total:= Total + Number, and repeated on several subsequent lines is a means of accumulating a total. It causes the value of Total to be replaced by its current value plus the value of the variable Number. Total is first set to zero on line {7} so that if Number was given a value of, say, 10, Total:= 0 + 10 = 10. If on line {11} Number was then given a value of 12, Total:= 10 + 12 = 22, and so on. In this way Total accumulates the values assigned to Number after each readln instruction.

Obviously this approach of writing a sequence of using a separate readln instruction and assignment statement for each value typed in would be completely impractical for, say, 1000 numbers, but the program in Listing 30.7, which is much shorter than Listing 30.6, uses a loop that allows it to handle as many or as few numbers as required.

```
{1}      program RunningTotal2(input, output);
{2}         {Program to add ten numbers }
{3}      var
{4}         Number          :real;
{5}         Total           :real;
{6}         Count           :integer;
{7}      begin
{8}         Total:= 0;
{9}         writeln('Enter ten numbers: ');
{10}        for Count:= 1 to 10 do
{11}        begin
{12}           readln(Number);
{13}           Total:= Total + Number;
{14}        end;
{15}        writeln('The total is: ', Total:10:2);
{16}     end.
```

Listing 30.7. *Using a loop to add numbers*

Listing 30.7 uses a for loop to repeat the two instructions which repeatedly read a number and add it to a running total. The for loop requires that a control variable, called Count in this example, is defined as type integer. The control variable is automatically given the first value specified (1 in this example) and, each time the statements within the loop are repeated, it is increased by 1 until it finally reaches the second value specified (10 in this example). Thus the same program, but with the value 10 replaced by the required number, could be used to add any number of numbers. Statements to be repeated are enclosed between begin and end.

Listing 30.8 is a further example of the use of the for loop.

```
{1}      program ConvTab(input, output);
{2}         {Program to display a conversion table for inches to
{3}          centimetres using a for loop}
{4}      const
{5}          CONVERSIONFACTOR =2.54;
{6}          MAXINCHES        =12;
{7}      var
{8}          Inches           :integer;
{9}          Centimetres      :real;
{10}
{11}     begin
{12}         writeln;
{13}         writeln('Inches':20,  'Centimetres':20);
{14}         writeln('------':20,  '-----------':20);
{15}
{16}         for Inches:= 1 to MAXINCHES do
{17}           begin
{18}             Centimetres:= Inches*CONVERSIONFACTOR;
{19}             writeln(Inches:17, Centimetres:20:2);
```

```
{20}          end;
{21}
{22}   end.
```

Listing 30.8. *Using a* for *loop to display a conversion table*

The output produced looks like this:

```
     Inches          Centimetres
    -------          -----------
       1               2.54
       2               5.08
      etc              etc

      12              30.48
```

Notice that the end value in the for statement on line {16} is a constant called MAXINCHES; this could also have been defined as a variable used in a readln instruction.

A slight variation in the format of a for statement allows the count variable to go down from a high value to a low value. For example, you could write

```
     for i:= 12 downto 1 do ....
```

which would cause the variable i to start at 12 and go down to 1 in steps of 1.

The for statement is a very useful means of implementing a loop, but certain programming problems require a different approach to repeating a set of instructions. For example, consider the following outline program description:

> *Read a set of real numbers representing the cost of a number of items. Accumulate the total cost of the items until a value of zero is entered, then display the number of items purchased and their total cost.*

Here it is not known how many times the loop is to be repeated: the user decides when to terminate the loop by entering a *rogue value*, (zero in this case). The rogue value is used in another type of loop instruction, the while instruction. Listing 30.9 shows how a while loop can be used in conjunction with a rogue value. The rogue value is defined as a constant on line { 5}. Because the user may want to terminate the program immediately, without entering any values, the program asks for a purchase amount before entering the loop starting on line {18}. The while instruction requires that a true/false expression is included after the word "while". Thus the expression, Amount > ROGUEVALUE, will be true if Amount entered is greater than zero, and it will be false if Amount is not greater than zero, that is if it is equal to, or less than zero. When the expression is true, the statements between the immediately following begin and end, that is lines {20} to {23}, will be executed; as soon as the expression becomes false, the loop terminates and the program goes on to line {26}.

Notice that the last instruction in the lines to be repeated is the readln instruction to read another value: this means that because the next instruction to be executed is the while instruction, the value typed in by the user is immediately compared with the rogue value. This ensures that the rogue value is not processed as an actual data item.

```
{1}    program RogueVal(input, output);
{2}       {program to illustrate the use of a rogue value
{3}          to terminate a loop}
{4}    const
{5}       ROGUEVALUE  =0;
{6}    var
{7}       Count          :integer;
{8}       Amount         :real;
{9}       Total          :real;
{10}
{11}   begin
{12}     Total:= 0;
{13}     Count:= 0;
{14}
{15}     write('Enter the cost of the first item, or 0 to end :');
{16}     readln(Amount);
{17}
{18}     while Amount > ROGUEVALUE   do
{19}      begin
{20}       Count:= Count + 1;
{21}       Total:= Total + Amount;
{22}       write('Enter the cost of the next item, or 0 to end:');
{23}       readln(Amount);
{24}      end;
{25}
{26}     writeln;
{27}     writeln(Count, ' items were purchased.');
{28}     writeln;
{29}     writeln('The total cost was: £', Total:0:2);
{30}   end.
```

Listing 30.9. *Using a* while *loop and a rogue value*

Here is a typical output from the program:

```
Enter the cost of the first item, or 0 to end :23.45 ⏎

Enter the cost of the next item, or 0 to end:6.12 ⏎

Enter the cost of the next item, or 0 to end:5.99 ⏎

Enter the cost of the next item, or 0 to end:0 ⏎

3 items were purchased.

The total cost was: £35.56
```

Notice that the assignment instruction on line {20}, `Count := Count + 1`, is used as a means of counting the number of times the loop is executed. The instruction simply adds 1 to the variable, `Count`, each time the instructions within the loop are repeated.

The true/false expression on line {18} in the `while` statement uses the *relational operator*, `>`, meaning 'greater than', to compare `Amount` with `ROGUEVALUE`. There are in fact six different relational operators that can be used in such logical expressions, and these are shown in Table 30.4.

Relational Operator	Meaning
>	Greater than
> =	Greater than or equal to
<	Less than
< =	Less than or equal to
=	Equal to
< >	Not equal to

Table 30.4 *Relational operators used in logical expressions.*

They are used according to the relationship between two values that is to be established. Whatever logical expression is used, the result of the comparison will either be true or false - if true, the `while` loop will repeat; if false the loop will terminate. More examples of the use of these operators is provided in the next section which deals with the use of logical expressions in making program decisions.

Decisions

Suppose a program is required to display multiple-choice questions with one correct answer out of three possible choices. For example, one of the questions could be:

```
A BYTE is the name given to

    (a)  Four bits

    (b)  Eight bits

    (c)  Sixteen bits

Your answer is:
```

The program is also required to display the message

```
Correct - well done!
```

if the answer is correct, and display a message such as

```
Sorry, the correct answer is (b)
```

if the answer provided is incorrect.

The program must therefore be able to take two alternate courses of action depending on the answer supplied. An `if` statement is one possible way of achieving this requirement. The appropriate form of the `if` statement is illustrated in Listing 30.10 which shows the Pascal code required to display the question above and provide the response appropriate to the letter 'a', 'b' or 'c', typed in.

```
{1}     program Decisions1(input,output);
{2}         {Program to illustrate the use of the if statement}
{3}     var
{4}        Answer         :char;
{5}     begin
{6}       writeln('Enter the letter corresponding to the ');
{7}       writeln('correct answer for the following question:');
{8}       writeln;
{9}
{10}      writeln('A BYTE is the name given to');
{11}      writeln(' (a)  Four bits');
{12}      writeln(' (b)  Eight bits');
{13}      writeln(' (c)  Sixteen bits');
{14}      writeln;
{15}      write('Your answer is: ');
{16}      readln(Answer);
{17}
{18}      if Answer = 'b' then
{19}         writeln('Correct - well done!')
{20}      else
{21}         writeln('Sorry, the correct answer is (b)');
{22}    end.
```

Listing 30.10. *Using an* `if` *statement*

The `if` statement extending over lines {18} to {21} shows how the program can take one of two possible courses of action depending on the value of a variable. We saw in the last section concerning the use of the `while` statement that logical expressions are either true or false. This is also the case with the logical expression `Answer = 'b'` in the `if` statement on line {18}. If the letter stored in the character variable `Answer` is the letter 'b', then the logical expression `Answer = 'b'` will be true, otherwise it will be false. If it is true, the statement following the word `then` is executed (that is, line {19}), otherwise the statement after `else` is executed (that is, line {21}).

The general form of the `if` statement is

```
if {logical expression} then
   {statement 1}
else
   {statement 2}
```

{statement 1} is the instruction that is performed if {logical expression} is true; {statement 2} is performed if logical statement is false. Note that either statement 1 or statement 2 or both of them can be a block of instructions enclosed between begin and end as illustrated below:

```
if Answer = 'b' then
   writeln('Correct - well done!')
else
   begin
     writeln('Sorry, the correct answer is (b)');
     writeln('There are eight bits in a byte');
   end;
```

Sometimes it is necessary to choose between more than just two courses of action in a program. For example, Listing 30.11 shows a program which converts a percentage mark to a pass, merit, distinction or fail grade. The program repeatedly accepts marks and converts them to grades until the mark entered is the rogue value -1 (or any negative integer value) signifying the end of the mark inputs. The rules that are used to determine the grade are as follows:

1. *For a distinction the mark must be over 80.*

2. *For a merit the mark must be greater than or equal to 60 and less than 80.*

3. *For a pass the mark must be greater than or equal to 40 and less than 60.*

4. *Below 40 is a fail.*

```
{1}      program Decision2(input, output);
{2}      const
{3}        DIST        =80;
{4}        MERIT       =60;
{5}        PASS        =40;
{6}
{7}      var
{8}        Mark        :integer;
{9}
{10}     begin
{11}        writeln;
{12}        write('Please enter the first mark(-1 to end): ');
{13}        readln(Mark);
{14}
{15}        while Mark >=0 do
{16}        begin
{17}          if Mark >= DIST then
{18}             writeln('Distinction')
{19}          else if (Mark >= MERIT) and (Mark < DIST) then
{20}                  writeln('Merit')
{21}              else if (Mark >= PASS) and (Mark < MERIT) then
```

```
{22}                        writeln('Pass')
{23}                    else writeln('Fail');
{24}          write('Please enter the next mark(-1 to end): ');
{25}          readln(Mark);
{26}      end;
{27}    end.
```

Listing 30.11. *The if..else if construction*

The if statement between lines {17} and {23} reflects this logic exactly. It is possible to chain if statements in this way to cope with quite complex lines of reasoning. Added flexibility is provided by the use of the logical and operator used for the the logical expressions on lines {19} and {21}. The and operator requires that both of the minor logical expressions it connects are true for the complete logical expression to be true. If either or both are false, then the whole expression is false. Logical operators are discussed in more detail in the next section.

Here is a typical output from the program:

```
Please enter the first mark(-1 to end): 46 ⏎
Pass
Please enter the next mark(-1 to end): 68 ⏎
Merit
Please enter the next mark(-1 to end):32 ⏎
Fail
Please enter the next mark(-1 to end):83 ⏎
Distinction
Please enter the next mark(-1 to end):-1 ⏎
```

Logical Operators

Logical operators allow you to combine logical expressions. There are three logical operators in Pascal : and, or and not. An example of the use of the and operator was provided in Listing 30.11. The and and the or operators are always placed between two logical expressions, and they each combine these logical expressions to produce a value of true or false. Table 30.5 shows the rules that are applied by Pascal to determine whether a compound logical expression is true or false. This type of table is usually called a *truth table*.

(Expr 1)	(Expr 2)	(Expr 1) or (Expr 2)	(Expr 1) and (Expr 2)
true	true	true	true
true	false	true	false
false	true	true	false
false	false	false	false

Table 30.5. *Truth table for the* and *and* or *logical operators.*

Referring back to Listing 30.11 in the previous section, on line {19}, where the compound logical expression (Mark >= MERIT) and (Mark < DIST) is used to determine whether the mark is equivalent to a merit grade. In the expression, (Mark >= MERIT) is an example of (Expr 1) and (Mark < DIST) is an example of (Expr 2) shown in Table 30.5. The next table shows how the and operator combines these two logical expressions for a number of cases:

Mark	(Mark > = MERIT)	(Mark < DIST)	(Mark > = MERIT) and (Mark < DIST)
45	false	true	false
86	true	false	false
67	true	true	true

Table 30.6 *Truth table for the* and *logical operator.*

Thus, both logical expressions must be true for the complete expression to be true; with the or operator, however, only one of the expressions needs to be true for the complete expression to be true. For example, consider the program in Listing 30.12 which reads some text and counts how many vowels it contains. The program uses a for loop to test each letter in turn in the text against each possible vowel. If the current letter is a vowel, that is 'a', 'e', 'i', 'o' or 'u', a count is incremented.

```
{1}     program Vowels(input, output);
{2}     var
{3}       VowelCount      :integer;
{4}       Letters         :string[80];
{5}       LengthOfText    :integer;
{6}       c               :integer;
{7}     begin
{8}       VowelCount:= 0;
{9}       writeln('Type text followed by ENTER: ');
{10}      readln(Letters);
{11}      LengthOfText:= length(Letters);
{12}
{13}      for c:= 1 to LengthOfText do
{14}         if (Letters[c] = 'a') or
{15}            (Letters[c] = 'e') or
{16}            (Letters[c] = 'i') or
{17}            (Letters[c] = 'o') or
{18}            (Letters[c] = 'u')
{19}         then
{20}            VowelCount:= VowelCount + 1;
{21}
{22}      writeln;
{23}      writeln('The text contained ', VowelCount, ' vowels');
{24}     end.
```

Listing 30.12. *Illustrating the use of the* or *logical operator.*

The text is held in a string variable called `Letters`. Each letter in `Letters` is accessed by specifying its position within the text. For example, if the text entered was the string 'hello there', then `Letters[1]` is the letter 'h', `Letters[2]` is the letter 'e', `Letters[3]` is the letter 'l', and so on. The `for` loop control variable, c, starts at 1 and goes up in steps of 1 to the length of the string (11 for the string 'hello there'). The length of the string is determined by the pre-defined Pascal function `length()`, on line {11}, which requires a string as its single argument. (See the later section on Pascal functions for more detail about functions).

Here is the output from the program when the string, 'the cat sat on the mat' is typed in:

```
Type text followed by ENTER: the cat sat on the mat ⏎

The text contained 6 vowels
```

Note that the program will only work with lower-case text. The reason is that lower-case letters 'a', 'b', 'c', etc are represented in a computer using a different set of codes from the equivalent upper-case letters 'A', 'B', 'C', etc.

The third logical operator is the `not` operator which simply reverses the logical value of a logical expression. Thus, the logical expression `not (x > 3)` is true only when x is less than or equal to 3. Similarly, the logical expression `not (Balance <= 0)` is true only when `Balance` has a value that is greater than zero. The truth table shown in Table 30.7 defines the operation of the not logical operator.

Expr	not Expr
true	false
false	true

Table 30.7

More control statements

Listing 30.13 draws together two further Pascal control statements, namely the `repeat..until` and the `case` statements using a progam which allows you to convert Pounds sterling into one of three foreign currencies: American Dollars, German Marks or French Francs.

The `repeat..until` statement provides a third method of constructing a loop. It is similar to the `while` statement in that it uses a logical condition to determine when to exit the loop, but the difference is that the condition appears at the end rather than at the beginning of the loop. This means that the loop will be executed at least once, which is appropriate for this example in which the loop repeatedly executes instructions which display a menu and ask the user to choose one of the menu options. In this example, the `repeat` statement repeats the statements between lines {13} to {63} until the condition following the word `until` is true, that is, when the user enters the letter 'X' or 'x' to indicate the desire to exit the program.

```
{1}    program menu1(input, output);
{2}    uses CRT;
{3}    const
{4}       DOLLARS      =1.5;
{5}       MARKS        =3.4;
{6}       FRANCS       =11;
{7}    var
{8}        Choice       :char;
{9}        Currency     :real;
{10}       Pounds       :real;
{11}   begin
{12}    repeat
{13}     clrscr;
{14}     writeln('Currency conversion program');
{15}     writeln;
{16}     writeln(' (M)arks');
{17}     writeln(' (D)ollars');
{18}     writeln(' (F)rancs');
{19}     writeln('e(X)it');
{20}     writeln;
{21}     write('Which currency do you want to convert to Pounds? ');
{22}     readln(Choice);
{23}     writeln;
{24}
{25}     case Choice of
{26}       'D', 'd':
{27}          begin
{28}            writeln('Enter the amount to convert to Dollars');
{29}            readln(Pounds);
{30}            Currency:=Pounds*DOLLARS;
{31}            writeln('You would get ',Currency:0:0, ' Dollars for',
{32}                       Pounds:0:0, ' Pounds');
{33}            writeln('Press ENTER to return to the menu');
{34}             readln;
{35}          end;
{36}        'M', 'm':
{37}          begin
{38}             writeln('Enter the amount to convert to Marks');
{39}             readln(Pounds);
{40}             Currency:=Pounds*Marks;
{41}             writeln('You would get ',Currency:0:0, ' Marks for ',
{42}                       Pounds:0:0, ' Pounds');
{43}             writeln('Press ENTER to return to the menu');
{44}             readln;
{45}          end;
{46}        'F', 'f':
```

```
{47}          begin
{48}            writeln('Enter the amount to convert to Francs');
{49}            readln(Pounds);
{50}            Currency:= Pounds*FRANCS;
{51}            writeln('You would get ',Currency:0:0, ' Francs for ',
{52}                        Pounds:0:0, ' Pounds');
{53}            writeln('Press ENTER to return to the menu');
{54}            readln;
{55}          end;
{56}        'X', 'x':
{57}            writeln('Exiting program..');
{58}        else
{59}          begin
{60}            writeln('Invalid option. Please try again');
{61}            writeln('Press ENTER to return to the menu');
{62}            readln;
{63}          end;
{64}
{65}   until (Choice = 'X') or (Choice = 'x');
{66}   end.
```

Listing 30.13. *Using the* case *and* repeat *statements in a menu program.*

The case statement is an alternative method to the if statement for choosing between alternative courses of action wihin a program. It has the following gerenral format:

```
case {variable name} of
   value list 1: statement 1;
   value list 2: statement 2;
   etc...
   ......
   else statement N
end;
```

The variable name after the word case can be of type integer, character or boolean; string and real variables ***are not allowed***. Pascal matches the value of the variable against the values specified on the subsequent lines; when a match is found, the corresponding statement is executed after which the case statement is immediately exited without considering any remaining values. If there are no values that match the variable, the case statement does nothing unless the else option is used in which case the supplied statement (shown as statement N above) is executed. Note that some versions of Pascal may not support the use of the else option: you may need to consult the language manual for your version of Pascal.

In Listing 30.13, the case statement is used to select the block of statements corresponding to the menu option chosen by the user. The user can choose one of four options using the letters 'D', 'M','F' or 'X'; to allow for the possibility of either upper or lower case letters being entered, both are included in the case statetment value lines.

Here are some program fragments which should help to clarify the use of the `case` statement:

Example 1

```
var
   Month, Days  :integer;
.......
.......
case Month of
   1, 3, 5, 7, 8, 10, 12  :Days:= 31;
   4, 6, 9, 11            :Days:= 30;
   2                      :Days:= 28;
end;
```

`Month` contains a number corresponding to the month of the year, where January = 1, February = 2 ..... December = 12. The `case` statement is used to store in the variable, `Days`, the number of days in the month whose number is stored in `Month`. Thus if `Month` contained the number 8 corresponding to August, `Days` would be assigned the value 31.

Example 2

```
var
   Smoker :boolean;
   ......
   ......
case Smoker of
   true   :writeln('Smoking seriously damages your health!');
   false  :writeln('Good for you!');
end;
```

If the boolean variable, `Smoker`, has been assigned a value of `true` prior to the `case` statement, the health warning will be displayed, otherwise the complimentary message 'Good for you!' will be displayed.

This is equivalent to using the `if` statement

```
if Smoker then
   writeln('Smoking seriously damages your health!')
else
   writeln('Good for you!');
```

Note that it is because `Smoker` is a boolean variable having a value of `true` or `false`, that it can be used as a logical expression in an `if` statement as illustrated above.

Example 3

```
var
   Letter            :char
   VowelCount        :integer;
   ConsonantCount    :integer;
.....
.....
case Letter of
   'a', 'e', 'i', 'o', u      : VowelCount:= VowelCount + 1;
   'A', 'E', 'I', 'O', 'U'    : VowelCount:= VowelCount + 1;
   ',', '.', ';', ':', '(', ')', ' ':{No action required}
   else    ConsonantCount:= ConsonantCount + 1;
end;
```

Here the program adds one to a vowel count if `Letter` contains either an upper or lower case letter; otherwise it adds one to a consonant count. Punctuation marks, brackets and spaces are ignored. Note that using `if` statements to perform this task would be much more difficult.

Arrays

An *array* is a data structure which allows you to store a number of items of data without having to allocate separate variable names to them. Arrays, like all other identifiers, must be declared before they are used. For example, the following declaration is for an array of five integers:

```
var
   Array1   :array[1..5] of integer;
```

This single declaration is in effect defining five variables called `Array[1]`, `Array[2]`, `Array[3]`, `Array[4]` and `Array[5]`, each of which can store a single integer value. The integer value inside the square brackets is called the array's index, and it is allowed only to take the range of values specified in the declaration (1 to 5 inclusive in this example). Each of these identifiers can be used just like any ordinary integer variable. For instance, to set each of them to zero could be accomplished as follows:

```
Array[1]:= 0;
Array[2]:= 0;
Array[3]:= 0;
Array[4]:= 0;
Array[5]:= 0;
```

However, we could accomplish the same operation by using an integer variable as an *index* and by putting a single assignment statement in a `for` loop:

```
for i:= 1 to 5 do  Array[i]:= 0;
```

Now the count variable i takes on the integer values 1 to 5 and again each element in the array is set to zero. The obvious advantage of using a variable for an index is that arrays can then be used very effectively within loops, and they allow the manipulation of as many or as few numbers as appropriate to the task in hand; notice that the same for loop could initialise 5000 array elements as easily as 5 elements:

```
for i:= 1 to 5000 do   Array[i]:= 0;
```

This would be an exceedingly difficult task to accomplish without the use of an array.

Listing 30.14 illustrates the use of an array of real numbers. The program reads ten numbers into an array and then finds the position within the array of the largest number. It then swaps this number with the frst number in the list before displaying the re-ordered array.

```
{1}     program TopList(input, output);
{2}     uses CRT;
{3}     const
{4}         MAXNUMS        =10;
{5}     var
{6}         Array1         :array[1..MAXNUMS] of real;
{7}         Temp           :real;
{8}         i              :integer;
{9}     begin
{10}      clrscr;
{11}      writeln('Enter ', MAXNUMS, ');
{12}      writeln;
{13}      for i:= 1 to MAXNUMS do
{14}        begin
{15}          write('Enter number ', i, ' and press ENTER :');
{16}          readln(Array1[i]);
{17}        end;
{18}      for i:= 2 to MAXNUMS do
{19}          if Array1[1] < Array1[i] then
{20}             begin
{21}                Temp:= Array1[1];
{22}                Array1[1]:= Array1[i];
{23}                Array1[i]:= Temp;
{24}             end;
{25}      writeln;
{26}      writeln('The new list is as follows:');
{27}      for i:= 1 to MAXNUMS do write(Array1[i]:10:2);
{28}    end.
```

Listing 30.14. *Using an array.*

Line { 2} contains a non-standard statement which allows you to clear the screen by using the pre-defined *procedure* clrscr shown on line {10}. You may have to omit these two lines if you are not using Turbo Pascal. Note that *procedures* and the uses statement are discussed later.

The program first defines a constant MAXNUMS to be the maximum size of the real array, Array1. Lines {11} to {17} are to read in the ten numbers with appropriate user prompts. Thus the first number is read into Array1[1], the second into Array1[2], and so on up to the last number which is read into Array1[10]. The second for loop starting on line {18} compares each number in the array in turn with the first number; if one is found that is greater than the first, they are swapped over. By the time the last number in the array has been compared with the first one, the largest number is in the first position in the array. The following table shows how the list 3, 6, 1, 7, 2, 9, 5, 8, 2, 4 would be processed:

						i				
Array1	*	**2**	**3**	**4**	**5**	**6**	**7**	**8**	**9**	**10**
[1]	3	6	6	7	7	9	9	9	9	9
[2]	6	3	3	3	3	3	3	3	3	3
[3]	1	1	1	1	1	1	1	1	1	1
[4]	7	7	7	6	6	6	6	6	6	6
[5]	2	2	2	2	2	2	2	2	2	2
[6]	9	9	9	9	9	7	7	7	7	7
[7]	5	5	5	5	5	5	5	5	5	5
[8]	8	8	8	8	8	8	8	8	8	8
[9]	2	2	2	2	2	2	2	2	2	2
[10]	4	4	4	4	4	4	4	4	4	4

The column labelled with the '*' shows the original list of numbers, and the subsequent columns labelled '2' through to '10' show the list as each number in turn is compared with the number in the first position of the array.

The table shows that when i is 2, 4 and 6 the first item in the array is exchanged with a larger value. Lines {20} to {24} perform the exchange. Finally, the new list, with the largest number in Array1[1] is displayed on the screen.

A typical output from the program might be as follows:

```
Enter 10 numbers

Enter number 1 :5.7⏎
Enter number 2 : 3 ⏎
Enter number 3 :9.1 ⏎
Enter number 4 :20 ⏎
```

```
Enter number 5 :98.4 ⏎
Enter number 6 :34.67 ⏎
Enter number 7 :23 ⏎
Enter number 8 :56.78 ⏎
Enter number 9 :0 ⏎
Enter number 10 :65.2 ⏎


The new list is as follows:
98.4   3   5.7   9.1   20   34.67   23   56.78   0   65.2
```

As a final example in this section on arrays, Listing 30.15 shows a program which uses a random number generator to select five lottery numbers in the range 1 to 49.

```pascal
{1}        program Lottery(input, output);
{2}        uses CRT;
{3}
{4}        const
{5}            NUMOFNUMS           =5;
{6}            MAXNUM              =49;
{7}        var
{8}            LuckyNums           :array[1..MAXNUM] of integer;
{9}            Num                 :integer;
{10}           i                   :integer;
{11}           Count               :integer;
{12}
{13}       begin
{14}          clrscr;
{15}          writeln('Lottery random number generator');
{16}          writeln;
{17}
{18}          randomize;
{19}
{20}          for i:= 1 to MAXNUM do LuckyNums[i]:= 0;
{21}
{22}          for Count:= 1 to NUMOFNUMS do
{23}            begin
{24}              Num:= random(MAXNUM + 1);
{25}              while LuckyNums[Num] <> 0 do
{26}                    Num := random(MAXNUM + 1);
{27}
{28}              LuckyNums[Num] := Num;
{29}              write(Num:5);
{30}            end;
{31}
{32}          writeln;
{33}          writeln;
{34}          write('Press ENTER to exit program');
{35}          readln;
{36}       end.
```

Listing 30.15. *Using random numbers and an array to generate lottery numbers.*

The random numbers are generated using the pre-defined function `random(N)` which produces a random number in the range specified by its single integer argument, `N`, within the brackets. For example, `random(11)` would produce a random number between 1 and 10 inclusively. Thus the statement

```
{24} Num:= random(MAXNUM + 1);
```

assigns a random number between 1 and 49 to the variable `Num`. The `randomize` instruction on line {18} simply initialises the random number generator so that it does not produce the same sequence of random numbers every time the program is run. Line {20} initialises each element to zero in the array `LuckyNums[]` which is to be used to store the five random numbers. The reason for the `while` loop on lines {25} and {26} is to ensure that the same random number is not used more than once. The loop keeps generating random numbers until it finds one that has not been generated previously. For instance, if the first random number generated on line {24} was the number 36, then this would be stored in `Num`. The `while` loop will only generate another random number if `Luckynums[36]` contains zero, showing that 36 has not previously been generated. As soon as the `while` loop finds an empty slot, the number is stored in the array and immediately displayed on the screen. The process repeats until five different numbers have been generated.

Pre-defined procedures and functions

High-level languages almost invariably provide libraries of useful pre-written programs that are available to the programmer. These programs, which are often termed *pre-defined procedures* and *functions*, have previously been written, compiled and thoroughly tested so that they can be used by programmers with confidence that they are error-free.

In Turbo Pascal such libraries of programs are declared with the nonstandard instruction, `uses`, followed by the name the library file, or *unit*, as it is called. We have already used a unit called `Crt` containing the procedure `clrscr` which was used to clear the display screen Some library programs require you to provide information in the form of *parameters* at the time they are called. An example of such a program is the `delay(T)` procedure which requires you to supply a delay, `T`, in milliseconds inside the brackets. Functions always return an item of information when they are used. For example, in Listing 30.15 we saw that the function `random(N)` returned to the calling program a random number in the range 1 to N-1, where `N` is an integer value. Whatever the version, however, Pascal always provides a number of *standard procedures* and *functions* which are available without the need to declare them in programs. They comprise procedures and functions which are considered to be the most frequently used. It was noted earlier that `readln`, `write` and `writeln` are in fact such standard procedures rather than instructions such as `for` and `if` which are integral parts of the Pascal language. Turbo Pascal keeps the standard procedures and functions, plus quite a few more, in a library unit called `System` which is automatically available when a program is compiled. Pascal's standard functions are described at the end of this chapter, and in addition we have provided further descriptions of a selection of procedures and functions that are available in some of Turbo Pascal's other units.

Simple user-defined procedures

Procedures are often called *subprograms* or *subroutines* because they form only part of a complete program. We saw in the previous section that Pascal provides a number of pre-written functions and procedures that you can use in your own programs, but it is also possible for you to write your own. These are called *user-defined* procedures and functions.

A Pascal procedure is very similar to a Pascal program, the main difference being that a procedure cannot stand by itself - it must form part of another program. Like identifiers such as constants and variables, procedures must also be declared at the beginning of the program before they are used. The structure of a program containing two procedures called Procname1 and Procname2 would have the outline structure shown in Listing 30.16

```
{1}     program Progname(input, output);
{2}     const
{3}        {Progname constants are declared here}
{4}     var
{5}        {Progname variables are declared here}
{6}
{7}     procedure Procname1;
{8}     const
{9}        {Procname1 constants are declared here}
{10}    var
{11}       {Procname1 variables are declared here}
{12}    begin
{13}       {Procname1 code goes here}
{14}    end;
{15}
{16}    procedure Procname2;
{17}    const
{18}       {Procname2 constants are declared here}
{19}    var
{20}       {Procname2 variables are declared here}
{21}    begin
{22}       {Procname2 code goes here}
{23}    end;
{24}    begin
{25}       . . . . . . . .
{26}       . . . . . . .
{27}       Procname1;
{28}       . . . . . . .
{29}       . . . . . . .
{30}       Procname2;
{31}       . . . . . . .
```

```
{32}     end.
```

Listing 30.16.   The structure of a program containing two procedures.

The two procedure definitions, shown in the shaded sections of the program, appear after the `constants` and `variables` declarations of the main program. The definitions of the procedures look exactly like a main program, each having their own constants and variables declarations (if required) and their own main code between `begin` and `end`. The program

Listing 30.17. illustrates the use of simple procedures to cycle through three rudimentary pictures of faces in order to give the appearance of a face winking alternate eyes. The program uses three procedures, `Face1`, `Face2` and `Face3`, each of which uses keyboard characters to display a face. The procedures are executed in the main program by simply naming them. Thus line {36} `Face1` causes the instructions in procedure `Face1` to be executed. The program then continues with line {37} `delay(500)`, a pre-defined procedure which causes a delay of 500 milliseconds.

```
{1}      program Winker(input, output);
{2}      uses CRT;
{3}      var
{4}        i                 :integer;
{5}
{6}      procedure Face1;
{7}      begin
{8}        clrscr;
{9}        writeln('     _ _      ');
{10}       writeln('   < 0 0 >   ');
{11}       writeln('    | ^ |    ');
{12}       writeln('     \_/     ');
{13}      end;
{14}
{15}     procedure Face2;
{16}     begin
{17}       clrscr;
{18}       writeln('     _ _      ');
{19}       writeln('   < 0 o >   ');
{20}       writeln('    | ^ |    ');
{21}       writeln('     \_/     ');
{22}     end;
{23}
{24}     procedure Face3;
{25}     begin
{26}       clrscr;
{27}       writeln('     _ _      ');
{28}       writeln('   < o 0 >   ');
{29}       writeln('    | ^ |    ');
{30}       writeln('     \_/     ');
{31}     end;
{32}
```

```
{33}    begin
{34}    for i:= 1 to 10 do
{35}      begin
{36}        Face1;
{37}        delay(500);
{38}        Face2;
{39}        delay(500);
{40}        Face1;
{41}        delay(500);
{42}        Face3;
{43}        delay(500);
{44}      end;
{45}    end.
```

Listing 30.17 . *Using procedures to make a face wink.*

Each of the procedures uses the pre-defined `clrscr` procedure to clear the screen so that the face stays in the same place and appears to wink. Notice that the logic of the main program is easy to follow by the use of procedures - this is one of their major advantages. Another feature of this program is that although the procedure `Face1` is used twice, the code required for it appears only once in its definition. This economical use of program code is another major advantage of using procedures in programs.

Global vs local variables

Earlier we said that a procedure is allowed to have its own `var` declarations. When this is the case, the variables declared in the procedure are termed *local* variables. This means that these variables only have values while the procedure is being executed; once the procedure has been completed and control has returned to the main program, local variables cannot be accessed. On the other hand, *global* variables, which are defined in the main program, are always available while the program is running, even to procedures. Note, however, that if a variable declared in a procedure has the same name as a variable declared in the main program, the local variable only can be used in the procedure. These ideas are best illustrated with the aid of an example such as that shown in Listing 30.18.

```
{1}     program Scope(input, output);
{2}     uses CRT;
{3}     var
{4}        Greeting1            :string[20];
{5}
{6}     procedure Proc1;
{7}     var
{8}        Greeting1            :string[20];
{9}     begin
{10}       Greeting1:= 'How do';
{11}       writeln('Proc1':15, 'Greeting1':15, 'local ':15, Greeting1:15);
```

```
{12}    end;
{13}
{14}    procedure Proc2;
{15}    var
{16}      Greeting2              :string[20];
{17}    begin
{18}      Greeting2:= 'Hi    ';
{19}      writeln('Proc2':15, 'Greeting2':15, 'local ':15, Greeting2:15);
{20}      writeln('Proc2':15, 'Greeting1':15, 'global':15, Greeting1:15);
{21}    end;
{22}
{23}    begin
{24}       clrscr;
{25}       writeln('Source':15, 'Variable':15, 'Scope':15, 'Value':15);
{26}       writeln;
{27}       Greeting1:= 'Hello ';
{28}       writeln('Main ':15, 'Greeting1':15, 'global':15, Greeting1:15);
{29}       Proc1;
{30}       Proc2;
{31}    end.
```

Listing 30.18. *A program to illustrate the difference between global and local variables.*

The program declares three string variables: `Greeting1` which is a global variable defined on line {4}, `Greeting1` a variable local to procedure `Proc1` and declared on line {8}, and finally `Greeting2` a local variable declared in `Proc2` on line {16}. The main program assigns a value ('Hello') to `Greeting1` on line {27} and displays it. Then when `Proc1` is executed, the local variable `Greeting1` is assigned a different value ('How do') on line {10} and then displays that string. Finally, when `Proc2` is executed, it displays the contents of the local variable `Greeting2` followed by the global variable `Greeting1`. Note that an attempt to include a line such as

```
    writeln(Greeting2);
```

after line {30} in the main program would result in an error since, once `Proc2` has terminated, the local variable `Greeting2` does not exist. Here is what the program produces as its output:

Source	Variable	Scope	Value
Main	Greating1	global	Hello
Proc1	Greating1	local	How do
Proc2	Greating2	local	Hi
Proc2	Greating1	global	Hello

Each line of the output indicates the source of the line, that is whether it is generated from the main program or from a procedure, the name of the variable whose value is being displayed, whether the variable is local or global, and the contents of the variable.

Using parameters in procedures

The 'wink' program shown in Listing 30.17 uses the simplest form of procedure which performs a task without any need to communicate with the main program. However, there will be many instances when you will want to use information available in the main program. As we saw in the previous section, global variables provide one means of accomplishing this, but for sound reasons current programming practice discourages the use of global variables for this purpose. Usually a much better method is to use procedures which have either *value parameters* or *variable parameters*.

Value parameters

Listing 30.19 is a modification of the program shown in Listing 30.17. Notice that another procedure, Wink(), has been included. This new procedure uses a *value parameter*, called Eye, which is defined within brackets after the procedure name on line {34}. A value parameter allows you to pass a value to a procedure from the main program or from another procedure. Thus, on line {47}, the value of the for loop variable k is passed to the procedure Wink. k takes the values 1, 2 and 3 which are used to decide which of the three procedures, Face1, Face2 or Face3 to execute. In effect, this causes each of the latter three procedures to be exected in turn. The outer for loop makes this cycle of three procedures to repeat ten times. When one loop is controlled by an outer loop in this fashion, they are called *nested loops*.

```
{1}      program Winker2(input, output);
{2}      uses CRT;
{3}      var
{4}        i              :integer;
{5}        k              :integer;
{6}
{7}      procedure Face1;
{8}      begin
{9}        clrscr;
{10}       writeln('     _ _     ');
{11}       writeln('   < 0 0 >  ');
{12}       writeln('    | ^ |   ');
{13}       writeln('     \_/    ');
{14}     end;
{15}
{16}     procedure Face2;
{17}     begin
{18}       clrscr;
{19}       writeln('     _ _     ');
{20}       writeln('   < 0 o >  ');
{21}       writeln('    | ^ |   ');
{22}       writeln('     \_/    ');
{23}     end;
{24}
```

```
{25}    procedure Face3;
{26}    begin
{27}      clrscr;
{28}      writeln('     _ _     ');
{29}      writeln('   < o 0 >   ');
{30}      writeln('    | ^ |    ');
{31}      writeln('     \_/     ');
{32}    end;
{33}
{34}    procedure Wink(Eye:integer);
{35}    begin
{36}      case Eye of
{37}        1  :Face1;
{38}        2  :Face2;
{39}        3  :Face3;
{40}      end;
{41}    end;
{42}
{43}    begin
{44}    for i:= 1 to 10 do
{45}        for k:= 1 to 3 do
{46}          begin
{47}            Wink(k);
{48}            delay(500);
{49}          end;
{50}    end.
```

Listing 30.19. *A program to illustrate the use of value parameters.*

The number of parameters that you can use in a procedure is not limited to one - you can use as many as you like as long as you declare them in the procedure definition and include them within the brackets when you call the procedure from the main program. For example, suppose that we wanted to include the pre-defined delay procedure on line {48} within the procedure Wink() as shown in the program fragment below.

```
procedure Wink(Eye:integer, Time:integer);
begin
  case Eye of
    1  :begin
          Face1;
          delay(Time);
        end;
    2  :begin
          Face2;
          delay(Time);
        end;
    3  :begin
          Face3;
          delay(Time);
        end;
end;
```

Now `Wink()` has two value parameters and these would both be included in any call to the procedure, as shown in the example below.

```
for i:= 1 to 10 do
    for k:= 1 to 3 do Wink(k, 500);
```

An important point about value parameters is that they provide a *one-way transfer of information* from the main program to a procedure. Variables used as value parameters when a procedure is called are unaffected by any processing that has occurred within the procedure; this is not the case, however, with *variable parameters*.

Variable parameters

Listing 30.20 is an example of a program which incorporates a procedure that uses a variable parameter.

```
{1}      program VarParam(input, output);
{2}      var
{3}         Smaller      :real;
{4}         Larger       :real;
{5}
{6}      procedure Sort(var a, b:real);
{7}      var
{8}         Temp :real;
{9}      begin
{10}        if a > b then
{11}          begin
{12}            Temp:= a;
{13}            a:= b;
{14}            b:= Temp;
{15}          end;
{16}     end;
{17}
{18}     begin
{19}        write('Enter two numbers: ');
{20}        readln(Smaller, Larger);
{21}        Sort(Smaller, Larger);
{22}        write('The sorted numbers are: ');
{23}        writeln(Smaller:10:2, Larger:10:2);
{24}     end.
```

Listing 30.20. *A program to illustrate the use of variable parameters.*

The program simply sorts two numbers into ascending order of magnitude using a procedure. The procedure has two variable parameters, a and b, which it compares: if a is greater than b, the values in a and b are swapped over. The main program asks the user to enter two numbers, it calls the procedure using the two numbers stored in Smallest and Largest, and then displays them when the procedure has finished. Here is a typical run of the program:

```
Enter two numbers: 34.6   17.32
The sorted numbers are:    17.32        34.6
```

Notice that the values contained in Smallest and Largest, which were exchanged in the procedure using the variables a and b, have been swapped over. Thus, *variable parameters allow a two-way exchange of data* between a program and a procedure.

User-defined functions

As well as being able to write your own procedures you can also devise your own functions. Functions also accept value or variable parameters, but in addition they require that you declare what type of value they return. So, for a function, you would need to write its first line using the following format:

```
function FunctionName(parameters):return type;
```

In addition, you must assign the return value to FunctionName somewhere within the function. For example, for a function called TriangleType which accepts three positive real numbers, in ascending order of magnitude, representing the three sides of a triangle and which returns an integer value of 0, 2 or 3 indicating how many of its sides are equal, the following function definition might be appropriate:

```
{20}    function TriangleType(a, b, c:real):integer;
{21}    var
{22}     Count      :integer;
{23}    begin
{24}     Count:= 0;
{25}     if a = b then Count:= Count + 1;
{26}     if b = c then Count:= Count + 1;
{27}     if c = a then Count:= Count + 1;
{28}     case Count of
{29}       0      :TriangleType:= 0;
{30}       1      :TriangleType:= 2;
{31}       2      :{not possible}
{32}       3      :TriangleType:= 3;
{33}     end;
{34}    end;
```

Listing 30.21. *A function which determines what type of triangle is represented by three numbers*

The three sides are passed as value parameters to the variables a, b and c. The if statements on lines {25} to {27} increment Count if any two sides are the same. The values that Count can assume are 0 for no sides equal, 1 if two sides are equal and 3 if all three sides are equal; a value of 2 is not possible when the three sides are arranged in ascending order of magnitude. The number of equal sides is stored in TriangleType by the case statement and it is this value which is returned by the function to the calling program. Note that because a function always returns a value it can be used like a variable in an arithmetic expression or in a logical expression or in a write statement. For example, it would be perfectly valid to write

```
if TriangleType(x, y, z) = 3 then
    writeln('Equilateral triangle');
```

Sorting a list of numbers

The program shown in Listing 30.22 is a further illustration of the use of a function, but this time using two variable parameters. The program uses a simple sorting technique called a *bubble sort* to arrange five numbers into ascending order of magnitude. It is called a bubble sort because, one after the other, it causes the next smallest number in the list to 'rise' to the front of the list. The program operates by repeatedly scanning through the list in 'passes', each pass causing the smallest number detected to move towards the beginning of the list.

For example, suppose we used the program to sort the numbers 4, 3, 2, 7, 9. A pass starts at the end of the list, comparing the last number with the preceding number, that is, it compares the number 9 with the number 7. If, as in this case, the two numbers are already in ascending order it leaves them as they are, but if they are not in ascending order it swaps them over. Then the next two adjacent numbers are compared, this time 7 and 2. Again, they are in ascending order and so they are not swapped. On the next comparison, however, when 2 is compared with 3, the two items are swapped so that they are in ascending order. The list of numbers then becomes 4, 2, 3, 7, 9. On the final comparison, this time using 4 and 2, the two values are again swapped to change the list to 2, 4, 3, 7, 9. Thus the smallest value, 2 has 'bubbled' to the top of the list. This set of four comparisons constitutes one pass. On the next pass, because the smallest number is in the correct position, it is ignored. The process of repeating passes terminates when a pass does not result in any swaps since this means that the list must be in the correct order. The table below shows how the numbers in the example list are processed over the three passes required to complete the bubble sort.

Original order	4	3	2	7	9
After pass 1	2	4	3	7	9
After pass 2	2	3	4	7	9
After pass 3	2	3	4	7	9

The shaded boxes show that the number of items used decreases by one after every pass. The program starts by asking the user to enter 5 numbers (the value of the constant, NUMS) using a read instruction. Read is very similar to readln, but it does not expect each item read to be terminated by pressing ENTER; items are separated with one or more spaces. If you were to type in more than five numbers separated by spaces, the extra numbers would be available for any further read instructions later in the program. In other words, inputs from a read instruction go into a buffer from which only the exact number of items required are extracted.

The program then goes on to perform a bubble sort on the numbers entered. The number of passes is controlled by a repeat instruction which terminates when a pass results in no swaps. The list of numbers is displayed after each pass to show how the list of numbers has been affected. After each pass the pass number, stored in the variable `Pass`, is incremented on line {48}. This is used to adjust the range of the control variable so that the number that last 'bubbled' to the top of the list is ignored in the comparisons made in the next pass. (See line {41}. The boolean function Swaps() on line {42} is used to determine whether it is necessary to swap two adjacent items. If a swap is necessary, it returns a value of `true`, otherwise it returns `false`. A swap within a pass indicates that the list may still not be fully sorted so the boolean variable `NoMorePasses` is set to false to ensure that at least one more pass is performed on the numbers.

```
{1}      program BubbleSort(input, output);
{2}      uses CRT;
{3}      const
{4}         NUMS            =5;
{5}      var
{6}         List            :array[1..NUMS] of real;
{7}         NoMorePasses    :boolean;
{8}         i               :integer;
{9}         Pass            :integer;
{10}
{11}     function Swap(var a, b:real):boolean;
{12}
{13}     var
{14}        Temp            :real;
{15}     begin
{16}        Swap:=false;
{17}        if a < b then
{18}          begin
{19}            Temp:= a;
{20}            a:= b;
{21}            b:= Temp;
{22}            Swap:=true;
{23}          end;
{24}     end;
{25}
{26}     begin   { *** Main program *** }
{27}        clrscr;
{28}
{29}        { *** Get numbers from the keyboard *** }
{30}        writeln;
{31}        writeln('Enter ', NUMS, ' numbers...');
{32}        writeln('... with a space between each number... '};
{33}        writeln('... and then press ENTER');
{34}        for i:= 1 to NUMS do read(List[i]);
{35}
{36}        { *** Sort the numbers *** }
{37}        Pass:= 1;
{38}        repeat
{39}          NoMorePasses:= true;
```

```
{40}            { *** Process complete list *** }
{41}            for i:= NUMS downto Pass + 1 do
{42}                if Swap(List[i], List[i-1]) then
{43}                        NoMorePasses:=false;
{44}            { *** Show result of this pass *** }
{45}            writeln;
{46}            write('Pass #', Pass, ':');
{47}            for i:= 1 to NUMS do    write(List[i]:10:2);
{48}            Pass:= Pass + 1;
{49}          until NoMorePasses;
{50}
{51}          writeln(' ... sort completed');
{52}        end.
```

Listing 30.22. *.A bubble sort program which uses a function.*

Writing programs using procedures and functions

Listing 30.23 illustrates the use of user-defined procedures and functions in a program which allows two people to use the computer to play noughts and crosses. The program illustrates the use of procedures and functions appropriate to a variety of situations. The main program alternately gets X and O moves, checking each time for a winning or drawn position. The program terminates when someone has won or after nine moves have been made.

```
{1}    program Oxo(input, output);
{2}
{3}    {-------------------------------------------------------------------}
{4}    { A program which makes use of functions and procedures to allow two  }
{5}    { players to play noughts and crosses. The computer checks for a win or}
{6}    { draw automatically, and makes sure that illegal moves are not made.  }
{7}    { The board is a grid numbered 1 to 9. Each Player in turn selects a   }
{8}    { number and the grid is redrawn with the X or O in that position.     }
{9}    { X always starts first.                                               }
{10}   {-------------------------------------------------------------------}
{11}
{12}   uses CRT; {The screen handling unit to allow the screen to be cleared}
{13}
{14}   var
{15}       Grid               :array[1..9] of char;
{16}       Move               :integer;
{17}       Count              :integer;
{18}       Winner             :boolean;
{19}       XMove              :boolean;
{20}
{21}   procedure InitGrid;
{22}   {-------------------------------------------------------------------}
{23}   { This sets up the board with the positions numbered from 1 to 9      }
{24}   {-------------------------------------------------------------------}
{25}
{26}   begin
{27}       Grid[1]:='1';
{28}       Grid[2]:='2';
{29}       Grid[3]:='3';
{30}       Grid[4]:='4';
```

```
{31}        Grid[5]:='5';
{32}        Grid[6]:='6';
{33}        Grid[7]:='7';
{34}        Grid[8]:='8';
{35}        Grid[9]:='9';
{36} end;
{37}
{38} procedure DrawGrid;
{39} {-------------------------------------------------------------------}
{40} { This draws the current board after every move                     }
{41} {-------------------------------------------------------------------}
{42}
{43} begin
{44}      clrscr;
{45}      writeln(' ',Grid[1], ' | ', Grid[2], ' | ', Grid[3]);
{46}      writeln('---|---|---');
{47}      writeln(' ',Grid[4], ' | ', Grid[5], ' | ', Grid[6]);
{48}      writeln('---|---|---');
{49}      writeln(' ',Grid[7], ' | ', Grid[8], ' | ', Grid[9]);
{50}      writeln;
{51} end;
{52}
{53} function CheckMove(Move:integer):boolean;
{54} {--------------------------------------------------------------------}
{55} { This validates every move to make sure that a number from 1 to 9 is }
{56} { chosen and that the selected position is not already occupied by an  }
{57} { X or O.                                                             }
{58} { Parameters:        Move    - integer value parameter              }
{59} { Return value:      boolean - true if valid move, false if invalid move}
{60} {--------------------------------------------------------------------}
{61}
{62} begin
{63}   CheckMove:= true;
{64}   if (Move < 1) or (Move > 9)
{65}   then begin
{66}        writeln('Invalid position - enter a number between 1 and 9');
{67}        CheckMove:= false;
{68}        end
{69}   else if (Grid[Move] = 'X') or (Grid[Move] = 'O')
{70}        then begin
{71}             writeln('This position has already been used');
{72}             CheckMove:= false;
{73}             end;
{74} end;
{75}
{76} function GetXmove:integer;
{77} {-------------------------------------------------------------------}
{78} { This accepts the X move from the player. If the move is invalid, the }
{79} { player is required to enter the move again.                        }
{80} { Parameters:        None                                           }
{81} { Return value:      Integer in the range 1 to 9                    }
{82} {-------------------------------------------------------------------}
{83} var
{84}    Xpos            :integer;
{85}    ValidXMove      :boolean;
{86} begin
{87}   repeat
{88}     writeln;
{89}     writeln('Enter position( 1 to 9 ) for X move');
{90}     readln(Xpos);
```

```
{91}          ValidXMove:= CheckMove(Xpos);
{92}       until ValidXMove;
{93}       GetXmove := Xpos;
{94}    end;
{95}
{96}    function GetOmove:integer;
{97}    {------------------------------------------------------------------}
{98}    { This accepts the O move from the player. If the move is invalid, the }
{99}    { player is required to enter the move again.                      }
{100}   { Parameters:        None                                         }
{101}   { Return value:      Integer in the range 1 to 9                  }
{102}   {------------------------------------------------------------------}
{103}   var
{104}      Opos         :integer;
{105}      ValidOMove   :boolean;
{106}   begin
{107}      repeat
{108}         writeln;
{109}         writeln('Enter position( 1 to 9 ) for O move');
{110}         readln(Opos);
{111}         ValidOMove:= CheckMove(Opos);
{112}      until ValidOMove;
{113}      GetOmove:= Opos;
{114}   end;
{115}
{116}   function CheckForWinner :boolean;
{117}   {------------------------------------------------------------------}
{118}   { This checks for a line of X's or O's in one of the 7 possible ways }
{119}   { It determines whether a row, column or diagonal contains the same  }
{120}   { character (ie an X or an O).                                     }
{121}   { Parameters:        None                                         }
{122}   { Return value:      Boolean - true if there is a winner, false herwise}
{123}   {------------------------------------------------------------------}
{124}
{125}   begin
{126}      if (Grid[1]=Grid[2]) and (Grid[2]=Grid[3]) or
{127}         (Grid[4]=Grid[5]) and (Grid[5]=Grid[6]) or
{128}         (Grid[7]=Grid[8]) and (Grid[8]=Grid[9]) or
{129}         (Grid[1]=Grid[4]) and (Grid[4]=Grid[7]) or
{130}         (Grid[2]=Grid[5]) and (Grid[5]=Grid[8]) or
{131}         (Grid[3]=Grid[6]) and (Grid[6]=Grid[9]) or
{132}         (Grid[1]=Grid[5]) and (Grid[5]=Grid[9]) or
{133}         (Grid[3]=Grid[5]) and (Grid[5]=Grid[7])
{134}      then
{135}         CheckForWinner:= true
{136}      else CheckForWinner:= false;
{137}   end;
{138}
{139}   begin    { Main program }
{140}      InitGrid;           { Call procedure to initialise the board }
{141}      Count:= 0;          { Counts the number of valid moves made  }
{142}      Winner:= false;     { Boolean variable which becomes true     }
{143}                          { when there is a winner                  }
{144}      XMove:= true;       { Keeps track of whose move it is:        }
{145}                          { true for X move                         }
{146}                          { false for Y move                        }
{147}      DrawGrid;           { Display the initial board position      }
{148}
{149}      { Loop to repeat the playing sequence                         }
{150}      while (Count < 9) and  not Winner do
```

```
{151}    begin
{152}      case XMove of
{153}        true:        { Do this if it is X's move               }
{154}          begin
{155}            Move:= GetXmove;   {Get the X move position         }
{156}            Grid[Move]:='X';   {Store it in the data structure  }
{157}            XMove:= false;     {Make it O's move next           }
{158}          end;
{159}        false:       { Do this if it is O's move               }
{160}          begin
{161}            Move:= GetOmove;   {Get the O move position         }
{162}            Grid[Move]:= 'O';  {Store it in the data structure  }
{163}            XMove:= true;      {Make it X's move next           }
{164}          end;
{165}      end;
{166}
{167}      Count:= Count + 1;    {Increment count after every move }
{168}
{169}      DrawGrid;                {Show the current board position  }
{170}
{171}      { Check to see if the game is a win or draw               }
{172}      Winner:= CheckForWinner;
{173}      if   Winner
{174}      then writeln('End of Game:', Grid[Move], ' has won')
{175}      else if   Count=9
{176}          then writeln('A draw');
{177}    end;
{178}
{179}    readln;
{180} end.
```

Listing 30.23. *Noughts and crosses game*

The two procedures, InitGrid and DrawGrid, and the four functions, CheckMove, GetXMove, GetYMove and CheckForWinner, used in the program are described in the following sections.

InitGrid

This procedure initialises the character array, Grid[], which is a global array used throughout the program by every procedure and function. The procedure is used only once and does not require any parameters.

DrawGrid

This procedure draws the current board position. Initially the board is displayed like this:

```
 1 | 2 | 3
---|---|---
 4 | 5 | 6
---|---|---
 7 | 8 | 9
```

The numbers are replaced by Xs and Os as the game progresses.

CheckMove

This function has a single integer value parameter called `Move` which represents the current player's choice of board position. The function first checks that the integer is in the range 1 to 9 before checking the contents of `Grid[Move]` to ensure that the position is not already occupied with an X or an O. If the move is valid, the function returns a boolean value of `true`, otherwise it returns `false`. `CheckMove` is used by the following two functions.

GetXMove

This function asks the X player to type in a number from 1 to 9 representing a board position. If the move is valid, the function terminates and the position entered by the player is returned as an integer value; if the move is invalid (see function `CheckMove`) the player is requested to try again.

GetOMove

This function asks the O player to type in a number from 1 to 9. Otherwise it is structurally identical to `GetXMove`.

CheckForWinner

This function checks individually the three rows, three columns and two diagonals that they contain the same character. If one of these lines does contain the same character, then one of the players has won. For example, if the diagonal represented by `Grid[1]`, `Grid[5]` and `Grid[9]` all contain an X, then the X player has won.

Advantages of using procedures and functions

All good programmers make full use of procedures and functions, and in fact their use is essential to the development of all but the most trivial programs. There are a number of good reasons for making this statement, including the following:

- They allow a large, complex program to be built up from a number of smaller of more manageable units. This facilitates a team approach to program development by allowing each unit to be written and tested independently of the rest of the program.
- They can reduce the amount of code required for a program. Once a subprogram has been developed, it can be used as many times as required within a program using the same code.
- They can reduce the amount of time required to write a program if libraries of re-usable functions and procedures are available. This is much the same as building electronic circuits using standard electronic components.

Validating input

Very frequently a program will need to be provided with data supplied by a user. Unfortunately, there is no guarantee that the user will always provide sensible data, so it is the responsibility of the programmer to *validate* input data, that is, check input data to ensure that programs do not attempt to process invalid data. The noughts and crosses program shown in Listing 30.23 incorporated two simple validation checks in the function `CheckMove` by ensuring that a player chose a number between 1 and 9 representing an unused position. However, there are many more possibilities for validating input.

For example, in typical stock control systems, transactions are details regarding the receipt of stock from suppliers, the issuing of stock to customers, deleting items of stock that are no longer provided, adding new items of stock and modifying stock details (such as cost). Even though these transactions may have been verified or subjected to other control procedures before entering the computer, they may still contain errors: some vital piece of information, such as the item's code number, may have been incorrectly typed or even accidentally omitted from a transaction, or an attempt might be made to add an item to the stock file using a stock code that already exists, or a field containing the cost of the item might be outside expected limits. There are many ways that invalid transactions can be presented to the computer for processing, hence the need for validation programming procedures to detect invalid data inputs. A number of common validation checks are described in the following sections.

Existence Test

It is often essential that certain data fields in a transaction are not left empty. For instance, if you go to a bank with the intention of depositing some money in your account, you need to fill in a credit transfer slip. This slip is the source document containing the details that the bank will use when it processes your transaction. Of course, the bank clerk that you see will probably notice if you forget to write your account number on the credit slip, but the computer system will also check that your account number is present before attempting to credit your account. In a stock control system, an order must show, in the quantity field, how many units of each item are required; if this field in the transaction details is blank then the transaction is invalid and some action must be taken.

Range Check

When applying for certain education grants, students must be a minimum age (18 for example) in order to qualify. A *range check* might be used by the computer system to determine that the applicant is no younger than the minimum age when processing the application. A mail order system might use a range check on numeric catalogue item codes to make sure that the codes entered in transactions are between known values. Range checks can be used whenever upper or lower limits are known for numeric fields.

Format Check

Quite frequently a field in a transaction is a code containing both alphabetic and numeric data. An example is a customer account number such as YG1232367, in which the first two characters must be alphabetic and they must be followed by seven numeric digits. A *format check* would be used to confirm that the code is correctly formed.

Combination Check

Combination checks validate fields that have some connection; that is, the value of one field in the transaction determines whether other fields are correct. For instance, a mail order company offering free delivery on orders over a certain value might cross check the order value with the field containing the postage charge; if the order value is below the limit for free postage, the postage field should contain a non-zero value. Public lending libraries usually allocate special membership numbers to junior borrowers; when a child borrows a book, a combination check could make sure that the type of book being borrowed is one that is allowed for juniors by examining the membership number in combination with the book classification.

Check Digits

Two of the most common errors that occur when data is being transferred from source documents to computer storage by means of a keyboard are *transcription* and *transposition* errors. Transcription errors are made by data entry persons accidentally making typing errors while copying source documents. For example, instead of typing the stock number 26573, the data entry person types 26513, mistaking the 7 for a 1.

The type of error illustrated above is not only very common, but is also difficult or even impossible to detect using the validation checks described so far. For these reasons, a special technique for numerical data is sometimes used, involving appending a specially calculated *check digit* to the end of a number. Calculating a check digit involves a number of steps which are illustrated below in the calculation of a check digit for the number 26573.

1. Multiply the rightmost digit by 2, then the next digit by 3 and so on:

original number:		2	6	5	7	3
multiply by:		6	5	4	3	2
this gives:		**12**	**30**	**20**	**21**	**6**

2. Add these values together:

$$12 + 30 + 20 + 21 + 6 = \textbf{79}$$

3. Divide by 11 and note the remainder:

$$79 \div 11 = 7 \text{ remainder } \textbf{2}$$

4. Subtract the remainder from 11 to give the final check digit:

$$11 - 2 = \textbf{9}$$

5. The number including the check digit is thus 26573**9**

In this example, the number 11 is called the *modulus* used to determine the check digit, and though 11 is frequently used, this need not be the case.

So how does this help with transcription errors? To illustrate, let's take another look at the two examples quoted earlier: firstly 26573 becoming 26513. We have seen already that the check digit for the number 26573 turns out to be 9 so that the number to be input to the computer by the data entry person is now 265739. It is a relatively simple matter to include in the computer program that processes the transactions, a validation check which repeats the check digit calculation on the first five digits of the number. This calculation, however, would be performed on the number 265139 which contains the transcription error. The calculation performed by the program would proceed as follows:

1. Multiply the rightmost digit by 2, then the next digit by 3 and so on:

original number:	2	6	5	1	3
multiply by:	6	5	4	3	2
this gives:	**12**	**30**	**20**	**3**	**6**

2. Add these values together:

$$12 + 30 + 20 + 3 + 6 = \mathbf{71}$$

3. Divide by 11 and note the remainder:

$$71 \div 11 = 6 \text{ remainder } \mathbf{5}$$

4. Subtract 5 from 11 to give the final check digit:

$$11 - 5 = \mathbf{6}$$

As you can see, the check digit is not the same as last time, and this means that the original number must contain an error. Though it is true that the length of numbers that use a check digit must be increased by one, this validation check greatly reduces the chances of errors entering an information system. Check digits are particularly useful for ensuring that important data fields such as customer, account or stock numbers are entered into the system without error. The program shown in Listing 30.24 illustrates the programming required to calculate a check digit for a five-digit number.

```
{1}   program CheckDigit(input, output);
{2}   {Produces a mod 11 check digit given a five-digit number}
{3}
{4}   var
{5}      Number       :integer;
{6}      Total        :integer;
{7}      Digit1       :integer;
{8}      Digit2       :integer;
{9}      CheckDig     :integer;
```

```
{10}    i                  :integer;
{11}
{12} begin
{13}    Total:= 0;
{14}    writeln('Check digit calculation.');
{15}    writeln('Please enter a five-digit number ');
{16}    readln(Number);
{17}
{18}    {Calculate the weighted total}
{19}    for i:= 1 to 5 do
{20}    begin
{21}      Digit1:= Number mod 10;         {Extract the least significant digit}
{22}      Total:= Total + Digit1*(i+1);   {Add it to a running total           }
{23}      Number:= Number  div 10;        {Remove the least significant digit }
{24}    end;
{25}
{26}    {Now calculate the check digit}
{27}    Digit2:= Total mod 11;
{28}    CheckDig:= 11 - Digit2;
{29}
{30}    {Display the answer and then wait for ENTER}
{31}    if    CheckDig > 9
{32}    then  writeln('Check digit not possible for this number')
{33}    else  writeln('The check digit is   ', CheckDig);
{34}    readln;
{35} end.
```

Listing 30.24 . A program to calculate a check digit

The for loop from lines {19} to {24} does most of the calculation. The least significant digit is extracted from the five-digit number using the mod function which, in this case, finds the remainder when the number is divided by ten. For example, again using the number 26513,

        26513 mod 10 = 3

This is then multplied by 2 (that is, i + 1) and added to a running total on line {22}. The least significant digit is then removed from the original number using

    Number:= Number   div 10;

on line {23}. This assigns 26513 div 10 = 2651 to Number, and the process repeats with the new least significant digit, 1. Thus the digits in the number are successively multiplied by 2, 3, 4, 5 and 6 and added to a running total. Lines {27} and {28} complete the calculation. Finally, because some numbers produce a check digit of 10 (as a result of using the remainder when the total is divided by 11), lines {31} to {33} determine whether a valid check digit has been obtained and, if so, display it.

Screen handling

Turbo Pascal's CRT unit contains a number of useful screen handling functions and procedures. We have already used two of the procedures in the unit: clrscr to clear the screen and delay() to make the computer pause while executing a program. More functions and procedures in the CRT unit are described below:

Window procedure

Defines a text window on the screen. The syntax of the procedure is

Window(X1,Y1,X2,Y2) where the four parameters are explained by the following diagram.

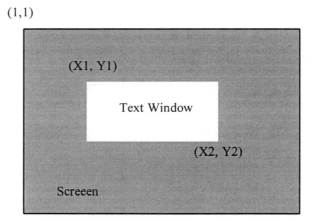

To set a text window containing ten lines at the top of the screen use

```
window(1,1,80,10)
```

To return the current window to the full screen size use

```
window(1,1,80,25)
```

ClrEol procedure

Clears all characters from the cursor position to the end of the line without moving the cursor. It uses the current text window.

DelLine procedure

Deletes the line containing the cursor in the current text window.

GotoXY procedure

Moves the cursor to X, Y, where X is the column and Y is the row relative to the top left corner of the current window which has the coordinates (1, 1). Thus to move the cursor to row 5, column 10, you would use GotoXY(10,5).

InsLine procedure

Inserts a line in the current text window above the line that the cursor is on.

TextColor procedure

This sets the colour for subsequently displayed text. There are sixteen colours and you can specify each one by name or by using the equivalent number as shown in the adjacent table. Thus, to set the text colour to red, you could use either

```
TextColor(Red) or
```

```
TextColor(4).
```

By using the pre-defined constant, blink, you can make the text flash eg TextColor(Blue + Blink).

Colour	Value
Black	0
Blue	1
Green	2
Cyan	3
Red	4
Magenta	5
Brown	6
LightGray	7
DarkGray	8
LightBlue	9
LightGreen	10
LightCyan	11
LightRed	12
LightMagenta	13
Yellow	14
White	15

TextBackGround procedure

This allows you to set one of sixteen different colours for the text background. The colours are shown in the table. Thus to set the background colour to light grey you could use either

```
TextBackGround(LightGray) or
```

```
TextBackGround(7).
```

Note that if you clear the screen using clrscr after setting the background colour, the whole of the current text window will change to that colour.

Example program 1

The example shown in Listing 30.25 illustrates the use of text windows and text colours by drawing random windows of different colours.

```
{1}    program Screen1(input,output);
{2}
{3}    {-------------------------------------------------}
{4}    { Illustrates some screen handling facilities by }
{5}    { drawing randomly sized and coloured windows    }
{6}    {-------------------------------------------------}
{7}
{8}    uses CRT;
{9}    var
```

```
{10}    x     :integer;
{11}    y     :integer;
{12}    i     :integer;
{13}
{14}  begin
{15}    textbackground(Black);{ Clear screen }
{16}    clrscr;
{17}
{18}    for i:= 1 to 100 do
{19}      begin
{20}      { Draw random windows }
{21}      x := Random(60);     { Random x position        }
{22}      y := Random(15);     { Random y position        }
{23}      window(x, y, x + Random(10), y + Random(8));
{24}      textbackground( Random(16) + 1);
{25}      clrscr;              { Set window to random color in }
{26}                           { the range 1 to 16        }
{27}      delay(200);          { Pause for 200 millisecs       }
{28}    end;
{29}
{30}  end.
```

Listing 30.25. *Using text windows*

KeyPressed and Readkey

Two other useful functions to be found in Turbo Pascal's CRT unit are `KeyPressed` and `ReadKey`. `KeyPressed` returns a boolean value of `true` if there is a character in the keyboard buffer and `false` if the buffer is empty. The keyboard buffer is simply an area of memory which is used to store, temporarily, characters entered through the keyboard. `KeyPressed` can therefore be used to detect any use of the keyboard. A common application of `KeyPressed` is as a means of terminating a loop, as illustrated by the following program fragment:

```
repeat
   {instructions to be repeated}
until keypressed;
```

Each time through the repeat loop `KeyPressed` tests the keyboard buffer: if a key has been pressed, tthe keyboard buffer will have at least one entry, `KeyPressed` returns `true` and the loop terminates, otherwise `KeyPressed` returns `false` and the loop repeats once more.

`Readkey` allows you to capture a keystroke by reading the first character in the keyboard buffer. If the keyboard buffer is empty, it waits until a character is available and then returns its value. The advantage of using `ReadKey` rather than `read` or `readln` is that it is not necessary to press < Enter >.

Example program 2

The program shown in Listing 30.26 echoes only numeric characters to the screen, ignoring characters that are not in the range 0 to 9. The repeat loop terminates as soon as the space bar is pressed.

```
{1}   program EchoNumbers(input,output);
{2}
{3}   {----------------------------------------------------------- }
{4}   {Program to display numeric digits entered at keyboard and to }
{5}   {ignore any other characters typed. The program terminates when}
{6}   {the space bar is pressed.                                    }
{7}   {-----------------------------------------------------------}
{8}
{9}   uses CRT;
{10}
{11}  var
{12}     key   :char;
{13}
{14}  begin
{15}    repeat
{16}      key:= readkey;
{17}      if (key >= '0') and (key <= '9') then write(key);
{18}    until key = ' ';
{19}  end.
```

Listing 30.26. *Using* readkey

Sound and NoSound

Finally, these two procedures allow you to use your computer's built-in speaker. Sound(Pitch) causes the speaker to emit a tone whose pitch is determined by the integer parameter, Pitch. Thus, Sound(500) produces a tone with pitch 500Hz. NoSound terminates the tone produced by Sound. Thus to produce a tone of 300Hz for half a second within a program you could use:

```
sound(300);
delay(500);
nosound;
```

Example program 3

As a final example Listing 30.27 uses all of the screen handling functions and procedures discussed in a program which measures how quickly you are able to press a key after being given a signal.

```
{1}   program reflexes(input, output);
{2}
{3}   {-----------------------------------------------------------}
```

```
{4}      { A program to illustrate some screen handling facilities.     }
{5}      { The user is invited to test his/her reflexes by pressing a key}
{6}      { as  quickly as possible. The average of three attempts is     }
{7}      { calculated and displayed in millisecond units.                }
{8}      {--------------------------------------------------------------}
{9}
{10}     uses crt;
{11}     const
{12}       ROW              =2;   { The row base position for screen text    }
{13}       COLUMN           =5;   { The column base position for screen text}
{14}
{15}     var
{16}       i                :integer;  { A for loop control variable         }
{17}       Total            :integer;  { The total time for the three attempts}
{18}     {...............................oOo.............................}
{19}
{20}     procedure FlushKeyboardBuffer;
{21}
{22}     {--------------------------------------------------------------}
{23}     { This makes sure that there are no characters in the standard  }
{24}     { input buffer. The function readkey removes a single character }
{25}     { from the keyboard buffer. Keypressed is true while there is at}
{26}     { least one character in the buffer                             }
{27}     {--------------------------------------------------------------}
{28}
{29}     var
{30}       key              :char;
{31}
{32}     begin
{33}       while keypressed do
{34}          key:= readkey;
{35}     end;
{36}     {...............................oOo.............................}
{37}
{38}     procedure PressAnyKey;
{39}
{40}     {--------------------------------------------------------------}
{41}     { A procedure that waits until a key is pressed before          }
{42}     { continuing with the next instruction                         }
{43}     {--------------------------------------------------------------}
{44}
{45}     begin
{46}       FlushKeyboardBuffer;        { Ensure that the keyboard buffer is }
{47}                                   { empty                              }
{48}       repeat until keypressed;    { Do nothing until a key is pressed  }
{49}     end;
{50}     {...............................oOo.............................}
{51}
{52}     procedure instructions;
{53}
```

```
{54}    {----------------------------------------------------------------}
{55}    { Displays the instructions for using the program               }
{56}    {----------------------------------------------------------------}
{57}
{58}    begin
{59}      window(10,10,70,20);        { Define the text window          }
{60}      textcolor(yellow);          { Text colour set to yellow       }
{61}      textbackground(blue);       { Background text clour is blue   }
{62}      clrscr;
{63}      gotoxy(COLUMN, ROW);
{64}      writeln('Put your finger on any key and as soon as');
{65}      gotoxy(COLUMN, ROW+1);
{66}      writeln('this window changes colour, press it');
{67}      gotoxy(COLUMN, ROW+3);
{68}      writeln('You will get three tries and the program');
{69}      gotoxy(COLUMN, ROW+4);
{70}      writeln('will calculate your average response time');
{71}      gotoxy(COLUMN +5, ROW+6);
{72}      write('Press any key to begin');
{73}      PressAnyKey;
{74}    end;
{75}    {.........................oOo.............................}
{76}
{77}    function Time(attempt:integer):integer;
{78}
{79}    {----------------------------------------------------------------}
{80}    { Uses the delay() procedure to determine the response time in   }
{81}    { milliseconds required for hitting the space bar.               }
{82}    {----------------------------------------------------------------}
{83}
{84}    var
{85}       Millisecs     :integer;
{86}
{87}    begin
{88}      clrscr;
{89}      textcolor(yellow);
{90}      gotoxy(COLUMN, ROW);
{91}      case attempt of
{92}        1:write('First attempt starting..');
{93}        2:write('Second attempt starting..');
{94}        3:write('Third attempt starting..');
{95}      end;
{96}     randomize;                  { Initialise the random number generator}
{97}
{98}      Millisecs:= 0;
{99}      delay(1000);                { Pause for one second before timing}
{100}     textcolor(red + blink);
{101}     write(' NOW!');
{102}     delay(random(5000));        { Random delay of up to 5 seconds  }
{103}     FlushKeyboardBuffer;        { Make sure that there are no       }
```

628   Skills Resource   *Chapter 30 Programming in Pascal*

```
{104}                                  { characters in the keyboard buffer }
{105}     textbackground(Red);
{106}     clrscr;                      { The signal to press the space bar}
{107}
{108}     repeat
{109}       delay(1);
{110}       Millisecs:= Millisecs + 1;{ Count how many millisecs expire  }
{111}     until keypressed;            { Look for the user hitting any key}
{112}       Time:= Millisecs;          { Return the time taken to respond }
{113} end;
{114} {...............................oOo.................................}
{115}
{116} procedure Results(Average:real);
{117}
{118} {-----------------------------------------------------------------}
{119} { Displays the average time taken over the three attempts         }
{120} {-----------------------------------------------------------------}
{121}
{122} begin
{123}     textbackground(LightGray);
{124}      textcolor(Black);
{125}     clrscr;
{126}     gotoxy(COLUMN, ROW);
{127}     write('Your average response time was ', Average:5:0,
{128}           ' milliseconds');
{129}     gotoxy(COLUMN, ROW + 5);
{130}     write('Press any key to continue');
{131}     PressAnyKey;
{132} end;
{133}
{134} begin
{135}   Total:= 0;                 { Set the total time to 0             }
{136}   for i:= 1 to 3 do          { Repeat the trial three times        }
{137}   begin
{138}     Instructions;            { Display the user instructions        }
{139}     Total:= Total + Time(i);{ Accumulate the time for each trial   }
{140}   end;
{141}   Results(Total/3);    { Display the result of the three trials}
{142} end.
{143} {...............................oOo.................................}
```

Listing 30.27. *Screen handling example*

The main program starts on line {134}. The procedure Instructions explains that the user is to press a key as quickly as he/she can when a rectangular window changes colour. The function Time() times how long it took to do so in milliseconds. This time is added to a running total which accumulates the times for three attempts. Results() displays the average time the user took to respond. The program makes good use of user-defined functions and procedures, and the comments in the program listing explain their operation, but it is worth adding some further explanation regarding the procedure `PressAnyKey` and associated functions and procedures. As mentioned earlier, the buffer memory associated with the keyboard temporarily stores the values of key depressions made while the program is running, and these values can be accessed using the `ReadKey` function which extracts the first available character in the buffer. By repeatedly using this function to read single characters until there are no more left in the buffer, `FlushKeyboardBuffer` empties the buffer in preparation for using the `KeyPressed` function. This is to ensure that `Keypressed` will detect only the next key depression and not any that have been made previously.

Records and Files

Many computer applications involve processing data which has already been stored as a *file* on a backing storage medium such as magnetic disk. A file is often organised as a sequential collection of *records*, each one containing information about the subject of the file. For example, a car file might contain details of a number of different cars, each record dealing with a single car and containing such information as make, model, engine capacity, number of doors, colour, insurance group, extras, and so on. *Sequentially* organised files contain records which can only be accessed in the order in which they were originally stored in the file, whereas *randomly* organised files contain records which can be accessed in any order. However, since standard Pascal provides facilities for processing sequential files only, the example programs in this section do not deal with Turbo Pascal's procedures and functions for processing randomly organised files.

Before we examine some file handling methods, however, it is necessary to discuss *user-defined data types*.

User-defined data types

As you know by now, every variable used in a program must be associated with a data type. Up to now the data types that we have used have been `integer`, `real`, `char`, `boolean`, `string[]` and `array[]`. However, Pascal allows us to create our own data types based on these. For example, suppose that within a program we wanted to use two similar arrays of integers, each containing ten elements. Then we could declare them as follows:

```
var
   List1 :array[1..10] of integer;
   List2 :array[1..10] of integer;
```

Another method of achieving exactly the same result is to use `type` to define a new data type called `List`, and then use it to declare the variables `List1` and `List2`:

```
type
   List  = array[1..10] of integer;
```

```
var
   List1, List2 :List;
```

The `type` declaration can also be used in conjunction with the reserved word `record` to define a more complicated data structure. For example, to define a `Car` type we could write

```
type
  Car  = record
   Make    :string[15];
   Model     :string[20];
   InsGp     :integer;
   Cost    :real;
           end;
```

and now we can declare variables to be of type `Car`:

```
var
   SportsCar, FamilyCar, HatchBack :Car;
```

In order to identify a variable (or *field*) within the record we must use the *dot notation*. For instance, to store information in the record variable, `SportsCar`, we could use the following instructions:

```
write('Make of car? ');
readln(SportsCar.Make);
write('Model? ');
readln(SportsCar.Model);
write('Insurance Group? ');
readln(SportsCar.InsGp);
write('Cost? ');
readln(SpotrsCar.Cost);
```

The field within the record is specified after the dot; this allows a number of related items to be grouped together as a unit (that is, as a *record*), while still allowing each part (or *field*) to be accessed separately. Now, to define a collection, or *file*, of such records, we need to use the reserved word `file`:

```
type
  Car  = record
   Make    :string[15];
   Model     :string[20];
   InsGp     :integer;
   Cost   :real;
           end;
  Cars = file of Car;
var
   Hondas   :Cars;
   Fords :Cars;
```

The type, Cars, is defined as a file of Car records and this allows us to assign this file type to our own identifiers Hondas and Fords. The programs in the following sections illustrate how files defined like this may be created, read and searched.

Creating a sequential file using `assign`, `rewrite` and `write`

The main program starting at line {59} in Listing 30.28 shows how a sequential file of car details can be created. The program shows that an `assign` statement is used to link the name of the file within the program (CarFile) with the name of the actual file stored on magnetic disk (FileName). The name of the disk file has been defined earlier in the program as the string constant 'a:\cars.dat'. This means that when write instructions are used later to store car records in the file, the data will be recorded using the filename 'a:\cars.dat'. Once this link between the internal and external files has been established in the program, it is then necessary to open the file for *output* using `rewrite(CarFile)`. This tells the system that the file, CarFile, is to be created.

```
{1}    program CreateFile(input, output);
{2}    uses CRT;
{3}      {-------------------------------------------------------------}
{4}      { A program which creates a car file containing a number of car}
{5}      { records.                                                    }
{6}      {-------------------------------------------------------------}
{7}
{8}    const
{9}        FileName = 'a:\Cars.dat';      {The name of the file on disk}
{10}
{11}   type
{12}      Car = record                    {The structure of each record}
{13}              Make    :string[10];
{14}              Model   :string[10];
{15}              InsGp   :integer;
{16}              Cost    :real;
{17}            end;
{18}      Cars = file of Car;
{19}
{20}   var
{21}      CarRec      :Car;
{22}      CarFile     :Cars;
{23}      Answer      :char;
{24}
{25}   procedure GetRec(var CarRec:Car);
{26}      {-----------------------------------------------------------------}
{27}      { Gets and returns the data for a single record.                  }
{28}      {-----------------------------------------------------------------}
{29}
{30}   begin
{31}       clrscr;
```

```
{32}        writeln;
{33}        writeln('Please enter Car details as follows:');
{34}        writeln;
{35}        write('Make(eg Ford): ');
{36}        readln(CarRec.Make);
{37}        writeln;
{38}        write('Model(eg Escort): ');
{39}        readln(CarRec.Model);
{40}        writeln;
{41}        write('Insurance Group(eg 7): ');
{42}        readln(CarRec.InsGp);
{43}        writeln;
{44}        write('Cost(eg 8450.50): ');
{45}        readln(CarRec.Cost);
{46}        writeln;
{47} end;
{48}
{49} procedure WriteRec(var File1:Cars; Rec1:Car);
{50} begin
{51}   writeln;
{52}   write('OK to save this record?(Y/N) ');
{53}   readln(Answer);
{54}   if upcase(Answer) = 'Y' then
{55}       write(File1, Rec1);        { Writes the record           }
{56}   writeln;
{57} end;
{58}
{59} begin
{60}   assign(CarFile, Filename);   { Links CarFile with the actual}
{61}                                { file held on backing storage.}
{62}   rewrite(CarFile);            { Opens the file for output    }
{63}   repeat
{64}     GetRec(CarRec);            { Gets the Car details         }
{65}     WriteRec(CarFile, CarRec);
{66}     write('Add another record to the file?(Y/N)');
{67}     readln(Answer);
{68}   until upcase(Answer) <> 'Y';
{69}
{70}   close(CarFile);              { Closes the file              }
{71} end.
```

Listing 30.28. *Creating a sequential Car file*

Most of the remainder of the program is within a loop which repeats the following sequence of operations:

1. Get the details for a car record, CarRec - this is accomplished using the procedure GetRec which asks the user to type in the appropriate information and returns the car record using a variable parameter.
2. Store the record obtained by the procedure GetRec. The procedure WriteRec first asks for confirmation before writing the record to the file. The whole record and the appropriate file are both passed as parameters; Rec1 is defined as a value parameter of type Car record but the file *must* be passed as a *variable* parameter. The format for the

instruction to write a record to a file is similar to the familiar write instruction we have used many times before; the difference is that the first item in the brackets must be the internal name of the file. Note that the function upcase has been used to force the user's answer to be an uppercase letter because the if instruction on Line {54} compares the answer typed in with the capital letter 'Y' only.

3. Ask the user if he/she wishes to add another record to the file. The program loop terminates when the user answers 'Y' to the question.

Finally, the close(CarFile) statement tells the system that no more records are to be added to the car file. It is important to note that if the file is now re-opened using rewrite, more records *can not be appended to the existing ones*; the file must be completely *recreated* since rewrite effectively causes the named file to be destroyed. Later in this chapter we describe a program which does allow you to add more records to a file.

Figure 30.1 shows the program running under Turbo Pascal.

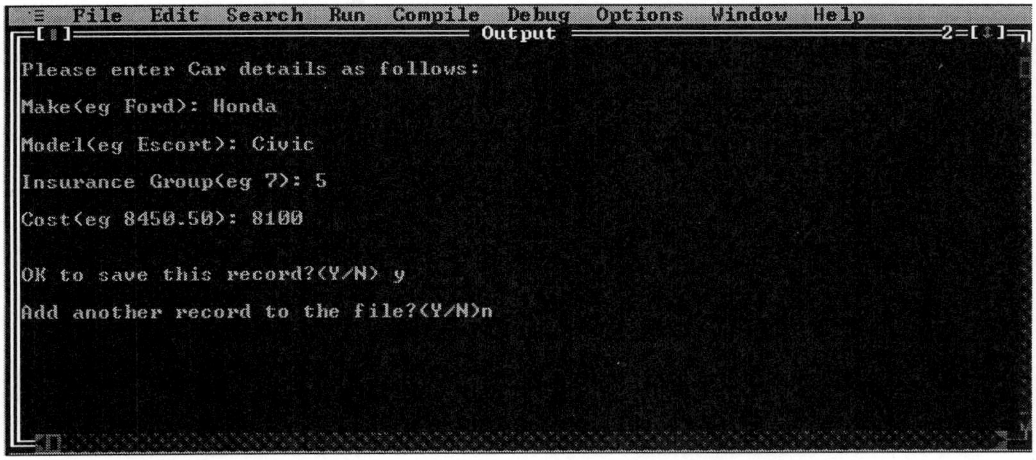

Figure 30.1. *The create program running*

Reading a file using assign, reset and read.

Whether a file is being created or read the same assign command must be used to link the internal and external file names. Thus before attempting to read the car file created by the previous program it is first necessary to use assign(CarFile, Filename) again. This appears on line {32} of Listing 30.29.

```
{1}     program File2(input,output);
{2}     {-----------------------------------------------------------}
{3}     { A program which reads a car file and displays and         }
{4}     { prints its contents.                                      }
{5}     {-----------------------------------------------------------}
{6}
{7}     uses CRT,
{8}          PRINTER;                    { To allow output to be printed}
```

```
{9}
{10}   const
{11}      FileName = 'a:\cars.dat';
{12}
{13}   type
{14}      Car = record                    {The record structure   }
{15}               Make    :string[10];
{16}               Model   :string[10];
{17}               InsGp   :integer;
{18}               Cost    :real;
{19}            end;
{20}      Cars = file of Car;
{21}
{22}   var
{23}      CarFile      :Cars;
{24}      CarRec       :Car;
{25}
{26}   begin
{27}    clrscr;
{28}    writeln;
{29}    writeln('Reading ', FileName, ' ....' );
{30}    writeln;
{31}
{32}    assign(CarFile, FileName);     {Links CarFile to the actual }
{33}                                   { file held on floppy disk   }
{34}    reset(CarFile);                {Open file for input         }
{35}    while not eof(CarFile) do      {Keep reading until no        }
{36}                                   { records are left           }
{37}     begin
{38}       read(CarFile, CarRec);
{39}       writeln(CarRec.Make:12,
{40}               CarRec.Model:12,
{41}               CarRec.InsGp:4,
{42}               CarRec.Cost:10:2);{ Display record on the  }
{43}                                 { screen.                }
{44}       writeln(LST, CarRec.Make:12,
{45}               CarRec.Model:12,
{46}               CarRec.InsGp:4,
{47}               CarRec.Cost:10:2); { Print record         }
{48}     end;
{49}    writeln;
{50}    writeln('End of ', Filename);
{51}    close(CarFile);               {Close the file         }
{52}    writeln;
{53}    write('Press <Enter> to continue');
{54}    readln;
{55}   end.
```

Listing 30.29. *Reading the Car file*

The reset instruction is used to *open a file for input*, that is, to enable it to be read. The records within the file are accessed using a read instruction which contains the name of the file to be read and the name of the record which is to receive the data obtained from the backing storage device: read(CarFile, CarRec). Once the data has been read from the file it is displayed using a `writeln` instruction which uses the dot notation to separate thefields within the car record. The `while` loop uses the `eof` (end of file) function to determine whether there are any more records left to be read from the file; when the end of the file is detected, the `eof` function returns a boolean value of `true`, otherwise it returns `false`. Thus the logical expression `not eof(CarFile)` has a value of `true` while there are more records to be read, and it has a value of `false` when the end of the file is reached.

Figure 30.2 illustrates typical ouput from the program when running under Turbo Pascal.

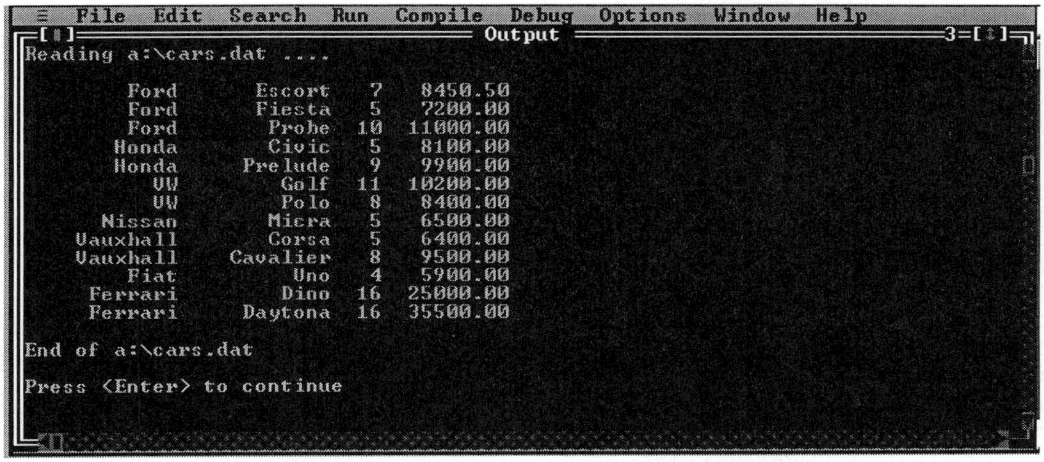

```
 ≡  File  Edit  Search  Run  Compile  Debug  Options  Window  Help
[■]══════════════════════════ Output ═══════════════════════════3=[↕]═
Reading a:\cars.dat ....

        Ford      Escort   7    8450.50
        Ford      Fiesta   5    7200.00
        Ford      Probe   10   11000.00
       Honda      Civic    5    8100.00
       Honda     Prelude   9    9900.00
          VW       Golf   11   10200.00
          VW       Polo    8    8400.00
      Nissan      Micra    5    6500.00
    Vauxhall      Corsa    5    6400.00
    Vauxhall    Cavalier   8    9500.00
        Fiat       Uno     4    5900.00
     Ferrari      Dino    16   25000.00
     Ferrari     Daytona  16   35500.00

End of a:\cars.dat

Press <Enter> to continue
```

Figure 30.2. *Reading the Car file*

Another of Turbo Pascal's units, `Printer`, contains procedures to enable information to be printed. Line {44} shows that by using `LST` at the beginning of the `writeln` instruction, the same results that are displayed on the screen can also be output to a printer connected to the computer.

Extending a file

There is no direct way in standard Pascal to extend a file that has already been created. However, there is a relatively easy way to overcome this shortcoming. The solution is to adopt the following scheme:

1. Make a copy of the file by reading each record and then copying them to a temporary file. The original file is therefore opened for input and the copy file is opened for output. After all of the records have been copied, the original file is closed but the temporary file is left open so that more records can be added to it.
2. The new records that are to be added to the original file are each read and then immediately written to the copy file. The copy file is closed when all of the new records have been stored.
3. The copy file is then opened for input and all of the records in it are written to the original file thus, in effect adding the new records to it.

The program shown in Listing 30.30 does exactly this. Understandably, the program makes use of a number of procedures that also appeared in Listing 30.28, a previous program to create the car file. The main additional procedure is called DuplicateFile which copies one file into another. It takes two variable parameters called SourceFile (the file to be copied) and DestFile (the file to which the records are to be copied). This means that the same procedure can be used to make a temporary copy of the original car file and also to transfer the new extended file in the copy back to the original file.

```
{1}    program File3(input, output);
{2}      {--------------------------------------------------------------}
{3}      { Appends a number of records to the end of a file.           }
{4}      {--------------------------------------------------------------}
{5}
{6}    uses CRT;
{7}
{8}    const
{9}       FileName = 'a:\Cars.dat';   {The name of the file on disk    }
{10}      CopyName = 'a:\copy.dat';   {The copy file name              }
{11}
{12}   type
{13}      Car = record                {The structure of each record    }
{14}             Make    :string[10];
{15}             Model   :string[10];
{16}             InsGp   :integer;
{17}             Cost    :real;
{18}           end;
{19}      Cars = file of Car;
{20}
{21}   var
{22}      CarFile      :Cars;
{23}      Copy         :Cars;
{24}      CarRec       :Car;
{25}      Count        :integer;
{26}      Answer       :char;
{27}
{28}   procedure DuplicateFile(var SourceFile, DestFile:Cars);
{29}   var
{30}      Count        :integer;
{31}
{32}   begin
{33}     reset(SourceFile);           {Open source file for input      }
{34}     rewrite(DestFile);           {Open copy file for output       }
{35}     Count :=0;                   {Record count variable           }
{36}
{37}     while not eof(SourceFile) do {Keep reading until no  more      }
{38}                                  { records left                   }
{39}       begin
{40}         read(SourceFile, CarRec);
{41}         write(DestFile, CarRec);
{42}         Count:= Count + 1;
{43}       end;
{44}
```

```
{45}     writeln;
{46}     write('Finished : ');
{47}     writeln(Count, ' records copied');
{48}
{49}  end;
{50}
{51}  procedure GetRec(var CarRec:Car);
{52}  {------------------------------------------------------------------}
{53}  { Gets and returns the data for a single record.                   }
{54}  {------------------------------------------------------------------}
{55}
{56}  begin
{57}      clrscr;
{58}      writeln;
{59}      writeln('Please enter Car details as follows:');
{60}      writeln;
{61}      write('Make(eg Ford): ');
{62}      readln(CarRec.Make);
{63}      writeln;
{64}      write('Model(eg Escort): ');
{65}      readln(CarRec.Model);
{66}      writeln;
{67}      write('Insurance Group(eg 7): ');
{68}      readln(CarRec.InsGp);
{69}      writeln;
{70}      write('Cost(eg 8450.50): ');
{71}      readln(CarRec.Cost);
{72}      writeln;
{73}  end;
{74}
{75}
{76}  procedure WriteRec(var File1:Cars; Rec1:Car);
{77}  begin
{78}    writeln;
{79}    write('OK to save this record?(Y/N) ');
{80}    readln(Answer);
{81}    if upcase(Answer) = 'Y' then
{82}        write(File1, Rec1); {Writes the record                    }
{83}    writeln;
{84}  end;
{85}
{86}  begin
{87}   assign(CarFile, FileName);
{88}   assign(Copy, CopyName);
{89}   clrscr;
{90}
{91}   writeln('Copying ',FileName, ' to ', CopyName,'...');
{92}   DuplicateFile(CarFile, Copy);
{93}   writeln;
{94}
{95}   repeat
{96}      GetRec(CarRec);                { Gets the Car details         }
{97}      WriteRec(Copy, CarRec);     { Writes the record to the file }
{98}      write('Add another record to the file?(Y/N)');
```

```
{99}        readln(Answer);
{100}   until upcase(Answer) <> 'Y';
{101}
{102}   writeln('Copying ',CopyName, ' to ', FileName,'...');
{103}   DuplicateFile(Copy, CarFile);
{104}   writeln;
{105}   writeln('Press <Enter> to continue');
{106}   readln;
{107}
{108}   close(CarFile);
{109}   close(Copy);
{110} end.
```

Listing 30.30. *Extending the Car file*

Notice that in this program two files, the original and the temporary copy, are open at the same time, but when one of them is open for output, the other is always open for input. The output from the program is shown in Figure 30.3.

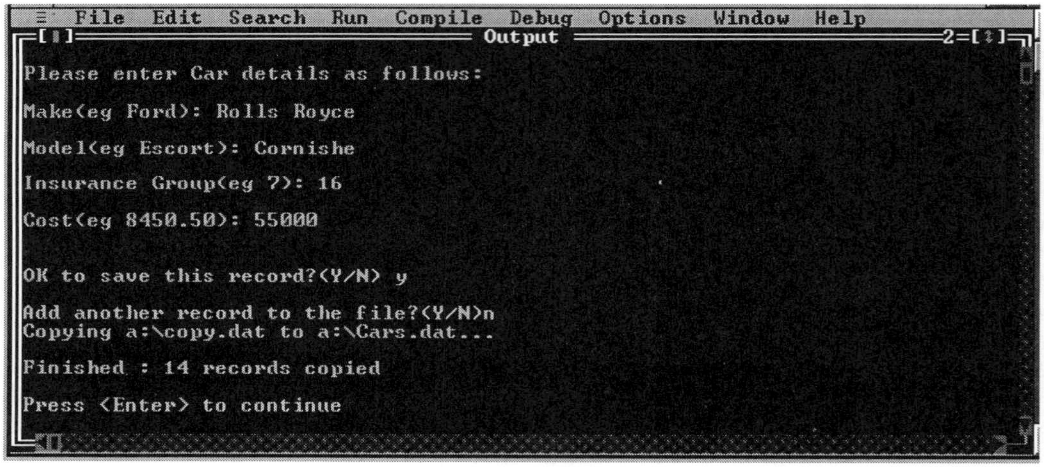

Figure 30.3. *Extending the Car file*

Searching a file

Searching a sequential file for certain records involves opening the file for input and then reading each record in turn and checking to see if it meets some criteria. For example, we might want to search the car file in order to extract all the cars made by Ford, or we might just want to find a particular car, such as a Fiat Uno. The program in Listing 30.31 allows the user to specify an approximate car price and then it searches the car file for all cars that cost within £1000 of the price entered. For example, if the user entered £8000, the program would print out all cars that cost between £7000 and £9000.

```
{1}   program File4(input,output);
{2}   {---------------------------------------------------------------}
{3}   { A program which reads a car file and displays details of  }
{4}   { cars which are within £1000 of a specified price          }
```

```
{5}     {----------------------------------------------------------}
{6}
{7}     uses CRT;
{8}
{9}     const
{10}        FileName = 'a:\cars.dat';     {The name of the file on disk}
{11}
{12}    type
{13}       Car = record                   {The structure of each record}
{14}              Make     :string[10];
{15}              Model    :string[10];
{16}              InsGp    :integer;
{17}              Cost     :real;
{18}          end;
{19}       Cars = file of Car;
{20}
{21}    var
{22}        CarFile     :Cars;
{23}        CarRec      :Car;
{24}        Price       :real;
{25}
{26}    begin
{27}      clrscr;
{28}      writeln;
{29}      write('Enter the approximate price of cars to be listed: œ');
{30}      readln(Price);
{31}      writeln;
{32}      writeln('Cars which are within £1000 of £', Price:0:0, ' :');
{33}      assign(CarFile, FileName);    {Links CarFile to the actual file  }
{34}                                    {held on floppy disk               }
{35}      reset(CarFile);              {Open file for input                }
{36}      while not eof(CarFile) do    {Keep reading until no records left}
{37}        begin
{38}          read(CarFile, CarRec);
{39}          if (CarRec.Cost >= Price - 1000) and
{40}             (CarRec.Cost <= Price + 1000) then
{41}            writeln(        {Display record on the screen }
{42}            CarRec.Make:12,
{43}                   CarRec.Model:12,
{44}                   CarRec.InsGp:4,
{45}                   '£':3,CarRec.Cost:0:0);
{46}        end;
{47}      writeln;
{48}      writeln('End of ', Filename);
{49}      close(CarFile);                  {Close the file            }
{50}      writeln;
{51}      write('Press <Enter> to continue');
{52}      readln;
{53}    end.
```

Listing 30.31. *Searching the Car file*

As you might expect, this program is very similar to the program which read and displayed the contents of the car file. The instruction which is used to identify and display the required records starts on line {39}:

```
    if (CarRec.Cost >= Price - 1000) and
       (CarRec.Cost <= Price + 1000) then
           writeln(          {Display record on the screen }
           CarRec.Make:12,
                   CarRec.Model:12,
                   CarRec.InsGp:4,
                   '£':3,CarRec.Cost:0:0);
```

The if statement contains two conditions connected by the and operator; if the cost of the car (CarRec.Cost) is both greater than Price - 1000 *and* less than Price + 1000, in other words within £1000 of Price, then the current record is displayed. The writeln instruction has been split over several lines for clarity. Figure 30.4 shows the program running.

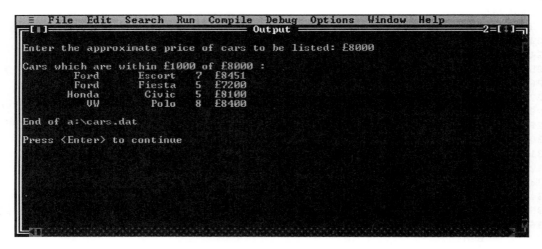

Figure 30.4. *The search program running*

Reference Section

This section describes a number of Pascal's standard functions and some of the additional functions provided by Turbo Pascal.

Standard Pascal functions

abs

Returns the absolute, that is unsigned, value of a real or integer value.

Examples

If x is a real variable then

1. `x:= abs(-3.7)`   gives   x = 3.7
2. `x:= abs(24.3)`   gives   x = 24.3

If i is an integer variable then

3. `i:= abs(-6)`   gives i = 6
4. `i:= abs(3.232)` is not allowed since the type of the returned value (real) is not the same as the type of the argument (integer).

exp

Returns the exponential of the argument, that is e^a, where a is the value of the parameter supplied in brackets and e is a mathemetical constant approximately equal to 2.72.

Example

If x is a real variable then

`x:= exp(2)`   gives x = 7.39 (that is, $x=e^2$)

ln

Returns the natural logarithm of the argument, that is, the inverse of the `exp` function.

Example

If x is a real variable then

`x:= ln(7.39)`   gives x = 2

sqr

Returns the square of the argument, that is x^2, where x is the argument.

Examples

If x is a real variable then

    1. `x:= sqr(-3.1)`   gives   x = 9.61

    2. `x:= sqr(3.1)`   gives   x = 9.61

If i is an integer variable then

    3. `i:= sqr(-6)`   gives i = 36

    4. `i:= sqr(3.232)`   is not allowed since the type of the returned value (real) is not the same as the type of the argument (integer).

Sqrt

Returns the square root of the operand, that is $\sqrt{x}$, where x is a positive valued argument.

Examples

If x is a real variable then

    1. `x:= sqrt(16.3)`   gives   x = 4.04

                            2. `x:= sqrt(-16.3)` is not allowed since x is negative

If i is an integer variable then

    3. `i:= sqrt(16)`   gives   i = 4

                            4. `i:= sqrt(-16)` is not allowed since i is negative

sin

Returns the sine of the argument which must be in radians.

Example

Since 1 radian = $\dfrac{180}{\pi}$ degrees, to convert an angle from degrees to radians we must divide the angle by $\dfrac{180}{\pi}$ where $\pi \approx 3.1416$

Thus if x is a real variable and we want the sine of 30°, then

    `x:= sin(30/(180/3.1416))`   gives x = sine(30°) = 0.5

cos

Returns the cosine of the argument which must be in radians. See `sin` above for converting degrees to radians.

Example

If x is a real variable and we want the cosine of 30°, then

    `x:= cos(30/(180/3.1416))`   gives x = cosine(30°) ≈ 0.87

Note that the `sin` and the `cos` functions can be used together for finding the tangent of an angle, since $\tan \theta = \dfrac{\sin \theta}{\cos \theta}$

arctan

Returns the arc tangent of the argument in radians. This is the inverse of finding the tangent of an angle.

Example

If x is a real variable and we want to find the arc tangent of 1 then

    `x:= arctan(1)*(180/3.1416)`   gives x = arctangent(1) = 45°

round

Returns the nearest integer type value to the real type value provided.

Examples

If i is an integer variable then

    1. `i:= round(34.3)`   gives i = 34
    2. `i:= round(34.8)`   gives i = 35

trunc

Converts a real type value to an integer type value by removing the fractional part of the real value.

Examples

If i is an integer variable then

    1. `i:= trunc(34.3)`   gives i = 34
    2. `i:= trunc(34.8)`   gives i = 34
    3. `i:= trunc(.975)`   gives i = 0

ord

This gives the ASCII numeric value for characters.

Examples

If c is an integer variable then

1. `c:= ord('a')`   gives c = 97

2. `c:= ord('A')`   gives c = 65

3. `c:= ord('?')`   gives c = 63

chr

Returns the character equivalent of an numeric code in the range 0 to 255

Examples

If c is an character variable then

1. `c:= chr(97)`   gives c = 'a'

2. `c:= chr(65)`   gives c = 'A'

3. `c:= chr(230)`   gives c = '?'

The following program prints the full character set:

```
program CharSet(input, output);
var
   c   :char;
   i   :integer;
begin
   for i:= 0 to 255 do
      writeln(i:10, chr(i):10);
end.
```

Odd

Returns TRUE if the argument is an odd number and FALSE if it is an even number. The argument must be an integer. The sign of the argument is ignored.

Examples

If t is a boolean variable then

1. `t:= odd(23)`   gives t = TRUE
2. `t:= odd(22)`   gives t = FALSE
3. `t:= odd(-23)`   gives t = TRUE
4. `t:= odd(0)`   gives t = FALSE
3. `t:= odd(7.5)`   is not allowed since the argument must be an integer

Some Turbo Pascal functions

These functions are always available in Turbo Pascal and do not require a `unit` declaration.

Length

Returns the length of a string.

Example

If `s1:= '1234567'` and `len` is an integer variable then
   `len:= length(s1)` gives len = 7;

Concat

Joins together a number of strings. The strings are provided as arguments to the function.

Examples

If string variables s1, s2 and s3 have the values
        `s1= 'One, two, three o clock '`
        `s2= 'four o clock '`
        `s3= 'rock'`
and s4 is another string variable then
        `s4:= concat(s1, s2, s3)` gives s4= 'One, two, three o clock four o clock
                                              rock'

Copy

This allows a set of characters, or a *substring*, to be copied from a string. It has the form:

    `copy(Str, StartChar, NumOfChars)`

   where `Str` is the string from which the substring is to be copied,
   `StartChar` is the position within `Str` from which to start copying and `NumOfChars`
   is how many characters are to be copied.

Examples

If `s1 = 'Copy me please'`
   1. `s2:= copy(s1, 6, 2)`   gives s2 = 'me'
   2. `s3:= copy(s1, 1, length(s1))` gives s3= 'Copy me please'

Pos

Returns the starting position of a substring within a string. Returns zero if the substring is not found.

Examples

```
1. p:= pos('Koteikan, Windsor Tce' ,  ',')   gives p=9
2. p:= pos('abcde', 'z')                      gives p=0
```

Upcase

Converts a letter to capitals, that is, upper case. Non letters are not affected.

Examples

1. `Capital:= upcase('x');`   gives Capital='X'

2. `Capital:= upcase('X');` gives Capital='X'

3. `Capital:= upcase('3');` gives Capital='3'

4. `readln(Answer);`

5. `if  upcase(Answer)  =  'Y'  then  writeln('The  Y  key  was  pressed');`

(This is a good way to ensure that pressing both 'y' and 'Y' can be detected)

Random

Generates a random number in the range 0 to n-1 where n is the integer value supplied to the function.

Example

`writeln(random(10) + 1)`   generates a random number between 1 and 10 inclusively

Randomize

This is a procedure used in conjunction with random function described above. It initialises the random number generator using the system clock so that each time a program is run it does not generate exactly the same set of random numbers.

Chapter 31

Information Technology Team Projects

Introduction

The word project can be used in two grammatical ways, as a noun and as a verb. When we use it as a noun we mean job, task, or piece of work. Used as a verb, one of its meanings is 'make plans for' and it is this meaning which is crucial to an understanding of project work. If you have to tackle a project on your own, you still need to do some planning, regarding, for, example, the time it should take to complete, the resources you need, analysis of tasks and the order in which they need to be done. Of course, you cannot plan until you have a clear idea of what you want to produce and usually, the requirements of other people need to be considered.

Suppose, for example, you want to arrange a reunion of around 18 people you knew at school. It is July 5th and you and many others are going back to college and university in September. The reunion will have to take place before the second week in September and some may be going away on holiday during the holidays. The reunion is your idea, but you still have to involve the people whom you expect to attend. You have the idea that everyone will join for a meal at a restaurant, but what will they do after the meal? Perhaps they would prefer to go to a club. It would be a pointless exercise to book a large table at a restaurant, on a particular evening, before you had asked everyone whether they wanted to and were able to come. You may decide that the first task is to telephone people, but then find that you don't have everyone's number. You see two of your old school friends quite frequently and after talking to them, find that they have the missing telephone numbers. It makes sense for them to do some of the telephoning, so you decide to contact 5 each. At first, you simply allocate 5 numbers for each of you to ring, but one of your friends says that he knows two of the people on your list particularly well. He thinks that they are more likely to come if he contacts them. You agree with this and take two other numbers from him. It is clear from pursuing this example, that many other issues would arise and that planning and cooperation would be needed to deal with them. For example, could you achieve a consensus regarding the type of restaurant, its location and the cost of the meal? Will the chosen restaurant be able to accommodate you all on the selected evening and will they ask for some notice and a deposit?

This example project is for a social event and the only consequences of its failure or poor execution are that people may be inconvenienced and that you may lose a few friends! Projects for the installation of, for example, IT-based administrative systems, require the involvement of corporate and departmental managers, operational users and specialists, such as systems analysts and programmers.

What is a Project?

A project is a relatively short-term activity, designed to achieve specific objectives. Working on a project team, therefore, is not usually a person's main job. For example, you may be employed as a programmer, systems analyst or computer technician, but are assigned to a project team as and when the need arises. Examples of information technology projects are:

- implementation of a new computerised payroll system;

- extension of a local area network to a new laboratory;

- introduction of a products database, through which customers can browse;

- a system to control a heating and ventilation system in a greenhouse.

Project Teams

A project team should comprise people with the necessary mix of personal qualities, skills and knowledge to achieve the objectives of the project. Departmental barriers should not restrict the choice of team members and where appropriate they should be selected from across the organisation and, if necessary, from outside it, as consultants.

Project Activities

Identifying a Project

Very often the need for a major new system, product or facility is identified by corporate management. This is because management has the benefit (or should have) of a 'bird's eye' view of the organisation, are responsible for decisions to move it in one direction or another, and control its resources, including finance, staffing, equipment and so on. Thus, a decision to computerise a personnel management system and the initiation of a project to achieve that objective is likely to be 'top-down'. Occasionally, needs are identified by staff working at an operational level, precisely because they have a more intimate understanding of the day-to-day problems they experience. In industries which have copied the Japanese style of management and team work, it is quite common for technician or operative level employees to have ideas which save the company thousands or millions of pounds. In fact, this can be a deliberate objective of teamwork; through daily experience of a particular aspect of an organisation's work, team members seek to improve, not only their immediate area of work, but to identify other areas of work which affect their own. For example, people working in Sales may be able to suggest improvements to the system used by Accounts, to provide them with credit limit information.

Identifying Project Objectives and Scope

The objectives of a project need to be clear, because they describe its main functions and what it seeks to achieve. Without objectives, the tasks of team members will be unclear. The scope of a project identifies its boundaries, so the limits of the project are set. For example, when identifying a project to install a new network, is it to be entirely separate from any existing network, or are they to be linked in some way? If so, this may mean a reassessment of the operation of the existing network.

Planning the Project

Before starting any project, a number of questions need to be asked.

- What results are wanted?
- When does it have to be completed?
- What resources, including accommodation, equipment, finance, components and people are needed to carry out the project?
- What are the main tasks?
- Can some tasks be progressed at the same time or be overlapped?
- Which tasks have to be completed before which others?
- In what order do the tasks have to be completed?
- When does each task have to be started and completed?
- How do the tasks relate to one another and contribute towards the successful completion of the project (see Co-ordination and Integration)?
- Who needs to be on the team?
- Who is responsible for dealing with each task?
- Is best use being made of each member's personal qualities, knowledge and skills?

All these questions point to the need for *planning* a project before it is started. Perhaps the most important questions are:

- What has to be done?

- What is the sequence of tasks and events?

- What time is needed to complete the tasks?

Why Plan?

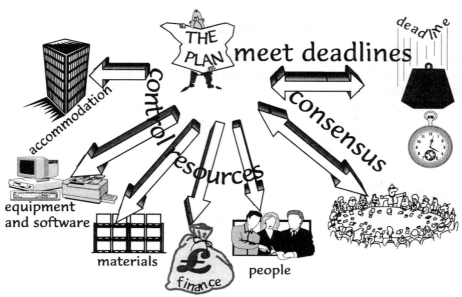

Figure 31.1. *The purposes of project planning*

Asked the question, "Why plan?", you would probably say something like, "It's obvious. If you plan something, you're more organised and more likely to achieve what you want." The social reunion example given in the introduction provides an illustration of the need for planning. To plan projects which cost time, money and other resources, we need to be a little more thorough. Figure 31.1 illustrates the main purposes of planning.

Figure 31.1 shows that *resources* include: people (members of the team and users and managers involved in the project); finance; materials (such as paper and other consumables); equipment (IT and any other special equipment); software (for example, word processor, charting and critical path analysis packages); accommodation (for planning work and team meetings). *Control* is needed, not only to ensure that necessary resources are made available, but also to promote efficiency in their use and keep the project within the planned budget. When referring to people as a resource, it is probably better to use the word *manage*. 'Control' suggests coercion, where staff are bullied and threatened as a way of ensuring compliance. More is said about this in the section on Assessing Team Performance.

Consensus shows a two-way arrow between the plan and the people involved in the project. To achieve consensus, requires that when feedback on progress is provided by participants, their comments are properly considered and, if necessary, used to modify the plan.

A plan also sets *deadlines*, dates or times when particular tasks should be completed. It is important that team members keep to deadlines. Each team member is given a role and some responsibilities and lateness is likely to prevent progress of dependent tasks, for which other team members are responsible. This delays the project and probably causes discord and resentment within the team. However, difficulties, unanticipated problems and modifications to the plan, are bound to result in changes to deadlines, hence the two-way arrow in Figure 31.1.

Analysing the Project

This requires a detailed analysis of the project objectives, to determine the solutions to achieve them. The detail of this work is covered in the chapter on Systems Analysis and design. To summarise, team members need to break the problem down into smaller component parts, suggest possible solutions, evaluate them and either accept or reject them. This will be an iterative process, as decisions on one aspect of the project may require a re-examination of other aspects. The formal method of analysing a problem into progressively smaller components is known as top-down design, which is dealt with in Chapter 29. Analysis also requires that a sequence of activities is identified for the achievement of each project component, as well as the resources which are needed at various points in the sequence. This is known as *scheduling*.

Co-ordinating and Integrating the Project

The aim of a schedule is to plan the timing of events, activities and resource usage, such that a particular aspect of a project is competed at a particular time. A project is likely to consist of several separate 'strands', each occupying different members of the team. The work of team members needs to be co-ordinated, or properly related. If we say that someone is uncoordinated, we mean that their various physical movements do not properly relate to one another. Lack of physical co-ordination manifests itself in clumsiness, and for example, an inability to dance or do gymnastics. Co-ordination of a project, therefore, means ensuring that the activities of team members and the tasks on which they are working, are related and complement one another. Loss of co-ordination may manifest itself in a team member working hard on a task, which bears little relation to and does not properly contribute to, the progress of the project. Co-ordination is necessary between team members, but also between the team and others who may contribute to the project (in other departments or from other organisations). For this reason, there should be *team* and *steering group meetings* (with user and management representatives and perhaps consultants from outside the organisation)

Integration is the fitting together of separate components. For example, if a joiner is making a table, the legs, the frame and the top should fit properly together. If the joints are poorly made, then the table will be spoiled, even if the separate components are beautifully carved. One particular kind of joint is called 'dovetailed' and this word is often used to describe the perfect integration of separate components. So, project components, which are being separately developed need to 'dovetail' or integrate to produce a complete product.

Budget Monitoring and Control

Every project has a budget, that is, a limited amount of money allocated for its development. The amount depends on the importance of the project to the organisation and the type of project. Not all projects proceed, perhaps because it is not seen to give value for money, or another project, viewed as more important, gains priority. For example, in a college, it may be highly desirable for maths and science students to have a new computer laboratory, but the travel and tourism courses attract far more students and their project for a travel agency office gains priority. The computer laboratory project may be cancelled or scaled down to half the number of computer workstations.

Cost Control

Given a financial budget, it is necessary to control money costs to stay within it. Careful thought needs to be given to what constitutes a cost. If you were asked to estimate the costs of installing a computer network, you may check catalogues for the prices of computer file servers, workstations, desks, printers, cabling, connectors and so on and come up with a total cost. You may also consider the costs of software and installation charges. Obviously, these are major items, but they do not reflect the complete cost of the project. You also need to consider staffing costs, not only those of the team, but also the salary of a  technician or network administrator who is to manage the network. If users are unfamiliar with the software, training charges will be incurred.

If the members of the project team are salaried employees of the organisation, the difficulty arises of separating their responsibilities to the project, from their other work. Members of a project team are rarely fully occupied by the project, and have other responsibilities. For example, a sales supervisor may be seconded to a sales marketing project team and spend approximately two days per week working on the project. It is more likely that the time given to the project will be highly variable, for week to week, depending on the stage reached. Despite this difficulty, efforts have to be made to calculate the cost of the sales supervisor's (and any other team members) secondment to the project. Otherwise, the actual cost may, in reality, veer drastically from the budgeted cost (although this may not be apparent at the time).

A large project will probably need a complex accounting and cost control system, but a smaller project can be measured by the number of people and the hours they spend working on it. To summarise, in seeking to control costs, you need to recognise what they are and the items in Figure 31.1 provide a useful checklist. Using the example of a computer network, we can identify the following likely costs:

- project team members' time, costed according to their hourly rate of pay;

- consultancy charges, both from outside the organisation and from other departments (if charged by them); this will be a corporate decision. If a department has a budget, it will need to charge other departments for work they do for them;

- computer and network hardware;

- software licences;

- carpets, air conditioning, blinds; tables, chairs, cable conduit.

- installation charges (unless carried out by the project team);

- training costs for users on use of new software;

- training/employment of network manager;

- accommodation, both for the project team and for location of the new network.

The team member with budget monitoring responsibility must record and monitor these costs as the project progresses. Costs give a guide to progress, in the sense that it is a measure of the value of work done. This is particularly so with tangible items, such as computer equipment. The accountant must also monitor the costs against the allocated budget and report to the project manager, or member of senior management, if the project is going over budget.

Project Implementation

This includes systems analysis, design, implementation and review, all of which are covered in the Chapter on Systems Analysis and Design.

Evaluating the Project

This activity is associated with the monitoring and review of the project, during and after its completion. Evaluation should include the following.

- Measuring progress against schedules and budgets. Has the planned stage been achieved at the budgeted cost?

- Are resources being used economically and effectively? If not, this may be because the strengths of team members are not being used in the most effective way. One person may be particularly skilled in one area, but is assigned a role, in which they are under-used or inadequate to the task.

- If the project is behind schedule, what are the causes? The problem may be inadequate definition of project, unclear solutions, lack of suitable resources, weakness of team member(s), either in commitment, knowledge or skills. Evaluation will tackle these problems and examine remedies which allow the project to progress (or if it is supposedly completed, correct the deficiency);

- The identification of potential problems and ways of avoiding them. In this way, the team should avoid 'management by crisis', by ignoring potential problems, hoping they will simply go away and only re-acting when forced.

- Analysis of alternative courses of action, referred to in spreadsheet jargon as 'what if' analysis (Chapter 22). In this way, likely effects of different approaches to the project can be anticipated. For example, during a project to install a computer network, consideration may be given to alternative shared printer solutions. The costs of these alternatives can be projected and a judgement made as to the project budget's sufficiency. If a more expensive printing solution is chosen, it may be that savings can be made in other areas of the project. Alternatively, an approach may be made to the project sponsor for an increase in the budget. However, this would require a submission of arguments as to the cost effectiveness of the change.

- Quality assessment. Measuring the quality of a product, such as a car, is fairly straightforward. The number sold in comparison with other cars in the same category and continuance of good sales over a long period indicates a high quality product. Measuring the quality of a service is much more difficult. Information technology systems provide services to fulfil the needs of various organisational functions and assessment of quality is sometimes highly subjective. Nevertheless, over time, the installation of a computerised sales order processing system can be evaluated in money terms. If, for example, a business increases its sales turnover by 50%, with no increase in staffing, or overtime costs, the contribution of the computerised system can reasonably be measured. If, on the other hand, a hospital installs a computerised appointments system, assessment of quality will come from different perspectives. It may make the lives of hospital administrators easier, but the experience of the patients may give a less favourable evaluation. Their experience of delays in seeing doctors and consultants may have little to do with a new computerised appointments system, but if the delays increase soon after its introduction, the blame is likely to be placed on the new system. To assess quality, you need to determine what features will indicate high quality and how you will measure it. The most important quality assessment is that of the project's customers; has the project achieved its objectives?

People, Roles and Responsibilities

Another word for 'role' is 'function'. Put another way, if your function is to take the minutes of team meetings, your role is 'minutes secretary'; in that role, it is your *responsibility* to take the minutes. The range of roles needed for a project will depend on its size, complexity and scope. Some roles can be regarded as *internal* and relate to the project team, whilst others are external; the latter may relate to people who are not directly involved in the project, but are affected by it, have an interest in its outcome and may be of occasional assistance to the project team. For example, a similar project may have been completed elsewhere (within the organisation, or outside it) and it makes sense to consult the people involved. If the project is being financed by a bank or other external agency, clearly the role of bank manager is going to impinge on the work of the team. Other team responsibilities include: resource allocation, monitoring of resource usage (records need to be kept) and monitoring of progress against schedules.

Team Building

Building a team involves the development of:

- ways of working to improve efficiency and productivity;
- relationships among members;
- mutual respect of each others' strengths;
- the team's adaptability to changes in circumstances, such as a cut in budget, or a reduction in the time allocation.

To begin with, team members may be very unsure how to proceed and may leave it to the leader to move things ahead. If the leader is not careful, this may be a permanent situation. Hopefully, as members get to know each other, they will be more willing to voice their opinions and reservations. They may suggest contributions from themselves or from others, if they feel they have more competence in a particular area. In this way the assignment of roles does not have to be dictatorial, but can come about through a process of negotiation.

As the project continues, and members experience some successes in working with each other, this tends to motivate them to achieve more. Conversely, if their methods of working are not co-operative and do not integrate, they are likely to experience frequent failures. Unfortunately, this will probably result in team breakdown and an incomplete project. If a team works successfully over a longer time (perhaps months, or years), or on different successful projects, the initial stages of team building should be unnecessary.

Achieving Consensus

Making decisions by consensus is desirable, but not always achievable, at least in the sense of absolute and unreserved agreement. Consensus can only be obtained when each member has clearly expressed his or her views and disagreements, listened to and understood those of the others, and presented any alternatives they wish to be discussed. When, through discussion and negotiation a decision, which everyone understands, is reached then we can say a consensus decision has been made.

To work towards consensus, members must avoid blind argument of their opinions, not agree, simply to "have a quiet life", or resort to measures such as flicking a coin or calling a majority vote. This way leads to resentment, loss of commitment and enthusiasm by those who appear to have 'lost' a decision. Of course, some decisions are not contentious and can be made by the team leader, or individual members. This is particularly the case when a member is delegated a task and limited decision-making is required to complete it, within the framework of the task.

Measuring Team Performance

Leadership

A team does not always have the same leader. Any team member must be willing to take that role. This is because, as a project progresses, different specialisms are needed. Thus, for example, during the analysis stage, when questionnaires are being drawn up and user interviews conducted, the team has a particular leader. When the project moves onto the production stage, entirely different talents are called for, such as technical knowledge of project equipment and computer software, and another member takes the team leader role. Teams should be democratic, so leaders should lead, not dictate.

Team Leader Role

A team leader should:

- gain consensus on the project objectives and clarify members' expectations of the project. If all the team are clear about the objectives, in the short and longer term, they are more likely to be able to co-ordinate and integrate their activities;
- make the best use of the available skills and talents. This means that task assignment must be carefully considered, so members work to their strengths and not their weaknesses;
- hold regular meetings to discuss progress and problems as they arise;
- monitor and give feedback on team and individual performance;
- ensure co-ordination and integration of separate tasks;
- ensure that the project is completed (as explained earlier, this is likely to be a stage or one aspect, as the team leader role may be occupied by different members, as appropriate).

Leadership Styles

Various leadership styles can be adopted, depending on the experience, competence and confidence of the team's members (and the team leader):

- lead by good example (but don't do it all);
- delegation and trust (assign tasks and leave them to get on with it, until the next review meeting);
- participate and support; this style may be appropriate where none of the members have strong experience of leading a team and need extensive support from one another. The team leader must still lead, otherwise direction and momentum are lost.

Co-operation, Enthusiasm and Adaptability

Co-operation means working together to achieve common objectives. It does not mean obeying orders from dictators! Enthusiasm comes from genuine interest in the work, so although people cannot always do what they most enjoy, they tend to be more enthusiastic when using their talents, rather than struggling with weaknesses. Enthusiasm also tends to come from previous success, and recognition by others of achievement. Adaptability is important, because a project will not go absolutely as planned. Members may have to learn new skills or extend existing ones (for example, a new version of a software package may be provided), work with different team members at various times and possibly, take the role of team leader.

Technical Knowledge and Competence

It is not necessary for every member of a team to be expert in the same technical areas. Each person is assigned to a team because they have a particular contribution to make; this contribution is likely to be a mix of the personal qualities already mentioned and competence in a particular area. For example, a team member with good communication skills may chair meetings, take minutes, or take the role of team leader. Of course, a team leader has to have the technical knowledge to understand the task or tasks for which they have responsibility. Some members of the team are likely to be, for example, better programmers than others and some may have highly developed design skills. The assignment of people to particular roles should take account of a range of factors, but technical knowledge and competence are fundamental to the production of a good product. It is useless to compose a team of good communicators, if their knowledge of the project subject is sketchy.

Effort and Efficiency

Non-productive effort is wasted. However, this does not mean that every effort should achieve instant success. By working on a task, finding that the results are unsatisfactory and repeating or modifying the work, we can learn and ultimately improve the end product. Of course, with proper preparation and planning, the chances of success are increased. For example, a programmer should not tackle a problem by immediately coding the program, but should follow a disciplined program design method (Chapter 29). Without this preparation, the program is likely to be difficult to debug and modify. Proper preparation and diligence are also likely to result in task completion by the required deadline. The project will be delayed if the necessary volume of work is not completed on time and rushing it will certainly reduce the quality. Efficiency comes from properly channelled effort. A good athlete uses energy efficiently through co-ordination of limb movements and breathing. To carry out a task efficiently requires that all the components (materials, tools, technical knowledge, accommodation and so on) are available as and when they are needed.

Project Management

Project management is concerned with the *planning* and the *control* of projects. Planning is mainly concerned with identifying the activities associated with the project, determining the order in which the activities are to be completed, estimating the length of time each activity will take to complete and what resources are required by the activity. Control takes place while the project is running: as activities are completed, resources can be reallocated to any remaining activities which are critical to completing the project on time.

Techniques such as PERT (*Project Evaluation and Review Techniques*) and CPA (*Critical Path Analysis*) use a branch of mathematics called *network analysis* to systemise and aid project management. Networks allow projects to be represented graphically as a series of activities connected by nodes representing their start and end points. Network analysis allows the crucial activities which determine the total duration of the project to be identified. The following case study uses a network to perform a critical path analysis of a project involving the installation of a LAN in a college.

Case Study: Installing a Local Area Network

A college has decided to install a local area network of PCs in a classroom. As well as obtaining and installing the network, the project involves refurbishing the classroom to be used - replacing the ceiling, redecorating, providing blinds on the windows, new carpets, air conditioning, benches for the workstations and chairs - and also appointing a technician who will help with the installation and testing of the network. It has been decided that tenders will be invited for suppliers of the network system and for the classroom conversion work. The suppliers of the office furniture and application software required - word processors, spreadsheets etc - will be selected and ordered by the college's computer manager directly. One of the first duties of the newly appointed technician will be to test the computer equipment before it is installed in the network room. Once the classroom has been converted, the office furniture and computer hardware will be installed and then the system will have to be tested and any faults corrected. Documentation will need to be provided for users of the network - one type for students and another for teaching staff - and finally, before staff start to use the network, they will need some training.

Identifying Activities

The first stage in managing a project such as this is to identify the activities involved and to assign a letter to each one. The list of activities for this project is as follows:

Activity

A	Carry out initial study of needs
B	Invite tenders from suppliers
C	Appoint suppliers
D	Obtain computer equipment
E	Convert classroom
F	Advertise for technician
G	Shortlist candidates and invite for interview
H	Interview candidates
I	Test computer hardware
J	Procure office furniture
K	Install office furniture and network system
L	Procure network application software
M	Prepare documentation for network users
N	Test network
O	Correct system faults
P	Train staff

At this stage it is not possible to assign a precise order to the activities since some of them can occur in parallel with others. The next stage is to estimate the length of time required to complete each activity. These estimates may be based on experience, discussions with prospective suppliers and building contractors, information obtained from equipment suppliers regarding probable delivery times, or from other sources. It should also be possible at this stage to identify, for each activity listed, which activity or activities must be completed before it can commence. For example, before tenders can be invited from network suppliers, the college must have conducted a study of its requirements so that the type and size of the network could be specified precisely. Similarly, before the network can be installed, the room must be ready and the equipment must have been delivered.

Activity dependence tables

An *activity dependence table* lists each activity together with activitities that must be completed before this particular one can begin. The activity dependence table for our case study is shown below. Included in the table is a column which shows the estimated amount of time required for each activity.

	Activity	Duration (Days)	Preceding activity
A	Carry out initial study of needs	15	None
B	Invite tenders from suppliers	19	A
C	Appoint suppliers	5	B
D	Obtain computer equipment	10	C
E	Convert classroom	40	C
F	Advertise for technician	21	A
G	Shortlist candidates and invite for interview	10	F
H	Interview candidates	2	G
I	Test computer hardware	10	H
J	Procure office furniture	20	A
K	Install office furniture and network system	15	D,E,I,J
L	Procure network application software	28	A
M	Prepare documentation for network users	15	K,L
N	Test network	10	K,L
O	Correct system faults	6	N
P	Train staff	10	M,O

Network Analysis

A common method of representing activities and how they relate to each other is by means of a *network* in which each activity is represented by an arrowed line and the starting point and finishing point are each represented by a circle called a *node*. The nodes are numbered such that the node at the start of an activity is always lower than the node at the end of the activity. The following diagrams illustrate how nodes and activities are drawn.

Activity B starts when activity A ends

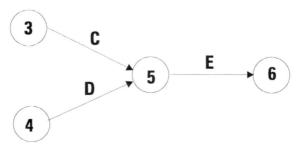

E begins when both C and D have finished

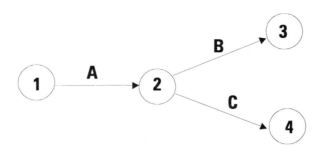

B and C can start when A is complete

Drawing the Network

A network diagram illustrates how all of the activities identified depend on each other. Note, however, that there are a number of rules to be observed when drawing the network:

1. There must be only one start node and one finish node.

2. No activities are allowed to have the same start and finish node.

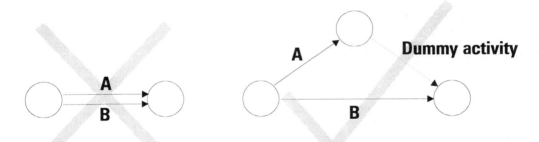

To avoid this, dummy activities, which have a duration of zero, are introduced as shown above.

3. Arrows should go from left to right.

Using these ideas, we can produce the network shown in Figure 31.2 for our case study project.

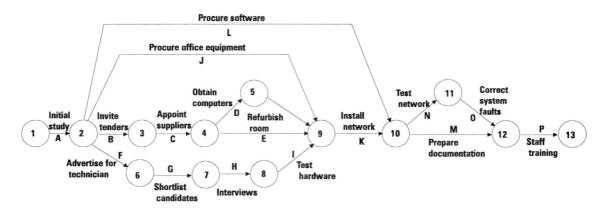

Figure 31.2. *The network for the project*

The diagram clearly shows the order of the activities, which ones can be undertaken at the same time and dependencies between activities. What we now need to detremine is how long the project will take overall.

Earliest starting times

Remembering that no activity can commence before all the activities which converge on its start node have finished, we can now determine the earliest starting times for each activity. This is shown in Figure 31.3.

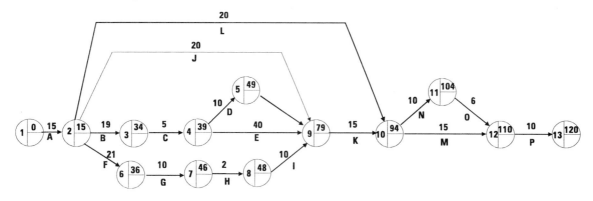

Figure 31.3. *Earliest starting times for the project*

The time taken for each activity is shown above the activity letter. The extra figure inside the node now shows the earliest day on which the project can start. Thus B starts 15 days after A has commenced, and since B requires a further 19 days for completion, C starts on the 34th day. Where two or more activities finish on the same node, for example on node 9, the highest accumulated figure is always shown. Thus, although activity I finishes after 48 days, D finishes after 49 days, and J after 35 days, it is the finish time of activity E, that is 79 days, which is recorded in node 9.

The diagram shows that the *total project time* is the longest path through the network, and it amounts to the figure shown in the last node, namely 120 days.

Latest Starting Times

We are almost at a position now to determine the *slack time*, or *total float*, for each activity. (see Figure 31.4). This will tell us by how many days each activity could be extended, or delayed, without delaying the whole project. In order to do this we must first calculate the latest starting time for each activity. Starting with the figure in the last node (120 days in this case), we work backwards through the network calculating the latest possible time each activity could commence without overrunning the time shown in its finish node. In practice this involves subtracting the duration of the activity from the latest starting time shown in its finish node and writing this in its start node. If a choice of two values occurs, the smallest figure is always chosen. For example, the latest start time of activity P is found by taking its duration of 10 days from the value 120 in its finish node. This gives a latest starting time of 110. For activity O, we subtract 6 from 110 to give 104; for N 10 from 104 gives 94. When we get to M, subtracting 15 from 110 gives 95, but activity N gave a value of 94 , which is smaller, so we use 94 as node 10's latest starting time.

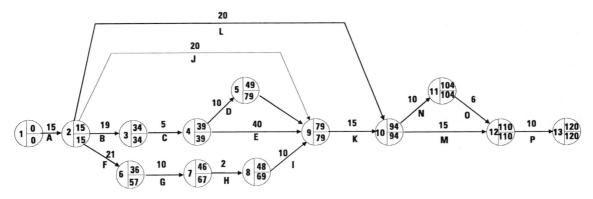

Figure 31.4. *Latest starting times for the project*

Slack Time

Slack time is the extra time that the activity could take without delaying the whole project. The diagram below illustrates how it is calculated.

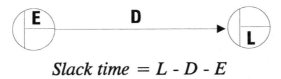

$$Slack\ time = L - D - E$$

Thus the slack time for activity I is 79 - 10 - 48 = 21 days. This means that testing the hardware could be allowed to take up to 21 days more to complete than was originally estimated without affecting the total project time. The following table shows the slack times for all the activities.

Activity		Duration (Days)	Latest start time	Earliest start time	Slack time
A	Carry out initial study of needs	15	0	15	0
B	Invite tenders from suppliers	19	15	34	0
C	Appoint suppliers	5	34	39	0
D	Obtain computer equipment	10	39	79	30
E	Convert classroom	40	39	79	0
F	Advertise for technician	21	15	57	21
G	Shortlist candidates and invite for interview	10	36	67	11
H	Interview candidates	2	46	69	21
I	Test computer hardware	10	48	79	21
J	Procure office furniture	20	15	79	44
K	Install office furniture and network system	15	79	94	0
L	Procure network application software	28	15	94	51
M	Prepare documentation for network users	15	94	110	1
N	Test network	10	94	104	0
O	Correct system faults	6	104	110	0
P	Train staff	10	110	120	0

Critical Activities

The critical activities are those with zero slack time. In other words, the total project time will be increased if any of these activities takes longer than was anticipated. For our network the critical activities are A, B, C, E, K, N, O and P.

Critical Path

This is the path, or paths, through the network consisting of only critical activities. In our example there is only a single critical path, but it is possible for other projects to have more than one critical path. The critical path is shown by the heavy line in Figure 31.5.

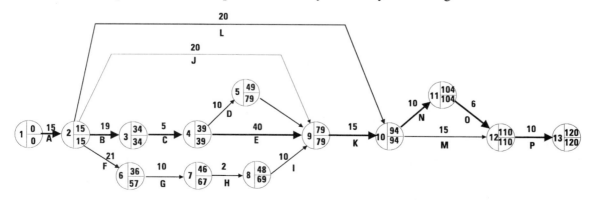

Figure 31.5. *The critical path*

The critical path is always the longest path through the network, and it tells us what the total time wil be for the project. During the course of a project, the critical activities will need to be monitored very carefully to ensure that they do not overrun and thereby increase the total project time. If this is in danger of occurring, it may be possible to divert manpower from non-critical activities in order to ensure that critical activities are completed on time.

Gantt Charts

A Gantt chart is a diagram which clearly illustrates when activities can start and finish. Each activity is represented by a solid line and any associated slack time by a dotted line as shown in 6 The start, end and duration of every activity can be read from the horizontal axis which shows the time scale in days.

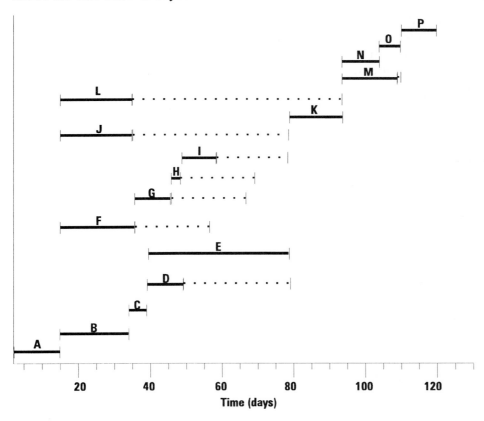

Figure 31.6. *The Gantt chart for the project*

Resource Scheduling

Resource scheduling is concerned with minimising the numbers of people required at any one time for the project. The Gantt chart shows us where overlapping activities can be moved to reduce the amount of overlap. For example, each of the activities D, E, G, H and I overlaps with one or more of the others, but D, G, H and I each have a considerable amount of slack time allowing them to be delayed. So, if, say D and G could each be carried out by one person, but not at the same time, then D could be delayed so that it starts when G finishes, thus allowing the person to do both jobs but one after the other.

In projects involving large numbers of human resources, this type of adjustment can result in a significant reduction in the number of people who need to be employed, and consequently result in a large reduction in cost.

Cost Scheduling

Cost scheduling uses the network to find the cheapest means of reducing the total project time. Activities can be shortened by, for example, using extra personnel, or by paying them overtime to work longer hours. This invariably incurs a cost penalty, but shortening some activities may be cheaper than others. The average cost of shortening each activity on the critical path by one time unit (a day for instance) can be calculated - this is called the *cost slope* of an activity - assuming accurate costing information is available. By repeatedly finding the critical activity with the least cost slope and reducing its duration, the overall project time can be shortened for the least cost.

Chapter 32

Developing Simple Control Systems

Introduction

Because of the enormous variety of devices used and the broad spectrum of applications of control systems, the approach that we have adopted in attempting to provide a practical guide to developing simple control systems is to emphasise the role of the computer rather than input and output devices. We describe the use of the National Instruments product LabVIEW which is a graphical programming language specifically designed for control systems. It provides interfaces for the serial port of a PC, for data acquisition devices, and for devices which use National Instruments own General Purpose Interface Bus (GPIB) which is designed to facilitate communication between computers and instruments. The examples described in this chapter have been developed using LabVIEW student edition (available from Prentice Hall) which contains the software to run a simplified version of National Instrument's graphical programming language and a comprehensive user's guide.

LabVIEW allows the student to read data provided by suitably interfaced external sensing devices (or to simulate such data), to simulate control panel devices such as meters, LEDs and switches, to process the data, display results and to transmit data and control signals to external devices. Thus, having specified the function of a specific control system, the student can construct and test the computer control aspect independently of the external sensing and control hardware.

Programs developed using LabVIEW are called *virtual instruments* (or *Vis)*. Virtual instruments can be considerd to be software versions of electronic devices used in control systems. Hardware devices are simulated by wiring together software components that perform input, processing or output functions. The major advantage of this approach for students is that with little experience in electronics they can quickly develop control systems that otherwise would be very costly to build and very difficult to test.

We illustrate the use of this software tool with a number of worked examples. The examples illustrate the use of the graphical programming language for simple control tasks. It is important to note, however, that we deal with only a very small subset of the large number of functions available in LabVIEW. We start by describing the program development environment for the creation and modification of VIs.

Using LabVIEW

LabVIEW provides two windows for you to use when creating a VI. The window shown Figure 32.1 is called the Panel window which is used to design control panels incorporating such things as as meters and switches. A number of these are shown.

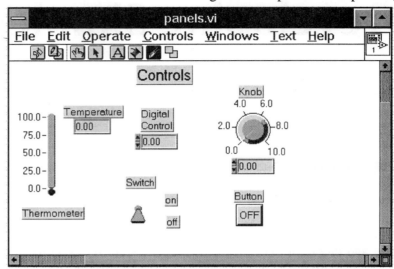

The window shown in Figure 32.1 is called the Diagram window in which you define the function of the device you are constructing in terms of components which are connected by lines representing wires. Objects which appear in the Panel window have a corresponding symbol in the Diagram window, but the reverse is not necessarily true as shown in Figure 32.2.

Figure 32.1. *The Panel window of LabVIEW*

The functions shown in the Diagram window do not have a counterpart in the Panel window. Functions can use controls and display data on controls, but they also provide sophisticated processing capabilities.

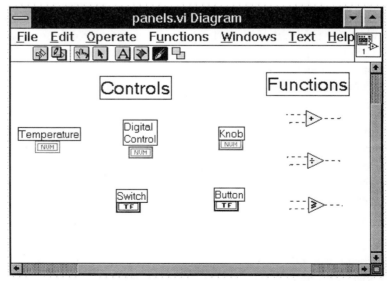

The menus in both windows allow you to select and display components, and subsequently you can adjust them, label them and connect them together. In addition, any VIs that you create can be saved and used again to create more complex instruments. This is the equivalent of using functions and procedures in high-level programming languages.

Figure 32.2 *The Diagram window of LabVIEW*

A Temperature Control VI

In this example we develop a simple device to read an external device which produces a voltage proportional to the temperature that it is detecting. The incoming signal is scaled up by multiplying it by 100 and it is displayed on a thermometer and a digital display. If the temperature falls below a certain value, an indicator is switched on. In order to test the device, the signal from the temperature sensor is simulated using a pre-written VI that is supplied with LabVIEW.

This simple control system is appropriate to the task of maintaining a tank of liquid at a constant temperature. The indicator light changing alternating between bright and dim represents the transmission of a signal to turn an external heater on and off.

The Front Panel

Figure 32.3 shows the Panel window of the VI. It comprises

- a switch to turn the device on and off;
- a thermometer and digital display to show the temperature being read;
- a dial for setting the minimum temperature below which a heater is to be activated;
- an indicator which illuminates when the heater is being activated.

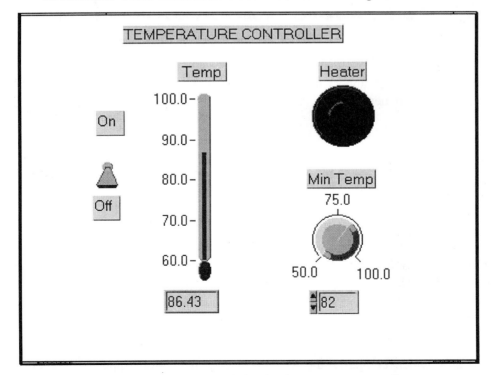

Figure 32.3. *The Panel window for the temperature controller*

The Wiring Diagram

The components shown in the Panel window are 'wired' together and combined with other processing components in the Diagram window which is shown in Figure 32.4.

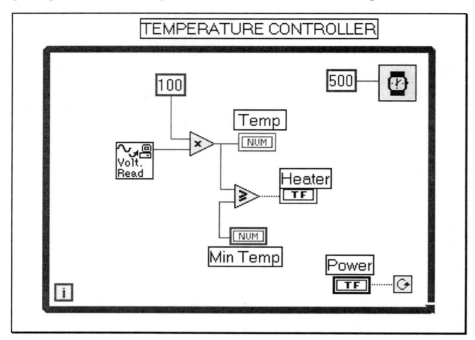

Figure 32.4. *The Diagram window for the temperature controller*

Notice that all the controls which appear in the Panel window also appear here in combination with a number of other components:

This is the component which simulates the voltage being produced by the temperature sensor. It is a sub VI which is provided with LabVIEW Student Edition.

This is a multiplication component which takes the voltage produced by the voltage simulator and multiplies it by 100. The value of 100 is classes as a numeric constant which passes its value to the component to which it is connected.

This is a comparator which compares the top input with the bottom input and outputs a boolean signal of TRUE if the top input is greater than or equal to the bottom input and FALSE otherwise.

This is a millisecond delay timer set here to produce a delay of 500 milliseconds, or half a minute. The size of the delay can be adjusted by changing the constant value shown.

This symbol represents a *while* loop. Everything inside is repeated until the signal connected to the circular arrow in the bottom right hand corner becomes FALSE. In this case, the device on/off switch is connected to it so that the instrument will continue to run until the switch on the panel is turned to the off position. The *i* symbol represents a counter which counts the number of times that the loop has repeated.

The Operation of the Temperature Controller

The signal from the voltage simulator (about .7 to .9 volts) is first scaled by 100, using a multiply component, to represent a temperature in the region of 80 degrees. The temperature is then linked to the temperature display symbol (that is, the thermometer) so that the value is shown in both digital and analog form on the front panel. The temperature also links to a comparator which compares it with the minimum temperature setting shown by the control knob and associated digital display. If the temperature is less than the minimum, the output from the comparator activates the heater indicator light, otherwise the indicator is unaffected. This process is repeated in a loop until the switch on the panel is turned to the off position while the device is operating. The VI is restarted by clicking the run icon on the toolbar of either the Panel window or the Diagram window. Note that the output from the comparator to the heater light could also be linked to the output port of the computer to activate an external heater which increases the temperature of the substance being monitored. This would then complete the feedback loop to maintain the temperature at a constant level.

A Car Park Monitoring system

This example simulates an automatic car park which detects the entrance and exit of cars. The number of cars in the car park is compared with its maximum capacity. When the car park is full, a status indicator shows the word 'FULL', otherwise another indicator shows 'SPACES'. A slider control allows the maximum number of cars allowed in the car park to be set. A push button enables or disables the monitor. In order to simulate the entrance and exit of cars, two random number generators randomly produce a value of one to indicate the presence of a car at an entrance or exit, or a value of 0 to indicate the absence of a car at an entrance or exit. The probability of each occurrence can be set using a numeric control on the front panel of the VI.

The Front Panel

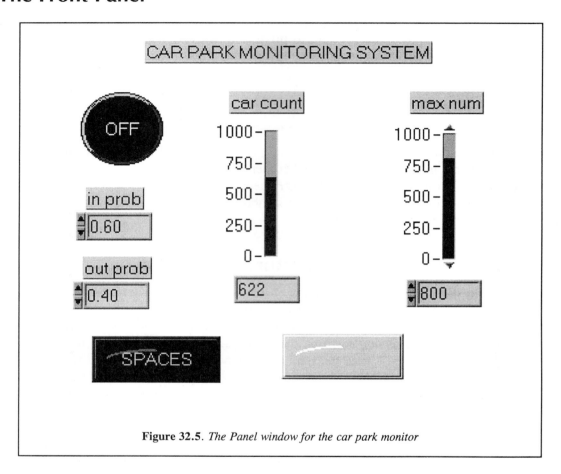

Figure 32.5. *The Panel window for the car park monitor*

Figure 32.5 shows the front panel of the Car Park VI.

The current maximum capacity is set at 800 and the count shows that 622 cars were in the car park. The probability of a car approaching an entrance during a set time period (one minute in this example) is shown as 0.6, and the probability of a car being at an exit is 0.4. This means that on average more cars would be entering the car park than leaving. These probabilities can be adjusted while the VI is running.

The Diagram Panel

Figure 32.6 shows that there are two new features in this VI, namely the use of a sub VI and a formula box.

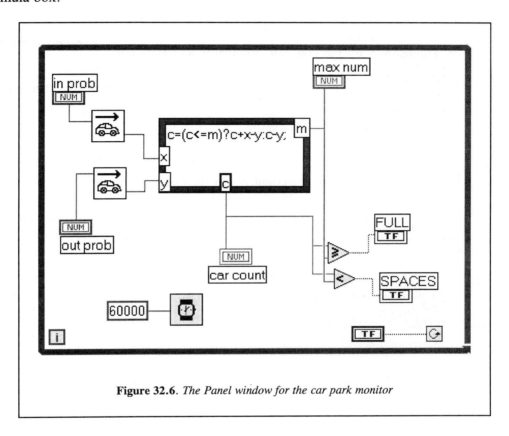

Figure 32.6. *The Panel window for the car park monitor*

The car symbol is a sub VI which has the following diagram:

The dice symbol is a random number generator which produces a random number in the range 0 to 1. The NUM box on the left represents the input to the sub VI and the NUM box on the right is the output. The input for the top car in the diagram is the *in prob* control on the front panel, currently set at 0.6. If the number produced by the random number generator is less than 0.6, the comparator outputs TRUE which is converted to a numeric value of 1 by the component attached to its output line, otherwise the comparator outputs FALSE which produces a value of 0 at the output. Thus, on average there should be more 1s generated than 0s. The bottom car symbol in the diagram is thus more likely to output a 0 than a 1, simulating fewer cars leaving than arriving.

The operation of the Car Park Monitoring system.

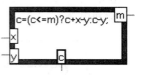

The cars are counted by the formula box shown on the right. The inputs to the formula box are variables x, y and m. These variables store the values provided by the components connected to them. Thus x has the value of 1 or 0 generated by the 'in car' simulator, y has the value 1 or 0 generated by the 'out car' simulator and m is the maximum capacity of the car park as set on the panel control. These values are used to calculate the value of the output, c, which is a counter. The expression for c is

$$c = (c <= m) \quad ? \quad c + x - y \quad : \quad c - y;$$

This is a conditional expression such that if $c <= m$ is true then $c = c + x - y$, otherwise $c = c - y$. This has the effect that if the current car count is less than or equal to the maximum capacity of the car park stored in m, then x is added to the count and y is subtracted from the count, simulating cars both entering and leaving. However, if $c <= m$ is false, indicating that the car park is full, only cars leaving the car park are subtracted from the count because no more cars would be allowed in.

Two comparators are used to activate the FULL and SPACES indicators on the front panel. They each use the c output from the formula box and the maximum capacity value to produce boolean outputs. The comparator activates the FULL indicator if c is greater than or equal to m; the comparator activates the SPACES indicator if c is less than m.

A value of 60000 input to the delay component produces a time period of one minute during which cars approach and leave the car park. All of the components are controlled by a *while* loop which repeats the monitoring process until the button on the front panel is set to OFF.

This VI also could produce output signals to control the operation of external devices such as automatic barriers at the entrances and exits. Sensors could be used to detect the presence of a car approaching a barrier and the VI could be used to produce a signal to raise the barrier. If the car park was full, the VI could prevent entrance barriers being raised until spaces became available. All of these functions could be programmed into the VI presented here.

Study Programme

Study Component 1
Word Processing

Aims

To develop word processing skills.

Resource Material

Chapter 21 in the Skills Resource.

Activities

All the activities in this Study Component are to be completed within the same document. Use the following settings and standards.

- The relevant page settings are as follows: *paper size* A4; *orientation* is portrait; *top margin* 2.49 cm; *bottom margin* 5.99 cm; *left margin* 3.5 cm; *right margin* 2.49 cm; *header* 1.25 cm from top edge; *footer* 1.25 cm from bottom edge.

- The *default font* is Times New Roman, *point size* 12 and *paragraph alignment* is justified (unless indicated otherwise in the text).

- Use only one space between words and after a comma and full stop.

- Leave one blank line after a heading or between paragraphs. Use single line spacing.

1. This activity covers a range of character formatting facilities, simple table construction, as well as general editing. There are two stages. First, enter the text labelled "Unformatted Text", as shown, computer spellcheck it and save the file as "baretext". Print the file and proof it against the original. Make any necessary corrections and save the file again.

Unformatted Text

Character Formatting

Apart from the daisy wheel printer, which only allows the use of one character set at a time, all dot matrix (impact, ink jet and thermographic) and laser printers allow the printing of a wide range of character styles. Some common examples are given below.

bold italic
strike-through
underline
bold-italic

For some word processing work, these variations are quite sufficient and your printer may well have a control panel to select a different font, but any such selection will be applied to the whole document. Typically, your printer may offer

courier, roman, condensed

Variable sizing of character fonts is a facility which, until recently, was associated with desktop publishing (DTP) software. Some examples are given below (size is measured in points).

This is Phyllis ATT 16.

This is Arial 14.

Using Character Formatting

You should use character formatting facilities sparingly. A business document can look very unprofessional, as well as a little silly, if you use too many different character formats. Thus, to emphasise, you may use bold or underlined characters. A quotation may be in italic print and headings in a report may be improved by using a larger font.

WYSIWYG Packages

WYSIWYG stands for What You See Is What You Get, which means that the results of paragraph and character formatting commands are seen on screen. Thus, lines can be seen as centred, characters can be viewed as bold, italic, underlined, or even in different sizes and fonts.

Apart from the package's WYSIWYG facilities, your screen must have the necessary graphics capability and resolution.

Bullets and Numbered Lists
Bullets and numbers can be used to emphasise or sequence items in a list. Two examples are given below. This pack includes the following items: assembly instructions; colour illustrations; components for assembly.

The tasks should be carried out in the following order: initial investigation; analysis; design; implementation.

In the second example, the numbering sequence is carried out automatically and a variety of number styles may be available, using Arabic or Roman numerals, or letters of the alphabet.

End of Unformatted Text

2. Load the file "`baretext`", completed in Activity 1 and format it to appear as shown in the following version, labelled "Formatted Text". Save the file as "`poshtext`" and print it. Compare it with the original, correct as necessary, re-save the file and print a finished copy.

Formatted Text

Character Formatting

Apart from the daisy wheel printer, which only allows the use of one character set at a time, all dot matrix (impact, ink jet and thermographic) and laser printers allow the printing of a wide range of character styles. Some common examples are given below.

Bold	*italic*	~~strike through~~		underline	***bold italic***

Create table with grid border   **Insert in table and format words as stated**

For some word processing work, these variations are quite sufficient and your printer may well have a control panel to select a different font, but any such selection will be applied to the whole document. Typically, your printer may offer

courier, roman, condensed

Variable sizing of character *fonts* is a facility which, until recently, was associated with desktop publishing (DTP) software. Some examples are given below (size is measured in points).

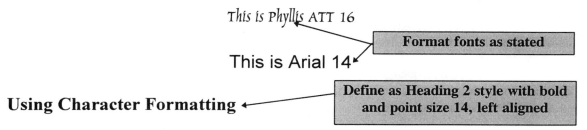

This is Phyllis ATT 16

Format fonts as stated

This is Arial 14

Using Character Formatting

Define as Heading 2 style with bold and point size 14, left aligned

You should use character formatting facilities sparingly. A business document can look very unprofessional, as well as a little silly, if you use too many different character formats. Thus, to emphasise, you may use bold or underlined characters. A quotation may be in italic print and headings in a report may be improved by using a larger font.

WYSIWYG Packages

Apply Heading 1 style, already defined

WYSIWYG stands for What You See Is What You Get, which means that the results of paragraph and character formatting commands are seen on screen. Thus, lines can be seen as centred, characters can be viewed as **bold**, *italic*, underlined, or even in

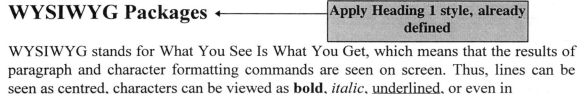

Arial 13; Arial 15; Desdemona 18

different sizes and FONTS.

Format fonts as indicated

Apart from the package's WYSIWYG facilities, your screen must have the necessary graphics capability and resolution

Bullets and Numbered Lists

Apply Heading 1 style, already defined

Bullets and numbers can be used to emphasise or sequence items in a list. Two examples are given below.

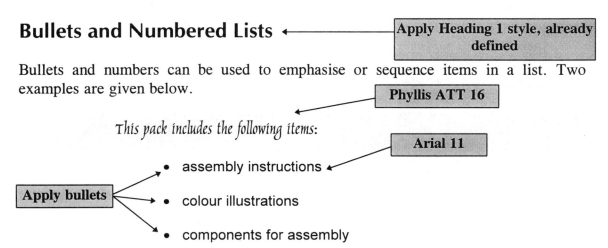

Phyllis ATT 16

This pack includes the following items:

Arial 11

Apply bullets

- assembly instructions
- colour illustrations
- components for assembly

The tasks should be carried out in the following order:

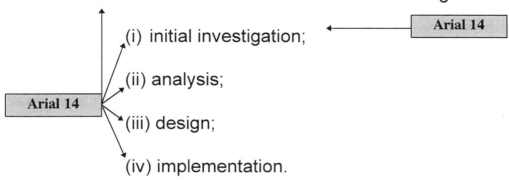

(i) initial investigation;

(ii) analysis;

(iii) design;

(iv) implementation.

In the second example, the numbering sequence is carried out automatically and a variety of number styles may be available, using Arabic or Roman numerals, or letters of the alphabet. Figure 24 shows a dialogue box for the selection of various bullet formats.

End of Formatted Text

3. Load the "poshtext" file and insert a right aligned title, using Arial, point size 18, bold. Insert page numbers to appear as a footer on the right hand side of each page. At the left side of the footer, insert your own name, the file name and the date on which you completed this document.

4. Create a new document and illustrate use of the various drawing tools (simple demonstrations of each will do) detailed in Chapter 21. If your word processor does not have drawing tools, you will have to use a graphics package and them import, or paste, the drawing into the document. Also insert a clip art image into the document. Use text boxes (as shown above), to annotate the drawings (for example, circle, square, ellipse and so on).

Performance Criteria

Activity number	Unit element
1-4	IT Core Skills

Study Component 2
Spreadsheets

Aim

To develop spreadsheet skills and the ability to apply them to problems.

Resource Material

Chapter 22 in the Skills Resource.

Activities

1. The proprietor of CompuSales wants to compare the profitability of each make of microcomputer which is sold by the firm. Use the following sample data to set up a worksheet to produce:

   (a) total sales revenue in respect of each model of computer;

   (b) total costs of the computers sold, in respect of each model of computer;

   (c) the gross profit (total revenue - total cost) in respect of each model of computer;

   (d) the gross profit margin (gross profit as a percentage of total revenue) relating to each model of computer;

   (e) the total revenue from and total cost of all computers sold;

   (f) the gross profit and gross profit margin on all sales.

Computer model	Unit sale price	Unit cost	Number sold
Dell 486/33	£1,400	£795	45
Dan 486/66	£1,700	£125	275
Compaq 386/25	£755	£375	95
Amstrad 486/33	£1005	£165	75
Viglen 486sx/25	£875	£725	30
CompuAdd 386/25	£988	£600	450
IBM PS2/70	£1,700	£1,350	35

2.   This activity relates to student attendance records. Each student's attendance details is to be held on a separate worksheet. Attendance is to be recorded for each separate class, identified by: day of the week; subject; start time; duration (in hours, with a maximum of two per class). The worksheet should allow the recording of attendance for a term of twelve weeks, beginning with Monday, 5th September. Some sample data are given below. Add your own to complete the week. **Design** the worksheet to allow entry of the student's *actual attendance hours* for each class throughout the term. Enter the necessary formulae to produce the following information:

(a) the total *possible attendance* each week;

(b) the total *actual attendance* each week;

(c) the *cumulative weekly variance* (the possible weekly hours minus the actual weekly hours; accumulate these variances from week to week).The possible weekly hours total is always the same, so use a single cell entry to store it. This will mean that, before you copy this formula to all weeks in the term, you will have to make the cell reference, for possible weekly hours, *absolute*.

(d) the total possible attendance over the full term, for each class; you can probably make use of the COUNT function in this formula;

(e) the total actual attendance over the full term, for each class;

(f) the total possible hours for all classes over the full term;

(g) the total actual hours attendance for all classes over the full term;

(h) item (f) as a percentage of item (g).

Day	Class	Start time	Duration (hours)
Monday	English	9.00 am	2
Monday	Maths	11.15 am	1
Monday	Maths	1.15 pm	2
Monday	French	3.30 pm	1
Tuesday	Physics	10.15 am	2
Tuesday	German	1.15 pm	2
etc.			

3.   In this activity, you are required to produce various figures concerning profit. **Create** a worksheet to permit the entry of:

(a) a single product name;

(b) a single product sale price;

(c) a single product cost price;

(d) the number of units of the product which are sold each month, for a period of 6 months;

(e) the monthly costs of overheads, including salaries, advertising, heat, light and transport.

Enter *formulae* to produce the following information:

(a) monthly sales revenue (units sold multiplied by product sale price); remember to use absolute cell referencing for the sale price, before copying this formula;

(b) monthly cost of sales (units sold multiplied by product cost price); use absolute referencing for the cost price;

(c) monthly gross profit (sales revenue minus cost of sales);

(d) monthly overheads (the sum of salaries, advertising and general overheads);

(e) monthly net profit (gross profit minus overheads);

(f) monthly profit margin (net profit divided by sales revenue).

4. MicroFile is a microcomputer dealer. It needs a bank loan of £30,000 and has to present to the bank, a forecast of its repayment plans. MicroFile's quarterly costs are: January to March, £10500; April to June, £11000; July to September, £11200; October to December, £11300. These costs remain the same for each year. During the first quarter, it will sell each computer for £800; the price will then be reduced by £25 in each subsequent quarter, until a base price of £675 is reached. MicroFile expects to sell 20 computers in the first quarter and 25 in each succeeding quarter. The sales revenue for each quarter, less the quarter's costs, is to be used to reduce the loan. The loan is to be taken on the 1st of January; repayments will be made on the last day of each quarter. Loan interest of 15% on the outstanding balance is charged to the loan account at the end of each quarter.

(a) **Set up** a worksheet to record this information. Following entry of the computer sale price for the first quarter, **use** a formula to produce the price for subsequent quarters. Enter formulae to calculate the gross revenue and the net revenue, which will be available for loan repayment, at the end of each quarter. Also **show** the amount of loan which is outstanding at the end of each quarter. **Show** when the loan will be fully repaid.

(b) The bank may require repayment of the loan within the year. **Use** the worksheet to determine the number of computers which need to be sold to clear the loan within that period.

5. In this activity, you make use of a number of statistical functions. Use the following student grades.

Assignment Grades	
Name	Marks (out of 75)
Smith	40
Erikson	34
Weber	50
Ricci	65
Clemenceau	27
Parker	44
Depardieu	50
Jones	70
Kahn	45

Singh	24
Lee	35
Shun	42
McDonald	51

Set up a worksheet to calculate:

(a) each mark as a *percentage*;

(b) the *range* of percentage marks; this is simply the difference between the highest and lowest values (you can use the MAX and MIN functions);

(c) the *mean* percentage mark (add them all together and divide by the number of marks; you can use the AVERAGE function here);

(d) the *standard deviation* (use the appropriate function).

(e) Of course, to make practical use of this information, you have to understand the significance of each statistic.

6. The Target Corporation wish to monitor certain aspects of the business's payroll. The following information is provided:

Employee Name	Standard Hours	Hours Worked	Basic Rate per Hour
Al-Fariz, A	35	42	£5.00
Crowley, M	38	38	£5.00
Guttuso, R	35	30	£7.50
Hideo, K	40	45	£7.50
Johnson, M	38	42	£6.00
Mackenzie, P	40	40	£6.00
Negewo, K	35	28	£5.00
Pascal, B	40	47	£7.50
Singh, H	38	39	£7.50
Weizman, E	38	33	£5.00
Wilson, H	35	39	£6.00

Create a worksheet which provides you with the following information, in respect of *each employee*.

(a) *Basic pay*. If the hours worked figure is less than that for the standard hours, the basic pay is calculated by multiplying the hours worked by the basic hourly rate. Otherwise, the standard hours figure is multiplied by the basic hourly rate.

(b) *Overtime rate*. This is one and a quarter times the basic hourly rate.

(c) *Overtime hours*. If the hours worked figure is greater than that for the standard hours, the latter is subtracted from the former. Otherwise, a figure of zero is to be displayed.

(d) *Overtime pay*. If overtime has been worked, multiply the overtime hours by the overtime rate. If not, display a figure of £0.00.

(e) *Gross pay*. This is the basic pay, plus the overtime pay.
Save the worksheet, then document it.

7. Adventure Holidays want to record details of holidays sold and the amounts charged. You are given the following data.

Adventure Holidays				
Client Name	Holiday Title	Cost per person	Number of persons	Discount code
Featherstonehaugh-Haugh	Andes	£1300	5	3
Cholmondley-Warner	Amazon	£1800	4	2
Isay-Carruthers-Oldbean	Serengeti	£2400	3	2
Scott-Oates-Gonout	Antarctic	£1400	12	1
Carter-Hayes	Atlantic	£1000	6	3
Badshow-Fortescue	Sahara	£1350	10	1
Cousteau	Undersea	£2000	2	1

Create a worksheet for entry of the above sample data and **enter** formulae to generate the following additional information.

(a) the gross cost of the holiday for each client;
(b) the discount to be deducted from the gross cost; this is calculated with the percentage discount rate. These percentages are to be held in a table and are identified by the discount codes as follow: 1 is 2.00%; 2 is 5.50%; 3 is 6.50%;
(c) an additional party discount. If the number of persons in the party is more than 4, then an additional discount of 3.00% is given. Otherwise, there is no party discount.
(d) the net cost to each client.

8. This activity concerns the calculation of income tax. **Create** a worksheet to allow the entry of the following details relating to a single employee: name; tax code (excluding the letter); gross annual salary; superannuation rate (percentage); national insurance rate (percentage). **Use** a *lookup table* to record the following tax rates, relating to gross annual salary.

Annual Salary	Tax Rate
£0 to £1999.99	0%
£2000 to £14999.99	20%
£15000 to £25999.99	25%
£40000 and more	35%

Design and **create** the worksheet to produce the following *monthly* figures:

(a) gross salary;

(b) superannuation (use the superannuation rate on the gross salary);

(c) national insurance (use the national insurance rate on the gross salary);

(d) taxable income (you need to deduct the superannuation and the month's tax allowance from the gross salary; remember that the tax code is 3 digits and has to be multiplied by 10 for the annual allowance);

(e) the amount of tax to be deducted (this is the tax rate pulled from the lookup table multiplied by the taxable income; remember that the tax rates in the table relate to annual taxable income). Of course, the taxable income would not all be taxed at the same rate; the first band is at 0%, the second at 20% and so on. For the purposes of this activity, assume that the extracted tax rate is to be applied to all the taxable income.

(f) the net salary (the gross salary, less the superannuation, national insurance and income tax).

NB Your tax calculation formula needs to be prefixed with an IF formula, to check that the taxable income is greater than or equal to £0.00. If you attempt to lookup a value less than £0.00 in the tax rate table the formula will not work; this is because the amount will be less than zero, which is not provided for in the table lookup ranges. In any case there is no point calculating tax for an employee who is not liable to it.

9. This activity concerns academic course fees, payable according to the *mode of attendance*. There are four modes: full-time (FT); part-time day (PTD); part-time evening (PTE) and block (BLO). **Create** a worksheet to allow the entry of a list of *student names*, *course titles* and *attendance modes* (by code). The worksheet should *automatically extract* the *fees* from a fee table (using the attendance code) and display them next to the relevant student records.

10. Suppose that you work for a small retail firm which does not make use of accounts software. Part of your job is to *monitor sales* and to *calculate revenue*. You want to use the spreadsheet to help you in this task and decide that the following information should be recorded about each sale. **Create** a suitable worksheet.

Product Code	Description	Unit Selling Price	Quantity	Total Price

Choose your own *product range*, *codes*, *descriptions*, *prices* and *quantities*. Bearing in mind that the details of each product will be held in a *lookup table*, it would be sensible to limit the number of products in the range to about five.

(a) **Set up** the vertical *lookup table* and the data entry area for the sales records. Remember to minimise the need for data entry. A user should only have to enter the Product Code and Quantity for an individual sale record. The other information should be generated automatically;

(b) **Enter** details for around thirty separate sales. This should ensure that each product code is entered several times, illustrating the savings in data entry time;

(c) **Enter** a formula to calculate the total sales revenue;

(d) **Save** and **print** the worksheet.

11. This activity is concerned with a *student tutoring system*. You have been asked to **develop** a *worksheet* which will allow the printing of student lists, including identification of the tutor for each student. There are 4 tutors. The lookup value for each student is to be Tutor Code (uniquely identifies an individual Tutor). Use of the lookup value enables extraction of the following information.

Tutor Name	Tutor Location (Room No)

    (a) **Set up** the *horizontal lookup table*. You will need three rows in the table (Tutor Code, Tutor Name and Tutor Location).

    (b) **Create** a *data entry area* to include the following headings: Student Name; Tutor Code; Tutor Name; Tutor Location. Enter the lookup formulae to produce the Tutor Name and Location for each student.

    (c) **Enter** the *details* for around *15 students* and **check** that the output is correct.

    (d) **Save** the worksheet and **print** the student list.

12. A particular examination board requires that assistant examiners award a percentage mark for each script they mark. These marks are submitted, together with the candidate number and name, to the examination board. They then need to be converted to literal grades (A, B, C and so on), using the following scale.

Percentage Range	Grade
85% to 100%	A
75% to 84%	B
60% to 74%	C
45% to 59%	D
40% to 44%	E
30% to 39%	F
Up to 29%	U

Set up the lookup table and a data entry area for the candidate details and marks. Enter the lookup formula to produce the literal grade for each candidate. Enter a number of candidate records and check the results. Save the worksheet and print the list of candidate results.

13. You work for a small, provincial theatre, called the Dominion and wish to calculate ticket costs for a new production. There are four seating zones in the theatre, labelled A, B, C and D. Each has a different standard seat price, £20, £18, £15 and £12, respectively. For senior citizens, the prices are cheaper, £14, £12, £9 and £6. For students, they are £10, £8, £6 and £4. **Design** and **create** a worksheet (using LOOKUP and IF function) to allow:

    (a) the entry of a person's *name*;

    (b) their *category* (standard, senior citizen or student);

    (c) the *seat area*;

    (d) the *number of tickets* required.

Generate a *total cost* for each ticket order.

Performance Criteria

Activity number	Unit element
1-13	IT Core Skills

Study Component 3
Spreadsheet Graphics

Aim

To develop spreadsheet graphic skills and the ability to apply them effectively.

Resource Material

Chapter 23 in the Skills Resource.

Activities

1. This activity can be used as an introduction to *break even analysis*, which is dealt with in Modelling and Simulation (Chapter 19). **Enter** the following data on production costs and generate a total cost for each level of output.

The Target Corporation - Production Costs		
Output in Units	Fixed Costs	Variable Costs
0	500	0
100	500	200
200	500	300
300	500	350
400	500	450
500	500	600
600	500	800

700	500	1050
800	500	1350
900	500	1700
1000	500	2100

Create a suitably labelled line graph showing the *fixed costs*, *variable costs* and *total costs* against each level of output. **Save** and **print** the graph.

2. A college wishes to show, pictorially, the relative number of students in each department, for particular academic years. A bar chart is chosen for this purpose. The following figures are provided.

Department	Number of Students			
	1990	1991	1992	1993
Business	850	957	1100	1365
Management	601	675	874	900
Science	512	475	264	276
Technology	300	465	477	523
Total	**4252**	**4556**	**4708**	**5057**

Use this data to construct a suitably labelled bar chart. Note that there are four data series to plot.

3. Before trying this activity, you should have produced the payroll worksheet in Activity 8 of the Spreadsheet Study Component. In that activity, the worksheet is designed to calculate payroll details for one employee at a time; it makes use of a lookup table to extract appropriate percentage tax rates. This graphics activity requires the production of pie charts to compare the amounts (in percentage terms) of superannuation, national insurance and tax paid by employees on several different levels of salary. Therefore, you will need to **modify** the payroll worksheet to permit the calculation of several payroll records. Also **modify** the worksheet with the following data. The tax rates are:

Range	Rate
£0 to £14999.99	0%
£15000 to £24999.99	15%
£25000 to £29999.99	25%
£30000 to £49999.99	40%
£50000 or more	50%

(a) There are 6 employees earning £18000, £28000, £45000, £60000, £80000 and £100000, respectively. Each has the same tax code of 512. National insurance is paid at 7% on the gross salary, with a maximum of £2600 per annum (you will **need to use** an **IF formula** to ensure the deduction is limited to that maximum figure). Superannuation is paid at 6% of the gross salary, with no upper limit.

(b) Once you have **calculated** the payroll details for each of the 6 employees, **produce** a pie chart for each, using the superannuation, national insurance and tax deductions, together with the net salary; the data series or range (the whole pie equates to the gross salary). Label the graphs and make observations on the varying proportions of these items at the different salary levels.

4. The next figure shows the inflows and outflows of male unemployment (the figures are monthly averages in thousands), for years 1970 to 1984.

Year	Inflow ('000s)	Outflows ('000s)
1970	248	244
1971	252	236
1972	226	235
1973	207	222
1974	222	215
1975	238	208
1976	218	214
1977	203	200
1978	189	197
1979	180	183
1980	217	173
1981	220	183
1982	222	214
1983	246	243
1984	248	241

(a) Enter the data (or obtain more recent figures) and then graph the inflow and outflow data series for the period covered by the figures. A line graph is probably the most suitable choice. Label the graph appropriately.

(b) Using stock market data from the financial newspapers, you can carry out a similar activity to show, for example, the comparative performance of particular shares and a unit trust over an extended period.

5. This activity concerns correlation; this is a measure of the strength of the relationship between two measurements. You need to know something about this topic before you can appreciate the results of this activity.

(a) **Collect** data relating to interest rates and share prices (using the Financial Times 100 share index and the Bank of England Base lending rate). To be of value, the data will have to cover an extended period. There are financial databases and publications which will provide this data for you. The aim is to measure the degree of correlation between movements in interest rates and the performance of shares. A *scatter* diagram is appropriate, because the two sets of data are associated. A scatter graph is another form of XY graph, except that no line is shown, only the plotted points. You may be able to select the scatter type of graph directly, from a range of options. However, as is the case with early versions of Lotus 123, you may have to choose an XY graph and then alter the line pattern, so that it is hidden. In this way, only the plotted points are displayed. If you do leave the line in place, it will be criss-crossing, because the values in the range are unlikely to be in any recognisable sequence.

(b) Repeat the exercise, perhaps with data relating to: the heights and weights of people; football statistics relating to a number of teams, such as the number of games won and the number of goals scored by each.

Performance Criteria

Activity number	Unit element
1-5	IT Core Skills

Study Component 4
Computer Installation

Aims

To demonstrate hardware connection, software installation and system configuration.

To review the system and make recommendations for its improvement.

Resource Material

Chapter 2 in the Knowledge Resource (primarily Operating Systems)

Activities

1. **Demonstrate** the connection of stand alone computer system components. The checklist which follows can be used by your assessor to check your performance.

Performance Criteria	Completed
Hardware Connection	
(i) Power cable to system unit.	
(ii) Keyboard to system unit.	
(iii) Mouse to system unit.	
(iv) Display to system unit.	
(v) Power cable to display	
(vi) Printer to relevant port in system unit.	
(vii) Power cable to printer.	
(viii) Connect power supply and power up.	

1. **Set up** and **configure** a computer system to a specification. This will detail the system's:

(a) *purpose* (for example, a drawing program);
(b) *inputs* (for example, parameters for shapes and colours, etc);
(c) *processing* activity (calculation of vector co-ordinates and screen drawing of images);
(d) *output* (screen and printer); required performance (for example, speed of screen re-draws, image resolution, colour definition, precision drawing).

3. The hardware or software components of the system will be deficient for the required specification in one or more respects. You will have to identify the deficiencies and suggest how the system can be improved. The activity has two main parts: *configuration* of hardware use by the operating system; *installation* and *testing* of software. Note that most software is automatically installed as you respond to a series of screen prompts, but this activity requires that you create the necessary directories/folders and copy the program files into them.

Performance Criteria	Completed
Configure operating system to use hardware	
(i) Install specified screen driver and check operation.	
(ii) Set memory configurations (e.g. files and buffers, HIMEM in *config.sys*, or virtual memory in Windows 3.1). Copy original settings first.	
(iii) Install mouse device drivers (possibly included in *autoexec.bat*).	
(iv) Set date and time (at MS-DOS prompt or in Windows Control Panel).	
Install application and test	
(i) Create directory to hold executable and other files for application.	
(ii) Copy application files from floppy disk into the new directory.	
(iii) If necessary, use Windows Setup to install application for Windows use.	
(iv) Run application and set defaults (e.g. work file locations, save options, tool bars displayed).	
(v) Enter test data, save and print.	
(vi) Assess performance, identify deficiencies and suggest how to improve (for example, faster processor, more memory, higher resolution screen).	

(a) **Configure** the system, **install** the software and **test** the system. The precise steps will depend on the specification and the equipment you are using, but you can use the following table as a checklist. **Keep notes** of **each step** you take and any *problems* which occur.

(b) **Produce** a short *report* on the procedures carried out in Activity 2, identifying any difficulties experienced, methods used to solve them and recommendations for improvement of the system.

Performance Criteria

Activity number	Unit element
1	1.4(1)
2	1.4(2), 1.4(3), 1.4(4)
3	1.4(5)

Study Component 5
Local Area Network Operation

Aims

To access a network in accordance with standards.

To prepare a user notice on standards.

To undertake file processing and management.

To access network applications.

To use electronic mail.

To install a new user and set initial access rights.

To modify access rights of other users to own files.

To prepare a simple user manual outlining specified operational procedures.

Resource Material

Chapter 8 in the Knowledge Resource and Chapters 21, 24 and 26 in the Skills Resource.

Activities

1. **Produce** a word processed, single page, summary description of the *access standards* used by the college (or, those of another system if you have such knowledge). This is to serve as a **notice to users**. In the absence of a standard, describe one which would be appropriate.

2. **Design** and **draw** a directory structure (a block diagram, using vector drawing tools), which subdivides your home directory on the network server. The design should correspond with the ways in which you want to divide your work.

3. **Demonstrate** *access* to the network, using the *defined standards* and carry out the processes listed in the next table (this will be used by the assessor as a checklist of your progress).

Performance Criteria	Completed
Network Access	
(i) login, using account name and password	
(ii) display required application, execute and then quit	
(iii)logout	

4. **Demonstrate** *file process* and *directory management* procedures, as listed in the next table (used by your assessor as a checklist). You will need the directory structure design you prepared in 2.

Performance Criteria	Completed
Directory management and file processes	
(i) Login with account name and password.	
(ii) Create designed directory structure within home directory.	
(iii) Access a specified application and set a default working directory within the package (selected from the structure created).	
(iv) Save a package file (e.g. spreadsheet document) into that directory.	
(v) Exit package and then reload.	
(vi) Select directory containing files saved in step (iv).	
(vii) Select file and open.	
(viii) Edit file and save.	
(ix) Quit package and logout.	

5. **Demonstrate** *file management* procedures, as listed in the next table.

Performance Criteria	Completed
File management and processes using file manager utility or operating system command line.	
(i) Login with account name and password.	
(ii) Access file manager utility (e.g. Windows File Manager) or operating system command line.	
(iii) Add another specified directory to the structure	
(iv) Within home directory structure, copy a specified file from its directory to the directory created in (iii).	
(v) Rename file in destination directory.	
(vi) Set attributes of new copy of file to 'read only'.	
(vii) Delete file in original directory	
(viii) Display contents of each directory (one at a time) within the structure, restricting the display, for example, to .doc files.	

(ix) Quit file manager utility and logout.	

6.   Demonstrate *installation of new user*, using steps in the following table. For this activity, you need to have been assigned additional network status by the network supervisor or administrator (for example, with the Novell Netware operating system, you could be given the security equivalence of Workgroup Manager (see Local Area Network Operation in the Skills Resource).

Performance Criteria	Completed
Installation of user and setting of initial access rights	
(i) Login with temporarily assigned user status, with one-time password.	
(ii) Access the appropriate network utility (e.g. SYSCON)	
(iii) Create new user.	
(iv) Assign specified trustee rights in home directory	
(v) Set specified account restrictions	
(vi) Create login script to map network drive to home user's home directory.	
(vii) Logout	
(viii) Login as newly created user, using appropriate name and password. Home directory is mapped to network drive.	
(ix) Logout	

7.   Demonstrate *allowing other users to access own files*, following the procedures listed in the following table. The person granting the rights is referred to as User 1(this is the person being assessed) and the user who is assigned rights is referred to as User 2.

Performance Criteria	Completed
Allowing other users to access own files	
(i) User 1 login with own user name and password.	
(ii) Grant selected trustee rights to User 2, in User 1 home directory.	
(iii) User 2 login and copy file from User 1 directory to their own directory.	
(iv) User 2 modifies file and saves it back to User 1 directory.	
(v) User 2 logout.	
(vi) User 1 revoke all User 2 trustee rights in User 1 directory.	
(vii) User 1 logout.	

8.   Demonstrate *using electronic mail.*

Performance Criteria	Completed
Using electronic mail	
(i) Login to electronic mail with user account and password.	

(ii) Select destination user.	
(iii) Send prepared message.	
(iv) Check own mail box and view contents	
(v) Logout of electronic mail.	

9. **Produce** a simple, step-by-step, user guide to *three* of the procedures followed in Activities 3 to 8. The guide should be *specific to the network system* you are using. The guide should be an A5, folded booklet (short edge to top), with title and contents page, page numbering and a footer detailing your initials and the date complete. The page numbering should start after the contents page. Use *vector graphics* and *bit map images* to **illustrate** the booklet. There should be one illustration to represent each topic covered in the booklet. Begin by **creating** a suitable *template* for page layout and heading styles.

Performance Criteria

Activity number	Unit element
1	2.1(1), 2.1(2), 2.2(4), 2.2(5), 2.2(6)
2	4.4(2), 2.2(1), 2.2(2), 2.2(5), 2.2(6)
3	4.4(1), 4.4(4)
4	4.4(1), 4.4(2),4.4(4)
5	4.4(1), 4.4(2), 4.4(4)
6	4.4(1), 4.4(6)
7	4.4(1), 4.4(3)
8	4.4(5)
9	2.1(1), 2.1(2), 2.1(3), 2.1(4), 2.1(5), 2.1(6), 2.2(1), 2.2(2), 2.2(3), 2,2(4), 2.2(6)

Study Component 6
Practical Data Communications

Aims

To describe system components of electronic communication systems.

To explain technical terms used in electronic communications.

To demonstrate preparation and connection of communications hardware and software.

To demonstrate configuration of control and protocol settings.

To undertake file transfer and interactive communications, maintaining a suitable log.

To use a word processor to present information in a tabular form.

Resource Material

Chapter 7 in the Knowledge Resource and Chapter 27 in the Skills Resource.

Activities

1. This activity is part of your preparation for the practical data communications work in Activities 2 and 3. **Using** the table facility in your word processor, **prepare**, **check**, **save** and **print** a glossary (including definition and purpose and example) of the following technical terms relating to this Activity and Activity 2 on file transfers (you should be prepared to explain these verbally to your assessor). In the table, **group** the terms appropriately into the categories of: system components; standards for data communications; protocols and parameters; terminal modes. The technical terms to be included are:

    data terminal equipment (DTE); data circuit terminating equipment (DCE); data representation; echo; wrap; terminal emulation; carriage return (CR); line feed (LF); transmission rate; data compression; flow control; start and stop bits; parity; null modem; modem; data bits; terminal software; communications port; binary transfer; carrier detect; text transfer.

2. This activity requires you to **demonstrate** the transfer of two types of file: binary and text (ASCII). The transfer should be between two computers connected by a null modem cable. The following checklist will be used by your tutor to check your demonstration as it proceeds.

Performance Criteria	Completed
Transfer of text file	
(i) Suitable text file prepared for transfer and stored on sending computer	
(ii) Connect computers with null modem cable through their serial ports	
(iii) Configure controls and protocols to match receiving computer	
(iv) Establish link and transfer file	
(v) View file on receiving computer and check properly transferred	
(vi) Close link	
Transfer of binary file	
(i) Suitable binary file prepared for transfer and stored on sending computer	

(ii) Configure controls and protocols to match receiving computer	
(iii) Establish link and transfer file	
(iv) Check integrity of file on receiving computer	
(v) Close link	

3. This activity requires you to **demonstrate** the **setting up** and **use** of an *interactive communications link* with a remote computer. The following checklist will be used by your tutor to check your demonstration as it proceeds.

Performance Criteria	Completed
Interactive communication	
(i) Access terminal software	
(ii) Configure controls and protocols	
(iii) Select destination, call and establish communication	
(iv) Retrieve information as required	
(v) Close link	
(vi) Check log and record in evidence portfolio	

Connect the necessary hardware and access the terminal software. **Access** and **adjust**, where necessary the various *terminal* and *communication* settings. **Establish** a link with JANET and retrieve information concerning HND and Degree courses in Computing and Information Technology offered by **three** universities in your region (use their BBSs). If your terminal software provides a communications activities log, check the entries when you are finished. **Close** the link and then **disconnect** the line. **Record** the details of each communication activity in your own evidence portfolio. The details should include: data; time; destination; BBS identification; purpose of activity. **Word process, check, save** and **print** a brief **summary** of the *facilities* provided by *JANET* and *similar network services* and outline the information you retrieved, concerning university courses.

Performance Criteria

Activity number	Unit element
1	4.1(2), 4.1(3), 2.1(3), 2.1(4), 2.1(5), 2.1(6)
2	4.2(1), 4.2(2), 4.2(3), 4.2(4)
3	4.2(1), 4.2(2), 4.2(3), 4.2(5), 4.2(6), 2.1(3), 2.1(4), 2.1(5), 2.1(6)

Study Component 7
Practical Systems Analysis

Aims

To allow investigation and practice of systems analysis methods and techniques.

To produce a feasibility report and a systems analysis report.

To develop skills in document, graphics and spreadsheet production.

Resource Material

Chapters, 11, 12 and 13 in the Knowledge Resource, Barford Properties Case Study in the Appendix and Chapters 21, 22, 23 and 24 in the Skills Resource.

Activities

These activities are based on the Barford Properties Case Study in the Appendix. To extend them you may carry out some additional research into the operation of an estate agency in your area. It is proposed that the Property Sales system is computerised.

1. **Produce** a plan of the *systems analysis stages*, which you will need to follow. **Explain** the purpose of each stage and the general activities it involves.

2. **Identify** the user categories who would be expected to have access to the records and **analyse** their requirements.

3. **Undertake** a *feasibility study* of the proposal. **Define** the *purpose* of the Property Sales System and establish its *objectives*. Other systems within the estate agency, which may interact with it, also need to be identified. **Produce** a word processed *feasibility report*.

4. **Briefly describe** the standard techniques for gathering users' system requirements, **select** the technique(s) you consider most appropriate for the estate agency proposal and **explain** your choice. **Design** and use appropriate software to **produce,** a *questionnaire* for gathering information from buyers. It should identify Barford Properties and establish a corporate style. The aim of the questionnaire is to establish which types of information on houses they most need in the initial stage of an enquiry and the form(s) in which they would like the information to be presented to them. You also want to know which types of house and price ranges are most in demand and the number of houses each respondent

has bought. Most people have bought at least one house, so you should **obtain** around 20 *responses*. You should make use of any software you consider appropriate to produce the questionnaire.

5.   **Use** a *spreadsheet* to **analyse** your findings and produce useful statistics. **Produce two** types of *chart* from these statistics, using *spreadsheet graphics* facilities.

6.   **Use** a suitable *graphics package*, to **draw** an *organisation chart* to represent the divisions of responsibility in the agency; it is likely to be a fairly 'flat' structure.

7.   **Draw** an *information flow* diagram (using vector drawing tools), showing the *functional* areas of the agency and the information flows between them. These should cover all the information systems in the agency, including property for sale records, viewing appointments, accounts, buyer and vendor records, and connections with outside bodies, such as solicitors, banks and building societies and the Land Registry.

8.   **Analyse** the Property Sales system, and **word process** a *system analysis report* (using the same corporate style, established in Activity 4). It must **include** a *data flow diagram* (computer produced and embedded in the document) in respect of the existing manual system. Your analysis should **detail** the current:

- data collection methods and inputs;
- documents used;
- operations and decisions;
- storage;
- system outputs.

Also, include in your report, *recommendations* for a computerised system. These should:

(a) **describe** the different types of system (for example, batch processing, transaction processing, information storage and retrieval) and make an argued recommendation for a particular type;

(b) **detail** *input* (including form, source and collection method), *processing* (form of processing activity), *storage* and *reporting* requirements of the system; you should also detail expected *volumes* of data and *frequency* of input and outputs;

(c) **identify** *expectations* of the system.

(d) *costs* and *savings* of a new system, identifying resources needed and any constraints on its development or use.

9.   **Obtain** user comments (this is likely to be your tutor) on your analysis and **make modifications**, as necessary.

Performance Criteria

Activity number	Unit element
1	5.1(3)
2	5.1(2)

3	5.1(2), 5.1(3), 5.2(1)
4	5.2(2), 2.1(1), 2.1(2), 2.1(3), 2.1(4), 2.1(5), 2.1(6)
5	2.2(1), 2.2(2), 2.2(4), 2.2(6), 2.3(4)
6	3.1(1), 2.2(1), 2.2(2), 2.2(5), 2.2(6)
7	3.1(2), 3.1(3), 2.2(1), 2.2(2), 2.2(5), 2.2(6)
8	5.2(1), 5.2(2), 5.2(3), 5.2(4), 2.1(1), 2.1(2), 2.1(3), 2.1(4), 2.1(5), 2.1(6), 2.2(1), 2.2(2), 2.2(5), 2.2(6)
9	5.2(5)

Study Component 8
System Specification

Aims

To describe the elements of a system specification.

To produce a system specification.

To develop skills in document and graphics production.

Resource Material

Chapters 13 and 14 in the Knowledge Resource, the Barford Properties Case Study in the Appendix and Chapters 21 and 24 in the Skills Resource.

Activities

These activities are based on the Barford Properties Case Study in the Appendix and builds on the feasibility and systems analysis reports produced in Study Component 7 - Practical Systems Analysis. These activities lead to the production of a system specification for the Property Sales system. To begin with, Activity 1 and 2 require you to demonstrate your knowledge of the terminology associated with this subject.

1. **Word process** (using table facilities) a *glossary*, **listing** and briefly **describing** the following elements of a system specification: *input specification; output specification; process specification; resources; constraints; first normal form (1NF) data model.*

2. **Word process** a similar *glossary*, **explaining**, with examples, the following types of processing activity: *sorting; selecting; merging; calculation; interrogation; repetition.*

3. **Produce a system specification** (word processed in the corporate style established in Study Component 7) in the following stages. At each stage, include an explanation of its purpose and the specification element(s) it comprises.

   (a) **Refine** and re-**draw** the *data flow diagram* produced in Study Component 7, Activity 8, and **identify** the *entities* which form the Property Sales system. **Produce** *data definitions* for each entity, and if necessary *normalise* to first normal for (1NF). **Establish** a *data dictionary* and **record** the details.

   (b) **Produce** an *input specification*, detailing data source(s), capture methods; screen layouts, verification, validation parameters.

   (c) **Produce** an *output specification*, with designs for screen and printed reports.

   (d) **Produce** a *process specification* (if appropriate, use decision tables to refine the efficiency of processes). Use at least one of the following methods to define the process(es): *structured English; structure diagram, flow chart.*

   (e) **Identify** and **describe** resource implications of the specification, including hardware, software, people, time scale for implementation and costs.

4. **Describe** the *alternative information technology methods*, which may be used to implement the specification and **suggest** for *which aspect of development* each may be appropriate (with reasons; otherwise indicate as inappropriate).

Performance Criteria

Activity number	Unit element
1	5.1(4), 2.1(2), 2.1(3), 2.1(4), 2.1(5), 2.1(6)
2	5.1(1), 2.1(2), 2.1(3), 2.1(4), 2.1(5), 2.1(6)
3	5.3(1), 5.3(2), 5.3(3), 5.3(4), 5.3(5), 2.1(1), 2.1(2), 2.1(3), 2.1(4), 2.1(5), 2.1(6), 2.2(1), 2.2(2), 2.2(5), 2.2(6)
4	5.1(1)

Study Component 9
Database Design and Use

Aims

To create a data model diagram according to a specification.

To define and create relational database structures to suit the data model.

To create entry forms to enable and control data entry according to specification.

To use a range of methods to query a database and produce reports.

To use information technology for a data handling activity.

Resource Material

Chapters 10, 14 and 17 in the Knowledge Resource and Chapter 25 in the Skills Resource.

Activities

1. This activity is based on the Barford Properties Case Study in the Appendix and the system specification produced for Property Sales in Study Component 8, Activity 3. Keep notes as evidence that you have completed the various requirements of this activity.

    (a) **Apply** the *second* and *third normalisation* rules (1NF and 2NF) to the data model from the Barford Properties specification, creating new entities as necessary. Ensure that the data definitions for each entity are as required for the specification.
    (b) **Draw** the *normalised entity relationship model* (ERM), using suitable graphics software.
    (c) **Produce** a *table definition* for *each entity*, identifying field names, lengths, types (for example, time, date, logical, character, number) and formats. Also identify primary (single or composite), and secondary keys (which may be used in queries, or to establish a relationship with another table).
    (d) **Update** the *data dictionary* to include, for each table: field names; synonyms; lengths; types; formats; and descriptions.
    (e) **Use your notes** to **append** the details of this data model to the system specification produced in Study Component 8.

2. This activity concerns creation and use of the database. Keep and file all the evidence produced in this activity.

    (a) Create a *database*, defining the tables with an RDBMS package and setting key fields and field properties, as specified in 1D. The properties should include *validation* settings and field *patterns* to help control data entered into the database. The validation settings should work in combination with the other controls, such as field types and field lengths.

    (b) Ensure that all table definitions comply with the data dictionary and **modify** as necessary).

    (c) Create a screen *input form* for *each* table in the database, using the design screen to modify them to *suit the specification*. **Save** the forms and use them to **enter** sample data (you need to produce this for testing purposes) into each table.

    (d) Create four suitable queries to service the report requirements *defined in the system specification*. **Two** should be created using *QBE* and two with *SQL statements* or *xBase commands*. **Save** the queries and **test** them.

    (e) Design and **save** the screen and printed report layouts as specified in the Property Sales system specification. This should detail: field order and position, spacing and layout. The layouts should define: pagination; footers; headers; data grouping (where appropriate); totals and calculated fields (where applicable).

    (f) Use the appropriate *report* to display or print the results of each *query*.

3. This activity is designed to cover the requirements of **Element 3.3 "Use Information Technology for a data handling activity",** and uses the database you have developed in Activities 1 and 2.

    (a) The work you do on this needs to be continued over a relatively long period of, perhaps, several weeks, to satisfy the performance criteria. During that period you need to gather evidence that you have used a number of file maintenance activities, data handling processes, report types, verification and validation checks. You will have used many of these during Activities 1 and 2, but you should use the following checklist to ensure that you use all those listed (make sure that you show contents of a table before and after any such changes, unless your work is observed).

    (b) Maintain a log, over an extended period of the *file saving* and *back-up* procedures completed, detailing operation, file names, date, location (directory or disk number). Also record details of any relevant *security measures* you have used (for example, passwords).

    (c) Write notes *evaluating* the *effectiveness* of the data handling system, in terms of its *speed*, *reliability*, *cost*, *benefits* to the organisation (Barford Properties) and the *volume* of data it can handle.

Performance Criteria	Completed
File maintenance activities	
(i) Data entry	
(ii) Amending records	
(iii) Deleting records	

(iv) Appending new records	
Data handling processes	
(i) calculating (numeric total fields)	
(ii) character conversion (amendment of field type)	
(iii) sorting (one field, multiple field)	
(iv) searching (using comparison and logical operators)	
(v) merging (query joining tables)	
(vi) grouping	
Report production	
(i) operational (this is any routine report for regular use)	
(ii) summary	
(iii) grouped	
(iv) exception	
Accuracy checks	
(i) verification (checking screen input against source document before entry)	
(ii) validation (you should have set validation parameters on several fields)	

Performance Criteria

Activity number	Unit element
1	7.1(1), 7.1(2), 2.2(1), 2.2(2), 2.2(3), 2.2(5), 2.2(6)
2	7.1(3), 7.2(1), 7.2(2), 7.2(3), 7.2(4), 7.3(1), 7.3(2), 7.3(3), 7.3(4)
3	3.3(1), 3.3(2), 3.3(3), 3.4(3)

Study Component 10
Industrial and Commercial IT

Aims

To describe and give examples of commercial and industrial systems.

To analyse and evaluate commercial and industrial systems.

Resource Material

Chapters 10 and 20 in the Knowledge Resource and Chapters 21 and 31 in the Skills Resource.

Activities

1. **Produce** *two tables* (use the word processor's table facility), **one** giving general descriptions of *commercial system* examples and the **other,** general descriptions of *industrial systems* examples. The commercial examples to be included are: *booking systems; electronic funds transfer; electronic point of sale; stock control; order processing; payroll processing.* The industrial examples to be included are: *design; process control; robotics; environmental control; traffic control.*

2. As a team of 4, **produce a report on two** *commercial* and **two** *industrial* systems. The report should:

    -   **analyse** each system, in terms of: purpose; hardware; software; data; people; processing activities; inputs; outputs; advantages; limitations; impact on environment.
    -   **evaluate** each system using the following criteria: comparison with an alternative system; costs; benefits (speed, efficiency, accuracy, quality), identification of potential improvements.

    (a) **Arrange** a team meeting to agree upon the *allocation of responsibility*.
    (b) You will have been given a deadline for the completion of the project, so you need to **prepare** a schedule of work to ensure, not only that the separate parts of the work are completed, but that there is sufficient time to integrate the separate contributions into a cohesive final report.

(c) As a team, **design** and **produce** a document template which you can all use. You need to agree at the outset on the format of the final document, so that each member's word processed document is consistent with the others when they are merged into one document.

(d) **Investigate** your assigned area (see Terms of Reference) and **prepare** your contribution (using the designed template).

(e) As the work progresses, team meetings should be used to **monitor** the team's work and comments should be sought from the tutor (and acted upon) on the work you have completed at that stage.

(f) **Merge** the separate documents into a single file, secure the new file and print it for submission.

(g) **Record** *your assessments* of your own contribution and those of other team members.

(h) **Study** the contribution of *another team member* and **use** *presentational graphics software* to **prepare** a presentation which summarises the main points of their contribution to the report. **Present** this to the rest of the class and be prepared to answer questions on the content.

Performance Criteria

Activity number	Unit element
1	1.1(1)
2	1.1(1), 1.1(2), 1.1(3), 1.1(4), 1.1(5), 2.1(1), 2.1(2), 2.1(3), 2.1(4), 2.1(5)

Study Component 11
Information Flows

Aims

To describe and give examples of types of organisations.

To explain the forms and types of information generated and used by functions in organisations.

To produce information flow diagrams.

To compare the types of information flow in different organisations.

Resource Material

Chapters 9 and 10 in the Knowledge Resource and Chapters 21 and 24 in the Skills Resource.

Activities

1. These activities require a general examination of a wide range of organisations and then a more in-depth study of two particular organisations.

   (a) Produce a table (use word processor table facilities) of various examples of *commercial*, *industrial* and *public service* organisations, for example: commercial bank; insurance company, chemical engineers; supermarket chain; leisure centre; accountancy firm; electricity generating company; university. **Include**, at least, *two* examples of each type. Also **indicate** whether the organisation *tends towards* a *hierarchical* or *flat structure*. The table should have three columns, headed: *example organisation*; *category* (industrial, commercial or industrial); *structure* (hierarchical or flat). **Save** two copies of the table, one with the organisations *sorted according to category* and the other *sorted by structural type*.

   (b) Draw, using vector drawing tools, *two* organisation charts, one showing a *hierarchical* structure and the other a *flat* or *'flatter'* structure. The charts should show *areas of responsibility* (which may be indicated by job title) and a *clear division* between *the major functional areas* (for, example, sales, personnel). Use two of the example organisations for this purpose. Each organisation chart should **include** features of its *corporate image*, including a *graphic logo*, *organisation title* and Head Office *address*.

   (c) Explain, by example, the *three* main forms of information: *verbal*, *documentary* and *electronic*. **Gather** examples of commonly used documents, for example: orders; invoices; account statement; price list. Store them in your file for use in Systems Analysis.

   (d) Select two organisations (of *different type*) from the table produced in A. For **each** organisation:

   (i) identify at least **three** *internal* and **two** *external* functions;

   (ii) identify *at least three types* of information, which are used by the selected functions. **You must include** at least one *example* for *each form* of information (one *verbal*, one *documentary* and one *electronic*).

   (iii) For **each** organisation **draw** (using vector drawing tools) **one** *information flow diagram*, showing *all the functions* identified in D; the information flows between them should include the example information types identified in D.

   (e) Present all your work in a word processed document, with embedded graphics and a consistent format throughout.

Performance Criteria

Activity number	Unit element
1	3.1(1), 3.1(2), 3.1(3), 3.1(4), 2.1(1), 2.1(2), 2.1(3), 2.1(4), 2.1(5), 2.2(1), 2.2(2), 2.2(3), 2.2(4), 2.2(5), 2.2(6)

Study Component 12
Data Handling Systems Theory

Aims

To explain methods of processing and types of data handling system.

To compare objectives of selected data handling systems.

To compare methods of data capture in the selected data handling systems

To examine data handling processes.

To review system performance against specified objectives and recommend improvements.

Resource Material

Chapters 5 and 10 in the Knowledge Resource and Chapters 21 and 31 in the Skills Resource.

Activities

1. These activities (which could usefully be undertaken as a team project) require some research into the functional areas of a **large clearing bank** (you can choose another type of large organisation, with which you are familiar) and thereby determine the range of data handling systems the bank is likely to use. For example, customer services comprises a number of different, but related systems: on-line telephone banking (touch tone or voice processing), account statement maintenance and production, charges calculation, personal insurance and mortgage services. Some of these services can be provided by home visits from a personal account manager, who will make use of a notebook computer for the provision of information and completion of application forms.

(a) Produce a table (using a word processor's table facility) of the systems you **identify** and for *each system*, **indicate**, with reasons, which processing method (*batch* or *transaction*) it would use. Use an example system to **explain** the batch and transaction processing methods and place the explanations beneath the table of systems already described.

(b) Using several bank system examples, **explain** what is meant by a *single user* and a *multi-user* system.

(c) Define the terms *centralised* and *distributed processing* and suggest reasons why modern banks favour a measure of distributed processing. Use the systems you have identified to support your suggestions.

(d) Explain the function and general operation of the following types of data handling system and **identify** the applications of these systems in the clearing bank organisation: *bookings, payroll, ordering, invoicing, stock control, personal records*.

(e) For each of the following methods of data capture, **identify** a bank system which could benefit from its use (briefly explain why it is used in preference to another method): *keyboard, mouse, keypad, bar code reader, OMR, MICR, magnetic strip reader, voice processor, touch tone telephone* (the list is not exhaustive and you should be able to identify others)

(f) For each of the following *methods of processing*, **identify** a bank system which would use it (the same system may use several). Briefly **explain** the *nature* of each processing method and its *application* in the identified system(s): *calculating, converting, sorting, searching, selecting, merging, grouping*.

(g) Select two data handling systems from those already identified and **compare** the data capture method(s) used. **Explain** how the data capture method used by each system contributes to the achievement of the identified system objectives. These should be drawn from the following: *speed, accuracy, cost, decision-making support*.

(h) Review the performance of both systems against their identified objectives and **suggest** how they might be improved.

(i) Present all your findings in a word processed report.

Performance Criteria

Activity number	Unit element
1	3.2(1), 3.2(2), 3.2(3), 3.2(4), 3.2(5), 2.1(1), 2.1(2), 2.1(3), 2.1(4), 2.1(5), 2.1(6)

Study Component 13
Security and Privacy

Aims

To identify reasons for the protection of data held on individuals and organisations.

To describe the obligations of system users.

To specify appropriate system security methods.

To contribute to a team project.

To use graphics software to deliver a slide show presentation.

Resource Material

Chapters 14 and 15 in the Knowledge Resource and Chapters 21, 24, 26 and 31 in the Skills Resource.

Activities

1. These activities require a *team* approach, to investigate and report on security and privacy issues. It also requires the *merging* of separate document files of a consistent format and the use of *presentational graphics* software to summarise main points in your investigation. A team could have three members, one being the team leader responsible for the co-ordination and integration of the work of individual team members. The **terms of reference** for the investigation are:

    *   the *types of data* held on *individuals* and *organisations* and the reasons for the protection of such data (confidentiality, legal, moral).

    *   *obligations of system users* (at least 4): confidentiality of data; accuracy; rights of individuals under personal privacy legislation; copyright protection for software and data; responsible attitudes to uncensored or private materials (consider difficulties of Internet).

    *   *System security methods* (at least 4) to: control access; identify users; prevent and recover from computer virus attacks. The methods should be appropriate to the threat

and the circumstances of the organisation and deal with, for example, back-up and recovery procedures, passwords, audit trails, forced recognition of security (official secrets legislation, signing non-disclosure agreement). Categorise the methods into logical and physical.

One area is allocated to each team member. Each team should **relate its investigation** to one, particular kind of organisation. In other words, although the investigation is wide ranging, comments should be included stating the relevance, or otherwise, of an issue to the chosen organisation. Examples are provided in the next table (this allows for six teams).

clearing bank	college or university
national manufacturing company	hospital
national estate agency chain	government department (e.g. Social Security)

(a) **Arrange** a team meeting to agree upon the *allocation of responsibility*. The *terms of reference* identify 3 areas of investigation.

(b) You will have been given a deadline for the completion of the project, so you need to **prepare** a schedule of work to ensure, not only that the separate parts of the work are completed, but that there is sufficient time to integrate the separate contributions into a cohesive final report.

(c) As a team, **design** and **produce** a document template which you can all use. You need to agree at the outset on the format of the final document, so that each member's word processed document is consistent with the others when they are merged into one document.

(d) **Investigate** your assigned area (see Terms of Reference) and **prepare** your contribution (using the designed template).

(e) As the work progresses, team meetings should be used to **monitor** the team's work and comments should be sought from the tutor (and acted upon) on the work you have completed at that stage.

(f) **Merge** the separate documents into a single file, secure the new file and print it for submission.

(g) **Record** *your assessments* of your own contribution and those of other team members.

(h) **Study** the contribution of *another team member* and **use** *presentational graphics software* to **prepare** a presentation which summarises the main points of their contribution to the report. **Present** this to the rest of the class and be prepared to answer questions on the content.

Performance Criteria

Activity number	Unit element
1	3.4(1), 3.4(3), 3.4(4), 2.2(1), 2.2(2), 2.2(3), 2.2(5), 2.2(6), 8.2(1), 8.2(2), 8.2(3), 8.2(4)

Study Component 14
Ergonomics, Health and Safety

Aims

To define health and safety issues for system users.

To use graphics software to produce an office layout design which addresses the health and safety issues.

To use graphics software to prepare a slide show presentation of the main ergonomic and health and safety issues.

Resource Material

Chapter 16 in the Knowledge Resource and Chapters 21 and 24 in the Skills Resource.

Activities

These activities require an assessment of current provision for system users and identification of the health and safety issues. Recommendations for improvement are then required.

Plumley Appleton is a long established firm of Solicitors who have become increasingly aware of the need to compete more strongly for business. This awareness has stemmed largely from the advertising campaigns undertaken by other firms and permissible under recent legislative changes. The partners are keen to remove the rather 'stuffy' image of their firm and at the same time make practical improvements in efficiency. With these aims in mind, they propose to make the general office and reception area open plan. Obviously, their own consulting rooms will remain separate. The client accounting systems are to be computerised and with the use of a Local Area Network, the office staff and the partners are all to have access to the computer facility. Each partner will have a workstation in his/her office. This will allow them to access the system during consultations with clients. A number of features concerning the present office provision have been identified:

- office desks and chairs are non-adjustable;
- floors are carpeted with a fairly cheap, nylon carpet;
- the main lighting in the office is provided by a single lamp in the centre of the ceiling;
- partners' consulting rooms have curtains at the windows;
- each partner has a heavy and highly polished oak desk;

- the main office desks have a shiny melamine 'teak effect' work surface;
- heating is provided by heavy cast iron radiators, two in the main office and one in each of the consulting rooms;
- cabling for the machines is trailing across the floor.

1. **Prepare** a *report*, (decide on a corporate style for the firm and use a template) which

   (a) makes some preliminary *recommendations* concerning new office furniture and equipment, relating to the installation of the new computers. The recommendations should detail commercial products and prices.

   (b) *identifies factors* to be considered when choosing the location and layout of the various workstations in the main office.

   (c) includes *layout plans* (**draw** with graphics software) for each of the offices, indicating workstation positions (showing which way the screen is facing and position of user), cabling, other work areas, seating, light and heat sources and location of window blinds.

2. **Prepare** a *slide show presentation*, summarising the main points (including graphical illustrations) in your report.

Performance Criteria

Activity number	Unit element
1	3.4(2), 2.1(1), 2.1(2), 2.1(3), 2.1(4), 2.1(5), 2.1(6), 2.2(1), 2.2(2), 2.2(3), 2.2(5), 2.2(6)
2	3.4(2), 2.2(1), 2.2(2), 2.2(3), 2.2(4), 2.2(6)

Study Component 15
Hardware and Performance

Aims

To describe the various types of hardware and their purposes.

To explain the effect of system specification on performance.

Resource Material

Chapters 5 and 6 in the Knowledge Resource and Chapters 21 and 24 in the Skills Resource.

Activities

1. **Produce** a **mail order catalogue** for HardSell, a company specialising in IT (not just computer system) hardware products. The specification is as follows:

    (a) The catalogue should be an *illustrated*, *multi-page* (3 or 4 pages) document, giving company details, ordering procedure and product details (code, description, unit price), *grouped* according to purpose: *data capture*; *processing*; *storage* (RAM, ROM and auxiliary); *output*.

    (b) Next to the details of each product, **describe** its *particular characteristics* and *purposes*. For example, a floppy disk and a hard disk have the same general purpose, but their specific purpose and applications are very different.

    (c) There should also be an *alphabetical index* to products. You should be able to find sufficient examples of such a catalogue in PC magazines. **Use word processing/DTP** software, together with **graphics** software and **import/embed** the graphical images into the catalogue document.

    (d) Before your begin the document, produce a template to establish consistent format and layout throughout the catalogue.

2. **Assess** and **report** on the *effects* of *upgrading* an existing microcomputer system to improve various aspects of its *performance*. The assessment is divided into three main areas:

    (a) system *speed*, *capacity* and *parallel processing* capability. The main concerns here are processor type and speed, RAM and cache size, disk capacity and access times, system bus standard.

(b) *sound*, *display* and *communications* capability. This will concentrate on the peripheral devices which can be attached and on expansion cards/boards.

(c) *control* capability.

In your report **select** a **purpose** (using an example application) against which *to measure* each category of *performance*. Example purposes are publishing, computer-aided design, photographic image processing, database system, traditional data handling activity, word processing, video capture and processing, multi-media presentations, data communications, network connection, process control, robot control. Also **comment** on the *quality* and *efficiency* of the upgraded system for the *selected purpose*.

Performance Criteria

Activity number	Unit element
1	1.2(1), 2.1(1), 2.1(2), 2.1(3), 2.1(4), 2.1(5), 2.1(6), 2.2(1), 2.2(2), 2.2(3), 2.2(5), 2.2(6)
2	1.2(2)

Study Component 16
Microprocessor Operation

Aims

To identify microprocessor system components and describe their function.

To describe the characteristics of memory.

To identify the main elements of a central processing unit (CPU).

To describe the machine instruction cycle and identify the components and elements used at each stage in the cycle.

To use vector graphics and slide show software to make a presentation of the machine instruction cycle.

Resource Material

Chapter 6 in the Knowledge Resource and Chapter 24 in the Skills Resource.

Activity

1. **Prepare** a *slide show presentation* incorporating the following:

   (a) Use *vector drawing* tools to **draw** a *schematic block diagram*, suitably labelled, showing the components of a microprocessor system and the relationships and connections between them. **Use** *shading* for each block to provide a 3-D effect. You should **also show** the *main elements* of the central processing unit (*ALU, control unit* and *clock*). **Use a key**, to provide a **description** of the function of each component, beneath the diagram.

   (b) Describe the *characteristics* of different *types of memory* and **describe** the *function* of each type.

   (c) Use graphics and text to **illustrate** *the machine instruction cycle* and the role of the various CPU registers in the cycle.

Performance Criteria

Activity number	Unit element
1	1.3(1), 1.3(2), 1.3(3), 1.3(4), 2.2(1), 2.2(2), 2.2(3), 2.2(4), 2.2(5), 2.2(6)

Study Component 17
Data Communications Theory

Aims

To investigate communication protocols and explain their function for error control.

To investigate the various modes of data communication and their relevance to different forms of communication.

To investigate network services and explain their function.

To process technical graphic designs

Resource Material

Chapter 7 in the Knowledge Resource and Chapter 24 in the Skills Resource.

Activities

These activities require reference to the Pilcon Polymers Case Study. The following activities concern the investigation of various aspects of data communications and networks, in the context of that case study. **Present** the information you gather, in the process of the following activities, in a word processed *report*.

1. **Use** a suitable package to **draw** a block diagram showing the various *data communications* and *network links* between the regional and continental centres of the business. Include the title "Pilcon Polymers - Communications" and a company logo (of your own design and produced with bit map software).

2. **Describe** simplex, half duplex, duplex and asymmetric duplex modes of communication and **explain** which modes are appropriate for the circumstances outlined in the case study. **State**, with reasons, whether serial or parallel communications would be employed between the offices and warehouses of Pilcon Polymers. Synchronous and asynchronous communications are also used in data communications systems. **Explain** the difference between these two forms and, by reference to the various needs of Pilcon Polymers, **argue** when each might be most appropriate. **Annotate** the diagram prepared in Activity 1 of this Study Component, to illustrate your explanation of these technical terms. You should use vector drawing tools. **Embed** the image as an object within the report document.

3. The criteria of transmission speed and data integrity (uncorrupted - without error) are vital to the usefulness of data communications. With reference to Pilcon and **using** example circumstances, **explain** why this is so. Also **explain** the role of modems and protocol parameters (flow control, stop bits, parity and other error checking techniques) in achieving speed and integrity.

4. Apart from data transfer, Pilcon want to make use of various network services. These include: electronic mail; video and teleconferencing; file transfer; bulletin board services (BBSs); databases, electronic data interchange (EDI); integrated services digital network (ISDN). **Briefly explain** the function of each of these services. **Identify** those services, which you judge could be of use to Pilcon Polymers, and **develop** your explanations with *example applications*.

Performance Criteria

Activity number	Unit element
1	2.2(1), 2.2(2), 2.2(4) 2.2(5), 2.2(6)
2	4.1(3), 2.2(1), 2.2(2), 2.2(3), 2.2(5), 2.2(6)
3	4.1(3), 4.1(2)
4	4.1(1)

Study Component 18
Computer Network Theory

Aims

To describe and give examples of types of networks.

To describe the components which form networks and the alternative topologies.

To describe the benefits of using computer networks.

To contribute to an information technology team project.

Resource Material

Chapter 8 in the Knowledge Resource and Chapters 21, 24 and 31 in the Skills Resource.

Activities

1. Use *vector* graphics drawing tools and bit map *clip art*, to **produce** a simple guide to network topologies. The guide should include text to annotate the graphics. The final product should fold into a multi-page, A5, booklet (short edge across the top) and include a title page.

2. This activity requires a *team* approach to **investigate** and **report** on computer networks. It also requires the *merging* of separate document files of a consistent format and the use of *presentational graphics* software to summarise main points in your investigation. A team could have four members, one being the team leader responsible for the co-

ordination and integration of the work of individual team members. The **terms of reference** for the investigation are:

- *types* of networks, with examples. Also describe the features of each and organisational types for which they are appropriate;
- network *components* and *topologies*, together with examples of network products, their topologies and the *protocols* they support (data flow control methods, such as CSMA/CD, token ring); network and PC magazines are a good source;
- benefits of the various types of network and the applications each has for particular organisations;
- network security methods and management activities.

Assuming that there will be several teams, each team should **relate their investigation** to a particular kind of user/system, for example:

bank or building society	college or university
DIY store	public - Internet, videotext
airline	government department

(a) **Arrange** a team meeting to agree upon the *allocation of responsibility*. The *terms of reference* identify 4 areas of investigation.

(b) You will have been given a deadline for the completion of the project, so you need to **prepare** a schedule of work to ensure, not only that the separate parts of the work are completed, but that there is sufficient time to integrate the separate contributions into a cohesive final report.

(c) As a team, **design** and **produce** a document template which you can all use. You need to agree at the outset on the format of the final document, so that each member's word processed document is consistent with the others when they are merged into one document.

(d) **Investigate** your assigned area (see Terms of Reference) and **prepare** your contribution (using the designed template).

(e) As the work progresses, team meetings should be used to **monitor** the team's work and comments should be sought from the tutor (and acted upon) on the work you have completed at that stage.

(f) **Merge** the separate documents into a single file, secure the new file and print it for submission.

(g) **Record** *your assessments* of your own contribution and those of other team members.

(h) **Study** the contribution of *another team member* and **use** *presentational graphics software* to **prepare** a presentation which summarises the main points of their contribution to the report. **Present** this to the rest of the class and be prepared to answer questions on the content.

Performance Criteria

Activity number	Unit element
1	4.3(3), 2.2(1), 2.2(2), 2.2(3), 2.2(5), 2.2(6)
2	4.3(1), 4.3(2), 4.3(3), 4.3(4), 4.3(4), 4.3(5), 4.3(6), 2.2(1), 2.2(2), 2.2(4), 2.2(6), 8.2(1), 8.2(2), 8.2(3), 8.2(4)

Study Component 19
Modelling and Simulation

Aims

To become familiar with the concept of mathematical models and computer simulations.

To develop simple computer models using spreadsheets.

To investigate the effects on output of changing computer model parameters.

Resource Material

Chapter 19 in the Knowledge Resource, and Chapters 22, 23 and 32 in the Skills Resource.

Activities

1. **Describe** three distinct areas that make use of computer models. Explain the purpose of each model and its benefits compared to alternative methods.

2. **Develop** a computer-based model to simulate customer queues at supermarket checkouts.

   (a) **Explain** the factors governing arrival rates, time taken to process purchases.
   (b) **Identify** other factors which may need to be taken into account when developing the model.
   (c) **Use the Monte Carlo method** to simulate your model on a spreadsheet.
   (d) Carefully **describe** the rules of operation of the model and how they have been represented in the spreadsheet.
   (e) **Explore the effects** on queue lengths of changing key variables such as average arrival rates, service rates and number of checkouts open.
   (f) **Use a graph** to show how the queue length at a typical checkout fluctuates over a period of time.
   (g) **Evaluate** the effectiveness of your simulation, commenting on any inadequacies and ways that it might be improved.

3. Investigate factors affecting the financial success of a social event such as a ceilidh (a ceilidh is a traditional Scottish dance), or a dance featuring a rock band. Food is to be provided and a bar is to be available. Assume that the caterers charge the following prices for meals:

No. of meals	Price per meal
Less than 50	£1.50
50 - 100	£1.25
Over 100	£1.00

(a) **Identify the various costs** involved (such as the fee for the band, catering) and sources of income (such as price of tickets, number of tickets sold).

(b) **Identify the variable parameters** of the model that can be altered to affect the profitability or otherwise of the event.

(c) **Construct** a spreadsheet model of the event to allow investigation of changing key parameters.

(d) **Explain** the calculations performed by the spreadsheet.

(e) Fix the ticket price and **determine** how many people would need to attend to (i) break even, and (ii) make a profit of £100.

(f) Limit the number of people attending to 75 and **determine** the minimum ticket price required to make a profit of £50.

Performance Criteria

Activity number	Unit element
1	2.3(1)
2	2.3(2), 2,3(3), 2.3(4), 2.3(5)
3	2.3(2), 2,3(3), 2.3(4), 2.3(5)

Study Component 20
Categories of Software

Aims

To identify and describe the categories of software.

To identify the typical uses of various types of sofware.

To identify the various modes of operation of software and those most appropriate to typical applications.

Resource Material

Chapters 2 and 5 in the Knowledge Resource. Skills Resource. Computing periodicals.

Activities

1. Briefly **describe** the software categories listed below and **identify** specific software products in each category:

   - applications software
   - operating systems
   - utilities
   - user interface software
   - computer languages
   - program generators
   - database management systems

2. **Describe** the purpose of each of the categories identified in activity 1 and give a specific **example of the use** of each.

3. Many software products allow the user alternative modes of operation - keyboard or mouse for instance. **Identify** the various **modes of operation** that are possible in general and also specifically with the products that you identified in activity 1.

Performance Criteria

Activity number	Unit element
1	6.1(1)
2	6.2(2)
3	6.2(4)

Study Component 21
Computer Programs

Aims

To investigate the features of computer programs.

Resource Material

Chapter 18 in the Knowledge Resource, Chapters 30 and 32 in the Skills Resource, Computer periodicals

Activities

1. **Provide examples** of one or more simple programs written in a high-level language such as Pascal which allow you to **identify** each of the following program features:

    (a) different data types such as integer, real and character

    (b) control structures such as selection and repetition

    (c) data structures such as strings, arrays and records

    (d) arithmetic, relational and logical operators

    (e) arithmetic expressions

    (f) conditional expressions

2. **Differentiate** between **compilers** and **interpreters** for high-level languages and **explain** why an interpreted program requires a run time system whereas a compiled program does not. **Give examples** of compiled and interpreted computer programming languages.

3. **Explain** the term *programming environment* and typically what features would you expect one to contain? Certain special programming languages such as Visual Basic and Visual C++ are becoming increasingly popular. What features are provided by the programming environments for these languages that are lacking in other program development environments?

Performance Criteria

Activity number	Unit element
1	6.1(3), 6.2(3,4,5)
2	6.1(3), 6.2(1,2)
3	6.2(1)

Study Component 22
Automated Procedures

Aims

To produce specifications for, create and evaluate two automated procedures.

Resource Material

Chapter 2 and Chapter 18 in the Knowledge Resource,

Chapters 28, 29, 21 and 22 in the Skills Resource.

Activities

1. With the aid of examples **describe** the purpose of automated procedures and what facilities are available for their creation.

Choose TWO automated procedures from the following (or devise similar procedures of your own):

(a) An operating system batch file which is required to

    (i) Create a directory with a specified name.
    (ii) Copy files of a specified type from a certain directory into the newly created directory.
    (iii) Delete the files in the original directory.
    (iv) Print the contents of the new directory.
    (v) Repeat **(a)** to **(d)** as many times as required.

(b) A mailmerge which generates personalised letters using a standard letter and a database containing information to be inserted.

(c) A macro which allows you to create a new document based on a choice of three different document templates. Each style of letter should contain

    (i) A header containing a graphics logo of your own design
    (ii) The current date
    (iii) A footer containing the names of the directors of the company

(d) A screen menu to allow you to run a specified item of software and return to the menu on its completion.

2. For **both** automated procedures chosen

    (i) Produce a detailed specification of its content and operation (ie how it is used).
    (ii) Create the automated procedures.
    (iii) Where possible **obtain hard copy** of the procedures created.
    (iv) Comment on their benefits in terms of speed and ease of use, any disadvantages you are aware of and possible ways that they could be improved.

Performance Criteria

Activity number	Unit element
1	6.3(1,2)
2	6.3(3,4,5) plus IT core skills

Study Component 23
Control Systems

Aims

To investigate the uses of process control systems.

To specify the operation of one or more computer control systems.

To construct simple computer control systems.

To evaluate the control systems constructed.

Resource Material

Chapter 20 in the Knowledge Resource and Chapter 31 in the Skills Resource.

Activities

1. For each of the control systems listed below **suggest** suitable input transducers/sensors, **suggest** appropriate outputs, **identify** processing requirements, and **explain** what **feedback,** if any, is involved.

    (a) A bowling alley
    (b) An anti-locking brake system (ABS) in a car
    (c) A household security system
    (d) A chemical process control system which maintains the concentration and temperature of a liquid in a tank
    (e) Traffic lights which also respond to requests from pedestrians
    (f) An automatic car park
    (g) A greenhouse with tempertaure and humidity controls
    (h) A machine which fills boxes with a fixed number of non-metallic objects moving on a conveyor belt.

2. **Choose** two of the systems above and, using a suitable computer control software environment (such as LabVIEW), **produce schematic diagrams** for them, **describing** the form of inputs required, **how** these inputs are processed, and what devices are to be controlled by output control signals. The systems that you have chosen should use **two** different types of sensors and **two** types of output device.

3.   **Identify** methods of testing your devices and **provide evidence** that they perform as specified.

4.   **Suggest improvement**s that could be made to your systems.

Performance Criteria

Activity number	Unit element
1	2.4(1,2)
2	2.4(3,4)
3	2.4(5)
4	2.4(6)

Study Component 24
IT Projects and Teamwork

Aims

To explore information technology team projects.

To contribute to an information technology team project.

To evaluate an information technology team project.

Resource Material

Chapters 6, 8, 9 and 16 in the Knowledge Resource and Chapters 21, 22, 24, 26 and 31 in the Skills Resource.

Activities

1. This team project concerns the development of a training programme for the use of the software available on a local area network used as a 'drop-in' facility within a college. A survey will determine how much the facility currently is being used, what software is being used most, what software is being under-used and what training students feel that they need to make more use of the facility. The survey will allow the project team to determine training needs, to subsequently plan the delivery of the training programme and to develop suitable support material such as user guides.

2. Before beginning the project, this activity aims to help you understand a range of associated concepts, which are dealt with in Chapter 31. By careful reference to the list of LAN project tasks (use examples to illustrate your understanding), produce brief notes to:

    (a) describe the purposes of planning the project;

    (b) describe what needs to be organised before the project begins, whilst it is progressing and when it is completed;

    (c) explain the various aspects of project scheduling;

    (d) explain the ways in which the project can be controlled.

3.   The project is to be undertaken by a team, and you should use the following list (this is not a precise sequence as some elements may occur in parallel) as a guide to the general progress of the project. Clearly, the precise detail will develop as you pursue the project tasks detailed at the start of this Study Component.

(a) **Arrange** a team meeting to agree upon the *allocation of responsibilities.*

(b) You will have been given a deadline for the completion of the project, so you need to **prepare** a schedule of work to ensure, not only that the separate parts of the work are completed, but that there is sufficient time to integrate the separate contributions into a cohesive final report.

(c) As a team, **design** and **produce** a document template which you can all use. This will ensure a consistent format for your separate contributions to the project documentation.

(d) **Investigate** your assigned area and **prepare** your contribution. This may include the use of a range of techniques and tools which form part of project *organisation*, *scheduling* and *control*. For example, you may use a spreadsheet to record, calculate and control costs. A calendar of events could be recorded in a word processor table to permit easy changes in the sequence. *Critical path analysis* may be undertaken manually or using a special software package.

(e) As the work progresses, team meetings should be used to **monitor** the team's work and comments should be sought from the tutor (and acted upon) on the work you have completed at that stage.

(f) **Record** *your assessments* of your own contribution and those of other team members. **Constructively comment** on the *performance* of your team and **suggest** how it might have been *improved* (these comments might arise as it progresses).

(g) **Study** the contribution of *another team member* and **use** *presentational graphics software* to **prepare** a presentation which summarises the main points of their contribution to the report. **As a team, present** these (with spoken commentaries) to the rest of the class and be prepared to answer questions on the content. The presentations should follow an agreed format and "hang together" in a co-ordinated and integrated way.

(h) **Obtain** and **record** the *evaluative comments* of your tutor and of those who viewed and listened to the team's presentation.

Performance Criteria

Activity number	Unit element
1.	8.1(1), 8.1(2), 8.1(3), 8.1(4)
2.	8.2(1), 8.2(2), 8.2(3), 8.2(4), 8.3(1), 8.3(2), 8.3(3)

Case Studies

Barford Properties

Barford Properties is a small firm of estate agents, operating in Barford. with three partners, each one specialising in a particular aspect of the business. The specialisms are:

- property valuation
- mortgage, insurance and conveyancing
- marketing

There are five sales negotiators and a potential buyer or vendor is assigned to one sales negotiator. The partner responsible for marketing has an assistant. These staff are directly responsible to the partners. An office manager is responsible for two accounts staff one administrative clerk. Two secretaries are also employed, with a range of duties including general correspondence, and the production of property descriptions (including photographs).

The agency operates a number of functions, as follows:

- Property valuations. When a client first approaches the agency with a request to handle the sale of their property, the responsible partner visits the property to assess its market value. The establishment of a selling price is usually a matter of negotiation. The client has a minimum figure in mind, which may coincide with the valuation assessment by the agency. If the valuation is less than the minimum figure put forward by the client, they are advised to lower the asking price accordingly. However, the final decision is made by the client. The asking price may be reviewed, depending on the response or otherwise of potential buyers. In making the assessment, the agency draws on its local experience, but also on data concerning regional and national trends in the housing market.

- Property sales. Once an asking price is agreed, fees are settled. Charges vary according to the value of the property, as the agency takes a percentage of the ultimate selling price, plus costs of advertising. Other charges for conveyancing work are also made. The sales negotiator assigned to a vendor handles their routine enquiries and correspondence to keep them informed of progress. If a client is not satisfied with progress are wants a different asking price, for example, he or she is referred to one of the partners.

- Marketing. This section deals with the placing of advertisements in local and national newspapers and property journals. It also organises the window displays and property details leaflets which are given out to interested buyers.

- Mortgage, conveyancing and insurance services (the agency acts as a broker). Buyers of properties handled by the agency are offered these services, and many clients make use of them, particularly if they are first-time buyers. The agency does not have Independent Financial Adviser status and mortgages are arranged with the Barford and Bamford Building Society. Property, mortgage protection and endowment insurances are obtained from the Buzzard Life Insurance Company.

- Financial accounting. This section handles all the customer accounts and deals with receipts and payments flowing between the agency, building societies, solicitors and insurance companies.

A brief outline of the procedures involved in a property sale is given below.

1. The initial request from a client wishing to sell a property is dealt with by the responsible partner, who makes an appointment to visit the property. Details of location, type, agreed asking price, number of rooms and so on are recorded. Photographs are also taken.
2. The property details are transcribed onto one of two standard forms, depending on whether the property is residential or business. This process is carried out in the Property Sales section.
3. The staff categorise the property according to basic criteria, including property location, type, size, quality, number of rooms and price range. These basic details are transcribed onto record cards, which are the initial point of reference when a potential buyer makes an enquiry.
4. To match prospective buyers with properties for sale, a Buyer Clients file is maintained. Details of suitable properties are sent (using a mailing list) to potential buyers.
5. When a buyer expresses an interest in a property, a viewing appointment is arranged between the buyer and the vendor (if the property is empty, one of the partners will accompany the buyer).
6. If a buyer expresses interest, they are asked to make an offer, which is then put to the vendor for consideration. Apart from the offer price, other factors are considered; for example, whether, the buyer has a property to sell.
7. Once a sale is agreed, solicitors take over the process of carrying out the various conveyancing operations and agreeing a completion date, when payment is made and the property ownership changes hands. When this is completed, the agency requests payment of the fees by the vendor. Buyers are not charged by the agency, although they do incur conveyancing costs.

Pilcon Polymers

Pilcon Polymers is a manufacturer of plastic containers of all kinds. Its Head Office, factory and main warehouse are in Peterlee, County Durham, but it also has distribution warehouses in Leeds, Birmingham, Milan and Cologne also The company also has regional office and wholesale outlet facilities in Glasgow, Leeds, Belfast, Swansea and Birmingham. Across the whole organisation, Pilcon employ 450 people, of whom 350 are in administrative, marketing, sales or clerical roles. The manufacturing processes are highly automated, so the factory only employs 50 people, whose main tasks relate to machine minding and maintenance. 25 staff are employed in warehouse operations and the remaining 25 research, design and develop new products. The UK centres each have a regional manager, who is responsible for the marketing, wholesale and distribution operations in his or her region. The Milan and Cologne centres have a warehouse and distribution manager who responds to instructions from Head Office in Peterlee. Physical stock control operations need to be carried out in the Milan and Cologne warehouses, but the records of stocks held of the continental warehouse stocks issues and receipts are all held by Head Office. Marketing and sales operations are all carried out from the UK, so the Milan and Cologne centres do not employ staff in these roles. Payroll and personnel management are functions handled by the Peterlee Head Office.

The main functions carried out in Peterlee are:

- research and development (R&D);
- product design and manufacture;
- product testing and quality control;
- sales and marketing;
- personnel;
- payroll;
- financial accounting (sales, purchasing and so on);
- stock control;
- sales order processing

The UK centres also take regional responsibility for these functions, except for R&D, product design and manufacture, product testing and quality control. Management information produced by these regional functions is regularly transmitted to Head Office, to allow assessment of regional efficiency and profitability, as well as a corporate view of performance to be obtained.

Each month, the warehouses in Milan and Cologne need to transmit their orders to replenish stocks; these order may involve several hundred different stock items. Goods are transported by rail and road. There may also be a need for an emergency order to be transmitted (the goods can then be flown out). Peterlee also wish to send information to Milan and Cologne, but the communications do not need be interactive (both ways at the same time). Local area networks are installed in all the United Kingdom offices and are linked across communications networks.

Borsettshire College

Borsettshire College of Further and Higher Education runs a wide range of vocational and non-vocational courses for both full-time and part-time students. It is generally accepted and often stipulated by external course validating bodies, such as BTEC, City and Guilds and RSA, that full-time vocational courses should include a period of relevant work experience for each student. Borsettshire College offers full-time vocational courses in, for example, catering, hotel management and reception, computing, information technology, business studies, nursery nursing and social work. During the year, the total number of students requiring work placement of one sort or another is around 500. Approximately 30 academic staff are involved in organising the work placements, and many use the same employers. At present, there is little or no co-ordination of work placement planning, each member of staff dealing directly with employers. This has lead to some embarrassing moments. For example, when one member of staff from the Catering Department telephoned the Personnel Manager of a local hotel to arrange a placement, she was told that one of her colleagues, from the Information Technology (IT) Department, was sitting in the Personnel Manager's office discussing a completely unrelated placement. Obviously, the Personnel Manager found it strange that neither member of staff, even though they worked at the same college, knew that the other was negotiating a work placement with the same employer.

At a recent staff meeting, it has been agreed that, as a first step, information on work placements should be centrally available to all interested staff. In addition, it has been agreed that a non-academic member of staff should keep such an information store up-to-date. Before approaching an employer, a member of staff would be expected to refer to the centrally held information, to see who else used the employer and to determine if there are likely to be any clashes. If any further information is required, the other member(s) of staff responsible for work placements with the same employer, can be consulted directly. It has been suggested by the academic IT and Computing staff that a relational database package may be the best solution, provided that money is available to pay for the services of a professional systems analyst/programmer. The person appointed to the task will be expected to consult the college staff on their requirements and to prepare for their approval, a system specification before programming starts. The database is likely to contain information concerning the employer, the type of work placements offered, official contacts and details of college staff involved.

Hailes Bookshop

Hailes Bookshop in Cambridge is internationally reputed to be one of the finest and largest bookshops in the world. The shop occupies a complete block of terraced Victorian buildings. There are three floors and each floor has several sections, divided according to subject. If a book is in print, Hailes will have a copy. Despite its volume of business, its only concession to automation to date has been to use electronic tills. All other tasks are carried out manually and communications between staff are generally face-to-face. There is a family atmosphere amongst the staff and management and the firm even employs a tea lady who wheels her trolley of tea and biscuits from department to department at break times. However, there is increasing competition from bookshops which adopt a supermarket approach. These 'book supermarkets' are highly automated and make extensive use of computers for almost all their data processing applications. Their staff have little or no knowledge of the products they sell and customers are left to sort out their own needs. In contrast, Hailes employs staff with specialist knowledge of books in a number of subject areas, but not popular fiction. It is in this area that Hailes is experiencing severe competition.

The directors of Hailes are willing to accept the idea that some applications and particularly stock control, could benefit from computerisation. A software consultancy, DataSoft, has been approached by the Hailes directors for advice on the best approach to computerisation. DataSoft have recommended the use of a Local Area Network, which they point out, will allow automation of a range of routine office tasks, apart from the standard data processing tasks envisaged by the Hailes directors. DataSoft have also emphasised the potential benefits of electronic messaging between the various departments of the shop and the provision of access to external E-mail systems. The Hailes directors are proud of the friendly atmosphere amongst staff and the frequent personal contacts. They are unwilling to sacrifice the 'personal touch' to the objective of automated efficiency, but are very conscious of the need to improve their competitiveness.

Index

D

Computing for A Level, BTEC and First Degree

Nick Waites Geoffrey Knott September 1992 608 pages ISBN 0 907679 40 4 Size 252 x 200mm Soft Cover £13.95

This text has been specifically written to cover the Advanced Level computing syllabuses of the major examining boards. It is also highly suitable for students of first year BTEC HNC/HND courses in computing and Part 1 of the British Computer Society. Examination practice is provided through a range of actual examination questions selected from a number of major examining boards. A Tutor's Manual containing suggested solutions is available from the Publishers for centres which adopt the book.

A disk produced by Microfile, the educational software house, containing software to supplement a number of selected topics from the text, can be purchased from the Publishers. The disk includes an integrated suite of programs for an assembler specifically designed for educational use, a number of programs to illustrate data structures and the source listings of a number of sorting programs described in the book.

Small Business Computer Systems

Second Edition Geoffrey Knott March 1994 284 pages ISBN 0 907679 60 9 Soft Cover £14.50

This text covers the Small Business Computer Systems stream of BTEC courses in Computer Studies and provides students with all the necessary source material. The programme of problem based assignments is designed to consolidate students' learning at every stage of the course and to cover the BTEC specific objectives.

The second edition extensively updates the material provided in the first, and reflects the most recent developments in microcomputer hardware and software. The book is also ideal for undergraduates and HNC/HND students of any discipline and for professionals who require a fundamental understanding of microcomputer technology and applications. Microcomputer users and practitioners, in both the small business and corporate fields, will find the book a highly readable and invaluable resource.

Information Technology Skills – a student guide

Geoffrey Knott June 1994 192 pp ISBN 0 907679 68 4 Size 252 x 200mm Soft Cover £7.95

This book is designed to meet the requirements of all students who need to develop their Information Technology skills. The text provides extensive coverage of the following types of software package:

- word processor
- spreadsheet (including graphics)
- database
- computer aided design
- graphic design (paint)
- desktop publishing

Guidance is also provided on:

- general microcomputer operation

- sharing data between applications
- health and safety issues
- error and fault management

Numerous, staged activities are included to encourage practise and consolidation of skills with each package type. Unlike books which guide the user through the precise use of a particular word processor or spreadsheet, this book is designed to provide knowledge and skills which are readily transferable from one package to another. The book is written in a highly readable and friendly style, which aims to give students a considerable degree of independence in the learning process.

An Introduction to Pascal

James K Morton June 1993 160 pp ISBN 0 907679 47 1 *Size 252 x 200mm Soft Cover* **£10.95**

This book has been specially written for those studying Pascal for the first time and assumes no prior knowledge of programming. The format of the book provides the student with a logical, step by step learning experience proven to be successful in practice.

The material included covers the programming requirements of BTEC National and First Awards, City & Guilds Modular Courses and GCE Advanced Level Computing syllabuses. BTEC National/First Award and City & Guilds students will find their requirements met by the material contained in chapters 1 to 5; Advanced Level students should include chapter 6 in their course of study. Undergraduate and HNC/HND students requiring a working knowledge of Pascal will find this an invaluable text. Chapters 1 to 5 provide the material necessary for a good, general understanding of the Pascal language and chapter 6 provides a platform for those students intending to pursue programming at a professional level.

The book contains a wealth of complete, ready-to-run programs along with numerous end-of-chapter practise programs, exercises and assignments designed to enhance understanding of the material presented in each chapter.

GCSE Information Systems

Nick Waites August 1994 320 pp ISBN 0 907679 71 4 *Size 252 x 200mm Soft Cover* **£11.50**

GCSE Information Systems has been written specifically for the National Curriculum Attainment Target 5: Information Technology Capability.

The material presented in the book covers the syllabus extensions for students who wish to obtain a GCSE in Information Systems.

The text, which covers all aspects of information technology and information systems, includes:

- basic computer operation principles
- hardware devices
- the different types of software
- problem solving techniques
- elements of programming in BASIC, Pascal and Logo
- systems analysis and design
- applications of computers
- social issues relating to computers
- glossary of commonly used computing terms

The text is supplemented with numerous diagrams and self-test questions and answers are provided at the end of each chapter. A number of model GCSE examination questions have also been included. These features combine to provide an excellent general introduction to computing for GCSE students or for people who out of interest, simply wish to learn more about this important subject.